Preface

With the appearance of Walter Lippmann's classic *Public Opinion* in 1922, the relationship of communication to politics began to intrigue not only journalists but politicians, publicity seekers, and social scientists as well. The publication of a seemingly unending number of specialized works treating public opinion, television's role in elections, the selling of candidates, government–press relations, political linguistics, and the effects of mass communication on political behavior is evidence that interest in the relationship continues unabated. In recent years this fascination has contributed to the gradual, yet steady, emergence of a cross-disciplinary field of political communication. Bearing sundry titles—including "public opinion," "mass media and politics," "politics and the press," "political persuasion," "public opinion and mass media," "political campaigns," and others—courses in political communication are now taught in departments of political science, sociology, mass communication, speech communication, journalism, and social psychology. Moreover, research in the field increasingly brings together the differing assumptions, perspectives, methods, and techniques of a variety of scholars sharing a common concern in a multidisciplinary endeavor. Formal recognition of the emergence of a teaching and research area transcending the boundaries of several academic disciplines came in 1973 with the establishment of a separate Political Communication Division within the International Communication Association.

Despite the growing interest in political communication by scholars and practitioners and the availability of specialized monographs and articles on aspects of politics and communication, there is as yet no single text which reviews and integrates the rich diversity that is the content of the emerging field. This book is a first response to that need. It differs from the large number of existing texts in public opinion in several respects. For one, although the topics contained in conventional texts are included—the nature of public opinion, the distribution of opinions, political socialization, political participation, voting, and the opinion-policy relation—they are discussed within the framework of the inherent political qualities of communication that involve leaders and followers in civic activities. Moreover, the bulk of public opinion texts place considerable emphasis on the role of the family, groups, and political parties in opinion formation; techniques, channels, and media of communication frequently receive cursory attention or are ignored entirely as merely reinforcing not altering political views. This text returns to an earlier tradition to take seriously what political communicators do to influence and respond to public opinion. There is a special effort to add the perspectives and findings of researchers in mass communication, speech communication, and sociology to those of political scientists in assessing the nature and effects of political linguistics, persuasion, and channels on mass, group, and popular opinion as well as policy making. Readers will also note that this text adopts a theoretical perspective, that emphasizing processes of symbolic interaction, and adheres to that viewpoint throughout in discussing the role of communication in creating political realities. Finally, those familiar with relevant works in the field, be they texts in public opinion or research monographs, will find another key difference in this volume, an effort to keep to a minimum discussions of research techniques that today's students often find more esoteric than enlightening, and to avoid inundating readers with tables of statistical data. Alternative ways of conducting research in political communication certainly are important; but a description of those matters has been placed in an appendix. For those interested in the reports of quantitative studies, bibliographical notes at the close of relevant chapters provide the necessary citations as do the extensive footnotes documenting various arguments.

The author's interest in political communication and in the preparation of this volume has provided the opportunity to become acquainted with investigators in disciplines outside of political science. Many of these scholars have published works and debts to them are acknowledged by citations throughout the text. However, a special acknowledgment is due to Keith R. Sanders of Southern Illinois University at Carbondale for calling attention to the vast number of relevant materials, published and unpublished, that comprise the literature of political communication. Two reivewers provided helpful

POLITICAL COMMUNICATION AND PUBLIC OPINION IN AMERICA

By
DAN NIMMO
UNIVERSITY OF TENNESSEE, KNOXVILLE

Goodyear Publishing Company, Santa Monica, California

For Greg, Vicky, and Larry—political talkers all.

Library of Congress Cataloging in Publication Data

Nimmo, Dan D
    Political communication and public opinion in
    America.

    Includes bibliographies.
    1.   Public opinion—United States. 2.   Communication
in politics—United States. I. Title.
HN90.P8N542   301.15′4   77-13143
ISBN 0-87620-682-8
ISBN 0-87620-681-X pbk.

Y-6828-1 (C)
Y-681X-4-(P)

ISBN: 0-87620-682-8 (C)
ISBN: 0-87620-681-X (P)

Current Printing (last digit):
10 9 8 7 6 5 4 3 2 1
Printed in the United States of America

Cover and Text Design: Russ Good
Production Editor: Pam Tully

comments on the manuscript prior to publication, Robert Meadows of The Annenberg School at The University of Pennsylvania and Deanna Robinson of The Ohio State University; perhaps had the author been receptive to all of their generous suggestions rather than those less ego-threatening, the text would have been improved. Discussions with James Combs of Valparaiso University and Harry Howard at Maryville College contributed greatly to developing an appreciation for the dramatic and symbolic dimensions of communication in politics. Ann Lacava and Paulette Acres were prompt in typing the manuscript. Several persons at Goodyear Publishing Company provided encouragement and assistance, especially James Boyd, political science editor, and production editor Pam Tully. But special thanks are due to one individual at Goodyear, to Dave Grady who first expressed interest in a project of this nature and continues to believe that in publishing the past need not dictate the present.

TABLE OF CONTENTS

chapter 1

Political Communication and Public Opinion: A Point of View

Consider the following:

> "Why do you believe *that?*"
> "You want *what?* Why?"
> "Why must you *act* that way?"

Such are the questions people face fairly often in their daily lives, indeed almost from the cradle to the grave. The inquisitors are all manner of persons—parents, offspring, relatives, spouses, teachers, fellow workers, and casual acquaintances. The queries come from friends and the not so friendly, the helpful and not so helpful, the interesting and the boring, the curious and the just plain nosy. At times the responses are open and generous; at others the interrogated suffer through the ordeal—or embarrassment—in polite toleration, occasionally retorting in exasperation, "Why not?" or more definitively, "None of your damn business!"

Perhaps less obtrusively (although that is not always certain), students of politics, communication, public opinion, and all varieties of human conduct ask the same questions—what people believe and why, what they want and why, and why they act as they do. Not so easily rebuffed by curt responses uttered in haste, desperation, or disgust, the social scientists keep asking, probing, and seeking to understand human beliefs, values, and actions. At least in one respect their persistence has paid off, for they have generated many (maybe too many) explanations. Despite the plentitude of diverse answers, it does no great violence to speak of three general interpretations behavioral scientists give to human activity.

UNDERSTANDING HUMAN BEINGS: SELF-ACTION, INTER-ACTION, AND TRANS-ACTION

The first interpretation is the notion that within each of us there is something that determines our conduct in any situation. Our behavior consists of *self-action* "where things are viewed as acting under their own powers."[1] These powers have many names—conscious and unconscious motives, attitudes, impulses, drives, capacities, and others. The sources of these powers are obscure. Investigators attribute a few to heredity, others to experience, and some simply to being human. In any case we need not dwell upon the controversies that exist over origins.[2] Rather we only note that it is popular to explain human conduct by identifying key factors present within individuals that stimulate resulting behavior. Thus greed results in avaricious pursuit of wealth, altruism in philanthropy. Or Johnny doesn't play with the neighborhood children because he is shy. And Ms. Doe thinks and feels about politics, discusses public matters, and votes as she does because she is conservative; Mr. Doe doesn't vote because he lacks efficacy ("the feeling that individual political action does have, or can have, an impact on the political process").[3] In short, we do what we do because we are what we are. In the words of Shakespeare's Cassius, "The fault, dear Brutus, is not in our stars but in ourselves."

A second interpretation looks at the stars, i.e., locates the forces that shape human conduct as outside the individual. A minimal inventory includes social and economic position, social roles, group demands, cultural prescriptions and proscriptions, customs, and laws. When a person interacts (as all do) with these factors, the resulting stimuli initiate and produce behavior. Some philosophers label this point of view as *inter-action* "where thing is balanced against thing in causal interconnection."[4]

As interpretations of human conduct, self-action and inter-action views, despite emphasizing different locations for what stimulates behavior, share certain assumptions. For one, there is the premise (whether implicit or explicit) that the causes of human conduct lie in the workings of selected factors or combinations thereof. Thus, whereas an exponent of self-action theory traces Ms. Doe's vote to a psychological input (i.e., deep-seated conservatism), the inter-action theorist attributes it to her high social status, class position, occupation, education, and income. The two views are not mutually exclusive; thus, a theorist might argue (and many do) that external social factors produce internal psychological demands guiding behavior, or that a person's attitudes mediate between external demands and the individual's response. Implied in all of this is a second assumption that as the magnitudes of internal or external factors change, conduct changes. For example, as one learns attitudes conducive to taking part in politics, the more apt that person is to participate; or, if higher income persons take a more active interest in public affairs, a rise in income prophesies increased political interest.

Although self-action or inter-action views do not ignore the meaning persons attribute to things in their environment, neither perspective stresses the *interpretative* processes from which meaning derives as the key to understanding human behavior. Instead both views regard the person as a neutral link intervening between the initiating stimuli and the conduct stimuli allegedly provoke. Sociologist Herbert Blumer has contrasted the way contemporary psychologists and sociologists regard human activity. He notes the tendency common to both schools to minimize an important aspect, "that human beings act toward things on the basis of the meanings that the things have for them." Said Blumer of psychological (self-action) and sociological (inter-action) approaches, "In the first . . . the meaning disappears by being merged into the initiating or causative factors; in the second . . . meaning becomes a mere transmission link that can be ignored in favor of the initiating factors."[5]

A third perspective, therefore, emphasizes that human conduct—what people think, feel, and do—arises out of the meaning persons give to physical, social, and abstract things, meaning derived through the social transactions people have with their fellows. Meanings do not arise in advance of relationships with others; rather, persons construct meanings through joint actions with one another. Thus, the "meaning" of some internal state (whether as specific as a headache or ambiguous as a feeling of loneliness) varies with the situation in which people take part with others. Similarly, people also derive the meaning of an external attribute (being rich or poor, a boss or an employee, a student or teacher, obedient or evasive of the law) through a process of interpretation in dealing with others. In sum, neither internal nor external variables cause human conduct; rather, *the key variable is the person,* or more accurately, the personal interpretative process by which one constructs meaning in a world of human relationships.

Meaning and action jointly influence one another; meaning does not cause a person's conduct, nor does that conduct cause meaning. Instead, the interpretative process involves ongoing, joint, mutual exchange of meaning and conduct, a transaction where cause and effect are indistinguishable. Blumer calls this third view "symbolic interactionism," i.e., "action on the part of a human being consists of taking account of various things that he notes and forging a line of conduct on the basis of how he interprets them."[6] Others distinguish it from self-action and inter-action as *trans-action.* Trans-actional accounts of human conduct point to aspects and phases of action occurring in continuous process. They attach no causal importance to elements either internal or external to persons; there is no isolation of presumptively detachable relations from detachable elements.[7]

The reader need not accept any of these three approaches to understanding human conduct (self-action, inter-action, or trans-action) as best, most useful, or clearly true in contrast to the others. To date no single interpretation of human beliefs, values, and activity tells us everything we wish to know. All have shortcomings; perhaps no single theory will ever suffice. Be that as it may, we put all three to work in the pages that follow in pursuing answers to a question central to the subject matter of this text: "Under what conditions do people take into account inner states and/or external influences in communicating about politics and formulating public opinion?" To approach that question we need first to consider in detail the relationship between communication and politics.

COMMUNICATION AND POLITICS

A major argument of this book is that to understand government and politics in the United States, close scrutiny of public opinion is required. To understand public opinion, it is helpful to know something about political communication. To get a start on all this, it is essential to ponder four questions: what is communication, what is politics, what is political communication, and what is public opinion?

What Is Communication?

Even at inflationary prices, definitions of communication are, as the saying goes, a dime a dozen. Depending upon the point of view, communication is: the transmission of information to elicit a response;[8] coordinating meaning between a person and an audience;[9] sharing information, an idea, or an attitude;[10] sharing elements of behavior, or modes of life, through sets of rules;[11] a "meeting of minds, a bringing about of a common set of symbols in the minds of the participants—in short, an understanding";[12] "a purely personal, internally experienced event" shared with someone else;[13] or "the transmission of information from one person or group to another (or others) primarily through symbols."[14] There are even definitions that state what communication is by saying what it is *not:* "Communication is not just the passing of information from a source to the public; it is better conceived as a re-creation of information ideas by the public, given a hint by way of a key symbol, slogan, or theme."[15] The reader will perceive some similarity in several of these definitions, as for example, an emphasis on sharing something between people—information, ideas, behavior, understanding, internal experiences, etc. Not so obvious are a host of other characteristics generally attributed to communication in these and other definitions. By specifying these attributes we will formulate a usage of the concept that is basic to this text.

Remember two points made earlier regarding trans-action as a mode of thinking about human behavior. First, the meaning of things to persons arises out of the joint actions of those people. Second, such action consists of taking account of various things and forging a line of conduct on the basis of personal interpretation. Here lie the key features of communication—people taking things into account, interpreting them, constructing meaning, acting upon that meaning, and, thus, expressing that meaning.[16] There are three kinds of things people take into account: (1) physical objects, ranging in diversity from chairs, plants, and automobiles to weather conditions; (2) social objects, whether other persons or oneself; and (3) abstract objects such as ideas, doctrines, feelings, and wishes. People perceive these objects as signs (say, a blinking light at an intersection), signals (a wink, a friendly gesture), and cues (a spoken utterance, etc.). Taking these signs, signals, and cues into account, they create meanings for objects. Through interpretation they formulate subjective images, remembering what objects have meant to them in the past, imagining future meanings once they act toward the objects, and thereby determining what objects mean in the present. Through symbols, spoken or unspoken, written and unwritten, people exchange or share their images and, in so doing, create new meanings. Communication is *the process of social transaction people use to construct meanings that constitute their images of the world (on which they act) and to exchange those images via symbols.*

Several implications of this view are noteworthy. Foremost is that human conduct considered as a process of communication is *creative.* Through social intercourse people derive and act out meanings that enable them to create and re-create their subjective world. Dean Barnlund notes this when he says "communication describes the evolution of meaning." "Meaning is something 'invented,' 'assigned,' 'given,' rather than something 'received.' " Thus communication "is not a reaction to something, nor an interaction with something, but a transaction in which man invents and attributes meanings to realize his purposes."[17]

Barnlund suggests other characteristics of communication implied by the above definition. Communication, he notes, is: (1) *dynamic*—a process of minded behavior of an active interpreter rather than of a mindless entity moved by internal mechanisms (self-action) or subject solely to external forces (inter-action);[18] (2) *continuous*—not a thing nor even a discrete act, but a continuing condition of life with no beginning or end; (3) *circular* in the sense that there is no linear sequence in the flow of meaning from one person to another—people engage in communication simultaneously *with,* not *to,* one another; (4) *unrepeatable* because the continuous re-creation of meaning implies changes in personal images of the past, present, and future that make it unlikely that people will give identical messages precisely the same meanings at separate points in time; (5) *irreversible,* because it develops in such a way that a message once uttered and interpreted can't be taken back from the mind of the receiver; and (6) *complex* in that it goes on in many different contexts and at many levels—intrapersonal, interpersonal, organizational, societal, and cultural.

Two other implications should also be noted. Any action a person takes in the presence of another (even silence, avoiding eye contact, or walking away, let alone speaking) has message value. That is, any act is something another person can take into account, interpret, read meaning into, and use to construct an impression or image. Put simply, *one cannot not communicate* when in the presence of another.[19]

Finally, the key notion of *process* which underlies our definition of communication must be taken seriously. Process is flow, change, and flux in the relation of activities to one another. In postulating what communication is all about (i.e., process), Barnlund describes the character of process itself—evolving, dynamic, continuous, circular, unrepeatable, irreversible, and complex. As process, communication has no starting or stopping point; it pervades personal interpretations, social exchanges, and politics endlessly. It has no readily discernible causes for observed effects. Given all this, it would be difficult for any text on political communication and public opinion to explain the causes of human behavior. Rather than explain *why* people behave, feel, and act as they do,[20] this text will describe *how* Americans communicate their political beliefs, values, and expectations and give meaning to public opinion.

What Is Politics and Political Communication?

As with communication, there are sundry definitions of politics. Politics is who gets what, when, how;[21] the authoritative allocation of values;[22] power and power wielders;[23] influence;[24] actions oriented toward the maintenance and/or extension of other actions.[25] Among all the diverse views there is general agreement that politics involves something people do; politics is activity.[26] And it is activity—differentiated (albeit not always successfully) from other activity—economic, religious, athletic, and so forth.

This text uses politics simply to mean *the activity of people collectively regulating their conduct under conditions of social conflict.* People differ from one another in many ways—physiques, talents, emotions, needs, aspirations, resources, behavior, and so forth. Sometimes these differences stimulate arguments, disagreements, and disputes. When people take these conflicts seriously, take account of them by making known the disputing interests, and settle them, this is political activity.

So viewed, politics occurs in any social setting marked by dispute, whether the setting is as large as a nation or as small as a poker-playing club or even two people. However, we shall use the term primarily in a narrower, conventional sense and speak of the regulation of social conflict by means of governmental institutions.

Politics, like communication, is process, and like communication, politics involves talk. This is not talk in the narrow sense of the spoken word but talk in the more inclusive sense, meaning all the ways people exchange symbols—written and spoken words, pictures, movements, gestures, mannerisms, and dress. Political scientist Mark Roelofs says simply, "Politics is talk; or to put the matter more exactly, the activity of politics ('politicking') is talking." He notes that politics is not all talk nor all talk politics. But "the essence of political experience, and not just its basic condition, is that it is an activity of communication between persons."[27]

Readers will find Roelofs's viewpoint in keeping with this work's perspective. Communication pervades politics. When people take conflicts into account, they derive meanings of the disputes through communication. When people settle their disagreements, those settlements also are things taken into account, interpreted, and exchanged through communication. Out of transactions we call political arise meanings of social disputes and their adjustments, and in the process, new conflicts are created. Constructed also are the ever-changing meanings citizens attribute to abstract ideas such as democracy, liberty, or justice; to key institutions such as the presidency, Congress, and courts; to political figures such as Jimmy Carter, Gerald Ford, or Richard Nixon; to the nation, its flag, anthem, monuments, political heroes, villains, and fools.

It is the presumption of this book, therefore, that many aspects of political life can be described as communication. It is a book of political communication, that is, *communication (activity) considered political by virtue of its consequences (actual and potential) which regulate human conduct under conditions of conflict.* But it is also a book of public opinion. How does that subject fit into all of this?

What Is Public Opinion?

"Public opinion," says the president, "is behind me on this matter." "Having just returned from my district," announces the leader of the president's opposition in Congress, "I can say that public opinion is dead set against the man in the White House." A headline touting the latest Gallup poll reads, "Public Opinion Divided." And, reports the CBS Washington correspondent, "It is clear that public opinion distrusts both the president and Congress."

Everybody, yet nobody, speaks for public opinion. In the wake of all this chatter, small wonder that democracy—often called "government

by public opinion"—was once described by critic H. L. Mencken in unflattering terms: "Democracy is the art and science of running the circus
from the monkey-cage."[28] Perhaps, however, the confusion belongs not
to the monkeys, but to those who purport to know what public opinion
is "really" all about. As with communication and politics, definitions
abound. Public opinion is: "the aggregate of views men hold regarding
matters that affect or interest the community";[29] "a short way of describing the belief or conviction prevalent in a given society that particular
laws are beneficial";[30] "a phenomenon of the group process";[31] and "those
opinions held by private persons which governments find it prudent to
heed."[32]

It has always been difficult to reach a suitable notion of what public
opinion is. Four decades ago a leading student of the phenomenon, Floyd
H. Allport, noted what he called "fictions and blind alleys" in talking
about public opinion (all of which are still with us). There is, he wrote,
a tendency first to personify public opinion by assuming a "soul" that
transcends the expressions of different groups on different issues; underlying diverse views is a single "voice of the people." A second fiction is
the tendency to personify the public as a "superorganic being . . . turning
its gaze now this way, now that, as deciding, and as uttering its opinion."
A third fallacy is to identify the opinion of a single group within a society
as the opinion of all persons, a "part of the whole" fallacy. Closely related
is a fourth blind alley of "partial inclusion," that of saying that those
individuals with a particular interest comprise the entire public. A fifth
dead end is public opinion as an "ideational entity" or essence that pervades the minds of everybody in an unseen way. Allport identified a
sixth fallacy, which is to regard public opinion as a byproduct of interactions between groups while ignoring the possibility that members of any
given group might not even share the views expressed by its leaders.
Finally, Allport noted the "journalistic fallacy," the confusion of public
opinion with public presentations of opinion in the news media.[33]

So much for alternative definitions, fictions, and fallacies. We cannot
resolve the confusion easily. At this point we will merely sketch a working
characterization of public opinion in keeping with the general view of
process used in describing communication and politics. Later, in Part
Three where it is more appropriate to do so, we examine the character
of public opinion in detail.

Recall that the underlying assumption of the discussion thus far is
that "human beings act toward things on the basis of the meanings that
the things have for them."[34] The relation between meaning and acting
is circular; people jointly act toward one another on the basis of the
meanings they attribute to their relationship, yet they continuously re-
create these very meanings through their transactions. Derived from each
person's learning experiences are *tendencies* that are basic to social transactions. Here we must be careful. For convenience it helps to think of these

tendencies as what a person takes *into* a social situation, but we must avoid two errors. First, tendencies do not exist apart from a person's conduct; they are not tendencies to act, but tendencies *of* activity: "One way of stating them is to call them 'tendencies of activity.' This contrasts them seemingly with the external activity and is a half-compromise with everyday speech. It will only be tolerable if we remember every time we use the words that these 'tendencies' are activities themselves; that they are stages of activity just as much as any other activity."[35] Second, tendencies *of* activity do not determine how a person relates with social comrades. Rather, a tendency "is merely an element that enters into the developing act—no more than an initial bid for a *possible* line of action ... what is crucial is not the tendency but the process by which the act is built up—not the attitude but the defining process through which the individual comes to forge his act."[36]

Three kinds of tendencies that suggest (but do not cause) a person's line of conduct are beliefs, values, and expectations. Much of scholarly literature labels these as cognitive, affective, and conative components respectively. Obviously, beliefs, values, and expectations overlap for any individual. Beliefs refer to what a person accepts as true or untrue about things; they are based upon images of past experience, current knowledge and information, continuing perceptions, etc. Values involve a person's likes and dislikes, love and hate, desires and fears; how a person evaluates objects and the intensity of his judgments—strong, weak, neutral—are at issue. Expectations consist of the person's image of what a situation will be like after acting; expectations derive from taking into account what has happened in the past, the current situation, and how things might turn out given certain possible lines of conduct.

Bearing these assumptions and distinctions in mind, only one more clarification is necessary before turning to a characterization of public opinion. What is an opinion? Simply put, an opinion is an act of expressing what a person believes, values, and expects with respect to specific objects and specific situations.[37] The act may be a vote, verbal statement, written document, or even silence; in short, any meaningful act is an expression of opinion. Put another way, a person expressing an opinion indicates the meaning that individual places upon things taken into account.

The *opinion process* is the relationship or linkage between (1) the beliefs, values, and proposals that private individuals express in public and (2) the policy choices public officials make in regulating social conduct under conditions of conflict, i.e., in politics.[38] There are three stages in that process:

> *Personal construction* is the stage in which individuals take things into account, interpret them, and construct private, subjective meanings of political objects.
> *Social construction* is the stage of public expression of private opin-

ions. That public expression takes three forms. (1) The give-and-take of private opinions within social groups results in the expression of a *group opinion.* (2) When persons express views not through organized groups but through the relative privacy of the voting booth, letters to congressmen, responses to an opinion pollster, etc., these choices made in isolation and separation from one another constitute *popular opinion.*[39] (3) *Mass opinion* is the generally diffuse, unorganized expression of views frequently symbolized as culture, consensus, and what politicians glibly refer to as "public opinion."

Political construction is the stage linking opinion publics, popular, and mass opinions to the activities of public officials (executives, legislators, administrators, and judges) sharing the responsibility for initiating, formulating, adopting, applying, interpreting, and evaluating policies.

As communication is key to politics, so it is to public opinion. When all is said and done, political and opinion processes are aspects and phases of communication. It is especially appropriate, therefore, to adopt a communication perspective in studying public opinion.

A COMMUNICATION PERSPECTIVE ON PUBLIC OPINION

In 1948 political scientist Harold Lasswell suggested that a convenient way to describe an act of communication is to answer the following questions:

> Who
> Says What
> In Which Channel
> To Whom
> With What Effects?[40]

This simple statement identifies the elements common to all communication: a source and receiver, message, medium of communication, and response. Whether elaborated in highly sophisticated theories of information transmissions[41] or in provocative sociopsychological views,[42] Lasswell's basic pentad provides a useful way of analyzing communication.

Its basic utility notwithstanding, as it stands Lasswell's formula is a little too simple for organizing a discussion of political communication and public opinion. With a few modifications, however, the formula will serve our purposes. As stated, the five basic questions imply that communication is a one-way street, *from* someone *to* someone. We have described communication, however, as joint action between and among persons who are not independent nor isolable from one another, but bonded through the meanings they derive from exchanging images through symbols. Source does not communicate to receiver followed by a role reversal (source becoming receiver and receiver becoming source). Rather the communication is *with* one another simultaneously. To be sure, only one person may be speaking at a time. Yet both (or all those involved in the transaction) continuously behave—responding; giving off signs through gestures such as a nod of the head, shrug of the shoulders, or smile; attributing meaning to one another's acts; and constructing meaning for the entire encounter. If we employ Lasswell's formula, then, we must bear in mind that the process of communication is not linear, but circular. As a reminder, we can make a small change in that series of questions: who says what in which channel *with* (rather than *to*) whom with what effect?

In addition to sequence and linearity, Lasswell's formula implies that communication is a structure of five elements. Although it enhances simplicity and clarity to think of communication as involving five separate components, as Barnlund argues, "a structural approach, with its static elements and terminal implications, does not fit a process like communication." Quoting Arthur Clarke, Barnlund makes the point that "There is," according to Clarke, "no demarcation of a boundary between the parts of a communication process." But Lasswell's formula delineates boundaries. To overcome that problem the reader must remember the oversimplification which is implied in the formula and apply Barnlund's admonition: "Linear causality, with its sharp demarcation of independent and dependent variables, no longer gives sensible structure to observation.[43]

Finally, "who says what in which channel with whom with what effect" will be more useful in organizing the chapters and discussion that follow, if we specify what kinds of things we will consider in this pentad of questions.

Who?

Prior to World War II there was considerable scholarly interest in how political leaders appealed to and mobilized support among followers. In part that interest grew out of the fascination and concern with the successes of a few notable revolutionaries and agitators in Europe, all of whom relied in large measure upon "powers of oratory" to "sway the masses"—Lenin and Trotsky in Russia, Hitler in Germany, Mussolini in Italy. For that matter oratorical eloquence always occupied a prominent place in American politics. Franklin Roosevelt (and Theodore before him), Woodrow Wilson, William Jennings Bryan, Albert Beveridge, the political stump speakers—all contributed to the building of a rich tradition of political oratory in our politics. Rhetorical skill often appeared to be a prerequisite for political leadership.

Moreover, in the years surrounding World War II, interest in political communication and communicators heightened as propaganda became as essential as armaments to modern warfare. During that conflict and the cold war that followed, analysis of propaganda (the type of "content analysis" described in the appendix) became a major enterprise of social scientists and propagandists themselves. At approximately the same period, commercial advertising on radio, and later television, seemed to have remarkable success in marketing consumer goods of all varieties. This sustained interest in the study of communicators and the content of their messages.

However, something happened to dampen that interest: the appearance one upon another of studies indicating that political communication and the communicators might not deserve much attention. They really didn't have, the research indicated, much effect upon audiences. Despite all the informative and pursuasive messages expounded by politicians, people turned out to be little involved and informed about politics. Moreover, effects of the mass media were filtered out by many other things—social groups, psychological states of mind, standing political loyalties. Appeals in campaigns had little to do with how people chose to vote.[44] Behavioral scientists began to turn away from the study of "who" communicates and to examine voters and nonvoters or participants and nonparticipants in the audience. Researchers asked how social class and position influenced political behavior; how people were socialized into politics; if democracy were possible if people did not take an active, informed, rational role in government; how an individual's personality shapes political conduct; or how organized interest groups affect policy making. This is not to say that interest in political communication and leadership vanished completely;[45] rather, it simply was no longer at the forefront.

We now have come, if not full circle, at least back to a renewed interest in "who says what." There is, for instance, renewed interest in pursuasive communications in winning electoral campaigns.[46] The role of mass media (especially television) in bringing home to Americans things remote from their lives—a war in Vietnam, the scandals of Watergate, urban riots, presidential nominating conventions—has increased interest in how professional communicators such as television journalists or anchorpersons influence what people believe, feel, and do about politics.

Chapter 2, "The Political Communicators" (and the whole of Parts One and Two), reflects the renewed and growing concern of students of communication in the question, "Who are our political communicators?" We identify three types of political leaders who, because of their active role in generating messages relevant to the regulation of conflict, are key political communicators. These political communicators are the "pols," politicians who make a living out of running for and serving in public office, the "pros," professionals who make a living out of manipulating communication, and the "vols," who are private citizens active in politics on a part-time, voluntary basis. We shall examine the nature of their political leadership, the dimensions of their role, their characteristics, their motives and intentions, and the problems associated with their activity.

Says What?

In the circular process whereby people define the meaning of things through their conduct, meanings which simultaneously affect that conduct in a reciprocal fashion, they use their imagination. Simply put, a person responds to an immediate stimulus on the basis of perception and interpretation of it. That orientation, as stated earlier, involves both recollection of past conduct relating to that stimulus (or a similar one) and how one imagines the future will be after responding to it. "Even in the simplest process of perception of a . . . thing the future as an image is already imbedded in the act. These futures are always hypothetical, because it is not until the act is carried out that the reality of the act is assured."[47] This business of *putting together the past, present, and future constitutes imagery,* i.e., *the image* (subjective understanding or interpretation) *of the act.* A person creates a host of images with respect to a wide variety of politically relevant objects (e.g., candidates for public office, political institutions, major issues, etc.). The stimuli which contribute to that imagery are *messages,* the "says what" of Lasswell's formula.

Chapters 3 and 4 examine the part messages play in the opinion process. Chapter 3, "Political Talk: Symbols, Languages, and Public Opinion," has a dual focus. A major portion of politics is talk. To understand the "says what" of political communication, it helps to look first at the language people use in talking, the phenomenon of political linguistics. Among our key concerns are exploration of the nature and uses of political language; types of language; and what we label semantics, syntactics, and pragmatics of political linguistics. Since messages reach us in symbolic form, the second focus of Chapter 3 is upon political symbols—what symbols are; the use of words, pictures, and actions as symbols; and the uses of symbols in enhancing politics as a viable means of making society possible. By joining a discussion of political language and symbols, the chapter explores meanings people attribute to political messages through imagery. Social scientist Kenneth Boulding has written that *"the meaning of a message is the change which it produces in the image."*[48] This message-image relationship is the object of inquiry in Chapter 3.

Political communicators employ languages and symbols both to inform and convince audiences. The emphasis of Chapter 4, "Political Persuasion:

Propaganda, Advertising, and Rhetoric," is upon the pursuasive aspects of political communication. There are currently three leading theories of how political leaders attempt to influence the conduct of followers by pursuasive messages. We shall examine each, note their differences and similarities, and see how they combine to suggest that, as singer Ray Charles has said, there are "different strokes for different folks." To the degree that it is helpful we shall note how pursuasion subsumes other types of communication—information, education, public relations, etc. Finally, we shall consider leading techniques of pursuasion directed at opinion publics and mass opinion. As noted later, however, we reserve discussion of the effects of pursuasive communications for Chapter 10.

In Which Channel(s)?

This portion of Lasswell's pentad pertains to the media. It is more aptly phrased in the plural, "in which channels," for there is a complex variety of media people use when communicating about politics. Part Two is an effort to simplify some of that complexity, first, by looking at three varieties of communication channels and, second, by exploring a few of the key facets and problems in the relationship between politics and the press in the United States.

The current fashion in many journalistic analyses of American politics attributes a significant, even determining, role to the mass media in shaping the political behavior of the average citizen. Certainly mass communications are a major source of the political messages people take into account in constructing their political conduct. Yet there are other media, and these too must be considered in any effort to understand contemporary political communication and public opinion. We endeavor to do this in Chapter 5, "The Political Media: Mass, Interpersonal, and Organizational Channels." As the title indicates, we distinguish three varieties of channels, examine theories pertaining thereto, and consider how each influences the political conduct of differing types of audiences.

What role do the news media have in providing the raw material from which citizens create their political images and construct their political behavior? That is the subject of Chapter 6, "Political News: Government and Press as Sources and Channels of Political Communication." If our political conduct derives from the meanings we attribute to political objects, then the news media occupy a significant position in the communication-opinion process by virtue of the fact that we obtain so much of our political information directly from television newscasts and newspapers. A nationwide survey conducted in 1972, for example, revealed that only one American in ten usually found out "what's going on in the world today" from a source other than television or newspapers, such as radio, magazines, or other people.[49] What newspersons define and distribute as "news" is a key element in the personal construction of opinion. In Chapter 6 we examine how people in the news business construct the meaning of news and "*the* news story." Moreover, we explore the relationships between reporters and public officials, how both are actively engaged in creating and making news, and the implications of their conduct for political communication and public opinion in America.

To (With) Whom?

Communication, we have said, involves the joint conduct, or trans-action, of source and receiver. The audiences of political communication are not passive receptacles into which political leaders with varying characteristics and motives simply pour diverse appeals by means of attractive language, symbols, devices, and media. Rather, the receivers are active participants in communication *with* sources—perceiving, interpreting, imagining, defining, and otherwise conducting themselves in ways that have message value. In this sense, therefore, the dichotomy between communicators and audiences, leaders and led, is false. At best the distinction is arbitrary; where everyone is, in effect, a political communicator of some variety it is a matter of perspective as to which party we designate "communicator" and which "communicatee."[50] But, if we—author and reader—are to communicate about political communication, then distinguish and designate we must. Hence, in Part Three we sort from the process of communication the members of the audience, the "with whom" of Lasswell's slightly modified formula.

Chapter 7, "Public Opinion: Mass, Publics, and Popular Expressions," distinguishes three ways citizens divide into audiences on the basis of their political beliefs, values, and expectations. Moreover, this chapter examines how mass opinion, opinion publics, and popular opinion form out of the articulation of individual views. In so doing it extends our concerns beyond the personal construction of private opinion to the social construction of public opinion.

During the last three decades a great deal of research has sought to find out what Americans think, feel, and want to do about their government. In Chapter 8, "The Distribution of Public Opinion: The One, Few, and Many," we summarize the most significant findings of that research and describe what is on the minds of members of various political audiences in contemporary America. We take a particularly close look at the notions of conflict and consensus in American politics, the role of organized and unorganized opinion, and the distinction between mass opinion, opinion publics, and popular opinion as manifestations of public opinion in America.

With What Effect(s)?

Again an alteration in Lasswell's formula is warranted. First, any act of communication can have numerous effects rather than one. Certainly plural effects are common with political communication. Second, it will not do, as with Lasswell's unmodified statement, to leave the impression that effects of communication derive from the interaction of three separable elements: the message, the audience allegedly to be influenced, and the resulting effects. Once more the overlap between message, human interpretation, and human conduct must be emphasized. "Effects" of "who says what in which channels with whom" are not established independently of the defining processes of—to borrow a term from a children's tale by Dr. Seuss, *The Grinch Who Stole Christmas*—all the Whos in Whoville that constitute the "whom" of the Lasswell formula. Effects, in short, are not established apart from interpretation: rather, effects are the continuous interpretative acts derived from the personal, social, and political construction of opinion.[51]

Within this context Part Four focuses upon four areas of such effects. The first deals with how and what people learn about politics throughout life—but especially in their pre-adult years—through communication. Chapter 9, "Learning About Politics: Consequences of Socializing Communications," deals with two facets of political learning. One consists of describing the general process of pre-adult political socialization; the content of beliefs, values, and expectations people learn; and the types of experiences people have (in the family, school, etc.) which influence learning. The second facet deals with the development of political personality and the relationship of psychological factors to political learning and the individual's construction of opinions.

Chapter 10, "Participating in Politics: Consequences of Politicizing Communications," extends the discussion of the preceding chapter. Two questions are uppermost in this account: what kinds of effects do the persuasive efforts of political communicators (discussed in Chapter 4) have upon changes in the thoughts, feelings, and plans of citizens; what considerations influence citizens' choices of whether to register those beliefs, values, and expectations through political participation? At this point, we thus make the transition from accounts of the personal and social to the political construction of public opinion.

Certainly one of the key ways to bring popular opinions to the attention of potential policy makers is through elections. Chapter 11, "Influencing Voting: Consequences of Electoral Communications," examines this aspect of the opinion process. Specifically it considers the relative impact of the factors people take into account in constructing their voting choices. We are especially concerned with the influence of persuasive communications within a political campaign in contrast to the alleged tendencies of voters' partisan, social, ideological, and policy preferences.

The final chapter, "Influencing Officials: Consequences of Policy Communication," explores the relation between public opinion and policy making in American government. At issue here is the representation of citizens' beliefs, values, and plans through policy making. We shall examine theories of representation and the alternative means of opinion representation in America. Of the extraconstitutional means we include the role of elections, political parties, organized groups, public opinion polls, the news media, and mass action. And among constitutional agencies of representation, we consider the presidency, Congress, administrative agencies, and courts in the opinion process. There is no presumption that the views of *all* private citizens are reflected in public policies; that is, there is no one-to-one relationship between personal, social, and political constructions in the opinion process. Contingencies rather than fidelity in communications are common. The sources of these contingencies occupy the discussion in the concluding section of this final chapter.

CONCLUSION

A quarter of a century ago political scientist Oliver Garceau wrote about the "political process" in ways that aptly summarize the view of this text regarding how political communication occurs within what we have labled the opinion process, which is the relationship between the beliefs, values, and proposals of private individuals and the policy choices public officials make. Said Garceau: "The political process may, therefore, be conceived and studied in terms of multiple, parallel, collaborating and competing patterns of inter-action linking citizen and active participants in key positions of decision-making." He noted that "some relations are indirect but constitute a reasonably continuous chain reaction spanning the whole political distance," yet "many meaningful patterns span only part of the way, from either pole or a segment without readily discernible impact at either pole." Still, "these segmental patterns overlap, and condition behavior and relationships in other segments." What it adds up to, Garceau concluded, is that "much of the time, indeed, the important processes of democratic politics may paradoxically consist of a discontinuous continuum of relationships."[52]

How can we view this "discontinuous continuum," or the opinion process? The individual citizen (but one of several million) constructs choices to participate or not participate in political activity. In the interpretative process of personal construction, the citizen takes into account several potential influences upon possible responses to political communications: social and socializing influences (fellows, family, peers, others regarded as significant in one's life, etc.); tendencies in beliefs, values, plans, and psychological makeup; and legal and constitutional factors. Through choices to participate or not, and how, the citizen also constructs and expresses opinions. The social construction of public opinion provides popular consensus on some matters (the one), opinions of diverse publics on the others (the few), and the sum of individually expressed opinions of the masses on others (the many). And through various representative devices, a political construction of public opinion occurs as policy makers take into account selected views in making choices under conditions of conflict.

Such are the various aspects of the opinion process examined in the following chapters. The word "aspects" is to be taken seriously, that is, to denote "the components of a full transactional situation, being not independents,"[53] the circular, overlapping, reciprocal, and transactional quality of the process alluded to in this entire discussion. Depending upon one's perspective, therefore, the flow of the opinion process may be viewed as from the activities of citizen to policy maker; but it is just as reasonable to view the process as flowing from policy maker to citizen. In any event, as Garceau stresses, there is seldom a direct sequence; multiple patterns sometimes parallel, sometimes overlap; segmentation interrupts continuity; and the continuum is discontinuous. In our desire to make sense out of a process with no discernible origin or terminus, design, or direction, we must guard against the tendency to see more order in the process than there may be, to overstructure and overinterpret political, communication, and opinion processes. The Greek playwright Aristophanes may have been correct: "Whirl is King, having driven out Zeus." Yet, even in the face of such chaos and bearing in mind such admonitions about the difficulties of doing so, it is time to obey the command of the King to the White Rabbit in *Alice in Wonderland:* "Where shall I begin, please your majesty?" "Begin at the beginning," the King said, very gravely, "and go on till you come to the end; then stop."

BIBLIOGRAPHY

The purpose of these remarks (and those that appear at the end of each chapter and in the appendix) is to suggest selected works that the reader will find useful in pursuing a more detailed understanding of political communication and public opinion in America. Moreover, along with works cited in the footnotes, the suggested readings provide readers with the sources of the key ideas incorporated into this text.

A work that receives all too little attention as a basis for developing the scientific study of human behavior is *Knowing and the Known* (Boston: Beacon Press, 1949) by John Dewey and Arthur Bentley. The book is in the philosophic tradition of pragmatism and the writings of Charles Pierce, William James, and George Herbert Mead. Dewey and Bentley offer the view that the process of knowing and what people know are twin aspects of common activity, knowings and knowns are derived from transactions of observers and observed, and the subject matter of study is activity itself. The authors devote a considerable portion of this complex treatise to problems of terminology, even attempting to generate a "trial group of names" to use and/or avoid in scientific investigation. The reader will find a lengthy discussion of process and the distinction between self-action, inter-action, and trans-action modes of interpretations. *Knowing and the Known* carries the perspective, tone, and style of both authors, but readers familiar with other works of Arthur F. Bentley—especially *The Process of Government* (Chicago: University of Chicago Press, 1908; now available in a 1967 edition through The Belknap Press, Cambridge, Massachusetts) and *Behavior Knowledge Fact* (Bloomington, Ind.: The Principia Press, 1935)—will note his influence. To place the Dewey and Bentley point of view within the development of philosophic analyses and communication study, the reader should consult, first, Charles Morris, *The Pragmatic Movement in American Philosophy* (New York: George Braziller, 1970), then Hugh Dalziel Duncan, *Communication and Social Order* (New York: Oxford University Press, 1962).

The whole question of the nature of knowings, knowns, interpretations, and scientific inquiry is one of continuing commentary. For a few of the perspectives underlying the argument in this introductory chapter the reader might turn to the following: Thomas S. Kuhn, *The Structure of Scientific Revolutions* (Chicago: University of Chicago Press, 1962); Karl Mannheim, *Ideology and Utopia* (New York: International Library of Psychology, Philosophy, and Scientific Method, 1936); and, of course, David Hume's *Inquiry Concerning Human Understanding*, available in many printings.

The point of view reflected in this introductory chapter derives from the general orientation of symbolic interaction. The basic statement of the symbolic interactionist position is George Herbert Mead's *Mind, Self, and Society* (Chicago: University of Chicago Press, 1934). Readable introductions to Mead's thought include Bernard N. Meltzer, "Mead's Social Psychology," in Jerome G. Manis and Bernard N. Meltzer, eds., *Symbolic Interaction* (Boston: Allyn and Bacon, 1967), pp. 5–24; Arnold Rose, "A Systematic Summary of Symbolic Interaction Theory," in Rose, ed., *Human Behavior and Social Process: An Interactionist Approach* (Boston: Houghton Mifflin, 1962), pp. 3–19; and Norman K. Denzin, "Symbolic Interactionism and Ethnomethodology: A Proposed Synthesis," *American Sociological Review*, 34 (December, 1969): 922–34. Two of the best statements of the application of the symbolic interactionist to problems of communication and opinion are Herbert Blumer, *Symbolic Interactionism* (Englewood Cliffs, N.J.: Prentice-Hall, 1969), a volume containing several of Blumer's previously published essays, and Peter M. Hall, "A Symbolic Interactionist Analysis of Politics," *Sociological Inquiry*, 42 (1972): 35–75.

Few fields of social inquiry spawn as many books published in a given year as the study of communication. A volume containing a diverse sampling of views is Lee Thayer, *Communication: Concepts and Perspectives* (Washington, D.C.: Spartan Books, 1967). See especially the essay by Harley C. Shands, "Outline of a General Theory of Human Communication: Implications of Normal and Pathological Schizogenesis," pp. 97–134. Three works provide an excellent orientation to communication as a transactional process: Dean C. Barnlund, "A Transactional Model of Communication," in Kenneth K. Sereno and C. David Mortensen, eds., *Foundations of Communication Theory* (New York: Harper & Row, 1970), pp. 83–102; Hans Toch and Malcolm S. MacLean, Jr., "Perception, Communication and Educational Research: A Transactional View," *Audio-Visual Communication Review*, 10 (July, 1970): 55–76; and William H. Ittelson and Hadley Cantril, *Perception: A Transactional Approach* (Garden City, N.Y.: Doubleday & Co., Inc., 1954). For a potpourri of what general areas concern students of communication, consult Ithiel de Sola Pool et al., eds., *Handbook of Communication* (Chicago: Rand McNally Publishing Co., 1973).

Many theories of communication exist, but it is convenient here to group them into two major categories. The first consists of information theories of communication. *The Mathematical Theory of Communication* (Urbana: University of Illinois Press, 1949) by Claude E. Shannon and Warren Weaver; J. R. Pierce, *Symbols, Signals and Noise* (New York: Harper & Row, 1961); Karl W. Deutsch, *The Nerves of Government* (London: The Free Press of Glencoe, 1963); and to a lesser degree in Colin Cherry, *On Human Communication* (New York: Science Editions, Inc., 1961). Generally the focus of works in this category is upon signal transmission, information processing, cybernetics, and communication engineering. A useful introduction is Wilbur Schramm, "Information Theory and Mass Communication," *Journalism Quarterly,* 32 (Spring 1955): 131–46. A second set of theories focuses upon human relational, entertainment and play aspects of communication. The best work is William Stephenson, *The Play Theory of Mass Communication* (Chicago: University of Chicago Press, 1967). See also George A. Miller, *The Psychology of Communication* (New York: Basic Books, 1967) and Paul Watzlawick et al., *Pragmatics of Human Communication* (New York: W. W. Norton, 1967). The place of other theorists, including Marshall McLuhan, we consider in Chapter 4.

There are numerous books currently available regarding the nature of public opinion. Curiously, the best remain those published some time ago. A case in point is Leonard W. Doob's *Public Opinion and Propaganda* first published in 1948, now available in a 1966 edition (Hamden, Connecticut: Archon Books). Readers will still learn a great deal from Walter Lippmann's classic *Public Opinion* (New York: Macmillan, 1922). And, although it has portions that now appear dated, the most comprehensive work by a political scientist concerned strictly with public opinion is V. O. Key, Jr., *Public Opinion and American Democracy* (New York: Alfred Knopf, 1961).

Viewed from the standpoint of process, any interpretation of political communication and public opinion is but one *possible* point of view. The observer of process takes to heart the uncertainty principle of Heisenberg, that at a point in space and time interpretations and images consist of but momentary perceptions of possibilities. Thus it is perhaps presumptuous to claim too much for a given interpretation and, more so, to overstructure and overinterpret indeterminate processes. Readers will find this possibility explored in Stanford M. Lyman and Marvin B. Scott, *A Sociology of the Absurd* (New York: Appleton-Century-Crofts, 1970).

NOTES

1. John Dewey and Arthur F. Bentley, *Knowing and the Known* (Boston: Beacon Press, 1949), p. 108.

2. For example, see Christopher Jencks, et al., *Inequality* (New York: Basic Books, 1972), Ch. 3.

3. Angus Campbell et al., *The Voter Decides* (Evanston, Ill.: Row, Peterson, 1954), p. 187.

4. Dewey and Bentley, *Knowing and the Known,* p. 108.

5. Herbert Blumer, *Symbolic Interactionism* (Englewood Cliffs, N.J.: Prentice-Hall, 1969), p. 213.

6. Blumer, *Symbolic Interactionism,* p. 15.

7. Dewey and Bentley, *Knowing and the Known,* p. 108.

8. J. L. Aranguren, *Human Communication* (New York: McGraw-Hill, 1967), p. 11.

9.   Melvin L. DeFleur, *Theories of Mass Communication,* 2nd ed. (New York: David McKay, 1970), p. 91.

10.   Wilbur Schramm, "How Communication Works," in Jean M. Civikly, ed., *Messages* (New York: Random House, 1974), p. 6.

11.   Colin Cherry, *On Human Communication* (New York: Science Editions, Inc., 1961), p. 6.

12.   John C. Merrill and Ralph L. Lowenstein, *Media, Messages, and Men* (New York: David McKay, 1971), pp. 5–6.

13.   Don Fabun, *Communications: The Transfer of Meaning* (Beverly Hills, Cal.: Glencoe Press, 1968), p. 15.

14.   George A. Theodorson and Achilles G. Theodorson, *A Modern Dictionary of Sociology* (New York: Thomas Y. Crowell, 1969), p. 62.

15.   William Stephenson, *The Play Theory of Mass Communication* (Chicago: University of Chicago Press, 1967), p. 8.

16.   Lee Thayer, *Communication and Communication Systems* (Homewood, Illinois: Richard D. Irwin, 1968), pp. 26–7.

17.   Dean C. Barnlund, "A Transactional Model of Communication," in Kenneth K. Sereno and C. David Mortensen, eds., *Foundations of Communication Theory* (New York: Harper & Row, 1970), pp. 87–8.

18.   George H. Mead, *Mind, Self and Society* (Chicago: University of Chicago Press, 1934).

19.   Paul Watzlawick et al., *Pragmatics of Human Communication* (New York: W. W. Norton, 1967), pp. 48–51.

20.   Norman Jacobson, "Causality and Time in Political Process: A Speculation," *American Political Science Review,* 58 (March 1964): 15–22. See also David Hume, "An Enquiry Concerning Human Understanding," in Edwin A. Burtt, ed., *The English Philosophers from Bacon to Mill* (New York: The Modern Library, 1939), pp. 585–689.

21.   Harold Lasswell, *Politics: Who Gets What, When, How* (New York: Meridian Books, 1958).

22.   David Easton, *The Political System* (New York: Alfred A. Knopf, 1953).

23.   G. E. G. Catlin, *A Study of the Principles of Politics* (New York: Macmillan, 1930); Robert A. Dahl, *Modern Political Analysis* (Englewood Cliffs, N.J.: Prentice-Hall, 1963).

24.   Edward C. Banfield, *Political Influence* (New York: The Free Press of Glencoe, 1961).

25.   Michael Weinstein, *Philosophy, Theory and Method in Contemporary Political Thought* (Glenview, Ill.: Scott, Foresman and Co., 1971).

26.   Arthur F. Bentley, *The Process of Government* (Cambridge, Mass.: The Belknap Press of Harvard University Press, 1967).

27.   Mark Roelofs, *The Language of Modern Politics* (Homewood, Ill.: The Dorsey Press, 1967).

28.   H. L. Mencken, *A Mencken Chrestomathy* (New York: Alfred A. Knopf, 1956), p. 622.

29.   James Bryce, *Modern Democracies,* vol. I (New York: Macmillan, 1924), p. 153.

30.   A. V. Dicey, *Law and Public Opinion in England* (New York: Macmillan, 1914), p. 3.

31.   Bentley, *Process of Government,* p. 223.

32.   V. O. Key, Jr., *Public Opinion and American Democracy* (New York: Alfred A. Knopf, 1961), p. 14.

33.   "Toward a Science of Public Opinion," *Public Opinion Quarterly,* 1 (1937): 7–23.

34. Blumer, *Symbolic Interactionism*, p. 2.

35. Bentley, *Process of Government*, p. 185.

36. Blumer, *Symbolic Interactionism*, p. 97 (emphasis added).

37. Compare Bernard Berelson and Gary A. Steiner, *Human Behavior* (New York: Harcourt, Brace & World, 1964), pp. 557–58.

38. Contrast the above discussion with that in Bernard Hennessy, *Public Opinion*, 3rd ed. (North Scituate, Mass: Duxbury Press, 1975), pp. 323–34, and James N. Rosenau, *Public Opinion and Foreign Policy* (New York: Random House, 1961), p. 16.

39. Stephenson, *Play Theory of Mass Communication*, p. 34. See also Herbert Blumer, "The Mass, the Public, and Public Opinion," in Bernard Berelson and Morris Janowitz, eds., *Reader in Public Opinion and Communication*, 2nd ed. (New York: The Free Press, 1966), pp. 43–50.

40. Harold D. Lasswell, "The Structure and Function of Communication in Society," in Lyman Bryson, ed., *The Communication of Ideas* (New York: Harper and Row, 1948), p. 37.

41. Claude E. Shannon and Warren Weaver, *The Mathematical Theory of Communication* (Urbana: University of Illinois Press, 1949).

42. See, for instance, Bruce H. Westley and Malcolm S. MacLean, Jr., "A Conceptual Model for Communication Research," *Journalism Quarterly,* 34 (Winter 1957): 31–8.

43. "A Transactional Model for Communication," pp. 90–1.

44. As an example of but one compilation of "effects" research, consult Joseph T. Klapper, *The Effects of Mass Communication* (Glencoe, Ill.: The Free Press, 1960), especially "The Bases of Pessimism," pp. 2–4.

45. Murray Edelman, *The Symbolic Uses of Politics* (Urbana: University of Illinois Press, 1964).

46. See Lynda Lee Kaid et al., *Political Campaign Communication: A Bibliography and Guide to the Literature* (Metuchen, N.J.: The Scarecrow Press, Inc., 1974).

47. Hugh Dalziel Duncan, *Symbols and Social Theory* (New York: Oxford University Press, 1969), p. 210. On this key feature of imagery as symbolic interaction consult Mead's "The Function of Imagery in Conduct," in *Mind, Self, and Society*, pp. 337–46.

48. Kenneth E. Boulding, *The Image* (Ann Arbor: University of Michigan, Ann Arbor Paperback, 1961), p. 7 (emphasis in original).

49. *What People Think of Television and Other Mass Media 1959–1972* (New York: The Roper Organization, Inc., 1973).

50. The limitations our language imposes upon us in trying to talk about communication are amply illustrated in Arthur F. Bentley, *Behavior Knowledge Fact* (Bloomington, Indiana: The Principia Press, 1935), especially Chs. 23–26.

51. Blumer, *Symbolic Interactionism*, Ch. 11.

52. "Research in the Political Process," *American Political Science Review,* 45 (March 1951): 69–85; the quotation is from the reprinted article in Heinz Eulau et al., eds., *Political Behavior* (Glencoe, Ill.: The Free Press, 1956), p. 44.

53. Dewey and Bentley, *Knowing and the Known,* p. 290.

part one

COMMUNICATING ABOUT POLITICS:
Who Says What?

chapter 2

The Political Communicators:
Leaders and Public Opinion

One of the characteristics of communication is that people can scarcely avoid taking part. Simply being in the presence and taken into account by another person has message value. In the most general sense, therefore, we are all communicators. By the same token anyone in a political setting is a political communicator. This extends from the unemployed craftsman standing in line for food stamps and complaining that "the president took my job when he closed the navy yard" to the president himself deploring the state of the economy. The communication-opinion process is so all-encompassing that each of us at least has the potential of being a political communicator. Our focus in this chapter, however, is not so broad. Although recognizing that everyone may communicate about politics, we accept the fact that relatively few do so, at least on anything like a regular, sustained basis. These relatively few persons not only exchange political messages, they are leaders in the opinion process. These political communicators, compared with the general run of citizens, are taken more seriously when they speak and act. In this chapter we shall identify three categories of these key political communicators, then examine the principal elements and aspects of their role as political leaders. Finally, we shall consider the contemporary uncertainties surrounding the role of political communicators in the United States.

IDENTIFYING KEY COMMUNICATORS IN POLITICS

Sociologist J. D. Halloran, a close observer of mass communication, has lamented that many communication studies lose sight of an important characteristic of the process, which is that communication occurs in a social matrix. The situation in which communication originates, develops, and continues is social: the relationships between communicators and audiences are an integral part of this social system. Simple though this notion is, notes Halloran, the insensitivity of many communication theorists has led to an "imbalance"; they devote far more attention to studying the effects of communication than to communicators. Too readily, theorists ignore "the mass communicator as one who occupies a sensitive central position in a social network, rejecting and selecting information in response to a variety of pressures all within a given social system."[1]

What Halloran says about the mass communicator applies equally to the political communicator. The latter plays a key social role, particularly within the public opinion process. Investigators once emphasized that role, perhaps too much. Karl Popper, for instance, notes that one entire theory of public opinion was built around it, the "avant-garde theory of public opinion." It asserts that leaders create public opinion because they "manage to get some ideas first rejected and later debated and finally accepted"; hence, "public opinion is here conceived as a kind of public response to the thoughts and efforts of those aristocrats of the mind who produce new thoughts, new ideas, new arguments."[2] Popper thinks the avant-garde theory overestimates the influence of "aristocrats of the mind." Indeed, the theory was such an oversimplification that it fell quickly before the onslaught of evidence generated by social scientific studies in the 1950s and 1960s into the effects of communications upon political participation, voting, learning about politics, public opinion, and policy making. Finding limited "effects" (something we shall examine in detail in Part Four), behavioral scientists discarded the avant-garde theory. But this created precisely the imbalance decried by Halloran. Although there have been studies of political leaders, elites, journalists, opinion leaders, and professional persuaders, they have not investigated the several levels of political communicators in anything like the detail in which political scientists have examined voters and opinion holders.

An advocate of greater understanding of the role of the communicator in the opinion process, Leonard W. Doob, suggests the kinds of things worth knowing about them: "The communicator can be analyzed in his own right. His attitudes toward his potential audience, the prestige he accords them as people, may affect the communication he produces; thus, if he thinks them morons, he is likely to pitch his message at a correspondingly low level. He himself has certain capabilities which can be conceptualized in terms of the resources he commands, his experience as a communicator with similar or dissimilar audiences, and the role which the motive to communicate plays within his personality."[3]

We cannot discuss all these features of political communicators, but we can start to understand some of them. The place to begin is by doing something urged by Doob: "Obviously the communicator or communicators must be identified and their status within the society determined."[4] For our purposes three categories of political communicators can be identified—that of the *politician* acting as a political communicator, that of the *professional* communicator in politics, and that of the *activist*, or part-time political communicator.

The Politician as Political Communicator

Persons who aspire to and/or occupy public office must and do communicate about politics. We label these aspirants and occupants as politicians no matter whether they are elected, appointed, or career officials, and regardless of whether the office is executive, legislative, or judicial. Their vocation is politics, and acting as political communicators is a featured aspect of the enterprise. Although politicians serve a variety of ends by communicating, two stand out. Daniel Katz points out that political leaders exert influence in two directions: "to affect the allocation of rewards and to change the existing social structure or to prevent such change."[5] In the first capacity the politician communicates as a *representative* of some group or clientele; the politician's messages advance and/or protect the cause of political interests; i.e., the political communicator represents group benefits. In contrast, the politician acting as *ideologist* is less centrally concerned with pressing the claims of a client, more devoted to defining broad policy goals, seeking reforms, and even promoting revolutionary change. The ideologist communicates primarily to convert people to a cause rather than merely to represent their interests in an arena of bargaining and compromise. Katz distinguishes between partisan representative and ideologist, but considered as political communicators, these are differences in degree rather than of kind. Both types of politicians influence other people; i.e., they act intentionally to affect the opinions of others. The partisan representative achieves a change or prevents a change in opinion by bargaining to make situations mutually advantageous to all parties as in the classical case of logrolling when legislators agree that "I'll vote for your bill if you vote for mine." The ideologist influences not by controlling a situation to the advantage of every interest, but by defining the goals of opposing and/or neutral interests and by bringing people around to one way of thinking. The representative is a broker inducing others to "go along to get along"; the ideologist is a debater offering a "better idea."[6]

In sum, politicians seek influence through communication. Who, then, are the principal politicians who act as key political communicators in our government? First are public officials, both elective and appointive, who communicate regularly about a large number of diverse political issues, items, and matters. This group includes what political scientist

James Rosenau labels "governmental opinion-makers" on "national, multi-issue matters."[7] Numbered in this category are executive officials (the president, members of his Cabinet, his chief advisors and White House staff, etc.); legislators (a U.S. senator, key leaders of the House of Representatives, etc.); and judicial officers, certainly including justices of the U.S. Supreme Court. Second are politicians at the national level who communicate regularly about a limited number of relatively narrow issues, what Rosenau refers to as national, "single-issue" opinion-makers. Among this group are assistant secretaries in various executive departments responsible for specialized areas of activity (for example, an assistant secretary in the U.S. Department of State for Latin American affairs); congressmen who specialize in selected areas of legislation as, for instance, policies related to energy, transportation, housing, etc.; or administrative law judges specializing in hearing and deciding citizens' claims against the government with respect to labor-management disputes, social security benefits, medical problems, etc. Just as at the national level there are two sets of elective/appointive/career officials serving as political communicators—one with respect to a multiplicity of issues and the other concerned primarily with single issues—there are also multi- and single-issue officials at state and local levels. For example, a governor or a city mayor, state legislators and city councilmen, local judges—all speak out on a variety of issues of a subnational nature; and the executive of a local development district, a school board member, a policeman—these are local officers concerned with a relatively specialized series of issues.

There are politicians who do not occupy public office; they too are political communicators about matters of national and nonnational scope, issues of multiple and narrow range. In 1976, for instance, former U.S. Senator Eugene McCarthy campaigned for the presidency as an independent third-party candidate speaking out on a broad range of domestic and foreign issues. Or consider key party organizers such as the national chairmen of the two major political parties, certainly examples of national-level, multi-issue political communicators. A person seeking appointment to a federal regulatory commission (perhaps the Federal Trade Commission or Federal Communications Commission) is concerned with relatively few, highly specialized kinds of issues. And on the state and local level it is easy to identify candidates for office (governors, mayors, state senators, etc.) and party leaders (state chairpersons, committee members) who communicate about many issues, in contrast to school board candidates or party precinct workers devoted only to restricted causes.

In sum, many kinds of politicians act as political communicators, as many as there are politicians, but it is convenient to classify them as (1) in or out of public office, (2) national or subnational in visibility, and (3) concerned with multiple or single issues. In describing the varieties of communications used by these politicians (Chapters 4 and 6), we limit our focus to multi-issue national-level politicians, in and out of executive, legislative, and judicial office. To enlarge our perspective we need now to turn to a second category, professional communicators.

The Professional as Political Communicator

Important though communication may be to success, the politician considers government, rather than communication, as the source of livelihood. This is not the case with the professional communicator, who makes a living by communicating whether in or out of politics. The professional communicator is a relatively new social role, a byproduct of a communications revolution that had at least two other major dimensions: the rise of the mass media that cut across racial, ethnic, occupational, regional, and class boundaries to heighten senses of national identity; and the simultaneous development of specialized media (e.g., special audience magazines, radio stations, etc.) creating new publics for consuming information and entertainment. Both the mass and specialized media rely upon the formation and management of meaningful symbols to appeal to nationwide and special audiences. Here enters the professional communicator "who controls a specific skill in the manipulation of symbols and who utilizes this skill to forge a link between distinct persons or differentiated groups." A professional communicator, says James Carey, "is a broker in symbols, one who translates the attitudes, knowledge, and concerns of one speech community into alternative but suasive and understandable terms of another community." "Professional communicators link elites in any organization or community with general audiences; horizontally he links two differentiated speech communities at the same level of social structure."[8]

The professional communicator, then, is a manipulator and broker of symbols who links leaders with one another and with followers. But the most "distinguishing characteristic of the professional communicator," according to Carey, "is that the message he produces has no *necessary* relation to his own thoughts and perceptions." The professional "operates under the constraints or demands imposed on one side by the ultimate audience and, on the other side, by the ultimate source."[9] That there is no necessary relation of the professional's views to performance does not mean that all professionals exclude personal opinions from their work; editorial writers, columnists, and commentators voice their views in their reports. What Carey calls particular attention to is that class of professionals that translate and interpret the message of one speech community (a client) into the idiom of another (the audience) without substituting their personal views, ideas, or thoughts for the source's or client's message. These professionals sell manipulative, brokering, linkage, and interpretative expertise to politicians and others. Some ply their trade without concern for liking or disliking either the client or audience. Others, such as leading political campaign consultant Joseph Napolitan, work for politicians only of a particular political party or ideological view.[10]

For the "pros," unlike the "pols," communication, not politics, is the profession. From what we have said we can designate two types. As in the case of politicians being partisan representatives and/or ideologists, the distinction is of emphasis, not kind. One set of professionals includes *journalists,* the other, *promoters.*

We speak of journalists as any persons associated with the news media in gathering, preparing, presenting, and delivering accounts of happenings (see Chapter 6). This extends to working reporters for newspapers, magazines, radio, television, or other media; television anchorpersons; publishers; news directors; executives of radio and television news stations or networks; etc.[11]

As professional communicators, journalists typically are employees of news organizations that link news sources and audiences. As we shall see in Chapter 6, they may allow governmental leaders to talk with one another (as when a congressional official finds out what is going on in the Department of State by reading the newspapers), link leaders to the general public (as when a newspaper reader finds out what the president did on a given day), join the general public to leaders (as when a congressman reads the results of the latest published Gallup poll), and help set issues and events on the agenda of public discussion.[12]

Promoters are persons hired to advance the interests of particular clients. Included among promoters are publicity agents of prominent public figures, public relations personnel of private or public organizations, public information officers of government agencies, presidential press secretaries, advertising personnel of corporate enterprises, campaign managers and publicity directors of political candidates, technical specialists (cameramen, film producers and directors, speech coaches, etc.) working on behalf of political candidates and other public figures, administrative assistants to congressmen, and all manner of similar symbol brokers.

Journalists and promoters differ from one another in degree in selected respects: the degree to which each works independently of employers' dictates; the extent that each has a primary obligation to enhance the interests of a news source (e.g., to tell only the client's version of a story) rather than reveal compromising information; the relative freedom, as Carey suggests, "of the communicator in creating a new message versus passively transmitting a preformed message";[13] and the degree that the journalist or promoter is more dependent on source or audience for professional livelihood. Not being in the pay of a news source frees the journalist to be an impartial reporter, at least when compared to the promoter who is acting as a paid cheerleader. But this is not always so. The roles of journalist and promoter often overlap (see Chapter 6). Take, for example, the editor of a local newspaper. Many local editors are members of the community power structure of businessmen, merchants, and government leaders. The pages of their newspapers are less apt to expose political and economic discord than to serve as a vehicle for promotion much like that of the chamber of commerce.[14]

In any event, being professional communicators rather than, as are politicians, professionals who must communicate, sets both journalists and promoters apart from other types of political communicators, especially the political activists.

The Activist as Political Communicator

A basic element in the politician's communication network is the formal governmental apparatus; he either is or aspires to be an occupant of a position within that network. By contrast, professional communicators act out roles either within networks of the mass and specialized media or linking government offices to the media, such as do public information officers in government agencies. Tied into these governmental and media networks are organizational and interpersonal channels that transmit a large portion of the information that the average citizen receives about politics. Serving as these organizational and interpersonal channels are two types of key political communicators.

First, there is the *spokesperson* for an organized interest. Generally this person neither holds nor aspires to public office; in this regard this communicator is unlike the politician for whom politics is a vocation. Nor is the spokesperson normally a professional in communication. Yet the spokesperson is sufficiently involved in both politics and communication to be labeled a political activist and semiprofessional in political communication. Speaking for organized interests is a role similar to that of the politician who is a partisan representative, i.e., representing claims of an organization's membership and bargaining for a favorable hearing. In another sense the spokesperson is akin to the journalist by reporting governmental decisions and policies back to an organization's members. There are many examples of such spokespersons—lobbyists before Congress and executive agencies, leaders of major organizations (George Meany of the American Federation of Labor or Leonard Woodcock, former president of the United Auto Workers, are illustrative), founders and leaders of social movements such as the late Martin Luther King, self-appointed crusaders such as Ralph Nader, and all varieties of rebels with and without causes. As with politicians and professionals, spokespersons of organized interests operate on national and subnational levels and deal with both multiple or single-issue concerns (contrast, for example, the National Commander of the American Legion concerned with many national-level issues with the local president of the Parent Teachers Association dealing with a restricted set of problems).[15] The communication techniques and audiences of such communicators vary: consultation, committee representation, and clientele relations directed at public officials; legislative testimony for Congress, press, and general public; press releases for the media and both their own and opposition group members; and specialized publications for public officials, experts, and organization stalwarts.[16]

Second, the interpersonal network includes another key political communicator, the *opinion leader*. A considerable body of research indicates that many citizens faced with making decisions of a political nature (such as for what candidate to vote) seek out the advice of persons they respect, either to find out what to do or to reinforce a decision already made. The individuals sought out for advice and information are "opinion leaders."[17] They perform in two capacities. In one they exert considerable influence on the decision of others; that is, like ideological politicians or professional promoters, they convince others to their ways of thinking. The proportion of such opinion leaders in the population varies from issue to issue and over time, but one estimate is that about one-fourth of the voters in Congressional elections go to others during the campaign and try to persuade them how to vote; about one-fifth report someone comes to them for advice.[18] In addition to advice, opinion leaders pass along political information from the news media to the general population. In this "two-step flow of communication" ideas "often flow *from* radio and print" (and today television) "*to* the opinion leaders and *from* them to the less active sections of the population."[19] Numerous studies verify the importance of opinion leadership through interpersonal communication as a means of learning about important events:[20] perhaps as high as 85 percent of some groups heard of the death of Franklin Roosevelt through interpersonal communication, and studies of how people learned of the assassination of John F. Kennedy indicated that far higher proportions of people obtained that information from interpersonal networks than from radio, television, or newspapers. The general proposition is that "the greater the news value of an event, the more important will be the interpersonal communication in the diffusion process."[21]

Who then are the key political communicators? There are three principal varieties—the politician, the professional, and the activist. Within each category are political communicators who perform representative and persuasive tasks. Emphasizing the representation of points of view between sources and audiences are partisan representatives, journalists, and spokespersons who define, describe, and change situations for diverse reasons. There are also communicators who persuade, i.e., change points of view within given situations—the ideologists, promoters, and opinion leaders. What distinguishes all of these political communicators from the general population of people who think, talk, and act about politics is their influence in the opinion process. Let us see how.

POLITICAL COMMUNICATORS AND POLITICAL LEADERSHIP

In designating one variety of political communicators as opinion leaders, we remind ourselves of the relation of communication to political leadership. To explore the overlap between communication, influence, leadership, and opinions, let us first look at the general nature of leadership and influence, then turn to selected elements of the role of political communicators acting as political leaders.

Characterizing Political Leadership

Cecil A. Gibb notes that the phenomenon called leadership has captured the attention of thinkers since at least the time of Confucius.[22] Out of all that thought have come numerous definitions of what leadership is (almost as many as thinkers) and several theories of leadership. For example, among the definitions consider the following: "a set of group functions which must occur in any group if it is to behave effectively to satisfy the needs of its members";[23] "the process by which one individual consistently exerts more influence than others in the carrying out of group functions";[24] leaders are members of society who occupy positions which enable them to transmit, with some regularity, opinions about issues to unknown persons;[25] the leader is "the individual in the group who has the task of directing and coordinating task-relevant group activities";[26] and leadership is a group process.[27] Another longtime student of leadership, Ralph M. Stogdill, has summarized these and other definitions by saying leadership involves group process, the effects of personality, the art of inducing compliance, the exercise of influence, persuasion, goal achievement, interaction, differentiated roles, and the initiation of structure in groups.[28]

In addition to numerous definitions of leadership there are several theories of what it's all about. Four, however, dominate the literature.[29] The first holds that leaders stand apart from the mass of people because they possess some single, highly prized trait or characteristic. All kinds of leaders in all kinds of settings and cultures possess this *unitary trait*. A variation on this theme is the Great Man theory, i.e., that men of extraordinary will, character, and ability appear from time to time in history destined to do great things—Napoleon, Gandhi, Jesus Christ, etc. A second variation is that there are three kinds of leaders possessed with certain traits that set them apart: supermen who break traditional rules and create new values for a people, heroes dedicated to great and noble causes, and princes motivated by the desire to dominate others.[30] The difficulty with these unitary trait theories is simply that scholars have not been able to discover a single unitary trait, or even a limited number of distinguishing traits, possessed by all leaders everywhere. This suggests a second view, the *constellation-of-traits* theory. In this theory a leader has the same traits anyone else has but combines those traits in a distinctive leadership syndrome. Hence, for example, the leader might be set apart by being taller, heavier, more energetic, more intelligent, self-confident, well-adjusted, etc. Stogdill in reviewing a wide variety of leadership studies notes that leaders do have some traits to a slightly higher degree than do nonleaders (for example, drive, tolerance of stress, originality in problem solving, etc.). He concludes, however, that this indicates only that personality is one factor in leadership differentiation; the presence of a given syndrome does not guarantee a person a leader role nor does its absence disqualify one for leadership.[31] Students of leadership have countered the trait approach to defining leaders (reflected in the unitary and constellation-of-traits theories) with a third theory, the *situationalist.* This simply holds that time, place, and circumstance determine who leads, who follows. Critics of the situationalist school, however, point out that the theory fails to account for variations in the types of leaders that emerge in different situations or why in some settings no discernible leaders can be identified. A fourth theory which receives wide contemporary acceptance is that leadership reflects the *interaction* of leaders' personalities with the needs and expectations of followers, the characteristics and tasks of the group, and the situation. Thus, it attempts to account for a variety of factors generally associated with defining leadership.

What can this digression into alternative definitions and theories of leadership tell us about the role of political communicators as leaders in the opinion process? Recall that in Chapter 1 we suggested that each of the three phases of the opinion process (personal, social, and political) involves people taking objects into account, interpreting them through their conduct toward those objects, and thus constructing meanings of them. The active process of interpretation people use to impart meaning to their world consists of constructing images of objects, images made up of one's beliefs, evaluations, and expectations regarding those objects. Certainly one kind of object that people take into account is other people. Not only do they take one another into account, they frequently attempt to influence each other. Influence refers to intentional efforts of people to weaken, reinforce, or alter others' beliefs, evaluations, or expectations. Put slightly differently, people not only construct and modify their own personal images of things, they influence one another's efforts at constructing those meanings.[32]

Despite the array of diverse definitions and theories of leadership reviewed above, there is a general consensus that *leadership* (and its inseparable corollary, followership) *is a relationship among people in a group in which one or more persons (leaders) influence others (followers) in a given setting.* We must be careful about what is involved in this influence relationship that designates some persons leaders, others followers. What is *not* involved is the notion that leaders with selected traits appear independently and exert or exercise influence over followers. What is involved is a social relationship where mutually held expectations emerge through communication to define and impart meaning to various roles. Stogdill puts it this way:[33]

> . . . the differentiation of member roles and the emergence of leadership in a group comes about as a result of mutual reinforcement of intermember expectations. One member, because of his initiative, interactions with other members, and contributions to the group task, reinforces the expectation that he will be more likely than other members to establish conditions which will promote task movement, member freedom and acceptance, and group cohesiveness. Other members, in deferring to him, reinforce his expectation that he should continue in the leadership role. Similarly, each member builds up expectations regarding the contribution he is to make. The reactions of other members to him confirm the expectation that he is to continue in the same role. Thus, the role system and the status structure of a group are determined by a set of mutually reinforced intermember expectations.

In sum, through communication people formulate expectations of one another; when this involves their adapting to and reinforcing the expectations of persons trying to affect group tasks and/or viewpoints, there is influence and the emergence of leader-follower roles. *Leadership followership is continuously defined and redefined through the communication process* cueing the construction and modification of interpersonal meaning. All leadership—including leadership in the opinion process—is a reciprocal, circular transaction between leaders and followers: "The leader's behavior conditions the response of the followers and the followers' behavior conditions the response of the leader."[34] "Conditioned" here does not imply that leaders and followers merely react to one another. Rather both are active participants in constructing the leadership-followership relation; that construction is a subtle and ongoing negotiation of mutual expectations and associated roles. It must be emphasized that the factors contributing to the emergence of leadership—the personality of leaders, the problems and needs of followers, the social structures and characteristics of groups, and the elements in the situation—do not define leadership. Rather, "it is not these variables per se that enter into the leadership relation, but rather the perception of the leader by himself, and others, the leader's perception of those others, and the shared perception by leader and others of the group and situation."[35]

Just as leadership arises out of communication, so does political leadership arise from the mutual construction, exchange modification, and sharing of political beliefs, values, and expectations though political communication. As key political communicators, politicians, professionals, and activists have the opportunity to influence political opinions. To the degree that they do so, they perform the role of political leaders. What then are the characteristics of the political communicator role when viewed from such a leadership perspective?

Political Communicators as Political Leaders

There are several aspects of the role of political communicators as political leaders that warrant consideration. We shall explore six: the dual nature of political leadership, types of leaders, the bond between leaders and followers, characteristics of political leaders, popular perceptions of political leaders, and the recruitment of leaders in politics.

The Task-Emotional Distinction in Leadership

What do leaders do? How do they behave? Are the distinctive acts that leaders perform different from nonleaders? Efforts to identify distinctive things leaders do have yielded mixed results. On the one hand, leadership theorists have been able to describe what leaders actually do. And they have observed differences in the way leaders and nonleaders act. Yet on the other hand, the boundaries between what make leaders and nonleaders are fuzzy; probably every member of a group acts "like a leader" in some ways at some time. Hence, leadership is shared behavior (a conclusion we would expect, given our view that leadership, by definition, derives from at least a minimal sharing of expectations).

Political scientist Lewis Froman summarizes the *tendencies* that distinguish leaders and nonleaders in a group.[36] Leaders (1) gain a wider variety of satisfactions from being group members; (2) are more intense in holding their values; (3) have more beliefs about the group and its relation to other groups, government, political issues, etc.; (4) are less likely to change their beliefs, values, and expectations through pressures brought upon them; (5) are more likely to make decisions concerning the group on the basis of their prior beliefs, values, and expectations; and (6) are more issue oriented, especially with respect to issues involving material gains rather than less tangible satisfactions or emotion laden questions.

Such a cataloging helps to distinguish leaders from nonleaders, but it is important to bear a few things in mind. First, since leadership is a relationship continuously redefined through the conduct of group members toward one another, it is well to regard these tendencies as really the differing expectations that persons in leadership roles develop toward nonleaders and vice versa. Second, in noting the greater range, intensity, and resistance to change in leaders' beliefs, values, and expectations (as contrasted to those of nonleaders), leaders articulate their thoughts, feelings, and proposals more clearly for all group members than do nonleaders. Perhaps leaders simply communicate greater clarity in the meanings they construct of group goals, members, and the situation. Third, there are two varieties of nonleader, and the above tendencies may not apply to both. There are some nonleaders who are truly followers, who take an active interest in the group, organization, or community and communicate about politics even though they might not be pols, pros, or opinion leaders. Then there are nonleaders who are actually uninterested or indifferent; they are neither leaders nor followers. The tendencies that distinguish leaders and nonleaders contrast leaders with indifferents better than they contrast leaders and followers: "the correlations for 'leader' and 'follower' are not of opposite sign and similar magnitude as would be expected of traits supposed to be antithetical. These may not be the opposite poles of a single underlying trait. It may be that the true antithesis of 'leader' is not 'follower,' but 'indifference,' i.e., the incapacity or unwillingness to lead or to follow."[37]

What then do leaders do that set them apart not only from the indifferents, or nonfollowers, but from followers as well? The answer to that question, "one of the most important achievements of leadership research,"[38] is twofold. One thing leaders do is to define and work toward the achievement of group goals, organize to get the job done (form committees and superior-subordinate relations, work out time schedules and deadlines, etc.), and establish performance standards for group members. These activities are *task* oriented. A second set of leadership activities is person, social, or *emotion* oriented. It consists of being considerate of the wants and needs of followers, establishing warm personal relations, fostering mutual trust, striving for cooperation, and achieving social solidarity.

The distinction posits two styles of communication in leadership: the task-motivated person communicates to get the job done, the relationship-motivated to achieve an emotional bond between group members. Both occur—perhaps must occur—in any group, organization, or community. This may give rise to two types of leadership roles, the task specialist and emotional specialist,[39] or a single individual may play both roles. For example, prior to the personal difficulties which led to his resignation as chairman of the House Committee on Ways and Means before the 94th Congress, Congressman Wilbur Mills of Arkansas had the reputation of being one of the most knowledgeable and powerful public officials in Washington, D.C. Mills was a dominant figure in shaping critical legislation concerning taxation, Medicare, and other issues. His effectiveness was a product of Mills' subtle intermingling of both task and emotional roles. Efforts to get key legislation passed, or blocked, gave rise to conflict among committee members; Mills responded to these byproducts of task efforts by doing things for committee members in a positive way, mending fences, identifying with other congressmen in a communal effort, and lending socioemotional support.[40]

Neither task nor emotional leadership is intrinsically superior. Whether the purposes of a group, organization, or community will be better served by the work-oriented or persons-oriented leader is very much like all things, in that it depends upon the situation. For example, suppose the leader feels accepted, the goals of the group are reasonably clear, followers are happy, and the situation is thus nonthreatening. In this fortunate circumstance the leader, whether normally prone to play a task or emotional role, can concentrate on the work at hand, simply assuming group acceptance has already been won and there is no immediate need to smooth social relations. But suppose the leader perceives the situation as unfavorable—he or she does not feel accepted, the task is vague, and things are threatening? The emotional leader is likely to work at improving interpersonal relations, the task leader upon getting things done.[41] Whether a selected strategy works in a given situation, of course, depends in a large measure upon whether leaders and nonleaders define that situation in the same way. Citizens who believe an economic crisis is so severe as to require drastic measures simply may not respond to a president's repeated appeals to "trust me" or assurances that the moral fiber of the people alone will help "weather this crisis."

It is tempting to assert boldly that the task-emotional distinction parallels distinctions among classes of political communicators—politicians as partisan representatives/ideologues, professionals as journalists/promoters, and activists as spokespersons/opinion leaders. Certainly, for instance, the partisan representative has the task of advancing constituent's interests, the journalist is task oriented in meeting deadlines, and the spokesperson lobbies for the organization's welfare. And many ideological politicians change people's minds by courting them, promoters often employ emotion laden appeals, and opinion leaders rely upon reputations for warmth and trust. Yet politicians, professionals, and activists more often than not combine task and emotional styles as political leaders. Thus, Wilbur Mills was both an instrumental and affective leader. Walter Cronkite delivers the news but assumes the stance of a reassuring personality as well, and Ralph Nader must be as concerned with being trusted in his role of consumer advocate as with being knowledgeable. If the parallels exist between task-emotional styles and classes of political communicators, they again are only tendencies. This is not to say, however, that the task-emotional distinction should be ignored. It is important. We encounter it again in Chapter 5 when we discuss the media of interpersonal political communication. And we shall see its implications even more immediately as we examine a second aspect of the leadership role of political communicators, the different performances of organization and symbolic leaders.

Organization and Symbolic Leaders in Politics

For a political communicator to be a political leader, he must behave in ways that people expect of leaders; followers impute leadership to one who fulfills their meaning of what a leader is. Some communicators are leaders because of the positions they occupy within a clearly defined social structure or organized group. Outside of the organization they may not mean much to people. We call such political communicators *organization* leaders. Other communicators, however, do not occupy clearly defined positions; or if they do, they are meaningful to people for reasons other than their organizational role. Political communicators who are leaders because of the meaning people find in them as persons, personalities, celebrities, and so forth, we label *symbolic* leaders.

Obviously a high proportion of our politicians, professional communicators, and political activists are organization leaders. Elective, appointive, and career officials hold formal positions of leadership in the organized networks of communication that constitute government. Professional communicators are frequently the employees of organizations; namely, the journalist works for a wire service, newspaper, television network, or other news organization and the promoter as a member of an organization publicizes the interests of a company, governmental agency, political candidate or party. The spokesperson as an activist communicator is, almost by definition, an organization advocate. Of the key political communicators described earlier, only the opinion leader operating through the intimacies provided by interpersonal communication networks lies primarily outside of formalized organizational structure.

That much of the leadership role of political communicators is organized carries important implications. As Gibb points out, communication is "*the* process by which one person influences another" and is thereby "basic to leadership." Organization "implies some restriction of communication, or at least a patterning in such a way that some communication channels are more readily available than others." These restrictions or patternings on communication "can affect perceptions of leadership."[42] In fact, a communicator's position within an organization determines in large measure the probability of one's being perceived as a leader. The more central one's position in the communication network, the greater the formal distinctions between a person's position and those of other members of the organization, and the greater one's freedom to communicate, then the more likely people expect the advantaged individual to influence others and thereby become a leader.[43] We see these organizational constraints defining leadership roles all the time. Political communicators who are "where the action is" within the organization—the president of the United States, a chairman of an important congressional committee, the chief justice, a television anchorman, the president's press secretary, or the president of the United Mine Workers— are, as Rosenau suggests, leaders by virtue of being "opinion makers." They *occupy positions which enable them to transmit, with some regularity, opinions about . . . policy issues to unknown persons.*[44]

Organized communication affords opportunities for *continuing* leadership,[45] leadership based upon the communicator's ability to anticipate correctly the likes and dislikes of followers, and hence their probable reactions to the leader's actions. To the extent that communicators correctly anticipate the expectations and responses of followers and are able to capitalize on them, the longer their tenure as leaders. Communication within an organized setting provides a predictable flow of accurate information about follower's likes and dislikes to which the leader can adjust. This "internal intelligence function" is more available to a leader within a formal organization than to one dealing with a mass audience. Precisely because of this, however, there is a recurring problem. Because it is relatively easier to assess how followers within an organized inner circle react than it is to gauge opinions of the general citizenry, a leader frequently places more reliance on "going over" with the inner faithful than with the public at large. Hence, for example, President Richard Nixon continued to think that he could weather the Watergate crisis, despite the fact that his standing in opinion polls deteriorated substantially, because he obtained reassuring feedback from his key aides. Small wonder that he at first discounted the report that a "cancer was growing" on the presidency, information that did not confirm the normal internal flow of intelligence. From that point on there was a growing tension between Nixon's leadership within his own "business as usual" organization and his weakened position as a leader of congressional and public opinion.

Organization leadership, by definition, works through the communicator's position in an explicit social structure. In contrast, says sociologist Orrin Klapp, "symbolic leadership works on masses and audiences prior to, without, and in spite of organization."[46] People find meaning in a symbolic leader who fires their imagination with a captivating outward appearance by symbolizing an attractive style of life. "The theory of symbolic leadership is that such leadership derives from meaning, and meaning is always extrinsic. If a man makes the right impression and does not contradict it publicly, he can become as a symbol almost anything he pleases (or that fortune pleases)."[47]

In order to draw the distinction between organization and symbolic leaders more clearly, and also to suggest the sources of symbolic leadership, it helps to examine two ways in which theorists have tried to answer the age-old question, "How is society (i.e., social order) possible?" (Recall the discussion in Chapter 1.) One view is that society comes about and continues through agencies of *social control*—organizations, educational institutions, governments making rules and laws, etc. Such task oriented agencies are the habitat of organization leaders. Public opinion and its leadership, as viewed by social control theorists, is the opinion of organized publics (usually special interest groups) influenced by controlled efforts to teach, inform, and propagandize. An alternative view rests upon the assumption that social order is not controlled or organized but emerges when separate, independent individuals among mass populations make personal choices from among a variety of options. When individuals make the same choice or choices, this is the phenomenon of *convergent selection,* the underlying factor in creating and re-creating social order. In this conception public opinion exists simply as the *consensus* of mass opinion, the product of independent beings freely reaching personal choices; each person is influenced by advertising working on individual consumers of the mass media rather than by propaganda reaching him as a member of social groups. Communications are less task oriented than directed at creating emotional bonds and through them the social groups of individuals previously isolated from one another in the mass.[48]

The symbolic leader is a product of convergent selections. An example is Eugene McCarthy during his pursuit of the presidency in 1968. For persons supporting his candidacy, he served the functions of a *condensation symbol*; that is, people simultaneously projected upon him feelings from their highly diverse experiences. McCarthy thus became a target for convergent selectivity; supporters from the mass rallied about him because of idiosyncratic attractions he held for each of them. For quite different reasons developed through quite different experiences, McCarthy symbolized a unifying emotional bond. A homogeneous mass (McCarthy supporters) derived from disparate, heterogeneous motivations of individuals responding to the candidate.[49]

Whether political communicators become symbolic leaders depends in part upon their ability to take advantage of the dramatic elements in the settings giving rise to symbolic leadership. Drama is a social process "in which things happen to audiences because of parts played by actors; the function of the actor is to transport an audience vicariously out of everyday roles into a new kind of 'reality' that has laws and patterns different from the routines of the ordinary social structure."[50] For people in the mass who perceive the world as cold, remote, complex, bewildering, and beyond their control, it is reassuring to fasten upon some abstract symbol to simplify, personalize, and provide an illusion of mastery over things. When an actor on the public stage appears to be in command of the situation and thus dramatizes competence to cope with insoluble problems, the performance projects reassurance—an illusion of control.

The leader "may maintain his 'symbolic leadership' through ascriptions of his ability to cope, through publicized action on noncontroversial policies or on trivia, and through a dramaturgical performance emphasizing the traits popularly associated with leadership: forcefulness, responsibility, courage, decency, and so on."[51]

Thus did President Gerald Ford act in 1975. Faced with what apparently were mounting frustrations of Americans at failures in international involvements—the fall of South Vietnam and Cambodia after a war involving the U.S. for a generation—Ford had to cope with the seizure of an American merchant ship by Cambodia. U.S. naval ships and a contingent of Marines landed on an offshore Cambodian island and after brief fighting rescued the ship and its crew. Although Americans later learned the Cambodian government had expressed a willingness to negotiate release of the crew and the operation could have probably been labeled a failure, since American lives were lost and Marines even invaded the wrong island, the crisis context at the time provided an opportunity for the president to dramatize control. A marked improvement in Ford's standing in public opinion polls followed the publicized act of symbolic leadership.

Chief executives such as President Ford are but one type of organization leader that function in the dual capacity of symbolic leader. Occupants of positions in highly visible organizations—government and the military, news networks, major industrial corporations and unions, etc.—have opportunities to dramatize qualities followers expect of leaders: that they can cope with crises, satisfy the individual and collective needs of the community, be believed in, and are protectors of the populace in times of distress.[52] Politicians such as Franklin Roosevelt, Dwight Eisenhower, and John Kennedy dramatized these qualities. So also have professional communicators as, for example, Dan Rather of CBS television news, who came to prominence for his coolness while reporting the events surrounding the assassination of John F. Kennedy in 1963 or when Tom Wicker was involved as both negotiator and reporter in the riots in Attica prison in 1971. And an interest spokesperson like Ralph Nader is both symbolic and organization leader.

In one respect organization leadership even provides the impetus to political communicators to become symbolic leaders. Because organizations pattern communication, they restrict maneuverability with chains of command, limits on information to be made public, etc. To break out of the organization the leader sometimes assumes a communication posture that yields celebrity status and creates a symbol of far-reaching acclaim. Edelman's observation, for example, could well be a description of Henry Kissinger as he worked to be something other than a "White House spokesman," a typical organization oriented national security advisor and later secretary of state: "In short, the difference between two political leaders in the same position today rests relatively little on differences in policy direction and very largely on other behaviors which we can label 'leadership styles.' Leaders rely increasingly on style differences to create and emphasize an impression of maneuverability, and the impression remains an important political fact even if the maneuverability is not."[53]

Symbolic leadership highlights the important interplay between what followers expect according to their image of leaders, and the impressions aspiring leaders attempt to leave with followers. This is but one element in yet another significant aspect of the role of political communicators as leaders, the bond between leaders and followers.

The Communication Bond between Leaders and Followers

Leadership and followership are complementary ways of viewing a single transaction: we cannot conceive of leaders without followers nor followers without leaders. The two terms remind us that persons in the alternating roles derive different things from their reciprocal leadership; for example, in exchange for popular support, the leader personifies and reifies remote processes for followers and supplies them with emotional reassurance in strange and foreboding situations. What other kinds of satisfactions do leaders and followers obtain from their transaction that strengthen the bonds between them?

For leaders there are several such rewards. For one, the leader has a greater opportunity to "call the shots" and to have control over his or her personal destiny. Beyond that there is something appealing in being able to influence others, assert dominance in a group, and even award benefits and deprivations. Then there are the economic rewards. Organization leaders usually occupy positions with attractive salaries; symbolic leaders frequently obtain the financial support of wealthy backers. Moreover, there are the benefits that accrue to having a higher status, both in the sense that group members stand in awe of their leader and in the sense that the leader commands sufficient resources through the backing of followers to negotiate as equal, or even superior, to leaders of other groups. A suite of private offices, staying at the best hotels, a cadre of secretaries and assistants, a private plane, people catering to every whim—all these can be heady stuff and constitute rewards in their own right. Finally, there are the satisfactions of accomplishing group goals—of getting a desired policy passed for the politician, of getting a news story first or promoting a new idea for the professional, or of changing people's opinions for the activist. Whether accomplishing a task or providing group solidarity, leaders can simply take pride in doing what is expected of them.[54]

Robert Salisbury likens the bond between leaders and followers to that between entrepreneurs and customers. The leader of an organized interest, for example, provides an impetus for creating the group by offering incentives to people to become group members, incentives exchanged for their "costs" in joining and lending support. Salisbury lists three chief benefits that followers derive from the leadership-followership transaction. First, there are *material* benefits consisting of the tangible rewards of goods or services—jobs, preferred tax rates, government contracts, improved roads, adequate housing, acceptable levels of prices and wages, etc. Then, there are *solidary* benefits. These include the social rewards of simply joining with others in a common enterprise—socializing, making friends, a sense of status, group identification, conviviality, and fun. Finally, there are *expressive* benefits—"those where the action involved gives expression to the interest or values of a person or group rather than instrumentally pursuing interests or values."[55] Some persons, for example, get satisfaction simply in supporting a political candidate as a means of saying to others that they oppose crime, or war, or poverty. Thus George Wallace ran for the presidency asking people to "stand up for America," an appeal to express their patriotism through him. Expressive satisfactions involve pleasures derived from vicarious identification with leaders, projecting dependency needs on the leader as a condensation symbol (remember the case of Eugene McCarthy), or simply being identified as a loyal and devoted follower.[56]

In sum, there is a bond between leaders and followers forged by the material, social, and emotional satisfactions that people derive from taking part in politics. These satisfactions, particularly those of the less tangible, socioemotional variety, arise in and through the communication process. Communication creates, enhances, or destroys a sense of solidarity among people and sense of personal satisfaction in expressing one's hopes and aspirations, fears and anxieties. To a very large degree, then, the bond between leaders and followers is one of communication. For this reason key political communicators play strategic roles, acting as political leaders transmitting messages followers find meaningful and satisfying. One measure of that meaning and satisfaction consists of the view non-leaders have of leaders. Let us turn to that aspect by examining the popular images of political leaders.

Popular Images of Political Communicators as Political Leaders

The philosopher Friedrich Nietzsche once wrote, "A great man, did you say? All I ever see is the actor creating his own ideal image."[57] If they aspire to organization or symbolic leadership, political communicators soon ask themselves what image followers hold of them. Although not always directly answering the question, there is a considerable body of evidence bearing on the popular images of key American political communicators. By a person's image we refer simply to the meaning one has for others, a subtle mental integration of the various attributes that the person projects and that people perceive and interpret in light of their beliefs, values, and expectations.[58] What, then, are the images of selected politicians, professionals, and activists as communicators?

Most politicians have great difficulty becoming sufficiently known even to have images. As a case in point consider the plight of various contenders for the 1976 Democratic presidential nomination less than eighteen months before their party's nominating convention. Such announced candidates as Representatives Morris Udall, former Governor of Georgia Jimmy Carter, Senator Lloyd Bentsen of Texas, and former North Carolina Governor Terry Sanford—each of whom had been in public life for several years—were known by less than a majority of those surveyed in a Gallup poll. Even Senator Henry Jackson, the most widely recognized of the announced candidates at the time, was unknown to more than four of ten polled.[59] Only such perennial possibilities as Teddy Kennedy, George Wallace, Hubert Humphrey, George McGovern, and Edmund Muskie were known by as many as eight in ten surveyed, and George McGovern, the 1972 nominee, was unknown to 20 percent! By the time of the nominating conventions only Jimmy Carter of the original aspirants had achieved outstanding success in fashioning a visible image.

An elected president has no problem of name recognition. The president is certainly the best known figure in American politics, probably the most prominent organization *and* symbolic leader. The qualities most expected of a president are honesty, intelligence, and independence, but citizens are ambivalent about how much power the officeholder should have; some studies indicate that Americans want to endow the president with considerable power, but evidence shows that Americans are always suspicious of granting power to their chief executives.[60] In any event, popular evaluations of the president's performance once he is in office fluctuate from time to time and group to group (see Table 2-1). Declines in presidential popularity flow from indications that he is failing in his task performance (for example, failing to maintain a healthy economy, to provide sufficient material benefits to interests among his winning coalition, etc.); that he lacks the personal qualities of integrity, intelligence, and independence; because people hold the president responsible for bad news; or simply because people in time grow disillusioned regardless of presidential performance.[61] In times of international crisis there is a strong tendency for confidence in the president to rise, especially if he is skilled in emotion-oriented leadership.

Popular images of federal appointees to the executive branch of government have been generally positive. A nationwide survey in 1960, for example, revealed that almost two-thirds of respondents had favorable impressions of federal appointees and gave them high ratings on "honesty," "ability," and "interest in serving the public."[62] Another survey found that Americans generally expected to receive equal and serious

Table 2-1   *Thirty-Five Years of Presidential Popularity*
                    1941–1976

President	Level of Popularity *(percent approving president's job performance)*		
	High	*Low*	*Average*
Franklin Roosevelt	84	54	75
Harry Truman	87	23	41
Dwight Eisenhower	79	48	64
John Kennedy	83	56	70
Lyndon Johnson	80	35	55
Richard Nixon	67	24	49
Gerald Ford	71	37	46

Source: *The Gallup Opinion Index*, Report No. 125 (November–December 1975);
        Report No. 138 (January 1977).

consideration from bureaucratic officials.[63] There is evidence, however, that public confidence in the executive branch, as distinct from federal employees, has declined. Pollster Louis Harris, for instance, noted that in 1966 41 percent of his nationwide sample expressed confidence in the "executive branch of federal government," but by 1976 only 11 percent did so. Harris did report a decline in confidence of career officials such as in the military—from 62 percent expressing confidence in the military in 1966 to less than one-fourth doing so a decade later.[64]

There is much less information available about the popular images of political communicators in legislative and judicial bodies. Devine finds that Americans prefer legislative rather than presidential predominance in deciding what the country needs in economic and budgetary matters and in declaring war or committing U.S. troops.[65] Apparently this is because citizens see the congressman as their "tribune," one who discovers, reflects, and advocates their needs and demands rather than one who acts independently of constituents' wishes.[66] As with the federal executive, there has been tarnishing of the popular image of Congress. Whereas in 1960, 62 percent of a nationwide sample held favorable views of congressmen, Harris reports that public confidence in Congress declined from a 42 percent level in 1966 to less than one in ten Americans expressing confidence in that instituiton in 1976. In the past the U.S. Supreme Court has had a favorable public reception, but not as favorable as that of the president or Congress. Here too, however, pollster Harris documents a decline of confidence, from a majority of Americans expressing confidence in the Court in 1966 to one in five in 1976.[67]

If we shift our attention from political communicators in public office to those aspiring to being elected, we focus upon the popular images of political candidates. A recent volume summarizing numerous studies of how voters perceive candidates suggests a division of the candidate's image that parallels the task-emotion orientation distinction in leadership generally. On the one hand, voters perceive traits associated with a candidate's political *role,* his experience and background (if any) in public office, experience and qualifications, record and associations in partisan politics, and other attributes associated with task-oriented performance. On the other hand, voters dwell upon a candidate's political *style.* This dimension consists of perceived personal attributes (honesty, intelligence, physical appearance, etc.) and skills as a dramatic actor (how he comes across in personal appearances, television presentations, debate, etc.). Generally voters tend to stress stylistic over role qualities in sizing up a candidate, in part because they look for an emotional tie between themselves and those seeking their support.[68] As evidence of the emphasis on style rather than substance, consider that surveys conducted during the 1976 presidential nominating primaries revealed that half of Jimmy Carter's supporters did not know where he stood on issues, a quarter had the wrong idea of his issue stands, and only about one in five could actually specify his views; 56 percent of those surveyed said Carter's personal characteristics attracted their support and only one-fourth said issues brought them to Carter.[69]

What of the images of professional communicators? Here there is relatively little evidence. What there is pertains primarily to journalists rather than promoters, and within that, emphasis is upon media forms rather than individuals (although we do know that some journalists such as anchormen Walter Cronkite of CBS or John Chancellor of NBC are more widely known than most politicians and, moreover, more trusted).[70] Surveys indicate that the most frequently employed media for political news are (in order) television, newspapers, radio, and magazines; the most believed media (in order) are television, newspapers, magazines and radio.[71] The public image of the most used and believed media, television and the press, is not as clearly on the decline as is that of the executive, Congress, and the courts. Harris reports that whereas the surveyed level of confidence in "press" declined from 29 to 20 percent in the period 1966–76, that in television news increased, reaching a high of 41 percent in 1973 before falling back to 28 percent in 1976. The only evidence pertaining to promoters rather than journalists as professional communicators concerns lawyers. Harris reports that public confidence in law firms is low (only 18 percent in 1974).[72] A survey commissioned by the American Bar Association indicated that majorities in a nationwide sample believed the legal system favors the rich and powerful, lawyers charge more for their services than they are worth, work harder for rich than poor clients, are not prompt in getting things done, and are not concerned about getting the "bad apples" out of their own profession.[73]

Finally, what of the images of spokespersons and opinion leaders, our activist political communicators. Little can be said of opinion leaders, most of whom have credence among their intimates but are not known outside that circle. In general, spokespersons for organized interests do not receive broad public approval, because in large measure, many of their organizations do not. Indications again are that fewer than one in four Americans express much confidence in organized labor or major business concerns, and the level of confidence in the medical industry has declined from 72 percent to 50 percent in the 1966–74 period. One spokesperson receiving public acclaim is Ralph Nader. A Harris survey reported in 1975 that 58 percent of those questioned approved of the job Nader was doing.[74]

In sum, there is considerable variation in the images of political communicators as leaders—by type of communicator, from one time period to another, and from group to group. Apparently all classes of political leaders and the institutions they lead today experience what Klapp calls "image trouble."[75] To the degree that there is declining confidence in them, nonleaders no longer assume automatically that leaders are trustworthy simply by asserting themselves to be, and communicators find it increasingly difficult to excite popular imaginations and create the illusion they are solving the insoluble, are in tune with, not to mention in control of the future, or personalizing the impersonal. There are undoubtedly a number of sources of this image trouble; one may be that people perceive that political leaders are simply too unlike themselves to empathize with their plight. This raises the question of what the social characteristics of American political leaders are, especially our key political communicators in that role.

Social Characteristics of Political Leaders

There is a considerable body of literature describing the social characteristics of American political leaders. The thrust of the findings is that in the aggregate, people who take the lead in politics are unrepresentative of the social diversity that marks the general population.[76] Compared to the general population, for instance, elective (executive and legislative), appointive (executive and judicial), and career officials are of a higher socioeconomic status (with higher incomes, better educations, and higher status occupations), disproportionately male, lawyers, and born into white, northern European, Protestant families.[77] Persons appointed to federal office also tend to be specific types: usually Protestants, well educated, frequently lawyers, and with previous business connections in large corporate or law firms. Similarly, career officials are typically middle-aged college graduates of higher status occupations and relatively secure income, thus differing considerably from the general run of citizens.[78]

Politicians not holding public office also differ from the general citizenry. Leaders of the major political parties, for example, have relatively high socioeconomic status, college degrees, and professional or managerial positions. There is a disproportion of lawyers among these party stalwarts. Politicians of the two parties differ from one another somewhat: in most regions Republicans are of higher socioeconomic status than their Democratic counterparts; Republicans have higher percentages of Protestants in contrast to higher proportions of Catholics and Jews among Democrats; Democrats are more frequently of Irish or Southern and Eastern European stock, Republicans of Northern and Western European heritage. And studies indicate that people who aspire to public office are generally more highly educated, from a higher class background, and from higher status occupations than those who do not seek office.[79] Even Black candidates in the American South have social characteristics which differentiate them from their constituents in similar ways.[80]

Professional communicators are scarcely more representative of the general population in social characteristics than politicians. Journalists, for instance, are far more likely to have completed college than is the average citizen; a recent nationwide survey of newsmen indicates that 86 percent had attended college, 58 percent were college graduates, and one in five had attended graduate school.[81] Promoters, as executive appointees or career civil servants in government, publicizers of organized interests, or even party workers, differ in social composition from the general population in ways typical of elective and appointive officials.

Spokespersons for organized interests are usually strikingly different from the general citizenry in social characteristics. For instance, business and corporate leaders are the upper crust of American society. A relatively few commercial leaders constitute an institutional elite in positions which control over half of the nation's total economic resources.[82] Although not possessing vast wealth, leaders of major trade unions are atypical of the general population. They are of higher income and status; many have college degrees and hold managerial positions. Lobbyists for organized interests also have a class bias in composition; Milbrath found, for example, that of the lobbyists he interviewed in Washington, D.C., three-fourths were upper-middle or upper class.[83] Finally, what of activists who are opinion leaders? Although the differences in social attributes between opinion leaders and followers are relatively slight compared with the differences observed among other classes of key political communicators, they are nonetheless measurable. Opinion leaders tend to be slightly better educated, with higher status occupations and larger incomes. Opinion leaders in one nationwide sample, for example, were more likely to be white than nonwhite, male than female, and of high occupational status.[84]

The same studies that find political leaders differ in social characteristics from the general population also find they differ in other respects—levels of political involvement, political beliefs, values, and expectations, and influence upon policy making. These are differences we shall
examine in Chapters 7, 8, and 12. Let us now move to the final consideration of political communicators in their leadership role—the general
question of how people select political leaders.

The Selection of Political Leaders

Organization leaders in public office reach positions of strategic importance in political communication by election, apppointment, or through
civil service procedures. We shall concentrate upon the elective mode
of leadership recruitment. There begins the biasing in social characteristics
that typifies relations between leaders and nonleaders in political
communication.[85]

Kenneth Prewitt has likened the process of selecting political leaders
to a Chinese box puzzle. The puzzle consists of several boxes of different
sizes; the smallest box fits into the next larger, that one into the next
larger, and so on until all boxes are in the largest one. To get to the
contents of the smallest box one must successively open each, largest to
smallest. In the case of leadership, the largest box consists of all persons
in the population, the smallest of leaders who govern. As the means for
choosing from among the many the few who govern, leadership is truly
selective; as we move from the largest box containing everybody to the
smallest containing the governors, a relatively small number of people
survive the sorting out to become the chosen few.[86]

The sorting is in many stages (or boxes).[87] The first stage sorts from
the general population the *eligibles,* all persons having the legal qualifications for taking part in politics and seeking office (citizenship, requisite
age, residency, etc.). From the eligibles comes a second sorting to select
the *availables,* or those persons with the necessary resources—primarily
social and economic—making for political involvement. Here enter the
social biases and the advantages that accrue to being white, male, Protestant, college educated, having a prestigious occupation, above average
income, a favored family background, and being of native stock. This
is not to say that only people with these characteristics are availables,
but rather that a disproportionate number are sorted into this smaller
box. The third stage involves entry into politics of a portion of the total
availables, the sorting out of political *participants.* Entry into this category
is for people acquiring political interest and motivation through childhood socialization; becoming politically concerned as an adult because
of some event or issue (as when a homeowner threatened with a drop

in property values because of rezoning starts attending city council meetings); or as a result of being thrust into politics because of one's occupation (as when a reporter receives an assignment to cover city hall, a marketing specialist writes advertising copy for a political candidate, a businessman bids for a contract before public officials, or a realtor is appointed to a government position). The intensity of political participation varies considerably, but most participants at least vote in elections on a regular basis (see Chapter 10). A fourth stage sorts from the estimated three-fourths of eligibles who become participants an even smaller group (about 10 percent of eligibles) of *consistents,* people with a continuing interest in politics who fit our description of key political communicators.[88] Here are the activists (spokespersons and opinion leaders), professionals (journalists and promoters), and the politicians who enter a fifth stage of the selection process, the *candidates* for public office. The source of their political candidacy may lie in the motivation to hold public office acquired from past experience (i.e., they may be "self-starters") or in the efforts of community sponsors to get them to run (the "recruits").[89] In either case they enter the election campaign, the final stage of the process for selecting organization leaders. Voters sort themselves out in support of competing candidates. Thus designating the contents of the smallest container in the Chinese box puzzle, the *elected.*

There are, of course, two respects in which the election is not the only or final stage in the selection of organization leaders. The first we have already alluded to; i.e., appointive and career public officials reach their positions as a result of preferences of those who win the election, or in the case of career officials, procedures designed to minimize the effects of who wins and loses. Second, for many public officials the election is but one step in being selected to ever higher and more prestigious offices, and thus being sorted into ever smaller boxes, such as those containing 435 congressmen, 100 senators, and ultimately a box with only one president. Ambition plays an important role in politics and influences political communication. For one thing, politicians with ever higher office goals typically adopt less strident and uncompromising, more bargain-oriented styles of communication aimed at negotiating differences, "a necessary requirement for success in politics in the pluralistic political system."[90] And political aspirations can produce more responsive and responsible modes of communication between leaders and nonleaders. Schlesinger, for example, speaking of the importance of ambition to representative government, notes that "the desire for election and, more important, for reelection becomes the electorate's restraint upon its public officials." Further, he argues that "no more irresponsible government is imaginable than one of high-minded men unconcerned for their political futures."[91]

In sum, political communicators who become leaders in public organization are not selected at random from the population at large. Rather they are recruited from even smaller groupings: eligibles, availables, participants, consistents, candidates, and the elected (and subsequently the appointed, careerists, elevated, and reelected). But what of those who become symbolic leaders? Does the analogy of the Chinese box puzzle still apply? The principal student of symbolic leadership, sociologist Orrin Klapp, offers a different metaphor—a tennis match.[92]

A symbolic leader, says Klapp, emerges from a dialectical process which, like the selection of organization leaders, has several stages. First, there is a "cooperative" exchange in which a person "has the initiative of hitting the first ball, as in a tennis game." Thus, for example, Jimmy Carter set out to tread the snow in 1976 in the New Hampshire Democratic primary, George Wallace tried to bar federal agents from integrating the University of Alabama in 1963 by "standing in the schoolhouse door," and Senator Joseph McCarthy early in his career brandished a list of alleged Communists in the federal government before an audience. Second, the audience, after the initiating act, return cues (shots) to the actor that provide the leader with a view of a popular image, i.e., how he looks to them. But third, "all shots are not returned"; perceptual and functional selection is such that "people see only what interests them and respond only to images that 'do something' for them." Thus, fourth, "the actor can accept or reject the cues returned, but he cannot make a shot from a position different from where he was when the ball came to him; that is, he cannot project a different image." For this reason, fifth, "even if he dislikes what is happening, he may not be able to prevent the game from going in a direction he does not choose," and he thereby "develops image trouble." "His lack of cooperation may make matters worse, and he may lose the game" (as did President Richard Nixon once the Watergate coverup began to unravel). Yet, sixth, Klapp notes that the actor can always capitalize on the existing situation by efforts to play it up, do trick shots (Nixon's release of tape transcripts in a television speech), elaborate on the gag (Nixon playing the piano and twirling a yo-yo in an appearance at the Grand Ol' Opry), or try to improve or change the trend, "so long as he works within the general framework in which the public will play ball and within the dimensions and rules of the court" (but Nixon finally had to yield for violating those rules). Finally, "his status—the symbol or image that emerges—is always a product of the game and cannot be surely set in advance." He may, notes Klapp, become a star (Sam Ervin of the 1973 Senate Watergate Committee), a hero (federal district judge John Sirica), a laughingstock (former Attorney General John Mitchell), a villain (White House aides John Erlichman and H. R. Haldeman) or a scapegoat (former FBI acting director Patrick Gray). But whatever he becomes, "he must wait until the game has been played to find out."

The symbolic leader emerges, then, when the communicator performs a dramatic act, selectively gleans an impression of an audience response, and then adjusts to and/or endeavors to live up to the popular impression. Members of the audience respond enthusiastically out of quite different, idiosyncratic, even conflicting, motives. What is important is that the leader symbolizes something to each of them individually. If so, the leader has made a personal-dramatic hit, and has become a symbolic leader. Whether one remains so depends in part upon whether the leader continues to act as expected. This does not mean conforming to type in every detail. Any symbolic leader builds up a few "idiosyncrasy credits" which permit a degree of communication "out of character."[93] Indeed, an occasional lapse may even endear a leader to followers (as when former Vice-President Spiro Agnew accidentally hit a fellow golfer in the head with a ball in a celebrity tournament). But behavior too divergent from the expected (as when evidence appeared that Agnew had accepted bribes) can destroy the image and the leader. Symbolic leaders may, however, simply fade away rather than destroy their own appeal. The once dramatic qualities the leader symbolized may simply become irrelevant or even unattractive to an audience. Thus a candidate with wide popular appeal in 1968 when running for vice-president on the Democratic ticket, Edmund Muskie, and who seemed even more "Lincolnesque" as a result of his campaign in the 1970 congressional elections, failed to spark popular imagination in the presidential primaries of 1972.

Whatever the means for selecting political leaders—the sorting of a box puzzle or the dialectic of the tennis match—it is clear that persons who take part in regular, sustained, widely broadcast political communication are more likely than those who do not to achieve organization and/or symbolic leadership. Thereby they influence the beliefs and values of others and reinforce the expectations of their followers that they are and should be their political leaders.

UNCERTAINTIES IN THE ROLE OF THE CONTEMPORARY POLITICAL COMMUNICATOR

We have looked with considerable detail at the identity and varieties of key political communicators, their role in influencing others, and their attributes as political leaders—as task and emotional leaders, as organization and symbolic leaders, the bond uniting them with followers, their images, social characteristics, and selection. We will close this discussion of the "Who" (that says what in which channel to whom with what effects) by introducing three areas of uncertainty in the activities of political communicators.

The first deals with the question of professionalism. A few scholars have grown concerned in recent years that political communicators have abandoned their clients, constituents, and audiences out of loyalties to impersonal, professional values. There is a paradox here, for professionalization of the public service and of the communications industry has long been a goal of political reformers and many educators of public administration, journalism, public relations, and advertising. Their rationale has been that professionalism promotes better government by emphasizing intellectual techniques, applications of a systematic body of knowledge, personal responsibility of the professional for judgments and actions, emphasis on service rather than private economic gain, and clear-cut ethical standards to measure performance. That there has been a marked professionalization in political communication is apparent from numerous studies that specify professional criteria and apply them to the performance of practicing politicians, government administrators, journalists, public relations men, etc. Research consistently identifies professionals and/or careerists as distinct from the semiprofessionals and/or amateurs.[94] The problem critics find in all this is that political communication has become so professional that its practitioners see things only from the narrow viewpoint of their own technical specialty and have a marked blind spot to anything outside their own perspective.[95] Thus the professional politician becomes wedded to acceptable policy rather than pressing for the ideal one, journalists to professional norms of what is news rather than describing events that do not conform to conventional definitions, and public relations personnel to the success of an information campaign rather than to the validity of the information. The consequence of overspecialization and overconformity to professional standards has made the political communicator in his leadership role "all too executive."[96] The emphasis is upon formalizing and structuring leader-follower relations so that the communicator simply "executes" a communication plan—a standard speech before campaign audiences, bland and noncommital responses in a presidential press conference, the advanced release of the text of a presidential address, a cover story prepared well before the event it describes, or the repetition of a single phrase, slogan, or gimmick ("Reelect the President," "Give Your Fair Share," or "We Try Harder"). In the world of the executive political communicator, the unexpected, unanticipated, and spontaneous has no place.

A second problem area arises from the characteristics of the communicators themselves. As noted earlier the social attributes of key political communicators scarcely reflect those of the rank and file of Americans. There are differences in status, levels of interest in politics, and amounts of time and effort devoted to political communication. These differences raise, as Prewitt notes, "the complex paradox of how public leaders can be both 'different' and yet 'representative,' different in the sense that they are unlike the population from which they are chosen and yet representative in the sense that they somehow act in accordance with the preferences of that populace."[97] In the sense Prewitt suggests, how representative are key political communicators of the opinions of the populace? We shall return to that question again in Parts Three and Four.

In addition to how professional and how representative political communicators are, there is a third major uncertainty about their role that we examine in detail in Chapters 3 and 4. That pertains to their motives. Certainly those motives are mixed. In some cases they are purposive—they *intend* to change popular beliefs, values, and expectations by informing, persuading, and entertaining. In other instances their motives are nonpurposive—they transmit messages to people with no intent to influence.[98] They may say something, write it, even portray it on stage or in film, purely to have an audience enjoy it for its own sake and not as a means of getting people to do anything with respect to something else. A painter, for instance, may put something on canvas solely for the enjoyment of expressing personal feelings, giving no thought to what it holds for a viewer. Or a president might slip in a few expletives in expressing his frustration to advisors at a series of events, again with no intent to influence and unmindful of how those remarks might be interpreted by outsiders if informed of it.

Whether their motives be purposive or nonpurposive, political communicators, using various forms of language, impart meanings to objects, events, and situations by giving them names, names that evoke beliefs, values, and expectations of people toward politics. Think of the difference a president can make by labeling the supply of petroleum as a "shortage" or "crisis," or by calling an economic downturn a "depression" rather than a "recession." Through the symbols they use, political communicators not only deal with political realities and reveal their motives toward them, but also create those realities and motives. To see how, we turn to the uses of political language, the "says what" of the Lasswell paradigm of communication.

BIBLIOGRAPHY

There is no single convenient source that discusses the role of political communicators in the opinion process. A reader interested in the topic must explore numerous books and journals containing both directly and marginally relevant chapters, articles, and fragments. An excellent place to begin is by consulting the listing of works in political communication provided in the volume by Lynda Lee Kaid et al., *Political Campaign Communication* (Metuchen,

N.J.: The Scarecrow Press, Inc., 1974). This bibliographical guide covers a much wider area of literature than works pertaining to political campaigning; in fact, at the time of its publication it was the most comprehensive such bibliography in political communication. As an aid to speculating about the varieties of key communicators in American politics, James N. Rosenau, *National Leadership and Foreign Policy* (Princeton: Princeton University Press, 1963) is helpful; also consult Chapter Two, "Identifying Public Leaders in America," in Wendell Bell et al., *Public Leadership* (San Francisco: Chandler Publishing Co., 1961).

But to get a full sense of the communication activities of the diverse kinds of actors in the opinion process, a reader must examine volumes devoted to each set of political communicators. But a few among the more relevant are the following. On public officials as communicators, consult Elmer E. Cronwell, Jr., *Presidential Leadership of Public Opinion* (Bloomington: Indiana University Press, 1965); Delmer D. Dunn, *Public Officials and the Press* (Reading, Mass.: Addison-Wesley Publishing Co., 1969); David T. Stanley et al., *Men Who Govern* (Washington, D.C.: The Brookings Institution, 1967); and Charles L. Clapp, *The Congressman* (Washington, D.C.: The Brookings Institution, 1963). On candidates as communicators see John W. Kingdon, *Candidates for Office* (New York: Random House, 1966); Robert J. Huckshorn and Robert C. Spencer, *The Politics of Defeat* (Amherst, Mass.: University of Massachusetts Press, 1971); and David A. Leuthold, *Electioneering in a Democracy* (New York: John Wiley & Sons, Inc., 1968). On professional communicators, in addition to the works cited in the bibliography for Chapters 5 and 6, examine Paul Halmos, ed., *The Sociology of Mass Media Communications* (Keele, Staffordshire: University of Keele, 1969); William L. Rivers, *The Opinionmakers* (Boston: Beacon Press, 1967); Martin Mayer, *Madison Avenue, U.S.A.* (New York: Pocket Books, 1958); Dan Nimmo, *The Political Persuaders* (Englewood Cliffs, N.J.: Prentice-Hall, 1970); David Lee Rosenbloom, *The Election Men* (New York: Quadrangle Books, 1973); O. J. Firestone, *The Political Persuader: Government Advertising* (Toronto: Metuchen Press, 1970); and Roy E. Hiebert and Carlton E. Spitzer, eds., *The Voice of Government* (New York: John Wiley & Sons, 1968). On interest spokespersons start with Lester W. Milbrath, *The Washington Lobbyists* (Chicago: Rand McNally & Co., 1963); Martin Mayer, *The Lawyers* (New York: Dell Publishing Co., 1966); and G. William Domhoff, *Who Rules America?* (Englewood Cliffs, N.J.: Prentice-Hall, 1967). And on opinion leaders, the standard work, although dated, is Elihu Katz and Paul F. Lazarsfeld, *Personal Influence* (New York: The Free Press of Glencoe, 1955).

Key political communicators are in strategic positions to play the role of leaders in the opinion process and, hence, many of the multitude of leadership studies apply to them. In recent years several volumes and articles have appeared which summarize the findings, both significant and trivial, of leadership studies. The best single volume is Ralph M. Stodgill's painstaking effort, *Handbook of Leadership* (New York: The Free Press, 1974), which comes close to telling the reader more about leadership studies than he ever wanted to know. A very readable and succinct statement of many of the same points is Fred E. Fiedler, *Leadership* (Morristown, N.J.: General Learning Press, 1971). If the reader thirsts for yet more, two summary articles are available: Cecil A. Gibb, "Leadership," in Gardner Lindzey and Elliot Aronson, eds., *The Handbook of Social Psychology* (Reading, Mass.: Addison-Wesley Publishing Co., 2nd ed., 1969) and Daniel Katz, "Patterns of Leadership," in Jeanne N. Knutson,

Handbook of Political Psychology (San Francisco: Jossey-Bass Publishers, 1973). A useful edited volume of the same nature is Glenn D. Paige, ed., *Political Leadership* (New York: The Free Press, 1972). All of the works mentioned explore the relationship of leadership to influence, alternative definitions and theories of leadership, and the task-emotional distinction. Although a few introduce the notion of symbolic leadership, the focus is primarily upon organization leaders, either within small groups or institutional settings. Two volumes provide highly readable introductions to symbolic leadership and the associated notion of charisma: Eugene E. Jennings, *An Anatomy of Leadership* (New York: McGraw-Hill Book Co., 1960), and Orrin E. Klapp, *Symbolic Leaders* (New York: Minerva Press, 1964).

A plethora of studies have by now demonstrated to everyone's satisfaction that the social characteristics of American leaders are no strict microcosm of those of the general population. As brief an introductory review of the findings of that literature as is available is to be found in Ralph M. Goldman's chapter, "Leaders in the United States," contained in his *Behavioral Perspectives on American Politics* (Homewood, Ill.: The Dorsey Press, 1973). Whether the social bias in American leadership adds up to rule by a single, concentrated elite or a pluralistic, fragmented elite is a bone of contention among elite theorists. The range of views on that question can be explored by consulting the following: Thomas R. Dye, *Who's Running America?* (Englewood Cliffs, N.J.: Prentice-Hall, 1976); C. Wright Mills, *The Power Elite* (New York: Oxford University Press, 1957); Suzanne Keller, *Beyond the Ruling Class* (New York: Random House, 1963); Arnold M. Rose, *The Power Structure: Political Process in American Life* (New York: Oxford University Press, 1967); and Floyd Hunter, *Top Leadership, U.S.A.* (Chapel Hill: University of North Carolina Press, 1959). The reader should also be aware of the relationship of the elitist-pluralist debate to studies of governance of local communities. A handy bibliography of this literature is Willis D. Hawley and James H. Svara, *The Study of Community Power* (Santa Barbara, Cal.: ABC Clio, 1972).

There is no comprehensive volume on how Americans view political leaders, but there are several works that explore facets of the popular images of leaders. Among these are Robert G. Lehnen, *American Institutions, Political Opinion, and Public Policy* (Chicago: Dryden Press, 1976); John E. Mueller, *War, Presidents, and Public Opinion* (New York: John Wiley & Sons, Inc., 1973); Dan Nimmo and Robert L. Savage, *Candidates and Their Images* (Pacific Palisades, Cal.: Goodyear Publishing Co., 1976); and Franklin P. Kilpatrick et al., *The Image of the Federal Service* (Washington, D.C.: The Brookings Institution, 1964).

Political scientist Lester G. Seligman has written numerous pieces summarizing and expanding what we know about the recruitment of political leaders. An excellent example of his thinking is his *Recruiting Political Elites* (New York: General Learning Press, 1971). The most complete statement on the subject is Kenneth Prewitt's *The Recruitment of Political Leaders: A Study of Citizen-Politicians* (New York: The Bobbs-Merrill Co., Inc., 1970). Klapp's *Symbolic Leaders* discusses how they emerge. Finally, after having perused so much serious talk about what political communicators and leaders are like and how they reach their positions, the reader might want to examine another little volume which he may or may not care to take just as seriously, Laurence J. Peter and Raymond Hull, *The Peter Principle* (New York: William Morrow and Co., 1969) wherein appears the flat statement that "in a hierarchy, every employee tends to rise to his level of incompetence." Perhaps it is as simple as that!

NOTES

1. "The Communicator in Mass Communication Research," in Paul Halmos, ed., *The Sociology of Mass Media Communications* (Keele, Staffordshire: University of Keele, 1969), p. 7.

2. *Conjectures and Refutations: The Growth of Scientific Knowledge* (New York: Basic Books, 1962), p. 349.

3. *Public Opinion and Propaganda* (Hamden, Conn.: Archon Books, 1966), pp. 559–60.

4. *Ibid.,* p. 559. See also Bruce Lannes Smith, "The Political Communication Specialist of Our Times," in Harold Lasswell and Ralph Casey, eds., *Propaganda, Communication, and Public Opinion* (Princeton: Princeton University Press, 1946), pp. 31–73.

5. "Patterns of Leadership," in Jeanne N. Knutson, ed., *Handbook of Political Psychology* (San Francisco: Jossey-Bass Publishers, 1973), pp. 206–7.

6. Talcott Parsons, "On the Concept of Influence," *Public Opinion Quarterly,* 27 (Spring 1963): 37–62.

7. *Public Opinion and Foreign Policy* (New York: Random House, 1961), p. 59.

8. "The Communications Revolution and the Professional Communicator," in Halmos, *The Sociology of Mass Media Communications,* p. 27. See also Harold D. Lasswell, "The Person: Subject and Object of Propaganda," *The Annals,* 179 (1935): 187–93.

9. Halmos, p. 28.

10. Joseph Napolitan, *The Election Game and How to Win It* (Garden City, N.Y.: Doubleday & Co., 1972).

11. For a discussion of the development of various facets of the journalist role see John C. Merrill and Ralph L. Lowenstein, *Media, Messages and Men* (New York: David McKay Co., 1971), pp. 106–110.

12. Maxwell E. McCombs and Donald L. Shaw, "The Agenda-Setting Function of the Media, *Public Opinion Quarterly,* 36 (Summer 1972): 176–187.

13. "The Communications Revolution," p. 28.

14. Clarice N. Olien et al., "The Community Editor's Power and the Reporting of Conflict," *Journalism Quarterly,* 45 (Summer 1968): 243–52. For a study reporting that local editors may not neglect their news role but be even more aggressive, see J. K. Hvistendal, "Publisher's Power: Functional or Dysfunctional?" *Journalism Quarterly,* 47 (Autumn 1970): 472–8.

15. Rosenau, *Public Opinion and Foreign Policy,* p. 59.

16. Ralph M. Goldman, *Behavioral Perspective on American Politics* (Homewood, Ill.: Dorsey Press, 1973).

17. Everett M. Rogers and David G. Cartano, "Methods of Measuring Opinion Leadership," *Public Opinion Quarterly,* 26 (Fall 1962): 435–41. See also Wendell Bell et al., *Public Leadership* (San Francisco: Chandler Publishing Co., 1961). pp. 23–8.

18. John W. Kingdon, "Opinion Leaders in the Electorate," *Public Opinion Quarterly,* 34 (Summer 1970): 256–61.

19. Paul Lazarsfeld et al., *The People's Choice,* 3rd ed. (New York: Columbia University Press, 1968), p. 151.

20. Lyman E. Ostlund, "Interpersonal Communication Following McGovern's Eagleton Decision," *Public Opinion Quarterly,* 37 (Winter 1973–74): 601–610.

21. Richard J. Hill and Charles M. Bonjean, "News Diffusion: A Test of the Regularity Hypothesis," *Journalism Quarterly,* 41 (Summer 1964), p. 342.

22. "Leadership," in Gardner Lindzey and Elliot Aronson, eds., *The Handbook of Social Psychology*, 2nd ed. (Reading, Mass.: Addison-Wesley Publishing Co., 1969), 4:205–82.

23. *Ibid.,* p. 205.

24. Katz, "Patterns of Leadership," p. 204.

25. James N. Rosenau, *National Leadership and Foreign Policy* (Princeton: Princeton Press, 1963), p. 6.

26. Fred E. Fiedler, *Leadership* (Morristown, N.J.: General Learning Press, 1971), p. 2.

27. Sidney Verba, *Small Groups and Political Behavior: A Study of Leadership* (Princeton: Princeton University Press, 1961), p. 118.

28. *Handbook of Leadership* (New York: The Free Press, 1974), pp. 7–16.

29. Gibb, "Leadership," pp. 267–71; Stogdill, *Handbook of Leadership*, pp. 17–23.

30. Eugene E. Jennings, *An Anatomy of Leadership: Princes, Heroes, and Supermen* (New York: McGraw-Hill Book Co., 1960).

31. Stogdill, *Handbook of Leadership*, pp. 35–91.

32. John W. Fox, "The Concepts of Image and Adoption in Relation to Interpersonal Behavior," *Journal of Communication*, 17 (June 1967): 147–51; Kenneth Boulding, *The Image* (Ann Arbor: University of Michigan Press, Anchor Books, 1961), p. 102; David A. Baldwin, "Money and Power," *Journal of Politics*, 33 (August 1971): 578–614.

33. Stogdill, *Handbook of Leadership*, p. 215.

34. *Ibid.,* p. 354. Also see Robert L. Kelley et al., "Role-Taking and Role-Playing in Human Communication," *Human Communication Research*, 1 (Fall 1974): 62–74.

35. Gibb, "Leadership," p. 268.

36. *People and Politics* (Englewood Cliffs, N.J.: Prentice-Hall, 1962), pp. 38–48.

37. *Handbook of Leadership*, p. 65.

38. Fiedler, *Leadership*, pp. 6–7.

39. Robert F. Bales, "Task Roles and Social Roles in Problem-Solving Groups," in Bruce J. Biddle and Edwin J. Thomas, eds., *Role Theory* (New York: John Wiley & Sons, Inc., 1966), pp. 254–62.

40. John F. Manley, "Wilbur D. Mills: A Study in Congressional Influence," *American Political Science Review*, 63 (June 1969): 442–64.

41. Fiedler, *Leadership*, p. 16.

42. Gibb, "Leadership," p. 242 (emphasis in original).

43. Alex Bavelas, "Communication Patterns in Task-Oriented Groups," in Daniel Lerner and Harold B. Lasswell, *The Policy Sciences* (Stanford: Stanford University Press, 1961), pp. 193–202.

44. Rosenau, *National Leadership and Foreign Policy*, vol. 6 (emphasis in original).

45. Karl W. Deutsch, *The Nerves of Government* (New York: The Free Press of Glencoe, 1963), pp. 157–60.

46. *Symbolic Leaders: Public Drama and Public Men* (New York: Minerva Press, 1964), p. 22.

47. *Ibid.,* p. 212.

48. Herbert Blumer, "The Crowd, the Public, and the Mass," in Alfred McClung Lee, ed., *New Outline of Principles of Sociology* (New York: Barnes and Noble, 1946), pp. 185–93.

49. Steven R. Brown and John D. Ellithorp, "Emotional Experiences in Political Groups: The Case of the McCarthy Phenomenon," *American Political Science Review*, 64 (June 1970): 349–66.

50. Klapp, *Symbolic Leaders*, p. 24.

51. Murray Edelman, *The Symbolic Uses of Politics* (Urbana: University of Illinois Press, 1964), p. 81.

52. Leon Dion, "The Concept of Political Leadership," *Canadian Journal of Political Science* 1 (March 1968): 66–78.

53. *The Symbolic Uses of Politics*, p. 75.

54. Fiedler, *Leadership*, p. 3; Gibb, "Leadership," pp. 248–51; Verba, *Small Groups and Political Behavior*, pp. 117–20.

55. "An Exchange Theory of Interest Groups," *Midwest Journal of Political Science*, 13 (February 1969): 16.

56. Gibb, "Leadership," pp. 252–54.

57. *The Philosophy of Nietzsche* (New York: Random House, 1927), p. 457.

58. Renato Taguiri, "Person Perception," in Lindzey and Aronson, eds., *Handbook of Social Psychology*, 3:432.

59. *The Gallup Poll*, May 25, 1975.

60. Roberta S. Sigel, "Image of the American Presidency," in Aaron Wildavsky, ed., *The Presidency* (Boston: Little, Brown and Co., 1969), pp. 296–309; Fred I. Greenstein, "Popular Images of the President," in Wildavsky, *The Presidency*, pp. 287–96; and Donald J. Devine, *The Political Culture of the United States* (Boston: Little, Brown, and Co., 1972), p. 155.

61. John E. Mueller, *War, Presidents, and Public Opinion* (New York: John Wiley & Sons, 1963); Richard A. Brody and Benjamin I. Page, "The Impact of Events on Presidential Popularity: The Johnson and Nixon Administrations," in Aaron Wildavsky, ed., *Perspectives on the Presidency* (Boston: Little, Brown, 1975), pp. 136–48; James A. Stimson, "Public Support for American Presidents: A Cyclical Model," *Public Opinion Quarterly*, 40 (Spring 1976), pp. 1–21.

62. M. Kent Jennings et al., "Trusted Leaders: Perceptions of Appointed Federal Officials," *Public Opinion Quarterly*, 30 (Fall 1966): 368–84; Franklin P. Kirkpatrick et al., *The Image of the Federal Service* (Washington, D.C.: The Brookings Institution, 1964).

63. Gabriel A. Almond and Sidney Verba, *The Civic Culture* (Princeton: Princeton University Press, 1963), pp. 108–09.

64. *The Harris Survey*, March 22, 1976.

65. Devine, *The Political Culture of the United States*, p. 163.

66. Roger H. Davidson, "Public Prescriptions for the Job of Congressman," *Midwest Journal of Political Science*, 14 (November 1970): 648–66.

67. Harris Surveys, however, suggest that the decline in confidence toward major institutions may be ending; see, for example, the Harris Survey, March 14, 1977, for evidence of a slight rise in confidence. Also consult Everett Carl Ladd, Jr., "The Polls: The Question of Confidence," *Public Opinion Quarterly*, 40 (Winter 1976-1977): 544–52, for the view that a decade of declining confidence in institutions has not necessarily produced a "legitimacy crisis."

68. Dan Nimmo and Robert L. Savage, *Candidates and Their Images* (Pacific Palisades, Cal.: Goodyear Publishing Co., 1976); Associated Press/Roper Survey, June 3, 1976.

69. The data come from a nationwide survey conducted for the Associated Press by the Roper Organization, May 8-15, 1976; a cross-section of more than 2000 Americans over age 18 were interviewed. The results were reported by Evans Witt, "Most Supporters in Dark on Carter's View on Issues," in AP dispatches of June 1.

70. *The Sindlinger Survey*, June 10, 1974; see also Leslie W. Sargent, "Communicator Image and News Reception," *Journalism Quarterly*, 42 (Winter 1965): 35–42.

71. *What People Think of Television and Other Mass Media 1959–1972* (New York: The Roper Organization, 1973).

72. *The Harris Survey*, September 30, 1974.

73. *National Opinion Research Survey*, 1974.

74. *The Harris Survey*, June 23, 1975; see also Louis Harris, *Confidence and*

Concern: Citizens View the American Government (Cleveland: Regal Books/King's Court Communications, 1974).

75. Klapp, *Symbolic Leaders,* pp. 101–20.

76. For recent summaries of such findings see Carol H. Weiss, "What America's Leaders Read," *Public Opinion Quarterly,* 38 (Spring 1974): 1–22; and Thomas R. Dye et al., "Institutional Elites in the United States," *Social Science Quarterly,* 54 (June 1973): 8–28.

77. For a comparison of the characteristics of political and nonpolitical leaders, see Thomas R. Dye, *Who's Running America?* (Englewood Cliffs, N.J.: Prentice-Hall, Inc., 1976).

78. David T. Stanley, *The Higher Civil Service* (Washington, D.C.: The Brookings Institution, 1964).

79. Stephen V. Monsma, "Potential Leaders and Democratic Values," *Public Opinion Quarterly,* 35 (Fall 1971): 350–57.

80. Lester M. Salamon, "Leadership and Modernization: The Emerging Black Political Elite in the American South," *Journal of Politics,* 35 (August 1973): 615–46.

81. See John W. C. Johnstone et al., "The Professional Values of American Newsmen," *Public Opinion Quarterly,* 36 (Winter 1971–72): 522–40; Merrill and Lowenstein, *Media, Messages, and Men,* pp. 110–18; and William L. Rivers, "The Correspondents After 25 Years," *Columbia Journalism Review,* 1 (Spring 1962): 4–10.

82. See C. Wright Mills, *The Power Elite* (New York: Oxford University Press, 1957), and G. William Domhoff, *Who Rules America?* (Englewood Cliffs, N.J.: Prentice-Hall, 1967) as examples of this point of view.

83. Lester Milbrath, *The Washington Lobbyists* (Chicago: Rand McNally, 1963).

84. Kingdon, "Opinion Leaders in the Electorate," p. 258; see also Bell et al., *Public Leadership,* Ch. 6.

85. Kenneth Prewitt and Heinz Eulau, "Social Bias in Leadership Selection, Political Recruitment, and Electoral Context," *Journal of Politics,* 33 (May 1971): 293–315.

86. Kenneth Prewitt, *The Recruitment of Political Leaders: A Study of Citizen-Politicians* (New York: The Bobbs-Merrill Co., Inc., 1970), pp. 6–8.

87. Compare the discussion to Lester G. Seligman, *Recruiting Political Elites* (New York: General Learning Press, 1971); and Herbert Jacob, "Initial Recruitment of Elected Officials in the U.S.: A Model," *Journal of Politics,* 24 (November 1962): 703–16.

88. Sidney Verba and Norman H. Nie, *Participation in America* (New York: Harper & Row, 1972), pp. 56–81; and Prewitt, *The Recruitment of Political Leaders,* p. 53.

89. Seligman, *Recruiting Political Elites;* A. Lee Hunt, Jr., and Robert E. Pendley, "Community Gatekeepers: An Examination of Political Recruiters," *Midwest Journal of Political Science,* 16 (August 1972): 411–38.

90. Gordon S. Black, "A Theory of Professionalization in Politics," *American Political Science Review,* 64 (September 1970): 865.

91. Joseph A. Schlesinger, *Ambition and Politics* (Chicago: Rand McNally & Co., 1966), p. 2. See also Michael L. Mezey, "Ambition Theory and the Office of Congressman," *Journal of Politics,* 32 (August 1970): 563–79; Gordon S. Black, "A Theory of Political Ambition: Career Choices and the Role of Structural Incentives," *American Political Science Review,* 66 (March 1973): 144–59; Jeff Fischel, "Ambition and the Political Vocation: Congressional Challengers in American Politics," *Journal of Politics,* 33 (February 1971): 25–56.

92. Klapp, *Symbolic Leaders,* pp. 34–5.

93.   E. P. Hollander, *Leaders, Groups, and Influence* (New York: Oxford University Press, 1964).

94.   Black, "A Theory of Professionalization in Politics"; C. Richard Hofstetter, "The Amateur Politician: A Problem in Construct Validation," *Midwest Journal of Political Science,* 15 (February 1971): 31–56; Jack M. McLeod and Searle E. Hawley Jr., "Professionalization Among Newsmen," *Journalism Quarterly,* 41 (Autumn 1964): 529–38; Ralph N. Dove and Otto Lerbinger, "Should a Public Relations Man Be the Mirror Image of His Boss?" in Otto Lerbinger and Albert J. Sullivan, eds., *Information, Influence, and Communication* (New York: Basic Books, Inc., 1965), pp. 75–86.

95.   John C. Merrill, *The Imperative of Freedom* (New York: Hastings House, Publishers, 1974), Ch. 6.

96.   Jennings, *The Anatomy of Leadership,* Ch. 2.

97.   Prewitt, *The Recruitment of Political Leaders,* pp. 205–06.

98.   Bruce H. Westley and Malcolm S. MacLean, Jr. "A Conceptual Model for Communications Research," *Journalism Quarterly,* 34 (Winter 1957): 31–8.

chapter 3

Political Talk: Symbols, Languages, and Public Opinion

Whether leaders be politicians, professionals, or active citizens, one thing that distinguishes them as political communicators is that they talk politics. For these communicators—the "whos" that "say" in our description of political communication—the "saying" consists of political talk. We examine that talk in this chapter. We will dwell here less on the *substance* of political talk (something of greater concern in Chapter 4) than on the *saying* itself: What makes talk political? What do words and word play have to do with politics? And what are the uses of political talk?

POLITICS AS TALK

If, as the saying goes, talk is cheap, it may be because there is so much of it. Certainly there is a lot of talk in politics, so much that it appears that politics *is* talk.[1] Consider, for example, how important talk is in the daily lives of politicians, both officeholders and office seekers. Most of us know the president either because of his talk (in press conferences, speeches, written statements, etc.) or what others say about him. Television, newspaper, and magazine journalists explore his every word for nuances, innuendos, and hints of things to come. A reticent president gets almost as much copy for *not* speaking (for example, "Silent" Cal Coolidge) as for what he says when he does. Through bureaus, committees, seemingly endless regulations, and the publication of all varieties of social, economic, and political information, the President's executive subordinates multiply many times over the amount of talk issuing from the administrative bureauacy. Members of Congress hardly shy away from talk either. The volume of words pouring forth from congressional debate, hearings, statutes, and items inserted into the *Congressional Record* is vocal, not silent, testimony that Congress is indeed a parlimentary body in the full sense of the French *parler,* to talk. The courts are also arenas of talk; there judges manage a process of speaking and counterspeaking between interested adversaries before finally rendering a verbal decision. And if talk occupies a large portion of the lives of executive, legislative, and judicial officeholders, think how essential it is to the candidate for office. An election campaign without political talk is inconceivable. But the total volume of political talk cannot be attributed solely to politicians. Professional political communicators, both journalists and promoters, contribute a vast portion, and as noted in Chapter 2, activists such as organizational spokespersons and opinion leaders are by definition practioners in verbiage.

The superabundance of political discourse is not the only reason to think of politics as talk. Talk includes far more than oral or written verbal activity. People talk to one another even if not a word is spoken. What we said about communication generally in Chapter 1 holds for talk as well; any act that is meaningful to one or more persons has message value. As popular aphorisms indicate, the idea is scarcely novel—viz., "money talks," "by their deeds ye shall know them," or, (as a recent Attorney General of the United States urged critics) "judge us not by what we say but what we do." Any act may communicate or say something; therefore any activity (including politics) is talk.

If all activity in the sense just described, however, can be viewed as talking, what is distinctive about political talk? We defined politics in Chapter 1 as activity of people regulating their conduct under conditions of social conflict, i.e., efforts to negotiate acceptable resolutions of disputes. Political negotiation aims at reaching a common understanding among parties as to what accepted terms of an agreement mean. They hope to create shared expectations regarding how parties will act respecting one another in the future. Negotiation involves people affecting one another's expectations. Talk that affects others, notes political scientist David V. J. Bell, "has by definition assumed political overtones." According to Bell three kinds of talk are of definite political significance and are distinctly political—power talk, influence talk, and authority talk.[2]

Power talk affects people through threat or promise. A typical form is "If you do X, *I* will do Y." Here "X" is the posture a talker desires of another person, "Y" is the declared intent to permit more (a promise) or less (a threat) enjoyment of something if that posture is forthcoming. The key to power talk is that the "I" has sufficient resources to back up either promise or threat and the other person expects the power wielder to do so. *Influence talk* takes place in the absence of such sanctions: "If you do X, *you* will do (feel, experience, etc.) Y." Promises, threats, bribes, and extortions are the currency of power communications; they yield to advice, encouragement, urgings, and warnings in influence communications. As Bell points out, power relations rest on the ability to manipulate positive or negative sanctions, but the influencer (because of his prestige or reputation) successfully manipulates another's perceptions or expectations of the contingencies of gains or losses. In effect, the influencer says, "If you do X, Y will happen," but it is beyond the control of the influencer to actually supply Y. Finally, *authority talk* is the discourse of command. Conditions are removed and the statement of authority is "Do X" or "Do not do X." One regarded as the legitimate ruler is the voice of authority and has the right to be obeyed. The sources of that legitimacy, and thus of authority, differ widely; examples are religious faith in the supernatural or superhuman qualities of the ruler, a ruler's personal attractiveness, custom, habit, or official position, and subjects' indoctrination to the view that certain officials ought to be obeyed. Whatever its source, authority talk poses an imperative rather than the contingent form so characteristic of power and influence.

For the nonce let us say that politics is a discourse of power, influence, and authority. It is also a discourse of conflict. Through talk political communicators adjust their differences by constructing a vocabulary of shared assumptions, meanings, expectations and commitments. That sharing, however, is only partial, never total. The vocabulary of political communicators contains nebulous terms such as "democracy," "freedom," "justice," with disputed meanings. These "essentially contested concepts" provoke and intensify contests central to politics.[3] We thereby have the intriguing paradox of politics; it is an activity of regulating conflict largely through talk, yet one that employs terms that are in dispute. Strangely enough politics adjusts conflicts through ongoing disagreements over words, conflicts which themselves must be accommodated.

Our modern political vocabulary of power, influence, authority, and conflict is of relatively recent origin. E. E. Schattschneider, for example, examined dictionaries published in the early 19th century and found that what we now accept as a language of politics scarcely existed in the 1800s.[4] What we currently regard as standard political words had far different meanings almost two centuries ago. For example, a ballot was defined as a ball, a lobby as an opening for a room, a campaign as the time an army keeps the field, a partisan as a kind of pike, an issue as an offspring, and electoral college was not even in the dictionary. By the eve of the Civil War, however, a distinctive political vocabulary was evolving; dictionaries not only defined terms such as those above in a more modern sense, but concepts such as presidential elector, speaker, and sovereignty were included. Yet a large number of contemporary political words still had not come into being in the mid-19th century—viz., apportionment, backlash, balanced budget, collective security, draft dodger, favorite son, landslide election, patronage, pressure group, voter registration, White House and many, many more. Indeed, Schattschneider provides a list of 500 terms in contemporary political parlance not defined in dictionaries of the last century.

As we see later, our available vocabulary helps shape our expectations and how we see, think, and feel about things. Thus the evolution of political language both reflects the changes in political thinking and influences perceived political options. Many people contribute to that evolution, but political leaders are especially active in coining new terms. With Franklin Roosevelt, for instance, came such coinages as forgotten man, New Deal, brain trust, and dollar-a-year man; Harry Truman provided Fair Deal and do-nothing, 80th Congress; the Eisenhower years witnessed the addition of domino theory, atoms for peace, brinkmanship, and massive retaliation; John F. Kennedy's administration supplied New Frontier, missile crisis, and others; with Lyndon Johnson came the war on poverty, nervous nellies, and credibility gap; and the Nixon years brought Watergate, stonewalling, and inoperative statement.[5]

Talk is thus important to politics, and broadly considered, politics is talk—an evolving discourse of power, influence, authority, and conflict. We qualify this claim for the political significance of talk in two respects. First, in spite of the importance of political talk in public life, relatively little of the talk of everyday conversation is *about* politics. A study of telephone conversations, for example, concluded that the subject of politics entered in less than one percent of the conversations; similarly, in general writing in English, perhaps less than one percent consists of politically relevant terms. In all, the bulk of our political language consists of terms which appear less often than one in ten thousand words. This relative lack of political terminology in conversation and writing is in part to be expected; given the fact that of all the words in the English language thirty of them account for half the words spoken and sixty-nine for half those written, it is unlikely that we would find a high usage of political terms. Yet even taking that into account, political talk is more the exception in every day life than the rule.[6]

Second, in stressing how important talk is to politics we should not ignore that politics is important to talk. In fact, one way to think of politics is that it is *talk to preserve talk,* i.e., the willingness of people to negotiate their differences through talk rather than resort to destructive combat for ending both the dispute and each other. Generically, then, political talk is not predisposed to serve any specific interest or end beyond the preservation of talk itself. Politics is a means to publicize interest conflicts and resolve them. If, as regulator of conflict, "political activity pertains to actions oriented to the maintenance and/or extension of other actions," political talk relates to ensuring and/or extending other talk.[7]

By considering politics as talk, then, we do not argue that all talk is political, for clearly it is not. Rather, political talk is talk that preserves and fosters talk about other matters. Specifically it is talk involving power, influence, authority, and conflict, a discourse with a continuously evolving vocabulary and one we want to explore in a greater detail.

THE CHARACTER OF POLITICAL TALK

To enhance our understanding of the relationship between talk and politics, we need to look at two facets of that association before examining how people use talk in politics. First, we consider the nature of political words; then, we explore the combinations of terms in the form of word play, the language of politics.

Symbolic Activity: The Words of Political Talk

If politics extends to any activity that regulates human conduct sufficiently to ensure that other, nonpolitical activities continue (and thereby if political talk is talk to preserve other talk), then the words of politics consist of far more than those listed in any dictionary. In a larger sense the "words" of politics extend beyond spoken and written utterances to drawings, paintings, photographs, film (the pictures allegedly worth a thousand words); and to gestures, facial expressions, and all manner of other actions (actions that proverbially speak louder than words). These other kinds of political "words" are *symbols*. In short, political talk is symbolic activity.

In Chapter 1 we touched upon the nature of symbolic activity. It is appropriate to review that discussion briefly. Recall that we said people take into account a variety of objects in the form of signs, signals, and cues. They interpret these objects in meaningful ways, thereby forming mental images of them. They exchange these images, or meanings, through symbols. Thus the primary elements in talk (i.e., communication) are (1) symbols, (2) the things symbolized, and (3) interpretation that creates meaningful symbols. The relationship between symbols, referents, and interpretation are depicted in Figure 3–1. The two solid lines in the triangle indicate that there is a direct relation between, first, the thought or interpretation and a referent (as when we think of a piece of cloth with alternating red and white bars and having in one corner 50 white stars on a blue background), and, second, between interpretation and symbol (for example, the symbol "U.S. flag"). Between symbol and referent, however, the relation is indirect, or imputed (indicated by the broken line). It reminds us that *the symbol is not a direct representation of the object;* without the active thought of a human being the flag is no flag at all, merely a piece of cloth. In sum, the "referent, thing, or object has uses, activities, or functions. These give rise to a person's thoughts about the referent. The symbol or word is the name ... which we give to the referent and the thought that is related to it."[8]

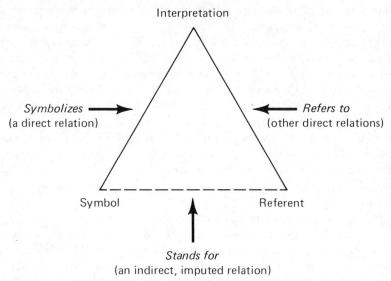

Figure 3-1:   The Relationship of Symbols, Interpretations, and Meanings

Adapted from C.K. Ogden and I.A. Richards, *The Meaning of Meaning* (New York: Harcourt, Brace and World, Inc., 1923), p. 11.

To say that political talk is symbolic activity, then, is to say that the words, or symbols, of political discourse have no intrinsic meanings independent of the thought processes of those who use them.[9] That various political communicators enter into a discourse using the same words to mean the same things is problematical. For it to happen, political talk must become an exchange of what George Herbert Mead called *significant* symbols. For Mead thinking always involved symbols. Any symbol is a significant symbol when it leads to the same response in another person that it calls out in the thinker. Significant symbols, then, are those with common meanings or understandings shared by all parties to a conversation. Common meanings, as we have said, are not givens; the meaning of and response to a symbol are not the same for everyone. Rather than existing in advance of discourse, significant symbols arise through mutual role taking, a process of social interaction. Thus, significant symbols that yield a shared political vocabulary evolve from continuous negotiation and renegotiation of political communicators. Through the social construction of significant symbols, political talk provides a common universe of discourse that preserves and enhances the opportunities for people to engage in furthur talk directed at adjusting their interest differences.[10]

There has evolved a large variety of significant symbols in politics. Some pertain to authority talk; they symbolize mutual understandings that people should revere and obey what they stand for: constitutions, laws, treaties, etc. Others symbolize power talk (for example, the annual

May Day parade of military armaments by the Soviets in Moscow). A large portion of significant symbols, however, are influence talk: party platforms, slogans, speeches, editorials, etc. Still others combine features of all three forms of political talk: memorial days, public monuments, music and anthems, ceremonies, artistic designs, flags, emblems, etc. It is helpful to classify political symbols in accordance with the types of objects symbolized: "Old Glory" and "democracy" pertain to the entire political community; "due process" symbolizes a rule or norm of the political regime; "the president" and "CIA" refer to formal political roles and institutions; "Gerald Ford" or "Jimmy Carter" symbolizes a particular government officeholder; "Ralph Nader," a nongovernmental personality. Finally, there are symbols of complex issues, such as the terms "busing" and "law and order."[11]

Whether we classify political symbols from the viewpoint of their usage in a particular form of political talk or the objects they presumably represent, political symbols normally blend referential and condensational qualities. *Referential* symbols indicate particular or general categories of objects, be those objects physical, social, or abstract, as described in Chapter 1. Referential symbols have denotative meanings, meanings that link the symbol to its referent. A *condensation* symbol is "a highly condensed form of substitutive behavior for direct expression, allowing for the ready release of emotional tension in conscious or unconscious form." Edward Sapir, the scholar who coined this distinction, provided an example: "telegraph ticking is a virtually pure example of referential symbolism; the apparently meaningless washing ritual of an obsessive neurotic, as interpreted by phychoanalysts, would be a pure example of condensation symbolism."[12] In furthur contrast to referential symbols, those of the condensational variety have more connotative than denotative meanings; the meanings associated with them consist of orientations toward the symbol itself rather than toward anything specific that it denotes. Citing our previous example, a flag may refer to a piece of cloth of specific design (referential/denotative) but also symbolize feelings people have for their nation (condensational/connotative). As noted, however, most symbolic activity combines both referential and condensation elements; for instance, a Jimmy Carter or Ralph Nader is a symbolic leader, for the name of the individual refers to a specific person who followers support as a target for projecting their deeply experienced emotional needs, demands, and expectations. In short, the meaning we find in such persons (and in other symbols as well) pertains to more than whatever qualities those persons possess apart from our perceptions of them; that meaning is also a function of the emotional outlet the person symbolizes for us.

Symbolic activity, then, consists of people constructing common meanings and responses to referential and condensation symbols manifest in words, pictures, and behavior. In saying that these meanings and responses flow from mutual role taking, we call attention to an important function of symbols, which is that they induce people to play roles (a feature that we shall find most relevant to our discussion of the effects of political communication in Chapter 10). This is as true for political symbols as for any other variety.[13] For example, a person moving to the occupancy of high political office (president, governor, congressman, etc.) assumes the title and trappings of the position; those symbols help shape the beliefs, values, and expectations of large numbers of people regarding how they should respond to that incumbent. Or take another example: people are likely to respond quite differently to a law that has been declared constitutional by the Supreme Court than to one not so labeled.

By inducing people to respond in certain ways, to play specific roles toward government, and to change their thoughts, feelings, and expectations, significant political symbols facilitate the formation of public opinion. As significant symbols of political talk, the words, pictures, and acts of political communicators are tipoffs to people that they can expect fellow citizens to respond to symbols in certain anticipated ways. For instance, political leaders throughout history have called out a spirit of self-sacrifice and collective dedication from their citizens by couching their appeals in significant terms, e.g., Winston Churchill's call for blood, toil, tears, and sweat from fellow Britons in World War II, and John Kennedy's ringing cry, "Ask not what your country can do for you, ask what you can do for your country." The absence of significant symbols, however, may impede emergence of a widely shared common response just as the presence of those symbols may facilitate it. Schettler notes that in China in an earlier era there was a common written but no common spoken language. Among the literate the exchange of significant symbols promoted common understanding, but public opinion scarcely developed among persons limited to oral communication.[14]

Significant symbols are important to the opinion process in another, albeit related, way. Recall that in our discussion of symbolic leaders in Chapter 2 we noted that theorists have argued that social order arises out of the controls leaders impose on followers (the social control view). The manipulation of significant political symbols to rally support is one variety of such social control. Another view, convergent selection or consensus, posits that discrete persons with sometimes overlapping, sometimes conflicting reasons and motivations, make identical choices (such as responding to a leader in the same ways, voting for the same candidate, tuning in to the same television program, etc.). Public opinion in this view is not so much managed, ordered, or mandated as derived from individuals freely responding in similar ways to significant symbols. We have now introduced a third view that social order results from mutual role taking, the construction and negotiation of significant symbols through social interplay. Regardless of whether one posits a social control, consensus, or negotiation model of what makes society and public opinion possible, however, political symbols, the essentials of political talk, play a critical part in achieving social order through the opinion process.[15]

Having examined the nature of political talk as symbolic activity and its relation to the opinion process, we need to consider but one other matter before detailing the political uses of talk. Language is the process of communicating meaning through symbols. To complement our discussion of political talk as symbolic activity, therefore, we explore the underlying character of political talk as language.

Language: The Word Play of Political Talk

Generically if symbols are the words of political talk, language is the word play of that discourse. In a semipopular survey of linguistics, Peter Farb likens talk to a game, not in the sense of a trivial pastime such as puns, puzzles, or jokes, but a serious game (more like war games). The game analogy is appropriate, says Farb, because (1) like any game, language requires players, (2) virtually any person within the vicinity of the game can be pressured to commit himself to play (remember our observation in Chapter 1 that one cannot not communicate), (3) prizes, tangible and intangible, are at stake, (4) each player has a distinctive playing style, (5) certain factors in the game are unpredictable (such as a player's moves or meaning of words), and (6) there are grammars for the language game peculiar to each speech community.[16] Farb is not alone in pointing to the gamelike features of language. Lyman and Scott describe all social situations in which two or more persons or groups communicate and engage in goal-directed action as games. Talk keeps social games going. For instance, by rendering accounts people explain their unanticipated or untoward behavior, such as a faux pas, accidents, or rudeness. Through excuses (admitting an inappropriate act but denying full responsibility for it, as in "the Devil made me do it") and justifications (admitting responsibility, but denying the pejorative quality of an act, or "it's really not all that bad"), people negotiate and enhance preferred identities vis-à-vis one another.[17] Lest the reader think such matters are irrelevant to politics, merely recall that in 1973 we witnessed a president, Richard Nixon, admit his culpability for acts surrounding the Watergate affair, but only to take the responsibility, not the blame (excuse); later when admitting responsibility for an act, he denied its seriousness with the disclaimer, "I am not a crook."

Most scholars of linguistics prefer more technical definitions of language than simply to refer to it as word play. Definitions vary, but there is consensus that language is a system of communication (1) composed of combinations of significant symbols (signs with common meanings and responses for people), in which (2) the significance of the symbols transcends the immediate situations where the language is used and (3) the symbols are combined in accordance with certain rules. Since at least the time of the Greeks people have been intrigued by the many functions performed by language. Greek philosophers viewed language as a means of discovering and expressing truth, a mode of artistic expression, and an instrument of persuasion. Shakespeare emphasized similar functions of language: to convey wisdom, win esteem, and convince. Contemporary linguistic experts provide a more detailed list of the social, psychological, and political functions of language.

W. P. Robinson catalogs the most important social functions of language.[18] They are noteworthy because they pertain to the political functions of talk as well. Briefly, Robinson lists these key functions of language:

1. *Avoidance of worse activity:* People use talk to escape unpleasant situations; we all know persons who prefer to talk rather than complete some assigned task, or who change the subject in a conversation rather than discuss an embarrassing problem. In politics think of how many officeholders and office seekers have perfected the art of using language to dodge questions they prefer to avoid.

2. *Conformity to norms:* Through speech and writing we indicate our acceptance or rejection of social rules. Politicians, for instance, are alert to remark that they adhere to the rules of fair play, openness, and free expression.

3. *Aesthetics:* Through literature, poetry, drama, novels, and rhetoric, people use language to express aesthetic values; a few politicians have, for instance, been well known for the aesthetic quality of their rhetoric—Abraham Lincoln, Franklin Roosevelt, Adlai Stevenson, and others.

4. *Encounter regulation:* Language is used for greetings and leave taking; in politics we see such encounter regulation in diplomatic circles, when campaigners "press the flesh," etc.

5. *Performatives:* People use language to make promises, assurances that acts will be performed. Obviously performatives are a large part of the linguistic hardware of the politician.

6. *Regulation of self:* Almost everyone talks to himself, either aloud or silently; we rehearse social situations before encountering, fantasize about things, or try to "psych" ourselves. Reporting an analysis of the contents of the conversations recorded between Richard Nixon and his top aides in the White House, Geoffrey Stokes indicated that the president used almost a third of such private talk to rehearse what he would later say in public.[19]

7. *Regulation of others:* We have discussed this earlier as power, influence, and authority talk.

8. *Expression of affect:* We all use language for exclamation ("Oh! My love!") and some of us, including presidents with "expletives deleted," even swear upon occasion.

9. *Expression of social identity:* Speech patterns frequently reflect social background, region of upbringing, etc. Certainly the clipped accent of John F. Kennedy differed from that of the mellifluous southern politician Jimmy Carter.

10. *Marking of role relationships:* Through talk people define one another as superior, subordinate, or equal in status.[20] As noted in Chapter 2 for example, leader-follower relations arise through an exchange of expectations, an exchange consummated through language.

11. *Reference to the nonlinguistic world:* Here Robinson speaks of the function of language in thought, problem solving, analysis, arguing, reporting, etc. Obviously this function is critical in politics, as in all endeavors.

12. *Instruction:* Language is vital to teaching and to the existence of an informed citizenry in any governmental arrangement.

13. *Inquiry:* Interrogation, whether it be in the form of the child's simple "Why can't I?" or the more involved confrontation between reporters and a president at a news conference, a congressional hearing, or the cross-examination of witnesses, points up the key function of language as a tool of finding answers to troublesome questions. In the Senate Watergate hearings of 1974, cochairman Howard Baker of Tennessee made a national reputation by reiterating the question, "What did the President know and when did he know it?"

There is controversy among students of linguistics regarding the psychological functions of language which centers primarily upon the Sapir-Whorf hypothesis. Benjamin Whorf, following up on earlier notions of Edward Sapir, asked questions such as: "Are our concepts of 'time,' 'space,' and 'matter' given in substantially the same form by experience of all men, or are they in part conditioned by the structure of particular languages?" He answered no to the first question, yes to the second.[21] Hence, the hypothesis states that language does not simply provide a means of expressing ideas, but rather that the words people use shape their ideas; that is, thinking is determined (and limited) by the language available to people in a speech community. Moreover, language governs perceptions of things, thus influencing what people see as well as how they conceptualize that reality.

What is at issue regarding the Sapir-Whorf hypothesis is how strongly language influences thinking. The strongest version of the hypothesis says, in effect, that any category of thought derives from the words we have available. Philosopher John Dewey put it thus: "Words are so loaded with associations derived from a long past that instead of being tools for thought, our thoughts become subservient tools of our words."[22] For instance, when the automobile was introduced, the Apache language had no word for such a machine. The Apache therefore applied existing terminology, thinking of the auto as the human body; their word for shoulder referred to the front bumper, for mouth the opening for putting in gasoline, for eye the headlight, and so forth. Such examples are relatively rare and scarcely support the proposition that a language forces people to think in certain ways. A weaker version of the proposition says that words influence perceptions, not conceptions. Thus, if only the words yellow and red were in our vocabulary, when confronted with orange-colored objects we might see yellow or red or one color tinged with another but not orange. This version of the hypothesis too is suspect because of results of scientific experiments. Finally, there is the third variation, that language has little or no direct influence on thinking or perception as such, but does influence how we remember. If people store information in their memories as words, the words available may influence what they can recall and how they remember it.

Regardless of which version of the Sapir-Whorf hypothesis one accepts (or even if one rejects it outright), it is clear that the labels we put on objects is one way of acting toward them, giving them meaning, and exchanging our beliefs, feelings, and expectations regarding what to do about them. Language is less a determinant of thought and action than a catalyst, something that helps precipitate, modify, and increase social transactions: "Language as symbol catalyses a subjective world in which uncertainties are clarified and appropriate courses of action become clear," because each symbol "condenses and rearranges feelings, memories, perceptions, and emotions, a structuring that varies with people's social situations."[23] Words and word play do more than designate objects; they also place a given object (for example, Ralph Nader) in a class of objects ("consumer advocate"), thereby providing guides for viewing, comparing, judging, and evaluating (can a consumer advocate be *all* bad?).

Thus far we have discussed the nature and functions of language from the perspective of oral and written expression. But there are *nonverbal* as well as *verbal languages* and what we have said of the latter also holds for the former. There is good reason to believe, in fact, that a large portion of the meaning and response given to a particular message flows from the interpretation people have of its nonverbal aspects. Psychologist Albert Mehrabian provides a formula for what each component of a message contributes to response: $Total\ Impact = .07$ verbal $+ .38$ vocal $+ .55$ facial.[24] (Of course, the formula does not apply to purely written messages.) Mehrabian's equation strikingly demonstrates that the overall effect of verbal symbols in our speech is relatively small compared to the effect of nonverbal symbols. The latter either reinforce or contradict the verbal message and are especially useful in symbolizing feelings, likings, and preferences. Sometimes nonverbal symbols *add* an entirely new dimension to a message, as when an administrative superior praises the quality of a staff member's work, yet nonverbally leaves the impression he does not like the subordinate.

The vocal aspect of nonverbal communication pertains to intonation, tone, stress, length and frequency of pauses in speaking, etc. Sarcasm, for instance, is a vocal way of indicating that the speaker does not really believe what he speaks, as when, in Shakespeare's *Julius Caesar,* Antony mockingly intones that Brutus is an honorable man. Or "ums" and "ahs," mispronunciations, and stammerings in speech may leave the impression that a speaker lacks confidence in what he is saying. President Dwight Eisenhower impressed reporters in press conferences partly because of the unexpected timing in his utterances and pauses; President Gerald Ford's speech writers, knowing that he had difficulty pronouncing such words as "judgment," purposely omitted difficult terms from his prepared addresses.

Silence, the absence of vocalizing, also performs linguistic functions. Silence between people who are close to one another often transmits feelings of affection and trust that strengthen the bond between them. Silence discloses some things (such as that something is troubling another person), and hides others. Through silence we also make judgments, as, for instance, when we take a person's silence as assent or disagreement with a statement. In the late 1960s political leaders spoke of the "silent majority," an alleged portion of Americans indicating support of policies respecting Vietnam, urban unrest, etc. by *not* speaking out one way or the other. Silence is also a means of impression management, which is a person's effort to influence what others think of him.[25] For instance, the speaker who pauses often leaves the impression of being thoughtful, reflective, and precise. Yet others may think him introverted, shy, and lacking in self-confidence.

The third element in Mehrabian's formula, the facial, refers to more than the expressions of just the face (which is capable of more than 250,000 different ones). Rather, it includes all other actions included in the category of nonverbal communication: body movements and changes in body position, touching, eye movements and head nods, gestures, self-manipulation (such as scratching, pulling one's ear), posture, the arrangement and spacing between people, costuming, etc. It is not hard to cite examples of political communication in this category. Consider proxemics, the study of the use and meanings people give to physical space. In government bureaucracy the general rule is that within an organization (such as the Department of Defense or State Department), the higher an official in the pecking order, the larger, more conveniently located, and sumptuous the office. Prestigious officials have reserved parking spaces, elevators for their private use, and the proverbial key to the executive washroom—visible symbols of superior rank. Another example involves a simple case of perspiration. In the 1972 presidential campaign, the Democratic vice-presidential candidate was Senator Thomas Eagleton of Missouri (ultimately replaced on the ticket). Shortly after a story broke that earlier in his career he had been hospitalized for mental depression, Eagleton appeared on a television network interview program. One of the reporters interviewing Eagleton noted that the candidate was perspiring heavily; was this a sign of nervousness, he asked, suggesting an inability to cope with tension? Eagleton denied that such a meaning should be read into glandular responses. Perhaps he should have simply replied, "Aw, hell; everybody sweats!"

In thinking about verbal and nonverbal languages two points should be remembered. First, communication, both verbal and nonverbal, is activity; whether it be a spoken word, silent pause, nod of the head, or other expression, it is an act which, when occurring in the presence of another who takes it into account, is interpreted. This leads to the second point. With respect to nonverbal modes of discourse, *"no position, expression, or movement ever carries meaning in and of itself"*; rather, as symbolic activity each acquires meaning from the context within which it occurs and the response people make to it, just as with messages transmitted verbally, whether oral or written.[26]

Verbal languages are discursive, i.e., the symbols that comprise them (words, phrases, mathematical notations, codes, points on a map, and similar things) help us to think precisely, make literal statements, and record information. There is a strong cognitive character about discursive languages. Nonverbal languages are nondiscursive; they help us express things that are hard to think about precisely—fantasies, emotional attachments, subtle nuances, mysteries, and other feelings which are difficult to state in a matter-of-fact way. Ritual is a case in point. Political rituals permit leaders and followers to commit themselves to one another in mystical ways, ways beyond the understandings that can be communicated discursively. The inauguration of the president of the United States, for example, is a ritual that melds a rich combination of significant symbols beyond the words of the administered oath: for example, the flag-draped setting on the Capitol steps, the presence of diplomatic dignitaries, the intonations of the chief justice administering the oath, the Holy Bible, even the mode and style of dress. All set the stage for a rite of passage, the bestowing of legitimacy upon the person elevated to presidential office, and his commitment (as Orrin Klapp says of all who take the oaths) that "Honestly, I'll really try. I'll never quit."[27]

Linguist Dell Hymes suggests a very convenient way of keeping in mind the various components that enter into the use of language.[28] His prescription provides an inventory of the kinds of things to keep in mind when analyzing word play; it can be especially helpful in thinking about political word play. Hymes suggests an acronym (SPEAKING); the letters of that acronym provide reminders of the components of any language situation: settings, participants, ends, act sequences, keys, instrumentalities, norms, genres. A shift in any of these elements may indicate changes in the goals, strategies, or intentions of political discourse.

> *Setting, or scene:* Communication occurs in a specific time period, place, and surroundings; it may be formal or informal, somber, gay, etc. An utterance in one setting may be interpreted differently in another. Thus, the meanings placed upon the taped conversations of President Nixon and his advisors concerning Watergate meant one thing within the Oval Office of the White House, and quite another when revealed to congressional inquirers.

> *Participants:* Each party responds meaningfully to a given message. Add or remove a participant and the shared meaning of things, i.e., the significant symbols, change. Imagine a conversation about U.S.-Soviet affairs between the secretary of state and the Soviet ambassador; then add the unlikely presence of a representative of the People's Republic of China. One suspects the shared meaning of "detente" between the three might differ from what it was between the two.

> *Ends:* Political talk normally has some desired outcome as its focus, some preferred end in the minds of its participants. A shift in ends (as when John Dean decided to warn President Nixon of the dangers of continuing to try to cover up aspects of the Watergate affair) can change the meanings and responses to messages.

> *Act sequence:* Written and oral discursive communication and the common forms of nondiscursive language (especially ritual) occur as a sequence of utterances and acts. An interruption of the sequence can disrupt meaningful responses. In the trial of persons indicted for conspiracy to incite riot at the 1968 Democratic convention, the interruptions of one defendant, Bobby Seale, were determined by Judge Hoffman as so disruptive that he ruled at one point Seale should be bound and gagged in the courtroom.

> *Key:* Key refers to Mehrabian's vocal and facial varieties of nonverbal expression. Such things as tone and mannerisms may enhance or even negate the verbal content of a message (as when a public official resolves in a subdued voice that he absolutely will not resign under fire, then resigns shortly thereafter).

> *Instrumentalities:* This refers to the type of language of a speech community. It can imply a specialized argot or jargon of a group (viz., the military argot of body counts, demilitarized zones,

search and destroy, etc.). Such jargon spoken before a group not familiar with it may be little more than a foreign tongue—as would be the case if a president were to urge all citizens to build fallout shelters to "avoid rads and rems of plutonium oxide."

Norms: Unspoken rules govern communication—the proximity as people face each other, eye contact between them, grammatical rules, rules against "talking nonsense," etc. President Lyndon Johnson was famous for encroaching on the territorial space of those he was trying to persuade—touching them, "pressing the flesh," etc. Those who experienced such tactics often were spellbound and persuaded by the performance.

Genres: Here we refer to categories of communication acts—speeches, prayers, jokes, proverbs, inquiries, greetings, farewells, etc. "My fellow Americans" is a ritualistic genre countenanced to identify the speaker as just "one of the boys and girls" of the U.S.

Semiotics: Meanings and Rules of Political Word Play

The acronym SPEAKING reminds us that language involves far more than merely setting down words on paper or voicing one's views. Any language, and political talk is no exception, consists of a rich interplay of significant symbols, both discursive and nondiscursive. The messages resulting from that interplay take many forms and yield diverse meanings, structures, and effects. The study of that diversity is one aspect of the science of semiotics, the general theory of signs and languages.[29] Semiotics examines the diversity of language from three perspectives: *semantics,* the study of meaning; *syntactics,* which deals with rules and structures relating signs to one another (for example, grammar); and *pragmatics,* analysis of the uses and effects of word play. In the next section we examine pragmatic features of the uses of political talk in detail; here it is appropriate to consider the semantics and syntactics of political language.

Political Semantics

Psychologist Hadley Cantril relates the following story of how three umpires described their job of calling balls and strikes in a baseball game:[30]

First Umpire: "Some's balls and some's strikes and I calls 'em as they is."

Second Umpire: "Some's balls and some's strikes and I calls 'em as I sees 'em."

Third Umpire: "Some's balls and some's strikes but they ain't nothin' till I calls 'em."

This little story will help us understand semantics. Recall that we have argued that meaning derives from the way people interpret and respond to symbols. Semantics is thus a study of the meanings things have for minded, responding people rather than a search for intrinsic, universal definitions of words or the essence of the objects so named. For the first umpire, balls and strikes exist as real entities independent of his being; he merely records the essence of things. The second umpire believes that there really are things called balls and strikes too, but he admits to judging which is which from his peculiar perspective. The third umpire regards definition as a *creative* act. There are not really such things as balls and strikes in nature, only motions of a thrown object through the air. Generations of umpires in accordance with shared convention have labeled some balls, some strikes. But for the third umpire, a single pitch is neither ball nor strike until he enters the process and so interprets it. He takes an act (the pitch) and assigns it a meaning (ball or strike) derived not from the essence of the act or even from the essence as viewed purely from his own perspective. He assigns meaning to an otherwise meaningless act by interpreting it in light of arbitrary, yet widely shared human understanding which helps create balls and strikes, i.e., the significant symbols of balls and strikes.

Are the semantics of political talk like this? We think they are. For example, imagine that we are all umpires in the game of politics. A presidential candidate speaks out on an issue. Is the position liberal or conservative? We could assume any issue position has an essential character that makes it liberal or conservative, thus calling the candidate as he "is." But yesterday's liberal measures ofttimes are today's conservatism (for instance, "fair trade" laws sponsored in the New Deal period to set a floor on prices as a means of protecting small businesses and consumer interests now operate to the consumer's disadvantage). If we can't "call 'em as they is," perhaps we should "call 'em as we sees 'em." After all, if the operetta composers Gilbert and Sullivan were correct, we are all either a little liberal or a little conservative (just as baseball players hint that some umpires are either ball or strike prone). Is whether the candidate's position is liberal or conservative, then, a matter of selective perception? We think not. The argument here is that to label the candidate's position as liberal or conservative consists of more than applying terms with unvarying meaning to acts (the first umpire) or registering our own biases (the second umpire). The candidate's position is neither inherently liberal nor conservative, but becomes something only when we assign a significant symbol to it; the candidate's position "ain't nothin' till we calls it."

But surely, the reader could argue, if significant symbols have widely shared, common meanings or understandings, then neither liberal nor conservative is a significant symbol so long as people scarcely agree upon what constitutes either. This is precisely the point: neither the word liberal nor conservative describes what an issue position "really" is; nor does either word say what a given person "really" is. Rather, each is a word used in similar ways by some human beings engaging in meaningful, symbolic activities. But to say that significant symbols are human constructs applied to objects by persons who share common meanings of what those symbols stand for is not to say that significant symbols reflect uniform behavior or likemindedness. Instead, writes Schettler, significant symbols "are the instruments through which the individuals who have some disagreements can work together in the organization of a public opinion which is representative of all of them."[31] If what Schettler says about the semantics of political talk has any merit, then we must be wary in political debate when our adversary dismisses the whole exchange as an argument over "mere semantics." Semantics it most certainly is; mere it is not. *Political talk involves semantic disagreement* in Schettler's sense—not over what democracy, equality, freedom, justice, majority rule, or minority rights *really are,* but over what people take each concept to mean and how they act accordingly. In sum, no act *is* anything until we "call it" (i.e., interpret it, understand it, and in the process respond to it); political talk is a means of resolving disputes over what to "call 'em."

But there is a problem. Although political talk negotiates shared beliefs, values, and expectations in situations of semantic conflict, like any talk it can also give rise to semantic confusion. The types of semantic confusion in politics are the same as in any variety of discourse. One is the problem raised by the *fallacy of the transitive verb.* Continuing with our baseball analogy, we can say "the pitcher throws the ball." The transitive verb "throw" conveys the notion that the pitcher does something to the ball and how well, how fast, and how accurately depends on the pitcher. But what if we say "the pitcher scares the batter"? The relation of pitcher to batter established by the verb "scare" differs from that of pitcher to ball conveyed in "throw." The former depends upon the separate and mutual goals, motives, and expectations of the players. Whether the pitcher scares the batter depends upon more than the desires and skills he brings to the mound. We encounter the fallacy of the transitive verb every day in political talk. A headline, for instance, reads "President Threatens Congress," or a reporter writes that a politician "molded" public opinion. The fallacy of the transitive verb distracts us from looking at what political communicators do reciprocally *with* one another and leaves the impression that politicians do things *to* constituents, fellow politicians, etc.[32]

A second type of semantic confusion is *to use a word or other linguistic symbol as if it were the object that it represents..* The word "Congress," for example, refers to a two-house legislative body composed of numerous individuals elected as representatives or senators (i.e., members of congress) and to the transactions between those members, their administrative staffs, employees, etc.—any one of whom may have views at variance with those attributed to "Congress." Congress is thus hardly the unitary object conjured up in such phrases as "President blames Congress for energy crisis" or "Congress refuses to back president on tax plan." The confusion raised by using symbols as substitutes for observable objects increases when symbols have no observable referents at all, as when they are purely condensation symbols. For instance, to label a man a "fascist" conjures up no image of a specific object in time and space familiar to the speaker and his listeners; instead it evokes an emotional response to the word itself.

The person credited with the founding of general semantics as a field of study, Alfred Korzybski, remarked on yet another key variety of semantic confusion, which he called *identification reactions*.[33] When persons respond in fixed ways to symbols, they treat as identical all of the quite different things they identify under a given label. Thus, all Democrats or mothers-in-law or capitalists or college professors or college students are alike. The differences in things falling under the same semantic label are dismissed even though no two Democrats, no two Republicans, no two Americans, or no two of anything are alike. Such semantic confusion leads to stereotyping and a misleading tendency to gloss over the rich diversity that is politics.

There are, of course, a number of reasons for the semantic confusions outlined. For one, people ordinarily respond to the law of least effort; it is easier to confuse symbols with things or processes they name than to draw the necessary distinctions. Moreover, people's mental worlds flow from everyday experiences and it is seldom easy, or even possible, to engage in activities that hint at the differences in various usages of words. (Few citizens actually have the opportunity to test what politicians say by accumulating evidence with respect to the controversies at issue.) Furthermore, there is a strong human tendency to assimilate the unfamiliar to the familiar, and thus to develop semantic categories for reducing threatening uncertainties through identification reactions. Finally, the structure of language itself contributes both to reification (speaking of abstract ideas as though they were observable entities, e.g., "communism") and personification (treating collectivities as individuals, e.g., "the State of Maine decided today to hold a presidential primary"). There is, observes one scholar, the natural tendency of languages to express any subject of a verb as a noun, as with the process of fire.[34] As we shall see later in this chapter and throughout Chapter 4, these types and sources of semantic confusion provide political communicators with ample opportunities for influencing public opinion.

Political Syntactics

In the early 1970s there appeared a movie entitled *Bang the Drum Slowly*. The plot concerned antics and tragedies befalling members of a major league baseball team. To pass the time while lounging around hotel lobbies between road games, the team members played a card game called Tegwar. Tegwar, it turned out, was an acronym for "the exciting game without any rules." In effect, with each player's turn, rules would be made up on the spot—rules defining who could lead a card, what card was trump, what card could capture another, overall scoring, etc. No rule lasted for long, scarcely beyond the playing of a single card, let alone for an entire hand or game. Tegwar was, in effect, a language game without rules, i.e., without syntax (aside from the understanding that there were no permanent rules!). To that degree Tegwar was scarcely a game at all, for, as Peter Farb argues, "any transaction between two human beings—an exchange of words, silence, or a mutually intelligible gesture such as the wave of a hand—conforms to rules and conventions understood by all members of that speech community. To have no firm rules at all is to have no language game at all."[35] Even to have rules and break them by lying or cheating merely confirms their very existence. Farb offers as demonstration the clever way the Marx Brothers departed from rules of the English language in their comedy routines. Or consider how to answer the question, "Why is an orange?"

Is there then a syntax that makes political word play possible in America? If Farb is correct that rule breaking at least demonstrates the presence of rules to break, then political talk is not altogether Tegwar. When speakers at political rallies in the 1960s charged that their rights of free expression were violated by hecklers, they called attention to the convention then in vogue that platform speakers were not to be interrupted. But rule breaking is not the only indication that some sense of political syntax exists. The U.S. Supreme Court through numerous decisions has, in fact, laid down rules pertaining to free speech, free press, and free assembly.

A syntax of political discourse must possess two basic rules if political talk is truly talk that ensures talk. The first is what Miller and McNeill call "the categorical imperative rule of any game—namely, that *you may make any move you would allow another player to make under similar circumstances.*"[36] Put another way, there must be constitutional guarantees of free expression that apply equally to everyone. If there are not, and one person can move to deny the talk of another, then political talk ensures not talk but enslavement. Second, there must be the understanding that all other rules of political syntax are subject to the first and thereby *always debatable, open to renegotiation and revision.* The reason is that one of the principal things that syntax does is draw a line between the speakable and unspeakable in a speech community, what is proper grammar and what is not, what is good English and what is not. Although a laudable and necessary purpose of syntax, if there is to be any language game at all, it raises complications when carried to extremes in political talk. What better way to exert control over opponents than to decree that they have violated rules of political word play—that a form for welfare assistance was not properly completed, that a last will and testament violated acceptable legalese, or that followers of a rival for a presidential nomination were out of order in raising a challenge in convention debate? Stokely Carmichael at the height of the Black protest movement in 1967, speaking of how words are defined said, "I believe people who can define are masters."[37] To define a person as a "nigger" was part of the language of white racism that kept Blacks "in their place." But not only are those who define words masters, so are those who define the rules of communication. In using obscenities in political discourse in the 1960s, protesters against the Vietnam war did so not only for shock value, but also to call attention that the convention against four-letter words could not apply to people who had no part in helping define the rules of word play. In sum, if political talk is to ensure and enhance peaceful resolutions of disputes, neither the meanings of significant symbols nor the rules of political discourse can be imposed; they must be open to negotiation by all citizens in the political speech community.

PRAGMATICS: THE USES OF POLITICAL TALK

To recapitulate, political talk is a dynamic discourse of power, influence, and authority that accommodates disputes through symbolic activity (the words of politics). But the meaning of political terms is itself a matter of dispute. As Jonathan Swift observed in recounting *Gulliver's Travels*, the only connection between a word and the thing it stands for is whatever association the speech community decides to make.[38] Political talk resolves social conflicts by negotiating definitions of meanings of contested words (semantics) and the rules of word play (syntactics). To complete our discussion of political talk, the middle term in the "who says what" of political communication, we now turn to its uses and potential effects in regulating social disputes (pragmatics).

Through political activity people derive benefits and suffer losses. The government that builds highways to ease travel imposes gasoline taxes increasing the burden of travel costs. There are many kinds of benefits and/or costs, but recall from our discussion in Chapter 2 that they fall into three general categories—material, solidary, and expressive. Political talk figures in the allocation of each. Without stretching the limits of each category too far, we discuss the political talk of material gain, status enhancement, and personal identity.

Mass Assurance and Arousal: The Political Talk of Material Gain

People get something special out of symbolic activity. Edelman writes, "Only man among living things reconstructs his past, perceives his present condition, and anticipates his future through symbols that abstract, screen, condense, distort, displace, and even create what the senses bring to his attention." Symbols make life meaningful; they join a person's world to one's behavior, one's behavior to the world. No less is true for political symbols; they make political life meaningful. We cannot explain politics merely as the interactions of people with fairly stable individual desires and tendencies. Rather, "Adequate explanation must focus on the complex element that intervenes between the environment and the behavior of human beings: creation and change in common meanings through symbolic apprehension in groups of people of interest, pressures, threats, and possibilities."[39]

Since symbols make experience meaningful and are thereby gratifying in their own right, they are especially useful as rhetorical devices in the struggle between social interests competing for material gain. "Everywhere," wrote Arthur Bentley, interests "are casting their demands absolutely against the social sky ... stating themselves in language-thought structures which split themselves off from their origin in activity and attempt to justify that from which they arise."[40] In short, private and governmental groups structure and limit political talk to advantage special interests. They accomplish this in two principal ways.

Assurance. First, political leaders use symbols to *assure* people that problems are solved even if current policies actually achieve relatively little. Hence, standing up for law and order leaves the impression of success even as the crime rate soars. At least espousing the ringing phrase "national self-sufficiency in energy by 1980" holds out the promise of low cost increases in living standards even though prices for heating oil, electricity, coal, and gasoline rise astronomically.

Private and government interests employ a variety of what Bentley calls "language thought-structures" to enhance their advantage. One example is the widely used language form, *euphemism,* the substitution of an inoffensive term for one considered offensively explicit. For example, in 1976 the Ford Administration's policy of easing tensions with the Soviet Union, called "detente," received widespread criticism; Ford dropped the word detente, kept the policy, and called it "peace through strength." The purpose was to make the bad actuality linguistically acceptable. Thus, unemployment becomes "nonpreferential leisure," a prison inmate is a "client of a social rehabilitation center," a bribe an "unsolicited contribution," an untruth an "inoperative statement," and rationing, "selective distribution." Carried to the extreme such euphemisms comprise bureaucratic jargon or political gobbledygook that are contradictions in terms. What sense, for example, can we make of phrases like those reported during the Vietnam War that there was "fighting in the demilitarized zone" or that military actions took place in the name of a "pacification program"? Or consider the following statement by Alan Greenspan, chief economic adviser to President Gerald Ford in 1974. Speaking of inflation he said:

> If you extrapolate the strains that we now already see as a consequence of what we have for an extended period of time, the institutions—economical, financial, structural—begin to break down because they are essentially developed over the decades in the context of low, single-digit inflation, and it's by no means clear or had not been clear, I should say, how significant this element was until we actually tested it, and having tested it, we found that it does not respond terribly well.

When submitted to a test to determine ease of understanding, this and other passages from Greenspan scored 13.6 on a scale where 85 rates easy, 65 standard, 40 difficult, and 15 impenetrable![41] The issue, however, is not Greenspan as such; rather it is that some political leaders consciously employ euphemisms, jargon, and gobbledygook to obscure actual conditions instead of clarifying them. The more obscure the symbolism, generally the greater the impression that things are very complicated and proposed solutions should be accepted without challenge.

Puffery is another language form relied upon by interests pursuing private material benefits at public expense. To puff is to "blow up, exaggerate, overstate, or state superlatives concerning matters of subjective judgment and opinion in the assessment of taste, beauty, pleasure, popularity, durability, and similar qualities." Puffery is a close cousin to what Arthur Herzog calls the "B.S. factor" or simply faking it.[42] We see puffery spotted throughout commercial advertising: "Bayer works wonders," "Things go better with Coke," "It's the real thing," "All my men wear English Leather or they wear nothing at all," and "What do you like, America? Baseball, hotdogs, apple pie, and Chevrolet!" Political puffery is equally easy to find. Think how many Fourth of July orations have used this puff: "Ours is the most advanced, most productive, richest, and most powerful society that humanity has seen since the dawn of history; it is a privilege to have been born here and to live here, taking the bad with the good." Namely, the deprived should not complain; things could be far worse in less advanced, productive, wealthy, powerful places.

A third major language form employed in the pursuit of material gain at the expense of less advantaged interests is *metaphor*.[43] A metaphor is a language device that explains the unfamiliar by identifying it with something more immediate, clear, and known. Metaphors in political talk call attention to desirable outcomes of proposed policies while glossing over less attractive consequences. A favorite phrase of military strategists during the prolonged Vietnam war was that the U.S. had "turned the corner and there is light at the end of the tunnel." However, the tunnel had no cc ners and no light; instead it was laid out in one vast circle and U.S. fortunes did little but go round and round in it. Or consider the phrase "war on poverty," which conjures up the imagery of marshalling forces to win victory in a short-term struggle. As in Vietnam, however, the corners were neither found nor turned; the end of that tunnel is not yet in sight. For a final example recall President Ford's 1975 declaration that "the recession has bottomed out," suggesting his administration's policies had turned the economy around. Yet large numbers of people remained without jobs, just as soldiers had died and the poor remained impoverished in the tunnels of the Johnson and Nixon administrations.

Do not be misled. Euphemism, puffery, and metaphor are not tools used solely by politicians to lull the masses. No, they are the discourse within the inner circle of political elites as well. The 1974 release of transcripts of President Nixon's conversations with advisers regarding the Watergate affair provided a rare backstage glimpse of the word play of politicians. Again the metaphor of war emerged. "This is a war," said Nixon to John Dean on September 15, 1972. "We take a few shots and it will be over. We will give them a few shots and it will be over." Later Nixon says, "It is better to fight it out"; Watergate is a booby trap ready to explode: "I think it's ready to do that right now. I think this would trigger it without question . . . cutting Bob and the rest to pieces." Surrender was unthinkable: "When you are in a battle, you are going to fight it to the finish." And, there were other metaphors: the gangster's mob, "Dean's not going to finger Magruder" and "beat the damn rap"; sporting talk, "he's a hell of a big fish" and "the ballgame's over"; and the use of "handle" as a synonym for manipulative control. Finally, as for what advisers said to Nixon, few will forget John Dean's prophetic statement of March 21, 1973: "I see . . . a cancer growing around the presidency."[44]

The function of political symbols in reassuring people is particularly important when governments undertake policies that distribute benefits to some groups, costs to others. So long as deprived groups respond to symbols of policy intent rather than ask how policies actually work, they "display little tendency to protest or to assert their awareness of the deprivation."[45] The progressive income tax is a case in point. Income taxes supposedly rest on the ability to pay; that is, persons with low incomes pay a smaller proportion in taxes than do those of higher incomes. Further symbolized is an ideal of redistribution of benefits and costs— benefits to low and middle income persons, costs to the wealthy. But numerous tax loopholes (frequently justified as stimulating investments in "national growth and prosperity") provide advantages to upper income groups, thus sharply reducing the progressive quality of income taxes. Add to that reduction the other taxes levied by federal, state, and local governments (sales, excise, and property taxes, to name only a few) and the overall tax burden is actually regressive—it falls out of proportion upon lower income Americans.

This example tells us something else about political symbols, that *government policies are symbolic* in the same sense as the language forms "law and order," "peace with honor," and "energy self-sufficiency." They help people believe government leaders serve a broad, public interest; meanwhile special interests often reap the harvest. Generally the political symbols that circulate among political leaders (especially key officeholders and spokesmen of dominant interest organizations) describe more accurately the full consequences of policies than do the symbols publicized at large.[46] This rule holds for symbols describing the functions of our key political institutions as well. For example, although election campaigns help citizens derive a sense of involvement, voice their discontents and satisfactions, and generally let off steam, they have little direct bearing upon policy making. Many a victorious campaigner ascribes his success to having received a policy "mandate," but such mandates guide relatively few elected politicians once in office (see Chapter 12).

Arousal.   Language forms, policies, institutions, and the acts of political leaders perform a second function serving private and governmental interests under the cloak of public assurance. They also *arouse* and mobilize support for action. Take as an illustration differences in popular response resulting from how political leaders label a particular set of circumstances. In 1972 and 1973, appeals to Americans to conserve gasoline had relatively little impact; few responded to the energy shortage. But when "shortage" became "crisis" with the refusal of oil producing nations to sell to U.S. buyers, Americans accepted irritations that were unthinkable earlier—long lines at gasoline pumps, restrictions on purchases, modified rationing, marked price increases, and fifty-five miles per hour speed limits. Whether a true crisis existed is not the point; nor did simply calling the problem a crisis mobilize support for new oil pricing and import policies. What the case illustrates is that in times of threat—wars, crises, emergencies—appeals to self-sacrifice induce the mass citizenry to accept and support restraints upon free choice and expression that otherwise would not be tolerated.

Myth and *ritual* are two language forms of particular value in arousing public action. The widely shared tendency of people to ascribe threatening or unforeseen calamities to a plot, conspiracy, or undefined enemy (i.e., the desire to find a scapegoat) is an example. In the 1950s Senator Joseph McCarthy rallied vast popular support by capitalizing on the myth of a communist conspiracy, one that allegedly had seriously undermined the U.S. power position after World War II. Or consider the myth that some people are inherently superior to others, a myth that fueled the fire of support for white racism for generations. The role of ritual is even more obvious. Political candidates, both Democratic and Republican, rally electoral support through standardized appeals to party loyalty. Ritualized hearings before congressional committees provide opportunities for proponents and opponents to "go on record" to support their cause.

Whether they contribute to popular quiescence or arousal, language forms, government actions, institutions, and procedures influence the beliefs, values, and expectations of a large numbers of people in ambiguous situations. For that reason politicians win popular acceptance and support as much because of emotional leadership as their ability to allocate material rewards. (Recall the discussion in Chapter 2.) The tangible gains that citizens actually accrue are less critical in affirming popular loyalties to regimes than what people think they get. We do not live by bread alone but by our illusions which sustain us. This conclusion challenges a leading proposition about politics, that "political arousal and quiescence depend upon how much of what they want from government people get." A more accurate view, says Edelman, is that *"Political actions chiefly arouse or satisfy people not by granting or withholding their stable substantive demands, but rather by changing the demands and their expectations."*[47] As we shall see, those demands are frequently less material than social.

Social Authority: The Political Talk of Status Enhancement

Stokely Carmichael was not the first to opine that mastery over people belongs to those able to define the meaning of things. In 1492 Queen Isabella, when presented with the first grammar written about a modern European language, asked, "What is the book for?" The Bishop of Avila responded, "Your majesty, language is the perfect instrument of empire."[48] Humpty Dumpty put it most clearly: " 'When I use a word,' Humpty Dumpty said in a rather scornful tone, 'it means just what I choose it to mean—neither more nor less.' " " 'The question is,' said Alice, 'whether you can make words mean different things.' " " 'The question is,' said Humpty Dumpty, 'who is to be master—that's all.' "

The lesson to draw from the Bishop and Humpty Dumpty is simple: although political groups talk to accrue material rewards, many interests are less concerned with deriving specific tangible benefits than in achieving ruling status in the social order. They use political symbols not only to distribute material goods but to distribute authority as well.[49]

Clearly, government policies extend beyond material allocations. More than material allocations are implied, for instance, in making the sale of alcoholic beverages or marijuana illegal, regulating massage parlors, prohibiting people from walking about nude in public, prosecuting sex offenders, outlawing obscenity, and so forth. At issue are decisions over legitimate social behavior and who has authority to decide what is moral and immoral, loyal and disloyal, punishable and not punishable. People use language to achieve status and authority; they ask governments to sanctify their views of legitimacy by making them mandatory for everybody.

The language devices that assist private and governmental groups in enhancing their special material interests are also valuable in getting people to submit to authority. Euphemism, puffery, metaphors, myths, and rituals define inferior stations in life and convince social subordinates that they profit from submissive status even though a factual description of conditions indicates otherwise. In the end the devices create and reinforce beliefs, feelings, and expectations that some people have a right to rule because they are more worthy than others. Other key language forms build a relationship between talk and status.

Labeling is one such form. It resembles euphemism, but there is a marked difference. Whereas euphemisms are inoffensive terms substituted for unappealing ones (e.g., "control and rehabilitation effort" for solitary confinement), labeling consists of applying offensive words to individuals, groups, or activities. In Nazi Germany, for example, the ruling elite as a matter of policy labeled Jews as "parasites," "vermin," and "bacillus," thus defining them not as humans but as pests to exterminate with little or no sense of guilt.[50] On our own shores are examples of labeling people unworthy and inferior. Few Americans would be unable to identify the referents of the following derisive and demeaning terms: nigger, darky, honky, white boy, the little woman, and broad.

Association is another linguistic device rich in possibilities for defining superior-subordinate relationships. It consists of equating a word denoting a positive or negative quality with a person, class, or set of actions. There is a tendency, for instance, to associate the word "black" with things foul, sinister, dark, and evil, and to associate "white" with purity, innocence, and cleanliness. It was not until the civil rights and black power movements of recent decades that we heard the slogan, "Black is beautiful." The woman's liberation movement called attention to the associations contained in sexist language. Words associated with women, noted dissident feminists, were seldom complimentary—such words as weakness, frivolous, timid, passive—whereas words equated with manhood were generally positive—courage, power, forceful, brave, etc. Some feminine terms (e.g., effeminate) were scornful slurs when applied to men. The fault, of course, lies not in the English language but in the way people use it. After all there are plenty of abusive words associated with males: cur, rat, bounder, rogue, stinker, etc. If every elderly female is a "little old lady," what of the tendency to associate elderly males with "dirty old man"?[51] Because usage rather than intrinsic qualities in words promote labeling and association, governing officials change language through decree. In the case of the Nazis the goals were malevolent. In other cases official policy may respond to interest groups who think language demeans them. In 1975, for example, the U.S. Department of Labor in deference to the woman's movement removed gender terms from the *Dictionary of Occupational Titles.* With a flick of a bureaucrat's pen, stewardess became flight attendant, garbageman emerged as garbage-porter, nursemaid appeared as child monitor, and charwoman became houseworker. One wit remarked that in the future Eugene O'Neill's famous play should probably be *The Ice Route Driver Cometh,* and Arthur Miller's work, *Death of a Sales Representative.*

In a remarkable essay written in 1946, "Politics and the English Language," George Orwell described several other devices, "tricks" as he said, to avoid clear prose and thereby fend off challenges to authority. "Political speech and writing are largely the defense of the indefensible," wrote Orwell. Dying metaphors, obscure phrasing, pretentious diction, and meaningless words are the first line of that defense.[52]

In the 1960s philosopher Herbert Marcuse reiterated Orwell's theme and argued that contemporary political talk is "the language of total administration," a discourse of manipulation and authoritarian control. In the language of total administration power, influence, and authority talk enhance the status of a ruling establishment by eroding critical think-ing. Marcuse cites several language devices of administrative talk. *Person-alized* language, for instance, comforts citizens by telling them that even if they do not directly affect policy making, "your" congressman does. The result is "your" highways, "your" country, "your" university, etc. The *inflectional genitive* reinforces images of legitimate authority by bonding individuals with an official position: viz., Energy Czar William Simon, Supreme Court's Warren Burger, Senate Watergate Committee's Howard Baker, State Department's Henry Kissinger, and U.N.'s Kurt Waldheim. *Hyphenized abridgements* force together terms designating quite different spheres of activity as though they were really a single whole: "the Presi-dent is off on a work-leisure holiday," he attended a "science-military get-together," or "he was greeted by a group of educational-industrial supporters." These other devices, says Marcuse, identify things with func-tions blotting out precisely the distinctions essential to critical understand-ing; mute acceptance supersedes effective challenge to authority: "the functionalized, abridged and unified language is the language of one-dimensional thought."[53]

Personal Expression: The Political Talk of Identity

Political communicators who pursue private, self-serving material and status benefits use symbols to get people to act in certain ways—quies-cently to accept policies from which they derive no tangible gains, perhaps even losses; to arouse popular support for more narrow causes; and to obey leaders in positions of high social status or governing authority. In this context political symbols are means to material and social ends; they are not ends in themselves. Yet there are large numbers of people, both leaders and followers, who talk about politics because playing with the symbols themselves provide considerable satisfaction. A person may take great pride, for instance, in announcing for all to hear, "I am a Democrat." Indeed, this may be the only political act one performs; a person might not vote, join political organizations, write a congressman, or attend political meetings, but just declare a partisan identification.

We shall see in Chapter 9 that politics provides each of us with some degree of self-expression, a way of negotiating and expressing personal identities: Who am I, what am I doing here, what sense does it all make, what do I need and want, hope for and fear, love and hate? Each of us continuously constructs, modifies, and presents a meaningful self-image through our communication with others, including our political talk. Expressive talk is a discourse disclosing our political identities. We display our country's flag, celebrate patriotic holidays, sing the national anthem, visit monuments, and engage in countless little rituals that symbolize something to us personally, that say "I am an American." In sum, political talk like any mode of expression provides us with a means for defining the *self as a significant symbol.*

Geoffrey Stokes' report on the 1974 White House transcripts provide valuable insights into how at least one political leader, Richard Nixon, engaged in expressive politics. Aside from his obvious desire to affirm his innocence, Nixon was also intent upon maintaining a particular self-image, that of the loner. Over and over again he imagined himself standing alone, fighting in isolation against various unnamed forces: "Nobody is a friend of ours. Let's face it." Nixon's focus on self contributed to an extraordinary tendency to emphasize the personal pronoun "I." In a hundred thousand words Nixon used "I" over four thousand times, a pattern Stokes finds quite remarkable in light of the fact that in normal usage the pronoun would not appear that frequently if more than a million words were spoken.[54]

As we said, the dividing line between political talk of material or social gain and expressive political discourse is whether people receive purely symbolic gratifications from talk—that is, they derive more satisfaction from contemplating and expressing the symbols of politics than in acting with regard to what these symbols stand for.[55] Since we have argued that all activity is in effect symbolic, this simply says that those people respond more to condensation symbols (ambiguous, vague, and emotion laden) than to referential symbols pertaining to more or less specific objects (people, places, events, acts, etc.). Herein is a key source of the capacity of political leaders to assure, arouse, and elicit obedience from a populace. When people pursue only symbolic gratifications they seldom demand clarification of the specific material and social costs implied in acquiescing to, rallying around, or obeying symbolic appeals. As we shall discuss in Chapter 4, many of the assumptions underlying theories and practices of political persuasion have this feature.

Public Discussion: The Political Talk of Informing

Having followed this outline of the material, social, and expressive aspects of political discourse, the reader may well wonder if something has been omitted. Do we not, one might ask, communicate simply to inform? Is it not a cynical view to say that political talk serves only selfish interests, status seekers, and the symbolically gratified? Are there not political communicators who identify pressing social problems, search out alternative solutions, and promote public discussion of preferred means and ends? To be sure, political talk can and is used to inform—to disclose who profits from material distributions, challenge authority and the status quo, and stimulate popular participation beyond expressive behavior. Such talk is important and should not be ignored. It too is a variety of symbolic activity, and the intelligence exchanged through it is crucial to the viability of any polity.

The argument here, however, is that, compared to the amount of talk devoted to matters of a material, status, and identity nature, there is relatively little *disinterested* communication in politics. Instead we have what Claus Mueller describes as forms of "distorted communication" which inhibit complete, comprehensive discussions of vital problems. Mueller speaks of three types of distortion, each of which parallels a form of political talk already discussed. First, there is *directed* communication; specific government policies attempt to structure language to legitimize the authority of a particular group and to institutionalize the subordinant status of all others (this is the political talk of status enhancement). Second, Mueller speaks of *arrested* communication; because of the nature of their linguistic environment people have not acquired the symbolic tools necessary to press for recognition of their demands, a distortion paralleling, but not identical to, the political discourse of the symbolically gratified. Finally, political communication is *constrained,* the use of political talk by self-serving elites to advance their material interests.[56]

Whether "distorted" is the appropriate term for describing the opinion process in American politics is debatable. But as we press on in our discussion of who says what in which channels to whom with what effects, we shall have ample opportunity to consider the degree of directed, arrested, and constrained language in our political talk.

POLITICAL TALK AND POLITICAL IMAGES

Through political words and word play we create images of things and conditions in our world of social conflict and cooperation. Some of those subjective pictures are accurate, vivid, and rich in detail; they help us adapt to the concrete realities of our experience. Others are misleading, ambiguous, and vague; if too illusory they portray a world of ghosts that does not exist. But whatever the images, they are meaningful for each of us.

Literary critic Kenneth Burke captured the quality of the role played by symbols, images, talk, words, and word play in human life in his "definition" of man. Writes Burke:

> *Man is*
> *the symbol-using (symbol-making, symbol-misusing) animal*
> *inventor of the negative (or moralized by the negative)*
> *separated from his natural condition by instruments of his own making*
> *goaded by the spirit of hierarchy (or moved by the sense of order)*
> *and rotten with perfection.*[57]

Burke's definition provides a convenient peg on which to hang a summary of the key points we have made in this chapter. Political reality for most of us is not something we experience firsthand but is conveyed through significant symbols. Politics is symbolic activity touching the lives of large numbers of people because persons find meaning in the symbol-using, symbol-making and symbol-misusing of political communicators. Within that context consider how important the negative, as Burke uses the notion, is to politics. "Laws," he remarks, "are essentially negative; 'mine' equals 'not thine'; insofar as property is not protected by the thou-shall-nots of either moral or civil law, it is not protected at all."[58] Moreover, the negative plays a vital role simply because it is the antithesis of the positive; through politics we symbolize such polar conditions as order-disorder, peace-war, victory-defeat, haves–have nots, pleasure-pain, and life-death. In short, through politics governments define and decree a vast portion of our public morals. But the specific political forms of society (its executive, legislative, or judicial institutions, partisan and interest organizations, general rules and procedures) are not given in nature. Rather, they are inventions, tools, or instruments of our fashioning for achieving adjustments of our social differences. Language also is a tool of sorts, or more precisely a species of social action that can be used as a tool, with instrumental value in allocating and justifying the distribution of social costs and benefits. Language assists us in achieving a sense of social order as well, a definition of rulers and ruled, leaders and followers, governors and governed that corresponds to the spirit of hierarchy (status) goading us all. Burke uses the term "rotten" with perfection in the same ironic way one might speak of a perfect fool or a perfect villain. Certainly there is a similar ever present irony about politics. The "perfect political solution" to a problem, as we shall see in Chapter 12, is seldom the solution that best responds to the substantive aspects of the problem itself; rather it is the "perfect" solution all parties are willing to accept. It is a solution derived from political talk that, as we have said before, permits other talk about the problem to continue. It is, in short, a solution "rotten with perfection."

BIBLIOGRAPHY

Although the character and use of talk and language forms is clearly a key feature of politics, there are few works by political scientists devoted exclusively to the subject. This makes David V. J. Bell's little volume, *Power, Influence and Authority* (New York: Oxford University Press, 1975) especially useful. Another with a focus almost exclusively on political language is Claus Mueller, *The Politics of Communication* (New York: Oxford University Press, 1973). Two works that also touch upon the subject less directly are William E. Connolly, *The Terms of Political Discourse* (Lexington, Mass.: D. C. Heath and Co., 1974), and Harold D. Lasswell and Nathan Leites, *Language of Politics* (Cambridge, Mass.: M.I.T. Press, 1949). A classic work written on political language from a postvisit theoretical perspective is T. D. Weldon, *The Vocabulary of Politics* (Baltimore: Penguin Books, 1953). Readers should also consult the scholarly and comprehensive analysis of Doris Graber, *Verbal Behavior and Politics* (Urbana, Ill.: University of Illinois Press, 1976).

There are several excellent treatises devoted to an analysis of the uses and abuses of symbolism in American politics. One of the most straightforward appeared some time ago, Thurman W. Arnold, *The Symbols of Government* (New York: Harcourt, Brace and World, Inc., 1935). But anyone seriously interested in the subject should not ignore the two major works of Murray Edelman: *The Symbolic Uses of Politics* (Urbana: University of Illinois Press, 1964) and *Politics as Symbolic Action* (Chicago: Markham Publishing Co., 1971). Both have chapters devoted to discussions of political language, especially the variety of language forms employed in politics. Readers concerned with the imagery surrounding political symbolism are invited to read Dan Nimmo, *Popular Images of Politics* (Englewood Cliffs, N.J.: Prentice-Hall, Inc., 1974). That volume raises many of the points introduced in this chapter and has an extensive discussion of instrumental, evaluative, and expressive symbolism in contemporary American politics.

Several works analyze the nature of symbolic activity. Three authors provide a perspective on the theoretical underpinnings of the subject. The first is George Herbert Mead and readers should consult his *Mind, Self, and Society* (Chicago: University of Chicago Press, 1934) for the classic statement of symbolic interaction. The second is Kenneth Burke who has written several volumes discussing symbolic action. Readers of this chapter will find two of those works most helpful. The essays in Burke's *Language as Symbolic Action* (Berkeley: University of California Press, 1968) provide the best single introduction to his thought. More complex is his *A Grammar of Motives* (Berkeley: University of California Press, 1969). The third author of special note in this area is Hugh Dalziel

Duncan. Two of his books are particularly relevant as background for the preparation of this chapter: *Communication and Social Order* (London: Oxford University Press, 1962) and *Symbols in Society* (New York: Oxford University Press, 1968). The first volume traces the development of a symbolic perspective in the writings of such theorists as Freud, Simmel, the pragmatists, Kenneth Burke, etc. The second of Duncan's works presents his own view of the role of symbols. Less directly relevant than the works of the three authors cited above, but still very helpful in understanding symbolic action as meaningful behavior are Peter L. Berger and Thomas Luckman, *The Social Construction of Reality* (Garden City, N.Y.: Anchor Books, 1975); Alfred North Whitehead, *Symbolism* (New York: G.P. Putnam's Sons, Capricorn edition, 1959); and Suzanne Langer, *Philosophy in a New Key* (Cambridge, Mass.: Howard University Press, 1942).

Linguistics is a growing area of study and the number of works pouring forth on its various theories and facets has been remarkable. An excellent and readable introduction to the area is Peter Farb, *Word Play* (New York: Alfred A. Knopf, 1974). A valuable survey of sociolinguistics is W. P. Robinson's *Language and Social Behavior* (Baltimore: Penguin Books, 1972). Psycholinguistics receives a comprehensive examination at the hands of George A. Miller and David McNeill in an essay of the same name contained in Gardner Lindzey and Elliot Aronson, eds., *The Handbook of Social Psychology,* Vol. III (Reading, Mass.: Addison-Wesley Publishing Co., 1969). An excellent introduction to general semantics is S. I. Hayakawa, *Symbol, Status, and Personality* (New York: Harcourt, Brace and World, 1953). The definitive statement of semantics is Alfred Korzybski's *Science and Sanity* (Lancaster: Science Press, 2nd ed., 1941). Another classic work in the field is C. K. Ogden and I. A. Richards, *The Meaning of Meaning* (New York: Harcourt, Brace and World, 1923). The works of Noam Chomsky have had a major influence on the study of syntactics in recent years. See especially his *Language and Mind* (New York: Harcourt, Brace and World, 1968) and *Cartesian Linguistics* (New York: Harper and Row, 1966). A more recent summary of the social implications of language is George Steiner, *After Babel: Aspects of Language and Translation* (New York: Oxford University Press, 1975). For an excellent discussion of pragmatic dimensions of talk see Paul Watzlawick et al., *Pragmatics of Human Communication* (New York: W. W. Norton and Co., Inc., 1967). Of course, in delving into the mysteries surrounding words and word play no reader should fail to reread any of the many existing editions of Lewis Carroll's *Alice in Wonderland.*

Several works already cited provide useful descriptions of the various ways talk functions in politics, i.e., the works of Bell, Edelman, and Nimmo. Two others that are valuable in this respect are Herbert Marcuse's *One-Dimensional Man* (Boston: Beacon Press, 1969) and Joseph R. Gusfield, *Symbolic Crusade* (Urbana: University of Illinois Press, 1966). Both focus upon the use of political talk as an instrument of social control. If the reader prefers a less painful introduction to some of these aspects of talk, there are several popularized accounts. Among these one might investigate Arthur Herzog, *The B.S. Factor* (Baltimore: Penguin Books, 1973), Edmond G. Addeo and Robert E. Burger, *Egospeak: Why No One Listens to You* (New York: Bantam Books, 1973) and Eric Berne, *What Do You Say After You Say Hello?* (New York: Grove Press, Inc., 1972).

Although this chapter contained a brief discussion of nonverbal communication, the primary emphasis has been upon the verbal aspects of political talk. For those readers interested in exploring furthur the possibilities of nonverbal talk and its relation to politics, a number of books are available. A nontechnical introduction to the possibilities of social control that exist in nonverbal exchange is Julius Fast, *Body Language* (New York: M. Evans and Co., Inc., 1970). A more scholarly introduction is Ray L. Birdwhistell, *Kinesics and Context* (Philadelphia: University of Pennsylvania Press, 1970). The relationship of nonverbal messages to expressive behavior is discussed in Jurgen Ruesch and Weldon Kees, *Nonverbal Communication* (Berkeley: University of California Press, 1972). Two recent issues of scholarly journals supply reports of empirical research into nonverbal communication; see Volume 22 of *The Journal of Communication* (December 1972), a special issue devoted entirely to the subject, and the issue of *ETC.*, Vol. 30 (September 1973) which also contains several studies in nonverbal communication.

NOTES

1. "Politics is talk" is a theme that resounds throughout the literature of political communication. See especially David V. J. Bell, *Power, Influence and Authority* (New York: Oxford University Press, 1975), p. 10; Mark Roelofs, *The Language of Modern Politics* (Homewood, Ill.: The Dorsey Press, 1967), Ch. 1; and Peter M. Hall, "A Symbolic Interactionist Analysis of Politics," *Sociological Inquiry,* 42 (1972): 51–54.

2. Bell, *Power, Influence and Authority,* pp. 15–69.

3. William E. Connolly, *The Terms of Political Discourse* (Lexington, Mass.: D.C. Heath and Co., 1974), p. 10.

4. E. E. Schattschneider, *Two Hundred Million Americans in Search of a Government* (New York: Holt, Rinehart and Winston, Inc., 1969), Ch. 6.

5. William Safire, *The New Language of Politics* (New York: Collier Books, 2nd ed., 1972), pp. iii–xviii.

6. For the results of studies exploring the usage of political terms in spoken and written English see Ithiel de Sola Pool, *The "Prestige Papers,"* (Stanford: Stanford University Press, 1952).

7. Michael Weinstein, *Philosophy, Theory, and Method in Contemporary Political Thought* (Glenview, Ill.: Scott, Foresman Co., 1971), p. 20; on this point also see Roelofs, *The Language of Modern Politics,* p. 41.

8. Clarence Schettler, *Public Opinion in American Society* (New York: Harper and Brothers, Publishers, 1960), p. 50. See also C. K. Ogden and I. A. Richards, *The Meaning of Meaning* (New York: Harcourt, Brace and World, 1923), Ch. 16 and the discussion of sign process in Rollo Handy and E. C. Harwood, *A Current Appraisal of the Behavioral Sciences* (Great Barrington, Mass.: Behavioral Research Council, 2nd ed., 1973), pp. ix–x.

9. See T. D. Weldon, *The Vocabulary of Politics* (Baltimore: Penguin Books, 1953).

10. *Mind, Self and Society* (Chicago: University of Chicago Press, 1934), p. 47; see also Anselm L. Strauss, *Mirrors and Masks: The Search for Identity* (New York: The Free Press, 1959); Peter L. Berger and Thomas Luckman, *The Social Construction of Reality* (New York: Anchor Books, 1967); and George Gordon, *The Languages of Communication* (New York: Hastings House, 1969), Ch. 4.

11. Roger W. Cobb and Charles D. Elder, "Individual Orientations and the Study of Political Symbolism," *Social Science Quarterly,* 53 (June 1972): 79–80.

12. "Symbolism," in the *Encyclopedia of the Social Sciences* (New York: Macmillan Co., 1930), pp. 492–495.

13. See Murray Edelman, *The Symbolic Uses of Politics* (Urbana: University of Illinois Press, 1964) and *Politics as Symbolic Action* (Chicago: Markham Publish-

ing Co., 1971) for a discussion of the relationship between social role taking and the meaning imputed to political symbols.

14. *Public Opinion in American Society,* p. 32.

15. See Hugh Dalziel Duncan, *Symbols in Society* (New York: Oxford University Press, 1968) for a discussion of the part played by symbols in achieving social order. A partial discussion of the social control, consensus, and interest theories of social order is Robert E. Dowse and John A. Hughes, *Political Sociology* (New York: John Wiley and Sons, 1972), Ch. 2.

16. *Word Play* (New York: Alfred A. Knopf, 1974), pp. 6–7.

17. Lyman and Scott, *A Sociology of the Absurd* (New York: Appleton-Century-Crofts, 1970), Ch. 5.

18. *Language and Social Behavior* (Baltimore: Penguin Books, 1972), pp. 50–51, 57–79; the social functions of language are also discussed by Allen D. Grimshaw, "Sociolinguistics," in Ithiel de Sola Pool and Wilbur Schramm, eds., *Handbook of Communication* (Chicago: Rand McNally, 1973), pp. 49–92, and Farb, *Word Play,* passim. For a listing and series of examples of political functions of verbal language in politics see Doris A. Graber, *Verbal Behavior and Politics* (Urbana: University of Illinois Press, 1976).

19. "The Story of P," *Harper's,* 249 (October 1974): 6–9, 12, 16.

20. Duncan, *Symbols in Society,* Ch. 3.

21. In J. B. Carroll, ed., *Language, Thought and Reality* (Cambridge: The M.I.T. Press, 1956), p. 138; also see Edward Sapir, *Language: An Introduction to the Study of Speech* (New York: Harcourt, Brace and Co., 1921).

22. "The Unity of the Human Being," in Joseph Ratner, ed., *Intelligence and the Modern World* (New York: Random House, 1939), p. 817. The three versions of the Whorfian hypotheses are discussed in George A. Miller and David McNeill, "Psycholinguistics," in Gardner Lindzey and Elliot Aronson, eds., *The Handbook of Social Psychology,* Vol. III (Reading, Mass.: Addison-Wesley Publishing Co., 1969), pp. 728–741. Other discussions of the hypothesis include S. I. Hayakawa, *Symbol, Status, and Personality* (New York: Harcourt, Brace and World, 1953), Ch. 10, and Farb, *Word Play,* pp. 180–187.

23. Murray Edelman, "The Political Language of the Helping Professions," *Politics and Society,* 4 (Sept. 1974): 299.

24. "Communication Without Words," in Jean M. Civikly, ed., *Messages* (New York: Random House, 1974), p. 87.

25. The concept of impression management is Erving Goffman's; see his *The Presentation of Self in Everyday Life* (New York: Anchor Books, 1959); on communication via silence see J. Vernon Jensen, "Communicative Functions of Silence," *ETC.,* 30 (September 1973): 249–257.

26. Ray L. Birdwhistell, *Kinesics and Context* (Philadelphia: University of Pennsylvania Press, 1970), p. 45 (emphasis in original). Also see Randall P. Harrison, "Nonverbal Communication," in Pool and Schramm, eds., *Handbook of Communication,* pp. 93–115.

27. *Collective Search for Identity* (New York: Holt, Rinehart and Winston, 1969), p. 121.

28. "Models of the Interaction of Language and Social Life," in John J. Gumperz and Dell Hymes, eds., *Directions in Sociolinguistics* (New York: Holt, Rinehart and Winston, 1972), pp. 35–63.

29. See Charles Morris, *Signs, Language and Behavior* (New York: Prentice-Hall, Inc., 1946). In "Psychology and Communication" in George A. Miller, ed., *Communication, Language, and Meaning* (New York: Basic Books, Inc., 1973), pp. 3–12, Miller offers a different division from that of semantics, syntactics, and pragmatics of Morris.

30. Hadley Cantril, "Perception and Interpersonal Relations," *American Journal of Psychiatry*, 114 (1957): 126.

31. *Public Opinion in American Society*, p. 31.

32. J. Samuel Bois, "The Power of Words," in Civikly, ed., *Messages*, pp. 81–86.

33. *Science and Sanity* (Lancaster: Science Press, 2nd ed., 1941).

34. See Murray Edelman's discussion in *The Symbolic Uses of Politics*, pp. 116–117; also Daniel Katz, "Psychological Barriers to Communication," in Civikly, ed., *Messages*, pp. 321–331.

35. Farb, *Word Play*, p. 24.

36. "Psycholinguistics," p. 667 (emphasis added).

37. Quoted in Haig A. Bosmajian, "The Language of Sexism," in Civikly, ed., *Messages*, p. 338.

38. Farb, *Word Play*, p. 28.

39. *Politics as Symbolic Action*, p. 2.

40. Arthur Bentley, *Relativity in Man and Society* (New York: G. P. Putnam's Sons, 1926), pp. 196–197.

41. Rudolf Flesch, *How to Write, Speak, and Think More Effectively* (New York: Harper and Row, 1960); see James J. Kilpatrick's syndicated column of October 10, 1974, "Greenspan True Expert at Gobbledygook." A critique of readability tests such as those cited is Theodore L. Glasser, "On Readability and Listenability," *ETC.* 32 (June 1975): 138–142.

42. Ivan L. Preston and Ralph H. Johnson, "Puffery—A Problem the FTC Didn't Want (and May Try to Eliminate)," *Journalism Quarterly*, 49 (Autum 1972): 558–568; Herzog, *The B. S. Factor* (Baltimore: Penguin Books, 1974).

43. Elliot Zashin and Phillip C. Chapman, "The Uses of Metaphor and Analogy: Toward a Renewal of Political Language," *Journal of Politics*, 36 (May 1974): 290–326.

44. Stokes, "The Story of P."

45. Edelman, *Symbolic Uses of Politics*, p. 25.

46. Harold D. Lasswell and Abraham Kaplan, *Power and Society* (New Haven: Yale University Press, 1950), p. 110.

47. Edelman, *Politics as Symbolic Action*, p. 7 (emphasis in original).

48. Farb, *Word Play*, p. 138.

49. P. G. A. Pocock, *Politics, Language, and Time* (New York: Atheneum, 1971), pp. 14–22.

50. Haig Bosmajian, *The Language of Oppression* (Washington, D.C.: Public Affairs Press, 1974).

51. Muriel R. Schulz, "Is the English Language Anybody's Enemy?," *ETC.*, 32 (June 1975): 151–153.

52. In George Orwell, *A Collection of Essays by George Orwell* (Garden City: Anchor Books, 1954), pp. 162–177.

53. *One-Dimensional Man* (Boston: Beacon Press, 1969), pp. 84–104.

54. "The Story of P," p. 8.

55. Ulf Himmelstrand, "Verbal Attitudes and Behavior: A Paradigm for the Study of Message Transmission and Transformation," *Public Opinion Quarterly*, 24 (Summer 1960): 224–250.

56. Claus Mueller, *The Politics of Communication* (New York: Oxford University Press, 1973).

57. *Language as Symbolic Action* (Berkeley: University of California Press, 1966), p. 16. (Emphasis in original.)

58. Ibid., p. 11.

chapter 4

Political Persuasion: Propaganda, Advertising, and Rhetoric

The political communicator not seeking to persuade others to his views is more rare than the whooping crane. Indeed, the failure to take part in persuasive communication may leave that person as close to extinction as the endangered species. Like talk, persuasion is essential to politics. It is the motivating aspect of "who says what" in political communication. This chapter explores the key features of political persuasion—what it is, its major dimensions, and linguistic techniques associated with it. We also review some ideas about selected effects of persuasive messages, at least insofar as those alleged effects figure into how political communicators frame persuasion compaigns. In Chapter 10 we ponder the more general consequences of persuasion upon political behavior.

THE PERVASIVENESS OF PERSUASION

George Gordon, long a student of the process, writes that the first human act of persuasion is recorded in *Genesis*, 3:6: "And when the woman saw that the tree was good for food, and that it was pleasant to the eyes, and a tree to be desired to make one wise, she took the fruit thereof, and did eat, and gave also unto her husband with her; and he did eat."[1] Much of the succeeding human drama consists of highlights of persuasion: the Socratic dialogues, Aristotle's *Rhetoric*, Sun Tzu opening the way for psychological warfare with *The Book of War*, the orations of Cicero, the speech Shakespeare provides Mark Antony in *Julius Caesar*, the writings of St. Thomas Aquinas, Machiavelli's admonitions in *The Prince*, *The Declaration of Independence*, and the modern day inspiration of Winston Churchill and diatribes of Adolf Hitler. Over the centuries persuasion pervades the history of man's activities and accomplishments, albeit under a variety of labels. In the world of commerce the principal variants have been advertising and public relations. In the political realm governments undertook campaigns of public information, psychological warfare, and the orchestration of events; partisan groups relied upon propaganda and electoral rhetoric. Added to these commercial and political verities were efforts of public service organizations in conducting information campaigns promoting causes such as the reduction of automobile accidents, the prevention of drug abuse, and fund-raising drives to fight killing and crippling diseases.

Characterizing Persuasion

What do all these variations on a theme have in common? What is persuasion? There are many proffered definitions: "changing people's attitudes and behavior through the spoken and written word,"[2] inducing a new opinion,[3] and a conscious attempt to change the attitudes, beliefs, or behavior of people through the transmission of some message.[4] We seek no final definition here, but prefer instead to outline a few of the chief characteristics of the persuasive process. Taken singly, none sets persuasion off from other modes of discourse; yet taken together they provide an insight into the nature of the process.

First, persuasion normally involves intent, an effort by a communicator to achieve some end through talk.[5] Persuasion is purposive, or interested, communication. The qualification "normally" needs to be taken seriously. As Leonard Doob notes in a classic work on the subject, there are unintentional as well as intentional modes of persuasion. As an example Doob makes a distinction between the advertising agent who wants to promote the sale of a product (intentional) and the housewife who spontaneously praises the product in the presence of a friend (unintentional).[6] Thus the conscious intentions of the communicator are a possible indicator of persuasion, but not the whole story. Unwittingly persuasion occurs even in the absence of a communicator's intent if the recipient of a message perceives some purpose in a communicator's motives and/or message and responds to it.

This introduces a second characteristic of persuasion, namely, that it is dialectical. It is erroneous to think that person A persuades person B when A simply appeals and B complies. Rather, people persuade each other in precisely the kind of mutual exchange that characterizes the influence process we described in Chapter 2. To be sure, as we shall see, an explicit persuasive appeal may be either a one-way, one-to-many, or two-way message. We can envision a president of the United States on nationwide television exhorting citizens to adopt energy conservation methods, or a two-way appeal in which a president sits down with congressional leaders and each implores the other to adopt a preferred energy program. In either mode, however, there is an exchange of symbols between communicator(s) and audience, involving all participants in a collective refashioning of images through the joint process of voicing and hearing appeals.

Persuasion, then, is a reciprocal process in which a communicator sets out, wittingly or unwittingly, to strike a responsive chord in others. The third element in that process is the form responses take. In keeping with the viewpoint developed in Chapter 1, those responses consist of people acting in ways different from the way they would have behaved in the absence of persuasive appeal. Most notably those actions consist of expressed opinions reflecting changes in perceptions, beliefs, values, and expectations. If, for example, people change their ideas about how things are (beliefs) as a result of new information, or misinformation, in the forms of facts, data, statistics, etc., this is persuasion; thus a person may learn that smoking cigarettes is conducive to lung cancer, or contrarily be convinced by evidence challenging that position. Or, if persons change their evaluations (values) of things—if they come to feel that an incumbent officeholder is not trustworthy upon hearing charges leveled by the official's election challenger—that too is persuasion. Again, if citizens predict an improvement in the economy after hearing a president speak optimistically of upturns in recent economic indicators (expectations), that too is persuasion.[7]

We can summarize by returning to our account in Chapter 3 pertaining to political talk. Political talk, we said, is purposive; that is, it is talk aimed at preserving and enhancing talk about other things. Persuasion is a mode of political talk. Unwittingly or not people who take part in politics intend to get others to act in ways that they might not act if there was no persuasion—to change perceptions, thoughts, feelings, and expectations. But persuasion is not power talk, not a threat that says "If you do (do not do) X, I will do Y." Power talk is closer to coercion and threat than it is to persuasion. Nor is persuasion the talk of authority that commands, "Do X." Rather, persuasion is influence talk, characterized by contingencies ("If you do X, you will do Y") identified through the mutual give-and-take of the parties involved.[8]

Identifying American Political Persuaders

Who then are the major persuaders in contemporary American politics? Simply put, they consist of all classes of political communicators described in Chapter 2. Certainly the politician plays the role of persuader be he the representative seeking benefits on behalf of his constituents or the ideologist advancing a cause (see p. 26). Both officeholders and office-seekers spend enormous amounts of money on essentially persuasive enterprises. There are hundreds of government bureaus, for example, which have an office of public information. As Herbert Schiller has pointed out, one reason for having these offices is to conduct public relations activities on behalf of bureau policies and programs; estimates of the amounts spent on such public relations ran as high as $400 million per year in the late 1960s, and one study estimated costs at twice the combined amount spent by the major wire services, three television networks, and ten largest U.S. daily newspapers to disseminate news.[9] Candidates for public office also spend large amounts persuading people to elect them as indicated by the $138 million guessed to have been budgeted for such purposes in the 1972 presidential campaigns.[10]

Professional communicators, like politicians, are skilled in the persuasive arts. The promoter (see pp. 28–30) we defined as a person who, because of skills at communication, receives pay from clients to advance special interests. Among promoters are press secretaries, publicity agents, advertising personnel, campaign consultants, etc. The second category of professional communicators, the journalists, engage in persuasion although less obviously. To the degree that they simply transmit information, even in an impartial and unbiased way, they still hope to be read or listened to and thereby to change the images their audiences have of the world. Some journalists—notably television commentators, newspaper columnists, many interpretative reporters, and magazine feature writers —deliberately try to persuade, a point we shall return to in Chapter 6.

Finally, the third major category of political communicators discussed in Chapter 2, the activist, is a persuader as well. The spokesperson for an organized interest and the opinion leader (see pp. 30–32) are purveyors of influence talk. Indeed, one could hardly write of political persuasion in contemporary American politics and ignore the considerable efforts of industrial, laboring, agricultural, and public service groups to achieve goals through propaganda, advertising, and rhetoric, the chief modes of political persuasion that we now examine.

PERSUASION IN POLITICS: CONTRASTING AND OVERLAPPING APPROACHES

There are three principal ways of thinking about persuasion as it occurs in politics. These approaches to political persuasion—propaganda, advertising, and rhetoric—are similar in several respects: all are purposive, intentional, and involve influence; all consist of reciprocal relations between people rather than one person dictating to another; and all result in varying degrees of change in personal perceptions, beliefs, values, and expectations. Yet there are ways in which the three differ. First, there is a difference between one-to-many and two-way emphases in transmitting messages. Second, there are differences in whether the approach is oriented toward individuals or groups. Third, each approach suggests a different view of what makes society possible. And, fourth, each implies a different focus in formulating campaigns of persuasion.

Political Persuasion as Propaganda

In the mid-1970s there appeared in movie theaters and on television a film entitled *Rollerball*. It depicted a world of the future, one in which (said the advertising) "wars will no longer exist, but there will be Rollerball." In that world, separate, multinational corporations supply every human need (food, clothing, transportation, shelter, energy) and want (notions, tranquilizing drugs, baubles, and sundries). Each major corporation is based in an important world city (New York, Rome, Tokyo, Houston and others); each operates a franchise in the exciting and brutal sport of Rollerball. But Rollerball is more than a sport; it is, remarked a member of the world's ruling elite, "a game devised to demonstrate the absolute futility of individual effort." The world of Rollerball is divided among a few dominant groups, each group maintaining its hold over its members by controlling what people talk about and the information they have available for forming opinions. This futuristic society is one of total propaganda, i.e., (1) one-to-many communication, (2) operating upon people who identify themselves as members of groups, (3) as a mechanism of social control using persuasion to achieve order. Jacques Ellul, French sociologist and philosopher, summarizes these traits in defining propaganda as communication which is *"employed by an organized group that wants to bring about the active or passive participation in its actions of a mass of individuals, psychologically unified through psychological manipulation and incorporated in an organization."*[11]

Propaganda as One-to-Many Transmission

The origins of the term propaganda to refer to social phenomena can be traced back three and a half centuries. In 1622 Pope Gregory XV convened a Committee of Cardinals, *Congregatio de Propaganda Fide*, to propagate the Christian faith among foreign peoples. Typically missionaries were dispatched to spread the doctrine, one missionary for each of several thousand desired converts. Here then originated not only the term but a key characteristic of the activity, that is, propaganda as one-to-many communication. The propagandist is a person or small group reaching a larger collective audience.

Examples abound of the one-to-many character of political propaganda. Stump speakers in bygone years addressed gatherings of their partisans; today the tradition lives on in the orations of candidates for president accepting their party's nomination before the convened faithful, their whistle stop and shopping center tours in front of sympathetic audiences, and other forms of party rallies. In his term as president, Gerald Ford initiated White House conferences, gatherings in various regions of local influentials. There Ford and his cabinet members would appear on behalf of programs and policies. President Carter's appearances before citizens in town hall meetings suggest his style of one-to-many persuasion. As Kecskemeti points out, even election canvassing—the door-to-door solicitation by party workers in search of funds and votes—is basically a one-to-many technique: "the canvasser presents an appeal to the members of a group successively rather than simultaneously, but this is just an alternative way of disseminating the center's message without the development of any significant dialogue between the source and the collective audience."[12]

The Group Orientation of Propaganda

As noted in Ellul's definition, propaganda is a means used by organized groups to reach individuals, psychologically manipulated and incorporated into an organization. For Ellul (and for other scholars as well) the development of groups takes place simultaneously with the development of propaganda.[13] Propaganda is a group phenomenon closely linked to "organization and action—without which propaganda is practically nonexistent." "Effective propaganda," writes Ellul, "can work only inside a group, principally inside a nation."[14]

Through manipulation of symbols, propagandists reach individuals as group members. In his carefully staged appeals before Nazi party rallies, Adolph Hitler exemplified the essential tie between organization and propaganda that is achieved through symbols. Speaking before huge crowds, surrounded by national and party banners, and using emotion laden oratory evoking a sense of identification, commitment, and loyalty from his audience, Hitler captured the person for the party and for himself: *"Ein Volk, ein Reich, ein Fuhrer"* (one people, one empire, one leader).

Political Propaganda: A Social Control Mechanism

The one-to-many and group aspects of propaganda separate the propagandist from the propagandee. The propagandist pretends to speak man to man, to leave the impression that leader and led are joined in a cooperative effort to the mutual benefit of both. Yet, argues Ellul, the propagandist is really nothing else nor more than a representative of an organization seeking to control its members, "a technician who treats his patients in various ways but keeps himself cold and aloof, selecting his words and actions for purely technical reasons."[15] The propagandist is, in short, a technician of social control.

The rationale for propaganda rests upon a theory of social control, that social order results from people continuously learning and reinforcing a shared political faith, religious belief, social outlook, customs, rules, and a basic way of life. But in a society based upon the premise that widespread popular participation in political affairs is desirable, no group simply can sit back and wait for favorable public opinion. Instead, under conditions of mass political participation and conflict with other groups, each organization actively mobilizes public support. It disseminates its ideology, awakens the awareness of vast numbers of people, establishes a close relationship with and among them, enlists their loyalties, and sustains their devotion. What holds for each group struggling with others in a society is equally the case for each nation in a conflictive world. Through a variety of techniques each nation's rulers, or aspiring rulers, employ propaganda as a mechanism of social control.

Types of Propaganda

Numerous writers endeavor to distinguish between intentional and unintentional propaganda. Thus the teacher of economics who deliberately indoctrinates students in Marxist views differs in intent from one who, responding to a question, spontaneously remarks on positive points in Marxist philosophy. Doob offers a related distinction between concealed and revealed propaganda.[16] In the former a propagandist masks intent, as when a president, for instance, holds a news conference ostensibly to respond to reporters' questions but turns each inquiry to his own advantage. Revealed propaganda discloses its purposes, as when a political candidate makes an open bid for votes.

Jacques Ellul suggests a typology of propaganda that is more complex than the distinctions between intentional-unintentional, concealed-revealed.[17] To begin with, there is political vs. sociological propaganda. The former involves the efforts of a government, party, administration, or pressure group to achieve strategic or tactical ends. It operates through short-term, specific appeals. Sociological propaganda is less apparent, more long term. Through it people are infused with a way of life; an ideology (such as "the American way of life") gradually penetrates economic, social, and political institutions. The result is a general conception of society faithfully adhered to by everyone except those few castigated as "deviants." Related to this is Ellul's distinction between the propaganda of agitation and integration. Agitation seeks to get people to make substantial sacrifices for immediate goals, to disrupt their lives in pursuit of a cause to be realized in a series of stages, goal by goal. Through agitation leaders maintain adherents' enthusiasm by achieving a specific victory, then offering a chance for respite followed by the pursuit of yet another in a chain of aspirations. Democratic and Republican candidates for their party's presidental nomination use agitation to sustain the energies of their partisans, moving from state to state in pursuit of a series of victories in primaries extending over six months of the election year. Propaganda of integration, on the other hand, enlists conformity in the pursuit of long-term goals. Through it people dedicate themselves to causes that may not be realized for years, not even in their lifetimes. Thus said President John Kennedy in setting goals for his administration, "All of this will not be accomplished within the first one hundred days, within the first one thousand days, or even within the lifetime of this administration. But let us begin!"

Ellul also distinguishes between vertical and horizontal propaganda. The former is one-to-many and relies particularly upon the mass media for dissemination of appeals. Horizontal propaganda works less from leader to group than among the membership of the group, less through mass communication than interpersonal and organization communication (see Chapter 5). Political parties have traditionally relied upon horizontal propaganda: canvassing within precinct organizations, drilling of the party cadres, conspiracies within the cell, etc.

Focal Points of Propaganda Campaigns: Who Says What in Which Channels?

In formulating persuasive campaigns, propagandists consider several factors. They are, of course, cognizant of the character of their enterprise (the one-to-many, group, and social control aspects) and the types of propaganda available. They are also aware of another feature of propaganda, namely, that the effectiveness of a campaign depends a great deal upon the stimuli presented to the audience. We shall see that propagandists, contrasted with political advertisers and rhetoricians, worry less about how the biases of their audiences restrict the effectiveness of persuasion than about using appropriate speakers, symbols, and media. Instead of trying to find out what audience predispositions are, then adjusting their appeals to them (an important feature of political advertising and rhetoric), propagandists simply assume a given bias associated with the membership of a specific group. Thus, whether for or against organized labor, the propagandist takes the prolabor biases of the trade union as given. For the propagandist the quality of the stimuli, not the predispositions of propagandees, counts most.

Social psychologists have been mildly helpful to the propagandist in this respect by providing studies documenting the relative effects of the communicator's qualities, message content, and type of media on the success of a persuasive appeal.[18] Although some of the findings of early research have been challenged (see Chapter 11), many propagandists take them into account and formulate campaigns accordingly. Here are some of the prime considerations:

Who? In pondering what advice to follow or give to another, the propagandist can turn to the following general principles derived from research pertaining to the effects of the communicator upon the success of persuasive efforts:

1. *The communicator's status:* Every person plays several roles occupying varying positions such as student, teacher, bank president, public official, journalist, etc. Each role carries status or prestige. Generally, the higher the status of a particular position and role, the more likely the communicator occupying it will be persuasive.

2. *The communicator's credibility:* Propagandees perceive communicators in several ways. To the degree that they perceive propagandists as possessing expertise, competence, reliability, trustworthiness, and authority, they regard the communicator as credible. Moreover, communicator credibility also includes perception of the source's intent (objective or biased, right or wrong, etc.). The general finding is that the more credible the propagandist, the greater the effectiveness of persuasion in the short run. But as time passes, persons distinguish between (1) what was said and (2) the credibility of the source, thus questioning the message content even though retaining a high opinion of the communicator.

3. *The communicator's attractiveness:* A communicator's status and credibility make him more or less attractive to audiences, but his personality, likableness, air of confidence, and the degree that people regard themselves as sharing certain desirable qualities posessed by the source also contribute to that attractiveness. Attractiveness enhances persuasiveness. This may be especially true of homophyly, the degree of perceived similarity in age, background, etc. between people. Persuasion succeeds in part to the extent that one perceives the communicator as being like oneself in salient, respected ways.[19]

We should keep in mind two points about these general principles. First, although the propagandist emphasizes the qualities of the communicator in formulating campaigns, it is not possible to ignore audience predispositions altogether. Each quality of a communicator—status, credibility, attractiveness—depends upon the perceptions of receivers, not solely or necessarily upon inherent characteristics of the source. The communicator's perceived attributes constitute an image; no image exists apart from how people perceive a communicator.[20] Second, the relationships described are not always consistent. For instance, a person responds more positively to a communicator with characteristics similar to one's own (homophyly); yet, if that person thinks the communicator knows more about the subject or has expertise, the person is likely to respond favorably even though a response to greater expertise would seem to run counter to the homophyly principle. We suspect in such cases perceived expertise is more important. As McGuire writes, "To paraphrase Groucho Marx's comment that he would not want to belong to a club that would let in a person like him, the average person usually may not care to listen to a source who knows no more about the topic than he himself does."[21]

Says What?   A variety of characteristics of a propagandistic message are related to its effectiveness:

1. *The content of the message:* Several aspects of a message relate to persuasiveness, but research findings equivocate with respect to precisely how. For instance, under some circumstances threatening people (fear arousal communications) persuades them to do things (as in raising the specter of dental cavities if residents do not vote to fluoridate the water supply); under other conditions, however, the threat boomerangs (some voters dismiss as scare tactics the politician's exhortations of dire consequences that will follow from his defeat). Moreover, there is no consensus on how much fear arousal is proper (mild or high) in cases where it does seem effective.

Research findings are a little more clear-cut (but still far from conclusive) respecting other aspects of message content: (a) any appeal must advocate some opinion change to be effective, but if the message differs too much from the audience's views it will be ignored—hence it is very difficult to get the lifelong, intense Republican to convert to the Democratic cause and vice versa; (b) a propaganda message should not be blatant, yet there tends to be more persuasion if the conclusion to be drawn from the appeal is made explicit rather than left for the audience to infer—thus, Richard Nixon in 1972 did not say directly that George McGovern was less qualified to be president, but merely used the explicit slogan "Reelect the President;" (c) before friendly audiences it suffices to present one side of the argument; before the unfriendly and uncommitted present both sides—i.e., damn the opposition before one's partisans, admit to, but do not show, one's warts before others; (d) metaphorical rather than literal expressions enhance persuasiveness,—Gerald Ford upon taking office in 1974 probably won more sympathy using an automotive metaphor to liken himself to "a Ford, not a Lincoln" than by saying, "I am of lesser quality than some other presidents;" (e) distractions—humor, anecdotes, etc.—often, but not always, increase the effectiveness of appeals; and (f) the jury remains out regarding whether appeals should be factual, emotional, or a combination of the two, for much depends upon the situation and the audience.

2. *The structure of the message:* As in the case of message content, there are no conclusive propositions regarding the relationship of a message's organization to how people respond. There are various possible orderings including climax ordering (placing the most important material last), anticlimax ordering (placing it first), and pyramidal ordering, (placing it in the middle). Differing structures give rise to the primacy-recency debate; i.e., is an appeal more effective if the most telling arguments

are stated early in the message or at the end? Research indicates that "it depends." Specifically, if the argument is over a familiar topic, the first points made are best remembered and perhaps most persuasive; if the topic is unfamiliar, the last-mentioned arguments are most telling. In either event, the arguments at beginning or end are usually remembered better than those appearing in the middle.

In Which Channel? A hallmark of contemporary propaganda is that it uses all channels of communication available—newspapers, magazines, radio, television, films, posters, rallies, door-to-door canvassing, direct mail, etc. The modern propagandist employs all three major types of channels (interpersonal, organizational, and mass) that we discuss in Chapter 5. The problem is not in deciding which media to employ, but in deciding which one for each aspect of a carefully programmed campaign in order to avoid a hit-and-miss, sporadic, haphazard campaign. In contemplating a full-fledged media campaign, three considerations are uppermost:

1. *What media do people use?* Survey researchers provide fairly reliable and consistent answers to this question over the years, at least insofar as which media people use to obtain political information.[22] About two-thirds of Americans use television to obtain information and one-third rely solely upon that medium. One-half use newspapers, but only about one-fifth do so exclusively. About one-fourth obtain information solely from a combination of television and newspapers. Radio, magazines, books, and conversations with people provide political information to relatively small proportions of Americans.

2. *What media do people believe?* About one-half of Americans regard television as the most credible medium, one-fourth opt for newspapers, and the remainder split fairly evenly over radio and magazines. If they could have only one of four media—television, newspapers, radio, and magazines—as a source of believable information, almost six of every ten would want television. Yet television as the most used and believable information source still does not inspire great confidence; Louis Harris found in 1977 that little more than a fourth of a nationwide sample placed confidence in television news as an American institution.[23]

3. *Which media for what?* Ellul points out that each medium is suited best for a different type of propaganda: movies and human contact serve best for sociological propaganda; public meetings and posters stress agitation; newspapers, radio and television are politically useful. Unfortunately, Ellul offers no empirical basis for his assertions, yet the major point is valid; i.e., "they must *all* be used in combination" for "the propagandist uses a keyboard and composes a symphony."[24]

Conceiving persuasion as propaganda, then, consists of emphasizing selected aspects of the process (one-to-many communication, group bases, aims of social control, and concerns with attributes of the communicator, message, and media). The study of propaganda, however, provides only a partial understanding of what political persuasion is all about. A more complete picture requires that we turn to a second approach, political advertising.

Political Persuasion as Advertising

If *Rollerball* provides insights into the character of contemporary political propaganda, then the 1970s movie *The Candidate* is an object lesson in the advertising dimensions of political persuasion. The film is about an attractive, intelligent, energetic young social activist who, when approached by a professional campaign manager, agrees to run for public office. The manager, in concert with his entourage of pollsters, film makers, advertising men, press agents, speech writers, makeup artists, and others, mold, package, and sell the candidate through a technically sophisticated mass advertising campaign. The worst fears of critics of contemporary political campaigns, that unknown products can be sold to an unsophisticated consuming electorate like deodorant, soap, or toothpaste, are confirmed in the closing scene as the victorious candidate anxiously contemplates whether he is actually qualitied for public office; he turns to his campaign manager, a hired gun already looking for new faces to sell, and says "But what do we do now?"

One-to-Many Individuals Communication

Like propaganda, mass advertising is one-to-many communication. But there is a distinct difference. Propaganda addresses persons as group members; advertising approaches them chiefly as single, independant individuals apart from whatever groups they identify with in society. Herbert Blumer makes the point by distinguishing between a public and a mass. (This is a distinction we shall return to again in Chapter 7.) A *public*, notes Blumer, refers to a group of people (a) confronted by an issue, (b) divided as to how to meet the issue, and (c) airing their differences through discussion. Propaganda is a principal means of manipulating that discussion, and through it, public opinon. A *mass*, on the other hand, consists of people from all walks of life and social strata whose concerns transcend their group memberships; the mass consists of anonymous persons (they do not, in contrast to group members, know one another), who rarely interact, are very loosely organized, and act not in concert but spontaneously as individuals. Advertising addresses each of these anonymous individuals: "The relation between the advertisement and the prospective purchaser is a direct one—there is no organization or leadership which can deliver, so to speak, the body of purchasers to the seller. Instead, each individual acts upon the basis of his own selection."[25]

Political Advertising: A Convergence Mechanism

This characteristic of advertising, that it operates as one-to-many communication upon individuals in a heterogeneous mass rather than as members of fairly homogeneous groups, distinguishes it from propaganda in another important respect. Propaganda is a social control mechanism employing symbols to promote social order through common beliefs, shared values, and overlapping expectations. The aim is to enhance members' identification with the group (nation, state, corporation, university, special interest association, etc.). Advertising works differently. First, its target is not the individual in a group but the independent, free person detached from the group. Second, the aim of that targeting is not to identify the person with a group, but to attract one's attention away from it, to get a person to act and choose separately from others. Whereas a group member is gradually stripped of his self-awareness through conformity-oriented propaganda, the individual in the mass is apt to be acutely self-conscious.

What happens, then, when advertising appeals to individuals detached from group identities, when it pitches individuality rather than conformity, when advertisers try to sell each person an automobile different from any other in its "options"? What happens is that each person acts not in concert with others but independently, freely, and spontaneously in making selections. When people acting independently arrive at the same choice, the individual selections converge—the phenomenon of convergent selectivity introduced in Chapter 2. In responding to the question, "What makes society possible?", proponents of the convergent selectivity thesis argue that a consensus of individual choices created by mass advertising, not the efforts of organized groups to exert control through conformity-oriented propaganda, is the principal answer.[26]

Following this line of thought yields a view of the purposes of political advertising. Governmental agencies, for example, institute advertising campaigns directed at getting individual citizens to conserve gasoline (Don't be fuelish), protect forests (Only *you* can prevent forest fires), and join the Army (We Want to Join *You*). Election campaign advertising establishes personal rapport between candidate and voter. In the age of candidate merchandising (as in *The Candidate*), victory depends less upon the efforts of party organizers and propagandizers than upon the converged selections of voters only weakly affiliated with political parties or calling themselves "Independents."

It is not the intent here to argue the accuracy of either the social control or convergent selectivity thesis of social order. It is sufficient at this point simply to note that propaganda and advertising as variants of political persuasion derive from these differing perspectives. Political persuasion as rhetorical process rests upon still a third thesis. Before elaborating that viewpoint, however, let us examine two remaining aspects of mass advertising relevant to politics.

Types of Advertising

One can distinguish between commercial and noncommercial advertising. The former, of no direct concern to us, includes consumer advertising (for selling products or services) and business advertising (aimed primarily at industrial management, professionals, occupational specialists, and wholesale or retail merchants). Noncommercial advertising is undertaken by charitable groups (public service advertising), governments, political groups (political parties, pressure groups, etc.), and political candidates.

However, a distinction borrowed from the realm of commercial advertising is quite relevant to noncommercial advertising, especially to political advertising. That distinction is between product and institutional advertising. Product advertising simply promotes the sale of goods or services. Its political counterpart is image advertising, appeals directed at building a public official's or office-seeker's reputation; informing audiences of a politician's qualifications, experience, background, and personality; and enhancing the election prospects of candidates or promoting specific programs and policies. President Gerald Ford's abortive 1974 campaign to "Whip Inflation Now" was an example of product advertising in politics; lapel pins, bumper stickers, posters, etc. bore the acronym WIN, a catchword designed to rally individual citizens in support of Ford's economic policies.

Institutional advertising seeks to promote the good reputation of an industry, firm, business, or other commercial enterprise. The assumption is that people are more likely to deal with an institution they trust rather than with one they do not; hence, institutional advertising seeks to convince people a reputable firm is behind the brand name (as when a consumer is implicitly invited to purchase a certain petroleum company's products because the corporation is "working to solve America's energy shortage"). The political variant of institutional advertising is conducted on behalf of a group, political party, or government agency. The national Democratic party, for example, has conducted nationwide telethons in recent years not only to raise funds but to promote the party as an institution. Or, consider the advertising campaigns conducted by various state governments to promote tourism and industrial growth for their commonwealths.

Institutional advertising bears some resemblance to public relations, but it is best to recognize key differences between these two modes of persuasion. Institutional advertising shares with all advertising the character of presenting and promoting an idea to a mass audience via paid, sponsored appeals. It is essentially an outward looking activity that promotes a product or institution to an audience whose members are rarely members of the promoting organization as well. In contrast, public relations conducts both internal and external communication campaigns for an organization. It is a function of management concerned with communication to groups within an institution, to groups outside that institution, and between internal and external audiences. The internal public relations program fosters morale, dedication, and a sense of purpose among an organization's membership. Externally it provides information and builds good will among nonmembers. Moreover, a public relations campaign relies not only upon paid advertising but even more so upon publicity, i.e., giving wide circulation to favorable facts about the institution through news releases, news stories, magazine articles, television documentaries, etc. Hence, public relations is akin to propaganda in its focus upon groups, akin to advertising when focused upon mass audiences. Government agencies, political parties, pressure groups, and the campaign organizations of office-seekers—all have public relations specialists devoted to internal and external promotions.[27]

Focal Points of Advertising Campaigns: To Whom With What Effects?

Of course, political advertisers scarcely ignore the considerations propagandists take into account respecting the relative impacts of communicator qualities, messages, and media upon the effectiveness of their campaigns (nor can propagandists simply ignore the predispositions of the audience in formulating appeals). But as a matter of emphasis, the focuses of mass advertising are more upon the qualities of the audience and the potential range of effects than upon other considerations. Planners of advertising campaigns are less prone than propagandists to think of a campaign's impact as direct influence (from communicator to audience); they accept the proposition that "little of what the communicator wants to get across does so unless the audience wants it to."[28] Stressing that the effectiveness of persuasion is determined as much by the perceiver as by the stimulus, exponents of advertising engage in motivation research (MR) to find out what turns an audience on and what kinds of effects are possible.

To Whom: Among the questions political advertisers need to answer in formulating campaigns are the following:

1. *What motivates audiences?* Numerous biases influence how people perceive political objects. Sears and Whitney note the tendencies that research reveals as particularly important. First, and to a declining degree, a citizen's affiliation with a political party shapes the existence, the manner, and the extent of response to persuasive messages from a party's leaders. The stronger one's party identification, the less likely the success of the opposition's appeal. Hence, political advertising focuses upon identifying weak partisans and independents. Second, Americans show a positivity bias, "a tendency to expect and prefer positive rather than negative stimuli in one's perceptions and a tendency to omit positive responses more often than negative."[29] This carries the implication that governmental leaders and office-seekers, at least in their advertising, should "think positively."

Moreover, it suggests that conflictive appeals (which carry negative over-tones) be avoided. Thus, the positivity bias works in concert with the influence of partisan identification to guide the political advertiser toward middle-of-the-road, noncontroversial, perhaps even bland messages that emphasize attractive personalities over divisive issues. In addition, there is evidence that persons with lower levels of information, less exposure to, and less commitment toward objects are most likely to be persuaded by political advertising. The problem is to get them to pay attention to appeals. This contributes to a tendency for political advertisers to formulate appeals with attractive, esthetic considerations in mind instead of providing information of a factual, utilitarian character.

2. *What are the personality and social characteristics of audiences?* Some re-searchers argue that persons with particular clusters of personality traits (see Chapter 9) are more susceptible to persuasion than people with other traits. For example, some studies indicate that people with low self-esteem are more persuasible than those with high self-esteem. Or the person with high neurotic anxiety is less persuasible than one who is not highly defen-sive about his place in the world. And persuasability is more probable for people who measure low on traits such as dogmatism and authori-tarianism.[30] Finally, some people are "levelers" (their cognitive processes emphasize similarities in things rather than differences) while others are "sharpeners" (those who think in particulars). The latter may respond more to detailed, logical presentations and the former to the high gloss appeal. To the degree that relationships between personality and per-suasibility hold, knowledge of how such traits are distributed among the audience assist a political advertiser to formulate a campaign. The prob-lem, however, is detecting such distributions.

Political advertisers are interested in the social characteristics of au-dience members for two reasons. First, there is the possibility that com-munication patterns are influenced by demographics; that is, people vary in, for example, television viewing habits by age, sex, education, occupa-tion, income, etc. An advertising appeal to a particular demographic group must employ the symbols and be programmed through media suitable for that audience. Second, although they differ from propagandists in that they do not filter their messages through organized groups, political advertisers do rely upon opinion leaders (see Chapters 2 and 5). What kinds of individuals in the mass occasionally take advice from others is an important consideration in formulating an advertising campaign.

With What Effects?   This is not the place to engage in a comprehen-sive discussion of the various effects persuasive campaigns have upon audiences. Although later in this chaper we offer a preliminary scheme for classifying such effects, we postpone a full discussion of communication effects until Part Four. Here we want only to suggest the kinds of effects that distinguish political advertising from propaganda.

Gerhart Wiebe, in discussing how people in a mass audience respond to television programming, delineates three kinds of messages affecting individuals:[31] (1) Using *directive* messages, communicators attempt to change people's beliefs, values, expectations, and behavior; (2) *Maintaining* messages preserve people's views; they do not change or convert but do reinforce; (3) *Restorative* messages appeal to a person's sense of individuality, direct attention, and commit one not to a single idea but to a range of *possibilities,* to a series of options (contrived though they may be) from which one freely and spontaneously chooses. In so doing they appeal to a person's desires to escape the beliefs, values, and expectations imposed by social conformity, offer the opportunity to release rather than control inhibitions. The emphasis in propaganda campaigns is to achieve directive or maintaining effects (i.e., to win people to a cause or sustain their faith in it) by identifying members with the nation, corporation, or other group. By focusing upon individuals comprising an aggregated rather than organized mass, the achieved effects of political advertising, however, are less likely to be directive or maintaining than restorative. Students of propaganda and public opinion conventionally examine the extent that symbol manipulation changes and/or reinforces predispositions; the focus is upon directive and maintaining messages and effects. Students of political mass advertising and behavior are more inclined to study restorative messages and effects. The focus is upon how persuasive communication engages people in creating anew their images of politics. In large measure, political persuasion as a form of advertising shares this characteristic with persuasion viewed from the perspective of rhetoric.

Political Persuasion as Rhetoric

Erle Stanley Gardner created a fictional character, lawyer Perry Mason, who became famous for persuasive exploits depicted in a series of popular novels and a longrunning television program. Mason was noted for his courtroom tactics—cross-examination of witnesses, verbal sparring with the prosecuting attorney, debates over points of law with the judge, and appeals to the jury. But most of all he was able to convince judge, jury, witnesses, and spectators alike that he had unraveled the truth of a case; the perpetrator of the foul deed, also persuaded, would rise and confess his crime, usually before the jury began its deliberations. Fictional though he was (Mason never really lost a case), Gardner's lead character did illustrate the basic character of rhetoric, a form of persuasion that highlights two-way communication, dialectics, negotiations, and drama.

One-to-One Communication

We have said that propaganda and advertising involve one-to-many communication. There is a conscious attempt by one individual (or group) to modify views of audiences through some appeal; those being persuaded don't try to modify the views of the persuader in return. Rhetoric is two-way, one-to-one communication in the sense that two or more persons (one person speaking with several as well as one to another) each consciously seek to influence the views of one another through mutual, reciprocal action. A Democrat trying to win a Republican's vote, a congressman seeking support for favored legislation over the objections of a fellow congressman, presidential counsel John Dean endeavoring to convince Richard Nixon that a "cancer" was growing on the presidency—all are examples of political rhetoric. The targets of mutual persuasion need not, of course, be limited solely to persons engaging in the debate; rhetoricians may seek to influence third parties as well. Consider, for instance, trial lawyers arguing before a jury or the justices of the Supreme Court, presidential candidates debating one another before a television audience, or debates on the floor of the House of Representatives or Senate.

Bearing in mind this transactional quality, we say that rhetoric employs symbols to identify a speaker with a hearer(s) through address. Its purpose is to assist the persuadee in constructing an image of the future in which to act; through rhetoric, persuader and persuadee collaborate with one another in formulating their beliefs, values, and expectations. This feature Kenneth Burke calls consubstantiality; men "acting-together . . . have common sensations, concepts, images, ideas, attitudes that make them *consubstantial.*"[32] Such a sense of identification is inherent in rhetoric. Identification is the process of evoking in an audience a sense of collaboration with the speaker so that the audience feels that it is participating with the speaker in creating and leading a cause. To evoke that sense rhetoric capitalizes upon symbols that induce cooperation from people who, by the very fact that they are symbol-using and creating animals (recall the discussion in Chapter 3), respond to symbolic appeals. Think of the number of presidential candidates who have likened their campaigns to crusades, of President Richard Nixon's exhortations to advisers to get on the "team" and follow the "game plan," of the battle cry of the civil rights movement of the 1950s and 1960s, "We shall overcome." All are symbolic statements of the cooperative, collaborative quality of political movements stressed through rhetoric.

Political Rhetoric: A Process of Negotiation

Political rhetoric differs from propaganda and advertising, then, in key respects: rhetoric is two-way, one-to-one rather than one-to-many communication; moreover, it works through the inherent interpersonal relations that link people rather than upon persons as group members (propaganda) or anonymous individuals (advertising). Rhetoric also rests upon a different mechanism for obtaining social order. Whereas propaganda implies social control mechanisms and advertising relies upon convergent selectivity, political rhetoric is a process of making society possible through negotiation.

Recall that we said that rhetoric uses language to identify speakers

and hearers through address. Address is as important a concept in analyzing rhetoric as identification or symbolism. Address is negotiation. It is
a creative, give-and-take process by which people construct common
meanings for words and other symbols, definitions of situations, opposing
and shared positions in debate, and their respective identities. Without
these agreements, shared understandings that are the foundations of consubstantiality, society would scarcely exist. By addressing one another
people disclose their respective views and create a common universe of
discourse. It is in this respect that persuasion is an essential feature of
politics; through address people reveal their disagreements and lay the
groundwork for regulating their joint conduct within the context of those
differences. Put differently, through political rhetoric we create society
by an ongoing negotiation of meanings of situations and our identities
within them.

Types of Political Rhetoric

In classifying the varieties of political rhetoric one can scarcely improve
upon Aristotle's typology in his *Rhetoric*. He identified three principal
modes—the deliberative, forensic, and demonstrative. Deliberative rhetoric is designed to sway people on matters of public policy by delineating
the relative advantages and disadvantages of alternative ways of doing
things. Its focus is upon what will happen in the future, given certain
policies. Thus it creates and modifies expectations of things to come.
We see deliberative rhetoric in all phases of politics—when a secretary
of defense calls for greater military spending to avoid threats from foreign
powers, a secretary of treasury calls for a tax increase to "dampen the
fires of inflation," mayors of large cities seek federal assistance to avoid
financial bankruptcy in metropolitan areas, etc.

Forensic rhetoric is judicial. It focuses upon what has happened in
the past in order to demonstrate guilt or innocence, responsibility, or
punishment and reward. Its normal setting is the courtroom, but it occurs
elsewhere. Hearings in the summer of 1974 before the Judiciary Committee of the House of Representatives regarding the possible impeachment of President Richard Nixon gave rise to forensic discourse, just
as do all proceedings before governmental regulatory bodies—the Nuclear Regulatory Commission hearings to license construction of nuclear
facilities, National Labor Relations Board hearings on labor-management
disputes, etc.

Demonstrative rhetoric is epideictic, the discourse of praise and blame.
Its intent is to amplify the good and bad qualities of a person, institution,
or idea. Political campaigns are filled with demonstrative rhetoric as
opponents challenge one another's qualifications for public office. Editorial endorsements by newspapers, magazines, television, and radio stations also follow demonstrative lines, amplifying the positive qualities
of the endorsed candidate and the negative attributes of the opponent.

Aristotle's typology suggests that a single kind of rhetoric may not be appropriate for persuading people in all situations. For example, judges view a demonstrative mode that devolves into name-calling as out of place in a courtroom (as evidenced during the trial of the Chicago Seven, in which the defendants were accused of conspiring to incite a riot at the 1968 Democratic National Convention; the presiding judge continually admonished defendants and their counsel against disruptive tactics). Efforts to adapt rhetorical modes to differing situations contribute to the development of political styles as mechanisms of persuasion, a topic we shall consider in discussing techniques of political persuasion.

Focuses of Rhetorical Campaigns: Creating and Courting Audiences

Drawing upon Kenneth Burke's theses regarding the nature of persuasion, sociologist Hugh Duncan developed a fivefold classification of the audiences persuaders take into account in rhetorical appeals.[33] Two points should be made regarding this typology: First, it is Duncan's view, following Burke, that persuasion is a process people use to court one another, that is, win each other's love, admiration, respect, and collaboration in a common enterprise. The persuader does not simply approach an audience and court it, however; through courtship one actually creates an audience by using symbols to make others get together and act together in concert in a way they would not in the absence of the appeal. Hence, Duncan's typology refers to audiences both created and courted, courted and created. Second, these audiences may be likened to the factors propagandists emphasize in formulating their campaigns (source, message, media) and advertisers stress (audience predispositions, types of effects). Empirical evidence about the characteristics of these audiences, however, is not sufficient to permit a detailed description equivalent to that supplied in talking about the focuses of political propaganda and advertising.

The General Public. This is the audience speakers symbolize by "They." It is the audience at large that a speaker imagines addressing when talking to and about "public opinion," "the public," or "my constituents." Communicators do imagine the character of their audiences. Pool and Shulman, for example, found that the accuracy of the news stories is in part influenced by whether reporters imagine that they are writing to a supportive or antagonistic audience and whether good or bad news will alter levels of that support.[34]

The Community Guardians. Persuaders also view themselves as members of an enlightened group of people who know and speak for the conscience of the community. This is the "We" so frequently cited in political rhetoric, people who are secure in the intuition that their course is righteous, that they have been called to govern, and thereby must convince others of the truth that has been revealed. Here is the source of much "I'd rather be right than president" rhetoric, the politician's claims that he stands by personal convictions "even if it costs me the election," and of many pious platitudes that resound through the halls of Congress.

Friends and Confidants.   Each political leader surrounds himself with an audience consisting of colleagues, trusted advisers, and close friends. The politician addresses this palace guard with the familiar "You" that sets apart members of the inner circle from outsiders. Rarely do we catch glimpses of how persuasion takes place between a political leader and his friends and confidants. When we do it is obvious that the language and appeals differ markedly from those used by the communicator before the general public or community guardians (take as an example the "expletives deleted" from the White House transcripts of conversations between President Nixon and his aides over the Watergate affair).

The Self.   All of us, and political leaders are no different, engage in soliloquies with our inner selves. This, says Duncan, is the "I" talking to the "Me." Through the conversations with self, we sharpen or obscure our motives, justify or rationalize our actions, and rehearse our public performances. Autobiographies of political leaders are replete with after-the-fact portrayals (often self-serving but not always) of the addresses made to the self by politicians faced with making decisions in time of crisis.

The Ideal Audience.   This audience consists of people in positions of authority who enforce society's laws, rules, and regulations. A prime example in America is the Supreme Court, whose justices symbolize the transcendent principles embodied in a sacred Constitution. This is the audience addressed as the ultimate source of social order, the "It" that may be a constitution, a way of life, a divine being.

We could find many instances of these five audiences being addressed in American politics, but since we opened this discussion of political rhetoric with the fictional Perry Mason let us keep to the courtroom. Mason is the audience of the self, the I of the drama. The You of the play consists of his confidential secretary, Della Street, and trusted private investigator, Paul Drake. The community guardians are the jury before whom Mason defends a client, the We with responsibilities for discovering truth which Mason shares. And since Mason's cases are always sensational, they receive widespread press coverage. Hence, there is also the court of public opinion, the "They" or general public for Mason's rhetoric. Finally, there is the audience of It, the repository of authority, the judge. But where do we place the prosecuting attorney, Hamilton Burger, and other of Mason's adversaries? As members of Mason's audience, they may be so courted and persuaded that they enter as community guardians agreeing with the jury's judgment. They may join the You audience, colleagues of Mason in solving the crime. And, as representatives of justice they symbolize the It of the law along with the judge. Viewed from his efforts in the persuasive process, of course, the prosecutor is an I. In sum, the ongoing two-way process of rhetoric offers no definitive delineation of audiences; rather people move from audience to audience as the drama unfolds.

POLITICAL PERSUASION: A SYNTHESIS

It should be obvious by now that, as we stated earlier in this chapter, the three ways of thinking about political persuasion that we have outlined overlap to a considerable degree. Without rehashing the details of the discussion, it is possible to summarize the most significant characteristics of the process and suggest an integrated picture.

As with all communication, persuasion is symbolic. Whether it be the one-to-many pattern of propaganda and advertising or the one-to-one mode of rhetoric, as Gordon indicates, "Little doubt exists, however, that the symbols are the major instruments of interpersonal or group persuasion.[35] To say that persuasion is symbolic activity simply reaffirms a major theme stressed before in this book, namely, persuasion is a creative transaction in which the persuadee takes active part in constructing meaningful responses to the symbols in the persuader's appeal. This view counters an argument stressed in much of the literature pertaining to political propaganda and mass advertising that persuasion is solely manipulative, i.e., that audiences react to symbols in automatic, conditioned ways like a dog salivating at the sound of a bell. A persuader need only discover which bells people resonate to and compose appeals accordingly.

The viewpoint of this book differs considerably from one that says political persuasion is mere manipulation. From our perspective persuasion is a process in which both persuader and persuadee are responsive, not reactive to each other; their behavior is constructive, interpretative, and minded rather than passive and mindless. In Kenneth Burke's terminology, persuasion of any kind is action, not motion. Motion is characteristic of inanimate things. Take, for example, a machine. We need not reason with a machine or persuade it to act; we merely operate it by levers, ignitions, programs, etc. Persons, however, act—they choose the manner of response, one not always predictable: "If one cannot make a choice, one is not acting, one is but being moved, like a billiard ball tapped with a cue and behaving mechanically in conformity with the resistances it encounters."[36]

It is in Burke's sense that the pursuadee is actively engaged in his own persuasion. Thus the notion of identification introduced to characterize rhetoric is really essential to understanding any form of persuasion. It implies the essential ingredient of a dialectic, that of joint participation and sharing in persuasion by both persuader and persuadee. "If the speaker wants to identify with his listener," writes Jane Blankenship, "he must appeal to him through language that the listener understands and to which he will respond."[37]

That persuadees are more than robots mechanically moved by political propaganda, advertising, and rhetoric has become apparent to an increasing number of students of the persuasive process. One such student, William McGuire, has developed a theory of how people interpret persuasive appeals.[38] For persuasion to occur McGuire believes that there must be six successive steps in an "information-processing" sequence: there must be a persuasive appeal, people must pay attention to it, they must comprehend its content, yield to it, retain the newly adoped opinion, and act further on the basis of the view.

We need elaborate upon each of these steps only briefly. That there must first be a persuasive appeal seems obvious enough; in Chapters 5 and 6 we will consider the extent that political communication channels provide citizens with such appeals from the various political leaders we described in Chapter 2. Second, it is also fairly obvious that people must take the appeal into account if it is to be relevant to their future behavior; here, of course, is where the first signs of the persuadee's active engagement in the process occurs. The third step, comprehension, requires even more action from audience members; comprehension consists of grasping the arguments and conclusions of the message. Yielding, the fourth step, consists of being convinced by the appeal; too often, says McGuire, students of persuasion treat this crucial step in the process as if it were the whole rather than but one stage. Retention, the fifth step, refers to a person staying with a newly acquired view for an extended period rather than simply asserting agreement and then forgetting the whole thing. (Let the reader recall how many times he or she has convinced someone of something only to find moments later that the adversary has not shifted views at all in spite of earlier signs of yielding.) The final step, acting in accordance with the persuasive appeal, is the practical payoff of the enterprise, as when a citizen actually votes for the candidate who has made the campaign pitch.

McGuire's six steps in persuasion, then, can be viewed as identifiable stages in the process by which the persuader (propagandist, advertiser, or rhetorician) and persuadee (group member, isolated individual, or collaborator) mutually construct a shared meaning, or image, of a persuasive message. The image results in the latter acting along lines intended by the former. Following McGuire we can combine these six stages of image construction with the five elements of political communication employed thus far: source (who?), message (says what?), channel, receiver (with whom?), and destination (with what effects?). The result is the scheme graphically portrayed in Table 4–1 for organizing and understanding political persuasion.

Table 4-1 *Dimensions of the Persuasion Process*

Phases of Image Construction	Phases of Communication				
	Source	Message	Channel	Receiver	Effects
Presentation					
Attention					
Comprehension					
Yielding					
Retention					
Compliant Response					

Source: Adapted from Figure 1, "Matrix of persuasive communication," in William J. McGuire, "Persuasion, Resistance, and Attitude Change," Ithiel de Sola Pool et al., eds., *Handbook of Communication* (Chicago: Rand McNally College Publishing Company, © 1973), p. 223.

The scheme is preliminary but suggestive. For one thing, it illustrates how complex persuasion is. Rarely does a political leader simply propose and a citizen dispose (i.e., power talk). Instead, the source's intentions filter through all stages of persuasion; each stage can influence whether one ultimately persuades oneself to behave as requested. At any stage the appeal may run afoul of complications. Take as an example appeals to Americans to conserve energy by using less electricity. Certainly messages are presented, many people pay attention and comprehend the long-run consequences of profligate electricity use, and they even yield to the idea of reducing consumption. Yet utility companies—the very sources of conservation appeals—offer competing messages that work against retention and compliance, namely, messages saying comsumers are proportionately charged less when using *increasing* amounts of electricity! In this instance, source, messages, yielding, and compliance combine to defeat the stated purposes of the conservation appeal.

There are, of course, other possible complications, so many that we can only suggest a few. Consider the presentation stage. Presidents of the United States—John Kennedy, Lyndon Johnson, and Richard Nixon are only the most obvious cases—have often complained of an unfavorable press. As political communicaters they have believed that their presentations of appeals have been ignored, downplayed, or even distorted by newspapers or television news commentaries. To remedy the situation they increasingly attempted to monopolize the presentation stage through televised presidential news conferences, thus hoping to "go over the heads" of reporters, editors, and news directors in order to reach citizens directly.

Or consider the relationship between source and channel, on the one hand, and retention, on the other. Edwin Diamond has commented upon the avid interest Americans have in the opinions (on a wide variety of matters, including political) of such celebrities as actors Burt Reynolds and Robert Redford, actress Jane Fonda, singer Cher, writer Erica Jong, or conductor Leonard Bernstein. Through media coverage and promotion these symbolic leaders (see Chapter 2) not only entertain, they offer homolies and hints for how to reform the political system, deal with the Middle East, Cuba, and Southeast Asia, and restore the two-party system. The interesting feature in all of this, points out Diamond, is that in spite of their buildups and widespread presentations (actress Liv Ullmann, for instance, was on the cover of both *Time* and *Newsweek* in a short period), the staying power of their utterances (i.e., retention) is relatively short. How many, for example, can now recall the messages of Dave Garroway, Hugh Downs, or Sally Quinn to which they might once have yielded? One suspects Mickey Mouse, Howdy Doody, and Captain Kangaroo received more retention.[39]

One final comment should be made regarding the "effects" aspect of the organizing scheme in Table 4-1. In evaluating the persuasiveness of appeals it is appropriate to distinguish between intended effects as viewed from the standpoint of the persuader and actual effects indicated by the persuadee's behavior. Intended effects may be achieved at one stage of the persuasion process, but not at another. For instance, take the case of Republican campaign appeals in southern states. Particularly in the 1950s there was a hope of reestablishing the Grand Old Party in the South. Seemingly the presidential candidacy of Dwight Eisenhower in 1952 and 1956 promoted this cause. Democratic voters in southern states attended the Eisenhower appeal, comprehended it, yielded and retained it, and crossed party lines to support Eisenhower in large numbers. Yet, the intended effects, if we assume they were meant to have immediate impacts below the level of presidential contests, were limited; that is, after supporting Eisenhower for president, Democrats returned to the fold in voting for statewide and local officials. The actual long-term, as contrasted with short-term effects, may have been something else again; viz., in the 1960s and 1970s the intended resurrection of the GOP became more of a reality. Yet, even then, the proportion of voters in the South identifying with the Republican party showed no consistent increase in the two decades between 1955 and 1975.

We will consider the range of effects of persuasive communications in greater detail in Part Four. Here it suffices to note that if we view persuasion as information processing by both persuaders and persuadees rather than as the simple manipulation of people by political leaders, a comprehensive picture of how it works must take into account all dimensions of image construction and communication as proposed in Table 4–1. In closing this discussion of political persuasion, let us focus upon a final element of the "says what?" aspect, the linguistic devices and styles contained in persuasive communications.

TECHNIQUES OF POLITICAL PERSUASION: LINGUISTIC DEVICES AND STYLES

With his formulation "Who says what in which channel to whom with what effect" Harold Lasswell provided a convenient organizing framework borrowed for this book. And, more specifically, William McGuire's presentation, attention, comprehension, yielding, retention, and overt behavior provide a way of teasing out the principal phases in the persuasion process. Without running the danger of having too many such formulas, we can add yet another, this time one that opens the door to the major aspects that must be considered in discussing the techniques of political persuasion. Three decades ago in discussing the relationship between communication and public opinion, Bernard Berelson offered the simple proposition that "some kinds of communication on some kinds of issues, brought to the attention of some kinds of people under some kinds of conditions, have some kinds of effects."[40] Hardly startling stuff, this, but at least a place to start. As noted, we have already touched upon kinds of effects and will probe that matter more deeply in later chapters; moreover, we shall dwell upon the issues, people, and conditions in public opinion in Part Three. What is particularly relevant to discussing political persuasion is the first element in Berelson's pentad, i.e., kinds of communication.

Persuasive campaigns in contemporary politics rely upon three techniques that shape the kinds of communications relevant to public opinion. First, since persuasion is a two-way, reciprocal process, the persuader must accommodate his appeal to the viewpoint of listeners since "the audience selects the communications which it finds most congenial."[41] To do that, the persuader gathers intelligence about what is congenial to audience members through polling techniques, an element of persuasion discussed in detail in Chapter 12 and the Appendix. Second, since persuasion is a one-to-many as well as one-to-one process, a persuader employs appropriate technology to disseminate a message to group members (in the case of propaganda), individuals (in the case of mass advertising), or potential collaborators (in the case of rhetoric). This involves choices between oral, print, and electronic technologies, between personal appearances, newspapers or magazines, and radio or television as media. (We discuss these techniques of persuasive communication associated with differing technologies and media in Chapter 5.) Finally, persuaders select appropriate linguistic devices and styles for couching their propaganda, advertising, and rhetoric.

Devices of Presentation

Persuaders since Eve have faced the task of formulating messages in ways to induce cooperation from other people. They have confronted problems of credibility, strategic and tactical matters, and how to use words, language, and logic effectively.

To Tell the Truth?

Critics of modern propaganda, mass advertising, and partisan rhetoric decry the deceit, falsehood, and just plain lying of persuasive campaigns. There are "credibility gaps" in what governments tell their people, cases of "faking it" to reconcile contradictions in logic and facts,[42] and of instances of "packaging candidates" to put each in the best light and not reveal "if the candidate has warts."[43] The Federal Trade Commission, a U.S. government agency charged with regulating the veracity of advertising claims made on behalf of products, regularly finds examples of misleading appeals, as when a safety razor was demonstrated on television as though able to shave sandpaper, when in fact it was being run over a piece of glass covered with lathered sand.

Yet it is erroneous to think that persuaders have no concern with truth or that they deliberately lie just for the sake of it. The relationship of persuasion to truth and falsehood is subtle indeed. The best way to put it into focus is to recall a principle enuciated by Joseph Goebbels, the Nazi Minister of Propaganda in Hitler's Germany often credited as the father of modern persuasive techniques. Goebbels, according to Leonard Doob, believed that credibility alone should determine whether propaganda should be true or false. Truth, Goebbels thought, should be told frequently to avoid having one's appeal exposed as falsehood; but if the credibility of a lie could not be challenged, or if the truth might not itself be believed, Goebbels would opt for falsehood as readily as for truth.[44] Adolf Hitler expressed the rule of expediency clearly in *Mein Kampf*:

> The truth must always be adjusted to fit the need. What should
> we say of a poster which purported to advertise some new brand
> of soap by insisting on the excellent qualities of competitive brands?
> We should naturally shake our heads. And it ought to be just the
> same in a similar kind of political advertisement. The aim of propa-
> ganda is not to try to pass judgment on conflicting rights, giving
> each its due, but exclusively to emphasize the right which we are
> asserting. Propaganda must not investigate the truth objectively,
> and, insofar as it is favorable to the other side, present it according
> to the theoretical rules of justice; it must present only that aspect
> of the truth which is favorable to its own side.[45]

The issue, then, is what will be believed, not accuracy or inaccuracy of detail. No better illustration of this principle exists than what Goebbels did with the case of Horst Wessel. Wessel was a tall, blond, broad shouldered, handsome storm trooper groomed by Goebbels as a symbol for the Hitler youth movement. But Horst met Erna Jaenicke, a prostitute, and lost interest in Nazi party activities when he found he could earn lavish profits as her pimp. Alas, Horst was shot through the mouth by Erna's former pimp, Ali Hoehler. Goebbels jumped at the opportunity to exploit the incident. He claimed (without mentioning Wessel's amours with Erna or his current occupation) that Wessel had been shot by a Communist. (Hoehler, in fact, was also a Nazi.) Goebbels embarked upon three weeks of highly publicized visits to Wessel's hospital bedside. When Wessel died, Goebbels concocted an elaborate plan to convert him into a martyr, even composing the "Horst Wessel March," which became a Nazi anthem.

Lest we leave the impression that Nazi propagandists alone had an expedient regard for truth and falsehood, let us consider the Allied persuasive campaigns of World War II. One study indicates that although there was a cardinal rule not to use detectable lies, the measuring stick was credibility; even true statements would be avoided if propagandists felt audiences might find them incredible.[46] R.H.S. Crossman, senior British officer in charge of Allied psychological warfare in Europe, emphasized that the basis for all successful propaganda was truth, but truth used to build the reputation of the propagandist as trustworthy: "The art of the propagandist is never to be thought a propagandist"; hence, the "first job is to build the credibility and authenticity of your propaganda, and persuade the enemy to trust you although you are his enemy."[47]

Strategic and Tactical Considerations

Goebbels, in thinking about the strategy of his persuasive campaigns, drew a distinction between influencing *haltung,* the behavior, bearing, and conduct of people, and *stimmung,* their morale, yielding, and retention of the persuasive appeal. Morale may have its ups and downs, but proper behavior must be maintained at all costs. To do so called for a persuasive campaign to achieve the long-term commitments of the population in contrast to those aimed principally at propping up the short-term *stimmung* of the people.

We see this distinction in contemporary persuasive campaigns as one between the Idea[48] that underlies appeals and the gimmicks adapted to specific situations. The Idea consists of an overriding theme in a campaign that unifies and coordinates all of the specific persuasive appeals in accordance with the intention of influencing ongoing behavior in a specific way. Take the example of Gerald Ford's effort to contrast himself with his predecessor. The Idea of the Ford administration was to build the popular impression of an open White House, one in which Ford would take the presidency to the people. The gimmicks to advance this Idea were a series of regional White House conferences held in various cities throughout the nation at which Ford would speak briefly and answer questions from an audience whose members had been given special invitations. The success of any given conference in building confidence in the Ford administration (the *stimmung*) varied from region to region, but the continuous news coverage of a series of such conferences provided the opportunity for public officials to conduct themselves (*haltung*) in a seemingly open manner.

Using (Misusing?) Words, Actions, and Logic

We have said that the persuader's stock in trade is symbols. Specifically, persuaders employ words, actions, and logic to advance their interests in hopes that audiences will respond accordingly. Prior to World War II a group of journalists and academicians organized as The Institute for Propaganda Analysis. That institute derived seven devices to summarize the principal propaganda techniques that take advantage of a combination of words, actions, and logic for persuasive purposes.[49] Those devices have appeared many times in basic texts for introductory courses in rhetoric, government, and public opinion. Old as they are and as widely publicized as they once were, they still warrant repeating. Briefly, the seven devices are:

1. *Name Calling:* Giving an idea, person, object, or cause a bad label to get people to reject it without examining the evidence (charging an election opponent with being a "coddler of criminals" is one example).
2. *Glittering Generality:* Using a "virtue word" to depict something so as to win support, again without investigating the appropriateness of the association. Thus, in 1972 both George McGovern and Richard Nixon utilized "God words" in their campaigns; McGovern, the former minister, urged the prodigal son to return with "Come home, America," and Nixon called for a "new majority," a "coalition of conscience and decency."[50]
3. *Transfer:* Identify a cause with a symbol of authority; thus, "Re-elect the President."
4. *Testimonial:* Obtain the utterances of respected or hated persons to promote or disparage a cause, a device we readily recognize in instances of political endorsements by newspapers, celebrities, etc.
5. *Plain Folks:* An appeal that says the speaker identifies with his audience in a common, collaborative effort, i.e., "I am one of you, just plain folk." While touring Europe in 1975 Governor George Wallace questioned America's policy of detente with the

Soviet Union by asking, "Why do they call it by a highfalutin French word like *detente* instead of saying we're trying to get together with the Communists?"

6. *Card Stacking:* Careful selection of accuracies and inaccuracies, logical and illogical statements, etc. to build a case (Goebbels's use of Horst Wessel is a prime example).

7. *Bandwagon:* The effort to convince audiences of the popularity and righteousness of the cause so that everyone will "get on board." Hence, everyone should join the cause of the candidate who is seeking the party's nomination in order to have a voice in affairs after his inevitable victory.

Such devices do not exhaust the techniques employed by persuaders to make self-serving use of words, actions, and logic. Consider, for instance, the persuasive uses of metaphor, sometimes a variation on name calling.[51] A president attacking Congress for failing to accept his programs need only refer to the "mulish" behavior of congressmen to conjure up the image of unreasoning stubbornness. Or, to say that the president "can't walk and chew gum at the same time" leaves an impression of a poorly coordinated leader indeed. Among actions to persuade is the time-honored technique of political candidates who ignore opponents. When an incumbent or more widely known candidate treats an opponent as a nonperson, or even nonexistent, he leaves the impression that his adversary is not worthy of challenging for the office. Richard Nixon in 1972 remembered well a lesson learned in 1960. In his first try for the presidency, then Vice-President Nixon agreed to debate his lesser known opponent, John Kennedy, on television, thus giving legitimacy to the Kennedy claim that he was sufficiently experienced to be a worthy challenger. In 1972 President Nixon simply ignored the Democratic nominee, George McGovern, as scarcely worth mentioning. Four years later Gerald Ford in debating his challenger Jimmy Carter implicitly recognized the need to try to overtake his challenger's early lead in preelection polls. Finally, there are all manner of liberties persuaders take with logic—making sweeping generalizations from a single case, ad hominem arguments, employing allegedly self-evident truths, using false analogies, misusing statistical evidence, and employing numerous other tricks known prior to Aristotle.

Styles of Presentation

Persuasive style is the arrangement of the parts of a political appeal—words, actions, logic, and associated symbols—communicators employ toward their subject matter and audience.[52] The style of political talk is a dimension of the syntactics of language discussed in Chapter 3 for style pertains to the rules, key, and tone involved in transmitting messages. The most general stylistic distinctions are between those that are terse or prolix, effect-modeling or contrasting, and hot or cool. A style that encompasses a large number of words, phrases, actions, intonations, circumlocutions, etc., is prolix; terseness minimizes the number and complexity of such symbols. Effect-modeling consists of setting an example for an audience to follow. For instance, President Lyndon Johnson went from room to room in the White House switching off the electric lights, thus allegedly exemplifying the desire of his administration to reduce unnecessary spending. Effect-contrasting occurs when a political leader distinguishes himself from followers by doing something they cannot, as when presidents bless citizens by striding through crowds shaking hands.[53] Finally, a hot style is one of high definitions. The speaker emphatically and precisely presents an appeal, sometimes to the point of becoming strident, even shrill. A cool style means a low profile, lowered voices, and calm, dispassionate presentations with sufficient ambiguity to permit an audience to interpret them in different, perhaps even conflicting ways.[54]

Lasswell and Leites speculate that persuasive styles vary according to the communicator's expectations about which combination of symbols will most economically achieve the intended effect. Those expectations in turn depend upon the communicator's assessment of his audience in different settings. For example, during periods of intense political crises— wars, economic depressions, domestic rebellions and protests—styles tend to be terse, repetitious, effect-contrasting, and hot. In more quiet times, say when routine policy matters are at issue, there is prolixity, diversity of statements, effect-modeling, and coolness. Compare, for example, the public utterances of a president in crises situations (viz., John Kennedy during the Cuban missile crisis in 1962 or Richard Nixon after the incursion into Cambodia and killing of students at Kent State in 1970) with their presentations of State of the Union messages before Congress. General persuasive styles also differ from one political regime to another; in authoritarian regimes effect-contrasting in public ceremonies, speeches, official regalia, and perquisites sets the ruling elites apart from the masses; in democratic regimes effect-modeling leaders follow common speech and manners.[55]

In addition to these general persuasive styles there are rhetorical styles for couching specific appeals.[56] The most common include the following:

1. *Exhortive:* Urging people that there is a problem, that something must be done, and that they must take the action (for example, arguing that busing black students to white schools and vice versa is wrong and that opponents should demonstrate their dissatisfaction on school grounds). Campaign speeches typify exhortive styles, typically employing metaphors to attract attention and support; thus party workers are exhorted to join the candidate's "team," follow the "game plan," and share in the victory.

2. *Legal:* The formal language of lawyers, judges, courts, statutes, constitutions, treaties, etc. symbolizing legitimate, sacred, immutable, rules

and decisions. Legal language is always open to differing interpretations and persuaders appeal to these differences in justifiying their actions and advancing their interests.

3. *Bureaucratic:* The technical jargon, or gobbledygook, associated with the rules, regulations, and discretionary actions of administrators vis-à-vis the general public and one another. As with the legal style, there tends to be prolixity providing opportunities for conflicting interpretations of highly ambiguous words, phrases, and procedures.

4. *Bargaining:* The give-and-take of political compromises, bartering, logrolling, and exchanges. Although frequently associated by citizens with partisan and/or congressional politics, bargaining styles occur as well among executive and judicial officials endeavoring to consummate workable and acceptable rather than perfect solutions to problems.

5. *Closed/Open:* The former refers to the guarded, aloof, effect-contrasting utterances of political communicators reluctant to surrender control over the release of information or hesitant to make full disclosure of their plans (an example is the politician fully intending to campaign for an office who continues to proclaim to be undecided and weighing all options); open styles are more spontaneous, less programmed, sometimes revealing and even disarming (as Jimmy Carter affected in the 1976 presidential campaign).

Such rhetorical styles involve the way persuaders use various types of exhortive, legal, bureaucratic, bargaining, and calculated words. As we noted in Chapter 3, however, verbal (in contrast to nonverbal) languages consist not only of words but of sounds; in fact, we noted that vocal dimensions of speech contribute five times more to the effects of a message than does the content of the words used. Sound is thus a significant element of style. Loudness, pitch, vocal pauses, punctuations, and voice quality all influence the meanings we read into a speaker's message. Consider the apocryphal story of the politician pressed for a decision as to whether to seek high office. The story goes that the response was, "I do not choose to run." But the way the politician said it brought different hopes and fears to his audience; "I do," he said with a long pause that brought cheers from supporters, "not" (again a pause interrupted by cheers from detractors) "choose (boos from one and all for indecisiveness) to run" (greeted by apathy since by this time the crowd had exhausted its interest and patience anyway). Finally, consider the relation of style to onomatopoeia, i.e., when words sound like things they refer to (zip, splash, clank, etc.). Even this element of style is politically relevant, since to apply a noxious sound to an otherwise neutral word conveys meaning. Let the reader ask, for example, how creepy was CREEP in 1972, the Committee to Re-Elect the President? After the Watergate affair many citizens came away with the impression that is was creepy indeed.

Caveat Emptor

Whether persuasive devices and styles clarify or distort, reveal or conceal, inform or confuse, authenticate or fake depends in any specific instance upon the intentions and intensity of the persuader, expectations of what audiences believe, the idea of the overall appeal, and audience response. Do all persuaders lie? No, but many do. Do all persuaders use words, actions, logic, and styles as mere hucksters' tricks to camouflage their intentions and the real facts? Again, no, but there are those who carefully highlight beauty marks and use cosmetics on warts. Is every Idea a sham and every gimmick bogus? Not necessarily, but let the buyer beware. Ultimately the success of persuasion depends upon the willingness of people to believe what they are asked without question, evaluate things in the lights provided by the communicator, and to accept another's expectations of the future. All of the persuasive techniques outlined above can be neutralized by persistently asking the questions (and demanding answers) we used in opening Chapter 1: "How do you *know* that?" "Why do you *feel* that way?" "Why do you *act* so?" Exasperating as they are to ask and answer, they yet provide a necessary and healthy skepticism to appraising political communicators, their talk and appeals. As we shall see in Part Two, these questions are also appropriate in appraising the channels of political communication.

BIBLIOGRAPHY

Two works provide general reviews of persuasion. The first is George Gordon's lengthy volume, *Persuasion: The Theory and Practice of Manipulative Communication* (New York: Hastings House, Publishers, 1971). Taking the position that "intention is probably a quality of all communication" (p. 37), Gordon ranges widely over the role of persuasion in society, touching not only upon politics but discussing persuasion and fear, sex, love, laughter, and a variety of other topics. A useful introductory text to the subject is Erwin P. Bettinghaus, *Persuasive Communication* (New York: Holt, Rinehart, and Winston, Inc., 2nd ed., 1973). Bettinghaus does a particularly good job of reviewing the impact of communicators, message coding and structures, channels, and social groups on the effectiveness of persuasive appeals. As a means of placing the study of persuasion into a theoretical context for the broader political process, readers should consult Harold D. Lasswell and Abraham Kaplan, *Power and Society* (New Haven: Yale University Press, 1950), especially Part Two.
Several works endeavor to identify and describe the role of political communicators as persuaders in contemporary America. The activities of governmental officials are described from a highly critical point of view by Herbert I. Schiller in *The Mind Managers* (Boston: Beacon Press, 1973). Schiller is particularly disturbed by government's role in manipulating people through what he calls "packaged consciousness." Three works discuss professional communicators as political persuaders: Stanley Kelley, Jr., *Professional Public Relations and Political Power* (Baltimore: The Johns Hopkins Press, 1966); Dan Nimmo, *The Political*

Persuaders (Englewood Cliffs, N.J.: Prentice-Hall, Inc., 1970; and David Lee Rosenbloom, *The Election Men* (New York: Quadrangle Books, 1973). A highly readable account of the persuasive efforts of journalists is William L. Rivers, *The Opinionmakers* (Boston: Beacon Press, 1965).

A large number of works deal respectively with propaganda, advertising, and rhetoric as modes of persuasive communication. No reader's understanding of propaganda can be complete without consulting Jacques Ellul's *Propaganda* (New York: Alfred A. Knopf, 1965). Ellul views propaganda as a mechanism of social control characteristic of a highly technological society; in his view propaganda is a mode of total communication that encapsulates people in myths and illusions. Less strident on the point, but still infused with social control assumptions, is a classic discussion by Leonard W. Doob, *Public Opinion and Propaganda,* first published in 1948 but now available in a reprinting (Hamden, Conn.: Archon Books, 1966). A brief introduction to propaganda and its relation to advertising, psychological warfare, and other modes of persuasion is Terence H. Qualter, *Propaganda and Psychological Warfare* (New York: Random House, 1962). A technical and theoretical discussion of the nature of mass advertising and convergent selection that is unsurpassed is William Stephenson, *The Play Theory of Mass Communication* (Chicago: University of Chicago Press, 1967). A popularized account of modern advertising is Martin Mayer's *Madison Avenue U.S.A.* (New York: Pocket Books, 1958). One of the best ways to get a balanced perspective pertaining to the diversity of activities that comprise public relations is to consult the variety of articles in the volume edited by Otto Lerbinger and Albert J. Sullivan, *Information, Influence, and Communication* (New York: Basic Books, 1965). A dated but still informative account of the place of public relations in government information programs is J.A.R. Pimlott, *Public Relations and American Democracy* (Princeton: Princeton University Press, 1951). Those readers interested in exploring the nature of rhetoric as the art of persuasion should consult two classics: Aristotle's *The Rhetoric,* which is available in many translations, and Kenneth Burke, *A Rhetoric of Motives* (Berkeley: University of California Press, 1969). Readers who would prefer not to tackle Burke's theory firsthand should consult Hugh Dalziel Duncan, *Communication and Social Order* (New York: Oxford University Press, 1962); Chapters 8–18 provide a summary of Burke's theory. A useful text that places rhetoric within the broader context of human communication is James C. McCroskey, *An Introduction to Rhetorical Communication* (Englewood Cliffs, N.J.: Prentice-Hall, 2nd ed., 1972). A brief work that focuses specifically upon a key Burkian notion, identification, is D. Byker and L. J. Anderson, *Communication as Identification* (New York: Harper and Row, 1975).

There have been numerous experimental, survey, and other studies devoted to discerning the effects of persuasion upon opinions and behavior. Many of these findings are summarized in the Bettinghaus volume alluded to above. Two other succinct, readable compilations of such findings include Marvin Karlins and Herbert I. Abelson, *Persuasion* (New York: Springer Publishing Co., Inc., 2nd ed., 1970) and Philip Zimbardo and Ebbe E. Ebbesen, *Influencing Attitudes and Changing Behavior* (Reading, Mass.: Addison-Wesley Publishing Co., 1969).

Most of the works that elaborate the techniques of persuasion center upon discussions of propagandistic devices, especially linguistic and logical tricks. A highly simplified account is William Hummel and Keith Huntress, *The Analysis of Propaganda* (New York: Harcourt Brace, 1939). Also helpful in this respect is Stuart Chase, *Guides to Straight Thinking* (New York: Harper and Brothers, 1956); Chase presents an entertaining introduction to the thirteen most common logical fallacies employed in persuasive appeals. Two works point with alarm to the growing use of persuasive techniques in contemporary American: Vance Packard, *The Hidden Persuaders* (New York: David McKay, 1957) and Arthur Herzog, *The B.S. Factor* (Baltimore: Penguin Books, 1973). Few political leaders have so intensively practiced the application of persuasive techniques as Joseph Goebbels and Adolf Hitler. A scholarly and readable view of the efforts of the Goebbels-Hitler duo is J. P. Stern, *Hitler: The Fuhrer and the People* (Berkeley: University of California Press, 1975). A summary of the techniques applied in a wide variety of persuasive campaigns—propaganda, psychological warfare, brainwashing, advertising, religious conversions, etc.—can be found in J.A.C. Brown, *Techniques of Persuasion* (Baltimore: Penguin Books, 1963).

NOTES

1. *Persuasion: The Theory and Practice of Manipulative Communication* (New York: Hastings House, Publishers, 1971), Ch. 4. On the distinctions between such variants of persuasion as advertising, propaganda, etc. see Reed H. Blake and Edwin O. Haroldsen, *A Taxonomy of Concepts in Communication* (New York: Hastings House, Publishers, 1975), pp. 57–66, Paul Kecskemeti, "Propaganda," in Ithiel de Sola Pool et al., eds., *Handbook of Communication* (Chicago: Rand McNally Co., 1973), p. 845.

2. William J. McGuire, "Persuasion, Resistance, and Attitude Change," in Pool et al., eds., *Handbook of Communication*, p. 216.

3. Carl I. Hovland et al., *Communication and Persuasion* (New Haven: Yale University Press, 1953), pp. 10–12.

4. Erwin P. Bettinghaus, *Persuasive Communication* (New York: Holt, Rinehart and Winston, Inc., 2nd ed., 1973), p. 10.

5. For a discussion of the element of intent in persuasion see Talcott Parsons, "On the Concept of Influence," *Public Opinion Quarterly*, 27 (Spring 1963): 63–82. The distinction between purposive and nonpurposive communication is developed in Bruce H. Westley and Malcolm S. MacLean, Jr., "A Conceptual Model for Communications Research," *Journalism Quarterly*, 34 (Winter 1957): 31–38. As treated here, of course, political persuasion is inherently purposive.

6. *Public Opinion and Propaganda* (Hamden, Conn.: Archon Books, 1966), pp. 245–46.

7. Some students of communication distinguish between information campaigns and information effects on the one hand, and persuasive campaigns and effects on the other. Thus a person may become more informed, but not change opinions. As viewed here, however, a change in information is a cognitive change (compared to an affective change) and thereby an aspect of opinion change. An example of those drawing the information-persuasion distinction is Lee B. Becker, Maxwell E. McCombs, and Jack M. McLeod, "The Development of Political Cognitions," in Steven H. Chaffee, ed., *Political Communication* (Beverly Hills, Cal.: Sage Publications, 1976), pp. 21–63.

8. Harold D. Lasswell and Abraham Kaplan draw the distinction between coercion and choice in *Power and Society* (New Haven: Yale University Press, 1950), p. 97.

9. *The Mind Managers* (Boston: Beacon Press, 1973), pp. 47–48.

10. See Herbert E. Alexander, *Financing Politics* (Washington, D.C.: Congressional Quarterly Press, 1976).

11. Jacques Ellul, *Propaganda* (New York: Alfred A. Knopf, 1965), p. 61 (emphasis in original).

12. "Propaganda," p. 862.

13. Ellul, *Propaganda,* p. 97. See also David B. Truman, *The Governmental Process* (New York: Alfred A. Knopf, 1951), Ch. 8.

14. *Propaganda,* p. 21.

15. Ibid., p. 24.

16. *Public Opinion and Propaganda,* p. 251.

17. Ellul, *Propaganda,* Ch. 1.

18. Among the works to consult for such research findings, see Marvin Karlins and Herbert I. Abelson, *Persuasion* (New York: Springer Publishing Co., 1970); David O. Sears and Richard E. Whitney, "Political Persuasion," in Pool et al., eds., *Handbook of Communication,* pp. 216–252; and Harvey London, *Psychology of the Persuader* (Morristown, N. J.: General Learning Press, 1973).

19. McGuire, "Persuasion, Resistance, and Attitude Change," p. 232.

20. Dan Nimmo and Robert L. Savage, *Candidates and Their Images* (Pacific Palisades, Cal.: Goodyear Publishing Co., 1976).

21. McGuire, "Persuasion, Resistance, and Attitude Change," p. 232.

22. Burns W. Roper, *What People Think of Television and Other Mass Media 1959–1972* (New York: The Roper Organization, 1973).

23. *The Harris Survey,* March 14, 1977.

24. Ellul, *Propaganda,* p. 10.

25. "The Mass, the Public, and Public Opinion," in Bernard Berelson and Morris Janowitz, eds., *Reader in Public Opinion and Communication* (New York: The Free Press, 2nd ed., 1966), p. 46. See also Jurgen Ruesch, "The Social Control of Symbolic Systems," *Journal of Communication,* 17 (September 1967): 276–301.

26. William Stephenson, *The Play Theory of Mass Communication* (Chicago: University of Chicago Press, 1967), Ch. 3.

27. Albert J. Sullivan, "The Tenuous Image of Public Relations," in Otto Lerbinger and Albert J. Sullivan, eds., *Information, Influence, and Communication* (New York: Basic Books, 1965), pp. 9–16.

28. Raymond A. Bauer, "Communication as Transaction," *Public Opinion Quarterly,* 27 (Spring 1963): 83–86.

29. "Political Persuasion," p. 272.

30. Bettinghaus, *Persuasive Communication,* Ch. 3.

31. "Two Psychological Factors in Media Audience Behavior," *Public Opinion Quarterly,* 33 (Winter 1969–1970): 523–536.

32. Kenneth Burke, *A Rhetoric of Motives* (Berkeley, Cal.: University of California Press, 1969), p. 21 (emphasis in original).

33. Hugh Dalziel Duncan, *Communication and Social Order* (New York: Oxford University Press, 1962), Ch. 21.

34. Ithiel de Sola Pool and Irwin Shulman, "Newsmen's Fantasies, Audiences, and Newswriting," *Public Opinion Quarterly,* 23 (Summer 1959): 145–158.

35. George Gordon, *Persuasion,* p. 21.

36. Kenneth Burke, *The Rhetoric of Religion* (Berkeley: University of California Press, 1970), p. 188.

37. "The Resources of Language," in Jean M. Civikly, ed., *Messages* (New York: Random House, 1974), p. 57.

38. See William J. McGuire, "Personality and Attitude Change: An Information-Processing Theory," in Anthony G. Greenwald et al., eds., *Psychological Foundations of Attitudes* (New York: Academic Press, 1968), pp. 171–196; and "Persuasion, Resistance, and Attitude Change," pp. 220–226.

39. "Starstruck: Would You Welcome, Please, Henry and Jackie and Liv and Erica," *Columbia Journalism Review,* 14 (Sept.–Oct. 1975): 42–46.

40. "Communications and Public Opinion," in Wilbur Schramm, ed., *Communications in Modern Society* (Urbana: University of Illinois Press, 1948), p. 172.

41. Ibid., p. 170.

42. Arthur Herzog, *The B.S. Factor* (Baltimore: Penguin Books, 1973).

43. Joseph Napolitan, *The Election Game and How to Win It* (Garden City: Doubleday and Company, Inc., 1972), p. 76.

44. Leonard W. Doob, "Goebbels' Principles of Propaganda," *Public Opinion Quarterly*, 14 (Fall 1950): 419–442.

45. Quoted in Alan Wykes, *Goebbels* (New York: Ballentine Books, Inc., 1973), pp. 39–40. See also J. P. Stern, *Hitler: The Fuhrer and the People* (Berkeley: University of California Press, 1975).

46. Daniel Lerner, *Sykewar* (New York: Steward Publishing, 1949).

47. Quoted in David Dinsmore Comey, "A Critic Looks at Industry Credibility," paper delivered at the topical conference, "Nuclear Power and the Public," Los Angeles, California, February 3–6, 1975.

48. Doob, *Public Opinion and Propaganda*, pp. 265–66.

49. Alfred McClung Lee and Elizabeth B. Lee, eds., *The Fine Art of Propaganda* (New York: Harcourt, Brace, 1939).

50. Bernard F. Donahue, "The Political Use of Religious Symbols: A Case Study of the 1972 Presidential Campaign," *Review of Politics*, 37 (January 1975): 48–65.

51. Elliot Zashin and Phillip C. Chapman, "The Uses of Metaphor and Analogy: Toward a Renewal of Political Language," *Journal of Politics*, 36 (May 1974): 290–326.

52. Compare Harold D. Lasswell and Nathan Leites, *Language of Politics* (Cambridge: The M.I.T. Press, 1949), Ch. 2, and George Gordon, *The Languages of Communication* (New York: Hastings House, Publishers, 1969), Ch. 13.

53. Lasswell and Leites, *Language of Politics*, p. 21.

54. Marshall McLuhan, *Understanding Media* (New York: Signet Books, 1964), Ch. 2.

55. Lasswell and Leites, *Language of Politics*, Ch. 2. See also Leon Dion, "The Concept of Political Leadership: An Analysis," *Canadian Journal of Political Science*, 1 (March 1968): 14–17.

56. Murray Edelman, *The Symbolic Uses of Politics* (Urbana: University of Illinois Press, 1964), pp. 134–151.

part two

PEOPLE, POLITICS, AND COMMUNICATION MEDIA
In Which Channels?

chapter 5

The Political Media: Mass, Interpersonal, and Organizational Channels

Political communicators, be they politicians, professionals, or activists, use persuasive talk to influence both one another and members of less politically involved audiences. The means, or avenues, they employ in sending messages are the *channels* of "who says what to whom." This chapter considers three items pertinent to understanding the channels of political communication. First, it examines the general nature and dimensions of communication channels. Second, we discuss the three principal types of channels of political communication—mass, interpersonal, and organizational channels. Finally, to see how political communicators employ channels for persuasive purposes, we explore the use of political communication in electoral campaigns.

CHANNELS OF POLITICAL COMMUNICATION

Chapter 3 noted that the symbols of political talk are words, pictures, and acts. Combinations of symbols produce narratives, photographs (both still photos and motion pictures), and dramatizations. Communicators transmit these symbolic forms and their combinations by a variety of techniques and media: orally via personal discussions, through print such as newspapers and magazines, and by electronic techniques such as radio or television. Conceived of broadly, communication channels consist of all such symbols, their combinations, and the techniques and media used to speak with audiences.[1]

Communication channels are thus instruments and devices that facilitate message transmission. Harkening back to Kenneth Burke's definition of man (Chapter 3), channels are inventions the symbol-using animal uses to expedite message exchange. Let us be wary lest this conception mislead. Certainly communication channels are inventions. But channels include more than instruments, devices, and mechanisms such as printing presses, radios, telephones, or computers. Taking precedence over all invented channels is one most fundamental to human communication, i.e., the human being itself. We must, as does psychologist George Miller, "consider the human being as a communication channel, with an input provided by the stimuli we present and an output consisting of his responses to these stimuli."[2] Unlike a megaphone, an instrument for magnifying sound, or a telephone that converts the human voice into electronic signals and back again into human sounds at the receiving end, people as channels transform inputs into outputs in strange, creative, often unpredictable ways. The human communication channel is not a high fidelity transmitter of serial information. Nor, like the telephone, is the human simply a link between other communicators. The human channel is active and selective, not passive and neutral. Human thinking recodes and transforms messages; it is not a mechanism for simple serial transfer.

Bearing in mind that people are channels as well as they are sources and receivers in communication, our primary emphasis is human channels of political communication. We will not ignore, however, the mechanical media, techniques, and devices that augment the human constructions of images through symbolic exchanges. But such instruments are precisely that; i.e., means of facilitating but not guaranteeing fidelity. In contrast, conceived of as basically human, "*communication channels,* then, are much more than mere points of contact; they consist of *shared understanding concerning who may address whom, about what subject, under what circumstances, with what degree of confidence.*"[3]

TYPES OF CHANNELS

Given the human character of communication channels, what are the principal types of channels of political communication? Chapter 4 distinguished between propaganda, advertising, and rhetoric by noting whether the persuasive talk was one-to-many or one-to-one communication. That distinction is relevant here. One major type channel emphasizes one-to-many communication, namely, *mass communication.* Depending upon how direct the one-to-many communication is, mass communication channels take one of two forms. The first consists of face-to-face communication, as when a political candidate addresses a public rally or a president appears before a large audience of reporters at a news conference. The second occurs when there is a mediary interposed between communicator and audience. Here enter the media, technologies, devices and other instruments of communication. An example of interposed mass communication is a presidential address to the nation (one-to-many) via television.

Interpersonal communication channels derive from one-to-one relationships.

They also take either face-to-face or interposed forms. A presidential candidate walking through a crowd shaking hands or a local candidate making door-to-door visitations in the suburbs exemplify face-to-face interpersonal channels. When Janet Gray Hayes, the first woman elected mayor of a city of over half a million population (San Jose, California) campaigned in 1974, she employed an interposed form of interpersonal channel. She instituted the "Hayes Hotline," a direct line telephone to her campaign office that permitted citizens to speak personally with her regarding issues of concern.

Finally, there is a third set of human channels in political communication. *Organizational communication* incorporates both one-to-one and one-to-many transmission. A president, for example, engages in face-to-face discussions with a subordinate, a member of his staff, or a chief adviser (as did President Richard Nixon with members of his White House staff concerning the Watergate affair from 1972 through 1974). But most political organizations are so large that one-to-one communication with all members is out of the question. Hence, there are devices for one-to-many, interposed communication within the organization: circulation of memoranda, assemblies, conventions (as, for instance, the quadrennial presidential nominating conventions of Republican and Democratic parties), in-house newspapers and newsletters, and training sessions.

Mass Communication

Recent years have witnessed widespread popular interest in the role mass communication channels play in politics. The reputations of politicians (Richard Nixon, Ronald Reagan, Jimmy Carter), professional communicators (Walter Cronkite, Harry Reasoner, Barbara Walters, David Broder), and activists (Ralph Nader, John Gardner) have been both enhanced and tarnished through symbols circulating in mass communication. Millions of Americans have vivid memories of man's first step upon the surface of the moon, the American debacle in Vietnam, the ascendencies, deaths, and resignation of presidents—all thanks to mass communication. Two aspects of mass communication concern us here—the general character of mass channels and theories of their social and political impact. Later we examine the mass communications in electoral campaigns.

The Mass and Minority Media

As with mass advertising discussed in Chapter 4, mass communication cuts across structural divisions in society such as race, occupation, region, religion, social class, and political parties to draw its audience from people acting primarily as individuals rather than group members. Writing two decades ago, sociologist Charles Wright argued that the mass media pro-

vide a special kind of communication involving three sets of special conditions: the nature of the audience, the communication experience, and
the communicator.[4]

The audience of mass communication, Wright said, is large, heterogeneous, and anonymous: too large for a communicator in a short duration
to exchange views with each audience member on a one-to-one basis;
heterogeneous in that the audience comes from all walks of life—all ages,
both sexes, many educational levels, etc.; and anonymous because audience members do not know one another, nor does the communicator
know each member.

In mass communications, the communication experience itself is rapid,
transient, and simultaneous. The transmission is rapid, whether instantaneous in radio or television or taking a few hours or days in newspapers
or magazines. Transience implies that mass communications are consumed
quickly, then replaced by other messages. Message transmission is essentially simultaneous; i.e., with little variation the mass message originates
at one time for all to attend simultaneously (copies of a metropolitan
daily may be sent to different sections of a city at slightly varied times,
television or network newscasts may be broadcast at different times to
adjust to the nation's time zones).

Finally, Wright argues that mass communication is organized. To be
sure, individual communicators are well-known celebrities, but mass communication generally requires a complex organization with a division
of labor and persons with varied skills performing specialized functions.
Organization and specialization imply a related characteristic of mass
communication—it is expensive. These qualities of the mass media exert
considerable influence over the kinds of political information available
through mass channels, a point we explore in detail reviewing the nature
of political news and government-press relations in Chapter 6.

The characteristics cited by Wright set mass communication apart from
other types of channels. Merrill and Lowenstein suggest four attributes
that distinguish various types of mass media from one another: (1) Reproduction refers to how messages are transmitted—as words, pictures, using
color, reproducing sounds, or employing motion. Print media (newspapers,
magazines, etc.) rely upon words, pictures, sometimes color; radio is a
sound reproducing medium; television combines various reproductive
modes. (2) Circulation denotes how the medium distributes messages, their
portability, reviewability, and simultaneity. Radio, for example, is a
highly portable medium in that it reaches an audience virtually anywhere
(some wags even suggest that children someday will be born with ear
plugs attached to their bodies, a Darwinian human adaptation to transis-
terized radio technology). Print is a review medium; a reader peruses
a newspaper or book at leisure and can reread portions as desired. And,
as noted earlier, each medium is more or less simultaneous in delivering

a message to audience members at a single instance. (3) Feedback consists of an audience's response to mass messages. Failure to purchase subscriptions, for example, is a way for newspaper readers to express dissatisfaction with the contents of the local daily. Letters to the editor, radio call-in shows, switching the television dial,—all are potential feedback. (4) Support pertains to the financial base of a mass media organization. The print media, for instance, rely chiefly upon single sales to individuals, subscriptions, and advertising. Radio and television are essentially advertising media. Public service radio and television rely upon a host of subsidies, government and corporate, for support.[5]

As Merrill and Lowenstein point out, the growth of the mass media occurs in stages.[6] In the elitist stage the chief consumers of media content are literate political and social leaders with the economic wherewithall to buy the media product. Think, for example, of communication in America during the Revolution, Confederation, and early days of the Republic. Relatively few Americans had access to newspapers, either because they could not read, could not afford, or simply could not find copies of papers in remote sections of the colonies. With the expansion of literacy and affluence, mass channels enter a popular state of development; large circulation dailies and magazines, radio, motion pictures, and television become widely available to large portions of citizenry. Finally, as education levels rise, affluence extends, more leisure time becomes available, and diverse interests grow within a nation, media development enters a specialized stage; there appear what observers refer to as "mini-comm"[7] or the "minority media." Specialized media appeal to highly fragmented, yet still basically large, heterogeneous audiences. Thus, *Field and Stream* appeals to hunters and fishermen; *The Nation* to liberals and *The National Review* to conservatives; FM radio stations cater respectively to followers of classical, jazz, country-western, rock, and other forms of music; AM radio stations become "all news" stations, others "Top Forty" stations, etc. Within a single medium develops an effort to reach specialized audiences with particularized material. For example, demographics—a term referring to the age, sex, occupation, and income makeup of audiences—is a strong influence on the development, placement, and cancellation of television programs. Networks seek young, affluent couples with children. Such people consume large quantities of goods and, hence, are ideal targets for the messages of advertisers. Older, less affluent viewers spend less. Although they may constitute a large audience for a popular show, it is not the "right" audience and, hence, the program may be cancelled.

Viewing the characteristics of the mass media and the stages of their development, James Carey argues that the overall consequences of mass channels on society are paradoxically both centripetal and centrifugal.[8] They are centripetal because mass communication enhances the opportunity of communicators in a nation's center to reach individuals directly rather than going through intermediary groups such as political parties, churches, or even the family. The link between leaders and followers is direct and immediate, uninhibited by pluralist forms of social organization. Moreover, within the mass society new communication channels develop as mass communicators, in search of ever larger and sustaining audiences, create and organize new centers of interest, confer national identity on previously disparate groups (hunters, fishermen, women's liberation groups, civil rights organizations, etc.) and nationalize related interests. In the long run, then, mass channels create new publics, the demands for media to serve them, and create a centrifugal impact upon society.[9] Carey's centripetal-centrifugal view of the forces of mass communication is but one theory of the role of the mass media. Let us turn to others.

Theories of Mass Communication

Theorists debate what impact communication channels have upon how people get involved in society and politics. We examine three general theories and the scholars associated with them.

A Social Theory.   A Canadian economist and historian, Harold Adams Innis, provided one of the most comprehensive statements of how the media affect forms of social organization.[10] Innis argued that any medium possesses either a time or space bias. For example, ancient media such as parchment, clay, and stone, although very permanent records of messages, were extremely hard to transport over long distances. Hence, they had a time over space bias. Print on paper, however, is easy to transport, yet far less durable than etchings on stone tablets. Here is a space over time bias.

Such biases, said Innis, affect social organization. As long as communication over vast distances is achieved easily (i.e., if media have a space bias) territorial expansion, population resettlements, and empires are possible. Media with a time bias, however, confine people in a limited sphere and give rise to close-knit groups influenced by history, tradition, religion, and family. Time bias leads to an emphasis on the past, the way things were, while space bias looks to the future.

In developing a theory of the social impact of mass communication, Innis focused upon two principal communication channels, oral and written communication. Each produces a distinct type of culture. An oral culture is ruled by tradition, elites, and elders of the tribe; it is a culture with a time bias, because oral communication transmits messages slowly over only short distances (distances limited by the capacity of the human voice). Narrative, folk tales, and myths preserve tried and true ways and the authority of the ruling elite. In contrast a written culture implies a much quicker and wider dissemination of messages. There are breaks with tradition; authority shifts from family and church elders to the nation state. Thus, Innis saw a clear relationship between how a society communicates and how it answers the question, How is social order possible? Modes of communication and the channels associated with them are instruments of social control creating various publics (depending upon oral or written communication, time or space bias) and fashioning governing regimes to regulate conflicts between them.

A Perceptual Theory.   Few theorists of communication have written so much, so breathlessly, or been so controversial as Marshall McLuhan.[11] In many respects McLuhan picks up where Innis leaves off. In others he sharply modifies Innis's intent. In still others he ignores Innis completely. As Carey argues, McLuhan takes a page from the Sapier-Whorf hypothesis (discussed in Chapter 3). Recall that this proposition says that the language people use determines the character of human thought; indeed the structure of reality presented to a person is very much influenced by the language available for conceptualizing the real world of one's perceptions. Whereas the philosopher William James wrote, *"The intellectual life of man consists almost wholly in his substitution of a conceptual order for the perceptual order in which his experience originally comes,"*[12] the Sapir-Whorf hypothesis offers a different emphasis, which is that the conceptual order is more than a mere substitute; it determines the perceptual order. James viewed neither perceptions nor concepts as determinant ("We need them both, as we need both our legs to walk with"); McLuhan adopts a more deterministic view, one of technological determinism.

For McLuhan any communication medium possesses a grammar. This is a set of operating rules closely related to the mixture of senses (sight, touch, sound, smell, etc.) associated with a person's use of a medium. Each medium's grammar is biased in favor of a particular sense (not, as in Innis, in favor of time or space). As people use a particular medium, they overrely on the sense associated with that medium. To this degree, then, the media are extensions of man's senses: speech an extension of the sense of sound, print an extension of the sense of sight, and certain electronic media—especially television—an extension of tactile sense (feel, touch, the nervous system).

Since each medium is biased toward a particular sense and the medium's use produces an overreliance, or bias, in the total pattern of the human senses, it follows that a medium can have profound consequences for the people who use it. In an oral culture, for example, the medium is speech and the bias toward sound. The results are a culture of social intimacy, people in and relying upon continuing communication as social beings. Along comes print and the biases change. Print, argues McLuhan, imposes a different conceptual-perceptual order: one in which people come to expect, look for, and demand linearity, a sequence, a feeling of coordination and order. Yet print is a highly individualizing sort of thing, because individuals, not groups, read and write and publish. The political upshot is a system of individual democracy emphasizing private capacities and points of view of individual citizens taking part in a process they seemingly can influence in an orderly manner (through voting, writing their congressman, and becoming well informed).

What speech is to social intimacy and print is to individual action, television, in McLuhan's theory, is to collective democracy. When McLuhan refers to television as a cool rather than hot medium, he says that people don't merely watch television, they engage in it. Television is a medium low in information: it simply presents to the viewer electronic impulses; he must interpret, detect a pattern, and make meaningful those impulses. A hot medium imposes a meaning upon the reader or listener (in the case of print or radio); a cool medium liberates the viewer from imposed patterns.

The distinction can be illustrated by considering a study undertaken in the late 1960s of two popular television offerings of that era, *Startrek* and *Mission: Impossible*. Audiences were played an audio tape of each episode but not shown the video portion. The audience had no problem detecting the story line, themes, development, and point of *Startrek*. In large measure *Startrek* was simply an illustrated radio serial, its story complete with only sound. As with radio, the voices, story sequence, and music supplied all the information necessary for audiences to interpret what was happening. *Mission: Impossible,* in contrast, was completely unintelligible without the visual images. There were long periods without dialogue or any identifying sound. *Startrek* was hot, *Mission: Impossible* cool.[13]

The sociopolitical consequences of the advent of cool media are not greater individualism, at least not for McLuhan. Rather, they are collectivizing consequences because people find joint communal meaning in messages, meanings that transcend their individual lives. The world becomes, thanks to television and McLuhan's theory, a global village of instantaneously transmitted and shared experiences. Social order arises from the transcendent meaning people derive from a common electronically mediated culture.

A Functional Theory.   Innis's theory is concerned primarily with effects of mass communication on social organization. McLuhan's examines effects of various media upon how people order their perceptions. In both theories the emphasis is primarily upon effects as what communication channels do *to* people. Yet in McLuhan's thesis there is a hint of a move away from examining *effects* to considering the *impact* of communication channels, that is, asking not what media do to people but what people get out of their communication and why. This is the focus of a functional theory of mass communication, which considers the kinds of functions the media have for readers, listeners, and viewers. There are several functional theories. We consider only the principal variants and they are not mutually exclusive.

Diffusion/Persuasion and Information Theory.   Why do people pay attention to mass media? One possible answer is that they seek to increase their store of knowledge (information) and/or to obtain guidance (opinions). Viewed from this function, the mass media diffuse information and persuade. As we saw in Chapter 4, the impact of diffusion and/or persuasion varies considerably and is generally more apparent in presenting messages and attracting attention than in achieving comprehension and yielding to appeals, more successful in bringing about comprehension and yielding than in producing message retention or overt activity in conformity to the informative or persuasive message.

Regardless of consequences, however, the notion of mass communication serving primarily a diffusion-persuasion function derives from distinct theory, the information theory of mass communication. In information theory, mass communications consist of a series of systems transmitting information in a serial, sequential fashion (1) from a source (2) through an encoder that translates the elements of a message into a series of signals (words, pictures, etc.) into electronic impulses (3) through a channel, (4) through a decoder, and (5) to a receiver. The theory defines information in terms of its ability to reduce uncertainty or disorganization of a situation at the receiving end.[14] If, for instance, one knows which side of a coin lies face up, that removes all uncertainty about which side is concealed. But if a person deals one card from a pack of fifty-two playing cards, there is considerable doubt which card might be the next dealt. In other words, the information about the coin is more useful in reducing uncertainty than that provided by the deck of cards. Other notions are important in information theory—entropy, redundancy, and noise. Entropy is the degree of uncertainty or disorganization in events; redundancy is the relative certainty in situations; noise is anything that interferes with information.

Do people engage in political communication to reduce uncertainty? Many do, of course, but others do not. The politician who seems to be on all sides of an issue, who never commits himself, who is vague and ambiguous in his utterances, apparently finds entropy far more suitable to his purposes than the removal of doubt. (Critics of Jimmy Carter's 1976 bid for the Democratic presidential nomination claimed that the candidate's selective ambiguity was in precisely this vein; supporters found no ambiguities, just no simple solutions to complex problems.) Or take a president who, when asked a particularly probing and embarrassing question at a news conference, replies that "I think it would be presumptuous of me to comment upon a matter currently pending before the Congress [or Court, staff, United Nations, etc.]." Such responses are like noise, i.e., they intrude upon the information the president is actually giving, namely, that he does not know the answer, does not want to reply, does not want to lie, or simply is embarrassed.

Play Theory.   Information theory says that people attend to communication to achieve a specific end, which is to exchange information and reduce uncertainty. Play theory, as formulated by psychologist William Stephenson, argues that we communicate simply for the pleasure we derive from the act itself. Play is activity people undertake for fun rather than, like work, to get something done. Play theory derives from the notion of *communication-pleasure,* the simple joy people get from conversing without expecting anything to come from it, the entertainment of aimlessly watching television, or the satisfaction in reading the comics or a column by Ann Landers. In contrast, information theory, suggests Stephenson, describes *communication-pain,* communicating to be better informed, educated, for problem solving, etc.

What does this have to do with political communication? For Stephenson, a great deal. Politics from the public viewpoint he sees as play: "The diplomats and politicians do the work; the public merely has something given to it to talk about, to give them communication-pleasure."[15] Political scientist Murray Edelman, in distinguishing between semantic and esthetic information, suggests the possible consequences of mass political communication are primarily play. Semantic political information is utilitarian: it is designed to advance an interest, get a candidate elected, pursue a policy goal. Moreover, it is information presented in a logical mode, in the deliberative style described in Chapter 4. Esthetic information, however, has no clear-cut intent; it pleases the person receiving it, but beyond this subjective pleasure it advances no decisions, no policies, no interests, no goals. In short, esthetic information, like play, creates states of mind-titillating, pleasurable, perhaps even shocking images. A high proportion of political communication, points out Edelman, is esthetic, especially mass political communication. A U.S. president visiting the Hall of the People in China, the trial of Patty Hearst, the unfolding of the Watergate drama, the color of a presidential election—each contains esthetic information about events that people use to construct images of politics. Exploiting the playlike and esthetic features of political communication, political leaders use mass channels to provoke popular arousal and quiescence to governmental decisions, the instrumental use of political symbolism described in Chapter 3.[16]

Parasocial Theory.   Another group of theorists argue that mass communications functions to satisfy human needs for social interaction. This is achieved when the mass media provide the opportunity for parasocial relationships, i.e., involving people in what seems to be the intimacy of face-to-face contact without the direct contact itself. Specifically, members of a radio, television, or film audience relate to a figure in the mass media more or less as if that person were actually present in their social circle.[17] Take as an example the talk shows that pervade late night, early morning, and morning television. Beginning with Dave Garroway, the star of NBC's *Today* show in the 1950s, there have been numerous, ongoing, daily relationships established between performers and audiences, relationships whereby audience members in the privacy of their living room sense they are active participants with the star in informal give-and-takes. The names of Jack Paar, Hugh Downs, Johnny Carson, Dinah Shore, Barbara Walters and others exemplify the celebrity side of parasocial relationships. With their supporting casts, guests, inside glimpses, and air of contrived spontaneity and congeniality, performers cue viewers when to laugh, sadden, cheer, approve, disdain, smirk, go to sleep and awaken.

Again, what has this to do with politics? The answer is that many of the formats used by political communicators build parasocial bridges between leaders and followers. Presidents since John Kennedy, for example, have chatted informally on hour-long television shows with a select group of two or three reporters (professional communicators such as Walter Cronkite, John Chancellor, and Howard K. Smith—political leaders in their own right as we noted in Chapter 2). Weekend long telethons to raise money for the Democratic party in the 1970s frequently employed talk show, parasocial formats. Some politicians make it a point to appear on popular talk shows, for example, both Robert and Edward Kennedy's appearing on *The Tonight Show,* Edmund Muskie on *Dinah's Place,* and Hubert Humphrey on the *Mike Douglas Show.* Finally, many public relations efforts of organized interest groups place their spokesmen on popular talk shows hoping to identify the show's host with such causes as environmental protection, prison reform, consumer boycotts, a halt to construction of nuclear power plants, etc.

Uses and Gratifications Theory.   Information, play, and parasocial theory consider possible reasons why people respond to mass communication channels. All point to specific needs which communications satisfy—information, pleasure, social interaction. This common focus upon people turning to the mass media to gratify various needs has been generalized into a fourth theory of mass communications, the uses and gratifications approach.

The uses and gratifications approach begins from the assumption that members of the media audience are active and selective participants in the total communications process.[18] They are not merely passive recipients of messages but purposefully enter communication experiences as goal-directed beings. Thus *no medium, such as television, uses people; people use television.* The audience member rather, than the communicator, chooses particular media to assuage salient needs. Mass media are but one way for people to achieve satisfaction of their needs. Actual social interaction, for example, may be the way most people achieve social intimacy, rather than through parasocial relationships.

There are various typologies of the kinds of needs allegedly gratified through the mass media, but a fourfold classification formulated by Mc-Quail, Blumler, and Brown summarizes the basic outlook of the approach. Mass communication functions on behalf of (1) diversion—to escape from boring, burdensome routine or from various problems, and to facilitate emotional release; (2) personal relationships such as companionship and social relations; (3) personal identity, including using the media to clarify some aspect of one's personal life, assist in exploring reality, and reinforcement of values; and (4) surveillance, i.e., information gathering.[19] It is not difficult to see the political relevance of each of these media uses. Following Stephenson and Edelman, for instance, the diversion function relates to the playlike features of politics salient to the populace. Or, respecting personal relationships many people use political figures as substitute companions (thus U.S. Senator Sam Ervin, in the 1973 televised hearings of the Senate Committee to examine the Watergate affair was the substitute for the yarn telling proprietor of the local grocery, John Dean the prodigal son returning home, or Maureen Dean the daughter of every mother once pleased when her child married an ambitious young lawyer).

The point of the uses and gratifications approach (and all other functional theories for that matter) is that in assessing the political effects of mass communication we must guard against the all too easy conclusion that the media play no role when we find the media change no votes, do not alter levels of public support for policies, or fail to increase the information people have about politics. The consequences of political communication (described in detail in Part Four) extend far beyond the diffusion of information, to diverting people from their daily routines, providing social companionship, and enhancing personal self-images. Interpersonal communication, like mass communication, is also important to politics. Let us see in what ways.

Interpersonal Communication

Mass communication extends to all impersonal, interposed means of reaching large noncontiguous audiences. Interpersonal communication consists of the word-of-mouth exchanges between two or more persons. In thinking about interpersonal communication in political matters we will explore the political importance of interpersonal contacts, the basic features of such communication, and factors that help shape the contours of the messages exchanged.

Personal Influence in Politics

In Chapter 2 we designated politicians, professionals, and activists as varieties of political communicators. In the activist category we spoke of opinion leaders, persons who pay attention to mass media, select messages, and transmit both information and opinions to friends, neighbors, coworkers, and others through face-to-face conversation. Through personal influence (which we estimated one-fourth to one-third of Americans try to exercise in major elections), opinion leaders are channels linking networks of mass and interpersonal communication.

Aside from the influence they exert upon political decisions through interpersonal contact, opinion leaders play a key role in the diffusion of political information. Research indicates, for example, that news about political events reaches a large portion of citizens through a *two-step flow* of information, i.e., many citizens hear about an event not directly from mass media but by talking with others who did learn of it through radio, television, or newspapers. The precise relationship of mass and interpersonal media in information diffusion is hard to discern. On the one hand there is the hypothesis that "the greater the news value of an event, the more important will be interpersonal communication in the diffusion process."[20] Supporting this contention are studies indicating, for instance, that when President Franklin Roosevelt died on April 12, 1945, 85 percent of Americans learned about it through interpersonal means; and when John Kennedy was assassinated in 1963, more people found out about it via personal contacts than from the mass media. Yet there is other evidence to indicate that in the case of many news events (such as the launching of the first Soviet satellite in 1957), 90 percent of Americans heard about it through the mass media; within 48 hours of a major news event all but 10 percent of citizens hear about it from the media (the remaining 10 percent are likely to remain uninformed permanently). In any case, interpersonal channels play a significant role in transmitting political information, although probably not a dominant one.[21]

Aside from its role in opinion leadership and information diffusion, interpersonal communication is important in politics for another reason. Despite the pervasiveness of the mass media, a great deal of political talk among politicians, professional communicators, and activists flows chiefly through interpersonal channels. Politicians, be they officeholders or office-seekers, communicate a great deal of the time on a one-to-one basis. Consider face-to-face communication on the floors, in the cloak rooms, in offices, and in committee hearings of Congress; briefings which agency public information officers give to journalists; the president's regular sessions with members of his staff; etc. Here are primary arenas of power, influence, and authority talk where the talk is by word of mouth rather than to mass audiences. Observers rightly argue that the behind the scenes talk between public officials provides a more accurate picture of what goes on in government than does what those officials say to mass audiences: "Political symbols circulating among the power holders," write Lasswell and Kaplan, "correspond more closely to the power facts than do symbols presented to the domain."[22] Those who doubt such an assertion need only compare the transcripts of President Richard Nixon's conversations with advisers about the Watergate affair in 1972 through 1974 to his public statements on the matter.

Characteristics of Political Conversation

Interpersonal communication about politics, or anything else for that matter, is a focused gathering,[23] that is, very few people take part, the parties grant each other rights of recognition and response in the exchange, and the conversation proceeds by people taking turns in saying things. This focused quality yields coorientation, gamelike, and negotiation qualities.

Coorientation.   This label simply denotes that people exchange views over time, the exchange generates a sequence of messages and acts, and through that sequence the participants simultaneously orient themselves to the object under discussion and to each other.[24]

The joint orientation to messages and participants of interpersonal communication implies that the messages exchanged have both content and relational dimensions.[25] The content of a message consists of information about the subject under discussion; thus a president of the United States and the foreign minister of Egypt discuss matters varying widely in content—sales of U.S. military arms, oil imports and exports, Arab-Israeli tensions, etc. The relational dimension carries information about how the participants in the conversation view each other. A smile or frown, the tone of voice, eye contact, body language—all are signs that people read to discern what impression they are having on others in the conversation.

Relational messages communicate both dominance-submission and affection-hostility.[26] Person A may, for example, defer to B's views, position, or forcefulness, thus suggesting B has superior judgment, status, or power. During the period in October 1962 when the U.S. government was attempting to get the Soviet Union to remove intercontinental missile bases from Cuba, advisers to President John Kennedy urged that he not "back down" for fear of giving the Soviets the impression of weakness. In addition to dominance-submission, relational messages communicate, directly or indirectly, how warmly or coolly people feel about one another. Many a meeting between rival politicians impresses us with marked cordiality ("My good and lifelong friend, Senator Smart"); but the coolness of relational communication often belies the warmth of the content message—the rivals turn their backs on each other, smile only when the television cameras are running, and end the meeting as soon as possible. Coorientation, then, suggests that interpersonal communication involves conversation about topics—taxes, energy policy, the cost of living, etc.— and subtle messages pertaining to how people feel about one another. Each communicator indicates whether he or she accepts, rejects, or simply ignores others; moreover, a person discloses whether he or she accepts, rejects, or feels apathetic about one's involvement in the discourse.[27]

Is the content-relational distinction politically relevant? Yes. For one thing, it says something about the sources of opinion leadership. We know that many people accept the political views of people they respect and/or like. Moreover, we shall see in Chapter 9 that when a person does not like the content of the views of one to whom he or she otherwise positively relates, that person uses subtle but complex means to resolve the inconsistency between what he or she hears and would like to hear. These efforts to resolve inconsistencies affect the degree and manner of people's participation in politics. In addition, consider the credibility and trust that political leaders place in the content of each other's opinions. These frequently depend as much on how they feel about one another as upon the topic under discussion. Many Republican members of Congress— Senator Hugh Scott and Senator Barry Goldwater among them—were reluctant to believe that President Richard Nixon shared any culpability in the Watergate coverup. They had known him too long, liked him too much, and respected his political acumen too readily. It took increasing evidence and a "smoking pistol" (irrefutable confirmation of Nixon's role) to shake that faith.

Conversations as Games. Numerous writers liken face to face communication to playing games. This is not to say they regard interpersonal communication as trivial. They distinguish between *phatic communion* (small talk, uninspired greetings, idle chatter, and pastimes) of lesser significance in human affairs and *games*, transactions in which the participants (1) have open and ulterior motives and (2) achieve payoffs or suffer losses in the process.[28] As defined in Chapter 3 a game is a communication interchange between people who are aware of each other, focus attention on each other, are aware that each party pursues certain goals, see a limited number of ways to achieve these goals, and follow a grammar (set of rules) in conversing. It is not hard to see how political conversations fit this definition: political communicators take account of each other and try to direct one another's behavior through distinctly motivated power, influence, and authority talk.

Lyman and Scott provide a fourfold typology of games suitable for illustrating the gamelike features of interpersonal political communication.[29] Games are distinguished according to the goals sought. *Face games,* for example, reflect efforts of participants to define their respective identities in valued ways. A face game may be defensive, in which a player tries to protect an identity from some threat. During the period in which he was under severe criticism from various members of the news media for failing to speak out on Watergate, President Richard Nixon visited Disney World amusement complex in Florida and held a televised news conference. Asked about charges that he had filed illegal deductions on his income tax returns and had inappropriately used government funds to make improvements on his Florida and California estates, Nixon announced, "I am not a crook!" In contrast to this form of defensive face game, there are also protective games, those which protect the identity of other persons. Politicians locked in heated debate in congressional committees ask, "Will the honorable senator from the great state of X yield?" The utterance is more than meaningless gesture; it is a recognition that disagreement or not, the opponent is a member of a respected legislative body and must be accorded the courtesy due that identity.

Exploitation games involve a participant trying to get compliance from another person or group. The linguistic currency of exploitation games is power talk, "If you do X, I will (or will not) do Y." Thus, during the administration of President Gerald Ford, the chief executive in meetings with congressional leaders repeatedly threatened to veto any legislation that did not conform with the administration's energy policy.

Information games occur when a communicator wants to uncover information from someone who wishes to conceal it. We scarcely need look beyond the confrontations between journalists and public officials to find examples of political information games. Many Washington correspondents, for instance, are skilled at making uncovering moves in the information game. A common tactic is to call a public official and tell the officeholder that a second official has made some charge. If the first official takes the bait and comments, the reporter calls the second, urging that a public statement might clear the air. Should the second official take the reporter's feint, the response yields a story revealing things the official might have preferred to keep quiet. In fact, of course, the reporter has made news through victory in an information game.

Finally, *relationship games* involve participants' approaching each other in a positive or negative manner in efforts to decrease or increase their social distance. At issue are both kinds of relationships we described earlier, i.e., relationships of dominance-submission and of affection-hostility. When a person makes a move in a relationship game, it induces a countermove from another. Dominance induces submission and vice versa. The moves and countermoves are complementary. But with respect to affection-hostility, the moves induce corresponding behavior—hate induces hate, love induces love.[30] President Lyndon Johnson was noted for his "flesh pressing" persuasive abilities in interpersonal communication. His political and physical stature communicated dominance and induced submission; his "politics of touch" communicated warmth. Once removed from the President's presence, many a visitor would leave the Oval Room of the White House, only to realize that Johnson had done a "job" on him.

> Johnson was that rare American man who felt free to display intimacy with another man, through expressions of feeling and also in physical closeness. In an empty room he would stand or sit next to a man as if all that were available was a three-foot space. He would flatter men with gestures of affection. The intimacy was all the more excusable because it seemed genuine and without menace. Yet it was also the product of meticulous calculation. And it worked. To the ardor and the bearing of this extraordinary man, the ordinary senator would almost invariably succumb.[31]

Negotiation Properties.   Interpersonal communication is a primary channel for achieving social order, the pattern, regularity, and consistancy in human affairs. Using face to face message exchange, people negotiate personal identities, social relationships, and meanings of political power.

Through interpersonal media people disclose their respective self-images, i.e., the picture each person holds of what he has been, is, and aspires to become. Communication involves, consciously or not, the continuous construction, presentation, enhancement, and protection of self-images. It carries reinforcements and threats to valued identities. The parties to a conversation confirm, disconfirm (ignore)[32] or reject each other's preferred identity. Through transactions with their political colleagues, journalists, and constituents, for instance, congressmen, governors, and cabinet officials negotiate an identity of presidential timber; others become powers behind the throne; still others become legislative, executive, or judicial experts: and still others vanish into the obscurity of nonpersons.

There are rewards and costs to any human transaction. People derive pleasures, satisfactions, and gratifications from interpersonal communication just as they do from mass communication; and there are costs in negative feelings, emotional stress, tension, boredom, and fatigue, just as with mass communication. Thibaut and Kelley use the notion of rewards and costs in interpersonal conduct to describe the negotiation of social relations.[33] Each person, they argue, has a feeling about what he or she deserves from any relationship. This feeling is that person's comparison level (CL), a personal standard for evaluating when a relationship is good or bad. Net outcomes (rewards minus costs) below the CL are unsatisfactory; outcomes above the CL are satisfactory. A person also compares outcomes he or she feels are deserved with alternative relationships for achieving them. One thus possesses a comparison level for alternatives (CL_{alt}), a standard for deciding to continue or terminate any relationship. If the outcomes a person receives from a relationship fall below what can be derived from another, the person will improve things by choosing the next best alternative. Take, for instance, the state legislator who no longer receives a sufficient return (in prestige, salary, influence, etc.) from office. If the legislator believes the costs of running for governor would be worth the increased rewards, the aspirant seeks higher office.

Through interpersonal transactions people negotiate three kinds of relationships, each politically relevant. In one a person's outcomes exceed the CL and CL_{alt}; moreover, the comparison level of the alternative also exceeds the CL. The person is, in short, in the happy position of being satisfied with a current situation, yet could move to the next best alternative and still be happy. The person is *independent* of any current relationship; the individual likes it, but even if this were not so the person could improve upon it. A second relationship is *dependent*. Here a person's outcomes from a relationship are above one's CL, yet the CL exceeds the CL_{alt}. If the individual leaves the satisfying relationship, taking the next best alternative produces an even worse situation. A person who enjoys being vice-president of the United States might well hope nothing happens to the president because the outcomes of the presidency might not be as satisfying. The third relationship is *nonvoluntary*. Here a person's CL exceeds both the outcomes derived from the relationship and what can be expected from any alternative. The person is, in sum, stuck. For example, an adviser to a political candidate is increasingly unhappy with low stature on the campaign staff, yet recognizes that like it or not, this is the only candidate, campaign, and job available.

Independent, dependent, and nonvoluntary relations are not static: they respond to distribution of rewards and costs that are continuously negotiated between the parties. What is independent today may become dependent, even involuntary tomorrow. There was speculation during the presidency of Richard Nixon that the relationship between the president and Henry Kissinger, first foreign policy advisor and later Secretary of State, shifted. In the beginning Nixon found the policy outcomes from his relationship with Kissinger satisfying, but there were other men of national stature that might also have proved satisfactory. As time progressed Kissinger built a reputation for policy success (opening relations with the People's Republic of China, negotiating a Vietnam settlement, etc.), and Nixon became bogged down in affairs surrounding Watergate. Alternatives to Kissinger seemed less attractive. As Nixon's reputation for statesmanship declined in contrast with Kissinger's successes, the outcomes of Nixon's relationship (at least in prestige) may have been below the Nixonian CL, yet the alternative of removing Kissinger from office was even less attractive. Independence had become dependence, dependence had become nonvoluntary. Contrast this with President Harry Truman's decision to fire the very popular military figure General Douglas MacArthur from command of United Nations forces in Korea. Apparently for Truman the outcomes of having MacArthur as commander were below the president's expectations; even though the alternative of removing MacArthur was unsatisfactory, Truman had no desire to perpetuate an involuntary relationship.

Dependent and nonvoluntary relationships are sources of political power and of power talk. So long as politician A can make B dependent on the relationship between the two and can keep B's outcomes above what B could get from an alternative, then A can decree that if B does X, A will (or will not) do Y. Many a congressman did not like President Franklin Roosevelt during the height of FDR's popularity but supported his proposals (which the congressman found unsatisfactory) rather than face the consequences of having to explain opposition to constituents. Out of such nonvoluntary power relations comes the old saying about how political party members regard their president, "He's a son of a bitch to be sure, but he's *our* son of a bitch."

Contours of Interpersonal Exchange

Several things influence the meanings people give to the messages that flow through interpersonal channels. We shall note three of the principal ones—homophyly-heterophyly, empathy, and self-disclosure.

The Homophyly Principle.   When people who engage in interpersonal communication are alike in key respects—opinions, ages, social status, education, sex, etc.—there exists homophyly; dissimilarities in these respects is heterophyly. Research suggests three general propositions which taken collectively, comprise the homophyly principle of communication: (1) People who are alike and who agree with one another communicate more frequently than people who are dissimilar in attributes and views; for example, during presidential campaigns persons of similar age and social status talk most frequently about the election.[34] (2) More effective communication occurs when source and receiver are homophyletic;[35] people who are alike tend to find common, shared meaning in the messages they exchange. (3) Homophyly and communication nurture one another; the more communication between people, the more likely they are to share views and communicate furthur.

The homophyly principle oversimplifies. For one thing, the more people are alike and agree with one another, the more redundancy to their communication. They may understand each other very well, but they may not be learning anything new in the process. Moreover, political leaders may communicate very well with one another, but that may not lead to greater mass understanding and, indeed, may insulate the leaders from the kinds of popular input necessary to innovative policy making. Finally, anyone who has watched a legislative session, committee meeting, or political convention realizes that an increase in communication does not always lead to shared views. Familiarity may breed contempt as often as it does homophyly.

Empathy.   The ability of a person to project himself into another's viewpoint, empathy, provides an opportunity for heterophyllous communicators to converse successfully. After all, Democrats do get through to Republicans from time to time, and vice versa; the president does negotiate common terms with congressional leaders of the opposing party upon occasion. By seeing how the other person in a situation feels and thinks, it is possible to share images and to construct messages that strike a responsive chord. But putting oneself in another's shoes is not easy, and empathy, like homophyly, may be enhanced or deterred through frequent communication. Empathy is a quality closely associated with a person's image of self and others[36] and is therefore itself a matter of negotiation through interpersonal media.

Self-Disclosure.   It is easier to see another person's viewpoint if that person tells you openly what it is. And to empathize with another, that person's personality must be accessible. Self-disclosure occurs when a person lets others know what he or she thinks, feels, or wants, the most direct means of revealing a self-image and valued identity.[37] Although self-disclosing communication probably enhances interpersonal understanding, it occurs relatively infrequently. Candid self-disclosure is even more rare in politics. Few political leaders make open statements of desires and intent. Many do not even do so in the privacy of conversations with advisers. President Richard Nixon's discussions with his staff regarding the Watergate affair were more revealing for the kinds of symbols and metaphors he used and for his tendency to rehearse privately what was later to be said in public than for self-disclosure. Nondisclosure, the communication strategies by which people avoid being known by others, is typical of interpersonal political communication.[38]

Beyond the participant's degrees of similarity-dissimilarity, empathy, and joint self-disclosure, other factors influence the nature of interpersonal communication. These include the situation surrounding the discourse, psychological needs and states of the participants, rules of the game, the proximity of persons to one another in time and space, and other considerations.[39] Since we have alluded to many of these factors in discussing how people impute meanings to symbols and messages (Chapter 3), we need not repeat that discussion here. Let us turn instead to the third principal channel of political communication, message exchange within organizations.

Organizational Communication

Communication networks of organizations combine features of mass and interpersonal channels. To explore that combination we consider the character and aims of organizations, why and how they communicate.

What Is an Organization?

A social organization consists of a collection of people possessing relatively stable relationships between individuals and subgroups. Organizations vary in how clear-cut those relationships are. The personal relationships of informal organizations develop spontaneously and persist through shared understandings, unspoken rules, rituals, and traditions. In contrast, formal organizations have explicit rules and regulations, precisely defined positions within the organization, and clearly designated rights and duties for members. Generally, the more complex the organization the greater the formal structure. Thus complex organizations develop elaborate standard operation procedures (SOPs) to routinize tasks, formal hierarchies of superior-subordinate relationships, divisions of labor for specialized tasks—managerial, clerical, technical, etc.—and performance criteria which dominate promotions, allocation of work loads, status, salaries, etc.

There are, of course, vastly different kinds of organizations, both informal and formal, in politics.[40] As we shall see in Chapter 9, one's family, peer groups, and coworkers are informal groups that play a significant role in developing a person's political opinions. More formalized groups include political parties and various special interest organizations such as labor unions, business associations, consumer advocates, civil rights organizations, and women's liberation coalitions. Finally, at the most formalized end of the continuum are bureaucratic organizations. Most of what we have to say about organizational media pertains to communication within bureaucracies.

A bureaucracy, defined in nonpejorative ways, is an organization that (1) is sufficiently large so that less than one-half its members know one another personally, (2) consists of full-time workers committed to and dependent upon the organization, (3) relies upon performance criteria in evaluating workers rather than ascribed characteristics (such as sex, or race) or popular election to positions of authority, and (4) has relatively little external evaluation of its product on a continuing basis by any accurate means.[41] (Thus, for instance, for a major commercial manufacturer, sales of products result in profit and loss statements, but external evaluation of the Central Intelligence Agency or Federal Bureau of Investigation, as indicated by congressional inquiries in 1975 and 1976, is a sporadic, imprecise, controversial effort.) Bureaucratic organizations try to achieve rationality, efficiency, and expertise in performing specific tasks.

Means to this end are attempts to control the definition of tasks and the work of organizational personnel through hierarchical structuring, efforts to preserve and enhance the identity and interests of the organization in conflict with rival bureaus, and means to socialize members in the doctrines and roles supportive of bureaucratic goals. Successful accomplishment of these efforts, in turn, requires organized communication.

Communication in and by Organizations

There are two general types of communication channels in organizational communication. One facilitates internal communication. The internal bureaucratic communication process has three aspects. First, persons must acquire information as a basis for making decisions. Second, decisions and their rationale must be disseminated to get the organization's members to carry them out.[42] Third, there are channels for "organizational talk," the daily conversation normal to the work setting, talk members engage in as they go about the everyday task of creating a meaningful membership in an ongoing social order.[43]

In addition to the internal channels, there are also media for external communication; in the case of government agencies, for example, this includes channels for communicating to the general citizenry, special interest clienteles, Congress, the president, and other governmental agencies.

Internal Channels. In complex organizations like governmental bureaucracies there is an impetus to formalize communication. The rationale is that informal, personalized, hit and miss exchanges fail to provide the information necessary for decision making, lead to serious biases and errors, and make it impossible to fix responsibility for decision making.[44] To guarantee that messages pass through planned, formalized channels, there are devices to control the flow of information. These include standardized forms (in multiple copies, bearing authorized signatures, and precisely routed throughout the hierarchy), periodic reports (daily, weekly, monthly, quarterly), specification of the content format of memoranda (the U.S. Army, for example, provides detailed instructions on paragraphing, etc.), and screening and clearance of messages throughout the chain of command to assure that no subordinate goes "over the head" of superiors or leaks information from authorized channels.[45]

But best laid plans of mice and men often go awry (anything less is bound to), and unplanned, informal arrangements subvert formalized channels of organizational communication. For one thing, day to day organizational talk structures personal relationships in nonhierarchical ways. People try to get along with one another on a routine basis. They often find formal procedures too tedious and time consuming to bother with, especially if a simple word-of-mouth exchange gets the job done without elaborate paperwork. Moreover, organization charts specify superior-subordinate roles, but in the everyday world people learn who is competent and incompetent, reliable and unreliable regardless of what the tables of organization say. Further, organizational tasks do not always lend themselves to formal communications: activities of workers are so interlocked that formal channels impede performance; uncertainty develops when workers faced with complex problems work out informal accords to get on with things; time pressures work against going through channels; and officials, trying to find out what is going on within their own organization, bypass immediate subordinates and go directly to the persons performing the tasks.[46] As anyone knows who has read Joseph Heller's popular novel of World War II, *Catch-22,* or viewed the 1970s television program *M.A.S.H.,* the vast majority of formal communication channels in complex organizations do not describe how the work gets done.

There are other factors that block channels of formal communication. For instance, requirements that messages be written rather than verbal often make it difficult for a communicator to use informal language readily understood by a receiver. If there is no immediate feedback, it is hard to gauge whether a message is misunderstood. And if our formula in Chapter 3 has any merit (i.e., the total impact of a message is 7 percent words, 38 percent vocal communication, and 55 percent facial symbols), then written communication ignores potentially meaningful dimensions. To be sure, formalized requirements seek to reduce misinterpretations: yet written words alone may impede rather than enhance organizational communications. When the language is "gobbledygook" (words with legalistic and technical auras), formal channels become even more obstructed.[47]

Victor Thompson points out that the dramatic qualities of organizational life also foul communication. Officials and subordinants employ informal devices to manage the impressions organization members have of each other. For example, they create an air of "busyness" to leave the impression that they are important people for, after all, important people are always busy, are they not? They surround themselves with signs of superior status—private office and secretary, carpeting, private telephone lines, and keys to the executive washroom. They have "management troupes," a coterie of advisers to assist in staging crucial performances; examples are Richard Nixon's reliance on H.R. (Bob) Haldeman and John Ehrlichman or any presidential candidate's staff of "insiders." Subordinates respond in a complementary way to managed dominance to leave the impression that they need to be bossed by following the superior's advice to the letter, recognizing the official's busyness by keeping conversations and memos infrequent and brief.[48]

Anthony Downs hypothesizes that the bulk of communication in large organizations is subformal.[49] The combination of formal and informal, planned and unplanned channels yields conditions that challenge rather than promote organizational rationality, efficiency, and expertise. Within the organization symbolic leaders emerge whose goals are not always compatible with those of the organization's designated task leader (see Chapter 2). Influence talk supplants authority and power talk; rhetorical persuasion is essential to getting things done; and the fidelity of organizational channels is increasingly problematic as information moves formally and informally back and forth through many officials (each of whom filters, condenses, interprets, and reconstructs it before passing it on to the next). The final message may differ substantially from the original input.

External Channels.   Organizations communicate beyond their own membership. Government organizations such as executive departments, agencies, and commissions do so for a variety of reasons. (1) They must consult with Congress to secure adequate operating budgets and respond to congressional oversight of their activities. (2) Aside from budgetary and operating considerations, most governmental bureaucracies want to influence policies. The Federal Communications Commission, for instance, is concerned with legislation pertaining to broadcasting (such as whether candidates for political office should be given equal time on the airwaves), and the Energy Research and Development Administration is vitally interested in policies dealing with allocations of resources to explore the uses of nuclear, solar, fossil, fusion, geothermal and other forms of energy. To influence policy, government organizations communicate with Congress, the president, the courts, and the general public. (3) Agencies communicate with one another to share information concerning activities one or more organizations might be undertaking; the Environmental Protection Agency, the Energy Research and Development Administration, and the Nuclear Regulatory Commission, for instance, are all concerned with the environmental impacts of building nuclear facilities to generate electrical power. (4) All agencies carry out public information programs to inform citizens of their respective functions and to build public support. (5) Some government organizations use external publicity as a way of enforcing regulations; the Federal Trade Commission, for example, reports and publicizes cases of misleading advertising to prompt advertising firms and their clients to conform to specific regulations.[50] (6) Government organizations communicate externally for internal reasons. One way to force bureau decisions upon recalcitrant subordinates is to announce policies as faits accomplis, hoping thus to cut off internal debate. The Department of Defense speaks through the secretary of defense regarding priorities in defense spending to quiet the internal wrangling between the military services over pet projects; the outcome, however, is rarely successful. (7) An organization's external communications may be prompted by the desire of the organization's chief officer to promote his personal political standing and career. There was much criticism of Secretary of State Henry Kissinger on grounds that he used the Department of State information machinery to enhance his personal prestige.

In addition to the seven reasons outlined above, there is another vital rationale for the external communications of government organizations, which is to carry out the responsibilities agencies have toward specific clienteles such as farmers, laborers, businessmen, consumers, and foreign governments. On a day to day basis the fundamental channel of external organizational communication consists of official-client contact. Whether the official is an auditor for the Internal Revenue Service or a street level bureaucrat for a welfare agency, at the official-client level, organizational and interpersonal communication mesh into a single network.

Katz and Danet provide a classification of the varieties of official-client relationships in political communication.[51] They stress that official-client communication varies depending upon the pressures and the official's response to them. When an official faces a client (say a government social worker considering an application to extend aid to a dependent mother), there may be pressures to grant a favor, pressures to discriminate negatively against the client, or no pressures at all. The official's response, in turn, may be positive, negative, or neutral. If there are no pressures and the official takes a neutral stand toward the client, communications conform strictly to rules, what Katz and Danet call a "pure" bureaucratic encounter. If an official is neutral in the face of pressures to grant favors, the bureaucrat adheres to the rules as a way of resisting the client's claims; the rules impersonalize the encounter. Should an official exercise neutrality in the face of pressures to discriminate, rules again provide an escape. In the face of no pressures but a desire to respond to a client positively, the rules offer no assistance; favors are dispensed on the bureaucrat's initiative. When pressures are to grant favors and the official accedes, this is political "pull," perhaps even corruption. If the pressures are to discriminate against the client but the official is positively inclined, the official may overcompensate by granting favors to prove resistance to external pressures. Finally, there are the cases where the official's responses are negative. If there is no pressure, the official rationalizes decisions by overconforming to the rules as a "typical bureaucrat"; if pressures are to grant favors, the official reacts in an opposite fashion to prove an ability to withstand it all; and if the pressures support the official's negative inclinations, the bureaucrat is free to discriminate.

Communication Channels: A Summary

Katz and Danet remind us that, ultimately, the external communication of even a large, complex organization involves individuals (officials and clients) negotiating specific outcomes. In the process they take into account a variety of things such as pressures, perceived facts, rules, and biases. This reminder provides the opportunity to summarize the common features of all communication channels—mass, interpersonal, and organizational.

Regardless of the channel (or of the technology, whether oral, print, or electronic), meanings flow not from the channels but are meanings created in the minds of receivers. Anything transmitted through a channel (even silence) is a potential message if people find meaning in it. This is not to say that the intent of a communicator's message and channel selection is not important; it is to say, however, that *the message received is the one that counts* and that a communicator's intent is important if it influences how people construct meanings of transmitted messages.[52] The process of constructing meaning, then, relates intended meaning and received meaning. It has marked consequences on forms of social organizations (as suggested by Harold Innis), individual perceptions (as urged by McLuhan), the images we formulate (as suggested by functional theories), how we approach one another, identify our self-images, and find satisfaction in human relationships, and how governmental organizations make decisions and enforce them. In short, how we construct meanings through communication channels is central to how we achieve social order. In this sense, therefore, *all communication channels are political by their very nature;* they are the means to negotiate a continuing regulation of social conflicts (see Chapter 1).

CHANNELS OF POLITICAL PERSUASION: THE CASE OF ELECTORAL CAMPAIGNS

Chapter 4 discussed the use of linguistic devices in persuasive campaigns. It is now appropriate to resume our consideration of political persuasion in light of the channels of communication available to political communicators. We do so by focusing upon persuasive channels employed in campaigns for electoral office. It is not the intention to provide a detailed description of the techniques of modern campaigning; this has been undertaken elsewhere.[53] Rather, this is a brief review of the character of electoral campaigns and their persuasive dimensions considered from the view of how they use mass, interpersonal, and organizational channels.

The Persuasive Character of Political Campaigns

People frequently think of electoral campaigns as elaborate efforts to propagandize potential voters. However, Jacques Ellul argues that the limited time period of a political campaign is scarcely sufficient for a full-fledged propaganda effort. "It is not surprising that such propaganda has little effect," he writes, "since none of the great techniques of propaganda can be effective" in a limited campaign.[54] There are elements of propaganda in any election (especially through organization communication via the political party), but the basic character of contemporary political campaigning lies in efforts to persuade through mass advertising (mass communication) and rhetoric (interpersonal communication) rather than propaganda.

There are many kinds of elections. We are interested here primarily in major partisan national (presidential and congressional) and statewide (gubernatorial) elections rather than party primaries, nonpartisan competition for office, or referenda elections (see Chapter 12 for a discussion of their role in the opinion process). In partisan contests the purpose of a compaign is threefold. First, there is an effort to evoke the natural loyalties of one's party followers and get them to vote accordingly; second, there are activities to locate citizens committed to no political party and, in Kenneth Burke's terms, to create identifiers out of independents; third, there is the campaign directed at the opposition, not designed to convert partisan beliefs and values but to convince people that in this one campaign they would be better off voting for the candidate of a different party.

The waging of a political campaign on three fronts requires commitments to both a *campaign plan* and the concept of a *total campaign*. Uppermost in careful preparation of a campaign plan is the formulation of the Idea of the campaign. Recall that in Chapter 4 we noted that a persuasive campaign usually has some overriding Idea to appeal to audiences and to galvanize campaign workers. John Kennedy in 1960, for example, offered the promise of a "New Frontier" (new, younger leaders pursuing innovative policies). Lyndon Johnson four years later called for a "Great Society." Slogans in 1976 were Jimmy Carter's "leadership, for a change" and Ford's "He's made us proud again."

The Idea, in short, is the organizing theme of the campaign; all slogans point toward realization of that Idea. Hence, Kennedy's slogan in 1960 to "Get America Moving" held out hope for progress toward new frontiers. The Idea also helps to define appropriate campaign gimmicks. In recent years several such gimmicks have come to the fore, including attention-getting devices such as candidates walking on foot throughout the state (as did Lawton Childs in winning a Florida Senate seat in 1970), working at low paying chores (bagging groceries in a supermarket to have the opportunity to meet voters, or, as Gerald Ford did when first running for Congress, helping to milk the farmer's cows and shovel manure), inviting all voters to the candidate's victory party (as did former Congressman William Roy in his election campaign in Kansas in 1970), and issuing ticket stubs to voters for a postelection drawing to see who would win the unused portion of the candidate's campaign fund (a tactic used by several candidates in 1974). The Idea of the campaign also defines the attributes a candidate publicizes to provide the raw material from which voters construct that candidate's image. It is not enough for the candidate simply to become known (i.e., to achieve name recognition); he must also become known in a unique way. Kennedy in 1960 accented youth, energy, and exuberance, all qualities relevant to moving toward new frontiers.

The campaign plan includes four features to execute the purposes underlying the Idea. First, there is early formation of a campaign organization consisting of experienced politicians (both public officials and party leaders), professional campaigners (including all manner of personnel ranging from campaign managers and consultants to specialists in polling public opinion, devising advertising messages, fund raising, making television commercials, writing speeches, and coaching the candidate in public appearances), and citizen volunteers (a host of people willing to make telephone calls, lick postage stamps, knock on doors, erect yard signs, etc.). In addition to establishing the campaign organization, the campaign plan details how funds are to be raised and expended, how to conduct research to supply necessary information on issues, voters, and the opposition, and how to transmit the candidate's message. The blending of these features of a campaign plan dealing with the Idea, organization, budgeting, researching, and communication components is not always the result of rational, comprehensive premeditation. Rather, the campaign plan often evolves in most instances in a hit and miss, trial and error, incrementalist fashion with adjustments to fit circumstances. Campaigners run around putting out many fires, throwing sand and water on sporadic blazes as best they can rather than execute a full-fledged fire protection plan.

It is the feature of the campaign plan pertaining to campaign communication that brings the concept of a total campaign into play. In recent years managers of successful political campaigns have been quick to attribute their candidate's victory to a host of factors: to television, grassroots volunteers, the organization, direct mail, or any one of many other possibilities. The impression is that a successful political campaign capitalizes upon but one communication medium. One political consultant even goes so far as to say there are two basic kinds of campaigns—those conducted through organizations and those conducted through the electronic media.[55] In contemporary America, however, most campaigns that achieve success blend diverse media into a balanced, total persuasive appeal.

There are several reasons for waging a total, comprehensive campaign not wedded to any particular communication channel. For one, there is not enough known about how people construct their images of politics to say that they take the messages from any one medium into account more than they do others in formulating beliefs, values, and expectations. Moreover, several features enter into the success of any given channel in delivering messages to people: the senses affected by the medium, the opportunity for feedback, the degree to which the audience controls whether it will pay attention, the way a medium codes messages, whether a message can be preserved (as in newspapers) or is transitory (as in television), and how media can be combined in intricate, appealing networks (as in the two-step flow of information).[56] Some media are superior in some respects to others. The tendency is to try to take advantage of the relative strengths of each medium by employing a combination. This increases the redundancy of appeals in hopes of assuring that voters will get the message.

In their calculations of a campaign plan, political persuaders look to specific mass, interpersonal, and organizational channels to accomplish different ends. The remaining part of this chapter explores the diverse uses of channels in campaigns for public office, and then draws a few tentative conclusions about the effectiveness of communication for political persuasion.

The Mass Campaign

We said earlier that mass persuasion is one-to-many communication. Mass appeals take place either through face to face contacts or the interposition of electronic, print, or poster type media.

Face to Face Campaigning

The political rally provides a key opportunity for a candidate to engage in face to face communication before a mass audience. For the most part, however, the crowds who show up to see and hear a candidate at a mass rally are predisposed toward him to begin with. Presidential campaigns may be an exception. Here the possibility of seeing a major public figure, be he Democrat or Republican, entices partisans from both parties. But even if the crowd is of mixed persuasion, the candidate's intent is not to convert the opposition but to reinforce the faithful, publicize a personal style, steal a few minutes on the evening network and television news programs, and assist in fund raising.

The rally, to accomplish these ends, relies upon preparation. This is a chief responsibility of the advance man, a member of the campaign organization who arrives in the city well before the appearance of the candidate to assure the proper staging of the event—to guarantee adequate facilities, prepare the site, produce a sufficient crowd, turn out the working press, supply the crowd with the candidate's posters and lapel buttons, and even provide the kinds of hecklers that the candidate can easily put down with a display of wit and charm.

A major element in planning the mass rally is preparation of the speech. The speech is an address the candidate delivers at numerous rallies throughout the district, state, or nation. Gerald Ford in his preprimary campaigning in 1975 delivered the same speech in various visits to midwest and western states. Jimmy Carter evolved a speech in the presidential primaries in 1976 which served him well in speaking to small-town audiences from January through October; his extemporaneous delivery, augmented by references to local matters supplied by advance men, provided a disarming, unprepared quality that went over well.

Interposing Electronic Media

Thinking of electronic media normally brings to mind radio and television, yet the telephone is also an important tool of political communication. Moreover, there are innovations in electronic communication that also have political consequences.

Telephones and Politics.   The telephone as a means of word-of-mouth, one-to-one communication serves several purposes in contemporary campaigns. For one, it is a useful device for personal contact when a campaign organization wants to raise funds. Either through calls to supporters or used in conjunction with telethons, the telephone reaches large numbers of constituents in a very short time. Telephone contact also increases voter turnout. This is particularly useful when a candidate wants high voter turnout in districts and precincts where he knows there is a latent sympathy for his candidacy. It is comparatively easy to target calls to reach pockets of Democratic, Republican, upper, lower, or middle class, or other composition. Telephone contact also introduces candidates to voters. The candidate records a message; the message then plays back to each telephone receiver after calls are placed through automated dialing. Appeals for votes also can be made via telephone calls, usually by a large staff of volunteer workers operating a bank of phones or by individual workers calling from their homes. The implicit message is that a volunteer cares enough about a candidate to make a personal call. Finally, telephones help survey the opinions of constituents; telephone polling, employing techniques of random digit dialing and using short, lively paced questionnaires, is a major survey procedure (see Appendix). Augmenting the telephone for each of these ends are several technical devices: with WATS lines it is possible to make numerous long distance calls at a fixed charge; with automated dialing machines, such as TELO/PLAY used in the 1972 campaign, a campaign worker can place 300 calls in five hours from a home phone; and recording devices play a candidate's message or take calls coming into campaign headquarters.

Radio Campaigning.   In his book *The Responsive Chord,* Tony Schwartz, who has created several thousand radio and television commercials for political campaigns, makes a strong case for radio in campaign communication. He argues that generations of Americans have grown up with radio; they take it so much for granted that it is a fixture of their natural environment. He reports that on the average Americans listen to radio twenty-one hours per week during working, commuting, and leisure time. Taking a page from McLuhan, he stresses that there is a resonance between radio and the human ear and mind, one that offers vast opportunities for radio campaigning.[57]

Beyond the tendency of radio to blend into the natural environment, the medium has certain advantages over other communication devices. It is less expensive than television or direct mail. In light of spending limitations set by the Federal Election Campaign Acts of 1974 and 1976 (a candidate should spend no more than $20 million on a presidential campaign in 1976, whereas George McGovern had spent $30 million in 1972 just to lose), radio has taken on a greater role. Additionally radio is both a mass and minority channel. Differing radio stations cater to specialized audiences. Instead of scattering appeals over wide areas and audiences that are irrelevant to his campaign, a candidate targets the most likely kinds of responsive voters.

Radio comes into play during an election in several respects. In 1972, for instance, Richard Nixon had a series of thirty-minute radio talks as a major thrust of his campaign. There are also prerecorded one-minute and thirty-second spot commercials as well as recorded five-minute conversations with the candidate. These commercials are paid advertising that add to campaign costs. There are ways, however, of using radio to garner free public publicity. One technique is to prerecord a public statement by a candidate or to record an event at which a candidate appears (for example, to tape a brief statement with a candidate as he shakes hands with workers leaving an industrial plant). Cassettes of these "news stories" go via mail to small-town or small-wattage radio stations; some stations, especially if they do not have their own news staffs, add these stories to regular newscasts.

Over the years rules of thumb have been formulated for candidates preparing radio presentations: (1) pick a familiar central theme for the radio talk, (2) open the broadcast with an ear-catching statement or idea to hold listeners, (3) present the speech in a logical sequence with simple words and simple, declarative sentences, (4) use as few statistics as possible, and (5) reach a definite conclusion.

Boob Tube Politics.   Few approaches to campaign politics have been so widely discussed in recent years as campaigning by television. There now seems to be an inexhaustible supply of books detailing the uses, techniques, merits, and evils, and needed reforms of television campaigning.[58] Rather than repeat the details of that commentary here, it is preferable to focus upon a few questions that are uppermost in the understanding the changing role of television as a channel of persuasive communication.

First, *how widely used is television in modern campaigning?* We need no dollars and cents figures to convince us that television campaigning has flourished in the last two decades, but such data are available. By the 1968 presidential election, more than $28 million was spent on campaign broadcasting, the bulk of that devoted to television. There are suggestions, however, that television campaigning is leveling off as a growth stock. Candidates in the 1972 presidential campaign spent only about half as much on political broadcasting as contenders did in 1968. In part this was because of restrictions placed by the Federal Election Campaign Act of 1971. But federal limits were not the sole reason for lessened interest in television; in fact neither major party's candidates came within $2 million of spending what they were allowed to devote to political broadcasting in 1972. Apparently there is growing awareness that in some types of elections the rewards of television campaigning do not warrant the costs, that there are other ways of spending campaign dollars provide a greater vote return on the investment. Diamond, for example, reports a study undertaken by Roland Cole of campaign expenditures of all the major party U.S. Senate candidates in 1972. Cole found that more money went for TV and radio than any other campaign activity, yet only 20 percent of expenditures were for broadcasting; the greater emphasis was for means of achieving free media coverage and heavy voter canvassing, i.e., spending on staff, telephones, campaign materials, and special events.[59] In presidential primaries and elections for lesser offices, where candidates are not as well known as in presidential or senatorial elections, television remains a major way of achieving name recognition.

In sum, television is still widely used as a channel of campaign communication. This introduces a second question, namely, *how is television used for campaign persuasion?* Here there is a shift in emphasis. In the decades of the 1950s and 1960s the stress in television campaigning was on *image making,* using the medium to project selected attributes of a candidate. Image making via video incorporated a clear-cut strategy. It involved placing televised appeals during time periods to achieve a maximum viewing audience; using formats of entertainment programming (such as twenty-, thirty-, and sixty-second spot commercials rather than half-hour televised addresses, and slick, diverting half-hour documentaries introducing the human side of candidates); and stressing only points relevant to the desired image rather than wasting time on discussing complex issues. Although there were techniques to build images through free publicity (staging campaign events for news coverage, engaging in televised debates, etc.), the emphasis was on paid television advertising.

The 1970s have witnessed changes in the general approach to television campaigning. For one thing, although image-making is not foresworn, there is more emphasis on articulating and discussing campaign *issues.*

(In fact, or course, when designed by a skilled practitioner of television politics such as Robert Goodman, Joseph Napolitan, or any one of a number of advertising agencies, an issue focus helps to create images.) This leads to more five-minute presentations with the candidate speaking directly to an audience (as in the early televised campaign of George Wallace in 1976). And in the face of both spending limitations and rising television costs, there are greater efforts to get free coverage through television news, interview programs, and talk shows.

Finally, *to what extent do voters take televised appeals into account in making up their minds?* The evidence is mixed. Research in the 1960s, for instance, suggests that televised campaigning affects chiefly the votes of persons who are self-classified independents, identified either weakly or not at all with either major party. In this respect brief (twenty-and thirty-second) image making spots were superior to longer five-minute, issue-oriented presentations. Conventional wisdom was that television news did more to influence voters than paid advertising. More recent research challenges these earlier thoughts. There is now evidence that political advertising informs voters about issues and may even influence their decisions more than does television news;[60] and that five-minute commercials are as suitable for image making as for issue discussion, especially when it comes to building name recognition, recall of candidate attributes, and enhancing voter turnout.[61] In sum, political campaigners are reevaluating television as a communication channel. One suspects that the reappraisal will contribute to changing patterns for several years with respect to how much television pervades election campaigns, the formats and techniques employed, and impacts on voters.

Innovations.   New electronic means of communicating develop and political campaigners adapt them for persuasive purposes. Community antenna television, such as cable television or CATV, strikingly increases the number of available television channels and opportunities for appeals. Possibilities exist for round-the-clock programming on special channels brought into the home on CATV. Electronic video recordings open other possibilities. A candidate, for example, can supply vast numbers of constituents with recorded television appearances suitable for viewing at their leisure through playback on home television. Some candidates use mobile electronic studios (Paxmobiles) that roam from city to city, as did Republicans in the 1972 campaign; containing telephone banks, audio and video recording equipment, and other electronic gadgetry, these vans supply campaign workers with a wide variety of instantaneous communications. And who knows what opportunities lie ahead for politicians able to take subtle advantage of the increasingly popular citizen band (CB) radios? In campaigning for her husband in the 1976 presidential primaries in

Texas, for instance, Betty Ford used CB with the "handle" of "First Mama." Telephone, radio, and television have but opened the way for what will be even greater electronic campaigning in the future.

Interposing Print

Electronic gadgetry aside, the printed word remains a chief means for a political candidate to communicate with mass audiences. Campaign literature (flyers, brochures, photographs, etc.) is as much a part of contemporary politics as were political stump speakers in frontier days. Two types of print media are of particular importance—that delivered by direct mail and newspapers.

Direct Mail.   In recent years the direct mail industry has commanded increasing portions of the candidate's campaign budget. Various commercial firms conduct direct mail campaigns and a few—particularly Richard Viguerie, who has been employed by numerous candidates—specialize in regional and nationwide mailings during elections. Direct mail campaigns aim at (1) fund raising, (2) building a candidate's name recognition and image, and (3) appealing for votes. In employing Viguerie to handle direct mail before the 1976 presidential primaries, George Wallace contracted to pay $2.5 million for his services. The purpose was primarily to raise funds by soliciting small donations. Candidates including Representative Morris Udall, Senator Lloyd Bentsen, and Senator Henry Jackson also spent vast sums on mass mailings in 1976. Most achieved success, but the cost was high. To collect one dollar in contributions via mass mailings, candidates were spending about sixty-seven cents. A better return on an investment in fund raising, but one which taps the wealthy rather than the small contributor, was the fund-raising dinner and cocktail party; there only eight cents had to be spent to collect each dollar. When it comes to building images and influencing voters, direct mail is apparently even less rewarding. Robyn and Miller examined the effects of a general mailing to 72,000 persons in 1974. They found that direct mail had scant effects on voter's information levels, views of the candidate, voting intention in the election, or choice of candidate.[62] In sum, the payoffs from direct mail don't always justify the costs.

Newspapers.   Three types of newspaper content act as vehicles for campaign communication—news items, editorials, and advertising. All assist in image building and presentation of issues. Image making, however, is primary. In a study of news coverage of the 1968 presidential election in major metropolitan dailies, for example, Doris Graber found that the focus was far more on personal attributes of candidates than on issues.[63] Newspapers provide readers with stories that build impressions of a candidate's importance, credibility, character, style, and reputation through such devices as story placement, headlines, content, and amount of coverage devoted to respective office-seekers. Editorial endorsements are more issue oriented, yet they too speak eloquently or disdainfully of the personal qualities of candidates. When Humke and his colleagues analyzed political advertisements in newspapers, they found that the principal themes concerned the candidate rather than issues.[64] A more comprehensive study conducted in twenty-three states during the 1970 elections revealed that less than one-half of the assertions in political newspaper advertising refer to issues rather than to candidates or their party affiliations.[65]

Political advertising serves other functions beyond image making and issue presentation. Political ads in newspapers, as well as those distributed by leaflets, brochures, and direct mails, bolster the morale of campaign workers: at least they receive the impression that money is being spent. The ads also provide workers with copy to point to when trying to persuade the uncommitted. Moreover, political advertising in print media is one way to sneak in an occasional ad which is too objectional to be placed on radio or TV. Typical of this type of ad is one listing names of individuals allegedly endorsing a candidate. Since some campaigners list names of fictitious persons or noted citizens who have not given their permission, newspapers must always check the authenticity of such claims.[66]

Important in weighing the role of newspapers in political persuasion is the impact of newspaper endorsements upon how people vote. Current research suggests that voters pay more attention to editorial endorsements than once supposed. In light of the fact that from 1940 to 1960 one-half to two-thirds of U.S. dailies endorsed the Republican presidential candidate and only twice was a Republican elected (1952 and 1956), it was easy to assume that endorsements carried little weight. However, drawing upon a nationwide sampling of Americans surveyed in the 1972 presidential campaign, John Robinson challenged that assumption. Controlling for such variables as the fact that newspapers overwhelmingly endorsed Richard Nixon in that contest, for partisan affiliations of voters, and for other confounding variables, Robinson established a clear link between newspaper endorsements and voting behavior: voters exposed to pro-McGovern endorsements voted accordingly; those reading pro-Nixon endorsements voted for Nixon; and voters exposed to uncommitted newspapers or none at all divided between the two candidates.[67] These findings, when added to evidence of substantial influence of newspaper endorsements in local elections, indicate that the editorial component of the newspaper is a significant channel of campaign persuasion.[68]

Interposing Posters

The political poster is one of the most colorful and arresting of techniques of campaign communication. Scattered across the landscape in any election, on billboards, trees, telephone poles, barn roofs, and building walls, are examples of this form of political advertising. Gary Yanker calls political posters "Prop Art," art used for propagandistic purposes.[69] As with the other media of political campaigning, posters seek broad support for a candidate, party, and platform; announce forthcoming political meetings and party rallies; assist in fund raising; criticize the opposition; build name recognition for obscure candidates; and bolster spirits of campaign workers. Widely distributed posters with artwork that captures the idea and themes of a campaign are daily reminders of the appeals voters encounter through telephone calls, radio announcements, television spots, and newspaper ads. Posters thus help tie together the diverse threads of a persuasive campaign; at a cost of twenty-five cents per one thousand voters exposed to the message, posters perform a useful function relatively inexpensively.

Yanker describes how prop art attracts voters. First, there is a recognizable sign included as a distinguishing element of the poster picture such as a raised hand, a striking pose, or the candidate with his coat slung over his shoulder and shirt sleeves rolled up. Through repetition, this "pre-motif" (to use Yanker's term) becomes a dominant symbol, universally recognized as standing for something, such as informal, hardworking, exhuberant initiative in the candidate with rolled-up sleeves. The symbol then acts as the motif for all future political advertising. Yanker's description parallels our account of the stages of persuasion described in Chapter 4: the presentation of a message, its impinging on the attention of people, comprehension of the message, popular yielding to it (perhaps because people find the visual or spoken advertising esthetically pleasing), retention of the message, and compliance.[70]

For each of the media of mass campaign communication—telephone, radio, television, direct mail, newspapers, and posters—paid specialists adjust the medium to the needs of any candidate-client. Matthew A. Reese and Associates is but one firm directing campaigns to increase voter turnout by way of telephone contacts; Tony Schwartz is a specialist in radio use; many agencies compose newspaper political advertising. With respect to posters, Yanker describes specialists versed in the PLANT approach (Perception/Precinct Level Attitude-Normative Technique). PLANT is a means of testing how people respond to various elements in political advertising—symbols they recognize, remember, identify with, and respond to. Yanker notes that different kinds of voters respond to different kinds of colors: moderates and conservatives to blue, sophisticated urban voters to black and white; reformists to yellow; radicals to red.

Orange on blue and red on black are the best color combinations for identifying unknown candidates.[71] The validity of such findings is conjecturable. However, political advertising, whatever the medium, is not hit or miss, but a business for trained specialists. As paid technicians, advertisers constitute a set of key political communicators in modern persuasive campaigns.

The Interpersonal Campaign

As with a campaign waged through the mass media, campaigning at the interpersonal level involves both face to face and interposed communication. Face to face contacts are of three types. First are the personal appearances that a candidate (or his wife, close relatives, and key spokesmen) make in relatively informal settings. Many a candidate awakens early to arrive at 5:00 or 6:00 a.m. for the change in work shifts at an industrial plant and shake hands with entering and departing employees. Others fill up on quarts of caffein at coffee klatches in the homes of neighboring admirers. Gerald Ford, when he first ran for Congress, arose before dawn to visit farmers as they began their daily chores of milking, feeding the chickens, and gathering the eggs. And we should not ignore the many sessions candidates have with members of the press as a mode of interpersonal informal exchange.

Second, there is the campaign through the good offices of opinion leaders. Candidates cultivate the good will of local, state, and nationally recognized notables. The active support of reputable clergymen, hardware salesmen, grocers, physicians, and teachers may be more valuable than all the paid advertising one can muster on a limited budget. Finally, there are all those people who volunteer to canvass during a campaign: they visit each residence in each precinct on behalf of a candidate. "Volunteer" is sometimes a misnomer. Many campaign workers are truly volunteers who receive no monetary reward for their efforts; but campaigns also utilize paid volunteers (most notably the campaigns of Nelson Rockefeller when he sought the governorship of New York and the nomination of the Republican party for president).

Channels can be of the interposed variety at the interpersonal level just as in mass communication. The telephone, for example, is used not for phone calls simply to reach mass audiences, but for conversations between campaign workers, calls to journalists, and friendly discussions between friends, neighbors, and coworkers supporting or opposing particular candidates. Another form of interposed media consists of personal displays—lapel buttons, bumper stickers, yard signs, hats, pens, pencils, match covers, streamers, ribbons, and other novelties. Lest one underestimate the use of such campaign paraphernalia, consider that when he first ran for the U.S. Senate in 1961, Edward Kennedy's organization provided supporters with more than one-half million bumper stickers so that they could advertise their personal loyalties (or at least the loyalties of their automobiles). Jimmy Carter in 1976 was a latter day Johnny Appleseed, scattering not appleseeds but peanuts across the land.

The Organization Campaign

In campaigns for major statewide and federal offices, various organizations take part. One is the candidate's organization described at the beginning of this section. A second consists of various and numerous special interest organizations that hold positions, contribute funds and other resources, mobilize their members, and bring pressures upon office-seekers: labor unions, business associations, agriculture groups, civil rights organizations, consumer lobbies, environmentalists, and others. These special interest organizations are vital links between a candidate and the group's members. For instance, during the 1968 presidential campaign, Democrat Hubert Humphrey feared that many blue collar laborers would defect to the third party candidacy of George Wallace. Humphrey's forces relied heavily upon leaders of the American Federation of Labor and Congress of Industrial Organizations to persuade union members to return to the fold; the leadership of the AFL and CIO accomplished this via various channels—union newspapers, meetings of union locals, brochures, flyers, personal contact, etc.

A third organizational form exists especially for the political campaign—the endorsement group. To give the impression of broad popular support transcending partisan, occupational, and ethnic lines, political campaigners establish associations to endorse and work on behalf of their candidate. For example, to take advantage of potential Democratic defections from the candidacy of George McGovern in 1972 Republicans organized "Democrats for Nixon," a group led by a former Democratic governor of Texas and secretary of treasury in the Nixon cabinet, John Connally (who, after the election, switched to the Republican party). Connally, under the auspices of the organization, made a half-hour television appeal to all Democrats and independents to join him in "reelecting the president."

Finally, there is the chief organization of American politics, the political party. The channels of party communication consist of specific party offices and party contact with constituents. Precinct, district, state, and national committees and conventions are principal levels of party machinery channeling messages to party members and supporters. In addition the party provides speakers' bureaus and information offices on behalf of its candidates. In recent presidential elections, for example, Republicans have employed "truth squads," usually Republican congressional leaders who trail the Democratic presidential aspirant to rebut his partisan contentions.

Political parties carry their messages directly to voters by means of canvassing. The proportion of citizens contacted by party workers has increased from 17 percent who reported contact by one of the two major parties in the 1952 presidential election to approximately 30 percent in 1972.[72] Generally parties follow the rule of "hunting where the ducks are"; that is, each party restricts canvassing chiefly to the areas of known sympathizers rather than foraging into the opposition's territory. Party contact and greater support for the party makes the effort go together, at least in influencing independents and party sympathizers.[73]

Consequences of Persuasive Communication in Political Campaigns

It is presumptuous, given the current state of scientific findings, to say exactly how specific channels of campaign communication influence voters. As Blumer has written, "whatever influence is exerted by the presentations of mass media depends on the way in which people meet and handle such presentations." The same observation holds for interpersonal and organizational media. What in media presentations people take into account and how they use it in constructing political images are things we need to know, but scarcely do, with respect to the consequences of persuasive communication.[74]

The conclusions we draw here about the consequences of persuasive communication in political campaigns merely preview what will be said at greater length in Chapters 10 and 11 on the subject. At the cognitive level of beliefs, thoughts, and information we can distinguish between immediate and long-term political consequences. In the short run, people do learn about politics during election campaigns; they acquire information both about candidates and issues through media presentations.[75] In the longer term between elections, media presentations place items on the agenda of public debate, filter out the views of numerous political communicators regarding the way things are and should be, and present a mediated, second-hand picture of political affairs.[76]

At the affective level of political values, judgments, wishes, and desires, the consequences of persuasive communications are less clear. Do persuasive appeals change what we want or don't want, like or don't like? The consensus of a host of studies is that voters are less likely to change judgements as a result of persuasion than to acquire information that reinforces predilections. Consider, for instance, the images of competing candidates. Surveys conducted from 1952 to 1972 suggest that people learn new things about political candidates as a campaign progresses, but they seldom translate that into more positive or negative feelings. The cognitive rather than affective dimension of candidate images shifts as a result of campaign communication.[77]

And, studies of voting in presidential elections since World War II strongly suggest that only a minority of persons decide whom to vote for (the conative dimension of images) as a result of the political campaign. On the whole, 40 percent of voters make up their minds before the nominating conventions, 25 percent once the candidates are nominated, and 35 percent during the presidential campaign. This 40-25-35 rule, derived from the study of presidential contests, cannot be generalized to local and state elections, party primaries, or nonpartisan elections. Moreover, the 40 percent who make up their minds prior to presidential nominating conventions do so primarily because of their party affiliations; as emotional ties to both political parties lessen (see Chapter 11) we may expect departures from the 40-25-35 pattern.

Finally, John Carey offers the view that the impact of political communication in electoral campaigns may depend less on how individual voters respond than on how the media shape the campaign and the actions of the campaigners. Carey reports that his study demonstrates that the news media focus sharply upon campaign tactics and evaluate candidates on the basis of their competence as tacticians. Politicians respond by engaging in "metacampaigns," attempts to demonstrate competence as campaign organizers, strategists, and tacticians. Instead of campaigning directly to and with voters, in other words, candidates play indirectly to voters by performing for the benefit of the media. Instead of proving to voters they would be good officeholders, they prove to the media that they are competent office-seekers.[78]

Carey's viewpoint raises the important question of the role played by the news media in political communication. It is to that role that we now turn by exploring the dimensions of government-press relations in American politics.

BIBLIOGRAPHY

Readers will find three general works particularly helpful in obtaining an overall picture of the various channels of communication. In *Communications and Media* (New York: Hastings House, 1975), George N. Gordon discusses channels of communication from several perspectives—the technology, media, audiences, economics, and legal considerations involved. John C. Merrill and Ralph L. Lowenstein in *Media, Messages and Men* (New York: David McKay Co., Inc., 1971) provide a very readable account of the elements and development of mass media channels, characteristics of communicators and audiences, and various problems associated with media ethics. J. L. Aranguren's *Human Communication* (New York: World University Library, 1967) is introductory in nature; Part 2 contains a detailed discussion of communication channels considered from a sociological viewpoint.

There are almost more works available discussing mass communication than one cares to count. One of the most succinct discussions is Charles R. Wright's *Mass Communication* (New York: Random House, 1959), now available in a second edition. Wright formulates a definition of mass communication that has become almost standard, then goes on to analyze mass media from a functionalist perspective. Wright's interest is that of a sociologist, as is that of most of the contributors to Denis McQuail's edited volume, *Sociology of Mass Communications* (Baltimore: Penguin Books, 1972). An excellent introduction to mass communication theories is a brief volume (172 pp.) by Melvin L. DeFleur, *Theories of Mass Communication* (New York: David McKay Co., Inc., 2nd ed., 1970). DeFleur presents information concerning the historical development of the media, the nature of the communicative act, and leading media theories—individual differences, social categories, social relationships, and cultural norm theories. For readers wishing to delve further into a few of the specific theories of mass communication discussed in Chapter 5, a good starting place is Marshall McLuhan's *Understanding Media: The Extensions of Man* (New York: The New American Library, 1964). Two volumes which summarize information theories of the media are J. R. Pierce, *Symbols, Signals and Noise* (New York: Harper and Row, 1961) and Colin Cherry, *On Human Communication* (New York: Science Editions, Inc., 1961). In contrast to information theory, William Stephenson formulates his play approach in *The Play Theory of Mass Communication* (Chicago: University of Chicago Press, 1967), a volume particularly recommended for those readers interested not only in the play theory but also in the nature of mass advertising, convergent selectivity, and mass opinion as contrasted with propaganda and public opinion.

Three brief texts offer readable introductions to the character of interpersonal communication. The first, Stewart L. Tubbs and Sylvia Moss, *Human Communication: An Interpersonal Perspective* (New York: Random House, 1974), is the more comprehensive in content. Also comprehensive, but more stimulating, is William A. Wilmot, *Dyadic Communication: A Transactional Perspective* (Reading, Mass.: Addison-Wesley, 1975). Also provocative is Matthew Speier, *How to Observe Face-to-Face Communication: A Sociological Introduction* (Pacific Palisades, Cal.: Goodyear Publishing Co., 1973). Speier offers a method people can use to increase their awareness of the social implications of everyday communication, a method drawing upon phenomenological and ethnomethodological assumptions (see Appendix). The relationship between interpersonal communication and opinion leadership is developed in Elihu Katz and Paul F. Lazarsfeld, *Personal Influence* (New York: The Free Press of Glencoe, 1955). Interpersonal communication has been examined most extensively from social psychological perspectives. Two valuable introductions are Kenneth J. Gergen, *The Psychology of Behavior Exchange* (Reading, Mass.: Addison-Wesley Publishing Co., 1969) and Richard C. Carson, *Interaction Concepts of Personality* (Chicago: Aldine Publishing Co., 1969). Also highly recommended is Paul Watzlawick et al., *Pragmatics of Human Communication* (New York: W. W. Norton and Co., Inc., 1967). Interpersonal communication is the focus of two popular best sellers of recent years: Eric Berne, *Games People Play* (New York: Grove Press, 1964) and Thomas A. Harris, *I'm OK, You're OK* (New York: Harper and Row, 1967).

The subject of organizational communication has spawned relatively few works devoted solely to it. An introduction to most of the key issues involving organizational communication is W. Charles Redding, *Communication Within the Organization* (New York: Industrial Communication Council, Inc., 1972); appended to the book is an excellent bibliography of related works. Another is Richard V. Farace et al., *Communicating and Organizing* (Reading, Mass.: Addison-Wesley, 1977). See also Harold Guetzkow's discussion, "Communications in Organizations," which is Chapter 12 in J. G. March, ed., *Handbook of Organizations* (Chicago: Rand McNally, 1955). How government organizations communicate with the public is the subject of two references: O. J. Firestone, *The Political Persuader: Government Advertising* (Toronto: Methuen, 1970) and the essay prepared by Elihu Katz and Brenda Danet, "Communication Between

Bureaucracy and the Public," Chapter 21 in Ithiel de Sola Pool and Wilbur Schramm, eds., *Handbook of Communication* (Chicago: Rand McNally and Co., 1973).

There are several works now available that describe the use of communication channels in political campaigns. A few of these report the actual experiences of political consultants: Joseph Napolitan, *The Election Game and How to Win It* (Garden City, N.Y.: Doubleday and Co., 1972); Gene Wyckoff, *The Image Candidates* (New York: The Macmillan Co., 1968); Hal Evry, *The Selling of a Candidate* (Los Angeles: Western Opinion Research Center, 1971) and Tony Schwartz, *The Responsive Chord* (Garden City, N.Y.: Anchor Books/Doubleday, 1974). Journalists have written their accounts of political communication in campaigns. One of the most widely read was Joe McGinniss, *The Selling of the President 1968* (New York: Trident Press, 1968). Readers will also find portions of Edwin Diamond's *The Tin Kazoo* (Cambridge: The MIT Press, 1975) entertaining. Social scientists also have examined the relationship of the media to elections. For a sampling see Kurt Lang and Gladys Engel Lang, *Politics and Television* (Chicago: Quadrangle Books, 1968); Harold Mendelsohn and Irving Crespi, *Polls, Television, and the New Politics* (San Francisco: Chandler Publishing Co., 1970); Dan Nimmo, *The Political Persuaders* (Englewood Cliffs, N.J.: Prentice-Hall, Inc., 1970); and James C. Strouse, *The Mass Media, Public Opinion, and Public Policy Analysis* (Columbus, Ohio: Bobbs-Merrill Publishing Co., 1975).

Increased interest in the effects of political communication on voting behavior has produced several significant works in recent years. Three that should not be overlooked are Sidney Kraus and Dennis Davis, *The Effects of Mass Communication on Political Behavior* (University Park: The Pennsylvania State University Press, 1976); take particular note of the abstracts and bibliographies following each chapter. Also valuable are Harold Mendelsohn and Garrett J. O'Keefe, *The People Choose a President* (New York: Praeger, 1976) and Thomas E. Patterson and Robert D. McClure, *The Unseeing Eye* (New York: G.P. Putnam's Sons, 1976).

NOTES

1.   For a discussion of the relationship between various techniques, media, and channels of communication, see George N. Gordon, *Communications and Media* (New York: Hastings House, 1975). Definitions of the notion of channels can be found in Reed H. Blake and Edwin O. Haroldsen, *A Taxonomy of Concepts in Communication* (New York: Hastings House, Publishers, 1975), p. 14, and Wilbur Schramm, "Channels and Audiences," in Ithiel de Sola Pool and Wilbur Schramm, eds., *Handbook of Communication* (Chicago: Rand McNally College Publishing Co., 1973), p. 116.

2.   George Miller, *The Psychology of Communication* (New York: Basic Books, Inc., 1967), p. 47.

3.   Tamotsu Shibutani, *Improvised News* (Indianapolis: The Bobbs-Merrill Co., Inc., 1966), p. 21 (emphasis in original).

4.   Charles Wright, *Mass Communication: A Sociological Perspective* (New York: Random House, 1959), pp. 13–16.

5.   John C. Merrill and Ralph L. Lowenstein, *Media, Message, and Men* (New York: David McKay and Co., Inc., 1971), pp. 18–32.

6. Ibid., pp. 33–41.

7. Gary Gumpert, "The Rise of Mini-Comm," in Jean N. Civikly, ed., *Messages* (New York: Random House, 1974), pp. 296–305.

8. James W. Carey, "The Communications Revolution and the Professional Communicator," in Paul Halmos, ed., *The Sociology of Mass Media Communications* (Keele, Staffordshire: University of Keele, 1969), pp. 23, 38.

9. Ibid., p. 27.

10. See Harold A. Innis, *The Bias of Communication* (Toronto: University of Toronto Press, 1951); the single best interpretative commentary is James W. Carey, "Harold Adams Innis and Marshall McLuhan," *Antioch Review* (Spring 1967): 5–39.

11. Marshall McLuhan, *Understanding Media: The Extensions of Man* (New York: Signet Books, 1964); also see Carey, "Harold Adams Innis and Marshall McLuhan."

12. Horace M. Kallen, ed., *The Philosophy of William James* (New York: The Modern Library, 1925), p. 77 (emphasis in original).

13. Anthony Schillaci, "The Now Movie: Film as Environment," *Saturday Review*, 51 (December 28, 1968): 9.

14. Wilbur Schramm, "Information Theory and Mass Communication," *Journalism Quarterly*, 32 (Spring 1955): 134.

15. William Stephenson, *The Play Theory of Mass Communication* (Chicago: University of Chicago Press, 1967), p. 60.

16. Murray Edelman, *Politics as Symbolic Action* (Chicago: Markham Publishing Co., 1971), pp. 34–41.

17. Karl Erik Rosengren and Swen Windahl, "Mass Media Consumption as a Functional Alternative," in Denis McQuail, ed., *Sociology of Mass Communications* (Baltimore: Penguin Books, 1972), pp. 166–194; Donald Horton and R. Richard Wohl, "Mass Communication and Para-Social Interaction," *Psychiatry*, 19 (1956): 215–229.

18. Elihu Katz, et al., "Uses and Gratifications Research," *Public Opinion Quarterly*, 37 (Winter 1973–1974): 509–523; Jay G. Blumler and Elihu Katz, *The Uses of Mass Communications* (Beverly Hills: Sage Publications, 1974).

19. Denis McQuail, et al., "The Television Audience: A Revised Perspective," in McQuail, ed., *The Sociology of Mass Communications*, pp. 135–165.

20. Richard J. Hill and Charles M. Bonjean, "News Diffusion: A Test of the Regularity Hypothesis," *Journalism Quarterly*, 41 (Summer 1964): 342. See also Elihu Katz and Paul F. Lazarsfeld, *Personal Influence* (New York: The Free Press of Glencoe, 1955), pp. 32–34; Steven N. Chaffee, "The Interpersonal Context of Mass Communication," in F. Gerald Kline and Phillip J. Tichenor, eds., *Current Perspectives in Mass Communication Research* (Beverly Hills, Cal.: Sage Publications, 1972), pp. 95–120 and Chaffee, "The Diffusion of Political Information," in Chaffee, ed., *Political Communication* (Beverly Hills, Cal.: Sage Publications, 1975), pp. 88–92.

21. Lyman E. Ostlund, "Interpersonal Communication Following McGovern's Eagleton Decision," *Public Opinion Quarterly*, 37 (Winter 1973–1974): 601–610; see, however, Percy H. Tannebaum and Bradley S. Greenberg, "Mass Communication," in Paul R. Farnsworth, ed., *The Annual Review of Psychology*, Vol. 19 (1968): 315–386; and David R. Segal, "Communication About the Military: People and Media in the Flow of Events," *Communication Research* 2 (January 1975): 68–78.

22. Harold D. Lasswell and Abraham Kaplan, *Power and Society* (New Haven: Yale University Press, 1950), p. 110.

23. Matthew Speier, *How to Observe Face-to-Face Communication* (Pacific Palisades, Cal.: Goodyear Publishing Co., 1973).

24.   Jack M. McLeod and Steven H. Chaffee, "Interpersonal Approaches to Communication Research," *American Behavioral Scientist,* 16 (March/April 1973):469–501.

25.   Paul Watzlawick, et al., *Pragmatics of Human Communication* (New York: W. W. Norton and Co., Inc., 1967), Ch. 2.

26.   Robert C. Carson, *Interaction Concepts of Personality* (Chicago: Aldine Publishing Co., 1969).

27.   Stewart L. Tubbs and Sylvia Moss, *Human Communication: An Interpersonal Perspective* (New York: Random House, 1974), pp. 307–309.

28.   Stanford M. Lyman and Marvin B. Scott, *A Sociology of the Absurd* (New York: Appleton-Century-Crofts, 1970); Eric Berne, *Games People Play* (New York: Grove Press, 1964); John C. Condon, "When People Talk with People," in Civikly, eds., *Messages,* pp. 27–40.

29.   *A Sociology of the Absurd,* Ch. 2.

30.   Timothy Leary, *Interpersonal Diagnosis of Personality: A Functional Theory and Methodology for Personality Evaluation* (New York: The Ronald Press, 1957); Uriel G. Foa, "New Developments in Facet Design and Analysis," *Psychological Review,* 72 (1965): 262–274.

31.   Doris Kearns, "Who *Was* Lyndon Baines Johnson?" *The Atlantic,* 237 (May 1976): 48.

32.   Watzlawick, et al., *Pragmatics of Human Communication,* pp. 86–90; John W. Kinch, "A Formalized Theory of the Self-Concept," in Civikly, ed., *Messages,* pp. 118–125; Thomas A. Harris, *I'm OK, You're OK* (New York: Harper and Row, Publishers, 1967).

33.   John W. Thibaut and Harold H. Kelley, *The Social Psychology of Groups* (New York: John Wiley and Sons, Inc., 1959); Carson, *Interaction Concepts of Personality,* Ch. 5.

34.   Paul F. Lazarsfeld, et al., *The People's Choice* (New York: Columbia University Press, 1948), pp. 137–139.

35.   Everett M. Rogers, "Mass Media and Interpersonal Communication," in Pool and Schramm, eds., *Handbook of Communication,* pp. 300–303.

36.   Daniel Lerner, *The Passing of Traditional Society* (London: The Free Press of Glencoe, 1958), pp. 49–52.

37.   Sidney M. Jourard, *Self-Disclosure: The Experimental Investigation of the Transparent Self* (New York: John Wiley and Sons, Inc., 1971).

38.   W. Barnett Pearce and Stewart M. Sharp, "Self-Disclosing Communication," *Journal of Communication,* 23 (December 1973): 426–445.

39.   For detailed discussions of other factors see Dean C. Barnlund, ed., *Interpersonal Communication: Survey and Studies* (Boston: Houghton Mifflin Co., 1968); R. D. Laing et al., *Interpersonal Perception* (New York: Harper and Row, 1966).

40.   See James Q. Wilson, *Political Organizations* (New York: Basic Books, Inc., 1973).

41.   Anthony Downs, *Inside Bureaucracy* (Boston: Little, Brown and Co., 1967).

42.   James E. Grunig, "A Multi-Systems Theory of Organizational Communication," *Communication Research,* 2 (April 1975): 99–136.

43.   Peter K. Manning, "Talking and Becoming: A View of Organizational Socialization," paper delivered to the Missouri Academy of Sciences, Columbia, Missouri, April, 1966.

44.   Richard M. Cyert and Kenneth R. MacCrimmon, "Organizations," in Gardner Lindzey and Elliot Aronson, eds., *The Handbook of Social Psychology,* Vol. 1 (Reading, Mass.: Addison-Wesley Publishing Co., 1968), pp. 581–583.

45.   Herbert Simon, et al., *Public Administration* (New York: Alfred A. Knopf, 1959) pp. 222–226.

46.   Downs, *Inside Bureaucracy,* pp. 113–115.

47. Simon, et al., *Public Administration*, p. 231.

48. Victor Thompson, *Modern Organization* (New York: Alfred A. Knopf, 1961), Ch. 7.

49. Downs, *Inside Bureaucracy*, p. 269.

50. Ernest Gellhorn, "Adverse Publicity by Administrative Agencies," report to the Administrative Conference of the United States, Washington, D.C., April 15, 1973.

51. "Communication Between Bureaucracy and the Public: A Review of the Literature," in Pool and Schramm, eds., *Handbook of Communication*, pp. 667–670.

52. W. Charles Redding, *Communication Within the Organization* (New York: Industrial Communication Council, Inc., 1972).

53. Dan Nimmo, *The Political Persuaders* (Englewood Cliffs, N.J.: Prentice-Hall, Inc., 1970).

54. Ellul, *Propaganda* (New York: Alfred A. Knopf, 1965), p. 19.

55. See Joseph Napolitan, *The Election Game and How to Win It* (Garden City, New York: Doubleday and Co., 1972).

56. Schramm, "Channels and Audiences," pp. 118–119.

57. Tony Schwartz, *The Responsive Chord* (Garden City, N.Y.: Anchor Books, 1974).

58. For a sampling see Edwin Diamond, *The Tin Kazoo* (Cambridge: The MIT Press, 1975); Joe McGinniss, *The Selling of the President 1968* (New York: Trident Press, 1969); Gene Wyckoff, *The Image Candidates* (New York: The Macmillan Co., 1968); Kurt Lang and Gladys Engel Lang, *Politics and Television* (Chicago: Quadrangle Books, Inc., 1968); Napolitan, *The Election Game*; Nimmo, *The Political Persuaders*, Ch. 4.

59. Diamond, *The Tin Kazoo*, p. 10.

60. Robert D. McClure and Thomas E. Patterson, "Television News and Political Advertising," *Communication Research*, 1 (January 1974): 3–31.

61. Lynda Lee Kaid, "Political Television Commercials: An Experimental Study of Type and Length," paper presented to the Political Communication Division, International Communication Association, Chicago, Ill., April, 1975.

62. Roy E. Miller and Dorothy L. Robyn, "A Field Study of Direct Mail in a Congressional Primary Campaign: What Effects Last Until Election Day?," *Experimental Study of Politics*, 4 (December 1974): 1–37.

63. Doris A. Graber, "Personal Qualities in Presidential Images: The Contribution of the Press," *Midwest Journal of Political Science*, 16 (February 1972): 46–76.

64. Ronald Gene Humke, et al., "Candidates, Issues and Party in Newspaper Political Advertisements," *Journalism Quarterly*, 52 (Autumn 1975): 499–504.

65. Thomas A. Bowers, "Issue and Personality Information in Newspaper Political Advertising," *Journalism Quarterly*, 49 (Autumn 1972): 446–452.

66. See Kenneth G. Sheinkopf, et al., "The Functions of Political Advertising for Campaign Organizations," *Journal of Marketing Research*, 9 (November 1971): 401–405; Scheinkopf, et al., "How Political Party Workers Respond to Political Advertising," *Journalism Quarterly*, 50 (Summer 1973): 334–339; and Scheinkopf, "Politicians Use Print Media for Most Objectional Ads," *Editor and Publisher*, (April 1, 1972): 17–18.

67. "The Press as King-Maker: What Surveys From Last Five Campaigns Show," *Journalism Quarterly*, 51 (Winter 1974): 587–594, 606.

68. Paul L. Hain, "How an Endorsement Affected a Non-Partisan Mayor Vote," *Journalism Quarterly*, 52 (Summer 1975): 337–340; James E. Gregg, "Newspaper Editorial Endorsements and California Elections," *Journalism Quarterly*, 42 (Autumn 1965): 532–538.

69.   Garry Yanker, *Prop Art* (New York: Darien House, Inc., 1972).

70.   Compare the stages in the persuasive process described in Harold D. Lasswell and Abraham Kaplan, *Power and Society* (New Haven: Yale University Press, 1950), pp. 112–113.

71.   *Prop Art,* p. 68.

72.   Dan Nimmo and Robert L. Savage, *Candidates and Their Images* (Pacific Palisades, Calif.: Goodyear Publishing Co., 1976), Ch. 6.

73.   John H. Kessel, *The Goldwater Coalition* (New York: The Bobbs-Merrill Co., Inc., 1968), pp. 287–289; Ted Bartell and Sandra Bouxsein, "The Chelsea Project: Candidate Preference, Issue Preference, and Turnout Effects of Student Canvassing," *Public Opinion Quarterly,* 37 (Summer 1973):268–275; John C. Blydenburgh, "A Controlled Experiment to Measure the Effects of Personal Contact Campaigning," *Midwest Journal of Political Science,* 15 (May 1971): 365–381; Gerald H. Kramer, "The Effects of Precinct-Level Canvassing on Voting Behavior," *Public Opinion Quarterly,* 34 (Winter 1970–1971): 560–573; Michael Lupfer and David E. Price, "On the Merits of Face-to-Face Campaigning," *Social Science Quarterly,* 53 (December 1972): 534–543; David E. Price and Michael Lupfer, "Volunteers for Gore: The Impact of a Precinct-Level Canvass in Three Tennessee Cities," *Journal of Politics,* 35 (May 1973): 410–438; William J. Crotty, "Party Effort and Its Impact on the Vote," *American Political Science Review,* 65 (June 1971): 439–450.

74.   Herbert Blumer, "Suggestions for the Study of Mass Media Effects," in Eugene Burdick and Arthur J. Brodbeck, eds., *American Voting Behavior* (Glencoe: The Free Press, 1959), p. 201.

75.   For a review see Maxwell E. McCombs, "Mass Communication in Political Campaigns: Information, Gratification, and Persuasion," in Kline and Tichenor, eds., *Current Perspectives on Mass Communication Research,* pp. 169–194, and Garrett J. O'Keefe, "Political Campaigns and Mass Communication Research," in Chaffee, ed., *Political Communication,* Ch. 4.

76.   Lee B. Becker, et al., "The Development of Political Cognitions," in Chaffee, ed., *Political Communication,* Ch. 1.

77.   Nimmo and Savage, *Candidates and Their Images,* Chs. 2 and 6.

78.   "How Media Shapes Campaigns," *Journal of Communication,* 26 (Spring 1976): 50–57.

chapter 6

Political News: Government and Press as Sources and Channels of Political Communication

People learn political goings-on from a variety of mass, interpersonal, and organizational media. On a day to day basis Americans rely heavily upon the press for their political information, information they receive in the form of news. The term "press" designates all of the news media, not only newspapers, newsmagazines, and related printed material. It extends to radio and television newscasts, documentaries, and all other organized means of relaying political information to mass audiences. We described in the last chapter how one breed of political communicators, politicians running for office, make wide use of the various news media for persuasive purposes. Once in office politicians continue to use the press as a vital means for communicating with citizens. We now examine the relationships between two sets of political communicators, public officials and journalists. Those relationships form a network involving officials in roles of news sources, journalists as communication channels. The resultant source-channel transactions constitute government-press relations. We explore that network with respect to the nature of political news, the role of the press in making news and of government in managing news, and the consequences of the newsmaking-management process for political communication.

What Is News?

Since news is the basis of so much political information people receive, it is a good idea to begin with asking what news is, look at what others have said, and attempt a tentative characterization of our own.

Alternative Views

In his analysis of the professional communicator in modern societies, James Carey depicts journalism as creative and imaginative working with symbols. A journalist "sizes up situations, names their elements, structure and outstanding ingredients and names them in a way that contains an attitude toward them."[1] Through naming the journalist makes news: like the third umpire in the anecdote related in Chapter 3 the reporter can say, "they ain't nothin' 'til I calls 'em." But to say news is what newspersons call it, is to choose but one of many proffered definitions.[2] The definition suffers from the obvious problem that it opens the way to having as many definitions of what is and is not news as there are journalists to make them. The result is a probable lack of consensus on how to draw the distinction between news and nonnews.

Another approach is to define news operationally as simply what the press publishes, broadcasts, or otherwise disseminates. This definition is also bothersome, for there is no specification of the standards for news that every journalist (or even a large portion) use for what they do.[3] It is easy enough to ask newspeople what criteria they use; when asked, they readily respond. A study of 35 members of the Washington press corps conducted in the early 1960s pinpointed the characteristics cited by journalists as features of a good news story: accuracy, comprehensiveness, interest to a reader, usefulness to a reader, and topicality.[4] A former managing editor of the *The New York Times* underscored the importance of topicality when he said, "News is anything you find out today that you didn't know before."[5] News, in short, is new—in August 1974 President Nixon's announced resignation was news; today it is not. Yet there remains a problem, which is that too often, stated criteria do not match what newspersons do; the contents of the news media are sometimes stale, inaccurate, partial, boring, and useless. Do we, therefore, watch what journalists say or what they do?

Still another approach to defining news is to shift from what news personnel say and do and depict news as what news organizations dictate. Following this line of thought involves two considerations. One is that news is what is permitted by the economics of the news business and the news organization's competitive position in it. Advertisers want to reach large audiences, so goes the argument; to do that a news medium must provide a salable product. News, then, is what sells newspapers, raises the audience ratings of newscasts, and produces advertising revenue. But what is that? Again the criteria are vague. What sells *Time* magazine may be a photograph of Cher on the cover; is that news? Is Walter Cronkite news? If reports of crime, violence, and mayhem sell newspapers to some readers, will they do so to all? Or are the gossip and exposés in the *National Enquirer* sufficient? Perhaps news is what Ann Landers advises or Dick Tracy and Steve Canyon do? Added to economics is a second consideration which pertains to technological matters. On any given day what is news on television may simply be anything it is possible to present visually in a thirty-minute period (minus commercials). For a newspaper, news is limited to the size of the day's news hole. But how are these decisions for filling time and space made, and on the basis of what criteria?

Without difficulty we could multiply definitions of news several times: news is not what all newspersons agree on, but what key functionaries in the press, "gatekeepers" such as influential correspondents, news editors, and wire editors, transmit:[6] or news is what journalists learn to agree on through socializing experience in the newsroom;[7] or news is what newsmen think interests their imagined audiences.[8] We need not go on. The point is clear that there is no agreed definition of news. At one and the same time news is all and none of these: what newspersons say, do, and sell within a framework of institutional, economic, technological, social, and psychological constraints. There are no criteria of what news is because news is not a fixed thing or a product; rather, news is the process of newsmaking.

News as Newsmaking

In a classic commentary on the nature of news written in 1922, Walter Lippmann designated the key phases in an ongoing process that continuously defines news. There are, he wrote, "circumstances in all their sprawling complexity, the overt act which signalizes them, the stereotyped bulletin which publishes the signal, and the meaning the reader himself injects, after he has derived that meaning from the experience which directly affects him."[9] Subsequent analyses have refined Lippmann's description, but its essential character is intact: news is a process (newsmaking) of negotiating meaningful reports of happenings.[10] It involves symbolizing (1) happenings and occurrences as events—the "overt act" that signals "circumstances in all their sprawling complexity"; (2) events as newsworthy through news and news stories—the "stereotyped bulletin which publishes the signal"; and (3) newsworthy events as meaningful to people in making adjustments in their lives—"the meaning the reader himself injects, after he has derived that meaning from the experience which directly affects him."

Happenings as Events

Happenings are all the things that go on in the world whether we are aware of them or not. Persons go about their daily chores; planes fly, automobiles move along expressways; and as humorist Will Rogers intoned, the grass grows and the water flows. To the extent that the vast bulk of happenings occur with little or no notice, they are routine. But now and then, to borrow the title of Joseph Heller's best selling novel, "something happens" that breaks the normal routine of life, something that is unusual, perhaps even shockingly extraordinary. People die, planes crash, autos collide, there are famines and droughts. Things are no longer routine; situations are problematic. We take these unusual happenings into account and they become occurrences, cognized happenings that mark shifts from the routine.[11] When these are important to several people, so important that people begin collectively to think and talk about them, there is a social redefinition. People interpret them as events, as meaningful in their experience. They demand more information about these events so that they can adjust to these nonroutine happenings that have assumed added importance.

Events as Newsworthy

An event becomes newsworthy when people deem information about it to be important; news, says Shibutani, "is more or less urgent information that men need in making adjustments to changed circumstances; it is sought, even at great sacrifice, because of the necessity of getting one's bearings in a rapidly changing world.[12] Here enters the journalist as a communicator who creates, by way of negotiating with the parties to an event and all potentially interested audiences, a meaningful construction of what happened. The reporter's account is not truth, nor is it rumor; rather it is a reality constructed for the practical purpose of relieving uncertainties in a nonroutine situation.

Newsworthy Events as News Stories

Molotch and Lester describe how an event becomes newsworthy. The process involves three sets of people. These are, first, persons who promote an event for some purpose, i.e., promoters such as described in Chapter 2; thus a political candidate's press agent promotes personal appearances as newsworthy, or a president holds press conferences to make news. Second, there are people who assemble and select information about the event (people choosing what to report and what not), the journalists. And, third, there are the consumers of the account—readers, viewers, etc. Using this classification Molotch and Lester classify news stories in four types: (1) routine stories are events that become news chiefly because persons involved in the happenings promote them into events, as when president Gerald Ford visited China in 1975 along with a full complement of press aides and representatives of the news media; (2) accidents are reports of unintended happenings promoted not by the parties to the happening but by assemblers largely independent of the persons involved in the happening, as when journalists reported information of Senator Edward Kennedy's automobile accident and the death of Mary Jo Kopechne in July, 1969; (3) scandals are happenings involving intent, but the reports are not promoted by those involved; the Watergate affair that disgraced a president pops readily to mind; (4) events of serendipity arise from unplanned happenings that a promoter endeavors to disguise as routine, as when U.S. setbacks during the Vietnam war were accounted for by military information officers as "routine withdrawals."[13]

Political events lead to all four types of stories; the bulk are routine but there are also stories of an accidental, scandalous, and serendipity nature. Any of the four types may be further labeled, as they are by newspersons, in other ways.[14] For example *hard news* concerns both unscheduled and prescheduled events, something that occurs unexpectedly (an assassination attempt) as well as a planned event (a political rally). The "hardness" refers to the quality of reporting the event in factual ways: the content of a president's off-the-cuff remarks or a prereleased State of the Union message. *Soft news,* in contrast, pertains primarily to unscheduled events reported for human interest quality, such as when First Lady Betty Ford, during her visit to China with the president in 1975, kicked off her shoes and danced with a group of school girls.

A second distinction is between spot and developing news. Both involve unscheduled events. *Spot news* is the initial, quick report of an event such as a bulletin unbacked by further elaboration or detail (the "breaking story"); *developing news* is an account that evolves over a long period. The first announcement of the assassination attempt against George Wallace in 1972 was spot news; in the hours that followed the story developed as reporters learned more of the identity of the person involved in the shooting and of Wallace's condition.

Finally, in contrast to unscheduled spot news and developing events as news, there is *continuing news,* a series of stories on the same subject based upon events occurring over a period of time. The continuing news story consists of a running coverage of separate events, piecing them together within the context of a unifying theme. Such a running account of events deemed newsworthy sustains the attention of an audience while serving the personal and corporate interests of the reporter, news organization, and other parties involved by winning bylines, increased circulation, and publicity. The continuing news story of the early 1960s was the civil rights movement; of 1967, unrest and violence in America's urban ghettos; of the late 1960s and early 1970s, Vietnam; of 1972 through 1974, Watergate; of 1975, investigations into operations of U.S. intelligence agencies; of 1976, the presidential election. Primary and general election campaigns are, of course, always subjects of continuing news.

News, Truth, and Rumor

News, then, is a meaningful account of an event, an account involving the choices of several persons (principally newspersons) who make selections that name, interpret, and give shape to occurrences. The definition of news, then, like the definition of any other word or symbol, is inherently political because it involves people making choices and, where there are conflicting selections, negotiating collective understandings. Joining Sigal, we think it advisable to distinguish between choices and decisions.[15] Decisions imply a conscious weighing of issues by people; choices are less calculated and involve selections from a variety of options, selections made under conditions of uncertainty regarding the precise consequences of choosing one alternative over another.

Because newsmaking involves the choices of many people, choices that frequently do not examine the underlying factors in an event, news must be distinguished from truth. The function of truth, wrote Lippmann, "is to bring to light the hidden facts, to set them into relation with each other, and make a picture of the reality on which men can act." News has a different function, "to signalize an event" in ways people find meaningful in their daily experience. News, said Lippman, is but a report extracted from a "sea of possible truths."[16] Men can and do act on the basis of news, but without foreknowledge of the hidden consequences of doing so.

If news is not truth, neither is it rumor. Rumor, however, serves a purpose similar to news. Thus Shibutani defines rumor as communication through which people caught together in an ambiguous situation attempt to construct a meaningful interpretation. In that sense, rumor is a form of news. But, says Shibutani, rumor actually is a substitute for news. When institutionalized channels for communication such as the press fail to provide information to help people remove ambiguity and reduce uncertainty, persons collectively satisfy their demand for news by constructing rumors.[17]

Perhaps the best way to think of news, truth, and rumor is that they are all derived from people's efforts to deal with the unexpected. In the process of making the unexpected routine, the credibility of the report—whether people believe it rather than its actual truth or falsity—is crucial. We act on the basis of our beliefs, values, and expectations, not always upon demonstrated truths.

MAKING POLITICAL NEWS: THE NEWSGATHERING ROLE OF THE PRESS

The process of political newsmaking develops through the overlap of a variety of influences. In this section we examine those derived from the activities of the press, specifically the influence of news organizations, the relationship between reporters and officials, newsgathering processes, and the presentation of news. In the following section we turn to a second key facet in the process of transforming events into political news, how governments manage information.

Organization Influences

A news organization is a corporate enterprise whose personnel collect, edit, and disseminate accounts and evaluations of events.[18] Although not so bureaucratic as typical government agencies described in Chapter 5, news organizations possess bureaucratic characteristics. Many news organizations are large, complex structures; certainly this is the case for the major radio and television networks (the National Broadcasting Company, Columbia Broadcasting System, and American Broadcasting Company), metropolitan dailies including the *New York Times* and *Washington Post,* and weekly news magazines such as *Time* and *Newsweek.* Each structure possesses a specialization and division of labor—separate roles and responsibilities in newspapers for the publisher, managing editor, editorial page editor, assistant editors, copy writers, reporters, printers, and distributors, and in news networks for producers, news directors, camera personnel, reporters, and anchorpersons. The organization of roles is hierarchical, both in structuring who reports to whom (a chain of command) and establishing a standard operating procedure, or "action channels,"[19] in covering stories (as, for instance, creating separate national, foreign, and metropolitan desks in large dailies and giving each specific gatekeeper responsibilities; thus, on the *Washington Post* in 1972 through 1974, the Watergate exposé was a metropolitan, not national story, because the break-in at Democratic headquarters was first covered as a common burglary having nothing to do with national politics.

Where news organizations depart from the bureaucratic model, as Tunstall notes, is in the nature of their work, which is to routinize the nonroutine. The action channels of a news organization are not an assembly line, nor even the formalized information routing procedures of a government agency; news is simply not a standardized industrial or government product.[20] In effect, notes Tunstall, news organizations are "nonroutine bureaucracies"; government-press relations are, at least partially, a network of transactions between routine and nonroutine bureaucracies. Several aspects of the news organization as a nonroutine bureaucracy affect its role in newsmaking—organizational values, procedures, rituals, conflicts, and economics.

Values

Implicit or explicit in the operations of every news organization are a set of dominant values which guide policy choices, especially in news selection. One organization, for instance, may be concerned primarily with building the size of its readership or audience ratings, another may pride itself on careful reporting ("get it first but get it right"), another on the overall quality of its craftsmanship ("the best edited paper in America"), or another on being a newspaper of record ("all the news that's fit to print"). Through on the job training within the parent organization, a journalist learns cherished values and at least unconsciously applies them.[21] A case in point was the failure of *The New York Times* to follow up on the Watergate story in 1972 until well after it had been scooped by *The Washington Post*. In a revealing examination of the *Times'* coverage, Philip Nobile points to the influence of organization values: " 'Philosophically, *The New York Times* is run by very cautious men,' declares a Washington Bureau editor and Watergate Complex victim. 'If Deep Throat had shown up in our office, we would have listened, thanked him and then sent him over to *The Washington Post*.' "[22]

Organizational values also enter into the processing of television news. For one thing, directors of news networks think in a dialectical mode. Hence, a good television news story possesses strong elements of conflict, of thesis versus antithesis. In defining news on an everyday basis, events possessing conflictual qualities receive priority attention—partisan, racial, legal, and other forms of dispute dominate nightly TV news. Dramatic values also enter into compiling television news stories. Epstein quotes Reuven Frank, former president of NBC News: "Every news story should, without any sacrifice of probity or responsibility, display the attributes of fiction or drama. It should have structure and conflict, problem and denoument, rising action and falling action, a beginning, a middle and an end. These are not only the essentials of drama; they are the essentials of narrative."[23] Finally, there is an emphasis on the abstract principle of political balance, the effort to treat events in such a way as, like Caesar's wife, to be above suspicion.

Ritualization of News

To avoid charges of political bias many news organizations insist that their journalists exercise "objectivity." In point of fact, as Tuchman argues, objective reporting is a ritual, a routine procedure that has little bearing upon removing partiality from newsmaking.[24] In an important sense any journalist filing a report exercises considerable discretion; the reporter's version of truth is only one subjective account. Journalism, as Lippmann stressed, is not a firsthand report of the raw material of happenings but a stylized report conforming to selected beliefs, values, and expectations.[25] There are strategies that stylize and ritualize newsmaking in accordance with organizational guidelines pertaining to objectivity:

1. *Presentation of conflicting possibilities:* On matters where reporters cannot uncover "facts," they maintain objectivity by providing conflicting accounts. For example, unable to prove or disprove whether the Soviet Union is complying with arms limitations treaties with the United States,

reporters first quote one official, say the Secretary of State, that they are, and another, the Secretary of Defense, that they are not. Senator Joseph McCarthy, in his efforts to ferret alleged communists out of government positions in the 1950s, exploited a similar reporters' ritual to make news. He would make a charge against an official, thus grabbing a headline and quote at the top of a story; the denial from the official (appearing much later in the account) seldom received much attention from readers.

2. *Presentation of supporting evidence:* This strategy consists of citing evidence commonly accepted as factual in support of an assertion whose authenticity is problematic. Tuchman relates the story of an editor who questioned the reference in an obituary to the deceased as a "master musician." Was there evidence that the deceased was not a "two-bit musician" instead? Reading down the obituary, the editor found reference to the deceased's having played with John Philip Sousa, a "fact" justifying use of the qualifier "master."

3. *Judicious use of quotation marks:* To journalists, supporting evidence consists largely of quoting other people's opinions. A reporter may want to write that the local mayor is disreputable but cannot say so. The reporter can, however, quote a local councilman to that effect, and thus maintain an air of objective reporting.

4. *Structuring a story in appropriate sequence:* A common practice in presenting news is the format of the inverted pyramid. Writers place the most important information about an event in the first paragraph with material of decreasing importance placed in each succeeding paragraph. Invoking the formula that information about "who, what, where, why, and how" constitutes the "material facts" of a story, the reporter introduces these elements early, reserving later paragraphs for more speculative assertions.

5. *The labeling of news analysis:* There are many instances where reporters, columnists, and editors make no pretense of being objective; they label such accounts as "commentary" or "news analysis." The implication, however, is that all stories not so designated are objective, impartial accounts.

The point of these various strategies is not that they achieve objectivity; they do not. Rather, they are convenient rationales journalists use to adapt to organizational pressures such as deadlines and injunctions to avoid libel suits, and provide responses in the face of reprimands from superiors. These *"news procedures exemplified as formal attributes* of news stories and newspapers *are actually strategies through which newsmen protect themselves from critics and lay professional claim to objectivity."*[26]

Processing the News

There are many procedural paths which news organizations follow in processing events into news. These too affect the nature of accounts. They include, first, procedures for assigning stories. In some instances reporters take the initiative in defining newsworthy events, either through their work as general assignment reporters or on specific events—a political meeting, a speech, an agency hearing, etc. There are also, second, procedures for editing news copy, whether the copy be presented via newspaper, newsmagazine, or television. And, finally, stories can be killed through a decision of management. Thus, for example, *The New York Times* prepared to publish an extensive account of the planned Bay of Pigs invasion on Cuba by U.S.-backed anti-Castro forces in 1961. Instead the upper echelon of the newspaper decided to kill the story, much to their own and the later regret of President John Kennedy.[27]

How stories are assigned, edited, and selected for publication or for the cutting-room floor gives an overall impression of a news organization. Where the reporter's initiative in selecting newsworthy events prevails, copy editors and rewrite personnel play passive roles, and the journalists' stories are published intact. Such an organization develops a reputation of being a "reporter's paper." An "editor's" paper implies that editorial and management choices predominate. Weekly newsmagazines and network television news programs are usually dominated by editorial considerations in the support of their respective news organization's values, rituals, guidelines for control, and economic positions.

Conflict and Control

As with any large scale operation, news organizations consist of networks of people, each person having his or her self-interests, aspirations, goals, needs, and desires. Sometimes interpersonal relations are cooperative, sometimes they are conflicting. The way in which news personnel relate leaves a mark on newsmaking in several respects. For one, consider the competitive quality of newsmaking. Only a limited number of stories can be published on any given day in a newspaper or newsmagazine or aired on a radio or television newscast. Reporters vie for space or time. Ultimately their livelihood depends upon bylines and visibility (salaries, assignments, rank in the hierarchy, promotions, and statuses). In 1974, for instance, CBS News had a staff of twenty-two journalists in their Washington bureau including such luminaries as Roger Mudd, Dan Rather, Daniel Schorr, Eric Sevareid, Lesley Stahl, and Fred Graham. Each evening these twenty-two competed for eight minutes of air time on Walter Cronkite's network news program. When so many compete for so little (and thereby so much!), the race affects judgment of newsworthy events.[28]

There are other kinds of conflicts beyond competition to be read, heard, and seen. As employees of a news organization, reporters, editors, broadcasters, and others do not always agree with organizational policies. A reporter might, as many do, feel confined by a newspaper's editorial stand or by editorial refusals to allow journalists to interpret events or advocate policies. To some degree the likelihood of conflict is relatively small because of the recruitment and socializing policies of the organization. In addition the organization insures conformity to policy norms by giving reporters the opportunity to shape their own roles within the organization (thus identifying themselves with news policy rather than in conflict with it), offering prized assignments, awarding promotions, and giving salary increases.

Journalists in conflict with organization goals and policies develop strategies for getting around controls and restraints. Faced with the refusal of the news director to provide ample time for airing a story on CBS-TV, for instance, a Washington correspondent may appeal (although not too often) to anchorman Walter Cronkite. Newspaper reporters resort to several strategems: claim the story is an exclusive that will scoop rival papers; save the story for a day when there is little in the way of competing copy; lobby with more sympathetic editors; go over the heads of editors to the publisher; leak portions of the story to rival news organizations, then publish the whole after it has broken; write the story for another publication on a free-lance basis; and adopt all of the strategies of objectivity already discussed.[29] In sum, the relationships of news personnel within the organization are every bit as political as the events journalists report. To get on with the business of newsmaking, superiors and subordinates negotiate means of regulating their disagreements.

Economic Considerations

Economic factors enter into newsmaking most obviously through the fact that news organizations are economic enterprises that sustain themselves primarily through sales of the product and advertising. Sigal points out that the profit motive influences newsmaking most when profit is least;[30] to stimulate an increase in readership and audience ratings it is necessary to liven up the news, provide more features and programming, and increase advertising revenue. But whether the profit is large or small, advertising revenue helps support the news organization to a considerable extent and thus influences how much space and time are available for reporting events. From 55 to 65 percent of the space of an American newspaper consists of advertising, leaving less than one-half for a news "hole"; much of that contains not political news but regular features—comics, advice on health, gardening, and romantic matters, etc. Advertising comprises a smaller proportion of a nightly network TV newscast, but the remaining twenty-two minutes of a half hour is scarcely suited to reporting much more than highlights.

Beyond their effects on allocating space and time for news, economic factors enter into newsmaking in other respects. The size, quality, and degree of a news organization's staff depends in large measure on how many persons can be employed. Some organizations have large budgets for news operations; others provide only sufficient amounts to subscribe to the various news wire services and make no pretense of gathering news via their own journalistic staff.

Finally, economics plays a major role in the kinds of special interests represented in the ownership and operation of America's news media. There are two points of view. One argues that media ownership lies within the hands of a relatively small group of corporate owners who control newspapers, newsmagazines, and broadcasting to their own advantage. A second view holds that media ownership is not highly concentrated and, even to the extent that there is any concentration at all, this scarcely demonstrates elitist control of the selection of newsworthy events, quantity of available news, or quality of news accounts. Despite considerable debate, however, there has been relatively little systematic appraisal of the discrepancies in the two viewpoints.[31]

Newsgatherers and News Sources: Relations of Reporters and Officials

Journalists do not gather news like a child plucking pansies from the meadow. Political news is the joint creation of the journalists who assemble and report events and other political communicators—politicians, professionals, and spokespersons—who promote them. On the national political scene these journalists comprise the corps of correspondents covering the White House, Congress, administrative agencies, and courts. Their sources include (1) elective and appointive officials in policy-making positions, i.e., policy officers such as the president, cabinet and agency heads and subordinates, congressmen and their aides, judicial officers, etc; (2) officials especially appointed to deal with the press, both political appointees and career civil servants—information officers variously labeled press secretaries, public information officers, press agents, public relations personnel, etc.; and (3) spokespersons of organized interests including lobbyists, leaders of public interest groups (e.g., Ralph Nader), corporate executives, chairmen and officials of the major political parties.[32]

Although there has been no comprehensive study of the backgrounds of the official and nonofficial news sources, they constitute a diverse group both socially and politically. We know only a little more about the characteristics of journalists. First, reporters traditionally have not come from racial and ethnic minorities, but recently active and less discriminatory recruiting by news organizations has gradually lessened the imbalance.[33] Second, whether journalists tend to be more liberal than conservative in political orientations is not clear; a 1960 study of Washington correspondents, however, found 55 percent to be liberal and 27 percent conservative, a finding supported by more recent investigation.[34] Finally, reporters are better educated than most Americans, at least as measured by number of years attending school. A nationwide survey of journalists in 1971 indicated that 86 percent had attended college and 58 percent had graduated; the 1960 study of Washington correspondents noted that 93 percent had been to college and 81 percent were college graduates (fewer than one-fourth of Americans go to college, and one in eight of the voting population are college graduates).[35]

Two general considerations enter into the day to day relations between news sources and gatherers. In turn those relations constitute a key aspect of newsmaking. One is the respective roles each set of actors plays in the news process. The other pertains to the conventions and routines of gathering news.

Source-Channel Roles

For purposes of delineating the roles of governmental news sources we confine ourselves to official sources, namely, to policy and information officers. Why do policy officials talk to journalists? One reason is to promote their political aims ahead of collaborating and competing interests. A tip to a journalist by a spokesman for the Department of Defense that the Soviet Union has superior naval forces may provide front page coverage and thereby provoke Congress into a higher budget for defense spending. Officials use the press for disseminating messages within the government to affect policy outcomes. Policy makers also use the press to influence public opinion outside government, to raise or alleviate public concern, build support, and advance both policy aims and political careers. And the audiences for both internal and external political communication extend beyond the domestic arena in efforts to affect the policy decisions of foreign nations.

The public information officer (PIO) is a professional political communicator working on behalf of policy officials. The rationale for the PIO's existence is the official's view that newsmaking is far too important to be left solely to the discretion and whims of the journalists. Working on behalf of an agency and its policy makers, the public information officer secures or avoids publicity for agency happenings. The PIO is no mere neutral conduit for messages (although some may regard themselves as such) but both a propagandist and a censor designated to control the flow of information to the press in accordance with a superior's interests. The president's press secretary, for example, be he Richard Nixon's Ron Ziegler, Gerald Ford's Ron Nessen, or Jimmy Carter's Jody Powell, is just that—the president's press secretary, not a secretary for the press.

Generally, then, both policy and information officers try to use the press to advance specific political interests. They are, in sum, political persuaders. But officers define their persuasive functions in different ways. Some official sources, for example, believe they should report all government happenings for public scrutiny. One press officer of an executive agency defined this *informer* role thus: "The function of the press officer of any governmental department is through the press to keep the public aware and acquainted with the operation of the department, and its programs, and its development of new programs, and the development within existing programs." Other official sources would go farther. For them their function is to be *educators* to press and citizenry. Take the policy and information officers of the Federal Communications Commission, National Labor Relations Board, or other regulatory agency. These agencies make significant decisions regarding highly complex, technical matters. Said an information officer with respect to his dealings with the typical newsman: "I don't mean to try to spoon-feed him but to provide a concise statement of the decisions of the board so that the newsman does not have to come in here and do all the case work himself." Finally, there are official sources who are straight out *promoters,* who would agree with one officer who said "I feel, and everyone in this office feels, that it is our duty to make this agency look good."[36]

Just as policy and information officers play the role of persuader as sources of news, so do many journalists when serving as news channels. Some journalists openly advocate particular ideas, policies, and programs because they are paid to take stands: editorial writers, newspaper columnists (such as conservative James Kilpatrick or liberal Tom Wicker), and noted television commentators (Eric Sevareid, David Brinkley, and Howard K. Smith). Other newsmen play the role of advocate in covering happenings as newsworthy events. They do not seek to report all sides of a story ("balanced" coverage), because they usually believe that balance is impossible, that they should redress the balance by telling only one side (since everyone else is telling the other), or that they know the truth and all other considerations are irrelevant. Carried to the extreme, the advocacy viewpoint contributes to what Merrill and Lowenstein call "propagandistic journalism." The journalist is a "propagandist with a belief, a program, and objective, and he systematically tries to implant it all in others."[37] In sharp contrast to the advocate's view is the journalist who limits the job to reporting the facts of a news event as the reporter sees them, quoting all points of view, and making no judgments about which ideas, policies, or programs should be followed. This journalist is neither critic nor supporter of government but only an impartial transmission link dispensing information to readers, listeners, and viewers. If the advocate regards the journalist as a participant in the happenings reported as newsworthy, the journalist defines his alternative role as that of a neutral observer and recorder of occurrences.

In 1971 three sociologists examined American journalists in participant and neutral roles. From interviews with a nationwide representative sampling of 1,313 journalists, they found more general support for participant than neutral orientations. For instance, more than three-fourths of the sample endorsed the idea that the news media should be a watchdog and "investigate claims and statements made by the government"; more than 60 percent thought the media should analyze and interpret complex problems; well over a majority (56 percent) felt it was proper for the news media to discuss national policy while it is still being developed; 60 percent dismissed the notion that the news media should concentrate on news of interest to the widest possible public, thus suggesting reporters should take the lead in defining newsworthy matters.[38] The results of this study suggest that journalists favor a role that lies somewhere between the most restricted neutralist and active advocate viewpoints. Journalists feel they should be investigative reporters, even critics and adversaries of government when they find policy makers making false or misleading claims. Yet, a majority agree that newspersons should stay away from stories where factual content cannot be verified. A high percentage of journalists thus probably define their role as professional communicators not in a fixed, static way but on a day to day basis, constructing it through what they do. Depending upon the circustances, they advocate, interpret, explain, record, investigate, or evaluate.

We can designate three principal roles of journalists suggested by current research. These shade into one another to form a continuum rather than standing in sharp contrast. The *recorder* plays the role of dispassionate observer and neutral channel of information; the *experimenter* tries out a number of approaches to his craft; the *prescriber* regards making judgments, criticizing, and advocating courses of action as legitimate. How then, do the persuasive intentions of governmental news sources combine with the journalistic orientations of news channels? We can only speculate, but the relationships probably go something like this:[39] recorders transmit the messages provided them by all categories of official sources (informers, educators, and promoters) without changing the content substantially. A wire service reporter, for instance, frequently records and transmits a president's remarks or the contents of a press release verbatim. The journalist of an experimentalist mind is more selective; endeavoring to put newsworthy events into perspective, the experimentalist quotes official sources but does not take their word at face value. Prescribers rely upon informers and educators for supporting materials, or upon promoters for opinions in building stories, but they have their own points of view; the prescriber's selections of what to include and exclude in accounts dictate which official sources to use, how much, and for what purpose. In turn, official sources exploit various journalistic orientations (recorder, experimental, and prescriber) as they manage the news for special advantage.

The Newsgathering Process

In the everyday world of government-press relations—as with any mode of interpersonal communication—officials and journalists negotiate mutually profitable ways of doing business. Practiced for long periods these become the *conventions* of newsgathering. "Objective reporting" is one such convention. We noted that to maintain at least the facade of objectivity, newsmen provide conflicting viewpoints, supporting evidence, judicious quotations, and appropriate formats. Policy and information officers know this and act accordingly. They seize any opportunity to gain entree to the press by offering spicy quotes, controversial statements: and inside dope.

Other newsgathering conventions are closely allied with "objective reporting." Consider (1) the rule of the authoritative source. News reporters know that an editor is more likely to notice dispatches that quote widely known, recognized, authoritative persons. In political matters, the more authoritative the source the greater the access to the press. A direct quote from the president provokes more interest than one from a bureaucrat buried in the subterranean depths of an executive department or agency. (2) It is conventional for a story to have some major point to attract reader or viewer interest. Quotations from authoritative sources constitute one form of news peg to hang a story on. Other pegs include conflict (violence, politicians attacking one another, debates), prospects for change (tax relief, new programs), and unique events such as a presidential visit to exotic lands or a noted senator being sued for divorce. Hence, politicians capture headlines by purposely calling each other names, proposing new programs, and touring exotic lands; fewer provoke their spouses into divorce. (3) The exclusive interview is a convention of newsgathering that is also a two-way street for reporters and officials; the reporter gets a story that no other journalist has and the official relates his persuasive message to a channel eager to hear and print it. (4) The constraints of space and time make it essential that journalists be brief, succinct, and concise. Short leads, simple paragraphs, exciting headlines, and conventional explanations assist journalists in adapting to these constraints. A congressman or other public official can exploit such constraints by being folksy, inserting a pithy comment or two, and employing slogans (energy "crisis," "war" on poverty, "rollback" of prices, "ceiling" on spending) to boil down complex issues into easily remembered symbols.[40]

The conventions of the news trade work to the advantage of both reporters and officials; so also do newsgathering *routines*. Most journalists don't like a daily diet of the unexpected any more than do other people trying to do their jobs and earn a livelihood. Hence, the bulk of the press corps pursue routine stories, accounts of events that become newsworthy because the persons involved (policy and information officers) promote them as such. Routine stories call for routine procedures: cultivating regular contacts among friendly officials and fellow journalists who provide news tips; making regular rounds of governmental offices, reading press handouts, attending press briefings, and relying on official accounts; or reading the newspapers and following news broadcasts to learn what stories are developing, then following up on a particular facet. As with the conventions of journalism, news sources are well aware of newsgathering routines and exploit them for advantage. Because they know newsmen must have daily rations of information, information officers schedule daily and twice-daily briefings and press releases; because they realize journalists have deadlines to meet, sources time their announcements and speeches to capture the afternoon headlines or a few minutes on the evening TV news. Or if they want to avoid publicity, they schedule announcements when the press is least likely to be paying attention (as when President Richard Nixon fired special Watergate prosecutor Archibald Cox in the "Saturday Night Massacre" of 1974, and later President Gerald Ford announced a major cabinet shakeup on a Sunday in 1975, the "Sunday Night Massacre"). Sources also cultivate friendships with reporters and feed them information when it is to their advantage to do so; officials identify opinion leaders among the press and give them special treatment in hopes that if key journalists are sympathetic with official positions, other reporters might follow the lead. And officials do favors for reporters (such as giving them tips, exclusives, background information) to obligate newsmen in exchange for guaranteed access by officials to the press at a later time when they may need it.[41]

Finally, journalists frequently adopt work and thought habits aside from the dominant conventions and routines already mentioned. These too can be used by news sources interested in promoting an official point of view. Think, for example, of how newsmen hedge their reports by employing qualifiers to cover the fact that their accounts are incomplete. Consider the number of news stories that have phrases beginning "According to" and end with any of the following: "official sources," "unofficial sources," "usually reliable sources," "well-informed sources," "unconfirmed reports," "reports reaching here," or "best available information." Or, consider the use of "It" as in "It was learned," or "appears," or "is reported," or "is confirmed," or "is known," or "is suspected," or "is alleged."[42] In thinking about events, journalists assume that all can be explained as flowing from the intentions of persons involved, intentions inferred from past acts and statements. In constructing elaborate explanations, reporters are prone to overstructure what happened; perhaps, for example, the nomination of George McGovern for president in 1972 did not reflect a "new mood" or "movement" in the Democratic party but just the cumulative failures of his rivals.[43]

In sum, newsgathering conventions, routines, work and thought habits provide ample opportunities for public officials to exploit the news media to their own advantage. The relationship between news sources and newsgatherers easily permits governmental dominance; reporters too easily become dependent upon official news sources. Before examining how officials explicitly try to take advantage of newsmaking by managing news, let us look at one other feature of newsgathering, how media present the news.

Presenting Political News: The Media and the Message

Any discussion of how the press presents political news must begin with the realization that items of political relevance comprise a relatively small portion of the daily fare of the media. One would think, for instance, that during a presidential election year nightly television network newscasts would provide the viewer with more campaign news than he could possibly want. The evidence suggests otherwise. In the ten weeks prior to the 1972 presidential election less than one-fifth of news stories covered by the three major networks in nightly telecasts concerned the campaign. Of course news of other political events received substantial air time (coverage of the Vietnam war, a wheat sale to the Soviet Union, etc.), so we cannot estimate the amount of televised political news solely on the basis of references to the campaign. And to be sure, television carries public affairs programs other than nightly and morning news shows—interviews, documentaries, specials, etc. Yet compared to sports and entertainment programming, relatively little of what appears on television has direct political content. Similarly, relatively little of the nonadvertising space of newspapers carries items of a political nature; 4 percent, for instance, is editorial comment, not all devoted to politics by any means, and 12 percent is comprised of columns that may or may not be political in content.[44]

Regardless of the quantity of political news presented, however, the culmination of the process relating government officials and journalists through the newsgathering process is the political news story. Its presentation to the reader, listener, or viewer is the result of a sequence of policy choices reached within the news organization regarding which items to present, how much space and/or time to devote to each, where to place each item (the page in the newspaper, the time period for radio and TV), which reporters to credit with stories, and other emphases. We have already reviewed the conventions that influence these choices for print media such as newspapers and newsmagazines—the inverted pyramid placing the most dramatic facts first, the search for a familiar news peg to anchor the story in the reader's understanding, and the focus on who, what, when, where, how, and (in the case of interpretive reporting) why.

News presentations vary from one type of publication to another. For example, suburban afternoon dailies rely heavily upon the wire services (Associated Press and United Press International) for daily news. The editorial staff is small, the time limited, the pressures considerable (a single working day results in the publication of the equivalent of a small book). Consequently there is little first-hand reporting, editing, or rewriting. Stories published in city and metropolitan dailies are products of a more complex sequence of operations involving large numbers of people in reporting, rewriting, copy editing, etc. The political news is itself a result of an intricate process of office politics. Finally, newsmagazines tailor their political coverage to particular audiences—*Time* and *Newsweek* to the upwardly-mobile, busy, relatively affluent American; the *Nation* to the liberal; the *National Review* to the conservative; etc.[45]

Challenging the print media as a major source of political news for most Americans is television. Ninety-seven percent of American homes have at least one television set and 50 million Americans watch evening newscasts. Although total newspaper circulation is well above 62 million, consider that three networks divide the TV newscast audience, while over 1700 dailies serve the readership of newspapers. Moreover, opinion surveys in recent years have noted that TV is the major source of news for most Americans and the one they regard most believable.[46] Certainly, there is a special quality to television news. For one thing, TV packages information in a condensed, digested, entertaining format. In addition, as we noted in Chapter 5, TV gratifies the needs of many people for parasocial intimacy; Walter Cronkite is as much a friend and neighbor as he is a mere anchorman. All in all, most Americans readily agree that TV news provides an appealing veritable "mirror of reality."

In recent years, however, critics of television news have questioned the mirror analogy. If TV holds a mirror up to the world, they noted, the resulting reflection is highly distorted.[47] Several factors underlie their criticism. First, there is a geographical imbalance in the number and types of stories in the nightly fare of network television news. The central headquarters for each of the three major television networks is in New York, a lesser bureau in Washington. The networks gather and report news chiefly from Washington, compile it in New York, but pay much less attention to happenings in other areas of the country. There are relatively few stories that originate with networks' affiliate stations and are fed into nightly newscasts. Those that do generally report events in urban areas, especially the urbanized population centers of the east and west coasts.

Second, although TV viewers feel closer to the action when they can see rather than merely read about events, the immediacy is largely manufactured and misleading. In efforts to routinize newsgathering and processing and to eliminate the unexpected, television networks employ several tactics. For instance, they concentrate heavily on planned and staged events to assure coverage by available camera and film crews. And they save film for several days, then run it on a nightly newscast without clarifying that the event did not occur that day. By keeping a bank of film strips, a network can build a story over time, piece together film taken at different times and places, and give the impression of related events occurring throughout the nation on a single day. Knowing, for example, that Congress is likely to adjourn within a short time, film crews throughout the country devote weeks recording interviews with state and local leaders regarding the success of the congressional session; on the day of the adjournment a televised story suggests widespread, simultaneous, immediate dissatisfaction with Congress. Yet another technique is to re-create and re-present happenings. Suppose that there is an attempt on the life of a prominent political figure, a happening not recorded on TV film. Film crews proceed to the place the incident occurred and film an interview with a witness. Given a subtle lead-in by the network's anchorman, the story gives a lingering impression to viewers of the network's having been on the scene when the assassination attempt occurred.

Third, TV news networks are more concerned with processing news than gathering it. With few exceptions the television networks use reports from the wire services for most of their stories; the exceptions arise from stories generated by the networks' White House, congressional, and other reporters on general or special assignment. Even when each network uses its own reporters to gather first-hand accounts, there is a remarkable sameness to the content of the three networks' newscasts. The reason for this is that the networks cooperate more than compete in newsgathering. Late each afternoon, representatives of ABC, NBC, and CBS exchange views on what stories they can cover jointly or "pool" coverage on for the next day. Pooled coverage cuts costs, provides an opportunity to plan the content of the nightly news in advance of happenings, and reduces the likelihood of a network's getting scooped.[48]

Finally, television is a visual medium and, hence, the newsworthiness of an event derives from whether or not it can be captured by the live camera or on film. Camera angles and the allowable length of a film report play an important part in defining what is news and how it is presented. During the 1968 Democratic convention one television network filmed a violent demonstration taking place outside the convention hall from three angles. Each film clip occupied several minutes of air time. The impression left upon the viewing audience throughout the nation (and in the convention hall) was that the riot was of long duration; in fact, viewers had seen the same brief demonstration repeated from three separate angles.

In sum, just as in the world of print journalism where specific conventions assist newspersons in deciding what is newsworthy, there are similar conventions in electronic journalism—the geographic location of news centers, controls for the unexpected, requirements of news processing, demands for visual content, dramatic formats, and considerations of cost. As a result the magic mirror presents selective reflections, an illusion of immediacy, warmed over and re-presented events, visual impressions, and a sense that things happening at widely dispersed places are really parts of a single urbanized, nationalized, politicized picture. It is possible that technological changes will modify the news presentation process in the future. For example, the "minicam" and "all-electronic coverage" affords the possibility of replacing unwieldy and slow film equipment with small videotape cameras that can be taken to any locale for live coverage of an event. It remains to be seen, however, whether such technological advances will actually produce greater immediacy in the news or, as politicians attending the 1976 Democratic and Republican nominating coventions said, will become merely a horde of restless cameras prowling the floor, panning the streets, invading privacy,. or being exploited by the publicity hungry.

We have considered separately a few of the considerations that enter into how news appears in the print and electronic media. To a substantial degree print and electronic journalism complement as well as rival one another. To be sure, about one-third of Americans receive their news solely from television and a fifth solely from newspapers; yet one of four Americans relies upon both as sources of information.[49] The fact is that people use different media for different purposes. For detailed accounting of events there is the newspaper: it has more stories, more details, and can be read and reread to aid understanding and recall. Electronic media, both radio and TV, provide quick, sketchy, almost bulletinlike announcements of happenings. Magazine journalism gives readers fleshed-out interpretations and an opportunity to relate events in a larger framework. Taken alone no news medium can gratify every citizen's desires for information, nor do all the news media collectively. Yet, each medium does play a distinct and key part in processing happenings into newsworthy events, news into news stories.

MAKING POLITICAL NEWS: THE MANAGEMENT ROLES OF GOVERNMENT

Just as the press makes, or defines, news through newsgathering, so does government, by managing the flow of information. And just as journalists employ conventions, routines, and habits that assist them in adapting to the unexpected in gathering news, public officials develop institutional devices to help them use, publicize, control, gather, and influence news for persuasive purposes. We label the activities of government officials directed toward achieving ends through the use of information *communication management*—the creation, processing, refining, and circulation of images to influence public opinion.

How Governments Use and Make News

We have seen that public officials use the press for a variety of reasons—to advance program and policy goals, further career ambitions, create and adjust to public awareness, and build popular support. In addition officials read, listen, and view the news to obtain information about what is going on that does not flow through routine government channels—to assess public opinion from published polls and editorials; to discover what public stance a superior announced in a reported speech; to learn who the influential people are in Congress, various agencies, and among lobbyists; and to find out what is happening and where the action is beyond the confines of their limited, perhaps parochial political worlds.

Because public officials pay attention to the press, news has an impact upon them. For one thing, officials get some measure of how well people are responding to policies by reading news items and gauging press opinion. This feedback suggests what kinds of adjustments may make policies more salable. Spurred by growing concern about economic downturns, for example, President Gerald Ford proposed measures to increase the buying power of American citizens in 1975. Moreover, the kinds of stories reported in the press hint at the types of questions politicians are likely to face when returning to their constituencies. In many respects, then, news stories define the limits of officials' acts, their available options, and the items on their policy-making agendas. Thus officials both use and respond to political news and thereby have vested interests in making it.

Presidential Newsmaking

Of all public officials, the President of the United States has the most direct and continuing access to the news media. Almost anything the president does makes news—what he says, how he says it, where he goes, who he sees, and even his mishaps (as when President Gerald Ford on a vist to Europe stumbled while disembarking from his airplane, a happening that got more news coverage than most of the other things he did on that tour). Not only does the press want to report presidential happenings, there are professional communicators working on behalf of any president to assure that he makes news—his Press Secretary, numerous press assistants and information officers, advance men, speech writers, specialists to answer presidential mail, etc.

Free and easy access of the president to news channels yields a "presidential theater."[50] Presidential theater consists of the president commanding simultaneous appearances on radio and television networks during prime hours when listening and viewing audiences are largest. These appearances permit the president to speak directly to the mass citizenry and, moreover, to capture front page headlines and news accounts following his presentation. Presidential theater is not limited to a personal address by the chief executive from the White House; it also includes prime time radio and television coverage of his public appearances, news conferences, conversations with representatives of the news media, etc. President Dwight Eisenhower once held a televised cabinet meeting. Before assuming the presidency in 1969 Richard Nixon appeared on television and formally introduced each of the members of his cabinet as a "team" of versatile men. Nixon also made wide use of network radio during his presidency and recorded several presidential addresses especially for radio so that they could reach members of select audiences—farmers, housewives, commuters, laborers, etc.—who could listen as they continued with their daily chores.

Presidential theater has increased steadily since the advent of electronic politics. As he was departing on a railroad trip, President Calvin Coolidge gave the first interview by a president for network radio. It was brief. Asked what message he had for the American people listening in for the first time on radio to such an event, Coolidge replied "Goodbye." Later chief executives have not been so terse. Franklin Roosevelt made considerable use of radio for "fireside chats," four in each of his first and second terms, twelve in his third. Each successive president has relied even more on presidential theater. By the time he had been in office for nineteen months, for instance, Richard Nixon had made fourteen prime time TV appearances (John Kennedy had made four and Lyndon Johnson seven during comparable periods of their presidencies). Jimmy Carter exploits TV, even holding fireside chats, and has added telephone call-ins on network radio.

Presidential theater serves three purposes. First, it permits the president to mobilize public opinion by appealing directly to citizens. Sometimes it works, sometimes not. For instance, in 1963 President Kennedy appeared on television to announce the signing of a nuclear test ban treaty with the Soviet Union; before the appearance polls indicated that 73 percent favored the treaty, afterwards 81 percent. In 1970 President Nixon explained on television why U.S. troops had been sent into Cambodia; before he did so, 7 percent favored the move, afterwards 50 percent favored. Yet, in 1973 when Nixon made his first televised disclaimer of blame in the Watergate affair, polls indicated no significant improvement in his standing as president; 50 percent rated his presidential performance as positive before the appearance, 48 percent did so afterwards.[51] Second, presidential theater is an attempt to influence Congress. For example, to get the Democratic majority in Congress to pass what he considered an acceptable energy policy in 1975, President Ford appeared early in the year in a prime time address blaming Congress for unnecessary delays. Yet by the end of the year, Congress still had passed no such legislation. Finally, presidential addresses on radio and television inform members of his administration of approved policy stands that they best adhere to in public pronouncements.

Congressional Newsmaking

Although the Washington press corps faithfully reports virtually every tidbit of information about congressional celebrities such as Senators Edward Kennedy, Hubert Humphrey, Howard Baker, and the majority and minority leaders of both houses and are quick to report the escapades of a congressional leader such as the Wilbur Mills-Fanne Foxxe flirtation of 1974 or the sex scandals in Congress in 1976, the fact is that the news media take remarkably little initiative in reporting about Congress. To begin with, 72 percent of the nation's more than 1700 dailies have no Washington correspondent or contact with the reporters of papers who do (more than 95 percent of radio and TV stations are in a similar position). Moreover, of approximately 1400 Washington correspondents about 400 cover Congress specifically but they concentrate on big issues and names; the vast majority of congressmen go unnoticed by the press.

In the absence of journalistic attention, most congressmen promote as newsworthy whatever events put them in the best light. One way is by employing former journalists as staff assistants. The assistants then are responsible for preparing news releases for publication in the local papers of congressmens' constituencies. Ben Bagdikian, a close observer and critic of the press, observes that "hundreds of press releases, paid for by the taxpayers, are sent to the media by members of Congress, and hundreds are run verbatim or with insignificant changes, most often in medium-sized and small papers, with only rare calls to check facts and ask questions that probe beyond the pleasant propaganda."[52] Members of Congress also use two televison and four radio studios (provided at a cost to taxpayers of $500,000) to film, tape, edit, and duplicate messages sent to local stations. The cost to the senator or representative for this service is one-tenth what he would pay if the materials were produced by a commercial firm. Again, TV and radio stations in medium-sized and smaller cities are the primary outlets for these "news" items, thus providing readily accessible channels of public communication for the more than 80 percent of congressmen who take advantage of studio facilities on a weekly basis. A congressman running for office, if he pays for the service out of his campaign funds, can use the congressional facilities for filming campaign appeals; during the 1972 presidential primaries, for instance, Senator Harold Hughes of Iowa filmed an endorsement of Edmund Muskie that eventually played on ten Iowa TV stations virtually verbatim.

Congressional newsmaking influences the nation's politics in numerous ways, but two stand out. First, when Congress offers its own persuasive messages as news, the resulting newspaper, radio, and television coverage advantages incumbents. Bagdikian found that in 1972 challengers to incumbents were significantly more likely to be successful if they were running in districts where the local media did have Washington correspondents providing direct coverage. Second, the congressional propaganda machine enhances the likelihood that a few congressional notables, usually senators, become suffficiently known (because of their own newsmaking efforts and the tendency of the Washington press corps to focus chiefly upon them) to seek the presidency. One reason the U.S. Senate has been the seedbed of so many presidential candidacies in recent decades has been congressional newsmaking.

Bureaucratic Newsmaking

We noted in our discussion of organizational communication (Chapter 5) that bureaucratic organizations use information and publicity to promote larger budgets from Congress, bypass presidential and congressional scrutiny by building close relationships with the clienteles served by the agencies, enforce their policies, and advance the political careers of agency chiefs. As with the bulk of congressional offices, the administrative departments, agencies, and regulatory commissions receive relatively little regular coverage from the news media. Hence, to promote their interests the agencies make their own news. For this purpose each government organization possesses a fairly elaborate information apparatus—an Office of Information staffed variously by an Assistant Secretary, Director, Deputy Director, and/or several public information officers. In Chapter 4 we reported a measure of the extent of bureaucratic newsmaking with an estimate that federal expenditures on public relations were more than double the newsgathering budgets of the two major wire services, three major television networks, and ten largest U.S. daily newspapers combined. In a three-year period, 1969 through 1971, the public relations activities of the Department of Defense alone, including Army, Navy and Air Force, cost more than $121 million.[53]

Bureaucratic newsmaking is in part a simple attempt to make information available to interested citizens—to announce regulations, respond to questions, and perform a public service (such as when the National Weather Service predicts temperatures, rain, sleet, or snow; the Bureau of Census compiles and releases demographic data; the Department of Agriculture explains how to candle eggs; or Americans receive instruction in the basics of the metric system). But agencies also try to curry public favor through elaborate public relations campaigns. Some of these have been notable: the campaign of the National Aeronautics and Space Administration to publicize its programs of manned space flights in the 1960s; the Department of Agriculture's campaign in 1962 and 1963 to counter the arguments against the use of pesticides raised by the publication of Rachel Carson's *Silent Spring;* the Navy Department's public relations efforts in the 1960s to improve the image of the Navy; the Department of Defense's cooperation in the filming of the popular movie, *Tora, Tora, Tora,* extolling the virtues of military preparedness; and the Energy Research and Development Administration's program in the 1970s to convince Americans of the virtues of building nuclear facilities to supply power for generating electricity.[54]

On a day to day basis bureaucratic newsmaking relies chiefly upon the press release to channel information to the news media. Information officers, whether informers, educators, or promoters in their views of how they should perform their jobs, prefer the news release as a means of providing information. The press release gives them control over information flows, provides an outlet for discussing complex matters, and is a scheduled, not unexpected, event. Journalists rail against "government by press release"; very few regard press releases as useful in newsgathering and, when asked, most deny that they even use them.[55] Yet the content of press releases still finds its way into news stories. A 10-week study conducted in 1972 of 26 daily newspapers (representing 20 percent of the total national daily circulation of newspapers in all major regions of the country) revealed that 52 percent of 528 releases of the Departments of Defense, State, Transportation, and Health, Education, and Welfare resulted in stories based upon those releases.[56] That a majority of releases from such agencies produced news stories indicates at least a partial, if not overwhelming, success for bureaucratic newsmaking.

The Supreme Court as Newsmaker

Of all of the bodies comprising four complexes of governing institutions which transact with the press in the newsmaking process—presidency, congress, bureaucracy, and courts—the Supreme Court is the greatest challenge to journalistic initiative. A number of factors make it difficult for newspersons to cover the Supreme Court. One lies in the nature of the decisions the Court makes; complex, often ambiguous, and highly technical verdicts on crucial social and political questions are not easily fit into the formulas provided by the inverted pyramid or who, what, when, where, how, and why. Second, reporters don't receive tightly worded, succinct press releases summarizing the principal points of each decision. The Court frowns on issuing releases for a couple of reasons: one is the fear that any interpretation contained in the release could later be treated as part of the decision; the other is that the justices often differ on what is a valid interpretation. Third, the reporter faces a deadline in his daily chores. Before meeting it, the journalist must not only analyze the complexities of Court decisions in the absence of helpful summaries but decide which of many decisions announced on a given day are most newsworthy. In 1962 on the day that the famous school prayer case was decided (*Engel* v. *Vitale*), for example, there were a total of 16 cases with opinion and 257 memorandum cases announced. Reporters scarcely had opportunity to read the list of cases, let alone the opinions, and then prepare a clear but detailed news account. Finally, the press simply devotes relatively few resources to Court coverage. Primary coverage for the bulk of newspapers, radio, and television media is via the wire services—Associated Press, United Press International, *New York Times,* etc. Few news organizations have correspondents in Washington with the training and experience to evaluate Court decisions. A reporter such as Fred Graham of CBS News is a rare exception; Graham has a law degree.

Given the problems associated with covering the Supreme Court, it is not surprising that the initial impression that news readers, listeners, and viewers receive of Court decisions is frequently misleading, sometimes erroneous, and almost always incomplete. A more comprehensive picture of what the Court decided in any given case must await subsequent reporting by more detailed accounts, official printed versions of the decisions, explanations by opinion leaders such as lawyers and government officials, and statements of organizations including bar associations, law enforcement agencies, and special interests. Many significant decisions, however, get lost in the shuffle and never make news.[57]

Techniques of News Management

There are three principal means employed by governments to capture the initiative in newsmaking and manage news.

Promotional Techniques

In discussing how reporters gather news we noted that there are several routine ways they go about assembling information. Each of these is also a way for official sources to disseminate information and thereby promote happenings into newsworthy events.

Press Conferences.   The open press conference is a primary newsmaking technique, one equally prized by newsmen and news sources alike. The most widely publicized press conferences are held by the president, but cabinet members, agency heads, other senior officials, and congressmen meet with accredited reporters for purposes of making announcements and responding to questions.

There are two major types of news conferences, the scheduled conference and the impromptu get-together with the press. The scheduled conference is a formal meeting between official and reporters, carefully organized and with as little as possible left to chance. Those with the president are most notable. On the official side presidential press aides go to elaborate lengths to assure that the president makes the planned impression. Where the conference occurs is a source of concern: President Kennedy preferred the auditorium of the State Department building where he could overlook and respond to each journalist in a formal, yet relaxed manner; Richard Nixon held news conferences in the White House in a relatively small room with a large blue drapery as a backdrop, thus giving a sense of closeness and intimacy to TV viewers; when Gerald Ford became President his aides moved him to the other side of the same room so that TV cameras could catch him standing in front of a doorway to a long hall, thus hoping to sustain the air of openness identified with his early regime. To have a rostrum or not is another concern: Kennedy used one, Lyndon Johnson employed a stand, Nixon faced reporters without "hiding" behind rostrum or stand. Moreover, aides brief the president regarding what questions to expect, appropriate responses, and what to do if caught in an embarrassing situation. And to enhance their control, presidential aides sometimes plant questions among White House correspondents to assure queries get asked. The journalists also routinize the press conference. The senior wire service correspondent controls its length with a "Thank You, Mr. President," a tip that the conference is over. Front row seats are reserved for press notables and the first few questions largely predetermined. In sum, the presidential press conference is less a spontaneous happening than a staged, newsmaking performance.[58]

Impromptu meetings with the press are also more standardized than implied by the term itself. Franklin Roosevelt called reporters into his office, to the swimming pool, or even to the side of his bathtub. In each instance he knew precisely what announcement he wanted to make, what questions he wanted to lead reporters to ask, and what headlines he wanted in the next editions of the newspapers. The White House rose garden has more recently been a place for presidents to meet correspondents in a seemingly informal atmosphere, thus building the image of always being available to the press.

Regardless of formats, official press conferences serve several purposes. First, they make news, usually the kind of news the official wants. Second, they provide the president and senior officials with opportunities to announce official stands, thus binding subordinates to similar positions. Third, they assure scheduling and control over the flow of information and thereby give officials rather than reporters the initiative in making news. Finally, they place an official in the limelight so that he can project his strengths and cover his weaknesses; even faced with probing questions many a president has appeared friendly, talked guardedly but seemingly candidly, and come across as gracious and cool under pressure.

Briefings. A news briefing is a relatively informal meeting between an official, either policy or information officer, and selected members of the press. It may be a regularly scheduled session or of the background variety.

Each of the major executive departments, agencies, and offices (including the White House) holds regularly scheduled press briefings. Their purpose is to make routine and special announcements and keep the working press informed about daily activities and plans. White House briefings are a case in point. These are usually conducted by the presidential press secretary or a chief deputy. What comes out of them depends upon what the press secretary knows, volunteers, answers, and the questions members of the White House press corps ask. These briefings are more effective tools of news management than of newsgathering. Reporters, for example, were highly critical of the briefings conducted by Nixon's secretary Ron Ziegler and deputy secretary Gerald Warren. White House correspondents charged that responses from the president's spokesmen were often purposely broad and meaningless, promises to seek out information but with no follow-up, references to previous official statements that actually did not exist, and efforts to send reporters on wild goose chases. But perhaps White House briefings provide little significant information because of lack of aggressiveness on reporters' part, their ritualistic adherence to a question-and-answer format, and the fact that—in many cases—a president simply does not confide in his press secretary.[59]

Background briefings are not as routine as those scheduled on a regular basis and may or may not be initiated by the news source. In some cases a small group of journalists instigates an informal meeting with a public official; in others an official sets up a private meeting with a select group of correspondents. Typical of the backgrounder is a set of understandings with respect to attributing information to the official news source in question. When the official speaks "off the record," this is a cue to reporters that the information is to assist them but is not to be reported in any form; for "background only," refers to information that can be reported but not attributed to its source; "deep background" indicates that the reporter should use the information as if it were solely his conclusion; and "not for direct quotation" means the information can be used and attributed but not via quotation or the official's precise wording. Thus, backgrounders serve both the interest of official and reporter: the former promotes a viewpoint without being directly accountable for what is published, the latter gets an insider's account that makes newsworthy copy. So long as the rules are clearly understood (which they sometimes are not) and obeyed (again, they sometimes are not), the backgrounder is a newsmaking tool for all concerned. However, many officials and reporters worry about being "used" and shy away.[60]

Interviews.   The interview is akin to the background briefing in certain respects: it may be instigated by either official or reporter, it is private, and there may be a variety of understandings with respect to what can emerge from it. Generally, however, the interview is a one-on-one exchange between a source and journalist that gives the journalist an exclusive and a news peg to assure publication or broadcast. The official gets direct access to the news media, often via a celebrated correspondent. Using the interview as a channel, a public official can announce decisions and plans, provide reasons and justifications for actions, respond to critics, agree or disagree with supporters, and put underlings on guard. In doing so the official is assured that the message will reach the public eye and, because the journalist wants to retain the official's good will, in a fairly sympathetic light.

Leaks. The leak is an institutionalized feature of newsmaking that serves the working needs of both the news source and channel. It is a covert means for an official anonymously to pass along to reporters information that other officials want kept private. Perhaps the most celebrated leaking of information in recent times came with the exposure of the circumstances surrounding the 1972 break-in at Democratic national headquarters in the Watergate apartment complex in Washington, D.C. Relying upon leaks provided by an informant identified only as "Deep Throat," investigative reporters Carl Bernstein and Bob Woodward of *The Washington Post* pieced together a story that ultimately included the resignation of President Richard Nixon.

Leaks serve news sources in various ways. Sometimes they permit an official who is prohibited by orders from his superiors from talking to the press to express dissatisfaction with various policies to newsmen. At other times they may be used for more venal purposes, such as to "get" people, forcing them to resign. For example, enemies of Secretary of State Dean Rusk within the administration of John F. Kennedy leaked a story that the president was looking for a new Secretary of State; the reporter who published the story was one of Kennedy's closest friends. Rusk said, "Washington is a very wicked city."[61] Leaks are valuable to newsmen because they contain tips that may develop into major stories, help them to get a jump on their competitors, and in instances of tight governmental secrecy and security are the only means of gathering news from other than formal channels. But when reporters depend constantly on leaks, serious questions arise with respect to what is proper and improper in handling leaks. Accepted in uncritical fashion, leaks simply turn reporters into tools of news management.

Publicity Devices. A wide variety of other techniques help government sources to promote what they do as newsworthy. One we have already examined, the *press release*. It has been estimated that one-fifth of the stories published in major dailies concerning foreign affairs, health, education, and welfare are traceable in whole or in part to releases or statements issued by the executive agencies involved.[62] *Public appearances* by government officials, staged to receive maximum news coverage, are also vital to news management. For example, when President Richard Nixon returned from his historical visit to China in 1972, his plane was deliberately delayed in arriving back in Washington until a full crowd of well wishers and media representatives would be there to greet and televise the President's "triumphant" return. Finally, government agencies use films, documentaries, television spots, magazine advertising, in short, all the means of *commercial promotion* to communicate through the news media. Thus through the good offices of Smokey the Bear, the typical American has heard, if not taken to heart, the message, "Only YOU can prevent forest fires!"

Governmental Secrecy

Promotion is a means of managing the flow of news by releasing information to the press under controlled circumstances. Secrecy is a technique of news management halting the flow of certain kinds of information altogether. In point of fact promotion and secrecy have always been closely linked in American political communication, but only since the advent of World War II has their connection with newsmaking been so clear.[63]

Traditionally government secrecy has taken two forms, *classification* and *withholding* of information. Classification is an administrative mechanism that designates certain kinds of information, generally sensitive military and foreign policy information as confidential, secret, or top secret on grounds that its disclosure would be harmful to national security interests. By executive order of the president, federal employees and military personnel are not permitted to release classified information to the general public; members of Congress and their staffs have limited access to classified information on a "need to know" basis.

Although journalists generally do not quarrel with the notion that material should not be released to the press when it would be detrimental to national security, they criticize abuses of the classification system. Testimony taken from governmental officials in the early 1970s, for example, revealed that the national archives contained more than 470 million pages of documents classified from 1939 to 1954, that 12 federal agencies having primary classification authority allow some 55,000 persons (since reduced by two-thirds) to classify materials, that well over 90 percent of classified material would not be prejudicial to national security if released, and that in four agencies alone the direct costs for classification run about $60 million annually.[64]

In recent years the news media have challenged the classification system. One of the most celebrated challenges came in 1971 when *The New York Times* and *The Washington Post* published extensive portions of a Defense Department study of the Vietnam war, the Pentagon Papers. The Nixon administration went to court in an attempt to restrain publication; ultimately the Supreme Court ruled against the government. Later in 1971 classified documents concerning the India-Pakistan war were leaked to columnist Jack Anderson who used them to report that despite claims by the Nixon administration of neutrality, U.S. policy favored Pakistan. It seems likely that classification will continue to be a major source of government-press tension in the future and that there will be other challenges by the press.

The other means of government secrecy is to withhold information for other than reasons of national security. On the grounds of "executive privilege," for instance, recent presidents refused to release certain kinds of information to Congress, arguing variously that the release of the information would serve no legislative purpose, that sensitive matters of a diplomatic, military, or law enforcement nature were involved, or that revelation would seriously undermine the methods by which the president seeks advice and counsel in policy making. The most dramatic confrontation over the issue came in 1973 when the special Senate committee investigating the Watergate affair subpoenaed documents and tapes pertaining to conversations held between President Richard Nixon and his White House aides. The president claimed executive privilege, later relented and turned over transcripts of some tapes, and finally obeyed a court order to release tapes requested during congressional hearings pertaining to possible impeachment.

But there are other instances of withholding information without any rationale, merely by simple refusals to release information to the press, public, or Congress. As a means of combatting this type of withholding, in 1966 Congress passed the Freedom of Information Act which went into effect July 4, 1967. The act decreed that all government papers, opinions, records, policy statements, and staff manuals be made available upon request unless falling into an excepted category (classified information, trade secrets, personnel and medical files, etc.). But the act had only marginal effects because government agencies used several tactics to get around its provisions—mixing unclassified material with classified material, requiring precise specification of the type of information being demanded, charging exhorbitant search and copying fees, designating information as a working paper and thereby in an exempted category, and other procedures. In 1975 Congress amended the law, over President Ford's veto, limiting exemption provisions, search and copying charges, the time an agency was permitted to take to respond, and other loopholes. Since its amendment the press has used the FOI Act to pry newsworthy information from formerly recalcitrant agencies.

One other means to withhold information is to discuss privately matters not formally recorded in proceedings of meetings. To overcome this practice several states have passed legislation requiring open meetings; these "sunshine laws" require that governmental bodies announce forthcoming meetings in advance and provide opportunities for public attendance and press coverage.[65]

Government Regulation

Through legislation such as the Freedom of Information Act and sunshine laws, governments regulate the relations between themselves and news media. Government regulation is thus another way of managing the flow of information and thus, newsmaking. The Failing Newspaper Act (the Newspaper Preservation Act of 1970) is an example of legislative regulation. Under the act a newspaper in financial difficulties may establish a joint newspaper operating arrangement with another local paper; both papers then have the same printing, advertising, and distribution facilities, but maintain separate news and editorial operations. The rational for the legislation, that one newspaper towns provide less diversity of news, may justify quasi-monopolistic enterprises, but the act is too recent to measure its consequences adequately.

In recent years there have been proposals for a form of legislative regulation that could have profound consequences for political newsmaking. The proposal is for "right of access" legislation seeking to guarantee freedom of expression by giving any political interest the right to voice its views in newspapers, radio, and television. Since most cities have but one newspaper and there are but three major broadcasting networks (so goes the argument) those who control the media control newsmaking. To assure greater diversity of opinion, therefore, groups should introduce their ideas into the media via assured access channels. In 1974 the Supreme Court decided a case arising out of Florida dealing with a state statute guaranteeing a political candidate a right to equal news space to reply to criticism and attacks on his record by a newspaper. The Florida Supreme Court had upheld the legislation on grounds that the First Amendment guarantee of a free press is for the benefit of all people, not just a protection of the property rights of media owners. The U.S. Supreme Court in *Miami Herald* v. *Tornillo,* overturned the decision of the Florida court saying: "The choice of material to go into a newspaper, and the decision made as to limitation on the size of the paper, and content, and treatment of public issues and public officials—whether fair or unfair—constitutes exercise of editorial control and judgment." Such control the Court deemed consistent with First Amendment guarantees. The Court concluded that it has yet to be demonstrated how government regulation in the area of access to the print media can be consistent with those guarantees.[66] With respect to the broadcast media, the situation differs. Broadcasters are required to give fair time for reply to people attacked on their stations even though newspapers are not obligated to give reply space.

It is obvious that the courts are major regulators of the newsmaking process; by defining the limits of freedom of the press the courts demarcate the boundaries of legitimate newsgathering and news management as well. We have seen that the Supreme Court did this with respect to censorship and classified material in the case of the Pentagon Papers, executive privilege in the case of Nixon and the Watergate tapes, and right of access in the Tornillo case. The Court has also dealt with other matters. Among these have been questions of libel (the press has broad latitude in criticizing public officials); relations between reporters and their news sources (newsmen have no blanket protection for the confidentiality of their sources but states may pass "shield" laws defining the limits of such protection); what the media may publish regarding persons accused of crimes without violating the rights of the accused to a fair trial; definitions of obscenity; and deceptive advertising.[67]

Finally, administrative regulation joins legislative and judicial action in guiding the newsmaking process. The principal administrative regulator is the Federal Communications Commission (FCC). The FCC consists of seven members (appointed by the president and confirmed by the Senate) serving staggered seven-year terms; not more than four commissioners may come from the same political party. Among the regulatory functions of the commission are allocations of broadcasting frequencies and channels, licensing, and decisions with respect to two rapidly growing means of communication—cable television and citizen's band radio. Three regulatory areas within the jurisdiction of the FCC are particularly important to processing political news: (1) the "fairness doctrine" says that when a broadcast station presents one side of a controversial issue, a reasonable opportunity must be afforded for the presentation of contrasting views; (2) the "equal time" provision of the Communications Act decrees that if a broadcaster permits any person who is a legally qualified candidate for public office to use a station, the broadcaster must afford equal opportunities to all other such candidates to use the station—but when a president campaigns as a candidate before announcing his candidacy, there is no equal time obligation; and (3) the "political party doctrine" requires that if one party receives or buys air time, the other major party must be given or allowed to purchase time.

Recent legislation and rulings have influenced portions of the regulatory areas just mentioned. For example, broadcast stations are now required to charge political candidates the lowest possible station rates for air time immediately before an election. Hence, if a station permits one candidate to use time, it must allow all other candidates the same amount at lowest rates, a situation producing the possibility of stations losing considerable money. To avoid selling large amounts of time to many candidates, some stations simply refuse to sell to any. This accounts in part for the relatively moderate use of television for campaigning we discussed in Chapter 5. Stations must also provide reasonable access to candidates for federal office but have no such obligation to state and local candidates. Another example of recent regulatory changes was the 1975 ruling by the FCC that permitted coverage of campaign debates and press conferences to be exempted from equal time requirements. This provided the opportunity for the 1976 presidential and vice-presidential debates, and for President Ford to hold press conferences without broadcast networks being required to provide equal time to Jimmy Carter and other challengers.

THE GOVERNMENT-PRESS RELATIONSHIP

Writing two decades ago Fred Siebert and his colleagues delineated four leading theories of relationships between government and the press: (1) the authoritarian theory that governmental power should be concentrated in a single person or elite and the press should serve as an instrument of social control to preserve social order and elitist rule; (2) the libertarian theory which argues that the press should operate in a laissez faire, unfettered manner to generate a pluralism of viewpoints providing independent checks on government and opportunities to explore all opinion freely and openly; (3) the communist theory which sees the press as an instrument for transmitting social policy on behalf of the ideology and goals represented by the Communist Party; and (4) the social responsibility theory which accepts the principle of a free press, but a press which performs a public service through responsible social criticism and education, under the presumption that a guarantee of a free press is a guarantee to a nation's citizens, not principally a protection of the property rights of press ownership.[68]

William Rivers points out that under our constitutional arrangement the relationship between government and the press is an anomaly; the Constitution delegates the function of informing citizenry to the press. "In effect, the press—privately owned, beyond official control—was incorporated into the machinery of government," yet it is "an information system that is *of,* but not *in,* the government."[69] If we accept the dictionary definition of an anomaly (a "deviation from the normal or common order, form, or rule") and the four theories of the press as possible "common orders," then indeed the situation is anomolous, for none of the theories describe the government-press relationship in the U.S. The press is not an instrument of social control (as in authoritarian theory) nor an institution that assures social order by providing all possible viewpoints from which people choose freely and promote order through the convergence of individual wills (libertarian theory).[70] The relationship of government and the press is not predetermined in fixed, static ways by the Constitution or any abstract theory. The Constitution left the relationship largely undefined, ambiguous, and open, thus subject to continuous negotiation in the multitude of cooperative, conflicting, and complementary situations news sources and channels find themselves in every working day. Sometimes the press is an honest broker of official information, gathering it from official sources, transmitting it to the citizenry, and returning citizens' responses to political leaders. At other times the press is an interpreter, weighing and evaluating what governments do, operating as a check and fourth branch of government. And at still other times the press is a proponent of ideas of one faction or another, inside and outside the halls of government, serving as as adversary on behalf of its own complex of diversified interests, those of other groups, and the perceived interests of whatever journalists symbolize as the public at large. But at all times the government-press relationship (and the distinctive, overlapping, co-operating, and competing interests that comprise it) is political, at least in the sense we have employed that designation in this book, i.e., as communication having consequences for the regulation of human conduct under conditions of conflict.

Bibliography

Anyone seriously interested in asking what political news is all about should begin by reading Walter Lippmann's classic *Public Opinion* (New York: The Macmillan Co., 1922). In this relatively brief and easily read book Lippmann develops several notions pertaining to news and its relation to public opinion. He explores stereotypes, interests, leader-follower exchanges, the self-centered man's role in democracy, the news enterprise, and the role social science can play in expanding the world of reportable truths. Another classic pertaining to the role of the press in politics is A. J. Liebling's *The Press* (New York: Ballantine Books, 2nd ed., 1975). Two other works provide valuable insights into the news defining process. An excellent account, but unfortunately available only through microfilm-xerography facsimile, is Gaye Tuchman's Ph.D. dissertation in sociology, *News: The Newsman's Reality* (Ann Arbor: University Microfilms, Inc., 1969). Tuchman's position is that news is a picture of the newsman's perception of social and political reality as shaped by ideas the journalists take for granted and by the organization of everyday work. She draws clear and significant distinctions between newspaper and television presentation of the news, distinctions that flow from the way each medium processes events to news. The other very worthwhile work is Tamotsu Shibutani's study of rumor as a form of news, *Improvised News* (Indianapolis: The Bobbs-Merrill Co., Inc., 1966). Shibutani is particularly interested in how people work out collective definitions of news, a process he views from the perspective of symbolic interaction.

Several excellent works provide the reader with a background pertaining to how journalists make news through newsgathering. Three that are particularly concerned with organizational influences on the process are Leon V. Sigal, *Reporters and Officials* (Lexington, Mass.: D.C. Heath and Co., 1973), which focuses primarily upon newspapers; Edward Jay Epstein, *News From Nowhere* (New York: Vintage Books, 1974), a study of television news; and, for comparative purposes, see Jeremy Tunstall, *Journalists at Work* (Beverly Hills: Sage Publications, 1971). For a sense of the internal politics of a major news organization, the reader can do no better than read Gay Talese, *The Kingdom and the Power* (New York: World Publishing Co., 1969), an entertaining account of *The New York Times*. Also highly relevant along these lines is Chris Argyris, *Behind the Front Page* (San Francisco: Jossey-Bass Publishers, 1974). The relationship of economics to the news process is a topic Martin H. Seiden discusses in *Who Controls the Mass Media* (New York: Basic Books, Inc., Publishers, 1974). Sigal's aforementioned volume also focuses upon the relationships between newsgatherers and their sources and the subsequent impact upon newsmaking. Three accounts by working journalists provide insights into these relationships as well. The best is Douglass Cater's *The Fourth Branch of Government* (Boston: Houghton Mifflin Co., 1959) but readers will also profit by consulting James Reston, *The Artillery of the Press* (New York: Harper and Row, Publishers, 1967) and Joseph and Stewart Alsop, *The Reporter's Trade* (New York: Reynal and Co., 1958). Readers will also want to look closely at William L. Rivers, *The Opinionmakers* (Boston: Beacon Press, 1965) for an account of the Washington press corps in newsmaking. The interaction between Washington correspondents and official news sources has been the subject of increasing empirical inquiry. Reporting the results of that research are Bernard C. Cohen, *The Press and Foreign Policy* (Princeton: Princeton University Press, 1963); William O. Chittick, *State Department, Press, and Pressure Groups* (New York: Wiley-Interscience, 1970); Dan Nimmo, *Newsgathering in Washington* (New York: Atherton Press, 1964); and a report by the American Institute for Political Communication, *The Federal*

Government-Daily Press Relationship (Washington: AIPC, 1967). For a case of investigative reporting on the Washington and national political scene see Carl Bernstein and Bob Woodward, *All the President's Men* (New York: Warner Paperback Library, 1975). Two studies examine source-reporter relations below the federal level: Delmer D. Dunn focuses on state politics in *Public Officials and the Press* (Reading, Mass.: Addison-Wesley Publishing Co., 1969) and Edie N. Goldenberg looks at how resource-poor groups gain access to local newspapers in *Making the Papers* (Lexington, Mass.: Lexington Books, 1975). Readers wishing to compare newsgathering in American politics with how it is done in Great Britain should read Jeremy Tunstall, *The Westminster Lobby Correspondents* (London: Routledge and Kegan Paul, 1970). And two works by journalists provide entertaining accounts of how journalists relate to news sources during presidential election campaigns: James M. Perry, *Us and Them* (New York: Clarkson N. Potter, Inc., 1973) and Timothy Crouse, *The Boys on the Bus* (New York: Ballantine Books, 1974); Perry and Crouse provide quite different pictures of how the campaign press corps covered the 1972 presidential election. An empirical examination of that election is the study by the American Institute for Political Communication, *The Presidential Campaign of 1972: The Nixon Administration-Mass Media Relationship* (Washington: AIPC, 1974).

In addition to Epstein's work on the presentation of television news, readers will want to consult each of the following: former CBS-TV News president Sig Mickelson's *The Electric Mirror* (New York: Dodd, Mead and Co., 1972); *The Tin Kazoo* (Cambridge: The M.I.T. Press, 1975), a study by Edwin Diamond; Edith Efron's highly controversial analysis of the content of TV news, *The News Twisters* (Los Angeles: Nash Publishing, 1971); Robert S. Frank, *Message Dimensions of Television News* (Lexington, Mass.: Lexington Press, 1973); C. Richard Hofstetter, *Bias in the News* (Columbus, Ohio: Ohio State University Press, 1976); and David L. Altheide, *Creating Reality* (Beverly Hills: Sage Publications, 1976).

Consequences of the overlap between newsgathering and news management upon newsmaking occupy the attention of several writers, although in varying degrees. Three edited works contain selections looking specifically at relations between the press and various branches of government: Robert O. Blanchard, ed., *Congress and the News Media* (New York: Hastings House, 1974); the brief volume edited by Richard W. Lee, *Politics and the Press* (Washington: Acropolis Books, 1970); and Harry M. Clor, ed., *The Mass Media and Modern Democracy* (Chicago: Rand McNally College Publishing Co., 1974). Also consult the series of case studies published by William L. Rivers, *The Adversaries* (Boston: Beacon Press, 1970); Hillier Krieghbaum's critical volume, *Pressures on the Press* (New York: Thomas Y. Crowell, Co., 1973); and John Whale, *Journalism and Government: A British View* (Columbia, S.C.: University of South Carolina Press, 1972). Presidential news management, especially with respect to the development of the presidential news conference, is explored by Elmer E. Cornwell, *Presidential Leadership of Public Opinion* (Bloomington: Indiana University Press, 1965). Also consult Newton N. Minow, et al., *Presidential Television* (New York: Basic Books, Inc., 1973).

Three useful guides to how governments combine promotional activities with secrecy and censorship to manage the news are Francis E. Rourke's *Secrecy and Publicity* (Baltimore: The Johns Hopkins Press, 1961), a study by a political scientist; Clark R. Mollenhoff's journalist's perspective in *Washington Cover-Up* (Garden City, N.Y.: Doubleday and Co., 1962); and the volume edited by Norman Dorsen and Stephen Gillers which contains selections discussing censorship, classification, freedom of information, the right to know, etc., *None of Your Business* (Baltimore: Penguin Books, 1974). That the press is too often a willing accomplice in news management is the burden of the argument in Dale Minor's *The Information War* (New York: Hawthorn Books, Inc., 1970). A comprehensive account of how journalists acting as war correspondents have often cooperated in news management is to be found in Phillip Knightley's *The First Casualty* (New York: Harcourt, Brace, Janovich, 1975). Finally, consult Stanley Cohen and Jock Young, eds., *The Manufacture of News* (Beverly Hills: Sage Publications, 1973). The response of one segment of the news media to news management is the topic explored by Robert J. Glessing, *The Underground Press in America* (Bloomington: Indiana University Press, 1970).

Theories of what is and should be the relationship between government and the press have concerned numerous writers. Two volumes provide useful summaries of such theories: Fred S. Siebert, et al., *Four Theories of the Press* (Urbana: University of Illinois Press, 1956) and John C. Merrill, *The Imperative of Freedom* (New York: Hastings House, 1975).

NOTES

1.   James W. Carey, "The Communication Revolution and the Professional Communicator," in Paul Halmos, ed., *The Sociology of Mass Media Communications* (Keele, Staffordshire: University of Keele, 1969), p. 36.

2.   Walter Gieber, "News is What Newspapermen Make It," in Lewis Anthony Dexter and David Manning White, eds., *People, Society, and Mass Communications* (London: The Free Press of Glencoe, 1964), pp. 173–182.

3.   Leon V. Sigal, *Reporters and Officials: The Organization and Politics of Newsmaking* (Lexington, Mass.: D.C. Heath and Co., 1973).

4.   Dan D. Nimmo, *Newsgathering in Washington* (New York: Atherton Press, 1964), p. 123; see also Reed H. Blake and Edwin O. Haroldsen, *A Taxonomy of Concepts in Communication* (New York: Hastings House, 1975), pp. 49–50.

5.   Quoted in Blake and Haroldsen, *A Taxonomy of Concepts in Communication,* p. 49.

6.   David Manning White, "The 'Gatekeeper': A Case Study in the Selection of News," *Journalism Quarterly,* 27 (Fall 1950): 383–90; George A. Donohue, et al., "Gatekeeping: Mass Media Systems and Information Control," in F. Gerald Kline and Phillip J. Tichenor, eds., *Current Perspectives in Mass Communication Research* (Beverly Hills: Sage Publications, 1972), pp. 41–70.

7.   Warren Breed, "Social Control in the Newsroom," *Social Forces,* 33 (May 1955): 326–35.

8.   Ithiel de Sola Pool and Irwin Shulman, "Newsmen's Fantasies, Audiences, and Newswriting," *Public Opinion Quarterly,* 23 (Spring 1959): 145–58.

9.   Walter Lippmann, *Public Opinion* (New York: Macmillan Paperbacks, 1960), p. 349.

10.   Harvey Molotch and Marilyn Lester, "News as Purposive Behavior: On the Strategic Use of Routine Events, Accidents, and Scandals," *American Sociological Review,* 39 (February 1974): 101–112; Herbert Altschull, "What is News?", *Mass Communication Review,* 2 (December 1974): 17–23.

11.   Molotch and Lester, "News as Purposive Behavior," p. 102.

12.   Tamotsu Shibutani, *Improvised News* (Indianapolis: The Bobbs-Merrill Co., Inc., 1965), p. 40.

13.   Molotch and Lester, "News as Purposive Behavior," pp. 103–11.

14.   Gaye Tuchman, "Making News by Doing Work: Routinizing the Unexpected," *American Journal of Sociology,* 79 (July 1973): 110–31.

15.   Sigal, *Reporters and Officials,* p. 2.

16.   Lippmann, *Public Opinion,* p. 358.

17.   Shibutani, *Improvised News,* Ch. 2.

18.   Malcolm Warner, "Decision-Making in American TV Political News," in Halmos, ed., *The Sociology of Mass Media Communications,* pp. 169–79.

19.   Sigal, *Reporters and Officials,* pp. 13–19.

20.   Jeremy Tunstall, "News Organization Goals and Specialist Newsgathering Journalists," in Denis McQuail, ed., *Sociology of Mass Communications* (Baltimore: Penguin Books, 1972), pp. 259–80.

21.   Breed, "Social Control in the Newsroom."

22.   Philip Nobile, "How *The New York Times* Became Second Banana," *Esquire,* 83 (May 1975): 99.

23.   Edward Jay Epstein, *News From Nowhere* (New York: Random House, 1973), pp. 4–5.

24.   Gaye Tuchman, "Objectivity as Strategic Ritual: An Examination of Newsmen's Notions of Objectivity," *American Journal of Sociology,* 77 (July 1972): 660–78.

25.   Lippmann, *Public Opinion,* Ch. 24.

26.   Tuchman, "Objectivity as Strategic Ritual," p. 676 (emphasis in original).

27.   For an account of this event as news and as non-news see Gay Talese, *The Kingdom and the Power* (New York: The World Publishing Co., 1969).

28.   Philip J. Hilts, "CBS: The Fiefdom and the Power in Washington," *The Washington Post/Potomac,* April 21, 1974, pp. 11–14, 26–27, 34–35, 42.

29.   Edie N. Goldenberg, *Making the Papers* (Lexington, Mass.: Lexington Books, 1975), p. 104; Lee Sigelman, "Reporting the News: An Organizational Analysis," *American Journal of Sociology,* 79 (July 1973): 132–41. For suggested ways to deal with such organizational conflicts see Chris Argyris, *Behind the Front Page* (San Francisco: Jossey-Bass Publishers, 1974).

30.   Leon V. Sigal, *Reporters and Officials,* pp. 8–12.

31.   For contrasting views see Martin H. Seiden, *Who Controls the Mass Media?* (New York: Basic Books, Inc., Publishers, 1974); Edward J. Weston, "Mass Media Ownership and Control," paper presented at the annual meeting of the Southern Political Science Association, Nashville, Tennessee, November 7, 1965; Ben H. Bagdikian, "Shaping Media Content: Professional Personnel and Organizational Structure," *Public Opinion Quarterly,* 37 (Winter 1973–1974): 569–79.

32.   For an analysis of how policy officers, information officers, and nonofficial news sources interact with journalists see William O. Chittick, *State Department, Press, and Pressure Groups* (New York: Wiley-Interscience, 1970).

33.   John C. Merrill and Ralph L. Lowenstein, *Media, Messages and Men* (New York: David McKay, 1971), pp. 110–12.

34.   William Rivers, "The Correspondents After 25 Years," *Columbia Journalism Review,* 1 (Spring 1962): 4–10; Edward M. Glick, *The Federal Government-Daily Press Relationship* (Washington: The American Institute for Political Communication, 1967).

35.   John W. C. Johnstone, et al., "The Professional Values of American Newsmen," *Public Opinion Quarterly* 36 (Winter 1972–1973): 522–41.

36.   These views of how official sources regard their roles are based upon Nimmo, *Newsgathering in Washington,* pp. 19–31.

37.   Merrill and Lowenstein, *Media, Messages and Men,* p. 104; see also Goldenberg, *Making the Papers,* p. 95.

38.   Johnstone, et al., "The Professional Values of American Newsmen," pp. 522–41; John W. C. Johnstone et al., *The Newspeople* (Urbana: University of Illinois Press, 1976).

39. For other speculations regarding the relationship see Bernard C. Cohen, *The Press and Foreign Policy* (Princeton: Princeton University Press, 1963); Jeremy Tunstall, *The Westminster Lobby Correspondents* (London: Routledge and Kegan Paul, 1970) and *Journalists at Work* (Beverly Hills: Sage Publications, 1971); Chittick, *State Department, Press, and Pressure Groups,* (New York: Wiley-Interscience, 1970); and Douglass Cater, *The Fourth Branch of Government* (Boston: Houghton Mifflin Co., 1959).

40. Delmer D. Dunn, *Public Officials and the Press* (Reading, Mass.: Addison-Wesley Publishing Co., 1969), pp. 25–26; Sigal, *Reporters and Officials,* Ch. 4.

41. Sigal, *Reporters and Officials,* p. 106.

42. Leonard W. Doob, *Public Opinion and Propaganda* (Hamden, Conn.: Archon Books, 1966), p. 271.

43. Sigal, *Reporters and Officials,* p. 74.

44. *The Presidential Campaign of 1972: The Nixon Administration-Mass Media Relationship* (Washington: The American Institute for Political Communication, 1974); Lee B. Becker, et al., "The Development of Political Cognitions," in Steven H. Chaffee, ed., *Political Communication* (Beverly Hills: Sage Publications, 1975), p. 21. See also Robert Cirino, *Don't Blame the People* (Los Angeles: Diversity Books, 1971) and Edith Efron, *The News Twisters* (Los Angeles: Nash Publishing, 1971).

45. William L. Rivers, "The Press as a Communication System," in Ithiel de Sola Pool and Wilbur Schramm, eds., *Handbook of Communication* (Chicago: Rand McNally Co., 1973), pp. 521–50.

46. *Trends in Public Attitudes Toward Television and Other News Media 1959–1974* (New York: The Roper Organization, Inc., 1975); Wilbur Schramm and Janet Alexander, "Broadcasting," in Pool and Schramm, eds., *Handbook of Communication,* pp. 577–618.

47. See especially Epstein, *News From Nowhere*: Diamond, *The Tin Kazoo;* Warner, "Decision-Making in American TV Political News"; and Gary L. Wamsley and Richard A. Pride, "Television Network News: Re-Thinking the Iceberg Problem," *Western Political Quarterly,* 25 (September 1972): 434–50.

48. Edwin Diamond, "Everybody into the Pool," *New York Magazine,* 8 (March 10, 1975): 68.

49. *Trends in Public Attitudes Toward Television,* p. 3.

50. Newton N. Minow, et al., *Presidential Television* (New York: Basic Books, Inc., 1973).

51. Diamond, *The Tin Kazoo,* p. 5.

52. "Congress and the Media: Partners in Propaganda," *Columbia Journalism Review,* 12 (January/February 1974): 5.

53. Hillier Kriegbaum, *Pressures on the Press* (New York: Thomas Y. Crowell, 1973), p. 210.

54. *The New Methodology* (Washington, D.C.: The American Institute for Political Communication, 1967), pp. 116–50.

55. Nimmo, *Newsgathering in Washington,* Ch. 6.

56. *The Presidential Campaign of 1972,* p. 136.

57. Chester Newland, "Press Coverage of the United States Supreme Court," *Western Political Quarterly,* 17 (March 1964): 15–36; David L. Grey, *The Supreme Court and the News Media* (Evanston, Ill.: Northwestern University Press, 1968); James E. Clayton, "News from the Supreme Court and the Justice Department," in Ray E. Hiebert, ed., *The Press in Washington* (New York: Dodd Mead and Co., 1966), 182–96; Stephen L. Wasby, *The Impact of the United States Supreme Court* (Homewood, Ill.: The Dorsey Press, 1970), pp. 83–99.

58. I. William Hill, "Report Urges Tougher Questions for President," *Editor and Publisher,* 108 (November 22, 1975): 17.

59. See Robert Walters, "What Did Ziegler Say and When Did He Say It?"

Columbia Journalism Review, 13 (September/October 1974): 30–35; Lou Cannon, "Nessen's Briefings: Missing Questions (and Answers)," *Columbia Journalism Review,* 12 (Nov./Dec. 1973): 39–43.

60. Ted Joseph, "How White House Correspondents Feel About Background Briefings," *Journalism Quarterly,* 50 (Autumn 1973): 509–16, 532.

61. Carl Rowan, "The 'Leak' Game," *The Chattanooga Times,* June 26, 1974, p. 14.

62. Glick, *The Federal Government-Daily Press Relationship,* p. 33.

63. See Francis E. Rourke, *Secrecy and Publicity: Dilemmas of Democracy* (Baltimore: The Johns Hopkins Press, 1961) and Dale Minor, *The Information War* (New York: Hawthorn Books, Inc., 1970).

64. William G. Phillips, "The Government's Classification System," in Norman Dorsen and Stephen Gillers, eds., *None of Your Business* (Baltimore: Penguin Books, 1974), pp. 61–92.

65. John B. Adams, *State Open Meeting Laws: An Overview* (Columbia, Mo.: Freedom of Information Foundation, 1974).

66. See the monograph entitled *Miami Herald v. Tornillo: The Trial of the First Amendment* (Columbia, Mo.: Freedom of Information Center, 1975), p. 33, and Jerome A. Barron, *Freedom of the Press for Whom?* (Bloomington: Indiana University Press, 1973).

67. Marc A. Franklin, "Freedom and Control of Communication," in Pool and Schramm, eds., *Handbook of Communication,* pp. 887–908; Donald M. Gillmor, *Judicial Restraints on the Press* (Columbia, Mo.: Freedom of Information Foundation, 1974); and David Gordon, *Newsman's Privilege and the Law* (Columbia, Mo.: Freedom of Information Foundation, 1974).

68. Fred S. Siebert et al., *Four Theories of the Press* (Urbana: University of Illinois Press, 1956).

69. Rivers, "The Press as a Communication System," p. 523 (emphasis in original).

70. John C. Merrill, *The Imperative of Freedom* (New York: Hastings House, 1974), Chs. 1, 4, and 5.

part three

AUDIENCES OF POLITICAL COMMUNICATION: With Whom?

chapter 7

Public Opinion: Mass, Publics, and Popular Expressions

In thinking about public opinion an old adage about the weather comes to mind: "Everybody talks about the weather but nobody does anything about it." Everybody, it seems, also talks about public opinion—politicians, members of the press, pollsters, even people sitting around complaining about taxes and assorted other problems. But unlike people who do nothing about the weather, many who talk about public opinion do something about it. The varieties of political communicators we described in Chapter 2, at least in part, can be distinguished by what they do about public opinion: politicians acting as representatives voice constituency opinion, ideologists try to forge it; in their capacity as promoters, professional communicators seek to change opinion, as journalists they inform it; and activists as spokespersons speak for group opinions, while as opinion leaders they guide the popular will. Moreover, the language of political communicators (Chapter 3), their means of persuasion (Chapter 4), and the media they employ (Chapters 5 and 6) all reflect efforts to do something about public opinion. In this chapter we try to clarify what all the talk and activity is about. We begin with a detailed look at the nature of opinions; then we consider the personal, social, and political processes of opinion formation that derive from the give-and-take of communication.

WHAT IS AN OPINION? A REVIEW AND CLOSER LOOK AT A PROCESS

In Chapter 1 we sketched a working characterization of public opinion, saying it is an aspect of political communication. Because that perspective is critical to the discussions in the remainder of this book, it is useful to recapitulate it in detail and elaborate upon points introduced earlier. We described public opinion as a process joining the thoughts, feelings, and proposals expressed by private citizens to the policy choices made by public officials charged with achieving social order in situations involving conflicts, disputes, and disagreements over what to do and how to do it. Like any process, public opinion changes and evolves. Again one thinks of the weather, "If you don't like the weather, just wait awhile, it'll change." There is a similar dynamic quality to public opinion, a quality traceable to a number of things. A key factor stands out, a factor discussed before, but one now deserving closer scrutiny: i.e., how people actively construct meaningful perceptions of political phenomena (their political images) and express those meanings through overlapping beliefs, values, and expectations (their opinions).

Tendencies of Opinion Activity

A central premise of our discussion of political communication has been that people act toward things on the basis of the meanings the objects have for them. But the meaning of an object, we have said, whether a person, place, event, idea, or word, is neither fixed nor static. People continuously construct meanings of things by dealing with them. In sum, they behave toward things by attributing meaning to them, meaning that in turn derives from their behavior as persons. Through this give-and-take between meaning and action, people acquire certain tendencies. These tendencies figure into their behavior when entering new situations. However, as stressed in Chapter 1, these tendencies are not predispositions to act in specific ways in new situations. Tendencies do not predetermine behavior. Rather, they are tendencies *of* activity. Tendencies suggest to a person a possible line of action, but not the sole line. What a person takes into account in finding meaning in a novel situation may be acquired tendencies, but this need not always be so. Moreover, as tendencies *of* activity rather than *to* activity, the tendencies themselves undergo change as a person constructs meaning in a subjective world and behaves accordingly.

Think of a tendency as a stage of an activity.[1] A person sits before a typewriter composing a letter to a friend. Assuming one has learned how to type well, the tendency to ready one's mind and fingers and to strike the proper keys in an appropriate sequence goes unnoticed. Yet the stages of the activity are there: tendency-strike-tendency-strike-tendency-strike and so forth. Similarly, driving an automobile consists of tendency-acts: a perception of traveling too fast, a tendency to ease up on the gas pedal, an easing up, perception of slowing down too much, a tendency to speed up, a pressing on the accelerator, and so on.

Miller, Galanter, and Pribram describe the relationship between tendencies and activities in a way that will help us understand the part played by tendencies in the activities of expressing personal beliefs, values, and expectations.[2] Activity is an intrinsic characteristic of any organism, including persons. Activities consist of three principal stages—images, plans, and operations. An *image* is everything a person has learned relevant to a situation and to acts that may occur within it. Included in an image is all one's knowledge (cognitions) whether correct or incorrect, all preferences (affects) attached to the particular stage of affairs that attracts or repels the person in the situation, and all expectations (conations) the person has of what may happen if he or she behaves in alternate ways toward objects in the situation. In sum, an image is a tendency composed of thoughts, feelings, and inclinations. Images change constantly with experience. *Plans* are represented in images and consist of the instructions a person gives himself by engaging in activity (for example, strike the letter *k* on the typewriter or ease up on the gas pedal). Sometimes plans are consciously and deliberately formalized and executed. But at other times plans are so routinized and habitual as to be undertaken unconsciously. A key aspect of plans is that they carry instructions not only of what to do but of the consequences of doing things; through plans an individual compares what was intended with what actually was achieved (as when a person perceives easing up too much on the car's gas pedal and must compensate by pressing down slightly). Finally, *operations* are the things people do, such as operating a typewriter, driving an automobile, etc.

Images, plans, and operations comprise a matrix of stages of activity, an ever changing situation within which a person originates, develops, and constructs behavior in a fashion that means something for him or her. In this matrix *"behavior depends on the image"*[3] and "the way in which the world is imagined determines at any particular moment what men will do."[4] But "depends on" and "determines" does not mean that fixed images, or tendencies, dictate acts. As Lippman avowed, "no statement of the end or any description of the tendencies to seek it, can explain the behavior which results." Rather, what men imagine guides "their effort, their feelings, and their hopes, not their accomplishments and results." Only in the sense that they are changing tendencies are images "a determining element in thought, feeling, and action."[5] Through plans people exploit their images. Plans tell one what to take into account in a given situation that might be relevant in making choices. Thayer states it thus: "The phenomenon basic to and underlying every situation in which human communication occurs is simply this: that an organism (an individual) took something into account, whether it was some observable event, some internal condition, the meaning of something read or looked at, some feeling intermingled with past memory—literally anything that could be taken-into-account by human beings in general and that individual in particular."[6] In sum, tendencies such as images and plans are stages of activity whereby people take-things-into-account

Table 7-1   *Tendencies, Acts, and Opinions*

Stages of Activity

Tendency <. . . . . >Act
Images < . . . . > Plans < . . . . >Operations
Images < . . . . >Interpretations< . . . . >Opinions
                             (taking into account)

and relate their thoughts, feelings, and inclinations to what they perceive
as relevant for responding to in a given situation.

Now, what does all this have to do with the opinion process? Simply
put, opinions are activities. People register their opinions by doing all
kinds of things—by voting or not voting, replying to a pollster's questions,
carrying picket signs, writing a congressman, obeying laws, disobeying
laws, going to court, donating money to a candidate's campaign, and
all manner of other acts. As activities, opinions incorporate images of
the political world, plans taking specific political objects into account,
and operations that are meaningful responses. A person's images of politics
consist of all thoughts, feelings, and inclinations that arise from, change,
and are exchanged through communication. One's plans consist of the
interpretative process when a person takes things into account in making
choices. Opinions are the beliefs, values, and expectations one voices
through behavior. We represent the stages of opinion activity in Table
7-1. Take particular note that the lines connecting tendency and acts,
images, plans, and operations, or political images, interpretations, and
opinions point in two directions. This is to emphasize that the relationship
in each instance is reciprocal. As stages of activity, tendencies and acts
shape one another; images, plans, and operations jointly influence each
other; and a person's subjective pictures of the political world, interpretations of what he or she takes into account, and opinions overlap. They
modify each other in a process that gives meaning to political objects
and actions. With that in mind let us look at each component of opinion
activity—political images, interpretations, and opinions—and elaborate
upon other details contained in Table 7-1.

Personal Images of Politics

The subjective thoughts, feelings, and inclinations that comprise a person's
images of politics are both useful and gratifying to the individual. They
are useful in at least three ways. First, no matter how correct or incorrect,
complete or incomplete may be one's knowledge about politics, it gives
that person some way of understanding specific political events. If, for

example, one knows something of executive-legislative relations, how committees of Congress work, and the role of pressure groups in American politics, a citizen can understand why Congress seldom complies when the president calls for massive cuts in federal spending. Or if one thinks all politicians are corrupt, that person also has at least one explanation for the same failure to cut spending and taxation. Second, the general likes and dislikes in a person's political images offer a basis for evaluating political objects. A person who prefers not to drink alcoholic beverages or consume drugs may also oppose legislation legalizing the sale of liquor or marijuana. Third, a person's self-image provides a way of relating one's self to others. One with a self-conception as a loyal, staunch American is more likely to find comfort in a patriotic, perhaps even chauvinistic organization than by identifying with a group committed to the cause of making the United Nations into a world government.

A person's images, then, assist in understanding, evaluating, and identifying with political events, ideas, causes, or leaders. Images help provide subjectively acceptable reasons for why things are as they seem to be, for political preferences, and for joining with others. But people not only have reasons for acting. People also have a need to act. Abraham Maslow theorizes that humans have a hierarchy of needs; as people fulfill the needs at one level, other levels of needs emerge. For Maslow the hierarchy consists of five levels of human needs:[7]

1. *Physiological:* food, clothing, shelter, air, water, reproduction, etc.
2. *Safety and security:* assurance of well-being, protection against attack, etc.
3. *Love and belongingness:* affection, being with others, etc.
4. *Esteem:* a feeling of personal worth and competence.
5. *Self-actualization:* a sense of self-fulfillment, control over one's surroundings and destiny, and ability to achieve desires.

Certainly images alone do not gratify human needs. Food, clothing, and shelter stem from more than human imagination; tangible goods are ulitmately essential to provide these necessities. If those tangibles are scarce, writes James Davies, the resulting deprivation "destroys politics for the needful."[8] Deprived people have their images and plans, but these are directed at achieving physical survival and only rarely pertain to politics. Generally people do not turn to politics for satisfying hunger or for love, self-esteem, or self-actualization. Instead they go to food markets, seek friends, and pursue other activities. It is when gratification of human needs is threatened by forces too powerful to be dealt with privately that we turn to politics and make demands upon governments for protection. Then political images come into play. People exchange those images through political communication as a way of regulating their disputes to assure a social order that preserves the opportunity to gratify physical, social, and psychological needs. As Langer notes, a person "can adapt himself somehow to anything his imagination can cope with; but he cannot deal with chaos."[9] Politics is a way of alleviating social chaos and the threats to the pursuit of basic needs associated with disruptions.

Once in politics, personal images help replace a perception of confusion with a sense of social order; moreover, popular images can even directly satisfy human needs, or at least yield the impression that they are gratified. Take as an example the need for self-esteem. The philosopher William James provided a formula for self-esteem: Self-esteem = Success/Pretensions.[10] The fraction (self-esteem) can be increased either by increasing the numerator (success) or decreasing the denominator (pretensions). Small wonder then that many a politician's subjective feelings of "success" and "pretensions" are quite as important in the leader's calculus of self-esteem as the achievements and aspirations others attribute to that politician. It is the same for all of us. We acquire a sense of physical comfort, well-being, belonging, esteem, and fulfillment through our imagined accomplishments as well as by enjoying the tangible rewards of our experience. As we saw in Chapter 3, political leaders understand that images gratify human needs, and they therefore couch their appeals in symbols to evoke sympathetic images among mass audiences. Millions of Americans remain unemployed and the cost of living continues to rise, yet a presidential announcement that "we have surmounted our economic difficulties" conjures up an image of better times ahead, perhaps even sustained approval of the incumbent administration. To the extent that political symbols do provoke gratifying images, those images, as the commercial for a leading soft drink says, are the real thing.

Personal Interpretations of Politics

Table 7–1 depicts a process whereby one relates personal images to private opinions through interpretation. By interpretation a person takes things into account, orders them, and responds to the most salient. Research indicates a number of things people routinely take into account in formulating their private political opinions and making them public. At best it is but a partial list, but here are a few possibilities:

1. *Inner states:* These refer to such things as the person's personality traits, predispositions, attitudes, emotions, wants, needs, moods, motivations, habits, and a host of other factors generally thought of as psychological and physiological.
2. *Demographic characteristics:* Here we include a person's age, sex, ethnicity, area of residence, social class (including income, education level, occupation), etc.
3. *Social characteristics:* These include the groups a person belongs to (family, friends, coworkers, church, peers, etc.), those one identifies with, respects, and looks to as models for what to do and how.

4. *Legal/formal considerations:* Governmental institutions, laws, rules, regulations, procedures, practices, and the cost or benefits of obedience or rebellion can all figure in the interpretative process whereby people formulate opinions.
5. *Partisan preferences:* Many people have long-term and enduring preferences for a political party, ideology, or cause, and these too may be taken into account through interpretation.
6. *Communication:* Here we must include who the sources of political communication are and what people think of them (see Chapter 4), the symbols and languages of their messages, the media they use, and the persuasive techniques they employ.
7. *Political objects:* People express opinions about something; some person, event, issue, idea, question, proposal, or other object is the focus and stimulus for opinion expression in the first place.
8. *Political settings:* The objects about which people express opinions appear in settings confined by time and space; people take these settings into account, sometimes as the background against which the object appears and at others as more important than the object itself (one might, for example, favor ending all U.S. assistance to Israel, but wish to continue it during an era of Arab-Israeli tensions).
9. *Options:* Here are included all of the available opinions one can express (favor, oppose, a middle position, no opinion, refuse to answer) and the means one can use to express them—voting, campaigning, donating money to a candidate, violent action, etc.

Obviously then there are many things people take into account in formulating private opinions and giving them public expression. That being the case, it is extremely difficult to say which factor or combination thereof is most influential in opinion making. As we shall see in Chapter 8, various factors correlate to some degree with the opinions Americans express on a wide variety of issues. The point here, however, is that none of these cause the opinions in question. Rather, in the tendency-act matrix (Table 7-1) that joins images, interpretations, and opinions, they are but possible things taken into account. In some instances a person's inner states are directly associated with expressed opinions; in others it is partisanship, perceptions of what governmental leaders are doing, response to a particular medium of communication, inability to express views clearly, and so forth. The interpretative process is not simply a passive link between inner states and a person's behavior.[11] Nor is it a mechanism merely activating predetermined, conditioned responses to proffered stimuli.[12] Instead, through interpretation a person exploits his thoughts, feelings, and inclinations in a minded, active fashion and responds to objects in settings in a subjectively meaningful fashion.

The Organization of Personal Opinions

An opinion is an active response to a stimulus, a response constructed through personal interpretation derived from and contributing to images. Any opinion reflects a complex organization of three components—beliefs, values, and expectations. These components overlap, but for purposes of understanding personal opinions as the building blocks of public opinion, let us consider each aspect separately before turning to their interrelations.

Personal Beliefs in Politics

The person who holds a belief perceives some relationship between two things or between a thing and a characteristic of it.[13] For example, in 1975 the Gallup poll asked a cross section of American adults if they thought a war would occur in the Middle East that year. Twenty-eight percent perceived such a relationship between war, the Middle East, and 1975; fifty-six percent did not; the remainder expressed no belief.[14] In 1976 the Harris Survey asked Americans if they perceived Ronald Reagan, then campaigning for the Republican presidential nomination, as an ordinary politician. A 45–25 percent plurality did not believe "ordinary politician" to be characteristic of Reagan.[15] Beliefs are thus closely associated with the cognitive, or thought, aspects of personal images and interpretations. They involve credulity, i.e., people either believe or disbelieve. Credulity varies in intensity from an unshakeable conviction to total disbelief. Finally, beliefs vary with respect to their salience for a person. One may, for instance, believe that the likelihood of there being a nuclear war during one's lifetime is fairly great, yet go about daily routine giving scarcely a thought to the matter; a second person holding the same belief may be so bothered by the likelihood of nuclear holocaust as to enjoy life to the fullest on grounds that tomorrow all may be dead.

Philosophers have long speculated over the sources of human beliefs and disbeliefs. Francis Bacon, who wrote in the early seventeenth century, spoke of four key sources as "idols," or false notions. People who follow the Idols of the Tribe accept the false assertion that the human senses and perceptions are adequate sources of belief; worshipers of the Idols of the Cave regard the private world of each individual rather than public exchange as the chief source of beliefs; persons who think that social intercourse alone is the source of beliefs follow Idols of the Marketplace; and people who take their beliefs from systems of thought passed down by tradition, philosophy, and even science embrace the Idols of the Theater.[16] The founder of American pragmatic doctrines, Charles S. Peirce, had a more straightforward list of the sources of beliefs. When faced with the tension produced by a state of doubt, people may fall back upon the unquestioned faiths they have learned in their lifetimes (the method of tenacity), accept the word of another person, group, or institution as to what to believe (the method of authority), or undertake a form of inquiry that checks beliefs against experience and reason (the scientific method).[17]

In probing the sources of politically relevant beliefs, social psychologist Daryl Bem distinguishes between what he calls primitive and higher order beliefs. Primitive beliefs are things we take for granted, scarcely noticing that we hold them at all. Perhaps the most important primitive belief is our unquestioned faith in the validity of our senses. Our sensory experiences are thereby a source of belief. Bacon might have regarded it as an Idol of the Tribe, but for most people, seeing is believing. Perhaps this is one of the reasons Americans opt for television as their most credible source of political information (see Chapter 4). A second key primitive belief is the tendency to accept without question the credibility of some external authority in fixing our views, a combination of Idols of the Marketplace and Theater. As Bem stresses, we not only experience our world directly, we are told about it as well: "It is in this way that notions about such intangibles as God, absent grandmothers, and threatened tooth decay first enter a child's system of beliefs."[18] So also, we might add, enter such authority figures as the president, policeman, and Democratic or Republican parties (see Chapter 9).

As noted above the central quality of a primitive belief is that it is unquestioned. As people grow up they become more cautious about believing everything they see or everything authorities say. For instance, instead of saying, "I know the recession is over because the president said so," a person more consciously thinks through the premises involved:

> The president says that the recession is over.
> The president is knowledgeable and trustworthy in
>   such matters.
> Therefore, it is true that the recession is over.

A belief derived from such reasoning, whereby one no longer treats the first premise as synonymous with the conclusion, is what Bem calls a higher order belief. Awareness of the fallibility of our sensory experiences or of external authorities permits us to question our higher order beliefs and take a skeptical stance toward political leaders trying to persuade us to their beliefs. Moreover, we can guard against the tendency to hold overgeneralized beliefs based on too limited a set of experiences (such stereotypes, for instance, as that the Democratic party is the party of war, the Republican, the party of depression). But it is not easy to be so thoughtful. Frequently, perhaps too frequently, we take our senses or authorities at face value, as valid internal or external sources of our convictions. One reason is that we want to do so because our beliefs are closely tied to cherished values, values that might be threatened by loosening the hold beliefs have upon us.

Personal Values in Politics

Values are simply preferences people have for certain ends or ways of doing things.[19] They are closely associated with the affective, or feeling, content of personal images which assist people in evaluating themselves and their environments. Like beliefs, values vary in direction (likes versus dislikes), intensity (strong, moderate, weak), and with respect to the salience any given value has for a person.

Psychologist Harry Stack Sullivan theorized that values stem from two principal human needs, the need to satisfy biological and physiological survival requirements and tensions, and the need to be secure from anxiety provoking social situations such as the disapproval of others.[20] These needs for satisfaction and security contribute to what Lasswell and Kaplan describe as two categories of values: (1) welfare values including the pursuit of well-being, wealth, skills, and enlightenment, and (2) deference values such as craving for respect, a reputation for moral rectitude, affection and popularity, and power.[21]

The welfare and deference values associated with gratifying satisfaction and security needs are terminal values or goals. They are ends sought that differ from the means to achieve those ends, which are instrumental values. In the late 1960s a study was undertaken to discover the terminal and instrumental values of Americans. The procedure was to ask a sampling of 1400 Americans over 21 years of age to rank separately, and in order of importance to each respondent, 18 terminal values (such as a comfortable life, an exciting life, a world of beauty, equality, etc.) and instrumental values (including ambitious, broadminded, capable, forgiving, imaginative, etc.). The terminal values ranked highest by the sample were a world of peace, family security, and freedom; ranked lowest was an exciting life; equality was ranked about midway in the list. Highest ranking instrumental values included honesty, ambition, and responsibility; among the lowest ranking were imagination, logic, and obedience. A replication of this study in the 1970s revealed no substantial change in Americans' ranking of values with the passage of time.[22]

Psychologist Milton Rokeach illustrates how different ways of ranking values provide clues to differing political views.[23] Rokeach took the values of freedom and equality as an example: people can value both freedom and equality, neither freedom nor equality, equality but not freedom, and freedom but not equality. Rokeach content-analyzed (see Appendix for details of content analysis) the writings of various political leaders: socialists Norman Thomas and Erich Fromm, Nazi leader Adolf Hitler, Bolshevik leader Nikolai Lenin, and conservative U.S. Senator Barry Goldwater. By comparing the number of favorable and unfavorable references to freedom and equality with similar references to fifteen other values, Rokeach was able to calculate the ranking of freedom and equality by the various political leaders. He found that the socialist writers valued both freedom and equality, ranking them one and two respectively. Hitler devalued both; freedom ranked sixteenth and equality seventeenth in his *Mein Kampf*. Lenin's writings rank equality number one, but freedom ranks last. In Goldwater's *Conscience of a Conservative,* in contrast, freedom ranks number one and equality is second to last. In the nationwide survey on values mentioned above, Americans ranked freedom third and equality midway among eighteen values, thus placing Americans much closer to the socialists or to Goldwater's rankings than to those of Hitler or Lenin.

Personal Expectations in Politics

In this discussion we have stressed the purposive quality of human behavior, i.e., that people act in ways meaningful to them to achieve ends that they regard valuable. In the process they make conscious and unconscious estimates of what to do, given their beliefs, to realize both instrumental and terminal values. They formulate expectations of what the future will be like when they carry out proposed courses of action in the present; they base those expectations on their experiences in the past. Thus, through personal expectations we construct our acts by bringing our pasts to bear upon the present in order to assess future possibilities. Expectations are associated with the conative, or inclining, aspect of personal images and the interpretative processes psychologists sometimes equate with impulse, desire, volition, and striving.

Personal expectations are of utmost importance in politics. People frequently judge a political event or a leader's performance on the basis of what they expected to happen. If expectations are high and an event or leader's conduct does not match them, people are disappointed or disparage a politician. If expectations are low and easily exceeded, they may be pleasantly surprised by even a poor showing. Candidates running in presidential primaries understand this phenomenon very well. As a means of influencing voters' expectations they poor-mouth their chances much like a football coach bemoans his team's lack of talent, the weather, time for preparation, and number of injuries before a big game so as not to get the fans' hopes up too much. Thus Ronald Reagan announced in 1976 that if he received 40 percent of the New Hampshire primary vote against President Ford, this could be considered a Reagan victory: George Wallace minimized his chances for success in the 1976 Massachusetts primary by stating that he did not expect more than 8 percent of the vote. By purposely underestimating his strength, a candidate and his supporters can claim victory even when failing to win a majority or even plurality of votes, a common tactic of campaign gamesmanship.

A key function of the press in the opinion process is to raise and lower expectations through their report of events. A case in point is the primary campaign conducted in New Hampshire in 1972 for the Democratic presidential nomination. Early in the campaign the press generally had designated Senator Edmund Muskie as the "front-runner." To retain that designation Muskie had to do well in New Hampshire. David Broder of *The Washington Post* set the tone of journalistic assessments by writing that the "acknowledged front-runner" would need to win "at least half" of the Democratic primary votes to claim victory, half in a field of more than half a dozen candidates. Why Muskie could claim victory only by achieving a majority in so crowded a race was left unsaid, but other reporters picked up Broder's theme. Moreover, a poll in early January estimated 65 percent support for Muskie and thus reinforced the expectation of a majority for the front-runner. In the unlikely event that one of Muskie's challengers (such as Senator George McGovern) could show "surprising strength" and keep the front-runner from receiving a majority, it would give such a challenger momentum in his nomination drive. Although Muskie attempted to lower such elevated expectations, the effort was to little avail. To be sure, a final preprimary poll reported signs that Muskie was in trouble: Muskie 42 percent, McGovern 26, others 12, and 20 percent of the respondents undecided. In the final election returns Muskie received 46 percent, McGovern 37 percent. Although winning more votes than his nearest rival, Muskie had not lived up to press expectations. Ironically, the leading vote getter suffered a "damaging loss," and a candidate receiving only slightly more than one-third of the primary vote (McGovern) claimed a "moral victory."[24]

Personal Opinions: Reflecting Systems of Beliefs, Values, and Expectations

Opinions combine beliefs, values, and expectations, usually in response to a single object (e.g., "I disapprove of the way the president is handling his job"). Such responses are generally not random reactions to things taken into account, but are embedded in reasonably coherent systems of beliefs, values, and expectations. In some people the coherence is the result of elaborate inductive and deductive reasoning. More typically, however, systems of belief, values, and expectations are less logical and rational than they are psychologically satisfying to the person who holds them. For example, there is a logical inconsistency when Joe Cool on the one hand believes strongly that gasoline and petroleum products must be conserved at all costs, and on the other, purchases an oversized automobile equipped with gas guzzling options that will result in less than ten miles to the gallon. But perhaps all Joe's friends are conservationists, and besides, it's fun to own a big car.

To speak of systems of beliefs, values, and expectations does not, therefore, imply a logical consistency in one's views. Instead there is an interweaving of perceptions, preferences, and plans in ways reflecting both logic and psychologic.[25] Partly as a result of the wedding of logic and psychologic, people differ in their belief, value, or expectation systems. Rokeach has noted the ways that personal belief systems differ.[26] Some

people, for instance, quickly see relationships between two or more of
their beliefs; others isolate specific beliefs from one another. We all know
of people who claim that their positive or negative beliefs about a particular party have nothing to do with their beliefs about the character of
a president who is a member of that party. They see no relationship
between their being Republican and their beliefs about the president,
be he Republican or Democrat, a typical case of isolation in belief systems.
Or some people have highly differentiated belief systems: they see a difference, for example, in thinking about a "female president" and about
a president who happens to be a female. Belief systems also vary in their
comprehensiveness; some systems cover only a limited number of things,
while others—communism, Taoism, some forms of Christianity—cover all
manner of beliefs and disbeliefs. We have already seen as well that people
differ with respect to how important, or salient, certain of their beliefs
are relative to others. Some beliefs may be so central and vital that if
badly shaken (such as a citizen's belief in the basic honesty of an incumbent president) they contribute to disillusionment with a wide range of
related beliefs (such as cynical distrust of all government). More peripheral beliefs, however, change without seriously threatening a person's
structure of fundamental convictions, as when one learns that a minor
presidential subordinate rather than the president is a crook. And belief
systems differ with respect to their focus on time: some people live in
the here and now, seldom looking back for fear, as Satchel Paige intoned,
"somethin' might be gainin' on you"; others confine their thoughts to
"the good old days" and the "way things used to be"; still others orient
their beliefs to the future, planning what life will be like "when my ship
comes in"; and still others carry out the vow of Dickens's Ebenezer Scrooge
after he had been visited by three ghosts in the classic *A Christmas Carol,*
to "live in the past, the present, and the future."

Belief systems may be opened or closed.[27] We say a person's belief system is open when he is able to judge the credulity and acceptability of a proposed idea independently of the source that proposed it. An open-minded
person, for instance, can evaluate a president's budget proposals on their
merits rather than accepting or opposing them because they are the president's. A closed belief system is characteristic of a person who cannot
differentiate between the merits of an idea and the source who advocates
it, as when a staunch Democrat believes everything said by Democratic
presidents but rejects anything said by a Republican president.

Sartori provides a typology of belief-value systems based upon whether
belief systems are open or closed and values are strongly or weakly held:
(1) a closed belief system combined with strongly held values is *adamant*;
(2) a *resilient* combination is one with closed beliefs but weakly held values;
(3) an open belief system unites with strongly held values to constitute
a *firm* ordering; and (4) an open belief system with weakly held values
is *flexible*. The adamant belief-value combination, suggests Sartori, is typi-

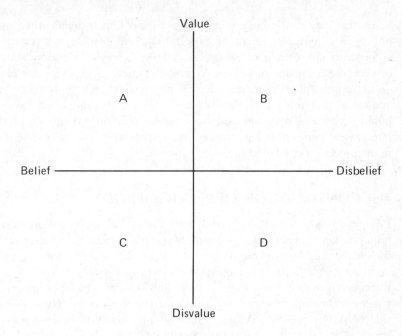

Figure 7-1   The Intersection of Belief and Value Systems

cal of people who are ideological in their orientation; their belief structures are closed and they are firmly attached to their convictions. The pragmatic orientation is just the opposite, a flexible combination of open cognitive structure and weakly held values. In Chapter 8 we shall explore the extent to which mass opinion in American politics is more typically ideological or pragmatic.[28]

Belief systems and value systems overlap in other respects. Consider Figure 7-1. The horizontal axis represents a continuum of belief-disbelief with one pole representing what people believe in most strongly and the other what they believe in not at all. The vertical axis represents a value-disvalue system running from what people prize most to what they find most repulsive. Everyone probably relates personal beliefs and values in one or more of the four possible ways suggested by Figure 7-1. A voter might, for instance, believe that an independent (say a George Wallace or a Eugene McCarthy) rather than one of the two-party candidates could be elected president; if one favors such an election, that voter falls into quadrant A. Or one might favor the election of an independent, yet think it impossible (quadrant B). In quadrant C, the voter might think such an election outcome likely but oppose it. Finally, quadrant D, one might oppose the election of an independent as president while thinking the eventuality improbable.

Another way of thinking about Figure 7-1 is that it depicts the possibilities in a person's system of expectations. An expectation system is an ordering of estimates of the probabilities of achieving what one values or avoiding what one disvalues. A person's system of expectations plays an important role influencing whether or not to express personal beliefs and values in a public way, that is, whether personal opinions will become public opinion. To understand how public opinion emerges from the interplay of personal beliefs, values, and expectations we must now turn to the process of constructing public opinion.

THE CONSTRUCTION OF PUBLIC OPINION

Private opinions consist of verbal and nonverbal activities presenting individual images and interpretations of specific objects in settings, usually in the form of issues, that people take into account. For those private opinions to constitute public opinion they must be widely shared through the collective activities of more people than the few who were the initial parties to the dispute or problem that gave rise to the issue. The construction of public opinion from private opinions involves the interplay of personal, social, and political processes (see Chapter 1). To examine that construction, let us look at the phases of opinion formation, the characteristics of public opinion, and the implications of personal, social, and political aspects of opinion construction.

Phases of Opinion Formation

The origin of public opinion on most matters lies in the emergence of some disagreement or dispute that has a potential for evolving into an issue that will capture the attention of many people. As Davison points out, the development of such disputes is much like that of seeds: of the thousands of them scattered over the landscape some fall on rocks and fail to germinate, others take root but die because the soil is of insufficient depth or because they are smothered by faster growing seeds, and only a few fall where conditions promote growth and multiplication. Similarly, virtually everyone has grievances, hopes, and aspirations; a large number lead to disputes. But, as Davison notes, most of these die away in mutterings or casual conversations: "An issue begins to take root only when it is communicated from one person to a second, who then carries it further in his own conversation."[29] Most potential issues never become things taken into account for very many people; only a few survive as the basis for public opinion.

When does an issue become a public issue rather than remain a private matter? The philosopher John Dewey offers a view close to that of Davison. There is the "objective fact," wrote Dewey, "that human acts have consequences upon others." Moreover, "some of these consequences are perceived" and "their perception leads to a subsequent effort to control action" to secure some consequences and avoid others. Dewey regarded two kinds of consequences as possible: "those which affect the persons directly engaged in a transaction, and those which affect others beyond those immediately concerned."[30] An issue is public, then, when the conflict giving rise to it extends beyond the parties immediately concerned with it.

The first phase of the publicizing of private conflict is the emergence of a dispute with issue potential; the second is the emergence of leadership to do the publicizing. Such leadership may be exercised by a party to the original dispute, someone who communicates beyond those he personally knows. When this occurs, usually "it is the *loser* who calls on outside help (Jefferson, defeated within the Washington administration, went to the country for support)."[31] Typically such leadership comes from the types of communicators who regularly exploit and publicize issues, whether for personal gain or more general interests—the politicians, professional communicators, and political activists described in Chapter 2. In leadership roles political communicators articulate the nature of disputes and issues, simplify their complexities by boiling them down into a few attention getting, resonant symbols, and generalize them to large audiences. Through all manner of influence talk and persuasion, the political leader formulates the issue so that it can be understood, is interesting, and reaches the lives of the largest possible number of people.

Once leadership stimulates communication about an issue through mass, interpersonal, and organizational channels (recall our discussion in Chapter 5), the way is opened for the third phase of opinion formation, the emergence of personal interpretation. We have already seen that through interpretation people take disputes and issues into account and bring their images to bear upon them. One set of images they formulate is a picture of what other people think, feel, and are inclined to do. Through "personal sampling" people learn about the opinions of others beyond their own immediate circle of acquaintances.[32] They may consciously strike up a conversation with a taxi driver, seatmate aboard a bus, train, or airplane, or the local pharmacist, grocer, or veterinarian. They may turn to newspapers, newsmagazines, and television for stories and published poll results. In a relatively short time (and after not too many conversations or too much effort), persons put together an image of how "everybody" or "people" or "the country" may be expected to behave with respect to an issue.

Personal sampling not only provides a picture of what others will do, but also calls to one's attention the range of options open to the individual. For example, an issue as complex as whether the federal government should regulate the sale of firearms raises the questions of what kinds of regulation are desirable; prohibition of all sales, registration and licensing of all firearms, prohibition only of handgun sales, sales only to selected individuals, and mandatory jail sentences for people convicted of crimes involving the use of guns are only a few of the options. Taking account of various options and the postures of others toward them is a process of social judgment described by Sherif and Hovland.[33] In their theory a person arrives at an opinion by reaching a "most acceptable position," that is, one deemed acceptable among several options, some of which are acceptable, others unacceptable. The most acceptable position constitutes a standard to compare related positions with. Social judgment is a process of making those comparisons. The positions close to a person's most acceptable position constitute his "latitude of acceptance"; those not agreeable form his "latitude of rejection." In addition there may be latitudes of noncommitment, positions on which a person does not feel strongly one way or the other. Into this image of acceptable, unacceptable, and noncommittal postures flow the pieces of information derived from personal sampling about what people are thinking, feeling, and doing. According to Sherif and Hovland the individual assesses this information through assimilation and contrast. If the information does not differ markedly from the positions constituting an individual's acceptance zone, he assimilates it as favorable to his image of things; if it does differ sharply, the person contrasts it with personal thoughts, feelings, and inclinations, perhaps even rejecting the information as incorrect, undesirable, or irrelevant.

In sum, personal interpretation provides a picture of available opinions, what others are likely to do, and what is acceptable to the individual. This leads to the final phase of opinion formation, the phase that adjusts each person's private opinion to his or her perceptions of wider, public opinion. This phase consists of the individual's choice to disclose private opinion or not. Through personal sampling a person arrives at a view regarding whether any privately acceptable opinions are also acceptable to a majority of what one perceives of as the public. In addition to an image of what the distribution of majority and minority sentiment is (i.e., the climate of opinion), the person also gets an impression of what the trend of opinion is, especially among those whose views he most respects. Noelle-Neumann hypothesizes that the willingness of people to expose their views publicly depends upon individual assessments of the climate and trend of opinion in each person's environment:

> It is greater if he believes his own view is, and will be, the dominating one or (though not dominating now) is becoming more widespread. There is less willingness if he feels that his own view is losing ground. The degree of willingness to express an opinion openly influences the individual's assessment of the distribution of opinion in favor of opinions most often shown publicly.[34]

Thus, if an individual perceives that his views coincide with the climate and/or trend of opinion, that person is likely to act in some public fashion to express personal convictions. This contributes to the collective construction of public opinion. The chances of one's being in the minority and thereby socially isolated is something a person deems remote. The self-image, at least as one sizes up the situation, will be reinforced rather than attacked. In short, the person riding with the flow of perceived opinion can express views secure in the thought that he is not embarking on an anxiety provoking voyage that will bring storms of disapproval from others. Instead, through opinion expression the individual derives precisely the kind of security that Sullivan theorized was an essential need of human beings.

But what happens if an individual perceives that the climate and/or trend of opinion is against her private views, that majority opinion falls into her latitude of rejection? In this instance, argues Noelle-Neumann, a person has a fear of isolating herself, both in the sense of receiving social disapproval and in that of beginning to question one's own capacity for judgment: "This is the point where the individual is vulnerable; this is where social groups can punish him for failing to toe the line. The concepts of public opinion, sanction, and punishment are closely linked with one another."[35] Facing the fear of isolation, then, a person is simply not likely to express an opinion at all. The citizen remains silent. If such a response is widespread, the result is what Noelle-Neumann calls a "spiral of silence," a phenomenon of increasing numbers of people hesitant to voice their views for fear of being in the minority. By not doing so they reinforce these with similar impressions that such views are indeed minority opinions. Quoting Tocqueville on how contempt of religion became a widespread view in eighteenth century France, Noelle-Neumann notes the consequences for gauging public opinion of the spiral of silence:

> People still clinging to the old faith were afraid of being the only ones who did so, and as they were more frightened of isolation than of committing an error, they joined the masses even though they did not agree with them. In this way, the opinion of only part of the population seemed to be the opinion of all and everybody, and exactly for this reason seemed irresistible to those who were responsible for this deceptive appearance.[36]

One of the framers of the Constitution of the United States, James Madison, made a similar point in writing in *The Federalist:*

> If it be true that all governments rest on opinion, it is no less true that the strength of opinion in each individual, and its practical influence on his conduct, depends much on the number which he supposes to have entertained the same opinion. The reason of man,

like man himself, is timid and cautious when left alone, and acquires firmness and confidence in proportion to the number with which it is associated.[37]

Thus, opinion formation is a four-phased process involving the overlap of personal, social, and political aspects through the emergence of (1) disputes with issue potential, (2) political leadership, (3) personal interpretation and social judgment, and (4) willingness to express private opinions publicly. That view carries several implications. Before noting them, however, two things need to be said. First, in attributing a key role to active, personal interpretation in opinion formation we are not repeating the essentials of the rational man model of human behavior (see Chapter 11). For one thing personal interpretation is seldom as conscious a process as the reader might want to infer from the above discussion. Much of interpretation takes place on a daily, routine, taken-for-granted basis without people really giving much thought to their personal samplings, social judgments, or estimates of what others are thinking, feeling, or doing. For another, although we argue that interpretation is purposive, we do not mean that the individual necessarily sets out a series of specific goals and rationally calculates optimum ways of achieving them on a cost-benefit basis. Rather, we are simply saying, as we have many times earlier, that people act toward issues on the basis of the meaning those things have for them, that there are both conscious and unconscious uses and gratifications from expressing or not expressing private beliefs, values, and expectations. The second thing that needs to be said about opinion formation before considering the implications of our views concerns the characteristics of opinions and of public opinion. Let us examine those briefly.

Characteristics of Public Opinion

We already have described the chief characteristics of any private opinion; opinions have content (they are about something), direction (believe-disbelieve, favor-oppose, etc.), and intensity (strong, moderate, or weak). Public opinion also possesses certain attributes. To begin with there is also content, direction, and intensity about public opinion. These features pertain to public opinion about political figures (usually public officials and candidates for office, but other kinds of political leaders, especially symbolic leaders as described in Chapter 2, become subjects of public opinion as well), parties, events, and all manner of issues that we will discuss in Chapter 8. Second, controversy characterizes public opinion; that is, it is about something over which people disagree. Third, public opinion has volume by virtue of the fact that the controversy touches all those people who feel the direct and indirect consequences of it even though they were not parties to the original dispute. Fourth, public opinion is relatively persistent. It is not possible to say how long, but a controversy yielding public opinion often endures for some time—as in election campaigns, civil rights issues of the 1950s and 1960s, the dispute over American involvement in Vietnam in the 1960s and 1970s, how to deal with tensions in the Middle East, etc. The distributions of majority and minority opinions often change as do individual views, yet public opinion persists. Despite this persistence of public opinion as an ongoing process, however, statements about what public opinion is on a matter must always be specific to a certain time and place. This injunction is in keeping with the realization that the proportions of people who notice the dispute, formulate private opinions, and are willing to express them in public vary from place to place and time to time.

In addition to the characteristics of public opinion listed above—content, direction, intensity, conflict, volume, persistence, and specificity—there is one other key attribute of public opinion, which is the pluralist appearance of public opinion. We recognize three faces of public opinion. The first face is that of *mass opinion,* the largely unorganized expression people talk about as the public, the community, background opinion, the consensus, or the public mood. Mass opinion flows from individuals reaching personal choices and the coincidences of these choices through the process of convergent selectivity, a means of achieving social order that we have noted is important in producing symbolic leaders (Chapter 2), mass persuasion (Chapter 4), and mass communication (Chapter 5). The second face of public opinion consists of all of the expressions on the countenances of diverse groups, the faces of *group opinions.* Business groups, labor unions, farm organizations, consumer groups, even government bodies—all take public stands on issues. Each group constitutes a separate public affected by the consequences of a given dispute in differing ways. This face of public opinion emerges both through the organized means of social control (such as propaganda as discussed in Chapter 5) and through the give-and-take of groups negotiating with one another. The third face of public opinion is *popular opinion,* the aggregated opinions of individuals as measured by political polls and surveys, other measurement tendencies (see Appendix), the buying choices of consumers, voting in popular elections, etc. It derives from processes of social control, the convergence of self-selections, and negotiation and is the joint product of the overlap of propaganda, advertising, and rhetoric (Chapter 4) of organizational, mass, and interpersonal media.

It is important to keep two things in mind with respect to the pluralist character of public opinion. To begin with, public opinion is not identical with any one of these three faces; it is the collective expression of personal beliefs, values, and expectations that appears through the interplay of all three manifestations. A full accounting of public opinion must take notice not only of the specific object, place, and time that forms the context of public opinion but also the overlap of mass opinion, the views of various groups, and popular opinion. The second point is that the three faces of public opinion may not be consistent with one another; that is, the mass opinion which leaders symbolize as the public, the stands of organized groups, and measured popular opinion may contradict one another.[38] Take again the issue of gun control. Speaking for what he seemed to view as mass opinion in his 1976 State of the Union message, President Gerald Ford proposed regulation of the sale of handguns but fell short of proposing more restrictive gun controls on grounds that the public did not want interference with the right to own guns. Opinion publics were divided on the matter; advocates of gun control lobbies insisted on registration of purchases of all guns but opponents of strict gun controls (such as the National Rifleman's Association) wanted to limit regulation chiefly to "Saturday night specials." And what was popular opinion during this period? A Harris Survey confirmed that popular opinion favored registration of "all gun purchases no matter where the purchases were made" by 73 to 24 percent, and 66 to 30 percent, that "a permit should be required by law in order for anyone to purchase a rifle."[39] As on so many issues, the three faces of public opinion regarding gun control wore different expressions.

Implications for Thinking about Public Opinion

Public opinion is a many faceted phenomenon constructed through the interplay of personal, social, and political processes and manifested in the form of mass, group, and popular activities. At the personal level the major implication of this characterization is that shifts in public opinion derive at least in part from changes in the images people have of their social environments. If the willingness of an individual to express a private opinion depends upon a perception of the climate and trend of opinion surrounding a person, it follows that shifts in the distribution of majority and minority opinion follow the willingness of people to add their individual voices to those who have already taken a stand. A corollary is that if people must take a stand when their private beliefs and values run counter to their expectations or to the temper of public opinion, the fear of isolation aroused may result in a change of personal opinions to conform with what seem to be majority views. Noelle-Neumann found, for instance, a change of individuals' voting intentions during an election campaign in favor of the opinion presented most forcefully in public.[40]

There are several social implications inherent in the view of public opinion taken in this chapter. One points to the role played by the mass media in the opinion process. In one sense, as noted in Chapter 5, the media help to create public opinion not so much by telling people *what* to think, but what to think *about*, the agenda-setting function of press. But there is also a sense in which the media do tell people what to think. Insofar as people rely upon any of the media—mass, interpersonal, organizational—for their personal sampling of what others think, the media offer pictures of social consensus. It is upon major issues of national concern that the mass media provide, through such pictures, the kinds of environmental pressures to which people respond with alacrity, acquiescence, or silence. To the extent that media pictures suggest that the views of a relatively few are what the majority believe and value, people hesitate to voice what the media portray as minority opinions: "the tendency of the majority to remain silent is considerable and gives the impression of a 'silent majority.'"[41] Corollary to this are other social implications suggested by Noelle-Neumann: (1) a current majority perceived to be a minority will decline in the future as the current minority perceived to be the majority grows; (2) a current majority divided in their expectations of what the future holds is more likely to decrease than one united in their expectations that they will remain a majority in the future; (3) when uncertainty rises about the future strength of prevailing opinion, this signals a change, perhaps reversal, of prevailing views; and (4) a faction more willing to publicize its views and able to leave the impression of being in a majority is more likely to have the future on its side.

We can draw many inferences about the political aspects of the construction of public opinion, but we will mention only two here and spell out others in later chapters. By now it should be clear that the opinion process is circular rather than linear. Public officials and other politicians playing leadership roles as political communicators articulate issues and disputes. Professional communicators and political activists bring the disagreements to the attention of large audiences whose members formulate personal opinions. If and when made public, these opinions reach policy makers through the mediation of political communicators acting as submitters of mass, group, and popular opinions. Governmental decision makers respond by taking opinions into account, representing some, disregarding others, and disputing those they find objectionable. The circular flow of decision making, conflict making, opinion making, and opinion submitting provides for the endless political construction of public opinion.[42]

The reciprocal nature of the opinion process contributes to a second feature of its political aspects, namely, the problematic character of the relationship between public opinion and public policy. A central and widely shared myth about American politics has been "that political institutions translate the will of the mass of people into public policies."[43] As we shall see in Chapter 12 there are, to be sure, many ways of representing public opinion to policy makers. However, the general rule is that many opinions are called, few chosen; there is never a one-to-one corre-

spondence between the beliefs, values, and expectations of all citizens
and the decisions made by public officials.

Writing of the relationship between public opinion and foreign policy,
Doris Graber draws a distinction between two functions public opinion
can play in policy making, those of initiative-advice and veto-support.[44]
Her observations can be extended to domestic policy making as well.
When the "people" play an initiative-advice role, policy officials consult
them for advice; citizens even initiate policies rather than merely choose
between broad, formulated policy alternatives. There is considerable
doubt in some circles whether the general citizenry can or should initiate
and advise on policy questions.[45] More typical than the initiation-advise
function is that of veto-support. Here the role of public opinion is to
acquiese to policies; widespread vocal dissent, particularly from influential
special interests, heralds withdrawal of support, a public veto of the policy.
The breakdown of *specific* support produces vetoes of objectionable policies; the loss of *diffuse* support (a reservoir of good will for the government
and its various institutions) suggests a deterioration in public confidence
and governmental stability.[46] (We shall examine diffuse support as reflected mass consensus in Chapter 8).

Also giving rise to the problematic relationship of opinions and policies
is the nature of political communication between public officials and
private citizens. As we noted in Part Two, government units undertake
elaborate public relations campaigns to merchandise their policies. By
propagating the illusion that policies correspond to a mythical public
will or interest, officials mobilize widespread specific and diffuse support.
In 1976, for example, no sooner had President Gerald Ford presented
his general budgetary plans to Congress than a carefully orchestrated
campaign started to sell his proposal to all Americans. Members of Ford's
cabinet lined up behind him and spoke firmly in support to leave an
impression of administration unity. The president faced journalists in
an elaborate news conference and answered probing questions with precise, detailed responses that indicated he had done his homework. In
comparison with what public officials can do to sell policies, the reverse
flow from public to policy makers is but a thin trickle, one that scarcely
provides a rounded picture of the diversity of views actually voiced, let
alone those masked by the spiral of silence. The means for gauging
public opinion are relatively crude when contrasted with the sophistica-
tion of modern techniques for opinion management. The result (as we
shall see in Chapter 8 and 12) is that few policies reflect mass opinion,
a larger number popular opinion; most represent the give-and-take of
group opinions.

This brings us to a final implication of the view expressed in this chapter
about the nature of public opinion, one that involves all of the personal,
social, and political dimensions of the opinion process. Public opinion

is a key indicator of social order; inquiries into what public opinion is in each of several specific places, at specific times, and with respect to diverse objects and settings helps us explore the nature of social order and project tentative answers to the question, how is society possible? We have previously offered three theories of how people achieve social order—through social control, converging self-selections, and negotiation. Public opinion, being the pluralist phenomenon that we have described, emerges from all three means of ordering society. Through tools of social control, including manipulation of appealing symbols, propaganda, public relations, and news management, groups inside and outside of government try, and frequently succeed, to influence personal sentiments and their public organization. By means of mass communication, media, and advertising, political elites not only reflect but help create mass expectations and widely accepted myths. But public opinion is not simply the product of a citizenry passively manipulated by means of social control of mass communication. People follow a minded process of interpretation that joins their images and opinions. They transact with their fellows, both those they come into daily contact with and the imagined persons presented through communication media. Out of these acts they negotiate a meaningful reality in which they contribute their beliefs, values, and expectations to the construction of public opinion, or by withholding them, nonetheless participate in formulating a picture of mass, group, and popular opinion. In sum, as Blumer wrote, "public opinion is formed and expressed in large measure through . . . ways of societal operation."[47] Public opinion, like society, is activity constructed through social control, coinciding personal choices, and personal and group transactions.

BIBLIOGRAPHY

A starting point for exploring more fully the view toward public opinion in this chapter and throughout this work consists of two articles written by Herbert Blumer and appearing in his *Symbolic Interactionism: Perspective and Method* (Englewood Cliffs, N.J.: Prentice-Hall, Inc., 1969). Consult his "Public Opinion and Public Opinion Polling" which describes public opinion as a social process and his "Attitudes and the Social Act," one of the few statements argued from the position that attitudes are activity rather than tendencies determining human acts. Two works will assist the reader in understanding the relationship between images and behavior. The first is Walter Lippmann's *Public Opinion* (New York: The Macmillan Co., 1922), particularly those portions discussing stereotypes and interests. The second is Kenneth Boulding's *The Image* (Ann Arbor: Ann Arbor Paperback, 1961). Boulding defines an image as the subjective knowledge a person takes to be true, spells out the relationships between images and behavior and between images and communication, and discusses the image at the biological level, in social life, economic life, the political process, and history. To gain a full understanding of how personal images combine thoughts, feelings, and inclinations (cognitive, affective, and conative dimensions) one must read George Herbert Mead's "The Function of Imagery

in Human Conduct," a supplementary essay to Mead's *Mind, Self, and Society*
(Chicago: University of Chicago Press, 1934). For readers interested in examining the contours of an image-based analysis of popular opinion, as distinct
from public opinion defined in this chapter, consult Dan Nimmo, *Popular Images
of Politics* (Englewood Cliffs, N.J.: Prentice-Hall, Inc., 1974).

Several authors have written about public opinion. The largest proportion focus
almost exclusively upon personal opinions and how people acquire them. Very
few think much about the nature of the public. One who did and thereby
formulated a classic notion of the public in the tradition of pragmatic philosophy was John Dewey. Two of his works are of special relevance in this respect.
In *The Public and Its Problems* (Denver: Alan Swallow, 1927) he defines the
nature of a public from a transactional perspective. In *Human Nature and Conduct*
(New York: Henry Holt and Co., 1950) he explores the social psychological
bases of the community and the public.

The belief, value, and expectation aspects of personal opinions are central concerns of several social psychologists. The most concise introduction to their
views is Daryl J. Bem's little book, *Beliefs, Attitudes, and Human Affairs* (Belmont,
Calif.: Brooks/Cole Publishing Co., 1970). Bem distinguishes not between beliefs
and values, as has been the case in this chapter, but between cognitive and
evaluative beliefs. He takes a look at the emotional, behavioral, and social
foundations of beliefs and the theory of cognitive consistency, and offers the
refreshing view (and inconoclastic to many social scientists) that "there is more
nonconsistency in heaven and earth than is dreamed of in our psychological
theories" (p. 39). Milton Rokeach has also written a great deal about beliefs,
values, and expectations. His *The Open and Closed Mind* (New York: Basic Books,
1960) has almost become a classic. In it he explores the nature of belief systems
and develops the notion of dogmatism. In *Beliefs, Attitudes, and Values* (San
Francisco: Jossey-Bass, 1968) Rokeach focuses more directly upon values, their
measurement, and distribution. Also instructive in understanding the functions
and dimensions of personal opinions is M. Brewster Smith, et al., *Opinions
and Personality* (New York: John Wiley and Sons, Inc., 1964).

Not a great deal has been said about attitudes in this chapter, yet a fairly large
number of scholars take the position that attitudes are key predispositions
shaping the way people behave in specific situations and toward specific
objects. Two edited volumes serve as excellent samplings of the literature:
Marie Jahoda and Neil Warren, eds., *Attitudes* (Baltimore: Penguin Books,
1966)—readers will find reprinted there Gordon Allport's highly influential
definition of an attitude as a neuropsychic state of readiness for mental and
physical activity—and Anthony G. Greenwald, et al., eds., *Psychological Foundations of Attitudes* (New York: Academic Press, 1968). Readers should also consult
William J. McGuire, "The Nature of Attitudes and Attitude Change," in
Gardner Lindzey and Elliot Aronson, eds., *The Handbook of Social Psychology*,
2nd ed. (Reading, Mass.: Addison-Wesley Publishing Co., 1968), 3: 136–314.
An excellent example of how political scientists employ attitudes to explain
political behavior is Jarol B. Manheim, *The Politics Within* (Englewood Cliffs,
N.J.: Prentice-Hall, Inc., 1975).

In recent years there have been more texts published by political scientists dealing
exclusively with public opinion than one cares to count. As is so often the
case, however, a few of the older works on the subject deserve to be read
before embarking upon more contemporary statements. One of these is George
Carslake Thompson's *Public Opinion and Lord Beaconsfield* (New York: Macmillan Co., 1886). Thompson clearly distinguishes between four major

characteristics of public opinion—diffusion, persistence, intensity, and reasonableness—and between the stages of activity that are opinions—general preferences, wishes for an end or course of action, and beliefs regarding how to achieve ends. Readers will surely note the indebtedness of the discussion in this chapter to Thompson's framework. Another older work that should not be ignored is A. Lawrence Lowell's *Public Opinion and Popular Government* (London: Longmans, Green and Co., 1913). More recent works, but still published prior to the spate of texts arriving in the last two decades, are Leonard W. Doob, *Public Opinion and Propaganda* (New York: Holt, Rinehart and Winston, 1948), now available in a second edition published in 1966 by Archon Books, Hamden, Connecticut, and Gabriel A. Almond's *The American People and Foreign Policy* (New York: Harcourt, Brace and Co., 1950). Almond makes an explicit distinction between values and expectations in his discussion of political mood, consensus, and opinion. An overall picture of the relationship of public opinion to voting is Philip E. Converse, "Public Opinion and Voting Behavior," in Fred Greenstein and Nelson Polsby, eds., *Handbook of Political Science* (Reading, Mass.: Addison-Wesley Publishing Co., 1975), vol. 4, chap. 2.

Among the more recently published texts dealing exclusively with public opinion that deserve perusal are Robert E. Lane and David O. Sears, *Public Opinion* (Englewood Cliffs, N.J.: Prentice-Hall, Inc., 1964); James J. Best, *Public Opinion* (Homewood, Ill., The Dorsey Press, 1973); Robert S. Erikson and Norman R. Luttbeg, *American Public Opinion* (New York: John Wiley and Sons, Inc., 1973); Bernard C. Hennessy, *Public Opinion*, 3rd ed. (North Scituate, Mass.: Duxbury Press, 1975); Alan D. Monroe, *Public Opinion in America* (New York: Dodd, Mead and Co., 1975), Dennis S. Ippolito, et al., *Public Opinion and Responsible Democracy* (Englewood Cliffs, N.J.: Prentice-Hall, Inc., 1976) and V.O. Key, Jr., *Public Opinion and American Democracy* (New York: Alfred A. Knopf, 1961). Readers will readily note that publishers of texts on the subject display relatively little variety in choosing titles.

Few works place the study of public opinion within the overall context of the communication process. Two that make a start in that direction are Ithiel de Sola Pool's essay on "Public Opinion" in the *Handbook of Communication*, edited chiefly by Pool and Wilbur Schramm (Chicago: Rand McNally Publishing Co., 1973), pp. 779–835, and the volume edited by Steven H. Chaffee, *Political Communication* (Beverly Hills, Calif.: Sage Publishing Co., 1975). A work that makes a less successful attempt in this respect is James C. Strouse, *The Mass Media, Public Opinion, and Public Policy Analysis* (Columbus, Ohio: Charles E. Merrill Publishing Co., 1975).

NOTES

1. Arthur F. Bentley, *The Process of Government* (Cambridge: The Belknap Press, 1967), p. 185.

2. George A. Miller, Eugene Galanter, and Karl H.Pribram, *Plans and the Structure of Behavior* (New York: Holt, Rinehart and Winston, Inc., 1960).

3. Kenneth E. Boulding, *The Image* (Ann Arbor: University of Michigan Press, Ann Arbor Paperbacks, 1969), p. 6 (emphasis in original).

4. Walter Lippmann, *Public Opinion* (New York: The Macmillan Co., 1922), p. 25.

5. Ibid., p. 27.

6. Lee Thayer, *Communication and Social Systems* (Homewood, Ill.: Richard D. Irwin, 1968), pp. 26–27.

7. Abraham H. Maslow, *Motivation and Personality* (New York: Harper and Row, 1954).

8. James C. Davies, *Human Nature in Politics* (New York: John Wiley and Sons, 1963), p. 16.

9. Suzanne K. Langer, *Philosophy in a New Key* (Cambridge, Mass.: Harvard University Press, 1942), p. 241.

10. Horace M. Kallen, ed., *The Philosophy of William James* (New York: The Modern Library, 1925), p. 145.

11. This being the case there is no reason to expect a one-to-one correspondence between a person's attitudes (his predispositions to behave in specific ways toward specific objects in settings) and opinions. A great deal of the research with respect to opinions, however, has been concerned with explaining the inconsistency between attitudes and opinions. For a review see Steven Jay Gross and C. Michael Niman, "Attitude-Behavior Consistency: A Review," *Public Opinion Quarterly*, 34 (Fall 1975): 358–368, and Howard J. Erlich, "Attitudes, Behavior, and the Intervening Variable," *American Sociologist*, 4 (February 1969): 29–34.

12. See Charles E. Osgood, "Behavior Theory and the Social Sciences," in Roland Young, ed., *Approaches to the Study of Politics* (Evanston: Northwestern University Press, 1958), pp. 217–244.

13. Daryl J. Bem, *Beliefs, Attitudes, and Human Affairs* (Belmont, Calif.: Brooks/Cole Publishing Co., 1970); Lester W. Milbrath, "The Nature of Political Beliefs and the Relationship of the Individual to the Government," *American Behavioral Scientist*, 12 (November–December 1968): 28–36.

14. *The Gallup Opinion Index*, Report No. 124 (October 1975), 12.

15. *The Harris Survey*, "Positive Response to Reagan," January 8, 1976.

16. Francis Bacon, "Novum Organum," in Edwin A. Burtt, ed., *The English Philosophers from Bacon to Mill* (New York: The Modern Library, 1939), pp. 34–35.

17. Charles S. Peirce, "The Fixation of Belief," in Philip P. Wiener, ed., *Values in a Universe of Chance: Selected Writings of Charles S. Peirce* (Garden City, N.Y.: Doubleday Anchor Books, 1958), pp. 91–112.

18. Bem, *Beliefs, Attitudes, and Human Affairs*, p. 7.

19. Milton Rokeach, *Beliefs, Attitudes, and Values* (San Francisco: Jossey-Bass, 1968).

20. Patrick Mullahy, *Psychoanalysis and Interpersonal Psychiatry: The Contributions of Harry Stack Sullivan* (New York: Science House, 1970).

21. Harold D. Lasswell and Abraham Kaplan, *Power and Society* (New Haven: Yale University Press, 1950), Ch. 4.

22. Milton Rokeach and Seymour Parker, "Values as Social Indicators of Poverty and Race Relations in America," *The Annals of the American Academy of Political and Social Science*, 388 (March 1970): 97–111; the follow-up replication is reported in Rokeach, "Change and Stability in American Value Systems, 1968-1971," *Public Opinion Quarterly*, 37 (Summer 1974): 222–38.

23. Milton Rokeach, "A Theory of Organization and Change Within Value-Attitude Systems," *Journal of Social Issues*, 24 (January 1968): 13–33.

24. James M. Perry, *Us and Them: How the Press Covered the 1972 Election* (New York: Clarkston N. Potter, Inc., 1973), Ch. 8.

25. Rokeach, *Beliefs, Attitudes, and Human Affairs*, p. 13.

26. Milton Rokeach, *The Open and Closed Mind* (New York: Basic Books, Inc., 1960), Ch. 2.

27. Ibid.

28. Giovanni Sartori, "Politics, Ideology, and Belief Systems," *American Political Science Review*, 63 (June 1969): 398–411.

29.   W. Phillips Davison, "The Public Opinion Process," *Public Opinion Quarterly,* 22 (Summer 1958): 93.

30.   John Dewey, *The Public and Its Problems* (Denver: Alan Swallow, 1927), p. 12.

31.   E. E. Schattschneider, *The Semisovereign People* (New York: Holt, Rinehart and Winston, 1960), p. 16 (emphasis in original).

32.   Davison, "The Public Opinion Process," p. 98.

33.   Muzafer Sherif and Carl I. Hovland, *Social Judgment: Assimilation and Contrast Effects in Communication and Attitude Change* (New Haven: Yale University Press, 1961).

34.   Elizabeth Noelle-Neumann, "The Spiral of Silence: A Theory of Public Opinion," *Journal of Communication,* 24 (Spring 1974): 45.

35.   Ibid., p. 43.

36.   Ibid., p. 45. The Tocqueville quotation comes from Alexis de Tocqueville, *L'Ancian Regime et la Revolution* (Paris: Michel Levy Freres, 1956), p. 259.

37.   James Madison, *The Federalist* (New York: The Modern Library, 1937), p. 329.

38.   Avery Leiserson, "Notes on the Theory of Political Opinion Formation," *American Political Science Review,* 47 (March 1953): 171–177.

39.   *The Harris Survey,* October 27, 1975.

40.   Noelle-Neumann, "The Spiral of Silence," p. 49.

41.   Ibid., p. 46.

42.   James N. Rosenau, *Public Opinion and Foreign Policy* (New York: Random House, 1961).

43.   Murray Edelman, *The Symbolic Uses of Politics* (Urbana: University of Illinois Press, 1964), p. 191.

44.   *Public Opinion, the President, and Foreign Policy* (New York: Holt, Rinehart and Winston, 1968), pp. 300–301.

45.   Walter Lippmann, *The Public Philosophy* (Boston: Little, Brown and Co., 1955).

46.   David Easton, *A Systems Analysis of Political Life* (New York: John Wiley and Sons, Inc., 1965), p. 273.

47.   Herbert Blumer, *Symbolic Interactionism: Perspective and Method* (Englewood Cliffs, N.J.: Prentice-Hall, Inc., 1969), p. 199.

chapter 8

The Distribution of Public Opinion:
The One, the Few, and the Many

The audience of political communication, which is the public that constitutes the "whom" of our organizing formulation in this book, is diverse.
In some respects it is an unorganized mass audience, in others a pluralist
audience of particularized publics, and in still others an audience composed of aggregates of individuals. This chapter takes a close look at the
distribution of each segment of public opinion—mass, group, and popular
opinions—on selected issues and questions of American politics. It proceeds by first examining the character of mass opinion as reflected in
our political culture and consensus. Then we will describe two aspects
of group opinion, that of organized special interests and that of unorganized, specialized publics. Finally, the discussion centers upon aggregates of popular opinion with respect to the hopes and fears of Americans,
key domestic and foreign issues, and the structuring of political opinions.

PATTERNS OF PUBLIC OPINION

The Greek philosopher Aristotle elaborated one of the earliest and still
one of the most useful means for classifying types of government.[1] His
scheme employed both quantitative and qualitative criteria. Depending
upon how many people took part in governing, Aristotle divided governments into "the One, the Few, and the Many." Each of these classes
had two variations pertaining to the quality of governing, essentially
whether the regime governed in the interests of the ruler(s) or of the
entire community. Thus government of the One could be either tyranny
(in the interests of the ruler) or kingship (in the interests of all). Similarly,
government by the Few was either an oligarchy or aristocracy, and by

the Many either democracy or polity. Aristotle's quantitative criteria provide a convenient way for classifying the three collective constructions of personal beliefs, values, and expectations that we call public opinion. Following such a scheme we label mass expressions the opinion of the One, group expressions the opinion of the Few, and popular expression the opinion of the Many.

The One: Political Culture and Mass Consensus

Both scholars and practicing politicians frequently liken public opinion to the unspoken and unquantified understandings and sympathies of a population. There are several variations on the theme. For example, more than half a century ago British author and political scientist Ernest Barker wrote about "national character" as the essential ingredient of public opinion. National character consisted of the sum of acquired tendencies which a nation derives from its racial blend, territory, and what Barker called the mass and social variety of its population. National character was neither measurable nor readily observed. It was formulated in unconscious ways by the minds and wills of a nation's members, made and continuously remade. For Barker the differences in political behavior of nations (France, Britain, Germany) derived from unique national characters.[2]

Other scholars describe public opinion of the One as the "community." In a classic treatise on public opinion also written more than a half-century ago, A. Lawrence Lowell argued that public opinion builds upon a people's common views of the desired ends of government and general acceptance of the proper means to achieve those ends.[3] More recently Robert Nisbet sounded the same note in distinguishing public opinion from popular opinion. Says Nisbet, "Not the people in their numerical total, not a majority, nor any minority as such represents public opinion if the individuals involved do not form some kind of community, by virtue of possessing common ends, purposes, and rules of procedure. Public opinion is given its character by genuine consensus, by unifying tradition, and by what Edmund Burke called 'constitutional spirit.' "[4]

Still a third view of the public opinion of the One, employed by scholars and politicians alike, is the notion of public opinion as the mood of a people. Political leaders refer to the public or the public mood as a way of associating self-interests with what they view as more widely shared and legitimate thoughts and feelings. In this context public opinion as mood is a linguistic symbol used for persuasive purposes. In contrast, political scientist Gabriel Almond employed the notion of public opinion as a mood to describe the context of making American foreign policy after World War II. For him basic values and tendencies during a particular era constituted the mood of the times, a factor conditioning policy alternatives.[5]

Or one may regard public opinion of the One as consisting of the overriding myths of a people, the general beliefs (valid or not) of a large number of people that give meaning to events and actions. Edelman catalogs a few myths of American opinion: that people determine what government does by means of elections, legislative actions, and opinion polls; that administrators simply carry out the will of legislators rather than make laws themselves; that popular support for a government indicates the government is meeting popular demands; and that government has the power and knowledge to produce the results people want.[6]

Closely associated with these views of public opinion as the translation of national character, community, mood, unifying symbol, and body of myth are two notions currently widely used by political scientists to describe mass opinion. These notions, of political culture and political consensus, warrant detailed consideration.

Political Culture

A significant way that public opinion affects what public officials do is by means of political culture. One student of public opinion suggests that "perhaps the greatest public opinion influence on governmental decision making" is "the sharing of a common political culture by the people and those whom they freely elect to public office."[7] Without going so far we can certainly say that political culture is sufficiently important to warrant scrutiny. What then is political culture and what are its characteristics?

Diverse definitions of political culture abound. One of the first was that political culture is a "pattern of orientations to political action."[8] With slight modification this view will assist our understanding of the phenomenon. Returning to a theme sounded in the last chapter let us speak of orientation *of* rather than *to* action. In this sense orientations are simply tendencies of activity, what we have alluded to as images. Basically, therefore, *political culture consists of a widely shared pattern of tendencies of beliefs, values, and expectations.* It is learned, fairly well diffused, and relatively stable, although continuously reconstructed.

Drawing a distinction very similar to that used by Lowell in describing the community basis of public opinion, Samuel Beer employs two conceptions to describe the content of any political culture. First, in any society there are general ideas about *how government ought to be conducted;* these are "conceptions of authority." Take, for example, the widely held value in the United States that there should be elections at stated intervals for legislative and various executive offices. Second, there are widely shared views regarding what authority should be used for and *what governments should do.* These are "conceptions of purpose." Examples include the views that government should provide defense against external enemies, build highways, and deliver the mail.[9]

Using these notions that political culture involves conceptions of authority and of purpose, several political scientists have differentiated the character of American political culture from others, delineated the principal concepts of authority and purpose in American politics, and measured how well Americans adhere to fundamental beliefs and values. Thus, in the late 1950s a team of political scientists conducted an extensive study of political orientations in five nations—the United States, Great Britain, West Germany, Italy, and Mexico.[10] The study utilized surveys of opinion to find out how much citizens in each nation knew, how they felt, and how they judged four types of political objects: (1) the nation's general political system—its history, size, location, power, constitution, etc.; (2) the ways policies get made and the citizen's role in the policy process; (3) the kinds of policies made and how they affect people; and (4) the degree of influence and capabilities people have as political activists. The study derived three types of political culture: the *parochial* culture in which people have limited knowledge and feeling for politics, the process of making policy, the impact of policy, and how to make themselves felt in politics; the *subject* culture where people know about and feel relatively strongly about their political system, but define their part in it as obedience to policy rather than as influencing politics; and the *participant* culture where citizens have positive views of themselves and the political system and believe that they can influence policy making. The political culture of the United States, concluded the study, was a participant civic culture as indicated by the following facts:

1. People feel emotionally involved and take great pride in the constitutional system.
2. The role of participant is highly developed and widespread; people are frequently exposed to politics, discuss politics, and take part in public affairs.
3. There is general satisfaction with specific governmental performance.
4. People believe themselves competent to influence government.

To say that the political culture of the United States accentuates participation, however, does not specify the conceptions of authority and of purpose associated with participatory orientations. In this respect Daniel J. Elazar's examination of the subcultures of this country is insightful. Elazar states that the American political culture consists of three discrete subcultures—the individualistic, moralistic, and traditionalistic. The purpose of government in the individualistic setting is to preserve the marketplace as an arena for promoting individual social and economic improvement. Authority is lodged in commercial interests and professional politicians; citizens accept policy decisions but take no effective part in shaping them. In a moralistic culture the purpose of government is to advance the shared interests of all citizens rather than special, private interests; the basic conception of authority is that all citizens should participate in politics. And in the traditionalistic culture, the purpose of government is to preserve the established social order on behalf of a small, paternalistic elite; this self-perpetuating elite has the "right" to wield authority. As conceived by Elazar the traditionalistic pattern has been common in southern states: the moralistic subculture pervades such states as Minnesota, Wisconsin, Oregon, Utah, and the areas of the Northeast; and the individualistic subculture appears in portions of the Midwest and East, sometimes in combination with moralistic tendencies.[11]

American political culture then suggests that the public opinion of the One emphasizes a general pattern of participation in the opinion process among sets of people with diverse conceptions of what government should do and how politics should be conducted. Bearing this general observation in mind, let us now consider the specific tenets—beliefs, values, and expectations—that comprise the political culture of the United States. In order to do so we need to introduce one other key idea pertaining to how scholars look at mass opinion, the notion of mass consensus.

Political Culture as Mass Consensus

We define consensus simply as a state of agreement among people with respect to some object that they take into account. To say that political culture exists at all asserts a fairly wide agreement among the mass of people on fundamental concepts of authority and purpose, i.e., political culture implies a level of political consensus. As a prelude to describing what a number of writers have said with respect to the quality of American political consensus, it is appropriate to bear three things in mind. Each will be relevant to the ensuing discussion:

1. The tenets that comprise the American political consensus are general, vague, abstract statements of principle frequently far removed from the everyday life of the average citizen. Such principles have the quality of being taken for granted rather than studied, reflected upon, and discussed. Hence, for instance, after having just completed a war to save democracy and the Bill of Rights, only one in five Americans surveyed in 1945 knew what the Bill of Rights contained.[12]

2. Because many of the principles comprising mass consensus are abstractions too removed from the daily lives of Americans to have practical bearing, they are rarely ordered into internally consistent belief and value systems. Thus Americans have no problems proclaiming government should be by majority rule, then saying that only taxpayers should vote in referenda on tax measures.[13]

3. As a result of the generality and inconsistency in American political views, the operating tenets of mass consensus are twofold: (a) the abstract principles Americans say they hold, and (b) the repeated, reaffirmed,

and reconstituted agreements, tacit understandings, and unspoken contracts that they negotiate in their daily encounters with specific situations
and unexpected contingencies.[14]

What principles meet these two tests, what are the abstract ideas that
Americans not only say they believe and value but that also operate
in the day-to-day workings of American politics? Political scientist Donald
Devine describes the character of such a mass political consensus in the
United States.[15] For Devine a political culture has four aspects. First
there is a community aspect—people think of themselves and attach
themselves as comembers to a common nation and political entity. A
political culture thereby requires a sense of national identity; not only
do its members realize their nation is distinct, they have a deep-seated
emotional affection for it. The indicators of such an identity include a
common name for the nation used both by citizens and outsiders
("America"), the organization of groups such as legislative bodies or political parties that transcend regional boundaries (as, for instance, the formation of the Continental Congress prior to the American Revolution), a
feeling of common union (members think in terms of "We" and "They"),
and an effective communication system linking the disparate parts of
the community (such as the American Committees of Correspondence).
Devine cites several studies to demonstrate in fairly convincing fashion
that residents of what was later to be the United States realized a common
nationality long before the Revolution, a sense of identity giving rise to
a common political tradition and a cooperative feeling of trust among
conationals.

The first element of political culture and consensus, national identity,
is sustained by a second, the development of unifying symbols with relatively common meaning for everyone. Americans certainly have such
symbols. These take the form of sacred writings, heroic figures, numerous
artifacts, and all manner of celebrated holidays. The Declaration of Independence and the Constitution are documents revered by most Americans. Devine reports that well over two-thirds of Americans questioned
in surveys about the Constitution believed it to be as "near perfect as
can be." Americans questioned in surveys say Abraham Lincoln and
George Washington were the greatest men who ever lived. Particularly
in their childhood years Americans acquire a particular fondness and
respect for salient political artifacts: as many as nine of ten schoolchildren
report that the best flag in the world is the American. Almost ten million
acres of land in this country are national parks and landmarks. Certainly
there is no dearth of national holidays, and the American bicentennial
was widely celebrated throughout the entire nation for much more than
the year 1976 itself.

For Devine the third key aspect of mass consensus that heralds a
common political culture is a shared set of rules for how government

should operate, which we have already labeled as common conceptions of authority. In large measure the conceptions of authority avowed and practiced by Americans derived from the republican principles enunciated by the English philosopher John Locke, and adapted to the American setting by the American colonists, revolutionaries, founding fathers, and succeeding generations of political leaders. To determine whether Americans believe and value these operating principles, Devine examines a plethora of opinion surveys of recent decades. Where he finds at least a majority favoring a principle and a substantial difference (at least twenty percentage points) between majority and minority positions, he considers there to be a political consensus. Using this measure he concludes that the liberal principles associated with Locke's representative democracy are far from obsolete, either in practice or in the lip service they receive from surveyed Americans. Specifically there is consensus on the following principles:

1. *Rules are necessary:* Americans support the notion that civil society can exist only with rules; they also show substantial support for obedience to rules (more than eight in ten believe even unjust laws should be obeyed and that the law should be upheld no matter what the reasons given for breaking it).

2. *The Constitution is the core of the rule system:* Not only should there be rules, but fundamental rules should be formalized in a written document.

3. *The basic rule is popular majority rule:* Americans prefer popular rule over a single ruler or ruling group; surveys indicate that more than three-fourths of Americans believe people can be trusted to make policy decisions, government pays attention to people, and elections help get government to pay attention.

4. *Popular rule should be qualified:* Popular majorities, as with all governments, should be restrained through the operation of formal institutions and procedures.

5. *The basic institution should be the legislature:* Although surveys indicate that support for specific legislative actions oscillates widely, diffuse support for the principle of legislative predominance (both with respect to Congress and state legislature) is well above the consensus level.

6. *There is guarded respect for executive and judicial authority:* There is substantial support for executive and judicial institutions as long as the people perceive that neither has violated that trust; specific violations (such as the Watergate affair in the second Nixon administration) contribute to short-term suspicion and distrust.

7. *Federalism is accepted:* There is wide support of the principle that there should be a division of authority between federal and state governments; in areas where the national government has not been given specific authority, the states receive support as preeminent.

8. *There should be a decentralized system of political parties:* Surveys reveal that, contrary to critics who say "the party's over," Americans support the two-party system that emphasizes localized and state influence in party affairs rather than accountability to national leaders.

9. *Terms of office should be limited:* There is support for the operating principle that legislative and selected public ,officials should be chosen by elections to limited terms of office as a means of reinforcing accountability to popular rule.

The fourth and final aspect of mass consensus contributing to political culture is agreement on fundamental values and goals, i.e., conceptions of purpose. Like conceptions of authority, those of purpose are very much in the Lockian tradition. They are summarized in the Declaration of Independence:

> We hold these truths to be self-evident, that all men are created equal, that they are endowed by their Creator with certain unalienable Rights, that among these are Life, Liberty, and the pursuit of Happiness.

As examined by Devine these fundamental values are: (1) men are created equal, (2) rights are bestowed by a Creator, (3) liberty is a prime goal; and (4) preservation of individual property provides the means for happiness. "In simplified form these resolve into belief in liberty, equality, property, and religion."[16]

Are these four principles also a part of mass political consensus in the United States? Devine offers evidence that they are. A variety of surveys indicate consensus on the concept of individual liberty as well as such cultural values as freedom of the press, speech and education. Consensus on equality is slightly more complicated. Americans support the notion of political equality—that is, equality before the law in the sense of equality of opportunity to vote or equal treatment by government officials—but reject notions of economic and social equality. Americans are also strongly committed to the value of personal property, a commitment reflected in measured preferences for private ownership of the means of production and the values of achievement. There is mass consensus favoring private ownership of factories, grocery stores, auto companies, coal mines, telephone and telegraph utilities, railroads, banks, etc. Finally, there is cultural consensus on two significant values marking the American religious commitment—a widely shared belief in God (more than 95 percent expressing that belief in polls) and support for the concept of a moral responsibility to promote the welfare of other members of the community (although this is translated more frequently into support for private, local, and state welfare programs than those of a federal nature).

Contemporary Dislocations in Mass Consensus: A Breakdown of the One?

Devine paints a picture of broad mass political consensus in the liberal tradition. Certainly the beliefs and values that constitute the four essentials of the political culture—national identity, meaningful symbols, conceptions of authority, and conceptions of purposes—are relevant to the daily operations of American government. Do they, however, serve as guides for Americans faced with responding to specific situations and unexpected contingencies in their everyday lives? Moreover, how stable is the contemporary political consensus even on general conceptions of authority?

Generalities versus Specifics.   The answer to the first question is that there are major differences, on the one hand, between the kinds of general principles that people believe in and value, and on the other hand, the principles they say they would apply in specific situations. Studies conducted over more than two decades underscore this difference. For example, a seminal study published in 1955 reported that significant proportions of Americans questioned in a nationwide survey would place restrictions on freedom of speech: almost one-third say they would not allow a socialist the right to speak in their community, one of five would deny the right to someone whose loyalty had been questioned even though that person was avowedly not a communist, and two-thirds would not permit a professed communist to make such a speech.[17] Similarly, a study published in 1960 noted that more than nine of ten persons sampled in two communities agreed with the principle that the minority has the right to criticize majority support; yet large percentages (ranging from 21 to 68 percent) favored barring an antireligious speech, a socialist speech, a communist speech, a black from running for office, and the candidacy of a communist.[18] A study published in 1964 revealed that almost 90 percent of a nationwide sample of the general electorate agreed with the statement, "I believe in free speech for all no matter what their views might be," but almost 40 percent also agreed that "a man oughtn't to be allowed to speak if he doesn't know what he is talking about."[19] One year later another study found that 60 percent of Americans agreed that people should be allowed to live where they please if they can afford it but 63 percent disagreed with "I would be willing to have a Negro family live next door to me."[20] Finally, in 1975 a Harris survey found that 56 percent of a nationwide sample favored desegregation of the public school system "as a matter of principle" but 76 percent opposed busing schoolchildren to achieve that end.[21]

In addition to a lack of consistency between views on general principles and specific applications, studies of mass consensus indicate that consensus is greater on some kinds of values than on others. In keeping with the findings reported in Chapter 7 regarding American preferences for liberty and equality, studies of mass consensus indicate that people give stronger support to principles of free speech, press, etc., than to notions about equal rights. Moreover, they have more positive feelings about political equality than about social, economic, or ethnic equality. And Americans adhere more strongly to conceptions of authority (such as free elections and majority rule) than conceptions of purpose reflected in the values of liberty and equality.

Another key finding with respect to the general principles versus specific applications question is that politically active members of the community are more likely than the mass of Americans to adhere both to abstract statements of principle and to the implied specifics. The activists comprise a class of "carriers of the creed," those more likely to espouse the democratic faith in word and deed.[22] A key reason for this may be the differences in communication patterns between political activists and the general citizenry. One observer remarks that "the actual consequences of communication, as well as the intended ones, are consensus-increasing."[23] Political activists communicate readily and freely with one another:

> Among many segments of the general population, however, communication on matters of political belief either occurs not at all or is so random and cacophonous as to have little utility for the reinforcement of political values. If Louis Wirth is correct in observing that "the limits of consensus are marked by the range of effective communication," it becomes easier to understand why the active minority achieves consensus more often than the voters do.[24]

Confidence in Government.   If governments are to achieve the values and goals reflected in both abstract and specific conceptions of purpose, people must have confidence in them; conceptions of authority must be positive and fairly stable. Devine's analysis and earlier studies of mass consensus suggest that Americans do agree upon basic rules of the political game and that they have confidence that political leaders play by them. However, recent studies suggest a weakening of the confidence Americans traditionally have placed in government. Significant portions of the mass public seem alienated from their political institutions, distrustful of what political leaders do, and cynical about politics.

Pollster Louis Harris has conducted regular surveys of Americans for more than a decade to detect changes in levels of alienation, or the sense that people feel powerless to change their lives and influence what government does. Harris asks people whether they agree or disagree with four statements: (1) "The rich get richer and the poor get poorer," (2) "What I think doesn't count much anymore," (3) "People running the country

don't really care what happens to me," and (4) "I feel out of things
going on around me." From 1966 to 1976 the percentage points increase
of agreement with each statement was 32, 37, 35, and 33 respectively.
By Harris's measure, alienation increased from 29 percent in 1966 to
58 percent in 1977.[25]

Since 1958 the Institute of Social Research of the University of Michigan has examined how much trust people have in government and levels
of cynicism about politics. Utilizing five questions in nationwide surveys,
researchers have constructed an index of trust-cynicism in government.
The questions pertain to (1) how much people can trust the government in
Washington to do what is right, (2) whether the government in Washington
is run pretty much by a few big interests looking out for themselves or
for the benefit of all the people, (3) if government wastes the money
we pay in taxes, (4) whether or not the people running the government
are smart and usually know what they are doing, and (5) whether or
not the people running government are a little crooked. On the basis
of their responses, people are either trusting or cynical; the percentage
of the latter is subtracted from the former to calculate an index. In 1958
the index of trust-cynicism was a +50 indicating a substantial trust in
government; by 1973 the index had dropped to −30, indicating a marked
decline in trust and increase in cynicism. Generally disaffection from
government increased across all ages and among both black and white
Americans. During the Watergate scandal of 1973 and 1974 cynicism continued to rise, but apparently the scandal itself had relatively little direct
relationship to the increase. Reasearch suggests that people perceived
Watergate as resulting from individual dishonesty rather than from weaknesses inherent in the political process; moreover, although two-thirds
of adults sampled were pleased that Richard Nixon resigned the presidency and 61 percent disapproved of President Ford's pardon of his
predecessor, they distinguished between the office and its particular incumbents, and any decline in confidence in the presidency did not reflect
simply the Watergate scandal.[26]

That there has been a general decline in mass confidence in political
institutions is apparent from Harris surveys (see also Chapter 2). In the
decade from 1966 through 1976 the percentage of Americans expressing
confidence in the executive branch of the federal government declined
from 41 to 11 percent, in Congress from 42 to 9 percent, and in the
Supreme Court from 51 to 22 percent. Upwards of 40 percent of those
interviewed by Harris in 1975 expressed the view that local and state
governments, the Supreme Court, Congress, and the White House did
not really know what people wanted and were mostly out of touch with
the people.[27]

In sum, as portrayed in studies of political culture and mass consensus,
the character of public opinion as the One emerges from a liberal demo-

cratic tradition that defines the boundaries of cultural conceptions of authority and purpose. Yet these cultural precepts of how government should operate and what government should do are abstract principles removed from the day-to-day lives of a large portion of Americans; consequently the tenets provide ambiguous guides not always adhered to in specific circumstances. Whether increased levels of alienation, distrust, and cynicism in recent years token a shift in the abstract liberal democratic consensus is hard to say. Perhaps contemporary disaffections may be nothing more than deviations from traditional patterns. In any case the future of mass consensus cannot be separated from the public opinion of the Few and the Many.

The Few: Unorganized and Organized Opinion Publics

"In any realistic sense the diversified interaction which gives rise to public opinion is in large measure between functional groups and not merely between disparate individuals."[28] The public opinion of the Few consists of the views held by major social interests and expressed in functional group form. Our focus is upon two types of groups, the unorganized and organized.

Unorganized Interests

A noted student of interest politics defined a group as "a certain portion of the men of society, taken, however, not as a physical mass cut off from other masses, but as mass activity, which does not preclude the men who participate in it from participating likewise in many other group activities." A group "is always so many men, acting, or tending toward action—that is, various stages of action. Group and group activity are equivalent terms."[29] Defined as activity, then, a group consists of people engaged in conjoint activity regardless of whether or not formal organization underlies that activity. In this sense people jointly acting in the opinion process, although not formally organized, constitute a group or opinion public. Three types of unorganized opinion publics are deserving of detailed consideration—the attentive public, the issue-minded, and the ideologues.

The Attentive Public.   Political scientists differentiate various levels of activity in the opinion process and the actors taking part in each.[30] The distinctions yield a picture of the process that resembles the pyramid depicted in Figure 8–1. Assuming that everyone communicates to at least a minimal degree in the opinion process (even indifferent subjects communicate quiescence), then the pyramid pictures the segmentation of the overall population of political communicators. At the top are the political

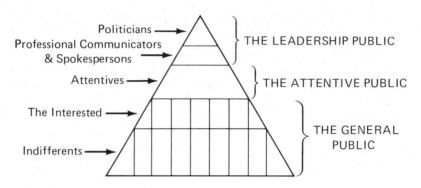

Figure 8-1:   The Segmentation of Political Communicators

leaders, politicians holding and seeking public office who either make
policies or aspire to that task. A second tier consists of political leaders
in the categories of professional communicators and group spokespersons
described in Chapter 2. A third tier is the attentive public comprised
of all citizens distinguished by virtue of their high levels of political
involvement, information, concern, and civic-mindedness. They are frequently the opinion leaders discussed in Chapter 2, persons to whom
the less politically informed and involved citizens go for advice and guidance. At the fourth tier, and comprising the largest grouping, is the general
public, normally the setting from which popular opinion emerges. As
indicated in Figure 8-1, members of the general public consist of both
politically interested (who vote but are not as involved in other ways
as the attentives) and indifferents.

The attentive public occupies an important position in the opinion
process. For one thing, the attentives act as channels of interpersonal
communication in the reciprocal flow of messages between political leaders and the general public. Attentives are key audiences for both mass
and organizational communicators. Second, attentives join political leaders as carriers of political consensus, i.e., persons described in the last
section who are more likely than others to support specific applications
of general democratic rules and values. Finally, the attentives constitute
a surrogate electorate in periods between elections; politicians frequently
perceive the currents of opinion flowing among the attentives as representative of what the general public (less likely to be interested in politics
during interelection periods) believes, values, and expects.[31]

The size of the attentive public is difficult to measure. Estimates suggest
that attentives comprise less than one-half of the adult population,
perhaps in the range of 10 to 15 percent. If an attentive is defined as
a fully active political citizen (i.e., one who not only votes but also campaigns for candidates, parties, and causes; contacts elected representatives
and appointive officials; consumes large quantities of political informa-

tion, etc.), then a variety of studies support the estimate of 10 to 15 percent.[32] Regardless of its size the attentive public is a distinguishable group. Research indicates that attentives, in contrast to the general public, pay more attention to political campaigns, talk about politics more frequently, follow politics more often through newspapers and magazines, and generally feel more efficacious about what they can accomplish in the political process. Generally attentives are persons of higher socioeconomic status than persons among the mass of the general public. However, attentives and members of the general public care about elections and voting to about the same degree and use television and radio as sources of political information to the same extent.

Attentives also can be distinguished by the political opinions they express. Examining the opinions of attentives through surveys conducted from 1952 to 1964 Devine found that the attentives differed from the general public in the following respects: on economic matters attentives indicated more support of the private sector from government interference; on welfare issues attentives were more likely to oppose federal aid to education and medical care; attentives were sometimes more opposed to the extension of civil rights, more supportive at other times, and hence, no clear pattern emerges; and attentives evidenced support for foreign aid and a strong foreign policy. There was relatively little difference between the attentive and general public with respect to the trust each placed in government.[33] In a study comparing the opinions of the most and least politically active citizens during the 1960s Richard Dawson also offers evidence of distinctive views of the attentive public. However, the differences were not overwhelming. The more active were slightly more supportive of Vietnam involvement and hard-line policy with respect to the war, less isolationist, and more supportive of foreign aid. The more active also gave slightly less support to government welfare programs, slightly less than the least active to the proposition that racial integration was moving too fast, and were more likely to support civil liberty positions and to tolerate dissent. Compared with nonvoters the most active were more trusting in government and more likely to believe that government benefits everybody; no such differences emerged when the most active were compared with voters not classified as active in other respects.[34]

In addition to the evidence that attentives differ from the general public in levels of political involvement and in opinion, there are also indications that attentives have greater influence in the policy process than do members of the general public (a topic we will return to in Chapter 12).[35] It suffices here to say that Devine argues that majority support from the attentive public is necessary if a policy is to be processed through political institutions. Moreover, the policies ultimately adopted by Congress tend to be closer to the positions voiced by attentives than those advocated by the generally involved or the indifferent. In part this reflects the tendency of policy makers to take the attentive public into account; it also reflects, perhaps, the tendency of attentives to respond positively to the persuasive appeals of policy makers already embarked upon a policy course.

The Issue-Minded Public.   The attentive public consists of people who pay fairly close attention to politics and play active roles regardless of the particular issues involved. Apart from these people there are others who pay attention to issues only when politics touch their particular interests. Such people make up the issue-minded public, that is, persons attracted by specialized issues rather than by politics in general. These specialized issue publics emerge from a process of selective convergence; a person makes an individual choice of what is salient and reaches conclusions regarding preferred courses of action with respect to a given issue. All persons converging on the same issue thus form a specialized public, a public that may ultimately organize into a formal group but need not. Hence, the elderly are interested in issues pertaining to medical care, retirement benefits, housing, and inflation whether or not they participate in organized groups to advance their interests. Similarly in the late 1960s millions of Americans between the ages of 18 and 21 were attracted to the issue of extending the franchise, and both black and white urban Americans formed issue publics with respect to the issue of civil disorder in urban areas.

Issue publics typically reflect the convergence of five kinds of interests. First, there are all the persons who have a special interest in a controversy (such as farmers concerned with price supports for their commodities, or truck drivers worried about speed limits on interstate highways). Second, with respect to the issue in question there are persons who have had considerable experience in dealing with it and are usually asked to make some dispassionate judgment about it (agricultural economists may be asked, for example, to comment upon farm prices, or energy experts, on the fuel savings derived from lowering speed limits). Third, there are the advocates for various positions; these may represent organized groups, but a private citizen might also emerge in a leadership role (say as a spokesperson for grain farmers or "the boys back at the truck stop"). Fourth, there are people not directly concerned with the issue but affected by its resolution (the average consumer must worry about farm prices, fuel prices, and highway speeds because higher costs for the producer or truck-driving middleman mean higher prices for the consumer). Finally, there are people who know relatively little about a matter, yet are called upon to express an opinion (through a survey, referendum, public meeting, etc.); once they do so, no matter how uninformed, they join one or another side of the issue public.[36]

When these five sets of interests converge into an interest public—the directly concerned, experts, spokespersons, indirectly affected, and ignorant—the issue that provoked their conjoint activity influences what they talk about, whether or not they organize, and how they vote. Specialized publics, for example, detect differences between the two major political parties on issues affecting the public; for such publics pertinent issues probably play a greater role in how members vote than do party loyalties, the personalities of the candidates, or more general "law and order," "bread and butter," or "peace and prosperity" issues.[37]

The Ideological Public.   In Chapter 7 we designated the ideologue as the person possessing a relatively closed belief system whose values are strongly held likes and dislikes. Moreover, the belief and value systems of members of the ideological public are internally consistent; that is, they hold beliefs and/or values that logically cohere rather than contradict one another (they do not believe in both A and non-A or value both A and non-A). How large is the ideological public of American politics? There is little agreement among observers. Some say the ideological public is large and growing; others argue that Americans have never been very ideological and are not likely to be more so in the future. A major source of the disagreement lies in how researchers measure ideology. Although most try to examine whether Americans are basically liberal or conservative in persuasion, students of public opinion differ widely on the best ways to find out whether people are one or the other.

A principal approach to measuring liberalism and conservatism in America is to ask people what they consider themselves to be. Pollsters have used this technique for several decades. Americans generally classify themselves as slightly more conservative than liberal, a tendency magnified in the early 1970s. For example, George Gallup found in 1976 that of those in a national sample 42 percent labeled themselves conservative, 31 percent liberal, 10 percent middle-of-the-road, and 17 percent had no opinion. Compare this with 1964 when the breakdown was 30 percent conservative, 26 percent liberal, 34 percent middle-of-the-road, and 10 percent unknown. Aside from the relative changes in the liberal-conservative split (and increase in conservative identifiers), the figures illustrate the tendency of large numbers of Americans to accept neither designation.[38]

A second approach to measuring ideology is to classify people as liberal or conservative on the basis of the positions they take on issues. For example, people can be asked their position on federal programs in the areas of reducing unemployment, spending for urban renewal, correcting poverty, building low-rent housing, etc. Studies using this procedure find Americans generally liberal in economic and welfare matters and conservative on issues of law and order, cracking down on drug abuse, etc.[39] Again, however, a large portion of persons take middle-of-the-road positions (one-fifth to one-third) and are not easily classified. Allied with this procedure is another which classifies people as liberal or conservative on the basis of their philosophical beliefs and values about government in general. For instance, people's views with respect to the following questions can be measured: does the federal government interfere too much in state and local affairs, with private enterprise, with property rights, etc. Using this technique the bulk of Americans emerge as conservative, about two in ten are liberal, and one-third again cannot be classified.[40] However, if specific rather than general questions are asked—such as if government should stop protecting consumers through the Food and Drug Administration—most Americans favor federal action. Moreover, it is very difficult, perhaps impossible, to distinguish liberals and conservatives on such matters. Liberals favor some federal programs such as spending to help the poor, but oppose others such as high defense budgets. Conservatives want the federal government to assist business but not the poor.

Measures of self, issue, and philosophical classification indicate that about two-thirds of Americans are members of the ideological public. A fourth technique casts doubt on such a large estimate. Using this procedure researchers measure the ideological content of people's open-ended responses to questions of what they like and dislike about each major political party and each party's presidential candidates, which party they consider more liberal or conservative, and what people have in mind when they say a party is more liberal or conservative than another. Procedures for defining the content of open-ended responses as ideological have varied from one researcher to another, yet there is agreement that the size of the ideological public falls considerably short of estimates based upon other techniques. In 1956, for example, less than 12 percent of a nationwide sample of voters could be classified as ideologues.[41] A follow-up study employing a less demanding definition of what constitutes ideological content in a person's response still found only 21 percent of those surveyed in 1956 to be ideologues; 27 and 35 percent of those surveyed in 1960 and 1964 respectively could be so classified.[42] Finally, attempting to estimate how much coherence there is to the understanding people have of the liberal-conservative distinction, Converse estimated that 37 percent of a national sample found no meaning in the distinction at all and that 20 to 25 percent made random guesses about the two labels, their meanings, and which to apply to the two major political parties. Only slightly more than one-half the sample, estimated Converse, had a reasonable recognition and understanding of the liberal-conservative distinction.[43] Differences among scholars on how large the ideological public is reflects, in part, a tendency to try to look for liberals and conservatives, a distinction that may mean something when applied to attentives but nothing when used to describe the general citizenry. Other modes of ideological thinking may well prevail, yet go undetected. Moreover, there are reasons to argue that the nonideological politics of the 1950s has been replaced by greater ideological awareness in the 1970s.[44]

In sum, there is an ideological public as well as attentive and issue-minded publics in the public opinion of the Few. How large such an ideological public is we cannot say; probably not as large as the two-thirds of Americans willing to classify themselves as liberal or conservative but not as small as the estimate of one in ten derived from studies in 1956. Moreover, the membership of all three publics—attentive, issue-minded, and ideological—overlaps to a considerable degree. Indeed, research suggests that attentives are more likely to be issue-oriented, think of themselves as liberal or conservative, and understand what they mean by those labels when applied to themselves, candidates, political parties, and other political objects.

Organized Interests

Writing two decades ago, political scientist David Truman noted the part interest groups play in the opinion process. For Truman an interest group was any group that, on the basis of one or more shared attitudes, makes certain claims upon other groups in the society for the establishment, maintenance, or enhancement of forms of behavior that are implied by the shared attitudes.[45] This definition reminds us that the interaction of groups pressing for recognition and acceptance of their respective opinions (i.e., the shared views of each group's members) influences public opinion.

We delay extended discussion of interest groups (organized interests) until Chapter 12. There we consider the role that interests play in the opinion-policy relationship. It is appropriate here to make a few preliminary observations. First, as examined by Truman and most political scientists, interest groups are membership groups. Put differently, interest groups are organized associations of people who engage in activities to influence government decisions. Approximately two-thirds of Americans are members of voluntary organizations (including social, fraternal, and church-related groups); only about four in ten join groups active in community affairs; and about one-third belong to groups in which political discussion occurs. Hence, for a large number of Americans, interest groups do not act as major formulators of political opinions.

Second, since group opinions are the summary statements of the individual opinions of members (usually represented by what group leaders profess as group opinion), the views of any single organized interest seldom offer an accurate reflection of the individual opinions of all group members. Thus, to say that any interest group involves the shared views of participants is not to say that everyone shares the same view.

Third, just as any group's opinion is not identical with the beliefs, values, and expectations of all members, so also is group opinion not identical with public opinion. "Broadly viewed," wrote Truman, "an interest group is a segment of a public that shares a similar view of . . . the consequences under discussion."[46] If, as noted in Chapter 7, a public refers to all persons affected by the consequences of a particular action, conflict, or issue, then any single interest group is likely to be but one organization so affected. Hence, an interest group is only one of many groups contributing to the public opinion of the Few. On any particular question the mythical public consists of the meld of organized interests, the views of unorganized interests, the sum of individual views, and the background opinion provided by mass consensus.

Finally, the diversity of members' opinions that comprise the shared view of the group and the diversity of group opinions that influence public opinion implies that, from the perspective of organized interests, public opinion results from a complex interplay of personal and group constructions. Internally the construction of group opinion involves (1) propaganda directed at molding group unity on behalf of the views of one or more leaders and factions and (2) the give-and-take negotiations between rival factions and leaders to forge a group consensus. Externally each group employs propaganda to influence the views of nongroup members while group leaders bargain with one another in pursuit of advantages and favorable government decisions. In short, just as the contribution of unorganized interests to public opinion is the product of a blending of negotiation and convergent individual choices, that of organized interests is a blending of negotiation with a technique of social control: propaganda.

The Many: Aggregates of Popular Opinion

Popular opinion on any matter is the sum of individual expressions; popular opinion thus includes the distribution of the total number and/or percentages favoring or opposing points of view. Although on a wide variety of matters individuals have relatively little information, most are still willing to state a preference when asked. The cognitive content of popular opinions is relatively low (a point we will return to in Chapter 10), but the affective content is high. Hence, the proportion of persons responding to a survey with question "no opinion" seldom exceeds one-fifth (normally it is more like one-tenth); frequently those who "don't know" or "don't care" express a view anyway. In addition to polls, the other major expression of popular opinion is through voting in primary, general, nonpartisan, and referenda elections for and against candidates, parties, and proposals (see Chapter 11).

People express their beliefs, values, and expectations about a broad range of political objects. When popular opinions pertaining to an object differ, resulting in a relatively persistent and visible dispute involving large numbers of people, there is a political *issue*. In our examination of the opinions of the Many we do three things: (1) explore the types of concerns of Americans that give rise to popular opinion, (2) define the principal issue domains and key issues that have provoked Americans to express popular opinions, and (3) examine the structuring and destructuring of contemporary popular opinion in the United States.

Popular Hopes and Fears

Since 1959 several researchers have conducted a series of nationwide surveys of Americans directed at finding out what concerns are uppermost in the minds of people with respect to their personal lives and America as a nation. The questions asked and the percentages of recurring hopes and fears mentioned in response to them are summarized in Table 8–1. It is apparent that the principal personal concerns of Americans pertain to their standard of living, economic well-being, and physical health. Their concerns for the nation have revolved about matters of war and peace, economic stability, and prosperity. As indicated by the marked variations in the percentage of mentions of such national hopes and fears as peace and war, economic stability and instability, and national unity and disunity, popular concerns follow the headlines. As the Vietnam war wound down, for example, war received fewer mentions as a major worry or fear of Americans.

In addition to probing the popular concerns of Americans since 1959 researchers have also tried to determine whether people think things have been getting better or worse for them and for the nation. Pollsters present survey respondents with a picture of a ladder, symbolizing a "ladder of life," with steps numbered from zero at the bottom, representing the worst possible life, to ten at the top, representing the best. Respondents indicate where on the ladder they are at the time of the survey, where they stood five years earlier, and where they expect to be five years after the year of the survey. Respondents also make the same ratings with respect to the nation—where it is at present, was five years earlier, and will be five years from the time of the interview.

Across five years (1959, 1964, 1971, 1972, and 1974) surveys have shown remarkable stability in how Americans assess their present, past, and future lives. The rating people have given to their current status in any given year has not varied significantly and has reflected moderate optimism. Similarly the popular views of the past have been stable, but people look back on the past as not as good a time as they find themselves in during the year of the survey. Generally, they have looked to the future with optimism. Thus Americans have indicated moderate optimism in their personal lives, expressing the belief that things have improved from past to present and that they expect things to get even better in the future. However, this optimism has not been reflected in popular assessments about the state of the nation. There was a gradual decline

Table 8-1   *Popular Hopes and Fears of Americans, 1959–1974*

Question and Concern	1959	1964	1971	1972	1974
Personal		(Percentage of mentions)			
"When you think about what really matters in your own life, what are your wishes and hopes for the future?"					
Better or decent standard of living	38	40	27	29	29
Good health for self	40	29	29	27	28
Aspirations for children	29	35	17	23	24
Peace in the world, no wars	9	17	19	32	16
Happy family life	18	18	14	18	15
Good health for family	16	25	13	12	11
Own a house or live in a better one	24	12	11	12	11
Good job, congenial work	7	9	6	10	11
"Taking the other side of the picture, what are your fears and worries for the future?"					
Economic instability, inflation	—	—	11	9	26
Ill health for self	40	25	28	21	25
War	21	29	17	28	18
Lower standard of living	23	19	18	18	16
Ill health in family	25	27	16	12	12
Unemployment	10	14	13	10	12
Inadequate opportunities for, unhappiness of children	12	10	8	8	10
National					
"What are your wishes and hopes for the future of the United States?"					
Peace	48	51	51	56	27
Economic stability	12	5	18	13	24
National unity and political stability	—	9	15	11	15
Improved standard of living in general, greater national prosperity	20	28	11	10	11
Employment, jobs for everyone	13	15	16	17	10
Better public morality	7	10	8	5	10

Table 8-1, cont.   *Popular Hopes and Fears*
of Americans, 1959–1974

Question and Concern	1959	1964	1971	1972	1974
National	(Percentage of mentions)				
"What are your fears and worries for the future of our country?"					
Economic instability, inflation, recession	18	13	17	13	28
War	64	50	30	35	24
Lack of law and order	—	5	11	16	13
National disunity or political instability	—	8	26	13	12
Threat of communism	12	29	12	8	8

Source: Adapted from Tables 8–12 in William Watts and Lloyd A. Free, *State of the Nation 1974* (Washington, D.C.: Potomac Associates, 1974), pp. 266–275. © 1974 by Potomac Associates.

from 1959 to 1974 in the ratings people gave the current state of the nation in any given year. Moreover, Americans tended to look back on the past as a better time for the nation than the present. Finally, American expectations of the nation's future have also declined. In 1959 Americans looked forward five years to 1964 with optimism. Looking forward in 1974, however, they anticipated little improvement for the nation by 1979, although a 1976 survey indicated slightly greater optimism.[47]

Issue Domains and Popular Opinions

Within the context of their general hopes and fears for themselves and the nation (and their image of whether those hopes and fears are realized in the past, present, and future), Americans show concern for certain kinds of issues. Gallup polls conducted over the course of more than four decades provide evidence of the general types of issues, or issue domains, that have troubled Americans in five recent historical periods: the period of a portion of the presidency of Franklin Roosevelt, 1937–1944; the period covering the presidency of Harry Truman, 1945–1952; the period of the Eisenhower presidency, 1952–1960; the Kennedy-Johnson years in the White House, 1961–1968; and the period of the Nixon-Ford incumbency, 1969–1976. With painstaking persistency during various years in each of these periods, Gallup's pollsters have asked, with some variations in wording, "What do you think is the most important problem facing the country today?" Figure 8–2 portrays five pie charts depicting the relative importance of key issue domains in each historical period. Each diagram represents the most prominent issues mentioned by people in response to Gallup's question and the relative proportion of mention of those problems. Other problems that sprang up from time to time but received few mentions in the historical period (space flight, specifics of the Watergate scandal, etc.) are not included.

Looking at Figure 8–2 we see that the key issue domains of the Roosevelt period were economic and foreign; Americans thus responded to issues pertaining to recovery from the depression of the 1930s and the nation's involvement in World War II. Matters of the postwar economy, growing tensions with the Soviet Union, and involvement in the Korean War resulted also in a focus on economic and foreign policies as issue domains in the Truman period; however, welfare questions (demands for better housing, issues surrounding a proposal for national health care, etc.) and social issues (principally the problem of race relations in postwar America) also came to the fore. In the Eisenhower era the principal concern of Americans was foreign affairs (receiving almost half the mentions as a "problem"), with economic, social, and welfare issues receiving less emphasis. Again, in the Kennedy-Johnson years Americans perceived foreign questions as principal problems; yet there was also considerable concern over social issues—civil rights, law and order, urban rioting, etc. Finally, in the Nixon-Ford era, economic, foreign, and social issues vied about equally for Americans' attention and a new issue domain appeared, the growing concern with threats to the very survival of the nation and humanity itself posed by environmental pollution and the inability to solve the world's energy needs.

The overall pattern is fairly clear; foreign and economic questions (peace and prosperity) recur as salient to Americans from one period to the next (see Table 8-2), social issues have become increasingly important, and over the course of four decades there seems to be an increasing variety of problems on the minds of Americans. Although the pattern is vivid, cetain points should be kept in mind. First, the relative emphasis Americans place on an issue area in any given period varies; Americans respond at different times in different ways depending upon events. Second, both Figure 8-2 and Table 8-2 mask the fact that from time to time Americans get very concerned about specific issues not easily reflected in any listing of their top concerns. From 1957 to 1961 for example, Americans expressed concern over the seeming inabilities of the nation to compete with the Soviet Union in exploring outer space (the Soviets launched the first satellite in 1957, well ahead of America's first successful launching of such an orbiting vehicle). The space program was a chronic, although not the leading, concern of Americans for several years. Moreover, by averaging the principal problems listed by Americans in historical periods, we also mask the fact that in any given survey a particular concern is actually of primary importance although it might not remain so for the whole period or even for a single year. For instance,

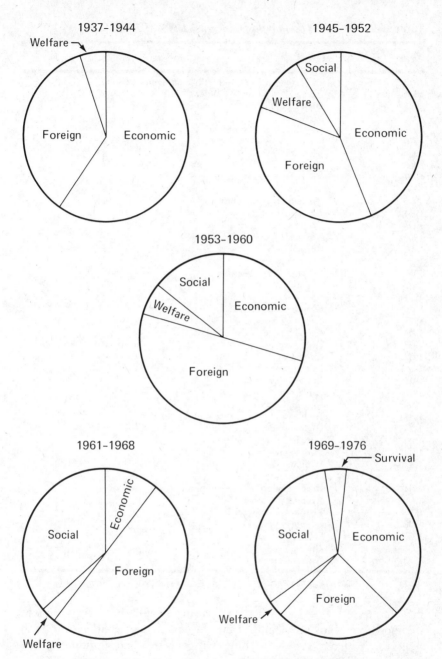

Figure 8–2:   Issue Domains of Recent Political Eras

Source: Constructed on the basis of mean percentages for each era as calculated from individual surveys reported in George H. Gallup, *The Gallup Poll* (New York: Random House, 1973), vols. 1–3.

Table 8-2   *Top Popular Concerns, 1935–1975*

Year	Concern
1975	The economy (high cost of living, unemployment)
1974	High cost of living, Watergate, energy crisis
1973	High cost of living, Watergate
1972	Vietnam
1971	Vietnam, high cost of living
1970	Vietnam
1969	Vietnam
1968	Vietnam
1967	Vietnam, high cost of living
1966	Vietnam
1965	Vietnam, race relations
1964	Vietnam, race relations
1963	Keeping peace, race relations
1962	Keeping peace
1961	Keeping peace
1960	Keeping peace
1959	Keeping peace
1958	Unemployment, keeping peace
1957	Race relations, keeping peace
1956	Keeping peace
1955	Keeping peace
1954	Keeping peace
1953	Keeping peace
1952	Korean war
1951	Korean war
1950	Labor unrest
1949	Labor unrest
1948	Keeping peace
1947	High cost of living, labor unrest
1946	High cost of living
1945	Winning war
1944	Winning war
1943	Winning war
1942	Winning war
1941	Keeping out of war, winning war
1940	Keeping out of war
1939	Keeping out of war
1938	Keeping out of war
1937	Unemployment
1936	Unemployment
1935	Unemployment

Source: *The Gallup Opinion Index,* Report No. 125 (November–December 1975), p. 93.

in February 1974, 46 percent of Americans viewed the energy crisis as the most important problem, but later events in the economy and with respect to Watergate tended to hide that concern when summing up the year and the Nixon-Ford era.

Popular Opinions on Salient Issues: The Pollsters' View

It is, of course, impractical to present here all of the specific issues and popular opinions on them that make up the economic, social, welfare, foreign, and survival domains that have concerned Americans for more than four decades. It is reasonable, however, to illustrate the content of each domain by discussing some of the more salient issues.

During the middle terms of the Roosevelt presidency, 1937–1944, polling was just getting underway as a systematic means of measuring popular opinion on issues. Professional pollsters not only measure the beliefs, values, and expectations of samples of the citizenry, but also define the issues which people respond to. Pollsters usually ask people about the issues that make news and, hence, share the function of setting the agenda of issues with the professional communicators of the news media. Such was the case in the 1930s and it has remained so since.[48]

Economic Issues.   What were the major economic issues that people talked with pollsters about during the Roosevelt presidency? Among the principal ones were labor-management relations. For example, Americans expressed strong support for the principle that workers have the right to organize trade unions to press for higher wages and improved working conditions; beginning in the 1930s no fewer than 60 percent of those surveyed approved of labor unions. Support for the concept of unionization extended into the 1970s as evidenced in 1975 by a survey indicating that well over a majority of popular opinions favored union efforts to organize farm workers on large California lettuce farms and vineyards. Moreover, surveys in the 1940s afford evidence of popular support for the right of organized labor to strike. And surveys in the period of the Roosevelt administration indicated solid popular support for compulsory arbitration to resolve labor-management disputes. Yet Americans opposed the closed shop (one that hires only union members) and about four in ten of those surveyed in the 1930s felt that the National Labor Relations Act should be revised because it was overprotective of the rights of labor. (Fifty-three percent of those surveyed in 1967 also favored revision of the NLRA.)

The period of the Truman presidency also emphasized labor-management relations as a major economic issue. The dispute was over passage of the Taft-Hartley Act in 1947, legislation placing restrictions upon organized labor (such as declaring the closed shop illegal). Surveys revealed a split in popular opinion over Taft-Hartley: approximately 40 percent favored its revision, 20 to 30 percent its repeal, and the remainder, that it be left alone. Yet there was wide support for certain provisions of the act: 78 percent favored the provision of a cooling-off period of 80 days before a union could strike, 84 percent favored the use of a secret ballot by unions to take a strike vote, and 60 percent liked the ban on featherbedding (the practice of a union exacting pay for members who had not performed any work). During the periods of the Eisenhower presidency, 1953–1960, and the Kennedy-Johnson years, 1961–1968, fewer polls focused upon the labor-management dimension of economic issues. A principal question asked in both periods, however, was whether Americans thought laws regulating labor were too strict, not strict enough, or about right. Generally about one in ten Americans responded that the laws were too strict, 35 to 45 percent found them not strict enough, 25 to 35 percent regarded them as about right, and the remainder had no opinion or declared they did not know.

Since World War II much of the expressed concern of Americans with the economy has pertained to how to confront recurring cycles of recession and/or inflation. Among the specific issues have been price and wage controls, federal spending, and dealing with unemployment. Americans have divided over price and wage controls. In 1958, for instance, by only a 47 to 43 percent plurality, popular opinions favored laws to keep prices and wages at current levels; asked about wage-price controls in 1971, 38 percent thought they should be more strict, 15 percent less so, and 37 percent left as they were. Americans have been relatively united in blaming government spending for perceived economic maladies, and generally favor a reduction in spending. In 1953 by a 60 to 22 percent majority Americans saw no reason why government spending could not be cut without sacrificing important services to the people; again in the 1970s, surveys indicated that approximately six of ten Americans believed a cut in federal spending was essential to control inflation. The issue of unemployment also divides popular opinion. A 1974 survey illustrates the division and how Americans relate government spending to unemployment. Asked if the level of government spending should be changed to alleviate unemployment, one in ten favored a spending reduction. A new wrinkle in how to deal with recession and inflation appeared in the 1960s with the proposal that government guarantee every family a minimum annual income. Since 1965 about twice as many Americans have opposed as have favored that idea.

Welfare Issues.   Over the past four decades the issues comprising the economic domain of popular opinion have been about the same: coping with recession and inflation; government spending and taxation; dealing with unemployment; and regulation of business, prices, wages, rents, etc. For most people such economic issues shade imperceptibly into welfare matters. To cut government spending to reduce unemployment, for example, may simply mean spending more on welfare programs. Pollsters recognize the relationship of economic and welfare issues, and hence many of the questions they ask take the overlap into account. Gallup, for instance, asked in 1975 that respondents choose between two hypothetical candidates, one who would cut government spending on welfare programs to balance the budget and another who would increase government spending to create employment and spur public buying. Faced with the alternatives, 42 percent opted for the first candidate, 46 percent for the second, and 12 percent were undecided. Given such a pattern one can scarcely say where Americans stand on government spending vis-à-vis such items as welfare programs, a balanced budget, stimulating consumer buying power, or unemployment.

To illustrate the kinds of issues that fall primarily into the welfare domain, however, we will look at popular opinion on selected issues in the five periods spanning forty years of professional polling. A key issue in the 1937–1944 period was that of social security, the program establishing government support for the aged, disabled, dependent children, etc. Repeated surveys indicated that more than 90 percent of Americans favored government financed old-age pensions and other portions of social security. A chief welfare issue in the Truman era concerned a proposal for compulsory national health insurance to provide government supported medical care for every American. Unlike social security, the medical care issue was hotly contested. Polls first indicated popular opinion evenly divided on the issue; later when the American Medical Association proposed a voluntary health insurance scheme, people favored it by a 47 to 33 percent plurality. The proposal for compulsory insurance died in Congress during the Truman era but was resurrected in different form in the 1960s with a plan to provide medical insurance under the social security program. Surveys in the 1960s showed popular opinion behind such a proposal about two to one.

A major issue arising in the Truman era and extending into the 1960s was federal aid to education. From 1948 through 1955 polls carried the question, "Should Congress provide money for public school aid, or should aid be left entirely to the states?" The results indicated substantial support for federal aid, as high as two-thirds. Americans balked, however, at the notion of using federal aid to induce local schools to integrate; surveys in 1956 and 1957 indicated that Americans thought federal aid should go to all schools, integrated or not. A final dimension to the federal aid to education issue has been whether aid should go to public schools or both public and parochial institutions. Asked in 1963 if they favored aid to both public and parochial schools, a plurality of 49 to 44 percent said yes. Seven years later, Americans provided almost an identical pattern of response when by a 48 to 44 percent plurality they opted for aid to public and parochial schools. In sum, Americans favor the concept of federal aid by a wide margin, but on the public-parochial issue, opinion has been markedly divided.

The 1960s witnessed a host of welfare and economic issues emerging in response to the Johnson administration's war on poverty. In the mid-sixties there was substantial popular support for federal welfare programs, both those directed at alleviating poverty and the more conventional kinds of programs associated with welfare policy. Thus, three-fourths of

Americans favored programs to do away with poverty, programs for federal housing, and programs for federal urban renewal; 78 percent favored federal programs to reduce unemployment; two-thirds favored federal aid to education; and two-thirds favored compulsory medical insurance for the elderly. Surveys of the mid-seventies show that popular support for such specific welfare measures has remained fairly stable. Well over two-thirds of those surveyed in 1974, for example, stated that government spending in the following areas should be kept at the present level or increased: programs to help low income families and the elderly, improve public housing and housing in general, urban renewal and urban problems in general, increased medical and health care for Americans generally, and aid to education.

Social Issues.   The domain of social issues consists of a variety of matters of increasing concern to Americans since World War II, especially those arising in the last two decades—race relations, the feminist movement, dealing with crime and assuring public order, coping with the increased use of drugs, and a perceived decline in public and private morality.

Race relations evoked attention in the 1930s and 1940s, but racial issues intensified when the U.S. Supreme Court declared school segregation unconstitutional in 1954. Immediately following that decision only a slight majority of Americans surveyed approved of the Court's action (54 percent), but by the opening of the 1960s approval stood at 62 percent. In the decade from 1956 to 1965 the percentage of Americans thinking whites and blacks should go to the same schools rose from a minority of 49 percent to a substantial 67 percent. Moreover, in the 1960s support increased for policies assuring equal voting rights, desegregation in transportation, housing, and public accommodations, and equal opportunities in employment. That the racial issue has not completely evaporated is illustrated by popular opinions on two items. First, a 1968 survey (conducted in a period following widespread riots in urban ghettoes) indicated that more than twice as many Americans thought that blacks rather than whites were responsible for the conditions blacks found themselves in. Second, there is substantial division on the issue of whether students should be bused to public schools in order to foster desegregation. When queried in 1975 whether they favored a constitutional amendment to prohibit busing of school children or supported busing to achieve racial integration, 72 percent favored the amendment, 18 percent busing, and 10 percent were undecided.

Women's liberation became a key social issue in the 1970s. Popular opinion divided in 1970 over the question, "Do you favor or oppose most of the efforts to strengthen and change women's status in society?" Opinion favored perceived efforts by 42 to 41 percent. However, in 1975, what had been a slim plurality five years earlier became a solid majority as people responded to the question 63 to 25 percent in favor. Moreover, by the mid-seventies popular opinion supported such propositions as, "This country would be better off if women had more to say about politics," and rejected the statement, "There won't be a woman president of the U.S. for a long time, and that's probably just as well." Two-thirds of Americans support establishment of child day-care centers where working mothers can leave children during the day. Finally, in the 1970s the popularity of a proposed Equal Rights Amendment increased. By 1975 polls indicated more than nine in ten Americans were aware of the proposal and a majority favored such an amendment.

Crime has been a major social concern for Americans for a long time. In the 1960s popular opinion supported the view that the courts were not harsh enough in handling criminals (63 percent of people so responded in a 1968 poll, and 75 percent did so in a 1969 survey). Moreover, opinion supported the proposal that persons committing a crime with a gun be given a double sentence and that second offenders be denied parole. Americans also favored the proposition that victims of crime or their families be compensated. In 1965, 62 percent of those polled approved the idea of making a financial provision for the family of an innocent person killed by a criminal. But popular opinion in the sixties was uncertain about the best ways to deal with crime in general; about equal proportions of people polled suggested correcting social and economic conditions, more parental control and less permissiveness, giving police a freer hand by removing court imposed restrictions, increasing the size of police force, and making penalties more severe. In the 1970s Americans generally believed that whatever measures had been tried to solve the crime problem had not worked. In 1967, 46 percent of Americans believed crime was on the increase; in 1975, 70 percent thought so.

Two of the principal crime related issues of the first half of the seventies were gun control and capital punishment. On gun control, surveys revealed that two-thirds of Americans favored registration of all firearms, but 55 to 41 percent opposed the prohibition of gun ownership except for authorized persons. By a 59 to 31 percent majority in 1973, Americans expressed support for the death penalty; substantial majorities thought the death penalty more effective in deterring crime than a life sentence with or without possible parole. But when Americans were asked if they would support the death penalty if it could be proved that long prison sentences were more effective deterrents, capital punishment was rejected 48 to 35 percent. Finally, Americans were sharply divided on what effects a possible death penalty would have on jury decisions. A 1973 Harris Survey revealed the proportions of popular opinion divided along the following lines:[49]

If guilt were proven, I could always vote guilty even
though the defendant would automatically receive
the death penalty 39%
I could not say that in all cases, even if guilt were
proven, I would vote guilty knowing the defendant
would automatically receive the death penalty. . 33%
I could never vote guilty, even if guilt were proven,
knowing the defendant would automatically receive
the death penalty 16%
Not sure 12%

Drugs and drug abuse also emerged as salient social issues in the 1970s.
In surveys in 1972 and 1974, 80 to 90 percent of respondents expressed
the view that current levels of government spending for preventing drug
abuse should be either maintained or increased. With respect to the use
of one drug, marijuana, popular opinions shifted. In 1969, 73 percent
thought marijuana smoking a very serious problem; six years later that
percentage had dropped to 58. Yet polls indicated no striking evidence
that Americans favored making the sale of marijuana legal in the 1970s.
A 69 to 25 percent majority opposed use of the drug. Opinions were
sharply divided on penalties for possessing the drug. By a 45 to 43 plurality in 1976, Americans opposed limiting penalties for possession of small
amounts of marijuana to a nominal fine and no jail term.

Two other issues also became a source of considerable social controversy
in the 1970s. First, there was the conflict over the desirability of abortion.
In 1975 surveys indicated sharp divisions on the abortion issue: 22 percent
responded that abortions should be illegal in all circumstances, 21 percent
favored the legality of all abortions, and 54 percent took the view that
abortion should be legalized under certain conditions (for instance, if
the life of the mother would be endangered by continuing the pregnancy).
Opinion divides more markedly when pollsters specify the circumstances
surrounding an abortion. Whereas 24 percent of those surveyed would
legalize all abortions in the first three months of pregnancy, only 10
and 7 percent respectively would do so in the second and third three-
month period of pregnancy; 56 percent would declare all abortions illegal
in the last three months of pregnancy.

The second issue concerns euthanasia, the ending of a person's life
to spare further suffering from an incurable illness. Asked their views
in 1975 with respect to euthanasia, Americans sampled opposed euthanasia by a 53 to 40 percent majority if the patient had an incurable disease
and opposed 51 to 41 percent if the person was "suffering great pain
and has no hope of improvement."

Survival Issues.   The convergence of three major concerns of Americans in the sixties and seventies contributed to the emergence of a relatively new issue domain. The principal survival issues concern the quality
of the environment, sources of energy, and population growth.

Pollution of the environment attracted considerable attention as an issue beginning in the late 1960s. By 1974 surveys gave evidence that upwards of 80 percent of Americans expressed substantial concern about water and air pollution, and by similar percentages favored maintaining or increasing the then current levels of spending to combat both. Americans, however, were pessimistic about how much influence environmentalists have on cleaning up pollution; only 15 percent in one survey described environmentalists as having a "great deal" of influence, whereas two-thirds attributed great influence to large corporations in policy making. Asked in 1974 how much progress had been made in cleaning up the environment, a majority thought progress had been achieved in combating air and water pollution but well over a third expressed the view that the country had stood still or even lost ground in the struggle.

Energy issues have had three focuses in recent years. First, with threats of embargoes by oil producing nations there has been the problem of what to do to assure oil and gasoline supplies. Provided with options in a survey in 1975, Americans preferred rationing to an oil imports tax by 2 to 1, a ten cents per gallon gasoline tax to an oil imports tax by 5 to 1, and were even more willing to have a twenty cents per gallon tax on gasoline than an imports tax by a 38 to 29 percent plurality. Support for the notion that removal of governmental regulation on domestic oil would encourage oil production increased from only 28 percent in 1974 to a majority in 1975. Moreover, by a 44 to 26 percent plurality in 1975, respondents approved the idea of decontrolling prices on domestic oil and natural gas; a 61 to 17 percent majority felt this would provide an incentive for companies to find new oil and natural gas resources. The second focal point of the energy issue concerned the development of new energy sources. Three-fourths of respondents in a 1974 survey approved the idea of increasing government expenditures to stimulate production of more domestic oil, gas, coal, and electricity. There was substantial agreement in the mid-1970s about which specific actions should be taken to exploit diverse energy sources: well over two-thirds in surveys favored speeding up construction of the Alaska oil pipeline, production of oil from shale in the western states, a speedup in building new nuclear power plants, and more offshore drilling for oil. A plurality also favored more strip mining for coal, exploitation of U.S. naval oil reserves for general consumption, and a phasing out of oil-fired electrical power plants. In favoring these measures, however, popular views opposed slowing down efforts to clean up air and water pollution by 65 to 26 percent.[50] The third focus of the energy problem was on the issue of conservation. In the early 1970s surveys indicated widespread support for conservation measures as ways of overcoming energy shortages. By 1975, however, surveys revealed that the dedication in the early years of the decade had waned. Specifically, the percentage of surveyed Americans who reported the following activities dropped: using fewer lights, lowering thermostat settings in winter, getting the auto tuned every 4000 miles, using electrical appliances less often, postponing long trips by car, limiting gasoline purchases to 35 gallons per licensed driver per month, using public rather than private transportation, joining a car pool, and improving home insulation.

Population growth, in the minds of many, is one source of both environmental and energy problems. Surveys of popular opinion in the last two decades reveal increasing support for limiting population growth, exercising birth control, and reducing the average size of the American family. In 1974 by a 54 to 37 percent majority Americans expressed that population growth should be regulated even if it mean less industrialization and potentially fewer jobs. And whereas in the 1940s, 40 to 50 percent of Americans responded that the ideal number of children in a family was four, by 1971 only one in four thought such a large number was ideal.

Foreign Policy Issues.   War and American commitments abroad have been the traditional concerns of Americans with respect to international issues. Although popular support tended to be reasonably high for Americans' participation in World War II (only 14 percent in a 1944 survey expressed the view that it was a mistake to enter the war), other wars have not fared so well in the popular mind. In retrospect, for example, two-thirds of Americans asked in 1937 if they thought it had been a mistake to enter World War I responded they thought so. The most unpopular wars in recent history were those in Korea in the early 1950s and in Vietnam in the 1960s. In both cases initial support for the war was high, with about 60 percent favoring involvement, but declined to about half that support as each war seemed to drag on without end and American casualties increased.[51]

The most recent American involvement on a large scale in Vietnam left a residue of hesitation and caution with respect to future American military commitments. Although Americans by a 53 to 37 percent majority in 1975 expressed willingness to maintain a policy of military strength throughout the world "in order to help governments that might be overthrown by communist-backed forces," Table 8–3 indicates that such a willingness does not always imply a willingness to commit troops. Yet Americans in 1975 were pessimistic about the possibilities of staying out of future wars. A survey published on Christmas day of that year revealed that by a 53 to 41 percent majority Americans do not think that "wars can be avoided."

The Issues of the Seventies: A Summary of the Opinion of the Many

As noted earlier, this discussion has suggested but a few of the specific issues that pollsters have asked Americans about over the last four decades. Another point should be made. The issues pollsters put to people are

Table 8-3   *Popular Opinion*
on American Military Commitments

"In the event a nation is attacked by communist-backed forces, there are several things the U.S. can do about it—send American troops OR send military supplies but not send American troops OR refuse to get involved. What action would you want to see us take if ____ is attacked?

Attacked nation	Send troops	Send supplies	Refuse to get involved	Don't know
West Germany	27%	32%	33%	8%
Israel	12	42	37	9
Japan	16	35	40	9
England	37	30	24	9
India	7	34	47	12
Mexico	42	25	23	10
Thailand	10	32	46	12
Brazil	15	33	39	13
Nationalist China	8	27	54	11
Canada	57	19	14	10
Saudi Arabia	7	27	54	12
Philippines	29	34	26	11
Turkey	9	29	49	13

Source: *The Gallup Opinion Index*, Report No. 121 (July 1975), pp. 16–28.

cues which each individual interprets and responds to with special, individualized meaning. Aggregating responses to survey questions necessarily obscures the richness of symbolic meaning that any single person finds in an issue. Whether the summation of individual pros and cons suffices as a measure of popular opinion is problematic:

> To reduce ambivalent, subtle, interacting, contingent responses to statistics is to abstract and simplify grossly but not randomly. It is to describe the responses that occur given existing circumstances, a useful enough enterprise. It is to ignore or discount *possibilities* and the response to changed perspectives that political acts might themselves create if the actors were less bemused by popularity polls.[52]

With the caveat that opinion polls measure possibilities in the present, not the certainties of future, it is appropriate to offer two items summarizing popular opinion in the 1970s. First, consider Table 8-4. It summarizes popular views on key matters contained within the various issue domains already discussed. Clearly the opinion of the Many is something of both conflict and consensus.

Table 8-4   *A Summary of Popular Opinion on*
                  Key Issues of the 1970s

Domain and Issue	Favor	Oppose
Economic		
Put wage-price controls back into effect	64%	36%
Welfare		
A 5% surtax on annual family incomes of over $15,000 to pay for programs for the poor and unemployed	45	55
Reduce spending for social programs such as health, education, and welfare	34	66
Aid to parochial schools	53	47
Social		
Busing to achieve better racial balance in schools	35	65
Death penalty for persons convicted of murder	64	36
Amnesty for Vietnam draft evaders and deserters	41	59
Registration of all firearms	72	28
Legalize use of marijuana	27	73
Legal abortions through the third month of pregnancy	51	49
Equal Rights Amendment	78	22
Foreign		
Resume diplomatic relations with Cuba	63	37
Reduce military-defense spending	55	45

Source: *The Gallup Opinion Index*, Report No. 113 (November 1974), pp. 4–17.

Second, we have learned from our survey of popular opinions that Americans generally support increased governmental activity and spending to solve a large number of problems. Yet the resources for dealing with salient concerns are limited. This means placing priorities on what should be done. Table 8–5 suggests popular priorities in the mid-1970s. It lists specific issues distributed across the various issue domains. Each

Table 8-5   *Support Priorities for Government Spending on National Issues*

Economic and Welfare

    2. Helping the elderly
    6. Making a college education possible for deserving young people
    7. Improving medical and health care for Americans generally
    8. Supporting and improving public schools
  11. Providing adequate housing for all the people
  12. Rebuilding run-down sections of our cities and meeting the overall problem of our cities
  15. Helping the unemployed
  18. Helping low-income families through welfare programs

Social

    3. Combating crime
    4. Coping with narcotic drugs and drug addicts
  17. Improving the situation of black Americans

Survival

    1. Developing greater self-sufficiency in energy supplies
    4. Reducing water pollution
    9. Reducing air pollution
  10. Providing better and faster mass transportation systems
  14. Establishing more parks and recreation areas
  16. Building better and safer roads, highways, and thruways

Foreign

  19. Total spending for defense and military purposes
  20. Economic aid and loans to less developed countries
  21. Contributing to the work of the United Nations
  22. Maintaining U.S. military bases throughout the world
  23. Providing military aid to some of our allies

Source: Adapted from Table 12 in William Watts and Lloyd A. Free, *State of the Union 1974* (Washington, D.C.: Potomac Associates, 1974), p. 275. © 1974 by Potomac Associates. (Note: two issues tied as the fourth place priority in the survey.)

issue has a number indicating its ranking as the concern Americans were most willing to spend governmental monies to deal with in the mid-1970s. As indicated, social and survival issues dominated popular priorities.

The Structuring and Destructuring of Popular Opinions

The emergence of social and survival issues in recent years is but one illustration that the popular focus is no longer limited to the traditional economic and welfare issues that concerned Americans prior to the mid-1960s. Political scientist Richard Dawson suggests that the pattern of popular views may be different in future years than it was in the past because new kinds of issues have emerged to break down the traditional structure of political views.[53]

Popular opinions have structure when identifiable segments of society express particular opinions while other social groupings express different opinions. For example, a majority of white Americans in 1974 said they opposed unconditional amnesty for Vietnam draft evaders and deserters; a majority of nonwhites favored amnesty. There is thus a structure of popular opinion on the amnesty issue along racial lines. Opinions on other issues may be structured in other ways, by social class, age groupings, sex, educational levels, region of residence, religious affiliation, or party loyalties. Prior to the 1960s popular opinion possessed a clear structure. For instance, measures of social class such as occupation and income were closely associated with opinions on a variety of matters, especially popular support for government regulation of business, increased levels of welfare spending, and the adoption of a plan for government medical insurance. Support levels increased as one moved down the occupational ladder from professionals and businessmen, to clerical and sales workers, to skilled workers, to unskilled workers, and to laborers.[54]

Dawson demonstrates that in the 1960s a "destructuring" of popular opinion began. Social, economic, demographic, and political categories of people differ less on opinions than in earlier decades. Traditional economic and welfare issues which once divided people along class lines no longer do so; fairly stable levels of support for both areas come from people in all levels of occupation, income, and education. Although regionalism persists in America, geographical and sectional cleavages also no longer structure the opinion of the Many on contemporary national issues. In spite of a great deal of talk in the sixties and seventies about the generation gap, Dawson finds that age is not significant in structuring conflict on a wide variety of issues. The only noteworthy difference in opinions by age groupings in the 1960s was among the oldest, not the youngest, generation: older Americans were more consistently opposed to Vietnam involvement, less supportive of civil rights, more disapproving of demonstrations, more negative toward U.S. involvement in foreign areas generally, and more unhappy with government. Nor do party loyalties structure popular opinion on the new issues confronting contemporary America. About equal proportions of members of both major political parties as well as persons independent of party affiliation favor government action to correct pollution, the use of force to stop student demonstrations, price and wage controls, cuts in defense spending, and doing everything possible to stop crime. The one factor that does clearly structure popular opinion in the 1970s is race. In the late 1970s surveys indicate that significantly higher proportions of blacks than whites favored government programs to promote medical assistance, provide jobs, increase standards of living, bring about school integration, and make aid available to selected foreign nations. Levels of trust in government are lower among blacks, and blacks are less likely to support the view that government supports all the people.

In addition to the destructuring of contemporary popular opinion there is also a fragmentation of the issue domains of American politics. As we saw in Figure 8-2, during the periods extending from the 1930s through the 1950s economic and foreign policy problems were the dominant concerns of Americans. Starting in the 1960s social issues competed with traditional economic and foreign policy items as perceived problems; in the 1970s survival issues came to the fore to rival other issues. Moreover, the variety of specific issues comprising various issue domains grows yearly, as illustrated by Table 8-4. No issue domain nor single issue dominates American politics, a fact that makes for a highly fluid, shifting, and dynamic process of opinion construction. In the realm of the public opinion of the Many, Whirl rather than Zeus bids to be king.

PUBLIC OPINION: AVOIDING THE REDUCTIONIST FALLACY

In Chapter 1 we repeated Floyd Allport's warning of four decades ago against reducing public opinion to the views of single entity, group, person, institution or personified public.[55] The three faces of public opinion—the One, the Few, and the Many—are additional reminders that the opinion process cannot be reduced to a single statement of what public opinion is or what the public thinks.

Public opinion involves organized community, political culture, and political consensus, all of which provide a contextual background and mythical general will permitting policy makers to act. In the absence of a public opinion of the One there could scarcely be legislation at all, for without a consensus that recognizes the legitimacy of what governors do, the governed are not likely to be bound by policy decisions. But

> the task of government ... is not to express an imaginary popular will, but to effect adjustments among the various special wills and purposes which at any given time are pressing for realizations. ... These special wills and purposes are reflected in the small cluster of opinions that develop within the larger uninformed and inattentive public.[56]

Because public opinion consists of special wills as well as a general consensus, we must take into account the interplay of opinions reflected in the activities of unorganized publics (attentives, the issue-minded, and ideologues) and organized interests. Yet in the clash of views between the Few, these special opinion publics appeal their respective cases to a wider audience. Thereby the opinions of the Many, popular opinion, round out a full picture of public opinion. And just as public opinion cannot be reduced solely to mass consensus or to group interaction, so also is it not solely popular opinion:

> Popular opinion is by contrast shallow of root, a creature of the mere aggregate or crowd, rooted in fashion or fad and subject to caprice and whim, easily if tenuously formed around a single issue or personage, and lacking the kind of cement that time, tradition, and convention alone can provide. Popular opinion is an emanation of what is scarcely more than the crowd or mass, of a sandheap given quick and passing shape by whatever winds may be blowing through the marketplace at any given time.[57]

Since public opinion has all three faces and all must be taken into account in describing the opinion process, the political communicator is never quite sure what his audience is, let alone what is on the audience's mind. Take the case of the political leader arguing for energy conservation. Americans will save gasoline, he says, if we but enforce a fifty-five miles per hour speed limit: "The public wants it done." But which public? If the politician is speaking of popular opinion, polls support him: 73 percent favored the fifty-five miles per hour limit in 1974. Or is his public the driving public, three in ten of whom reported in 1974 they had not reduced their speed in keeping with the limit?[58] Is his public a special interest? If so, did the protest lodged by truck drivers against the imposed speed limit suggest that the truck-driving public wants the limit enforced? Or is it the mythical general public of the One, which wants all laws enforced, at least in principle?

In sum, the burden of Part Three has been to urge that the audience of political communication, i.e., the public and public opinion, is entirely too diversified for us unthinkingly to accept glib assertions about what the public wants or rejects, whether those glib assertions emanate from politicians, journalists, professional hucksters, pollsters, group spokespersons, alleged opinion leaders, or even (especially?) social scientists.

Bibliography

Public opinion viewed from the perspective of the One, the Few, and the Many receives considerable attention from social scientists, professional pollsters, and journalists, although not many are likely to speak precisely of those three divisions. With respect to the One, public opinion understood as a cultural phenomenon and manifested as organized community and political consensus, the most useful single examination of American political culture is Donald J. Devine, *The Political Culture of the United States* (Boston: Little, Brown and Co., 1972). Devine musters vast quantities of survey data to test the presence and strength of consensus on national identity, symbols, rules, and underlying values. More speculative but equally worth examination is Daniel J. Elazar's *American Federalism* (New York: Thomas Y. Crowell, 1966) wherein the author develops the notion of three subcultures peculiar to American politics—the traditionalistic, moralistic, and individualistic. An excellent inquiry into the roots of disaffection with government, both in the United States and other political systems, is Giuseppe Di Palma, *Apathy and Participation* (New York: The Free Press, 1970). A key dimension of political consensus involves the levels of tolerance in a community for dissent. A seminal study on the topic is Samuel A. Stouffer, *Communism, Conformity and Civil Liberties,* first published in 1955 but available in a 1966 paperback edition published by John Wiley and Sons, New York. Readers should also consult two recent studies: Angus Campbell et al., *White Attitudes Toward Black People* (Ann Arbor, Mich.: Institute for Social Research, 1971) and Monica D. Blumenthal et al., *Justifying Violence* (Ann Arbor, Mich.: Institute for Social Research, 1972).

Four major works will assist the reader in coming to grips with contemporary opinion publics such as the attentives, issue-minded, and ideologues. Donald J. Devine presents a succinct analysis of the concept of *The Attentive Public* (Chicago: Rand McNally and Co., 1970) and explores the opinions of attentives as revealed in various surveys. James N. Rosenau traces the interelection role of attentives in *Citizenship Between Elections* (New York: The Free Press, 1974). A comprehensive, perhaps exhaustive, examination of the social class bases of the issue-minded is Richard F. Hamilton's *Class and Politics in the United States* (New York: John Wiley and Sons, Inc., 1972). And a useful description of the ideological views of Americans in the 1960s (as well as an introduction to the various ways ideologues may be identified) is Lloyd A. Free and Hadley Cantril, *The Political Beliefs of Americans* (New Brunswick, N.J.: Rutgers University Press, 1967).

Several works explore the part played by organized interest in the opinion process. The basic text on the subject remains David B. Truman, *The Governmental Process* (New York: Alfred A. Knopf, 1958). A related effort is Harmon Zeigler's *Interest Groups in American Society,* available in a second edition with C. Wayne Peak as coauthor (Englewood Cliffs, N.J.: Prentice-Hall, Inc., 1972). A valuable examination of the internal processes of constructing group opinions is James Q. Wilson, *Political Organizations* (New York: Basic Books, Inc., Publishers, 1973), especially Part 3.

The various data from public opinion polls and surveys used in Chapter 8 to illustrate the domains of popular opinion on salient issues were extracted from several volumes that make poll and survey results readily available to interested readers. To begin, the reader should consult the three volumes of George H. Gallup, *The Gallup Poll: Public Opinion 1935-1971* (New York: Random House, 1972). These volumes bring together the published polls of the Gallup organization on a day-to-day, year-to-year basis. For poll results after 1971 the reader may consult the monthly publication, *The Gallup Opinion Index.* Two books describing the results of Gallup surveys for various periods are John N. Fenton, *In Your Opinion* (Boston: Little, Brown and Co., 1960) and George Gallup, *The Sophisticated Poll Watcher's Guide* (Ephrata, Penn.: Princeton Opinion Press, 1972). Results of *The Harris Survey* are available from Louis Harris and Associates, Inc. on an irregular basis. In addition there is a compendium of Harris surveys for 1970, *The Harris Survey Yearbook of Public Opinion 1970* (New York: Louis Harris and Associates, Inc., 1971). Readers will also want to consult Louis Harris, *The Anguish of Change* (New York: W. W. Norton Co., 1973) for the pollster's interpretation of what his survey results imply for the future of American politics.

Potomac Associates have undertaken to measure popular opinions on key issues with a survey conducted every two years. Basic questions tapping the hopes and fears of Americans, assessments of living conditions, perceived progress in solving national problems, and preferred levels of support for government programs are asked in each survey so that the data may be compared over time. The volumes reporting the results of the Potomac surveys are Albert H. Cantril and Charles W. Roll, Jr., *Hopes and Fears of the American People* (New York: Universe Books, 1971); and the two volumes by William Watts and Lloyd A. Free: *State of the Nation* (New York: Universe Books, 1973) and *State of the Nation 1974* (Washington, D.C.: Potomac Associates, 1974).

Two useful books that summarize the results of surveys of popular opinion in past decades are Rita James Simon, *Public Opinion in America: 1936–1970* (Chicago: Rand McNally College Publishing Co., 1974) and Richard E. Dawson, *Public Opinion and Contemporary Disarray* (New York: Harper and Row, 1973). Simon brings surveys conducted by seven major polling organizations to bear upon the question of what longitudinal changes in popular opinion there have been on salient domestic and foreign policy issues. Dawson relies upon surveys, primarily of the Survey Research Center/Center For Political Studies of the University of Michigan, to examine opinions on traditional versus newer issues and to explore the destructuring of American popular opinion. Readers interested in the summary results of SRC/CPS surveys, conducted especially during years of presidential and congressional elections since the 1950s, should examine the Center's published codebooks. Finally, a useful source of survey results on key questions is a regular section, "The Polls," published in the professional journal *Public Opinion Quarterly*.

Notes

1. Ernest Barker, trans., *The Politics of Aristotle* (London: Oxford University Press, 1952), pp. 114–115.

2. Ernest Barker, *National Character* (London: Methuen Company Ltd., 1948); see also George Santayana, *Character and Opinion in the United States* (New York: George Braziller, 1955).

3. A. Lawrence Lowell, *Public Opinion and Popular Government* (New York: Longmans, Green, 1913).

4. Robert Nisbet, "Public Opinion Versus Popular Opinion," *The Public Interest,* 41 (Fall 1975):168.

5. *The American People and Foreign Policy* (New York: Frederick A. Praeger, 1960).

6. *The Symbolic Uses of Politics* (Urbana: University of Illinois Press, 1964), p. 191.

7. Doris A. Graber, *Public Opinion, The President, and Foreign Policy* (New York: Holt, Rinehart, and Winston, 1968), p. 363.

8. Gabriel A. Almond, "Comparative Political Systems," *Journal of Politics,* 18 (August 1956):396. For a review of alternative definitions of political culture see Young C. Kim, "The Concept of Political Culture in Comparative Politics," *Journal of Politics,* 26 (May 1964):313–336.

9. Samuel H. Beer and Adam B. Ulam, *Patterns of Government* (New York: Random House, 1962), Ch. 3.

10. Gabriel A. Almond and Sidney Verba, *The Civic Culture* (Princeton: Princeton University Press, 1963).

11. Daniel J. Elazar, *American Federalism: A View from the States* (New York: Thomas Y. Crowell, 1966).

12. Survey, National Opinion Research Center, November, 1945.

13. James W. Prothro and Charles M. Grigg, "Fundamental Principles of Democracy: Bases of Agreement and Disagreement," *Journal of Politics,* 22 (Spring 1960):276–94; see also Herbert McClosky, "Consensus and Ideology in American Politics," *American Political Science Review,* 58 (June 1964):361–82.

14. Peter M. Hall, "A Symbolic Interactionist Analysis of Politics," *Sociological Inquiry,* 42 (1972):43–45.

15. Donald Devine, *The Political Culture of the United States* (Boston: Little, Brown and Co., 1972).

16. Ibid., p. 184.

17. Samuel A. Stouffer, *Communism, Conformity, and Civil Liberties* (New York: Doubleday and Co., 1955).

18. Prothro and Grigg, "Fundamental Principles of Democracy."

19. McClosky, "Consensus and Ideology in American Politics."

20. Frank R. Westie, "The American Dilemma: An Empirical Test," *American Sociological Review,* 30 (August 1965):532. See also Lawrence J.R. Herson and C. Richard Hofstetter, "Tolerance, Consensus and the Democratic Creed: A Contextual Exploration," *Journal of Politics,* 37 (November 1975):1007–32.

21. *The Harris Survey,* October 2, 1975.

22. V.O. Key, Jr., *Public Opinion and American Democracy* (New York: Alfred A. Knopf, 1961), pp. 51–53.

23. Theodore M. Newcomb, "The Study of Consensus," in R. K. Merton, et al., eds., *Sociology Today* (New York: Basic Books, 1959), p. 280.

24. McClosky, "Consensus and Ideology in American Politics," p. 375. The quotation from Wirth is in *Community Life and Social Policy* (Chicago: Univ. of Chicago Press, 1956), p. 201.

25. *The Harris Survey,* March 25, 1976. See also *The Harris Survey,* "Confidence and Concern: Citizens View American Government," published in pamphlet form (Cleveland: Regal Books/King's Court Communications, 1974); Louis Harris, *The Anguish of Change* (New York: W. W. Norton and Co., 1973), pp. 10–14; and *The Harris Survey,* Jan. 3, 1977.

26. "Trust in Government Falls," *IRS Newsletter,* Vol. 1 (Winter 1974):6; "Americans' Trust in Government Falls Sharply, Blacks Rapidly Lose Faith in Political System," *IRS Newsletter,* Vol. 1 (Spring–Summer 1973):4–5; "Watergate Crisis Had Indirect Impact on Deteriorating Trust in Government," *IRS Newsletter* 3 (Summer 1975):4–5.

27. *The Harris Survey,* March 22, 1976 and October 16, 1975. For a less alarmist view of such poll results see Everett Carll Ladd, Jr., "The Polls: The Question of Confidence," *Public Opinion Quarterly,* 40 (Winter 1976–77):544–52.

28. Herbert Blumer, *Symbolic Interactionism: Perspective and Method* (Englewood Cliffs, N.J.: Prentice-Hall, Inc., 1969), p. 200.

29. Arthur F. Bentley, *The Process of Government* (Cambridge: The Belknap Press, 1967), p. 211.

30. See Almond, *The American People and Foreign Policy;* James N. Rosenau, *Public Opinion and Foreign Policy* (New York: Random House, 1961); and Key, *Public Opinion and American Democracy.*

31. James N. Rosenau, *Citizenship Between Elections* (New York: The Free Press, 1974).

32. See Richard E. Dawson, *Public Opinion and Contemporary Disarray* (New York: Harper and Row, 1973), pp. 138–39; Sidney Verba and Norman H. Nie, *Participation in America* (New York: Harper and Row, 1972), pp. 79–80; Rosenau, *Citizenship Between Elections,* Ch. 2.

33. Donald J. Devine, *The Attentive Public* (Chicago: Rand McNally and Co., 1970).

34. Dawson, *Public Opinion in Contemporary Disarray*, Ch. 6.

35. Devine, *The Attentive Public;* Verba and Nie, *Participation in America.*

36. William Stephenson, "Application of Q-Method to the Measurement of Public Opinion," *Psychological Record,* 14 (1964):265–73.

37. David E. Repass, "Issue Salience and Party Choice," *American Political Science Review,* 65 (June 1971):389–400: Ruth S. Jones and E. Terrence Jones, "Issue Saliency, Opinion-Holding, and Party Preference," *Western Political Quarterly,* 24 (September 1971):501–509.

38. *The Gallup Opinion Index,* Report 137, Dec. 1976. p. 41.

39. See Richard M. Scammon and Ben J. Wattenberg, *The Real Majority* (New York: Coward-McCann, Inc., 1970).

40. Lloyd A. Free and Hadley Cantril, *The Political Beliefs of Americans* (New Brunswick: Rutgers University Press, 1967).

41. Angus Campbell, et al., *The American Voter* (New York: John Wiley and Sons, Inc., 1960).

42. John Osgood Field and Ronald E. Anderson, "Ideology in the Public's Conceptualization of the 1964 Election," *Public Opinion Quarterly,* 33 (Fall 1969):380–398.

43. Philip E. Converse, "The Nature of Belief Systems in Mass Publics," in David Apter, ed., *Ideology and Discontent* (New York: The Free Press, 1964), pp. 206–56.

44. For recent and contradictory views, see Arthur H. Miller et al., "A Majority Party in Disarray: Policy Polarization in the 1972 Election," *American Political Science Review,* 70 (September 1976):753–78, and the comments on that article by Samuel Popkin et al., pp. 779–805, by Frederick T. Steeper and Robert M. Teeter, pp. 806–13, by David E. Repass, pp. 814–31, and the rejoinder to those comments by Arthur H. Miller and Warren E. Miller, pp. 832–49.

45. David Truman, *The Governmental Process* (New York: Alfred A. Knopf, 1958), p. 33.

46. Ibid., p. 218.

47. William Watts and Lloyd A. Free, *State of the Nation 1974* (Washington, D.C.: Potomac Associates, 1974), pp. 7–18; Ladd, "The Polls: The Question of Confidence," p. 547.

48. A documentation for each survey or poll noted in this section would be as tedious as it is unnecessary. The reader is advised to turn to the bibliography for this chapter which lists the principal compilations of public opinion surveys from which the data used in this section are drawn.

49. *The Harris Survey,* June 14, 1973.

50. *A Survey of Public and Leadership Attitudes Toward Nuclear Power Development in the United States* (New York: Louis Harris and Associates, Inc., 1975).

51. John E. Mueller, *War, Presidents and Public Opinion* (New York: John Wiley and Sons, Inc., 1973).

52. Murray Edelman, *The Symbolic Uses of Politics* (Urbana: University of Illinois Press, 1964), p. 119 (emphasis in original).

53. Dawson, *Public Opinion in Contemporary Disarray.*

54. Key, *Public Opinion and American Democracy,* Ch. 5–8.

55. Floyd H. Allport, "Toward a Science of Public Opinion," *Public Opinion Quarterly,* 1 (1937):7–23.

56. John Dickenson, "Democratic Realities and Democratic Dogma," *American Political Science Review,* 24 (May 1930):291.

57. Robert Nisbet, "Public Opinion versus Popular Opinion," *The Public Interest,* 41 (Fall 1975):168.

58. *The Gallup Opinion Index,* Report 115 (January 1975), pp. 22–25.

part four

CONSEQUENCES OF POLITICAL COMMUNICATION:
With What Effects?

chapter 9

Learning About Politics: Consequences of Socializing Communication

People are not born with political beliefs, values, and expectations. Rather, they construct them in ongoing ways when confronted with political stimuli. One stage of this personal construction phase consists of the things people learn about politics through political communication. Political learning continues throughout the life of the normal human being, through a process called political socialization. In this chapter we examine the political consequences of socializing communication. First we look at the relationship between learning and communication in general. Then we explore the role of one's personality, which is learned, in politics. From there we consider one aspect of the human personality that is particularly significant, that is, the political self. Finally, we describe the communication sources, channels, and messages of political learning.

LEARNING AS A COMMUNICATION PROCESS

In Chapters 1 and 7 we discussed how people over time acquire and display recurring tendencies in responding to objects in their surroundings. The adoption of response patterns and changes in them in the face of new experiences is what we call learning. Learning is minded activity that involves modifying and reorganizing behavior, including one's images and interpretations and the beliefs, values, and expectations associated with them.

A Cybernetic View

There are a number of ways to think about learning and to describe it. We find it useful to focus upon two which emphasize the communication aspects of learning. The first, following political scientist Karl Deutsch's lead, is to think of learning as cybernetic activity.[1] Cybernetics is the study of communication among persons, animals, and machines, that is, among self-controlling systems. A self-controlling system (also regarded as a self-modifying communications network, or "learning net") possesses organization, communication, and control regardless of how it operates or exchanges messages—whether through words, as among people in a social organization, the nerve cells and hormones of a living being, or electronic signals as in a computer. The key feature of a cybernetic system is that it learns via feedback. It is "a 'communications network that produces action in response to an input of information, and *includes the results of its own action* in the new information by which it modifies its subsequent behavior."[2]

There are two types of learning for a self-controlled person. One is simple learning. In simple learning a person adjusts responses to reach goals; goals which continue unchanged throughout one's life. One example is the politician bent upon becoming president of the United States. The goal is fixed but the politician adjusts to advance toward it, perhaps attempting to win lesser offices as stepping stones and, if defeated, advancing in other ways. John F. Kennedy endeavored to become the Democratic nominee for vice-president in 1956 in hopes of advancing toward the presidency. After failing, he did not surrender the goal but pursued it by first wrapping up a landslide victory in his race for reelection to the U.S. Senate in 1958, thus putting himself in good stead to seek the Democratic presidential nomination in 1960.

The other type of learning is complex. It involves goal changing rather than simple goal seeking. Twice defeated for the presidency in the 1950s Adlai Stevenson turned from pursuit of elective office to advancing the causes of world peace and American foreign policy, aims he strived to achieve in his capacity as U.S. Ambassador to the United Nations in the administrations of John Kennedy and Lyndon Johnson.

Viewed as cybernetic in character, learning thus consists of changes in one's thoughts, feelings, and proposals for the future, changes reflected in making different responses to repeated stimuli. Learning is responsive rather than reactive. A person who learns adjusts means and ends to perceived changes in surroundings; in contrast, fixed attributes (social characteristics, partisan loyalties, ideological surroundings, commitments, etc.) alone move the reactive individual (see Chapter 11). To understand learning from a cybernetic view is to consider how people transact with their environment, especially how they exchange messages and use communication to modify their surroundings, behavior, and goals.

A Symbolic View

A second perspective that calls attention to the communication aspects of learning emphasizes the active rather than reactive character of the process. It views learning as symbolic activity and borrows from the thinking of George Herbert Mead.[3] According to Mead human activity is essentially social and, being social, is learned. Social life consists of each person taking others into account, ascertaining the intentions of others, and responding on the basis of that perceived intention. Note that humans do not simply respond directly to the acts of others in Mead's theory. Rather, they respond to what they *believe* to be the intentions of others, their *evaluations* of those intentions, and what they *expect* to be the future, intended behavior of others.

But how do people estimate one another's intentions? They do so by exchanging significant, or meaningful, symbols. As we noted in Chapter 3, gestures, utterances, words, and pauses are signs which people interpret. Interpretations make signs meaningful symbols. Through communication (and the process of negotiation that communication facilitates) people work out shared, commonly understood meanings for significant symbols. Learning, then, amounts to people "internalizing" the jointly understood meaning of symbols and, thereby, responding to themselves as others respond—or at least as they imagine their responses to be shared with others—and responding to the intentions of others as presented in significant symbols.

The cybernetic and symbolic character of learning suggests that it may be fruitful to consider political learning as a process of communication whereby people adopt and adjust response tendencies.[4] In addition to the adoption and adjustment phases of political learning we will want to inquire into its specific communication aspects: what is the socializing content of what people learn and the content of the messages that make learning possible; and what are the communication sources and channels that transmit messages of political learning? In exploring these phases and aspects of political learning, let us turn first to the content of political personality, and then to the content of the political self.

PERSONALITY AND POLITICS

Among students of politics there is a school which argues that once a person acquires a personality there is a strong likelihood that it will be projected upon political objects, thus coloring one's political perceptions and determining political behavior.[5] Harold Lasswell offered a variation on this theme by deriving a formula for what he calls "Political Man": p] d] r = P. Translated, it says that private motives (p) are transformed (]) and displaced (d) into the public arena, then rationalized (r) in terms of the public interest and/or widely accepted community values.[6] It is not the intention here to affirm or refute the validity of such a perspective. Rather, because personality is both a product of and an influence upon political learning, we need to explore the relationship of personality and politics and the implications which that relationship has for the consequences of socializing communication in politics. Hence, we will examine: (1) alternate views of personality, (2) theories of personality in politics, and (3) the question of the role of personality in shaping political behavior.

What Is Personality?

It seems there is no end to possible definitions of "personality." Four decades ago one authority listed fifty different definitions and the number has grown since.[7] We need not enter far into that conceptual jungle. Instead it will suffice to examine two general categories of definitions, that is, deterministic and behavioral. Deterministic definitions speak of personality as an internal state of an individual, as an organization of processes and structures inside a person: "Personality is what determines behavior in a defined situation and in a defined mood."[8] Or, as Allport notes, personality lies *behind* specific acts and *within* the individual"; and "the systems that constitute personality are in every sense *determining tendencies.*"[9] So defined personality is: (1) an organized set of internal tendencies and dispositions to behave in certain ways; (2) an entity inferred from behavior rather than directly observable; (3) fairly stable and consistent over time and triggered by functionally equivalent stimuli; (4) a force that mediates between a person's appraisal of the world and activity in a situation; and (5) assists the individual in screening reality, expressing feelings, and identifying the self to others.

The key element in deterministic definitions is something we have seen in our earlier discussions in Chapters 1 and 7. That is the view that personality consists of stable tendencies *to* behave, that personality *causes,* or at least explains, regularities in a person's responses to diverse stimuli. The alternative category of definitions, the behavioral, posits a view of personality much like that we have introduced in defining opinions; that is, personality is a tendency not *to* behave but *of* behavior. Expressed slightly differently, personality is an observed pattern of regularity in one's behavior, not a cause of such a pattern: "Personality is the totality of the behavior of an individual with a given tendency system, interacting with a sequence of situations."[10] How then does personality differ from opinion?

An opinion is a response tendency (that is, stage or pattern of activity) a person constructs in a specific situation toward a specific object. Personality is the relatively organized configuration of typical patterns of beliefs, values, and expectations—recognized by the person and others—across a wide range of settings and toward diverse objects; personality is the general pattern of how an individual thinks, feels, and acts.[11] Given the preference expressed in this volume for the view that opinions and behavior are the constructed, subjectively meaningful responses of people to objects in the world as they perceive and imagine them, it stands to reason that we also favor a behavioral definition of personality. Bearing that in mind, let us examine various theories of how personality emerges in politics.

Theories of Personality in Politics

There are as many theories as there are definitions of personality. We shall focus on but a few of them, but most specifically upon those that suggest ideas about political learning.

Need Theories

We introduced the notion of psychological needs in Chapter 7. Need theories posit that human beings have a hierarchy of physiological, safety and security, affection, self-esteem, and self-actualization needs. Human behavior reflects efforts to gratify these needs. Unless people satisfy certain basic needs—for food, clothing, shelter, energy, reproduction, etc.—there is little likelihood that they will think, feel, or act in a political fashion. People turn to politics only after gratifying basic physical and social needs; "Without enough to eat there is not a society. Without a society, the adjective 'political' has no noun to modify."[12] Moreover, need theorists argue that much of what a person learns about politics depends upon the personality the individual acquires as a child while attempting to gratify basic physiological and social needs early in life. So important are personality patterns learned before the child begins formal education, writes Knutson, that "the personality of the individual, as it is shaped in the first few years of his life, will be *a more important though less obvious* source of his 'information, values, or feelings vis-a-vis' the basic ground rules by which *all* human systems—social, political, and economic—work and relate to him than will the concurrent and later manifest socialization to which he is subjected."[13] In sum, needs make the child the father of the political man.

Psychoanalytic Theories

Two varieties of psychoanalytic views offer suggestions for how personality influences political learning and behavior—personal and interpersonal.

Personal. The personal school of psychoanalytic theory is in the tradition of Sigmund Freud. Freud argued that people act upon the basis of motives of which they are unaware, as well as upon conscious and partly conscious thoughts, feelings, and inclinations. Freud spoke of three processes central to the functioning of personality: (1) the id, the process of a person striving to satisfy the urge for pleasurable things; (2) the ego, the means used to appraise the person's surroundings, or realities; and (3) the superego, the person's derived notions (usually through experiences with parents) of what is good and bad. The pleasure-seeking processes of the id and the feelings of right and wrong reflected in the superego frequently compete. The ego resolves these conflicts through a variety of defense mechanisms. These include repression (forcing a threatening belief, value, or expectation out of consciousness), displacement (transferring emotional reactions from one object to another), sublimation (finding acceptable ways of expressing otherwise unacceptable drives), projection (shifting one's faults or one's virtues to others), rationalization (giving questionable reasons to justify behavior or relieve disappointment), regression (reverting to immature behavior), reaction formation (going from one extreme to the opposite), introjection (adopting another's viewpoint as one's own), or identification (increasing one's feelings of strength, safety, and/or security by taking on the qualities of another).[14]

Carried into the political realm psychoanalytic theory suggests that unconscious defense mechanisms block adaptive political learning. For example, children learn to repress the thought that nuclear war is possible in their lifetimes; adults displace their emotional outrage at paying higher taxes upon the "welfare chiselers" supported by tax monies; aggressive impulses may be sublimated and transmuted into military careers or law enforcement; voters project their faults and virtues upon candidates for public office, assuming a candidate is "just like me"; a public official caught in election wrongdoing rationalizes it as advancing the reelection chances of his superior; and some adults, frustrated in dealing with a public official, regress to earlier stereotypes such as "What can you expect of a female cop anyway?" Today's arch liberal may become tomorrow's reactionary conservative. This is a case of reaction formation. In addition, many citizens introject or identify with the beliefs and/or qualities of a respected president, congressman, or nationally known television journalist. As in the case of need theories, the personal variant of psychoanalytic theory views much of childhood learning (especially acquisition of feelings of right and wrong) as influencing later socialization and behavior. Once more, the child is the father of the political man.

Interpersonal. The interpersonal variant of psychoanalytic theory stems largely from the work of Harry Stack Sullivan. In Sullivan's words, "Personality is the relatively enduring pattern of recurrent interpersonal situations which characterize a human life."[15] Sullivan accepted the view that a human being possesses innate biological needs—for food, water, warmth, and elimination. In addition, humans possess an innate need for contact with other people. Assuming such an interpersonal need led Sullivan to posit the notion discussed in Chapter 7, namely, that people need security from anxiety-provoking experiences with others as well as satisfaction of their biologically derived tensions. However, achieving security and satisfaction is not easy. Frequently, in efforts to reduce their anxieties and satisfy biological urges, people end up in distorted and complicated relationships with others. In these situations people develop defense mechanisms, or what Sullivan called "security operations," to preserve a feeling of security with their fellows. Sullivan emphasized four such operations: (1) sublimation, which is similar to the defense mechanism recognized in Freudian theory; (2) obsessionalism, the tendency for an idea or impulse to grow so persistent and intrusive that an individual cannot eliminate it from consciousness (in some instances, these impulses assume the form of ritualistic verbalism with an almost magical quality—as when the child thinks that by repeating "I'm sorry" his transgressions will be forgotten, or former President Richard Nixon's repetition of "Let me make this perfectly clear" before obscuring a response to a reporter's question at a news conference); (3) dissociation, the mechanism of keeping conflicting thoughts apart; and (4) selective inattention and its complement selective enhancement, or, the practice of seeing what we wish to see and avoiding threatening information.

Dissociation and selective inattention have a direct bearing upon political communication and the opinion process. We noted in Part Three, for instance, that many Americans express political views which, to the observer, contradict one another (this is the case when an individual claims to believe in free speech for everyone but favors a denial of a communist's right to speak at a public forum). This is an example of political dissociation. Moreover, a large body of research notes the popular tendency to select information from a political campaign which reinforces partisan biases, a case of selective inattention and enhancement (see Chapter 11).

One other aspect of Sullivan's thought is also particularly relevant in any discussion of political learning. Students of political socialization emphasize that one of the key ways children acquire political beliefs and values is through a process of interpersonal transfer. For example, the experience and relationships children have with authority figures in the home (i.e., mother and/or father) influence their concepts of authority when they become adults. It will affect their perception of the president of the United States. They may perceive him as being benevolent or malevolent as was the father in the home. Sullivan stressed that the interpersonal experiences of the child color subsequent perceptions and operate as a possibility throughout adulthood; for Sullivan the precedents of the past always influence a person's thoughts, feelings, and actions in the present.[16] Once more, the child is the father of the political man.

Trait Theories

Theories in this category focus upon tendencies or predispositions which determine how people behave. Each personality consists of a unique, individual set of traits. Hence, people can be compared with one another on the basis of differences in their traits—differences measured on scales indicating how much of each trait a person possesses. Examples of personality traits measured by such scales include whether one is adaptable or rigid, emotional or calm, conscientious or unconscientious, conventional or eccentric, prone to jealousy or not jealous, polite or rude, quitting or persevering, tender or tough, self-effacing or egotistical, and languid or energetic.[17]

A number of social scientists explain politics as the reflection of personality traits. One study, for example, related political behavior to authoritarianism, a complex of traits including the general tendency to defer to authority figures, adhere rigidly to middle-class values, emphasize power and toughness, think in stereotypes, project faults on others, and be preoccupied with sexual "goings-on" in life.[18] Another study sought to specify the traits comprising the conservative personality.[19] Rokeach endeavored to specify the traits comprising the open and closed mind (see Chapter 7). Also, as noted in Chapter 8, studies of public opinion argue that there is a breakdown in American political consensus and trace that decline, in part, to increased levels of traits such as cynicism and alienation, and a general sense of loss of personal efficacy.

Typal Theories

These theories classify people into categories on the basis of dominant characteristics or central themes that recur in their political behavior. Although most attempts to describe political personalities that have applied typal theories have focused upon characters and styles of political leaders,[20] our interest here is upon those that have used typal theories to account for how the audiences of political communication learn to respond in various ways. A prime example of such an analysis explored the differences in personalities of groups of younger Americans responding to major disruptions on college campuses in the 1960s.[21] The study identified five groups of students, then typed the behavior of each group on the basis of differences in the influences parents had upon the students' personalities.

1. *Inactives* were students with no participation in political or social organizations in college; inactives shared a common type of parental upbringing. Their parents were anxious about their children's health and welfare while also insisting upon obedience, conformity, and docility to parental demands.

2. *Conventionalists* consisted of members of sororities and fraternities. These students had relatively little political involvement and were conventional "Joe College" stereotypes; the parents of conventionalists generally adhered to traditional social values such as responsibility, conformity, achievement, and obedience and demanded socially appropriate behavior

of their children. These parents invoked physical and psychological punishment in rearing their children.

3. *Constructivists* worked in social service projects but were seldom participants in organized protests; their parents emphasized discipline, achievement, and dependability, restricted self-expression, and used nonphysical punishment. They were more warmly regarded by their children than were parents of conventionalists.

4. *Activists* protested their dissatisfaction with perceived ills of society and also joined in social service projects to correct those ills; their parents had encouraged their children to be independent and responsible, encouraged self-expression short of physical aggression, and emphasized discipline less than the groups described above. Yet, activists recalled their relations with parents as tense.

5. *Dissenters* were those involved only in organized protests. This group's parents were inconsistent in child-rearing practices. They were permissive in certain areas and highly restrictive in others; they emphasized independence and early maturity less than did parents of other students, yet demanded achievement through competition. Dissenters were far more likely to protest as a form of rebellion against parents than were students in other groups.

The merits or inadequacies of such a typology are not at issue here. Rather, it is but an example of how scholars sometimes attempt to explain politics as a reflection of personality. Unlike trait theories, typal views do not specify tendencies that determine behavior but focus instead upon configurations of behavior which set people off from one another. In both trait and typal theories, however, childhood influences play a major role in shaping political expression. The theme that the political man is born of the child recurs once again.

Phenomenological Theories

We have seen that most personality theories emphasize the influences of childhood development upon personality. Although not ignoring the influence of early learning, phenomenology is the view that the role of personality in behavior (including personality in politics) can be best understood by describing people's immediate experience—that is, the processes they use to attend to and grasp phenomena presented directly to them. Phenomenological theories, therefore, stress that the way in which a person subjectively experiences the world—the sensations, feelings, and even the fantasies involved—is the starting point for examining how people respond to objects.

Two major lines of thinking reflect a phenomenological approach. The first is the Gestalt theory of perception. Gestaltists argue that a key aspect of personality is how people organize perceived experience into patterns or configurations. Gestaltists stress the principle of simplicity in organizing perceptions. For example, let us say that we are viewing a political candidate. If he is new and unknown to us, we formulate an overall, or holistic, image of the candidate that consists of something more than simply the sum of individual traits we perceive. We formulate this view by noting the candidate's similarity to other political figures of our experience, the candidate's social proximity to us (that is, does he seem intimate or far removed from our personal lives), by exercising closure (i.e., imagining and assuming what certain qualities of the candidate must be like even though there is no information about these missing elements), and by projecting qualities we see in ourselves upon the candidate. Moreover, in constructing such an image, we view the candidate against the background provided by the setting the candidate is in—as someone depicted on the evening television news as smiling and shaking hands among members of a friendly crowd, and as a person facing a TV camera from behind a desk flanked with flags and photos of former presidents such as Washington and Lincoln. Thus, we form an overall impression of a figure and the ground on which it sits. This is called figure-ground. It is a fundamental tenet of Gestalt theory. Obviously, if theses derived from Gestalt theory about human perception are correct, then there are lessons in them for political candidates who desire to appear as appealing as possible to voters.

The second major phenomenological approach is field theory.[22] Field theory argues that personality (a learned and enduring pattern of behavior) alone cannot explain how people behave. Each person has a life space composed of a field of forces. In acting, an individual approaches or avoids forces and objects in his life space as he understands these forces at the time of acting. Past experiences may well constitute a force within that field but they do not determine how the person will act toward objects in specific situations. Field theory rejects the notion that causes for human action lie in each individual's distant past; rather, the field at the present moment is a product of the field as it was at a time just past. Distant experiences contribute to the present field indirectly over time, but immediate experiences provide surer explanations of why people behave as they do in the present field.

Field theory has spawned two notions which are of special political relevance. The first is that political learning is a cumulative process, that one's current experiences help a person differentiate the diffuse beliefs, values, and expectations adopted in childhood. The political man teaches the former child by engaging in new, previously unaccounted for experiences. Second, one group of social scientists used field theory to orient their research into American voting behavior.[23] If distant events (such as being unemployed in the depression years of 1933) influence current behavior (such as deciding to vote Democrat), then the influence must be present in some form in the here and now (such as a suspicion of Republican economic policies). If not present in measurable form, it is not possible to demonstrate that a person's current voting behavior is the product of past experiences. As we shall see in Chapter 11, the early childhood and adolescent experiences of many Americans are distilled in a fashion that does influence their voting behavior in the present. It is distilled through an emotional attachment to one of the major political parties, and involves a sense of partisan identification.

Is the Child the Father of the Political Man?

The thrust of the theories reviewed above is that people acquire personality—a recurring, patterned way of viewing, facing, and doing things—early in life; personality influences their beliefs, values, and expectations thereafter. For trait theorists, personality determines much of behavior while phenomenologists believe that personality is more distantly related to a person's contemporary activity. Hence, given the variety of notions posed in theories of personality, the question, "Is the child the father of the political man?" is better expressed: "When do patterns of activity learned early in life, that is, personality, intrude into one's current expressions of political opinions?"

Political scientist Fred Greenstein assesses the impact of personality on politics by specifying the influences that individuals have on political events, the effect that variations in personal characteristics have on behavior, and the influence that personality needs have on political activity. He provides the following listing.[24]

1. The likelihood of the actions of single individuals influencing events increases according to the degree that the situation can be manipulated by people, i.e., is not fixed, ritualized, or highly institutionalized; that the individual is in a position to take action (a president is in a more strategic position than a freshman member of the House of Representatives); and that the individual possesses the appropriate skills to meet the situation. (Franklin Roosevelt's forensic talents were well-suited to restoring public confidence in the 1930s.)

2. Different people placed in identical situations will act differently to the degree that acts are peripheral rather than central to what goes on (that is, personal styles, enthusiasm, and expressions differ more than simply voting yea or nay on a roll call); that acts are demanding rather than perfunctorily performed; that the behavior is spontaneous rather than ritualized; that situations are ambiguous rather than well-defined; that sanctions are not available to enforce conformity; that people make up their own minds rather than conforming to the advice of others (in other words, are "inner" rather than "other" directed); that people are emotionally involved in what is taking place; and that the person is acting

in a situation where others do not have elaborate expectations of what should happen (as when a military leader is free to adopt a battle plan rather than pursue a routine maneuver).

3. Personality needs are more likely to color political behavior on emotion-laden issues (capital punishment, abortion, and amnesty for war evaders and deserters) if a person has strong ego-defensive needs, and when the situation permits an open expression of emotion or frustration. (For instance, a protest march is more expressive than pulling a lever on a voting machine.)

In sum, the child is the parent of the political adult in some circumstances but not in others. Personality, then, does not always intrude upon current political activity but it is one factor a person unwittingly takes into account. This raises a related question: If personality only sometimes influences politics, does politics affect personality? There are three points of view on this issue. In Chapter 1 we discussed three general ways in which social scientists think about human behavior: (1) self-action, where things act under their own powers, (2) inter-action, where things are independent of one another but produce changes when they are in each other's presence; and (3) trans-action, where things are inseparable and jointly change to develop or regress.[25] Applied to the relationship between personality and politics, the self-action view simply says that, once formed, personality is fairly firm and immutable; that is, we can take the boy out of the country, but we can't take the country out of the boy. Thus, personality influences politics but politics does not change personality. An inter-action view argues that environment and experience change one's way of acting and, hence, personality; in other words, if we take the boy out of the country, we also take the country out of the boy.[26] We suspect, however, that a trans-action viewpoint is more descriptive—that boy and country are inseparable and that personality and politics jointly affect one another. One way they do this is through the development of the political self.

THE POLITICAL SELF

We have taken the view that personality is the totality of the behavior of an individual manifested in recurring, patterned tendencies across a variety of situations and with respect to a variety of objects. One object that a person acts with respect to on a daily basis is one's self. Just as in acting toward others, one may praise and encourage oneself or become disgusted, blame, and punish one's self. By treating oneself as an object a person formulates answers to such basic questions as "Who am I?" (develops a self-concept), "Who do I want to be?" (an ideal self), and "What am I worth?" (self-esteem). The self is thus an aspect of personality that a person treats as an object in regularized ways in various situations.[27]

Many people acquire a *political* self, that portion of the self consisting of "an individual's package of orientations regarding politics ... political socialization produces a political self."[28] There are several theories regarding how this happens. Let us examine each briefly, and then pose the notion that the development of a political self is a process of communication, i.e., of symbolic activity.

Theories of Adoption

Given their interest in how people acquire thoughts, feelings, and inclinations, social psychologists offer a variety of models describing the acquisition of "all knowledge of the world, correct or incorrect, that the particular organism—let us say the person—possesses" and of "the affective significance, on a scale of desirability versus indesirability, which he attaches to any particular state of affairs."[29] The general label applied to these models is social learning theory. Social learning theory attributes the acquisition of personal beliefs, values, and expectations to an individual's experiences with other persons, objects, or events. There are two types of such experiences—direct and indirect.

Direct Learning

Through direct learning a person acquires orientations that constitute the political self by: (1) imitating the thoughts, feelings, and actions of people the person is in contact with—as when a child parodies the political preferences of the parent; (2) anticipating what others expect in certain situations—as when, in law schools, students begin to think, feel, and talk like lawyers; (3) direct education—when the student learns about politics in the civics class; and (4) direct experiences—as when many younger Americans learned about political campaigns through direct involvement in the election efforts of Barry Goldwater in 1964, Eugene McCarthy and Robert Kennedy in 1968, George McGovern in 1972, and Jimmy Carter and Gerald Ford in 1976.

The two key models of how direct learning occurs are those of classical and instrumental conditioning. Both pertain to how people adopt affective (values) and conative (expectations and actions) responses to stimuli. Classical conditioning emphasizes the pairing of an object with a stimulus to evoke an affective response. Thus, a child wishes the approval of a teacher. To win it the child tries to answer exam questions correctly, perhaps reciting the names of the United States presidents. In the vernacular of classical conditioning the teacher's approval, as evidenced by direct, verbal praise of the child is an "unconditioned stimulus"; it is a goal prompting the child's effort to make correct responses. If the child gives the correct answers, the teacher's verbal praise rewards, or reinforces, that behavior. Now suppose the teacher pairs that praise with a letter grade of "A." Over time, the student associates the letter grade with the teacher's approval and responds to win good grades as well as direct praise. The student is now conditioned to value the "A" as symbolizing direct praise and coveted approval of the instructor.

Instrumental learning, in contrast to classical conditioning, emphasizes conative (expectations) over affective (evaluative) responses. Let us assume that the child in the classroom displays a varied repertoire of activities—the child may be boisterous, sleep, fly paper airplanes, listen attentively, argue, talk to a classmate, etc. If the student is attentive, the teacher approves (positive reinforcement); if the student is boisterous, the teacher punishes (negative reinforcement). Not surprisingly, the child habitually expects rewards for being attentive; these rewards may take the form of direct verbal praise or high letter grades for "deportment." Note that in instrumental learning the teacher's approval (which serves as a stimulus for the student to seek correct answers under classical conditioning) comes only after the student evidences various behaviors. The student's actions occur without being prompted by a specific goal, but approbation or reprobation following each action serve as reinforcement. The reward or punishment is contingent upon what one does. Thus, when people learn in an instrumental fashion, the political orientations they acquire are those which are reinforced. For example, a person who avoids paying income tax can expect to face government action against the violation; or the citizen who is so conditioned can expect times to improve by voting Democratic or Republican, depending upon his experience with each party in the past.[30]

Indirect Learning

In contrast to direct learning, the indirect mode results from personal experience with surrogates of persons, objects, or events rather than direct encounters with people, places, and things. For instance, a person may model behavior after an idealized image of someone he has never met—as when the small boy learns to be a cowboy, astronaut, or race car driver not by meeting such a person but by seeing how they are portrayed in books, films, or on television.[31]

Direct and indirect learning are often coupled in what theorists call secondary learning. An example of this coupling provides a clue as to how cognitive (beliefs) rather than affective (values) or conative (expectations) responses develop. Assume that our budding scholar associates "A's" on the report card with direct teacher praise to the degree that "A's" become the overriding goal even in the absence of congratulations from authority figures. The symbol "A" is now its own reward. The student formulates beliefs regarding how a high grade can be achieved. He may decide that, since grades appear to be based as much on demeanor as knowledge, it is better to keep silent rather than disagree with the instructor's views. In any event, a person can learn beliefs about appropriate strategies through the coupling of direct and indirect experiences.

Implications of Social Learning

Our presentation of the character of social learning is oversimplified and, hence, a few comments are in order. First, we should not press too far the distinction that affective learning derives from instrumental conditioning, and cognition from secondary learning. There is considerable overlap and at best the distinctions are matters of convenience rather than inherently being part of learning. Second, whether direct or indirect, social learning theory emphasizes the influence of external factors on how people adopt thoughts, feelings, and inclinations. Much of social learning theory implies a copy of the world. But copying is not the whole of learning; people actively construct images of their surroundings and adapt to things through those constructions, not directly to the objects in settings themselves. "Knowledge is not determined by the knower, or by the objects known, but by exchanges . . . between the knower and the objects."[32] Social learning theory tells little about the nature of these mental exchanges. Finally, social learning theory does suggest the origins of a common political phenomenon—i.e., the fact that political symbols are often their own rewards and something people can enjoy in their own right (see Chapter 3).

Theories of Change

Social learning theory emphasizes the possible ways that people adopt their initial thoughts, feelings, and inclinations. As noted, however, it says very little about the mental processes involved. Nor does it explain changes in initial opinions. Consistency theory is a set of models focusing upon opinion change. These models take into account that a person not only perceives a sign, or stimulus—a basic point of social learning notions—but also interprets and responds to the sign on the basis of that interpretation. All models recognize distinctions between cognitive, affective, and conative aspects of learning.[33] The question each poses is under what conditions and by what means are a person's beliefs, values, and expectations consistent. This question is explored in a tentative way in Chapter 7. The basic thesis of all models is that when one's thoughts, feelings, and inclinations are inconsistent, the person experiences tension, there is a "strain toward consistency," and changes occur; i.e., the self learns by adjusting inconsistent views. Each model—balance, congruity, dissonance, and discrepancy—offers a different view of the interpretation process.

The Balance Model

This view focuses primarily upon inconsistencies in a person's beliefs and values.[34] The assumption is that when a person believes things to be alike, the individual evaluates them in similar ways. If Harry likes Jerry and also likes a particular object, then everything is balanced so long as Harry believes Jerry also likes that object. Thus, if a person approves of President Jimmy Carter and knows that a close friend also approves of Carter, the person's views of Carter and of friend are balanced. But if the person hears that the friend opposes the president, there is imbalance. The balance model holds that when views are inconsistent they are unstable. As a result changes occur. Specifically, when feelings about an object change, beliefs change as well, i.e., changes in affects make for cognitive shifts. Hence, a person who becomes more critical of the president becomes more apt to believe stories critical of the chief executive.

The Congruity Model

The focus here is upon inconsistencies between evaluations, not between beliefs and values as in the balance model.[35] Thus, assume a Democrat favorably regards candidates of the Democratic party. Assume also that the partisan dislikes war. The citizen reads in the newspaper that a Democratic candidate proposes warlike policies. The congruity model argues that when political communication produces incongruity between how a person evaluates a communication source (the candidate) and message (the warlike stance), there will be a change of views. The type of change depends upon what evaluations are involved and how strongly the person feels in each instance. Hence, if our citizen has a strong positive attachment to the Democratic party, the opposition to warlike policies will weaken.

The Dissonance Model

This model calls attention to changes resulting from inconsistencies in beliefs.[36] Dissonance exists when a person's beliefs, or cognitions, conflict with each other. For instance, if A implies B, then holding A and the opposite of B makes for cognitive dissonance. Dissonance motivates a person to change beliefs to reduce the conflict. The more important the beliefs are to the individual, the greater the proportion of one's beliefs in conflict, and the more one perceives conflicting beliefs as related, the greater the likelihood of change. Consider again the case of the hawkish Democratic candidate. A Democratic loyalist may believe that no candidate of his party could or would propose war. And our loyalist may also believe that newspapers normally publish the truth. Faced with a news story that the Democratic candidate is offering hawkish ideas, our partisan suffers dissonance. This can be resolved by believing the news account (thus learning that Democrats do make such proposals) or by rejecting the validity of the newspaper, thus changing one's beliefs about the press. Forced to vote for or against the candidate, the partisan's experienced dissonance becomes particularly salient. If one votes for the Democrat, still believing the candidate a dove, then a loss of faith in the press will probably endure since, according to the dissonance model, completed behavior (the vote) cannot be changed but beliefs can (faith in the press). Finally, if the partisan believed there was a genuine choice, that is, that he could have voted for a dovish Republican but did not do so, the loss of faith in the press would probably be even greater. In sum, the greater the contradiction in beliefs, commitment to one belief over another, or choice open to a person, the greater the likelihood of learning new views.

The Discrepancy Model

In this model, opinion change is a function of the discrepancy one perceives between personal views and the views expressed through political communication.[37] We have discussed this model earlier, i.e., in Chapter 7, as accounting for a key phase in the personal construction of opinion. To review, a person wittingly or unwittingly compares what political leaders communicate with what the individual already believes, values, or expects. Views falling within the person's latitude of acceptance are likely to be adopted; those in the person's latitude of rejection dismissed. The more concerned a person is about an issue (say smoking of marijuana), the greater that individual's zone of rejection contrasted with the range of acceptable views. Faced with the appeal "Legalize Pot," the person neither accepts nor rejects it out of hand (i.e., does not respond directly to the stimulus). Instead, the individual contrasts the proposal with acceptable and unacceptable alternatives. Although the proposal may fall into the individual's latitude of acceptance, the person may take no action toward it since it is not the most favored of the individual's favored views. (The person might, for instance, want to legalize marijuana, but only in the sense of making possession a misdemeanor rather than a felony.)

Role Taking and Role Playing: Learning a Political Self

Social learning theory emphasizes the copying aspects of learning. Consistency theory emphasizes the kinds of interpretations people make of what they perceive, interpretations suggesting that learning is more than direct or indirect copying. In formulating a synthesis to describe how people learn a political self, it is useful to introduce the notion of learning as a process of role taking and role playing, symbolic activities flowing out of communication. *Political learning is thus a process of adopting and adapting the political self to the expected and ongoing actions of others through role taking and role playing.* Several aspects of this characterization warrant elaboration.

First, political learning is interpersonal. This aspect introduces role taking and role playing. To think of one's self as an object is like thinking of any other object. That is, it requires taking the object into account, characterizing the self from one's own point of view, and defining the self from the imagined perspectives of other people. Role taking is the mental activity of a person imagining the beliefs, values, and expectations others have of him, comparing those inferences with one's own point of view, and adapting behavior accordingly. Role taking necessarily involves communication and vice versa. It is through language (that is, significant symbols of any type) that one expresses a personal point of view and estimates the definitions of situations made by others. This holds for politics as well as any activity; hence, political talk is crucial to learning a political self because it allows one to adopt political roles (see Chapter 3). Communication is also essential to role playing—the observable behavior of a person that is appropriate in a given situation (as in playing the role of legislator, political reporter, candidate, or campaign manager). Role taking is basically mental activity. It involves the imaginative construction of the roles of self and others. Role playing is overt; it is observable rather than imagined.[38]

Second, political learning is accumulative. In other words, like any learning, political learning occurs in stages. The earliest stage is the preparatory stage during the child's infancy, from approximately zero to two years of age. Role taking as such scarcely happens. But by relatively meaningless mimicry (such as looking at the newspaper as if "reading" it) the child incipiently takes the roles of those around it. The child "is on the verge of putting itself in the position of others and acting like them."[39] The way is thus prepared for two key stages in the development of the political self:

1. *Pretending.* This stage, sometimes referred to as the play stage,[40] covers the period of two to seven years of age and involves the child in acting toward itself as it conceives "mother" or "teacher" would act. However, the role taking is confused; lacking a fully developed, unitary self (and hence standpoint), the child passes from one role to another in diffuse, inconsistent ways. Moreover, this is a period of assimilation. The child is relatively egocentric—ignoring the arguments of others, rejecting evidence, reasoning intuitively and often in a contradictory way, and unable to cooperate with others. The child cannot fully take the other's viewpoint but assimilates everything to its own way of thinking, feeling, and acting. The world is as the child pretends and imagines: a stick is a gun, a cardboard box a house.

2. *Imitating.* Beginning around seven years of age and extending to about eleven is a period in which the child becomes more accommodating. It begins to incorporate the views of others, taking and imitating the standpoints of others in a more organized, consistent role taking and role playing fashion than ever before. Here begins what Mead calls the game stage, the "completing period of the self." Each person is as a player in a game, simultaneously visualizing and estimating the intentions and expectations of other players. Egocentrism gradually yields to sociocentric behavior. The child not only takes the role of individual persons, but also abstracts more generalized roles of collectivities of people. Thereby emerges the child's "generalized other," a generalized perspective from which the child views the developed self and its behavior. With respect to political learning, this is the stage when the child learns about political figures, institutions, and rules and shares the consensus of what government should do and how it should do it, the "generalized other" discussed in Chapter 8 as political culture.

Third, through role taking, role playing, and the development of a generalized other, political learning is adaptive. The minded citizen with a fully developed political self adapts views and definitions of the situation to changes in the political environment, changes the individual takes into account by being open to political communication. In turn, the person also adapts political surroundings to personal political beliefs, values, and expectations.

The capacity for adaptive learning is particularly important to the political communicator, be it the politician, professional communicator, or political activist. Adaptive learning makes possible the kind of identification discussed in Chapter 4 as a key aspect of political persuasion. Recall that a leader adapts to an audience of followers by identifying interests of the audience with his own, something possible only if the leader can take the generalized viewpoint of the audience (that is, by taking the role of the audience). So also must followers take the role of the leader, identifying the leader's interests as their own. The process is two fold: (1) identification *of*—by both leaders and followers—the attributes in one another then can be shared, and (2) identification *with* those attributes by both leaders and followers in order that all parties appear to share the same interest. It is in this sense that a political candidate "projects" an image; that is, he identifies attributes that he can share with voters; voters, in turn, "project" an image on the candidate. They perceive attributes in the candidate they like or dislike in themselves and others.

But not all citizens continue their political learning to the point of completing a fully developed political self. Moreover, different people learn different beliefs, values, and expectations from political communication. How well each citizen develops the political self, and the content of each political self depends in large measure upon the sources, channels, and messages inherent in political communication.

POLITICAL COMMUNICATION AND POLITICAL LEARNING: SOURCES, CHANNELS, AND MESSAGES

Once it is developed, the political self helps a person to relate to politics in three principal ways: (1) to express a personal identity—as a conforming or dissenting citizen, a member of a political group and/or party, as a leader, follower, or nonfollower, etc.; (2) to evaluate political objects, accepting or rejecting political leaders, groups, parties, policies, and authorities; and (3) to understand how best to achieve tangible goals in an instrumental way by influencing government. The reader will recall that these three functions of the political self—expressive, judgmental, and instrumental—are similar to the ways people use symbols in politics (Chapter 3). In fact, learning a political self is largely a matter of adapting to the polity's significant symbols (in other words, symbols significant in Mead's sense of conveying the same meaning for all parties in communication)[41] and being able to use them effectively. Acquiring the content of a political self, then, consists of adopting and modifying significant symbols to enhance expressive, judgmental, and instrumental behavior. That content derives from one's participation in interpersonal, organizational, and mass communication.

Socializing Content of Interpersonal Communication

There are two principal channels of interpersonal communication that contribute to political learning, the family and the person's circle of close friends and intimates known as peers. Conventional wisdom once said that "the unquestioned fact remains that the family is the primary social institution in all lands."[42] The general conclusion was that the family was the most important source for political learning. Supporting this were findings of a considerable similarity between the political orientations of parents and offspring. Recent research, however, indicates that previous discussions of political learning probably overrated the part played by the family, particularly as compared with that of peer groups and the mass media.[43]

The Family as Political Communicator

In assessing the part played by the family in political learning, we need to consider both the things learned in the family and how that learning occurs. With respect to the content of family socialization, the emphasis is upon acquiring orientations that assist later expressive and judgmental rather than instrumental behavior. In the family, for example, children acquire a sense of national identity, an emotional attachment to the nation. Although probably not knowing fully what it means to others, the child learns to be an "American" rather than "British," "Russian," or some other nationality. This initial labeling of the political self appears in one's early identification of the stars and stripes not simply as "my" flag but as *the* flag; the typical child of five, for example, is unaware of other flags and nations and it is only gradually that a less chauvinistic view emerges.[44]

Family socialization also contributes to children learning to identify with groups, especially with one of the two major political parties. Research indicates that at one time at least one-half of American children reaching the age of seven were likely to think of themselves as Republicans or as Democrats. The patterns were fairly clear. Among children reared in middle-class households where both parents identified with the same political party, the probability was very high that the child would copy the parental partisan preference. Where parents differed in partisanship, the evidence was less clear-cut; early studies tended to indicate the child would acquire the father's partisanship, but later evidence indicated the the mother was also an influential socializing force. In any case, unless politics within the family led to bitter parental quarrels—thus contributing to some children withdrawing from the dispute by adopting no partisan preference at all—the general pattern was for early learning of parental partisan loyalties.[45] More recent research, however, indicates a marked rise in political independence of younger people. A survey conducted in 1973, for example, indicated that of those reaching voting age about one-half considered themselves independent; moreover, compared with a similar survey in 1965, the proportion with strong party allegiances had dropped to almost one-half of what it had been. In sum, the previous pattern of partisanship emerging fairly quickly in life as a result of transmission across generations no longer holds.[46]

As part of its influence over the child the family also communicates political judgments. For example, notions of "government" and "law" are generally too abstract for very young children to grasp. Partly as a result of the give-and-take in the family, children learn to personify these abstractions, thinking of government as the person of the president, and of law as the policeman. Young children (white, middle-class more so than poor and/or black) give high marks to both officials—expressing faith, respect, and warmth in the president while regarding him as hard working, honest, friendly, and knowledgeable, and viewing the uniformed policeman as dependable and trustworthy.[47]

In light of recent political history, two comments should be added regarding children's faith in the president and policeman. First, although the evidence is sketchy, the events of recent years, especially American disillusionment with the war in Vietnam in the late 1960s and early 1970s, and the Watergate scandal touching the Nixon presidency in 1972–1974, have helped decrease the average child's respect and affection for the president as a figure of political authority. For instance, one survey comparing the views of second through sixth graders in Tacoma, Washington during two years, 1962 and 1974, found a substantial decline in the proportions of children in all grades saying that the president is "my favorite of all" or "almost my favorite of all"; the president "would always, or almost always, want to help me if I needed it"; the president "knows more than anyone" or "more than most people"; and the president "always, or almost always, keeps his promises."[48] If the president is regarded as less popular, benign, knowledgeable, and reliable, so also is there a marked decline among young people in political trust and a corresponding rise in political cynicism. This is a trend children share with parents. Second, views of the local policeman are not the same for both blacks and whites. Although both black and white children learn very early to respect the policeman, that respect erodes considerably more among blacks as they grow older than it does among white children. This difference in judgment reflects in part the differences in experiences with the police of the two groups in the periods of urban unrest of the 1960s.[49]

In addition to communicating symbols of national identity, political preferences, and authority that form the basis of the child's expressive and judgmental behavior, the family also imparts political information. There is marked overlap between the level of political knowledge held by the parent and by the child. The fact that more knowledgeable children are members of families where the parents are also knowledgeable suggests a transmission from parent to child. Actually, however, studies indicate that both parent and child learn in parallel rather than from one to the other and that the fact that parent and child share the same social status better explains corresponding political beliefs and values than does simple transmission.[50]

Generally, then, family communication fosters a degree of sharing of significant political symbols among family members. But the sharing results less from one-way parent-to-child guidance than from the fact that the communication itself occurs within a context of shared social advantages (or disadvantages) and psychological support (or lack thereof). The influence of family upon socialization is more indirect than direct; that is, the content of parental communication is less important than the openness to the child's response. Children from families which encourage self-expression and exposure to conflicting political ideas, while deemphasizing deferential and conformist social relations, tend to be more knowledgable about politics, more likely to get politically involved, more politically trusting, more realistic in admiration of political leaders, and more interested in politics generally than are children from other types of families.[51]

The Peer Group as Political Communicator

A person's circle of friends and those perceived "like" the individual are important to political learning throughout life. In early childhood years, peer groups come primarily from one's neighborhood, church associates, and friends in the primary grades. These neighbors and friends usually share the child's social status, relative affluence, and activities. Peer groups therefore have a reinforcing, supportive influence on the child's general political outlook to the degree that politics is at all a relevant topic of discussion. For the middle-class child this means reinforcing middle-class beliefs, norms, and expectations acquired in the family. Children reared in the ghetto or poverty areas, in contrast, are unlikely to acquire such middle-class outlooks from their peers; in fact, research indicates that they grow up with less trusting views of political institutions and leaders.[52]

Peer groups during the years of secondary education (and during college for those who go beyond high school) also play a role in socialization. There is some evidence, for example, that one's secondary school peers are more important than the family or the civics curriculum for the person who acquires through the school experience a sense of civic obligation and some understanding of how politics works. One study indicates that high school peer groups are particularly important in helping the child acquire a sense of political efficacy and in influencing views on political issues that are particularly salient to younger people (such as views in the 1960s regarding whether eighteen-year-olds should be permitted to vote).[53] Finally, there is evidence that if a person reaches high school with no clear sense of partisan loyalty, school friends influence the partisanship acquired in these years if any identification with party occurs at all.[54]

Peer groups also influence political learning to the degree that they provide a person with guidance through membership in voluntary associations, civic clubs, or with fellow workers in a company, union, or other place of occupation. Because a person usually joins groups whose aims and views are compatible with his own, the probabilities of such associations changing political opinions are decreased. Although it is not always the case, the general tendency is for persons to adjust their political beliefs, values, and expectations to their peers so as to increase the likelihood of being accepted as an equal and to retain the friendships implied by being a peer.

Socializing Content of Organizational Communication

The principal organization that purports to influence early political learning is the school. After completing his schooling, a person may become a member of a variety of organizations—religious institutions, political parties, civic groups, pressure groups, and work groups—all of which influence political learning in adulthood. The precise consequences of organizational channels beyond school years, however, is a relatively little researched subject. Most of what can be said about organizational communication outside of the school we have reviewed in our discussion of propaganda (Chapter 4) and of organization channels (Chapter 5). Therefore, we will focus here upon the consequences of the school as a political communicator.

The Elementary School

In contemplating the part schools play in political learning, we must recognize the importance of the total school experience as well as the influence of the politically relevant curriculum. The total school experience refers to the student's exposure to a social climate of peers, the informal give-and-take among students outside the classroom, and the closeness of the relationship, between ideas the student encounters in the school and the family. The overall school experience is particularly noteworthy in appraising the role of primary schools as political communicators. The neighborhood school which draws its student body from a relatively homogeneous social environment reinforces many of the beliefs, values, and expectations about politics the child learns in the home. Under such conditions there is fairly continuous development of the political self from home to school in several respects: reinforcement of the early attachment of the child to the nation, a pariotism supported by displaying the flag, pledging allegiance, and singing patriotic songs; a tendency in the later elementary years to join with the family in introducing the child to partisan affiliation; and reinforcement of the notion that it is proper to comply rather than disobey established rules and authorities.[55] By and large, then, during the primary years, the family-school tandem operates uniformly in homogeneous neighborhoods to provide a common basis for the child's expressive and evaluative aspects of the political self.

There are many instances, however, when the social background of the elementary school's clientele is diverse. In such cases, lower-, middle-, and higher-class children get thrown together. Thus the student encounters a range of opinions that may differ from the family's convictions. When this occurs there is evidence that the socializing consequences are far from random. Lower- and working-class students are far more likely to be resocialized in the direction of middle-class values than for there to be a shift in middle-class orientations.[56]

If the social experience of the primary grades has an expressive and evaluative tone, the formal curriculum stresses more instrumental political learning. Civics courses in the elementary grades assign importance to topics dealing with both political persons (president, mayor, and congressman) and government institutions (Congress, and the Supreme Court). Children's positive feelings about the president decline with age, but it is difficult to say that this is a result of formal instruction. Moreover, although teachers place equal importance upon persons and institutions in curriculum topics, research indicates that older children attach greater importance to political institutions and a decreasing importance to persons. That the child's view of government grows more institutionalized and depersonalized is clear but that this is a result of civics instruction is less so.

Both the overall school experience and the curriculum during the primary grades inform the child of strategies for political participation and influence. The emphasis is upon *individual,* not *collective* action. For instance, children entering elementary school take relatively little interest in voting; by the eighth grade, however, voting has become a significant symbol of the citizen's obligation to take part in politics and of how to influence government. Children however, acquire little appreciation of how collective efforts may influence government: "Children's evaluation of pressure groups is generally negative, and knowledge of the most efficient channels of influence is limited. They believe in *individual* access to power—an unrealistic viewpoint, particularly in a rapidly expanding society."[57]

The Secondary School

As with the primary grades, the total social experience in secondary schools is probably as important as formal instruction in contributing to political learning. It may even be more important. We have already noted, for example, that peer groups are important socializers during adolescence. The efforts undertaken in American high schools to indoctrinate students with democratic values have mixed results. For most high school students the civics curriculum is not a major source of political socialization. But the consequences of the curriculum on political learning differ according to the social class of the student. As middle- and upper-class students entering high school, many young Americans have already formulated a view of how political participation can contribute to their lives; formal courses add or detract relatively little from these beliefs, values, and expectations. But children entering high school from lower- and working-class families bring limited political interest, information, and involvement from their family and primary school backgrounds. They are more likely to respond to civics courses than those of higher socioeconomic backgrounds. Research indicates that this is especially true among black youths. In several cases the civics courses move blacks to a position of information and involvement similar to that of whites, one relatively congruent with the stated goals of civic education.[58]

If the civics curriculum is not a major source of political learning for most Americans, neither are the civics teacher's personal political beliefs and values in the classroom. For one thing, despite fears among some segments of Americans that teachers express alien ideas in their classes, few teachers are avowedly partisan.[59] Most take the required textbooks as their guides, texts that have been approved for purchase by higher authority for reasons of economic cost and convenience as well as content. Moreover, there is no evidence that high school students display that much interest in the teacher's political views, let alone adopt them.

Of course, the textbook is a primary means of communication within both primary and secondary schools. Required texts can become the focal points of political controversy. In Kanawha County, West Virginia, in the mid-1970s such a controversy erupted when parents, instigated by a member of the local school board, protested that the texts used in the schools lacked taste, served no real purpose, and denounced traditional institutions. A committee of dissidents demanded banning of 180 texts but the school board refused, agreeing to place the thirty-five most controversial books in the school library to be read only with parental permission. Such antitextbook controversies are but one illustration of the general belief that somehow texts are important socializers. Textbook publishers accept the notion of the importance of their wares. In the mid-1970s, for instance, publishers of many texts undertook a quiet campaign to rid schoolbooks and children's literature of stereotypes thought to foster unflattering images of selected groups: that boys are brave, girls timid; a good family always has a father, mother, big brother, little sister, pet, house, and car; any nonwhite is disadvantaged; old people are pleasant nuisances; mothers are always in the kitchen; all American Indians once lived in tepees; etc. Whether removal of the stereotypes from texts will alter such images and whether texts were responsible for the images in the first place remains to be seen.

College Communication

In considering the socializing consequences of college on political learning, one must remember that the bulk of Americans do not receive college educations. Among voters in the 1970s, for example, fewer than one in three had attended college. For those who do attend college it is difficult to appraise the results for political learning. The young adult attending college encounters diverse ideas and acquaintances, opportunities for political instruction, and challenges to compare the perceived world with the academic conception of it to a degree unprecedented in most primary and secondary school experience. On the surface this all seems to make a difference: persons with college educations have a higher sense of civic awareness and competence than other citizens; are far more likely to vote; have a greater tendency to be independents rather than party loyalists; and are more likely to split their tickets between parties in voting. The problem, however, in attributing these differences to a college education is that high school graduates who go to college already differ in many of these respects from their classmates who do not do so. Hence, differences in the political learning of high school-educated vs. college-educated adults can probably be attributed as much to the lingering social class differences of those going to college as to the college experience.

Research provides some indication that within any single generation of Americans, regardless of the educational levels its members have attained, once formal schooling ends, the changes in later years in popular political beliefs, values, and expectations touch all members of the generation about the same. In 1965, Jennings and Niemi interviewed a cross-section of more than 1600 high school seniors; eight years later they reinterviewed more than one thousand of the original sample. They found that 40 percent had no college after high school, 26 percent went to college but did not graduate, and 34 percent received college degrees. Jennings and Niemi asked what changes took place in the eight years with respect to the sample's interest in politics, following public affairs in the mass media, partisanship, perceptions of the political parties, voting, information about politics, trust in government, opinions on issues, and other political orientations. To be sure, they found differences but the three educational subgroups tended to move in tandem from 1965 to 1973. "Thus regardless of whether the drift was down, up, or stable, the direction of the drift tended to be very much the same for all three." Changes were "not a function of one subgroup performing at odds with another nor of widely disproportionate contributions from the college educated."[60] These findings suggest that persons in a single generation experience the events and issues of their times in ways that transcend many of their intragenerational differences in family backgrounds, peer groups, and schooling. One way that people experience such political happenings is through the media of mass communication.

Socializing Content of Mass Communication

Part two discussed the characteristics of mass channels of communication, including the politically relevant activities of the news media. We noted that the mass media do several things—help set the agenda of issues for public debate, define the contexts for popular evaluations of occurrences, transform happenings into events, influence popular expectations of how events will turn out, and portray the images of political leaders in various ways. In Chapter 10 we will explore the consequences persuasive campaigns conducted through the mass media have for changing opinions. Presently our concern is with the consequences of the mass media for initial political learning.

Studies of political socialization undertaken in the 1950s and early 1960s played down the influence of the mass media upon political learning; they emphasized instead the importance of the family and school in developing the political self. Recently there has been a revision of earlier thinking. For one thing, it is now apparent that the mass media provide a major source of politically relevant information for children, especially for those of elementary school age. Approximately one-third of younger children and two-thirds of older ones in elementary school watch nightly television newscasts; a majority of children of all ages watch the Saturday morning "In the News" formats sandwiched between televised cartoons. Moreover, several studies report that when asked, children cite television as their most important source of political information. Typical is the finding that children rate the mass media as their major source of information with teachers, parents, and friends trailing well behind; as sources of opinion, the mass media lead and parents, teachers and friends follow in that order.[61]

Although studies disagree as to precisely how close the association is between mass media usage and levels of political knowledge (some reporting the association substantial, others moderate, still others mild), the consensus is that exposure to television and newspapers correlates positively with the amount of information young people have about politics, whether the young be elementary or high school students.[62] Usage of the news media especially enhances knowledge of political objects to which the child has a sense of attachment (such as a political party) or objects that are a part of the child's local community. In addition, following television news or reading about politics in the newspapers assists in the development of the child's concept of government as an institutional process rather than something involving only personalized authority figures.[63]

Affective as well as cognitive orientations result from exposure to the mass media. For example, a survey of 400 junior and senior high school students in North Carolina revealed that adolescents using television rather than newspapers as a primary news source tended to think more favorably about government.[64] A study of elementary and junior high school students in the San Francisco Bay area during the Watergate scandal in 1973 concluded that because of media coverage children *could not avoid* hearing and knowing about Watergate; given the nature of much of that inescapable information, children's affective orientations toward the president, and to some extent government generally, suffered considerably. Additionally, the children's faith in their own ability to have much effect on government decreased markedly.[65]

The evidence is that the mass media probably have less influence upon developing a person's overt political behavior than upon one's information and evaluations of politics. There is a relationship between a person's general interest in politics and the manner in which he follows it in the mass media. However, the relationship between media exposure and taking part in election campaigns or making voting decisions appears relatively weak. In this respect, the association between print media use and political activity is greater than that between using the electronic media and taking part in politics.[66]

Communication, Socialization, and Politicization: A Summary and Look Ahead

Most scholars who study political learning agree that the political beliefs, values, and expectations acquired in childhood have important implications for adult behavior. From our focus in this section primarily upon the child's exposure to politically relevant communication—interpersonal, organizational, and mass—we can make a few tentative conclusions about the consequences of socializing communication. Generally, through interpersonal communication the child learns to express national and partisan identities and evaluate politics, government, and authority figures. Through organizational communication, principally in the school, the child reinforces learned identities and evaluations, adds factual information, acquires a sense of personal rather than collective civic obligation, and may become more interested in politics. Through mass communication the child follows politics as news, acquires political knowledge, develops some evaluative orientations, and (more rarely) starts to take part actively in politics.

We have also seen that the development of the political self is a continuing process; political learning goes on beyond childhood. The focus of adult political learning, however, incorporates less the consequences of socializing communication than those of specific political appeals, that is, the consequences of persuasive (or politicizing) communication on opinions. We consider those consequences in the next chapter.

BIBLIOGRAPHY

There are many works summarizing various theories of learning. Few, however, accent the communication aspects of learning. Two that focus directly upon learning as a communication, although from quite different perspectives are: Karl Deutsch, *The Nerves of Government* (New York: The Free Press of Glencoe, 1963), which applies a cybernetic model to examine how men and machines learn, and George Herbert Mead's *Mind, Self, and Society* (Chicago: University of Chicago Press, 1932), which discusses the symbolic interactionist approach to human learning. Readers interested in reviewing leading learning theories should consult Ernest R. Hilgard and Gordon H. Bower, *Theories of Learning* (New York: Appleton-Century-Crofts, 1966); B. F. Skinner, *Science and Human Behavior* (New York: The Free Press, 1953); and Alfred L. Baldwin, *Theories of Child Development* (New York: John Wiley and Sons, Inc., 1968).

There are many reviews of theories of personality. The perspective that dominates the writing of this chapter is described in J. Milton Yinger, *Toward a Field Theory of Behavior* (New York: McGraw-Hill Book Co., 1965) and Robert C. Carson, *Interaction Concepts of Personality* (Chicago: Aldine Publishing Co., 1969). Carson's work contains a very useful summary of the personality and learning theories of Harry Stack Sullivan. A brief, succinct survey of leading personality theories appears in Albert Mehrabian, *An Analysis of Personality Theories* (Englewood Cliffs, N.J.: Prentice-Hall, Inc., 1968). A major problem in studying personality is how to measure the phenomenon. Two works that provide an introduction to conventional techniques are Raymond B. Cattell, *The Scientific Analysis of Personality* (Chicago: Aldine Publishing Co., 1965) and Donald W. Fiske, *Measuring the Concepts of Personality* (Chicago: Aldine Publishing Co., 1971). However, one should not conclude a review of techniques without consulting William Stephenson, *The Study of Behavior: Q-technique and its Methodology* (Chicago: University of Chicago Press, 1953). In recent years studies of politics have emphasized the psychological and personality-based aspects of political behavior. A good place to begin a review of those studies is with the various selections included in the *Handbook of Political Psychology* (San Francisco: Jossey-Bass Publishers, 1973) edited by Jeanne N. Knutson. Readers will also find three general surveys useful: Fred I. Greenstein, *Personality and Politics* (Chicago: Markham Publishing Co., 1969); William F. Stone, *The Psychology of Politics* (New York: The Free Press, 1974); and Anne E. Freedman and P. E. Freedman, *The Psychology of Political Control* (New York: St. Martin's Press, 1975). Several studies incorporate specific theories of personality into their political analyses. Freudian notions appear in Paul Roazen, *Freud: Political and Social Thought* (New York: Alfred A. Knopf, 1968); Harold D. Lasswell, *Psychopathology and Politics* (New York: The Viking Press, Compass Ed., 1960); and Robert E. Lane, *Political Thinking and Consciousness* (Chicago: Markham Publishing Co., 1969). H. J. Eysenck's *The Psychology of Politics* (London: Meuthuen and Co., 1954) offers an example of the application of trait theories to political analysis. M. Brewster Smith, et al., *Opinions and Personality* (New York: John Wiley and Sons, Inc., 1956) exemplify the uses of functional analysis. Finally, in surveying psychological approaches to politics one should not overlook Harold D. Lasswell's *Power and Personality* (New York: Viking Publishing Co., 1948).

The notion of the development of the self, and particularly that of the political self which is employed in this chapter stems from the perspectives of three writers. The first is George Herbert Mead of which the aforementioned *Mind, Self, and Society* is an example. The second is Harry Stack Sullivan; readers should pursue Patrick Mullahy's *Psychoanalysis and Interpersonal Psychiatry: The Contributions of Harry Stack Sullivan* (New York: Science House, 1970) for a comprehensive and voluminous introduction to Sullivan. The third is the developmental psychologist Jean Piaget. Piaget has written extensively on the subject of child development; for an introduction to his theories readers should consult Hans G. Furth, *Piaget and Knowledge* (Englewood Cliffs, N.J.: Prentice-Hall, Inc., 1969).

Students of political socialization have published almost more reviews of the subject and relevant research findings than one could want to read. Among those that nevertheless provide useful introductions are Herbert Hyman, *Political Socialization* (Glencoe: The Free Press, 1959); Richard E. Dawson and Kenneth Prewitt, *Political Socialization* (Boston: Little, Brown and Co., 1969); Kenneth P. Langton, *Political Socialization* (New York: Oxford University Press, 1969); Dean Jaros's attempt to use a different title, that is, *Socialization to Politics* (New York: Praeger Publishers, 1973); Robert Weissberg, *Political Learning, Political Choice and Democratic Citizenship* (Englewood Cliffs, N.J.: Prentice-Hall, Inc., 1974); and Michael P. Riccards, *The Making of the American Citizenry* (New York: Chandler Publishing Company, 1973), a volume employing a developmental model influenced by the writings of Erik Erikson.

In addition to the general surveys of research findings in political socialization there are a few works reporting results of major research projects. Among the significant volumes are David Easton and Jack Dennis, *Children in the Political System* (New York: McGraw-Hill Book Co., 1969); Fred I. Greenstein, *Children and Politics* (New Haven: Yale University Press, 1965); Robert D. Hess and Judith V. Torney, *The Development of Political Attitudes in Children* (Chicago: Aldine Publishing Co., 1967); Charles F. Andrian, *Children and Civic Awareness* (Columbus, Ohio: Charles E. Merrill Publishing Co., 1971); Herbert Hirsch, *Poverty and Politicization* (New York: The Free Press, 1971); and M. Kent Jennings and Richard G. Niemi, *The Political Character of Adolescence* (Princeton University Press, 1974).

NOTES

1. Karl Deutsch, *The Nerves of Government* (New York: The Free Press of Glencoe, 1963).

2. Ibid., p. 88 (emphasis in original).

3. George Herbert Mead, *Mind, Self and Society* (Chicago: University of Chicago Press, 1934).

4. John W. Fox, "The Concepts of Image and Adoption in Relation to Interpersonal Behavior," *Journal of Communication,* 17 (June 1967): 147–151.

5. For a review of the literature see Fred I. Greenstein, "Personality and Politics," in Fred I. Greenstein and Nelson W. Polsby, eds., *Handbook of Political Science,* Vol. 2 (Reading, Mass.: Addison-Wesley Publishing Co., 1975), pp. 1–92.

6. Harold D. Lasswell, *Psychopathology and Politics* (New York: Viking Press, Compass Ed., 1960), p. 75.

7. Gordon Allport, *Personality* (New York: Henry Holt and Co., 1937), pp. 24–54.

8. Raymond B. Cattell, *The Scientific Analysis of Personality* (Chicago: Aldine Publishing Co., 1965), p. 27.

9. Allport, *Personality,* pp. 49, 218.

10. J. Milton Yinger, *Toward a Field Theory of Behavior* (New York: McGraw-Hill Book Co., 1965), p. 141.

11. George A. Theodorson and Achilles G. Theodorson, *A Modern Dictionary of Sociology* (New York: Thomas Y. Crowell, 1969), p. 296.

12. James C. Davies, *Human Nature in Politics* (New York: John Wiley and Sons, Inc., 1963), p. 17.

13. Jeanne N. Knutson, *The Human Basis of the Polity* (Chicago: Aldine-Atherton, Inc., 1972), p. 263. See also Robert E. Lane, *Political Thinking and Consciousness* (Chicago: Markham Publishing Co., 1969).

14. A. A. Brill, ed., *The Basic Writings of Sigmund Freud* (New York: The Modern Library, 1938).

15.   Harry Stack Sullivan, *The Interpersonal Theory of Psychiatry* (New York: W. W. Norton Co., 1953), pp. 110–111.

16.   Robert C. Carson, *Interaction Concepts of Personality* (Chicago: Aldine Publishing Co., 1969), Ch. 2.

17.   Cattell, *The Scientific Analysis of Personality,* pp. 63–64.

18.   T. W. Adorno, et al., *The Authoritarian Personality* (New York: John Wiley and Sons, Science Editions, 1964).

19.   Herbert McClosky, "Conservatism and Personality," *American Political Science Review,* 52 (March 1958):27–45.

20.   James David Barber, *Presidential Character* (Englewood Cliffs, N.J.: Prentice-Hall, 2nd ed., 1977).

21.   Jeanne H. Block et al., "Socialization Correlates of Student Activism," *Journal of Social Issues,* 25 (1969): 143–177.

22.   Kurt Lewin, *Field Theory in Social Science* (New York: Harper and Row, 1951).

23.   Angus Campbell, et al., *The American Voter* (New York: John Wiley and Sons, 1960), Ch. 2.

24.   Fred I. Greenstein, *Personality and Politics* (Chicago: Markham Publishing Co., 1969), Ch. 2.

25.   John Dewey and Arthur F. Bentley, *Knowing and the Known* (Boston: Beacon Press, 1949).

26.   Peter McKellar, *Experience and Behavior* (Baltimore: Penguin Books, 1968).

27.   Arnold M. Rose, "A Systematic Summary of Symbolic Interaction Theory," in Arnold M. Rose, ed., *Human Behavior and Social Processes: An Interactionist Approach* (Boston: Houghton, Mifflin, 1962), pp. 3–19.

28.   Richard E. Dawson and Kenneth Prewitt, *Political Socialization* (Boston: Little, Brown & Co., 1969), p. 17.

29.   Carson, *Interaction Concepts of Personality,* p. 83.

30.   B. F. Skinner, *Science and Human Behavior* (New York: The Free Press, 1953), Anthony G. Greenwald, "On Defining Attitude and Attitude Theory," in Greenwald, et al., eds., *Psychological Foundations of Attitudes* (New York: The Academic Press, 1968), pp. 361–390.

31.   A. Bandura and R. H. Walters, *Social Learning and Personality Development* (New York: Holt, Rinehart and Winston, 1963), pp. 48–50.

32.   Albert Mehrabian, *An Analysis of Personality Theories* (Englewood Cliffs, N.J.: Prentice-Hall, Inc., 1968), p. 134.

33.   A full review of consistency theory is available in Charles A. Kiesler, et al., *Attitude Change* (New York: John Wiley and Sons, 1969); Daniel Katz, "Attitude Formation and Public Opinion," *The Annals of the American Academy of Political and Social Science,* 367 (September 1966):150–162; and Robert B. Zajonc, "The Concepts of Balance, Congruity and Dissonance," *Public Opinion Quarterly,* 24 (Summer 1960):280–296.

34.   Fritz Heider, "Attitudes and Cognitive Organization," *Journal of Psychology,* 21 (1946):107–112; John P. Robinson, "Balance Theory and Vietnam-Related Attitudes," *Social Service Quarterly,* 51 (December 1970):610–616.

35.   Charles E. Osgood, "Cognitive Dynamics in the Conduct of Human Affairs," *Public Opinion Quarterly,* 24 (Summer 1960):341–365.

36.   Leon Festinger, *A Theory of Cognitive Dissonance* (Evanston, Ill.: Row, Peterson Co., 1957).

37.   Carolyn W. Sherif, et al., *Attitude and Attitude Change* (Philadelphia: W. B. Saunders and Co., 1965).

38.   Robert L. Kelley, et al., "Role Taking and Role Playing in Human Communication," *Human Communication Research,* 1 (Fall 1974):62–74.

39.   Bernard N. Meltzer, "Mead's Social Psychology," in Jerome G. Manis and Bernard N. Meltzer, eds., *Symbolic Interaction* (Boston: Allyn and Bacon, 1967), p. 10.

40.   Mead, *Mind, Self, and Society*; see also Jean Piaget, *Play, Dreams, and Imitation in Childhood* (New York: W. W. Norton and Co., 1962).

41.   Mead, *Mind, Self, and Society*, pp. 71–72.

42.   J. Gillespie and Gordon Allport, *Youth's Outlook on the Future* (New York: Doubleday and Co., 1955), p. 8.

43.   Frank R. Scioli and Thomas J. Cook, "Political Socialization Research in the United States," in Dan Nimmo and Charles M. Bonjean, eds., *Political Attitudes and Public Opinion* (New York: David McKay, 1972), pp. 154–174.

44.   Eugene A. Weinstein, "Development of the Concept of Flag and the Sense of National Identity," *Child Development*, 28 (June 1971):167–174.

45.   M. Kent Jennings and Richard G. Niemi, "The Division of Political Labor Between Mothers and Fathers," *American Political Science Review*, 65 (March 1971):69–82.

46.   "Generation Gap Narrow on Political Issues, Ideology," *IRS Newsletter*, 4 (Winter 1976):3, 6. see also M. Kent Jennings and Richard G. Niemi, "Continuity and Change in Political Orientations: A Longitudinal Study of Two Generations," *American Political Science Review*, 69 (December 1975):1316–1335.

47.   David Easton and Jack Dennis, *Children in the Political System* (New York: McGraw-Hill, 1969).

48.   Steven H. Chaffee and Lee B. Becker, "Young Voters' Reactions to Early Watergate Issues," *American Politics Quarterly*, 3(October 1975):360–385; see also Fred I. Greenstein, "The Benevolent Leader Revisited: Children's Image of Political Leaders in Three Democracies," *American Political Science Review*, 69 (December 1975): 1371–1398.

49.   Edward S. Greenberg, "Orientations of Black and White Children to Political Authority," *Social Science Quarterly*, 51 (December 1970):561–571.

50.   Jack McLeod, et al., "Adolescents, Parents, and Television Use," in G. Comstock and E. Rubenstein, eds., *Television and Social Behavior* (Washington, D.C.: U.S. Government Printing Office, 1972), vol. 3, 173–238.

51.   Steven H. Chaffee, et al., "Family Communication Patterns and Adolescent Political Participation," in Jack Dennis, ed., *Socialization to Politics* (New York: John Wiley and Sons, 1973).

52.   Herbert Hirsch, *Poverty and Politicization* (New York: Free Press, 1971).

53.   Suzanne Koprince Sebert, et al., "The Political Texture of Peer Groups," in M. Kent Jennings and Richard G. Niemi, *The Political Character of Adolescence* (Princeton: Princeton University Press, 1974), pp. 229–248.

54.   Martin L. Levin, "Social Climates and Political Socialization," *Public Opinion Quarterly*, 25 (Winter 1961):596–606.

55.   Robert D. Hess and Judith V. Torney, *The Development of Political Attitudes in Children* (Chicago: Aldine Publishing Co., 1967).

56.   Bernice L. Neugarten, "Social Class and Friendship Among School Children," *American Sociological Review*, 51 (January 1946):305–313; Kenneth P. Langton, "Peer Group and School in the Political Socialization Process," *American Political Science Review*, 61 (September 1967): 751–758.

57.   Hess and Torney, *The Development of Political Attitudes in Children*, p. 67 (emphasis in original).

58.   Jennings and Niemi, *The Political Character of Adolescence*, Ch. 7.

59.   Harmon Ziegler, *The Political Life of American Teachers* (Englewood Cliffs, N.J.: Prentice-Hall, Inc., 1967).

60. Jennings and Niemi, "Continuity and Change in Political Orientations," p. 1320.

61. Steven H. Chaffee, et al., "Mass Communication and Political Socialization," *Journalism Quarterly*, 47 (Winter 1970): 647–659; for an excellent review of studies reporting rates of children's exposure to the mass media see Charles Atkin, "Communication and Political Socialization," *Political Communication Review*, 1 (Summer 1975):2–6.

62. Atkin, "Communication and Political Socialization".

63. M. Margaret Conway, et al., "The Relation Between Media Use and Children's Civic Awareness," *Journalism Quarterly*, 52 (Autumn 1975):531–538.

64. Gary C. Byrne, "Mass Media and Political Socialization of Children and Pre-Adults," *Journalism Quarterly*, 46 (Spring 1969):140–142.

65. Robert Parker Hawkins, et al., "Watergate and Political Socialization," *American Politics Quarterly*, 3 (October 1975):406–422; David H. Weaver, et al., "Watergate and the Media: A Case Study of Agenda-Setting," *American Politics Quarterly*, 3 (October 1975):458–472.

66. Steven H. Chaffee, "Mass Communication in Political Socialization," in Stanley A. Renshon, ed., *Handbook of Political Socialization* (New York: The Free Press, 1977).

chapter 10

Participating in Politics: Consequences of Politicizing Communication

Through socializing experiences a person develops politically relevant beliefs, values, and expectations. Whether this results in the adult's taking an active part in politics depends upon the person's exposure and response to politicizing as well as socializing communication. This chapter describes the relation between political communication and political participation. Our focus is not upon the political demands and preferences people express through politics. We consider these matters in subsequent chapters dealing with the consequences of electoral and policy communication for voting and influencing public officials. Rather, here we look at the types of people who take part in politics, how they do so, and the factors associated with encouraging or diminishing their political activity. Finally, we examine one factor in detail, that is, how participants respond to political communication.

POLITICAL COMMUNICATORS AS POLITICAL PARTICIPANTS

In Chapter 2 we described the types of people—politicians, professionals, and activists—who play leadership roles in political communication. As politicians, both representatives and ideologists communicate either in behalf of their constituents or a cause. Professional communicators, both promoters and journalists, communicate to persuade and inform. Spokespersons for organized groups and opinion leaders play considerably more active roles in political communication than the average citizen.

Although in Chapter 2 we emphasized the leadership roles of political communicators, we also noted that political followers are communicators as well. Moreover, we distinguished between people who are political followers (those who take an active interest in politics) and nonfollowers (persons oblivious to political affairs). Later, in Chapter 8 we introduced an added distinction between the politically attentive, interested, and indifferent (refer to Figure 8-1): attentives take part in politics in a variety of ways, the interested limit their involvement primarily to keeping informed and to voting, and the indifferent are a core of political nonfollowers. Our concern in this chapter is with followers who are attentive and interested—those we label political participants—rather than with either political leaders or nonfollowers. In political communication, participants are active members of the audience who not only take into account what political leaders say, but respond and exchange messages with those leaders. In sum, political participants share with political leaders a common activity, that is, both are political communicators.

James Rosenau calls attention to two key sets of citizens who comprise the audience of participants in political communication.[1] The first consists of persons who pay close attention to politics, not only during the election years but between elections as well. These *observers* of politics serve as an unorganized audience for the appeals of political leaders; they watch televised news, read newspapers, go to lectures, ask questions of leaders, talk about politics with friends and acquaintances, write letters, and read books. Through these activities observers remind political leaders that they are being watched and evaluated. In addition, political leaders test their appeals out on this audience of observing participants; the participants form a surrogate electorate the leader uses to estimate the probable success of policies, programs, and candidacies. There are other participants, however, who do more than just observe and evaluate; they are thereby more than an unorganized audience or surrogate electorate. These are people who contact and exchange messages with governmental and nongovernmental leaders. Political leaders, in turn, mobilize these participants in support of or in opposition to proposed policies and causes. This second set of participants, then, consists of those who not only are interested and attentive, but *mobilized* as well. To get a better idea of what these observing and mobilized participants do in politics, let us take a closer look at the activities that make up political participation. We examine first the dimensions of political participation, the major types of participation, and the factors influencing whether and how people engage in politics.

Dimensions of Political Participation

People take part in politics in different ways. These differ in three major respects, or dimensions: the general style of participation, the motives underlying their activity, and the consequences of participation for the individual's role in politics.[2]

Styles of Participation

As noted in Chapter 3, style refers both to what a person does and how the person does it. Just as styles of political talk vary (as between terse and prolix) so do general styles of participation.

Actual/Vicarious. Some people involve themselves in ongoing encounters with political figures—calling them on the telephone, writing them, and visiting governmental offices. Still others act *toward* politicians, but not *with* them; for example, they vote to elect public officials they have never seen nor met. Still others watch television to learn who was elected president or mayor, in a contest they were not moved enough to vote in, thus vicariously taking part by finding out who won. Whereas interpersonal communication with an officeholder requires an actual encounter, mass communication assumes the vicarious character of the parasocial relationship we described in Chapter 5.

Tangible/Intangible. As pointed out in Chapters 3 and 9, when a person utters a political opinion it may enhance the likelihood of achieving material gain (as when supporting a political candidate in exchange for appointment to public office). The style involves tangible, instrumental gain. Some participation is less instrumental, and more intangible and evaluative, such as efforts to demonstrate superior status to one's fellows. Consider the opinionated college teacher who impresses students with a superior level of knowledge and information. The teacher says, in effect, "You must value my views more than yours for I am better informed." Finally, participation may be even more intangible and expressive, as when calling a politician a "crooked liar" out of earshot; the person feels better for having said it but it changes nothing in the politician's behavior.

Individual/Collective. We saw in Chapter 9 that the emphasis in childhood socialization, particularly in the primary grades, is upon individual styles of participation (voting, writing a letter to an official, etc.) rather than joining organized groups or demonstrations to exert collective pressure on policy making. In adulthood more collective styles may emerge—joining a political party, working for a political candidate, becoming active in a labor union, Common Cause, or the P.T.A.

Systematic/Random. Some individuals participate in politics to obtain specific goals; they act not out of impulse but on the basis of calculation; their thoughts, feelings, and proposals for doing things are consistent rather than contradictory; and their action is continuous and persistent rather than sporadic or of varied intensity. Such people display a systematic rather than random style.

Overt/Covert.   A person who expresses political opinions openly and without hesitation, and who employs a variety of observable means of doing so, is overt in style of participation. Others are very guarded in their views, never confiding their votes, for example, and extolling the secrecy of the ballot. As the Watergate scandal of the early 1970s demonstrated, covert activities have played an important part in the participation not only of followers, but in the styles of key political leaders including a president of the United States.

Committed/Uncommitted.   Citizens vary in the intensity of their political participation. One who feels strongly about a cause, candidate, policy, or program acts with a fervor and enthusiasm not characteristic of a person who views an election as a choice between Tweedledum and Tweedledee.

Pain/Pleasure.   We saw in Chapter 5 that a person may pay attention to politics and get involved because political activity is enjoyable for its own sake. Others want to achieve something beyond politics through participation. They may want to become better informed, win an argument, elect a public official, or promote better schools. People interested in advancing both tangible and intangible aims through politics may experience what Stephenson calls communication-pain; those who enjoy following politics just for the fun of it and without more long-range goals reap rewards of communication-pleasure.[3]

Motives for Participation

Various factors elevate or depress levels of political participation. One such set of factors pertains to people's motives for taking part. These motives, like the styles of participation to which they contribute, vary in several respects.

Intentional/Unintentional.   Some citizens seek out political information and events to accomplish specific ends. They may have a desire to become informed, influence a legislator's vote, or guide an administrator's discretion. For them politics is purposeful and intentional. Others undertake political activity almost by chance, perhaps falling into a political story, finding a campaign sticker affixed to the automobile bumper, etc. Circumstance, not intention, produces participation for these persons.

Rational/Emotional.   The individual desiring to achieve specific ends who carefully weighs alternative means of achieving those goals, and then selects the most favorable from the viewpoint of its costs and benefits is rational in motivation. Alternately, some people act without thinking, simply out of impulse. Unspecified anxieties, fears, frustrations, biases, prejudices, hopes, aspirations, and other feelings motivate emotional participation (frequently conducted in the expressive style alluded to earlier).

Psychological/Social Needs.   We noted in Chapter 9 that people sometimes project their psychological needs upon political objects, as, for example, in supporting a political leader out of a deep-seated need to defer to authority, or when projecting their own inadequacies upon various classes of perceived political "enemies"—minorities, foreign nations, or politicians of the opposition party. Others use politics to promote social camaraderie, identify with persons of desirable status, or promote the position of their social group in relation to others.

Inner/Other-Directed.   Closely related to psychic vs. social motivations for political participation is the inner/other directed distinction. The inner-directed person is self-actional, that is, orientations and tendencies acquired from parents guide behavior: "Since the direction to be taken in life has been learned in the privacy of the home from a small number of guides and since principles, rather than details of behavior, are internalized the inner-directed person is capable of great stability."[4] The other-directed person, in contrast, is more cosmopolitan, responding on the basis of orientations acquired from a far wider circle than simply parents. Morals and principles motivate the inner-directed; a desire to conform and be on the inside socially goads the other-directed.

Minded/Mindless.   People vary in how aware and conscious they are in constructing political acts. Minded behavior implies active interpretation of one's actions and an estimate of the consquences of those actions for one's self and for others (the role-taking process described in Chapter 9). Mindless activity—such as being swept up in a crowd, aimless rioting, violence or parroting partisan and ideological slogans—implies little thought on the individual's part. For instance, a person may never have intended to join a violent demonstration, yet finds himself carried along by circumstances and events.

Consequences of Participation

Discussion of the minded, interpretative aspects of political participation in contrast to the less thoughtful, more unconscious variety of mindless politics raises the question of what consequences participation has for the individual's role in politics generally.

Functional/Dysfunctional.   Not every form of political participation advances one's goals. If, for example, a citizen's goal is to discharge a perceived civic obligation, voting is a functional way of doing that.

However, if the citizen wants to overthrow the entire governmental apparatus, voting contributes relatively little to that end; at least as generally practiced in the United States, popular voting has not advanced the cause of revolution.

Continuous/Discontinuous.   When a person's political participation contributes to prolonging an existing situation, program, government, or state of affairs, the consequences are continuous. If participation disturbs an existing balance of forces, disrupts routines and rituals, and threatens stability, it is discontinuous. Electoral participation is generally continuous; blowing up an airliner, kidnapping, or assassination as political protests have discontinuous consequences.

Supporting/Demanding.   Through some types of acts people demonstrate their support for the existing political regime—by voting, paying taxes, obeying the laws, singing the national anthem, pledging allegiance to the flag, and so forth. Through other actions they make demands upon public officials—petitioning congressmen with letters, visits, and phone calls; lobbying; or withdrawing financial support from a candidate's campaign.[5]

The Types and Distributions of Political Participation

Although our list of the styles, motives, and pragmatics of participation appears long, it is hardly complete. What it suggests is that in examining the various ways people participate in politics, as well as how many take part, we need to remember that people performing the same kinds of political acts differ widely in their political demeanor and motives, and derive differing gratifications and irritations from politics. We shall examine two principal types of political participation—electoral and nonelectoral—and the specific political acts associated with each.

Electoral Participation

The most widely publicized and studied type of political participation of people is taking part in elections by voting. However, there is a continuum of possible electoral acts ranging from the easiest to perform to the most difficult in expenditure of time, money, and energy.

Identifying with a Political Party.   Over the course of recent decades substantial proportions of Americans have expressed an affective tie to one or the other of the major political parties. They simply think of themselves as Democrats or Republicans. We will see in Chapter 11 how partisan affiliation figures into a person's construction of a voting decision. Here we are interested simply in the fact that Americans emotionally identify with a political party, that is, they possess partisan self-images.

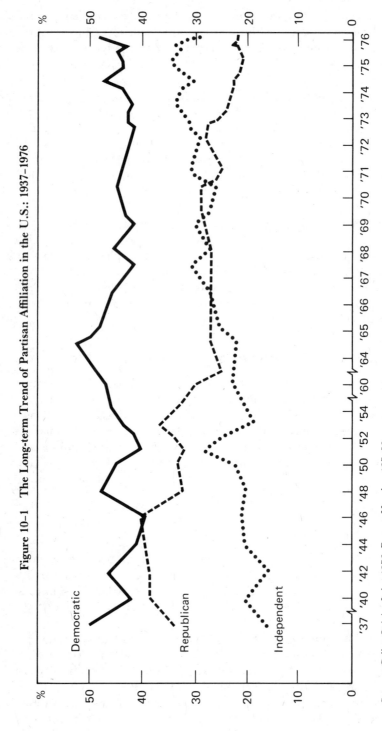

Figure 10-1 The Long-term Trend of Partisan Affiliation in the U.S.: 1937–1976

Source: *Gallup Opinion Index*, 1976, Report Number 137, 50.

Figure 10-1 summarizes the results of four decades of the Gallup Poll measuring partisan affiliation in this country. A number of points should be noted. First, higher proportions of Americans have identified themselves as Democrats than as Republicans since the mid-1940s. Second, there has been a long-term decline in the proportions of Americans declaring themselves as Republicans. Third, there has been almost a steady rise since the 1950s in percentages of persons identifying with neither party but as political independents. In fact, by the start of this decade greater percentages of Americans were thinking of themselves as independents than were affiliating as Republicans. As the presidential election year of 1976 began, the percentage distribution between Democrats-Republicans-independents had become 45-22-33.

The partisanship of Americans varies in intensity as well as direction of affiliation. Table 10-1 summarizes the percentages of Americans identifying themselves at various levels of partisan intensity in recent decades. Again we note the decline in Republican identification and the increase in independence. Added to that, however, is evidence of the erosion of the strength of party identification, both among Democrats and Republicans. We will spell out the implications of this erosion in our discussion in Chapter 11 of the consequences campaign communication has on voting.

Registering to Vote. In most states and localities a person must formally register to vote, thus demonstrating to authorities his citizenship, requisite age, residency, etc. Substantial percentages of Americans otherwise qualified to vote do not because they have not surmounted the preliminary obstacle of registration. At mid-decade of the 1970s, for example, a Gallup Poll reported that 30 percent of Americans were not registered. Of persons not voting in the 1968 presidential election, one-third did not because they were not registered or could not meet residency requirements; that percentage was 28 in the 1972 presidential election and 38 percent in the 1976 election.[6]

Voting in Elections. Turnout rates among the voting age population vary from one level of election to another. Since World War II the highest level of voting turnout in a presidential election was 64 percent in 1960; the lowest came in 1976 when the turnout was 53 percent. Voting rates in years when Congress but not the president is elected fall off sharply; in 1974 only four in ten eligible voters exercised the franchise. Statewide elections for governors, lieutenant governors, etc. vary in turnout rates from state to state, usually falling somewhere between the voting percentages of presidential and congressional elections. Voting turnout in local elections drops in some sections of the country below one-third of qualified voters.

TABLE 10-1   The Distribution of Partisan Self-Images in the United States, 1952–1974

Question: "Generally speaking, do you usually think of yourself as a Republican, a Democrat, an Independent, or what? (IF REPUBLICAN OR DEMOCRAT) Would you call yourself a strong (R) (D) or a not very strong (R) (D)? (IF INDEPENDENT) Do you think of yourself as closer to the Republican or Democratic Party?"

	Oct. 1952	Oct. 1954	Oct. 1956	Oct. 1958	Oct. 1960	Nov. 1962	Oct. 1964	Nov. 1966	Nov. 1968	Nov. 1970	Nov. 1972	Nov. 1974
Democrat												
Strong	22%	22%	21%	23%	21%	23%	26%	18%	20%	20%	15%	17%
Weak	25	25	23	24	25	23	25	27	25	23	27	21
Independent												
Democrat	10	9	7	7	8	8	9	9	10	10	11	13
Independent	5	7	9	8	8	8	8	12	11	13	13	15
Republican	7	6	8	4	7	6	6	7	9	8	10	8
Republican												
Weak	14	14	14	16	13	16	13	15	14	15	13	14
Strong	13	13	15	13	14	12	11	10	10	10	10	8
Apolitical, Don't know	4	4	3	5	4	4	2	2	1	1	1	4
Total	100%	100%	100%	100%	100%	100%	100%	100%	100%	100%	100%	100%
Number of Cases	1614	1139	1772	1269	3021	1289	1571	1291	1553	1802	2697	2512

Source: Center for Political Studies, The University of Michigan.

Taking Part in Campaigns.   Finally, people take part in elections by contributing money to candidates, attending campaign rallies and meetings, working for the political parties or candidates, displaying campaign buttons and stickers, canvassing neighbors in support of candidates, and through other means. This type of activity enlists far fewer Americans than do other forms of electoral participation. Although as many as one-third typically try to persuade others how to vote through personal conversations, less than one in ten is regularly more active on behalf of parties and candidates.

Nonelectoral Participation

Nonelectoral participation includes all political activities people take part in during and between election years with little direct bearing upon campaign politics, that is, such things as expressing political opinions, keeping abreast of political events, being active in civic and political organizations, and contacting public officials. Chapter 8 dwelled at length upon opinion expression as a mode of participation for the interested, attentive, and general citizenry. Hence, we will not discuss that matter here. Rather we will concentrate upon participation through keeping informed, taking part in political organizations, and contacting public officials.

Keeping Informed About Politics.   The rank and file of Americans are only moderately informed about politics, especially in nonelection years. For example, in a comprehensive survey of citizens' knowledge about public affairs conducted in 1973, pollster Louis Harris found that no more than four in ten Americans considered themselves up-to-date on political developments in the nation's capital. Less than 60 percent could name one U.S. Senator from their state, and barely half could say what political party the senator represented. Less than 40 percent could name both of their U.S. Senators. Fewer than 50 percent could name their congressman in the House of Representatives. Approximately one-half of Americans had difficulty naming even one member of the U.S. Supreme Court. Only governors of states are relatively well-known political figures; nine of every ten people surveyed correctly identified their governor. Adding to the generally poor showing in political knowledge, 38 percent did not know that Congress consists of both the House of Representatives and Senate; 20 percent thought Congress included the Supreme Court as well as House and Senate and 8 percent simply had no idea of the make-up of Congress.[7] Political ignorance of this sort, of course, is not universal. Being more informed about politics is precisely one thing that sets off the interested, attentive, and mobilized publics from the general citizenry (see Chapter 8).

We already know, based upon evidence discussed in Chapters 4 and 5, that most Americans get their political information from television.

Approximately two-thirds rely upon television as a news source, half use newspapers, and smaller percentages include radio and newsmagazines as sources of their information. The more interested, attentive, and mobilized publics, however, rely less upon television and more on print. For example, the 1973 Harris Survey revealed that of the most politically active citizens surveyed, almost as many used newspapers as a news source as used television, and four in ten relied on news magazines; moreover, Rosenau found in his survey of attentive and mobilized Americans that about one-third relied on opinion magazines, as well as other media, for information about foreign affairs.[8] Hence, although fewer than 10 percent of adults "very carefully" read about politics on a day-to-day basis, the politically involved turn regularly to the print media as a source of information.[9]

Joining Civic and Political Organizations. As reported in Chapter 8, many Americans are members of voluntary organizations: almost two-thirds are members of some organization, four in ten belong to more than a single organization, an equal proportion identify themselves as active in their organizations, more than 40 percent belong to organizations active in civic affairs, and about one-third belong to organizations where political discussion occurs.[10] Compared with the general population, the rate of organizational participation among the more politically involved segment of the citizenry is, as expected, markedly higher. Of those classified by Rosenau as attentive and mobilized respectively, 81 percent of the former and 90 percent of the latter belonged to organizations expressing viewpoints on national or international problems. Eighty percent of both groups were members of two or more such organizations. Attentives and the mobilized not only join political organizations, they take an active part: 22 percent of attentives and 30 percent of the mobilized attended organization meetings at least once per month; 47 percent and 58 percent of attentives and mobilized respectively joined the deliberations of organizations taking stands on public issues.[11]

Contacting Public Officials. Americans petition public officials at public meetings, in offices, through telephone calls, by writing letters, and during private social gatherings. In some cases the reason for the contact is to get the official to deal with a problem that touches only the individual or the family of the person involved—to redress an error in social security payments, to free a relative from foreign imprisonment, or to demand that officials catch dogs upsetting the citizen's garbage cans. Particularized contact is normally routine and something many Americans do from time to time. Of wider political relevance is contact with public officials to advance a social cause—to influence pending legislation, protest American involvement in a war, insist that the official take a stand against abortion, legalization of marijuana, construction of a nuclear facility, or whatever. This generalized contact involves fewer Americans than routine, particularized efforts.

We get some estimate of the proportions of Americans that contact public officials by looking at two areas. First, consider the letter-writing proclivities of citizens. Estimates are that less than 15 percent of the citizenry write letters to congressmen or senators and only about 3 percent do so regularly. Although not a general practice, politically involved citizens do express their opinions to officials via letters. In examining his sample of attentives, for instance, Rosenau classified one-third as nonwriters, half as sporadic or occasional writers, and 15 percent as frequent or steady writers. Comparing those figures to his sample of mobilized persons (that is, those who not only observe politics but can be goaded to take action for specific causes), Rosenau reported only 5 percent of nonwriters among the mobilized, 60 percent in the sporadic and occasional writing category, and more than one-third who were steady or frequent writers. Essentially, then, letter writing as a means of contact must be motivated, either by a high general interest in politics or by organized effort; it is not the normal political activity of Americans.[12]

Second, Verba and Nie provide data that compares contacting public officials with other forms of electoral and nonelectoral participation. Utilizing a nationwide survey Verba and Nie reported that 20 percent of adults stated they had at some time or another contacted a local official about some issue or problem; 18 percent had contacted a national official. Thus, about one-fifth of Americans probably utilize some form of contact as a mode of political participation. However, those who contact officials also vote, join organizations, and sometimes campaign. What percentages of Americans perform but one or some specific combination of these activities? Verba and Nie made the following estimates: (1) about 11 percent are complete activists; that is they engage in all types of electoral and nonelectoral activity with great frequency—voting, campaigning, contacting, communal activity, etc.; (2) another 21 percent are voting specialists who do not campaign, contact public officials, or engage in organized community affairs; (3) 15 percent are campaigners who are active in political campaigns but do very little else in the way of contacting officials or communal activities; (4) 20 percent are communalists who work with others to solve local problems, are active in problem-solving organizations, organize groups, and contact local, state, and national officials for general purposes; (5) another 4 percent are parochial participants, that is, persons engaging solely in particularized contact for personal reasons; and (6) the inactives are that remaining 22 percent of the Verba-Nie sample who take almost no part in political life. Seven percent of the Verba-Nie sample could not be classified.[13]

To Participate or Not? Opportunities, Resources, and Motivations

The Verba-Nie study suggests that there is a sizable core of one-fifth of Americans who play no active role in politics. Others confine most of their attention to specific roles: specializing in voting, campaigning, acting in the community, or engaging in particularized contact with officials. To take part in politics or not, and how, is a witting or unwitting choice that each person makes just as he makes other choices; in other words, each constructs his degree of participation by taking a variety of factors into account, interpreting them, imagining how others behave, and responding accordingly. For many people, political participation takes very low priority compared with other possibilities in their daily lives. For them the opportunities, resources, and motivations for taking part in politics do not intrude upon their imaginations; others construct images of fruitful political action through their participation. Let us look at the various factors people take into account in participating in politics.

Legal Opportunities

Provisions of the U.S. Constitution, and their interpretation by the Supreme Court, help guarantee a broadly based and diversified opportunity for Americans to participate in politics. Consider the varieties of participation promoted by the First Amendment, which guarantees that "Congress shall make no law": (1) "respecting an establishment of religion, or prohibiting the free exercise thereof," thereby opening the way for free formulation and statement of private convictions; (2) "or abridging the freedom of speech," which assures the opportunity to express opinions; (3) "or of the press," which promotes the opportunity to keep politically informed; (4) "or of the right of the people peaceably to assemble," which enhances the organization of political groups, including political parties; and (5) "to petition the government for a redress of grievances," which fosters contact with public officials.

Other constitutional provisions and laws make possible participation in elections: provisions for the popular election of members of the House of Representatives (and the Seventeenth Amendment for popular election of Senators); articles and amendments dealing with the election of president and vice-president; amendments prohibiting denial of voting rights to citizens on grounds of race, color, previous condition of servitude, sex, failure to pay a poll tax or other tax, or age; and the Fourteenth Amendment definition of national citizenship and guarantee of equal protection of the laws that opened the door to passage of voting rights acts. Current suffrage opportunities extend to all citizens 18 years of age and older. But, as noted earlier, various legislative requirements limit voting considerably, especially requirements of residency and registration. If adopted, a proposed universal voter registration system would remove some of these restrictions. Miscellaneous restrictions limit the voting opportunities of such persons as inmates of penal institutions or mental institutions.

Social Resources

Although there are relatively few legal restrictions on widespread political participation, the fact is that fewer Americans take part than have the opportunity. A chief reason is that not all Americans possess the social and economic resources associated with political activity. Levels of participation vary from one social class to another, and from one demographic grouping to another.

Social Class.   There are many ways to determine what social class a person belongs to, but generally class is a function of one's occupation, income, and education. Members of upper and upper-middle classes are of professional/managerial occupations with high incomes and have college educations; those in the middle classes may be relatively well-paid white collar or skilled workers, often, but not always, possessing a college degree; lower classes include wage-earning blue collar employees with high school and lesser education, the unemployed, and the impoverished. The general rule is that persons from higher social classes participate in politics far more often than do those from lower social strata. Having the time, money, energy, and other means to do so, middle- and upper-class Americans engage in a variety of electoral and nonelectoral activities.

With respect to electoral participating, voting rates are generally higher as one moves up the social ladder. Whereas about six of ten persons with only grade school educations normally vote, almost nine of ten college graduates do so; from one-half to two-thirds of unskilled workers vote in presidential elections compared with the 80–90 percent of those in white collar, professional, and managerial occupations; and, persons earning $10,000-$20,000 per year are more likely to vote than those earning less than $10,000. What holds for voting rates also holds for registration. In the mid-1970s, 70 percent of Americans registered to vote; this overall percentage included 77 percent of professional and business persons compared with 61 percent of manual laborers, 79 percent of persons earning $20,000 or more per year compared with 59 percent of those earning less than $3,000, and 77 percent of the college-educated compared with two-thirds of those whose formal schooling ended with grade school. Moreover, affiliation or nonaffiliation with a political party is roughly associated with social class. In the mid-1970s almost four in ten college graduates were political independents, less than one-fourth of the grade school-educated were independents; more than one-third of persons earning $10,000 did not identify with a political party but three-fourths of those earning less did so; and, 38 percent of professionals, businesspersons, and skilled workers were independents compared to 30-35 percent of farmers and unskilled workers. Of those who identify with a political party, Democratic loyalists were more likely to be of lower status occupations, educations, and incomes.[14] Finally, the Verba-Nie study reported a correlation of .30 between socioeconomic status and campaign activity, thus indicating the higher the social class of persons generally, the more apt they were to take part in political campaigns.[15]

Nonelectoral participation is also a function of social class. Verba and Nie report a correlation of .33 between communal activity and social class. They also note that 56 percent of persons in the lowest socioeconomic category were not members of political organizations compared with only 20 percent of those in the upper classes who are nonjoiners.[16] Levels of political information are also higher among persons of better occupations, income, and educations. And the persons comprising Rosenau's sample of attentive and mobilized publics between elections were better educated, wealthier, and composed of more professional and managerial persons than in the population as a whole.[17]

Demographic Differences.   There is a clear upper- and upper-middle-class bias to political participation in America. There are also differences in participation among people in various demographic categories, i.e., those of age, sex, race, region of residence, religion, etc.

Americans over thirty years of age take part in politics in higher rates than do younger citizens. In the mid-1970s more than one-half of those under thirty were not registered to vote, about a fourth of those over thirty were not registered. Upwards of 70 percent of adults over thirty vote in presidential elections but only about one-half of those under that age do so. The under thirty group is only slightly less campaign-oriented than those over thirty. And, in the mid-1970s almost one-half of those under thirty were political independents whereas almost two-thirds over that age identified with either the Democratic or Republican parties.[18] Nonelectoral activities such as participation in organizations, working to solve community problems, and contacting public officials are more likely to be the activities of older rather than younger citizens.

Men participate more widely in politics than do women, but the gap is relatively narrow. In the mid-1970s the men vs. women rates of registration were 70 and 69 percent respectively, men vote in presidential and congressional races in only slightly higher rates than women, men are more likely to be political independents (38 percent of men in 1975 contrasted with 30 percent of women), and are more likely to take active parts in campaign politics.[19] Women, on the other hand, are slightly more likely to write letters to the editor, but less likely to write letters to public officials.[20] Verba and Nie, examining the range of potential political participation, conclude that "Men are somewhat overrepresented in the more activist groups, but not to a very great degree."[21]

There are clear differences among blacks and whites in levels of political participation. Blacks are less likely to register to vote, to be politically informed, to be communal activists, and mobilized citizens. These differences, however, cannot be attributed to "blackness" or "whiteness" but to the generally lower social class standing of blacks in American society. Among blacks and whites of the same social standing, differences in participation are substantially less; in some elections, for instance, blacks vote in higher rates than whites and are more likely to be campaign partisans.

Generally, regional differences also exist in participation. Rates of voter registration are lowest in the South as are the levels of voter turnout and political information, and the proportion of attentives and mobilized citizens. Residents of rural areas are less politically active in virtually all respects than are persons living in cities and suburbs. In one area of political activity, that is, identifying with a political party, regional and rural-urban differences are minimal. It is generally the modes of participation requiring the greatest expenditure of time, effort, and money where such differences emerge.

Finally, the general pattern of participation by religious groups is mixed. Slightly higher percentages of Protestants than Catholics were registered to vote in the mid-1970s (71 vs. 69 percent), but Catholics usually vote in slightly higher rates. Verba and Nie found that Catholics were more likely to participate in electoral activities, Protestants in nonelectoral activities.[22] Persons of the Jewish faith are most active, especially in voting (upwards of 85 percent in presidential elections), in identifying with a political party (two-thirds with the Democratic party), and in comprising the membership of the attentive and mobilized publics.[23]

Personal Motivations

We saw earlier that the motives underlying one's political activity vary considerably. Motives may be intentional or unintentional, rational or emotional, psychologically or socially inspired, inner or other directed, and minded or mindless. There are also motives prompting a person *to* participate as well as *how*. Most of these we have reviewed in earlier chapters, as, for example, in our discussion of personal needs satisfied through politics (Chapters 7 and 9), of aspects of personality projected into the political arena (Chapter 9), of the satisfactions and gratifications obtained by following politics in the mass media (Chapter 6), of responding to the sense of civic obligation derived from childhood socialization (Chapter 9), and of changing levels of trust and distrust in politics and government (Chapter 8).

Political scientist Roberta Sigel suggests a way to summarize many of the personal motives that underlie a person's choice of whether or not to participate in politics and, if to participate, how.[24] She relies on the concept of locus-of-control developed in psychology. Locus-of-control refers to whether people believe they can cope effectively with their lives and the situations they enter. Some persons are "internals"; they are confident that they can control themselves and their destinies. Others are "externals" who believe they are the pawns of fate. Sigel defines these two general types of tendencies in political terms: externals do not get politically involved because they consider it futile to try to influence government by taking part; internals, because they feel themselves in control, participate. Using a scale to measure the degree of a person's internality and externality, Sigel examined the association between the locus-of-control and three dimensions of political involvement. She stud- ied the cognitive, affective, and activist tendencies of individuals. The cognitive tendency is closely related to the person's interest in politics, the amount of political information he has acquired, and his understand- ing of politics in general. The affective tendency refers to each person's sense of personal efficacy (the feeling that one can do something to change things politically), cynicism about politics, and feelings about the rele- vance of government. The activist tendency determines the likelihood that a person will take part in politics. Among her sample of 346 public school sophomores and seniors she found that internals are politically more involved, provided they regard government as relevant to their personal lives; this is especially true for cognitive and affective dimensions of involvement. Relevance of government made no difference to externals; their sense of powerlessness inhibits their capacity and/or willingness to take part in politics along any dimension.

Sigel's study not only implies a relationship between personal motiva- tions and political involvement, it also cautions that acquired personality traits such as a sense of locus-of-control are but one set of factors involved in political participation. She notes that much of what people do or don't do is related only tangentially to their personalities; the situations they must cope with and the options they have and take into account are also important: "The options they notice and the ones they bypass are partially determined by an individual's personality. It is the concept of *partial* determination which is important."[25]

HOW PARTICIPANTS RESPOND TO POLITICAL COMMUNICATION

Sigel's reminder that personality is but a partial explanation for why people get politically involved holds for legal and social factors as well. Into the matrix of perceived legal opportunities, social resources, and personal motivations comprising the individual's world, enter messages about politics carried through political communication (Figure 10-2). Those messages contain information about the options people have. Which options they take into account—i.e., those they respond to rather than react toward—make a difference in their political activity. How,

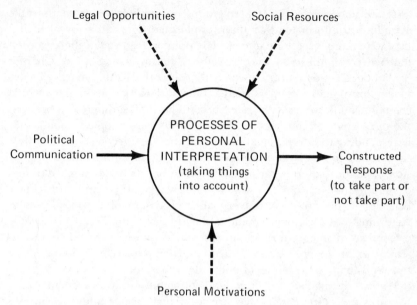

Figure 10-2   Influences on Political Participation

then, do people respond to political communication? To answer that question we need first to conclude this chapter with a review of the consequences of political communication upon participation; in the remaining two chapters we explore the specific consequences on voting and policy making.

In closing our discussion of political persuasion in Chapter 4, we cited Bernard Berelson's formulation concerning the relationship between communication and public opinion. Wrote Berelson three decades ago: "Some kinds of *communication* on some kinds of *issues,* brought to the attention of some kinds of *people* under some kinds of *conditions,* have some kinds of *effects.*"[26]

The formulation is a masterpiece of reserved, qualified, and cautious commentary. Some might consider it obvious. Yet, it does pinpoint the aspects one must recognize in assessing how people respond to political communication.

Kinds of Communication

In Berelson's formulation, "kinds of communication" refers to the channel of communication (interpersonal, organizational, or mass) as well as to the content of communication. With respect to channels, research conducted after World War II stressed that "the more personal the media, the more effective it is in converting opinions."[27] Because people trusted their personal informants, wanted to conform to the opinions of close associates and members of favored groups, or simply felt more comfortable attending to informal rather than formal media, research revealed that they were more responsive to personal "opinion leaders" in the "two-step flow" of communication than directly to the mass media (see Chapter 2). Although contemporary research allocates considerably more influence to organizational and mass media than did earlier findings, personal communication strikes its own responsive chord. The differences between the three kinds of channels tend to lie in the *ways* people respond, that is, responding to interpersonal communication in affective ways to adjust their values to others, to mass media in cognitive ways to increase their store of political information and adjust their beliefs, and to organizational communication in cognitive ways to alter expectations and adjust their behavior to perceived collective goals and actions of the organization. Returning to the argument made explicit in discussing Figure 4-1, people respond to all media forms, but different channels have different consequences for the presentation, attention, comprehension, yielding, retention, and compliance phases of political persuasion.

We can distinguish two basic kinds of communication content. Some messages are *informational*. They try to change beliefs and expectations rather than likes or dislikes, preferences, or values. For example, a message summarizing research findings with respect to the correlation between cigarette smoking and the incidence of lung cancer seeks to change people's levels of information about the problem. This is not to say that information campaigns are nonpersuasive in intent. Any campaign directed at changing beliefs, values, or expectations is persuasive. Rather, the primary focus of information messages is cognitive in contrast to the second kind of messages, *promotional* messages. Promotional efforts try to change preferences and values as, for instance, changes in preferences of voters or consumers. Since discussion of voting in Chapter 11 concerns the consequences of communication that promotes various candidates, issues, and political parties, we will dwell here only on how people respond to information campaigns. Many of the points made, however, apply to promotional campaigns as well.

Three decades ago two students of public opinion, Herbert H. Hyman and Paul B. Sheatsley, spelled out the reasons why they thought it naive to expect a perfect correspondence between the nature and amount of material presented in an information campaign and what people absorb.[28] For one thing, they pointed out, not everybody is a good target for an information campaign. There are some people who simply know nothing about *any* event no matter how widely publicized. An event occurring early in this decade illustrates that the point Hyman and Sheatsley were making in the 1940s is as valid now as it was then. In 1971, *The New York Times* and *The Washington Post* published a series of articles revealing how the U.S. became involved in the Vietnam War. The articles were based upon documents classified as secret, documents the newspapers acquired without government sanction. The government took legal action against the newspapers. Ultimately the Supreme Court decided in the widely celebrated case of the "Pentagon Papers" on behalf of the *The New York Times* and *The Washington Post*. At the height of the controversy a Gallup poll revealed that 45 percent of Americans had not even heard about the matter![29] That so many were unaware of the event is not unusual. As Hyman and Sheatsley point out, there is a hard core of chronic "know-nothings" that virtually no information about public affairs penetrates.

In addition to the know-nothings, there are many other people who have virtually no interest in politics or public affairs. Those who are interested tend to seek information congenial to their existing beliefs, values, and expectations. Often, people acquiring the same information interpret it in different ways. Through interpretation, people alter the symbols they perceive in messages, thereby reading different meanings into what they see. Sometimes these altered meanings change prior opinions, sometimes they do not. In sum, for Hyman and Sheatsley, the likelihood of information campaigns succeeding was remote; stepping up the amount of information available to people would not make them more informed unless campaigners could do something about the chronic know-nothings, the disinterested, people who perceive selectively, and those who read unintended meanings into the information they acquire.

Until relatively recently, the Hyman and Sheatsley view of why information campaigns fail was the conventional wisdom regarding how people respond to communication. Granted, however, the general resistance to information campaigns, does this mean that such campaigns are always doomed to failure? Does it mean that people never respond? Recent research reveals otherwise. Summarizing the findings derived from several specific efforts to inform people on a variety of matters, Harold Mendelsohn provides three guidelines for achieving successful information campaigns.[30] First, information campaigns must be planned with the assumption that most of the people they try to reach will be only mildly or not at all interested in the communication. Second, within the context of general disinterest, campaigners need to establish modest, middle-range goals adjusted to the everyday lives of the audience rather than try to convince people of things remote from their imaginations. For example, Mendelsohn reports that in a campaign dealing with traffic safety, audiences would resist messages aimed at saying they were bad drivers. Instead, let drivers learn for themselves what bad driving habits are and if they practice them. Hence, in 1965 "The National Drivers Test" aired as a nationwide television program as a means of having drivers test their own driving skills and information. The program had an audience of 30 million and CBS News received mail responses from nearly half a million viewers. Third, after setting middle-range objectives, campaigners should specify the kinds of people best suited as targets of the communication, that is, campaigners should delineate those most likely to respond in accordance with their social class and demographic attributes, personal motivations, life styles, beliefs, values, expectations, and media habits. In short, the information campaign should be adapted to the character of the audience rather than trying to adapt the audience to the information.

Kinds of Issues

People respond in different ways to alternative communication channels and content. Part of the content of communication, of course, deals with issues. Views with respect to how people respond to political issues have changed with increased research on the subject. Social scientists long ago rejected the classical democratic model of popular response to issues. That model depicted the democratic citizen as interested, motivated, and knowledgeable about issues, bent upon discussing issues and matters of principle, and capable of rationally selecting the most appropriate means to reach desired ends. But voting research and opinion studies uncovered a different and more dominant strain of democratic citizen—disinterested, uninformed, and emotion laden[31] (see Chapter 11).

Rejection of the classic model of the democratic citizen, combined with research findings of the 1950s, led to the following conclusions regarding how people respond to issues: (1) People are more likely to respond to communication and formulate or change their views if the issues are relatively new, unstructured, or remote. For example, people in the 1950s were more apt to be persuaded by the president's views on issues pertaining to the Soviet Union, Cuba, or other nations than they were on issues of a domestic nature such as unemployment or inflation. Foreign policy issues are remote and firsthand information is unlikely; on domestic issues, people weigh persuasive appeals against the evidence accumulated from their daily lives. (2) Communication about issues is more effective on peripheral than central issues; the more salient the issue to the individual, the more likely the person's opinion will remain stable in the face of counterarguments. Hence, it is easier to persuade people to a point of view regarding the U.S. position on granting commonwealth status to the Mariana Islands than it is on an issue such as busing children to achieve racial balance in schools. (3) Communication about issues as such is less likely to be effective than communication about persons *as* issues. Abstract notions about the economy or foreign affairs are less likely to attract attention than are views with respect to a controversial secretary of the treasury (as, for example, John Connally in the Nixon Cabinet) or a controversial secretary of state (such as Henry Kissinger). (4) People simply do not recognize differences between politicians and political parties on basic issues. They may see no difference between a Republican and Democratic candidate, for example, on issues of federal aid to education, dealing with the Soviet Union, proposals to deal with inflation, recession, etc.

Such were the propositions regarding popular response to issue communications derived from research rejecting the classic democratic model of the citizen. However, beginning in the late 1960s evidence accumulated that these propositions required qualification. As we shall see in Chapter 11, voting studies revealed an increasing tendency for people to be interested in the issue stands of candidates, to detect differences between Democrats and Republicans on issues, and to vote on the basis of issues. In sum, voters are more likely than they used to be to scan political communication for information on issues and to respond to it on the basis of what they perceive.

Kinds of People and Conditions

Implicit in this discussion of the kinds of communication and its issue content is the view that the consequences of political communication vary from one person to another. Ball-Rokeach and DeFleur present a useful view of the varying ways in which people respond to communication.[32] One reason researchers don't know more about how people respond to communication, say Ball-Rokeach and DeFleur, is that simplistic learning theories too often guide research. Researchers often adopt a stimulus-response view of learning, either of the classical or operant conditioning variety discussed in Chapter 9. This leads investigators to posit that people should respond to selected communication stimuli in certain ways under certain conditions. When experimental subjects do not respond in these ways, researchers conclude that it is because people filter and re-create media messages to conform to their own predilections. This conclusion is consistent with the explanation that Hyman and Sheatsley offer for why information campaigns fail. Hence we get the proposition that communication has only minimal consequences for what people do; personal predispositions determine behavior.

One can take a different stance toward such research findings. What these findings suggest is that people actively involve themselves in communication, that they are not reacting objects, but respond as a part of a total communication experience. Their responses are as much a form of communication as the messages that reach them from external sources. The proper question to ask, then, is not how communication influences behavior, but rather, under what conditions do people take into account available messages in constructing their opinions rather than reacting on the basis of past experience, personal inclinations, social standing, demographic characteristics, legal status, etc.?

Borrowing from the sociological writings of Durkheim, Marx, and Mead, Ball-Rokeach and DeFleur offer a "dependency" model to answer the question posed. They start from the premise that people's social realities flow from their life histories, current activities, and connections to the structural conditions of the society in which they live. As society becomes more complex, people have fewer opportunities and resources for firsthand experience with it; that is, they are less and less aware of what takes place beyond their own immediate social environs. Here enter the communication media, especially the mass media. For Ball-Rokeach and DeFleur, the mass media not only promote products and entertain, they provide information joining the media with audiences and the social order. To explore how people respond to the communication media in the social setting requires considering how they depend upon communication for information about the larger social world:

> It is not sufficient to attempt to account for media alteration effects solely in terms of the audience's psychological characteristics, prior socialization, ongoing group associations, or their social characteristics. . . . The conceptualization stresses as a central issue the *dependency* of audiences on media information resources—a dependency that leads to modifications in both personal and social processes.[33]

As Ball-Rokeach and DeFleur approach the problem, then, the consequences of communication on participation in social affairs—and in politics as one variety of social encounter—vary with the degree of dependency of people on the communication media under different conditions. Dependency is a relationship in which the satisfaction of needs or attainment of goals of one party is contingent upon the resources of another. (Readers will note that this definition bears a resemblance to the thinking described in the uses and gratifications view of media functions described in Chapter 5.) So defined, dependency on media information resources is a ubiquitous condition in modern society.

What variations can we expect in people's response to communication? Ball-Rokeach and DeFleur offer three propositions:

1. The more dependent people are on media for information, the more likely they will change their beliefs, values, and expectations as a result of the information communicated.
2. The more essential the information delivered by a medium to audiences, the greater the dependence of people on that medium and, hence, the more likely people are to change their views as a result of attending to that medium.

3. The more developed a society's media of communication, the more people depend upon the media as social conflict and change increases.

In sum, the dependency theory implies that people will take into account political communication (that is, information and promotional appeals of candidates, public officials, leaders of special interest groups, and professional communicators) in constructing opinions about politics (that is, their political participation) to the degree that: (1) they depend upon political media for a broad range of unique and essential information, and (2) the media supplies needed information under conditions of social instability, change, and conflict. Given this view, the next question is, What kinds of effects can be expected?

Kinds of Effects

A wide variety of scholars have summarized the diverse types of consequences of communication for human behavior.[34] Having demonstrated a preference for thinking of three overlapping components of opinions, i.e., beliefs, values, and expectations, and having described the Ball-Rokeach and DeFleur dependency theory as congenial with that outlook, it is appropriate to summarize the potential political effects of communication using the cognitive, affective, and behavioral categories employed in the dependency model.

Cognitive Effects

We saw in Chapter 6 that one of the functions of political news is to provide information that people need when confronted with ambiguous situations. When something happens and people lack sufficient information to understand it, or have conflicting information regarding the happening, the consequences of communication can be twofold. First, communication supplies the initial, bulletin-like information that *creates* the ambiguity (as, for example, the bulletins on November 22, 1963 announcing that President John F. Kennedy had been shot in Dallas, Texas). Second, communication provides more detailed information that *lessens* or *resolves* the ambiguity.

Whether a situation is ambiguous or not, communication assists people in defining it. As Ball-Rokeach and DeFleur argue, the media do not determine that everyone interprets an event uniformly; however, "by controlling what information is and is not delivered and how that information is presented, the media can play a large role in *limiting the range of interpretations* that audiences are able to make."[35]

By responding to communication, people *expand perceived political realities* as well as interpret ambiguous and routine situations. Think, for example, of the problems that have entered the consciousness of Americans during the last few years, issues about which they had no beliefs prior to the communication that transmitted the relevant events to them—the crisis over declining energy resources, consequences of nuclear proliferation, environmental pollution, the Vietnam war, the Watergate scandal, and many, many more.

Related to the expansion of people's political worlds is the media's role in *agenda setting*. Topics selected for presentation through the media, as we saw in Chapter 6, are not ordained solely by what politicians would like discussed nor by what audiences want to read, hear, and view. Rather, there is a complex interplay of politicians, professional communicators, political activists, and participating audience members that influences the content of media presentations. That content, in turn, helps set the agenda for further debate; as we said before, it does not necessarily tell people what to think but what to think about. Reporter, journalist, and author David Halberstam summarizes the agenda-setting effects of all media when he writes of television's impact beginning in the 1950s:

> In the decade beginning with the mid-fifties television began to change, and change quite drastically, the nature and pace of American life. It speeded the pace of social protest. Television had a great deal to do with the surge of the civil rights movement. It brought black people into white homes and white people into black homes. Television simplified events and conditions; at the same time it was deeply dramatic. . . . Television heightened interest in the war in Vietnam, heightened for a time the enthusiasm for it, probably hastened the demise of it, and left people exhausted and disheartened by it long before it was in fact over.[36]

In addition to creating and resolving ambiguities in people's minds, providing raw material for personal interpretations, expanding social and political realities, and setting agendas, the media also play upon the belief systems of people. Recall in Chapter 7 that we said one person's political belief system may be rich, diverse, and range over almost innumerable matters while another's is narrowly focused and barren of detail. Exposure to communication by media-dependent persons provides them with information to *enlarge belief systems* and include a wider variety of political objects (as, for example, incorporating issues and policies as well as personalities and political parties).[37]

Affective Effects

There is a general consensus that political communication is more likely to be taken into account by people in constructing their political beliefs than in their political values.[38] It is increasingly clear, for example, that the mass media influence the amount of information people hold about politics, in part because of the cognitive effects of the media during childhood socialization (see Chapter 9) and those fostered by the dependency relationship we have been discussing in this chapter.[39] It is much less apparent, however, that people rely upon the communication media for guidance in formulating preferences and values. Four potential affective consequences flow from political communication.

First, a person may *clarify,* or crystallize, political values through political communication. Recall, for instance, that in Chapter 7 we noted that Americans prize both freedom and equality as terminal values. But, forced to choose between the two, which do they value more? When the media of political communication portray controversies in which those values conflict (as in the civil rights movement) there is an opportunity—perhaps even the strain toward consistency discussed in Chapter 8—for the media-dependent person to reduce the conflict through value clarification. Similarly, for some business leaders the ecology movement poses a conflict between economic well-being, survival, and esthetic values.[40]

Second, one may *reinforce* values through political communication. Research indicates that this is perhaps the most frequent affective consequence of communication as people selectively attend to messages congenial to their views, perceive message content as nonthreatening, and recall messages that confirm prior evaluations of political objects.

Third, political communication may *diminish* held values. A prime example has been the growing sense of alienation among Americans. This has been remarked upon by many writers in the 1970s and discussed at length in Chapter 8. Although there is evidence that increases and decreases in citizens' political morale flow in part from the kinds of messages about politics in the media (emphasis upon war, scandals, corruption, failures to achieve reform, etc.), researchers disagree as to whether the media foster a disillusionment with political authority. Shosteck, for example, found that both blacks and whites residing in Indianapolis, Indiana depended considerably upon television for their news about civil unrest. Television fostered black unrest by serving as a source of unfulfilled expectations; that is, television held out the hope of participating in economic affluence, yet with reduced opportunities and resources for adequate economic and political participation these expectations went unfulfilled for many blacks. A potential consequence was lowered morale, disillusionment, and civil unrest.[41] If media fare does contribute to the denigration of political authority, however, it is less likely to be a direct effect of the contents of political news than the more indirect type of relationship depicted by Shosteck. Pride and Richards analyzed the content of randomly selected evening newscasts of the three major television networks over a period covering 1968–1970, a period of considerable political unrest in this country. They found relatively few messages in television news that might contribute to a lowered sense of the legitimacy of government by audiences: "Neither the symbols of political authority nor those of academic authority are overwhelmingly presented as unresponsive, inefficient, weak, or dishonest. It seems reasonable to speculate that the likelihood of generalized public disaffection as the result of exposure to television news is lessened by the absence of televised, heavy criticism of authority over time."[42]

Researchers also ponder the possibilities of a fourth variety of affective consequence of political communication, namely, do political appeals *convert* people from one persuasion to another? Do Republicans respond to political communication by becoming Democrats? Do Democrats become Republicans? The evidence is not clear-cut. As we shall see in Chapter 11, many people make up their minds whom to vote for on the basis of their partisan identification very early in a political campaign. Yet, Democrats frequently vote for Republicans and vice versa. This, however, is not conversion so much as it is defection from the party ranks. There is reason to believe that relatively little conversion from one persuasion to another results from a single campaign or appeal. What is more likely is that the converting effects of political communication are indirect, long-term, gradual, and incremental. Rather than dwell upon the possibility here, however, we postpone that discussion to the following chapter.

Participation Effects

Exposure to political communication can influence a person to get actively involved in politics; on the other hand, political communication may depress political participation.

Whether activating or deactivating, the consequences of political communication may be primary or secondary. A *primary* effect takes place "when the person affected has himself been involved directly in the communication process."[43] That participation, say Ball-Rokeach and DeFleur, derives from a chain of effects. First the media attract the attention of people to a variety of causes—to political candidates, the women's movement, civil rights movement, environmental concerns, or antinuclear protests. In the initial stages of their involvement, people often respond with bewilderment since the nature of the candidate or cause is ambiguous ("Jimmy Who?" people asked when Jimmy Carter, former governor of Georgia, announced his candidacy for president). But communication helps to resolve as well as form issues, and to build as well as present candidates. For the media-dependent person, the process assists in the formation of new perceptions, beliefs, and evaluations: "The culmination of this chain of effects is a felt need to act."[44] This need finds expression through participation in the opinion process.

A *secondary* consequence of communication occurs when people not involved directly in communication are affected by changes in people who are. Seymour-Ure points to the conduct of the war in Vietnam by the administration of Lyndon Johnson as an example. On the one hand, television coverage probably had some primary effect on viewers by creating, confirming, or converting beliefs, values, and expectations. But it also had a secondary effect; it decreased the administration's capacity and conviction to fight the war on a maximum scale. That secondary effect, of course, affected the prospects of Americans who might otherwise have participated in the conflict as well as those engaged in the combat.

Primary and secondary consequences of political communication are particularly apparent in political campaigns. Some individuals who hear a candidate's appeal respond in a primary way by taking part in his campaign; others not involved in that communication detect that the candidate has "momentum" and, hence, decide that there is no point in actively opposing him. Such was the developing plight of Morris Udall in his 1976 quest for the Democratic presidential nomination. Unable to win any of the early primaries, Udall suffered a secondary consequence and found it increasingly hard to mobilize voters who were losing interest in his campaign.

Consideration of the consequences of communication in political campaigns raises the question of how voters respond to campaign media and messages. We turn to that question in the next chapter.

BIBLIOGRAPHY

Works dealing with the general topic of political participation fall into two categories. The first includes the numerous textbooks and other surveys of political participation and behavior. One of the most useful surveys is that which was published in 1959 by Robert Lane, *Political Life* (Glencoe: The Free Press). Lane provides information not only on who participates and why, but also discusses the role political institutions play in stimulating political activity and the general community dimensions of participation. Another highly useful survey is Lester W. Milbrath, *Political Participation* (Chicago: Rand McNally and Co., 1965, 1977). Milbrath considers participation as a function of stimuli, personal factors, social position, the political setting, etc. He provides a fairly comprehensive listing of the various dimensions of participation. Readers will find a similar listing in Jarol B. Manheim's *The Politics Within* (Englewood Cliffs, N.J.: Prentice-Hall, 1975). This brief and lucid primer is a handy introduction to many of the topics relevant to considering political behavior. Other books which explore participation in the behavioral tradition of political science include Don R. Bowen, *Political Behavior of the American Public* (Columbus, Ohio: Charles E. Merrill Publishing Co., 1968); H. T. Reynolds, *Politics and the Common Man* (Homewood, Ill.: The Dorsey Press, 1974); and Dean Jaros and Lawrence V. Grant, *Political Behavior* (New York: St. Martin's Press, 1974).

The second category of works dealing with political participation are reports of specific research projects. One with a comparative intent is the five-nation study by Gabriel A. Almond and Sidney Verba, *The Civic Culture* (Princeton:

Princeton University Press, 1963). This volume reports survey data from the United States, Great Britain, West Germany, Mexico, and Italy regarding the obligation to participate, levels of participation, and political cognitions and affects. Giuseppe Di Palma undertakes a secondary analysis of the Almond-Verba data to measure levels of political satisfaction and disaffection. See his *Apathy and Participation* (New York: The Free Press, 1970). A widely acclaimed study of political participation is Sidney Verba and Norman H. Nie, *Participation in America* (New York: Harper and Row, 1972). The authors employ a model of the participation process linking socioeconomic factors, civic attitudes, political organizations and parties, and participation. Also emphasizing the relationship of social class and participation is Richard F. Hamilton, *Class and Politics in the United States* (New York: John Wiley and Sons, 1972). In *Citizenship Between Elections* (New York: The Free Press, 1974) James N. Rosenau uses data collected from a mail survey of members of a political organization to distinguish between the participation patterns of the attentive and mobilizable publics. To examine factors associated with the participation of black Americans, readers should consult Donald R. Matthews and James W. Prothro, *Negroes and the New Southern Politics* (New York: Harcourt, Brace and World, 1966). In addition to the above works readers will find that many of those cited in the bibliographical note appended to Chapter 11 dealing with voting, pertain to more general political participation as well.

Most of the published books concerning how people respond to political communication as political participants focus almost solely upon the effects of communication. An early survey of mass communication was Joseph T. Klapper's still useful volume, *The Effects of Mass Communication* (Glencoe: The Free Press, 1960). Klapper reviews such effects as reinforcement, minor change, opinion-formation, and conversion as well as the factors which tend to mediate between communication and behavior. Klapper weighs the effects of mass communication by drawing upon the findings of both survey and experimental research. A more recent and equally valuable assessment dealing more directly with politics is the volume by Sidney Kraus and Dennis Davis, *The Effects of Mass Communication on Political Behavior* (University Park, Pa.: Penn State University Press, 1976). A major work reporting the results of research in the experimental tradition is Carl I. Hovland, et al., *Experiments on Mass Communication* (New York: John Wiley and Sons, Science Editions, 1965). The work was first published in 1949 following research conducted during World War II. Like Kraus and Davis, a volume that deals specifically with political communication is Colin Seymour-Ure's *The Political Impact of Mass Media* (Beverly Hills, Ca.: Sage Publications, 1974). Part One discusses the context of potential media effects; Part Two consists of case studies selected from the British setting. Readers should also consult the essays in Steven H. Chaffee, ed., *Political Communication* (Beverly Hills, Ca.: Sage Publications, 1975): especially useful are those of Lee B. Becker, et al., on the development of political cognitions, Chaffee's essay on the diffusion of political information, and Garrett J. O'Keefe's review of political campaigns and mass communication research.

Four essays provide a particularly useful review of media effects. The first three include Percy H. Tannenbaum and Bradley S. Greenberg, "Mass Communication," in Paul R. Farnsworth, ed., *The Annual Review of Psychology,* Vol. 19 (1968), pp. 351–86; Otto N. Larsen, "Social Effects of Mass Communication," in Robert E. L. Faris, ed., *Handbook of Modern Sociology* (Chicago: Rand McNally Co., 1964). pp. 349–81; and Walter Weiss, "Effects of the Mass Media of Communication," in Gardner Lindzey and Elliot Aronson, eds., *Handbook of Social Psychology* (Reading, Mass.: Addison-Wesley, 2nd ed., 1969), Vol. 5, pp.

77–195. The fourth takes a very critical look at research into the "effects" of communication, a critical posture from the symbolic interactionist viewpoint: Herbert Blumer, "Suggestions for the Study of Mass-Media Effects," in Eugene Burdick and Arthur J. Brodbeck, eds., *American Voting Behavior* (Glencoe, Ill.: The Free Press, 1959), pp. 197–208.

NOTES

1.   *Citizenship Between Elections* (New York: The Free Press, 1974) Ch. 1; Rosenau distinguishes between The Attentive Public (observers) and The Mobilized Public (observation plus more active following).

2.   A more detailed summary of many of the dimensions listed here is available in Jarol B. Manheim, *The Politics Within* (Englewood Cliffs, N.J.: Prentice-Hall, 1975); see Ch. 7 for Manheim's inventory of modes, motives, and substantive aspects of participation.

3.   William Stephenson, *The Play Theory of Mass Communication* (Chicago: University of Chicago Press, 1967), Ch. 4.

4.   David Riesman et al., *The Lonely Crowd* (New York: Doubleday Anchor Books, 1955), p. 41.

5.   David Easton, *A Systems Analysis of Political Life* (New York: John Wiley and Sons, 1965).

6.   *The Gallup Opinion Index,* Report Number 137 (November-December 1976), p. 12.

7.   Louis Harris, *Confidence and Concern: Citizens View American Government* (Cleveland: Regal Books/King's Court, 1974), pp. 17–18.

8.   Rosenau, *Citizenship Between Elections,* pp. 226–31.

9.   V.O. Key, Jr., *Public Opinion and American Democracy* (New York: Alfred A. Knopf, 1961), p. 353.

10.   Sidney Verba and Norman H. Nie, *Participation in America* (New York: Harper and Row, 1972), p. 176.

11.   Rosenau, *Citizenship Between Elections,* p. 222.

12.   Ibid., pp. 207–19; see also Key, *Public Opinion and American Democracy,* pp. 418–19; Emmett H. Buell, Jr., "Eccentrics or Gladiators? People Who Write About Politics in Letters-to-the-Editor," *Social Science Quarterly,* 56 (December 1975): 440–49; and Leila Sussmann, *Dear FDR: A Study of Political Letterwriting* (Totowa, N.J.: The Bedminster Press, 1963).

13.   Verba and Nie, *Participation in America,* pp. 79–80.

14.   *The Gallup Opinion Index,* p. 83, 91.

15.   Verba and Nie, *Participation in America,* p. 132.

16.   Ibid., p. 204.

17.   Rosenau, *Citizenship Between Elections,* Ch. 7.

18.   *The Gallup Opinion Index.*

19.   Ibid., p. 336.

20.   Buell, "Eccentrics or Gladiators?", p. 445.

21.   Verba and Nie, *Participation in America,* p. 101.

22.   Ibid., p. 336.

23.   Rosenau, *Citizenship Between Elections.*

24.   Roberta S. Sigel, "Psychological Antecedents and Political Involvement: The Utility of the Concept of Locus-of-Control," *Social Science Quarterly,* 56 (September 1975): 314–23.

25.   Ibid., p. 323.

26. "Communication and Public Opinion," in Wilbur Schramm, ed., *Communication in Modern Society* (Urbana: University of Illinois Press, 1948), p. 172 (emphasis in original).

27. Ibid., p. 172.

28. "Some Reasons Why Information Campaigns Fail," *Public Opinion Quarterly*, 11 (Fall 1947): 412–23.

29. American Institute of Public Opinion, news release, July 6, 1971.

30. "Some Reasons Why Information Campaigns Can Succeed," *Public Opinion Quarterly*, 37 (Spring 1973): 50–61.

31. Bernard B. Berelson, et al., *Voting* (Chicago: University of Chicago Press, 1954), ch. 14.

32. S. J. Ball-Rokeach and M. L. DeFleur, "A Dependency Model of Mass-Media Effects," *Communication Research*, 3 (January 1976): 3–21.

33. Ibid., p. 5 (emphasis in original).

34. See Percy H. Tannenbaum and Bradley S. Greenberg, "Mass Communication," in Paul R. Farnsworth, ed., *The Annual Review of Psychology,* Vol. 19 (1968), pp. 351–86; Otto N. Larsen, "Social Effects of Mass Communication," in Robert E. L. Faris, ed., *Handbook of Modern Sociology* (Chicago: Rand McNally Co., 1964), pp. 349–81; Walter Weiss, "Effects of the Mass Media of Communication," in Gardner Lindzey and Elliot Aronson, eds., *Handbook of Social Psychology*, Vol. 5 (Reading, Mass.: Addison-Wesley, 2nd ed., 1969), pp. 77–195; Joseph T. Klapper, *The Effects of Mass Communication* (Glencoe, Ill.: The Free Press, 1961); and Bernard Berelson and Gary A. Steiner, *Human Behavior* (New York: Harcourt, Brace and World, 1964), Ch. 13.

35. Ball-Rokeach and DeFleur, "A Dependency Model of Mass-Media Effects," p. 10 (emphasis added).

36. "CBS: The Power and the Profits," Part Two, *The Atlantic,* 237 (February 1976): 70.

37. Ball-Rokeach and DeFleur, "A Dependency Model of Mass-Media Effects," p. 13.

38. Dan Nimmo, *The Political Persuaders* (Englewood Cliffs, N.J.: Prentice-Hall, 1970), Ch. 5.

39. See Lee B. Becker, et al., "The Development of Political Cognitions," in Steven H. Chaffee, ed., *Political Communication* (Beverly Hills, Ca.: Sage Publications, Inc., 1975), pp. 21–64.

40. Ball-Rokeach and DeFleur, "A Dependency Model of Mass-Media Effects," p. 13.

41. Herschel Shosteck, "Some Influences of Television on Civil Unrest," *Journal of Broadcasting,* 13 (Fall 1969): 371–85.

42. Richard A. Pride and Barbara Richards, "Denigration of Authority? Television News Coverage of the Student Movement," *Journal of Politics,* 36 (August 1974):660; see also a contrary view relying on different evidence in Michael J. Robinson, "Public Affairs Television and the Growth of Political Malaise: The Case of 'The Selling of the Pentagon,'" *American Political Science Review* 70 (June 1976): 409–32.

43. Colin Seymour-Ure, *The Political Impact of Mass Media* (Beverly Hills, Ca.: Sage Publications Inc., 1974), p. 22.

44. Ball-Rokeach and DeFleur, "A Dependency Model of Mass-Media Effects," p. 16.

chapter 11

Influencing Voting: Consequences of Electoral Communication

Election campaigns afford excellent opportunities to examine the consequences of persuasive communication. Related to voting and the voting act are the efforts to persuade people through propaganda, advertising, and rhetoric described in Chapter 4; the techniques of campaign persuasion outlined in Chapter 5; the roles and activities of members of the news media discussed in Chapter 6; the opinions and concerns of mass audiences listed in Chapters 7 and 8; and the socializing and politicizing effects of communication presented in Chapters 9 and 10. We now explore the convergence of these various lines of persuasion in the setting of electoral politics. The emphasis is twofold, first upon the character of voting as the active personal and social construction of political opinion, and second, upon the ways voters take campaign communication into account in fashioning their behavior.

Voters and the Voting Act: Alternative Views

Armed with a variety of aggregate and survey research techniques, political scientists and communication scholars have studied the voting patterns of the American electorate for several decades. As Abrams notes, many of the earliest of the voting studies explained behavior in socio-psychological terms, i.e., by emphasizing group influences on, and political predispositions of, voters.[1] Studies of the Bureau of Applied Social Research (BASR) of Columbia University offered a typical conclusion that "voting is essentially a group experience."[2] A second set of researchers, the Survey Research Center (SRC) of the University of Michigan, stressed psychological factors as voting determinants, especially voters' enduring political attitudes including their affective ties to one or the other major political party.[3] Neither BASR nor SRC studies viewed political campaigns as a particularly significant influence upon voting. The general conclusion was that persons most exposed to persuasive communication in a campaign were those most likely already to have arrived at a voting decision; those most likely to be influenced by persuasive appeals were precisely those least interested in politics and, hence, least likely to pay attention to campaign communication. In recent years, however, a third trend in voting studies has emerged, a revisionist perspective that assigns an important role to campaign communication. These recent studies focus upon the uses and gratifications that communication media have for voters (see Chapter 5), why people attend to campaigns, and the relationship between voters' expectations of possible influences and their actual voting behavior.[4]

From these sociopsychological, psychological, and communication oriented traditions in voting studies we can derive four alternative ways to think about how voters act. These perspectives assist us in formulating a view of voting as a communication act.

The Rational Voter

BASR and SRC studies of voting raised a direct challenge to the view of the voter associated with classical democratic theory, a view we touched upon briefly in Chapter 10. The rational voter is essentially self-actional, i.e., qualities intrinsic to each voter's personal character contribute most to the citizen's voting decision. The rational person: (1) can always make a decision when confronted with alternatives; (2) ranks alternatives so that each is either preferred to, indifferent to, or inferior to others; (3) ranks alternatives in a transitive way: if A is preferred to B and B to C, then A is preferred to C; (4) always chooses the alternative with the highest preference ranking; and (5) always makes the same decision when confronted with the same alternatives.[5]

So characterized, rational action consists of calculating appropriate means to achieve desired ends. Whether the goals of action are rational is not at issue; we are concerned only with the means of achieving them. Placed within the political arena the notion of rational action establishes stringent requirements to qualify as a rational voter: the rational voter is always motivated to act when faced with political options, takes an active interest in politics so as to become informed and knowledgeable about alternatives, discusses politics as a means of arriving at some ranking of alternatives, and acts on the basis of principle, "not fortuitously or frivolously or impulsively or habitually, but with reference to standards not only of his own interest but of the common good as well."[6] So self-motivated, informed, and principled, the rational voter acts consistently in the face of political pressures and forces.

The blow dealt by the voting studies to the rational voter conception of electoral behavior was well nigh mortal. Surveys of the voting age population conducted in the 1950s and early 1960s documented repeatedly an electorate only mildly interested in politics, seldom motivated to vote, rarely discussing issues and candidates, doing so only in superficial ways, poorly informed (recall the discussion in Chapter 10), and prone to precisely the fortuitous, frivolous, impulsive, and habitual ways of approaching politics deplored in classical democratic theory. It was then a small step to the formulation of a new view of the American voter, that of the reactive voter.

The Reactive Voter

The portrait of the reactive voter is not flattering. It derives from physicalistic assumptions that human beings react to stimuli in passive, conditioned ways. Candidates and parties in a political campaign provide cues setting voters in motion by triggering long-term factors determining the direction of voting behavior. As noted above, the early voting studies conducted by the BASR viewed these factors as primarily social. Researchers amassed an impressive inventory of the social and demographic attributes correlated with voting decisions—measures of social class including occupation, education, and income, and attributes of age, sex, race, religion, region and locale of residence, etc.[7]

As an example of the view that voters react to elections on the basis of long-term social and demographic factors, i.e., that voting is again self-action, consider the Index of Political Predisposition, a formulation of one of the earliest voting studies.[8] The index consisted of a set of sociodemographic categories—religion, socioeconomic status, and rural-urban residence—that helped researchers explain the vote. Depending upon one's position on the index it was possible to say what direction the person's vote would take: Democrat if Catholic, of lower status, and urban residence; Republican if Protestant, upper status, and rural residence. Fixed attributes were thus thought to move people in a predictable partisan direction. If voters possessed characteristics predisposing them in one direction, but other characteristics predisposing them in the opposite (e.g., the Protestant, urban, blue collar worker), these "cross pressures" provoked vacillation and indecision. In a sense, then, demographics were destiny.

Voting studies in the 1950s and early 1960s moved away from an emphasis on demographic correlates toward a view that attitudes working in tandem with attributes predispose voters to behave in given ways. Mentalistic "mediating variables" (attitudes, predispositions, identification, loyalties, etc.) functioned as intervening constructs in a cause-effect sequence that portrayed the voter as decidedly passive and mechanistic:[9]

Social &
physical
properties ⟶ Mentalistic constructs ⟶ Passive motion
(attributes)   (attitudes)   (voting)

Of the constructs linking social influences to voting, the most important for the reactive voter was an emotional attachment to a political party: "In the competition of voices reaching the individual the political party is an opinion-forming agency of great importance." SRC studies characterized emotional attachments to party as "party identification," a key source of the self-action of the reactive voter: "Merely associating the party symbol" with a candidate's name "encourages those identifying with the party to develop a more favorable image of his record and experience, his abilities, and his personal attributes." Hence, "identification with a party raises a perceptual screen through which the individual sees what is favorable to his partisan orientation. The stronger the party bond, the more exaggerated the process of selection and perceptual distortion will be."[10] Surveys indicated that three-fourths to four-fifths of Americans possessed partisan identifications; those that did not were unlikely to vote anyway. Thus, again it was not difficult to paint a portrait of the American voter as a passive machine moved primarily by forces stimulating latent predispositions.

The focus upon the attribute-attitude link as the key cause of voting evoked skepticism of the capacity of political communication in campaigns to have more than a minimal, triggering effect. Party loyalty, for example, had little basis in any alleged electorate's concern with issues or policy matters. Rather, partisanship derived from an emotional attachment to symbols acquired early during the socialization process. In campaigns, the reactive voter applauds or decries proffered symbols but largely ignores issues or policy positions of the parties. Moreover, as noted, this voter selectively perceives qualities of competing candidates rather than rationally appraising pluses and minuses. Small wonder then that most voters decide fairly early in a campaign whom to vote for, then employ political communication to reinforce that decision.

Beginning in the mid-1960s an increasing number of scholars moved to challenge the reactive voter portrait of the electorate just as the voting studies that gave rise to the reactive model had earlier confronted the portrait of the rational voter. For one thing, the outcome of a large number of presidential elections deviated from what researchers expected based upon presumptions that people vote mainly on the basis of enduring social attributes or partisan loyalties. In a succession of presidential contests, short-term factors specific to the election provided better explanations of what happened than did long-term factors—the marked appeal of Dwight Eisenhower (a Republican) in winning the votes of Democrats in 1952 and 1956; the failure of many Democrats to support John Kennedy because of his Catholicism in 1960; the defection of Republicans from the candidacy of Barry Goldwater in 1964; and the failure of the party with the majority of identifiers, the Democratic, to win in either 1968 or 1972. Still another indication that fixed attributes do not always influence the partisan direction of the vote was the fact that voters in virtually all social and demographic categories shifted their support between the parties from one election to another to about the same degree (see Table 11-1). In addition, surveys indicated that people were taking increased interest in both issues and policies and often aligning themselves behind candidates on the basis of their perceptions of those candidates' issue positions and personal qualities. Finally, studies indicated that the tendency of Americans to identify with the two major parties was on the decline. (Recall the data in Table 10-1 and Figure 10-1.) More and more people labeled themselves independent and even demonstrated that independence through increased split-ticket voting. Prompted by evidence that changes are taking place in electoral politics, observers formulated yet another view of what voters are like, that of the responsive voter.

The Responsive Voter

Political scientist Gerald Pomper draws a portrait of the responsive voter.[11] Whereas the character of the reactive voter (what Pomper calls the "dependent" voter) is fixed, stable, and enduring, that of the responsive voter is impermanent, changing with the times, political events, and shifting influences on voting choices. There are other ways, writes Pomper, that responsive and reactive voters differ:

1. Although responsive voters are affected by their social and demographic characteristics, these essentially permanent attributes are not deterministic. As Key and Munger argue,[12] these characteristics "move in and out in the zone of political relevance" and insofar as they "determine political preference they encounter considerable friction."

2. The responsive voter also has party loyalties, but these affiliations again do not determine electoral behavior. In fact, partisan attachments are more rational than emotional, for by associating parties with issues, the responsive voter rationally reduces the personal costs of participation (e.g., the voter uses party as a shortcut to gather information on issues) and effectively expresses personal interests. Whereas the reactive voter identifies with party as a substitute for exercising independent judgment, the responsive voter's party identification assists the choice-making task.

3. Responsive voters are influenced more by short-term factors salient in specific elections than by long-term group and/or partisan loyalties that transcend all elections. Many citizens shift their partisan choices from election to election as a function of their positions on issues and appraisals of the capacities of the candidates. Pomper approvingly quotes V. O. Key, Jr., to the effect that the portrait of the responsive voter "is not one of an electorate straitjacketed by social determinants or moved by subconscious urges triggered by devilishly skillful propagandists. It is rather one of an electorate moved by concern about central and relevant

TABLE 11-1

Vote by Groups in Presidential Elections Since 1952

	1952		1956		1960		1964		1968			1972		1976		
	Stevenson %	Ike %	Stevenson %	Ike %	JFK %	Nixon %	LBJ %	Goldwater %	HHH %	Nixon %	Wallace %	McGovern %	Nixon %	Carter %	Ford %	McCarthy %
NATIONAL	44.6	55.4	42.2	57.8	50.1	49.9	61.3	38.7	43.0	43.4	13.6	38	62	50	48	1
SEX																
Male	47	53	45	55	52	48	60	40	41	43	16	37	63	53	45	1
Female	42	58	39	61	49	51	62	38	45	43	12	38	62	48	51	–
RACE																
White	43	57	41	59	49	51	59	41	38	47	15	32	68	46	52	1
Nonwhite	79	21	61	39	68	32	94	6	85	12	3	87	13	85	15	–
EDUCATION																
College	34	66	31	69	39	61	52	48	37	54	9	37	63	42	55	2
High School	45	55	42	58	52	48	62	38	42	43	15	34	66	54	46	–
Grade School	52	48	50	50	55	45	66	34	52	33	15	49	51	58	41	1
OCCUPATION																
Prof. & Business	36	64	32	68	42	58	54	46	34	56	10	31	69	42	56	1
White Collar	40	60	37	63	48	52	57	43	41	47	12	36	64	50	48	2
Manual	55	45	50	50	60	40	71	29	50	35	15	43	57	58	41	1
AGE																
Under 30 Years	51	49	43	57	54	46	64	36	47	38	15	48	52	53	45	1
30–49 Years	47	53	45	55	54	46	63	37	44	41	15	33	67	48	49	2
50 years & older	39	61	39	61	46	54	59	41	41	47	12	36	64	52	48	–
RELIGION																
Protestants	37	63	37	63	38	62	55	45	35	49	16	30	70	46	53	–
Catholics	56	44	51	49	78	22	76	24	59	33	8	48	52	57	42	1

TABLE 11-1, cont.

Vote by Groups in Presidential Elections Since 1952

	1952		1956		1960		1964		1968			1972		1976		
	Stevenson %	Ike %	Stevenson %	Ike %	JFK %	Nixon %	LBJ %	Goldwater %	HHH %	Nixon %	Wallace %	McGovern %	Nixon %	Carter %	Ford %	McCarthy %
NATIONAL	44.6	55.4	42.2	57.8	50.1	49.9	61.3	38.7	43.0	43.4	13.6	38	62	50	48	1
POLITICS																
Republicans	8	92	4	96	5	95	20	80	9	86	5	5	95	9	91	—
Democrats	77	23	85	15	84	16	87	13	74	12	14	67	33	82	18	—
Independents	35	65	30	70	43	57	56	44	31	44	25	31	69	38	57	4
REGION																
East	45	55	40	60	53	47	68	32	50	43	7	42	58	51	47	1
Midwest	42	58	41	59	48	52	61	39	44	47	9	40	60	48	50	1
South	51	49	49	51	51	49	52	48	31	36	33	29	71	54	45	—
West	42	58	43	57	49	51	60	40	44	49	7	41	59	46	51	1
Members of Labor Union Families	61	39	57	43	65	35	73	27	56	29	15	46	54	63	36	1

Source: *The Gallup Opinion Index*, Report No. 137 (December 1976), pp. 16–17.

questions of public policy, of governmental performance, and of executive personality."[13]

A dominant portion of the background of Pomper's depiction of the visage of the responsive voter consists of the options from which the electorate can choose in any given campaign: "The variation in the stimuli provided by political leadership, parties, and candidates is particularly important in this view of the voter, for the popular response will be strongly *conditioned* by these stimuli." Hence, "the behavior of the voters varies with the character of the available choices."[14] Again evoking Key, Pomper quotes: "The voice of the people is but an echo." But Pomper includes only the last three sentences of what Key went on to say:

> The output of an echo chamber bears an inevitable and invariable relation to the input. As candidates and parties clamor for attention and vie for popular support, the people's verdict can be no more than a selective reflection from among the alternatives and outlooks presented to them. Even the most discriminating popular judgment can reflect only ambiguity, uncertainty, or even foolishness if those are the qualities of the input put into the echo chamber. A candidate may win despite his tactics and appeals rather than because of them. If the people choose only from among rascals, they are certain to choose a rascal.[15]

Pomper urges that there is no single answer to the question, "Who is the American voter?" The quotation from Key illustrates the problem of trying to find such an answer. Key and Pomper seem to be saying that although voters are responsive rather than dependent, conditioned, passive, and reactive, they are nonetheless limited to responding to the influences objectively available and predefined in a campaign. Voters are active to the degree that they "selectively" reflect upon "the alternatives and outlooks presented to them," yet a strong hue of passivity colors the portrait of the responsive voter. Voters respond to political communication, but ultimately the "voice of the people is but an echo" and "the output of an echo chamber bears an inevitable and invariable relation to the input." But if the input-output relation of the echo chamber is indeed inevitable and invariable, how does it differ from the mechanistic cause-effect sequence contained in the attribute-attitude-behavior relation in the portrait of the reactive voter? In short, there is the suggestion here that even the responsive voter is dependent, or at least only as independent as the options objectively available permit. If the portrait of the reactive voter relies upon self-actional qualities to explain electoral behavior (social, demographic, and partisan determinants in the voter's makeup), that of the responsive voter focuses upon inter-actional qualities, that is, voters and campaign options are viewed as independent parts of a machine operating with "considerable friction." However, what if voters are not simply chambers echoing inputs as outputs but are active beings who interpret and thereby transform inputs into outputs in a fashion neither inevitable nor invariable? In sum, what would a portrait of the active voter look like?

The Active Voter

We return to a theme that we have reiterated many times, that human beings act toward objects on the basis of the meanings those objects have for them. On first blush it appears that there is little difference in regarding human beings as either reactive or responsive agents. But Blumer sees a fundamental difference:

> Instead of being regarded as merely an organism that responds to the play of factors on or through it, the human being is seen as an organism that has to deal with what it notes. It meets what it so notes by engaging in a process of self-indication in which *it makes an object of what it notes, gives it a meaning, and uses the meaning* as the basis for directing its action. Its behavior with regard to what it notes is not a response called forth by the presentation of what it notes but instead is an action that arises out of the interpretation made through the process of self-indication. In this sense, the human being who is engaging in self-interaction is not a mere responding organism but an acting organism—an organism that has to mold a line of action on the basis of what it takes into account instead of merely releasing a response to the play of some factor on its organization.[16]

So viewed, the active individual confronts a world that must be interpreted and given meaning in order to act rather than an environment of prearranged options to which one responds because of the nature either of individual attributes and/or attitudes or the limited range of stimuli. Certainly political campaign stimuli which provoke responses cannot be presumed uniform in people's minds. Some pay close attention to the campaign, perhaps even get actively involved; others glance only at the headlines or the evening televised news; many give it no heed at all. People thus sort themselves out with respect to what in a campaign they take into account; as more than mere echo chambers they transform meaningless inputs into political symbols with meanings that grow, remain constant, contract, or even vanish as they reach different sectors of the public.[17]

Regarded in this light the stimuli, or options, provided voters in a political campaign are no more fixed or evenly distributed throughout the electorate than the social attributes and predispositions of the electorate. Rather, the content of campaign communication varies in its presentation by the media, in the responsiveness of people to it due to intervening processes of definition, and in the range of richness perceived among alternatives by voters:

> In a political campaign the various media are participating in a total evolving process, treating to a large extent the same events and responding to one another's presentations. What they present is filtered and organized in diverse ways in the experiences of people, with much of it picked up and used in the arena of local communication. This intertwined, interacting, and transforming makeup of the communicative process stands in noticeable contrast to a scheme wherein each form or channel of communication is regarded as exercising a distinct influence that can be kept separate and measured in some parallelogram of forces.[18]

Put simply, a political campaign takes form and acquires meaning for voters through communication. Voters' involvements are limited neither to registering fixed attributes and/or attitudes nor to responding to predefined campaign appeals. Active involvement extends to people interpreting events, issues, parties, and personalities, thus defining and constructing as much as accepting a range of given options. Voters formulate images of what they take into account, images that vary enormously and continually. Voting is thereby a communication act.

CAMPAIGNS, COMMUNICATION, AND VOTERS

Voting is one of the final acts in an election campaign, a lengthy and sometimes heated series of exchanges which constitutes a process of communication. To grasp the basic character of a political campaign as a communication process it helps to review briefly our basic perspective on human activity. Recall that social behavior is a complex of interactions. There are two varieties of these interactions, nonsymbolic and symbolic. Nonsymbolic interaction occurs when people respond to objects, including one another's behavior, directly without interpreting the stimulus. A boxer automatically raising his arm to ward off a blow acts in a reflexive way; he simply reacts to the gesture of his opponent. Similarly the voter who unthinkingly pulls the levers beside a list of unknown candidates also engages in nonsymbolic behavior, a "conversation of gestures" in which a sign (in this case a candidate's name) evokes a meaningless reflex.[19]

In contrast, symbolic interaction derives from people interpreting objects and actions. Nonsymbolic behavior involves *direct* response to things, symbolic behavior to the *meanings* of things (recall Chapter 3). The boxer automatically jousting his opponent reacts nonsymbolically; however, if he foresees the opponent's blow as a feint designed to trap him, he is acting symbolically.[20] In a like manner the voter reflecting upon various aspects of candidates, imagining what each is like, then voting, engages in symbolic behavior. Through symbolic interaction people reply not to meaningless gestures but to what Mead called "significant symbols" (see Chapter 3).

A political campaign is a continuous exercise in the creation, re-creation, and transmission of significant symbols through communication. Campaigns incorporate the active participation of both campaigners and voters. Campaigners—candidates, advisors, consultants, and others described in Chapters 2 and 5—try to manage the impressions voters have of them by expressing symbols they hope will appeal to the electorate. The media employed by campaigners, promoters, and journalists acting in media roles add to the producing and modifying of significant symbols. Voters selectively attend to certain things in the campaign, take them into account, and interpret them. Consequently, the campaigner's appeal is more than an imprint upon the voter's nervous system; voters do more than just open their eyes so that sensations can rain down on their retinas. Voters' choices are not immediate, direct, and habitual but delayed; voters inhibit their reactions and try out various responses in their imaginations. Voters thereby construct images of campaigns and campaigners, images that lend significance to proffered symbols.

So viewed, the task of understanding the consequences of campaigns upon electoral behavior involves more than describing techniques and channels of campaign communication as we did in Chapter 5. It involves taking seriously the possibility that voting is *minded* behavior that

> consists of presenting to oneself, tentatively and in advance of overt behavior, the different possibilities of alternatives of future action with reference to a given situation. The future is, thus, present in terms of images of prospective lines of action from which the individual can make a selection. The mental process is, then, one of delaying, organizing, and selecting a response to the stimuli of the environment. This implies that the individual *constructs* his act, rather than responding in predetermined ways.[21]

Minded behavior, however, is not synonomous with the rational behavior described earlier in this chapter; nor is the active voter identical with the rational voter. No presumption is made, as in the case of rational behavior, that minded people have clear-cut goals and behave to optimize those ends. Nor is there any presumption that the process of delaying immediate action by trying out various responses in the imagination is rational, i.e., that a person contemplates a full range of alternatives, ranks alternatives in order of preference, even has preferences that are transitive, or consistently chooses the most preferred action (at least from an observer's viewpoint). Rather, minded behavior involves selective attention, imagining alternatives, and the construction of meanings for things that have no intrinsic meanings of their own. This characteristic, as already noted, also sets the active voter off from the responsive voter: "The 'audience' or people must be viewed not as responding to stimuli but as forging definitions inside their experience."[22]

To understand the relations between campaigns, communication, and voters, therefore, we ask first what possible things voters take into account in fashioning their images of a campaign, including their own attributes, perspectives, and perceptions. Then, we examine the role of campaign communication in providing the raw materials for image construction. Finally, we consider the cognitive, affective, and conative effects of campaign communication.

Constructing the Voting Act

Many considerations figure into the process voters use to make up their minds. Three are particularly significant in forming the background against which voters perceive communication about issues and candidates received during a campaign—the voters' attributes, perspective, and perceptions.

The Voters' Attributes: Social and Demographic Characteristics

Chapter 10 has already described the general relationship between socio-demographic factors and political participation. The traditional pattern has been that the persons most apt to take part in politics are of middle-class occupations or higher, educated, earning moderate incomes or better, middle-aged, white, and generally Protestant. Such persons pay more attention to politics than people with other characteristics, are more apt to register to vote, and to vote in higher rates. As voters, however, do people of differing social and demographic attributes act differently in elections?

Consider first the inclinations of American voters to think of themselves as Democrats, Republicans, or independent of partisanship. Generally both major political parties, and independents as well, are basically heterogenous; that is, they number among their loyalists large proportions of diverse people of differing educational levels, occupations, religions, etc. Democrats, Republicans, and independents each contain substantial numbers of blue and white collar workers; the young, middle-aged, and old; blacks and whites; and so on. There are, to be sure, some differences between the groups. For instance, more than one-half of whites in the South with grade school level educations identify with the Democrats; only two in ten of Protestant college graduates who are white and living outside of the South call themselves Democrats; almost one-half of all Jews think of themselves as Democrats; etc. Such tendencies, however, do not override the basically diversified social and demographic character of major party loyalists.

Many of the early voting studies distinguished the social and demographic attributes of partisan and independent voters. Studies conducted prior to the mid-1960s revealed that independents were predominantly persons concentrated toward the bottom of income, occupational, and educational ladders, precisely those people least likely to participate in politics at all. More recent investigations suggest that there are at least two sets of independents: the first comprised of nonparticipants in lower status socioeconomic categories and the second of individuals with educations beyond high school, in middle-income groups, and in white collar occupations.[23]

Analyzing trends they thought could be projected for the entire decade of the 1970s, DeVries and Tarrance distinguished from both the "old" and "new" independents yet another group, a "new force in American politics."[24] This force was voters who professed to split their tickets rather than vote straight party ballots in elections. Younger, more likely male, and more affluent than the "new" independents, ticket-splitters had above average educations (beyond high school), earned middle and higher incomes, were employed in professional, technical, and managerial occupations, were middle-aged or younger, usually Protestant (but numbering more Catholics than were among independent voters), and married, homeowning American-born white males with families. Ticket-splitters, noted DeVries and Tarrance, were more interested in politics and campaigns than other voters, more active politically, and—a point returned to later—consumed more information about politics from the mass media.

Turning from professed partisan identification or independence to actual voting behavior the picture is again of heterogeneous support for the two parties. To begin, as noted in Table 11-1, it is rare that any subgroup in American society (other than party identifiers) consistently supports a single party across several presidential elections. Bloc voting for either party is more the exception than rule; moreover, no subgroup is sufficiently unified to shift all of its votes from one party to another between elections (note, for example, that members of labor union families, the alleged "organized labor bloc," divided their votes 54–46 between the parties in 1972).

Yet, as Robert Axelrod has demonstrated, there are significant differences between the electoral coalitions of the two major political parties. It is incorrect to claim that there is not a "dime's worth of difference" in the parties. Examining the electoral coalitions of the Republicans and Democrats from 1952 through 1968, Axelrod profiles the Republican coalition as composed of the nonpoor, whites, nonunion families, Protestants, Northerners, and people living outside the central cities of metropolitan areas. Democrats have mobilized the working class (but not consistently the poor), blacks, union members, Catholics, Southerners, and people living in the central cities. Axelrod cautions that these coalitions are very loose; group loyalties are not total, not constant from one election to another, and shift in response to national trends rather than for reasons specific to each group.[25]

There has been an increasing tendency in recent presidential elections for voters to discern differences between parties and candidates on election issues. For this reason it is wise to qualify Axelrod's view that voting groups in society shift their support from one to another party or candidate mostly in response to national trends rather than for reasons touching specific groups. Specialized publics do spot differences between the major political parties on issues that are important to them. Thus, for instance, the elderly see partisan differences on social security and health care issues; businessmen discern differences on economic measures; blacks note differences on civil rights and employment issues; etc. When the issues are salient to people of specific social attributes, pertinent issues rather than national trends explain the response of members of social groups to competing parties and candidates.[26] In such instances, a person's social and demographic attributes inform the voter's perspective.

The Voters' Perspectives: Evolving Political Self-Images

We have seen in earlier chapters that people learn to identify with significant symbols through political talk, persuasion, socialization, and opinion formation. Thus, for instance, one reaches the point of claiming "I am an American" or "I am a fan of the Washington Redskins." These identifications[27] contribute to the continuous development of self-images, the aspects of one's personality described in Chapter 9. Moreover, these beliefs regarding what *to be* combine with personal values and expectations to form outlooks on what goes on in the world. People entering a political campaign, for example, take with them various viewpoints closely tied to their political self-images; not only do they see things happening (their short-term images, or perceptions, of political objects), they observe them from individual points of view (their long-term political self-images, or perspectives). Among the vantage points voters take to a campaign that are derived from their evolving political self-images, we shall examine five: (1) partisan identification, (2) social class, (3) ideological leanings, (4) conceptions of desired qualities in ideal officeholders, and (5) personal concerns.

Partisan Self-Images.   The discussion in Chapter 9 made the point that one of the consequences of socializing communication is that Americans learn to identify with a political party. That many people do was illustrated by Table 10–1 depicting the distribution of partisanship in the United States as measured by opinion surveys conducted in recent decades. Advocates of the reactive voter view of electoral behavior focus upon the relative constancy of partisanship portrayed over time and argue that partisan self-images either condition voting irrespective of changes in issues, candidates, and events, or so shape the citizen's perspective that the voter views all political stimuli in conformity with party identification, by screening out information at odds with partisanship and selecting only communication that reinforces the partisan bias. Scholars who regard voters as responsive or active rather than reactive find other lessons in the distribution of partisan self-images. A particularly noteworthy indicator of how Americans are becoming liberated from partisan ties, for example, is the decline in the relative proportions of strong Democrats and Republicans since the 1960s and the relative rise of percentages of persons identifying as independents of one stripe or another.

Other evidence alluded to earlier in our discussion can be mustered to show that party identification is neither an all-determining nor all-coloring perspective for contemporary voters. For one thing, although voters generally evaluate political objects in partisan terms, this is not always the case. For example, in response to open-ended questions soliciting their likes and dislikes about the presidential candidates in 1960, almost one-half of the remarks made by Democrats about Richard Nixon were positive (almost two-thirds of the remarks made by weak Democrats were positive); by contrast in 1972 less than one-half of the remarks of Democrats about George McGovern were positive.[28] Second, both strong and weak partisans are less likely to vote for their party's candidates in presidential contests than they once were. For instance, from the 1950s to 1960s the defection rates almost doubled among strong Democrats (from 4.3 to 8.0 percent) and strong Republicans (from 3.7 to 7.2 percent); defection rates among weak Democrats and Republicans also increased across the decades. Third, not only are more people identifying themselves as independents than was earlier the case, but those independents cast a greater share of the total vote (almost doubling in a two decade span from 1952 to 1972). Finally, Democrats, Republicans, and independents vote split tickets; in 1976 alone one-half of Republicans, 45 percent of Democrats, and 83 percent of independents split their tickets.[29]

If the bonds of partisanship are loosening, does this argue that party identification is less a factor in voters' constructions of meanings of political communication? Relatively few studies address this problem. Those that do posit an affirmative answer. First, there is evidence that the growing availability of mass media, especially television, and the use of the media by candidates (see Chapter 5) penetrates all segments of the electorate—partisan, "old" and "new" independents—both during and between elections.[30] As Mendelsohn and O'Keefe illustrate in their study of the 1972 presidential election, partisans are no longer the most exposed to and dependent upon television for campaign information; there were scarcely any differences among Democrats, Republicans, and independents in television usage.[31] Second, early voting studies suggested that those most likely to be exposed to political communication during a campaign were least likely to defect from their basic partisanship; those least exposed were least likely to vote their party self-images. Yet the correlation between party identification and party voting has been declining with each passing presidential election since 1952 regardless of level of media exposure. And in 1972 Mendelsohn and O'Keefe found no significant differences among Democrats, Republicans, and independents in the degree that they reported being influenced in their voting by events reported in the media. In sum, the perspective provided by party self-image has a diminishing direct influence upon voting and declining indirect influence in shaping voters' images of campaign stimuli.

Class Images.   Class image refers to the social class that a person identifies with and considers himself to be a member of—upper, middle, lower, propertied, working, etc. Richard Hamilton observes that the distribution of the class images of Americans has been fairly stable in recent decades.[32] Given the options of calling themselves upper, middle, working or lower class, fewer than 1 to 2 percent say they "don't know" their class, and fewer than 5 percent designate either upper or lower class; about one-third of the remainder view themselves as middle class and two-thirds as working class. When given simply middle or working class options, the proportions are about 1 to 2, respectively.

What has not been convincingly demonstrated as yet, however, is that Americans evaluate political objects and approach voting along lines of class awareness. There are two reasons for this. The first lies in the fact that associating the basic middle and working class categories with voting reveals no consistent pattern of support for parties or candidates by middle-class or working-class identifiers. The second lies in the fact that most arguments regarding "class voting" in the United States examine not class awareness but such measures of class as occupation, education, and income, not the class a person identifies with, but the social category the voter fits. Gerald Pomper, however, has looked at the relationship of class awareness and class position to voting behavior. He observes that even when people are aware of their social class they don't divide their votes between Democrats and Republicans by class; that is, the working-class identifiers do not vote Democratic, the middle-class Republican. Rather than polarizing the vote, class consciousness tends to increase

Democratic voting among both middle- and working-class identifiers. Nor does class position as measured by a person's manual or nonmanual occupation contribute to marked class voting in presidential elections, although within a single election class voting may be greater than other types (such as when political leaders deliberately stress class-based issues).[33]

Ideological Self-Images.   Just as Americans identify themselves as partisans or members of a social class, so also they locate themselves along an ideological continuum. In 1974, for example, Potomac Associates asked a cross section of Americans to place themselves at one of five points on a liberal-conservative scale. The results were that one-third classified themselves as "middle of the road," about one in twenty classified themselves as either "very liberal" or "very conservative," and about one-fourth of the sample selected "moderately liberal" or "moderately conservative."[34]

Like social class, ideology may be measured in a variety of ways. And, as with class consciousness, when measured in the form of ideological self-images it has been difficult to discern a direct relationship between one's ideological perspective, evaluation of political objects, and voting behavior. This stems partly from the fact that only relatively recently have Americans perceived ideological differences projected by parties and candidates (indications are that they did so most sharply in 1964 with the candidacy of Barry Goldwater and again in 1972 when George McGovern emphasized ideological differences). Moreover, it has been only recently that voting studies yielded evidence that a voter's ideological self-image conformed to the voter's stands on political issues. Earlier studies pictured a voter willing to identify with an ideological label, yet without a coherent ideological viewpoint to support it. Although the conclusion is very tentative, current research suggests the development of more coherent ideological perspectives among voters, perspectives which seem to be congruent with partisan self-images: "Most voters not only know their place, but are in the right place. More than four times as many liberals are in the Democratic party as are Republicans, while there are half again as many conservatives as in the opposition."[35]

Images of Ideal Officeholders.   Many voters bring to an election campaign a conception of the qualities they most desire in public officeholders and the characteristics they find most objectionable. The evidence is that these images of the ideal officeholder provide a base line, or standard, voters use to compare and evaluate the traits they perceive in candidates actually running for office.

What are the traits of the ideal officeholder? Several studies report similar findings. Voters look for such abstract qualities as maturity, honesty, sincerity, strength, activity, and energy. The composite is virtually that of a political hero.[36] Granted that it hardly is news that voters look for heroism in their candidates, nonetheless it is possible to explain the choices of a large proportion of voters simply by comparing their images of the ideal with the images they construct of competing candidates. Miller and Jackson, for example, compared the ideal images of voters with their perceptions of candidates for governor and congressman. They found that (1) the structure of people's images of the ideal officeholder are quite stable; (2) such images have clear dimensions including how people imagine the ideal candidate's personal qualities, professional background, party affiliation, and ideological stance; (3) the advantage one candidate has over another in voters' minds is largely a function of how each candidate measures up to the ideal; and (4) a comparison of voters' ideal images with their perceptions of candidates on the dimensions of personal qualities and professional background provides an accurate prediction of the election's outcome.[37]

Voters formulate their perspectives of what officeholders should be like on the basis of their childhood experiences in the family and school as well as through their personal experiences with government. Gene Wyckoff, a radio, television, and film producer who has worked on behalf of a number of political candidates, credits the mass media with inculcating such images in the form of "media predispositions." Television, he notes, creates a symbolic language of its own that builds stereotypes of good guys and bad guys; the medium teaches voters on a year-round, unceasing basis what images embody personifications of universally admired or detested characters in the popular American culture:

> All television viewers, to a greater extent than they might suppose, would seem to have mental picture galleries in their heads, the walls of which are hung with portraits of heroes, lovers, villains, stooges, fathers, statesmen, politicians, comedians, and other stereotype characters in television's commedia dell'arte. With little conscious effort—or perhaps in spite of conscious effort viewers probably match the images in their mental picture galleries against the images of candidates seen on television and derive an impression of the candidates' characters accordingly.[38]

Personal Concerns.   As we saw in Chapter 8, Americans have a variety of concerns about economic, social, welfare, foreign, environmental, energy, and other matters. Moreover, they have concerns about whether political leaders and institutions are credible, honest, trustworthy, and responsive. One of the tasks of the political candidate is to tap these lingering concerns in hopes of generating support. For instance, a newsletter from a leading campaign consulting firm summarized survey data on the eve of the 1976 presidential election; it argued that Americans felt there was something deeply wrong with their country, thought things were moving in the wrong direction, were alienated from politics, and that the federal government could not be trusted. In such speculation there is a question worth raising: Was such a perspective of pessimism and distrust the precise backdrop against which voters constructed images of issues and candidates in the 1976 campaign so that a virtual unknown, Jimmy Carter, rose to a presidential nomination simply by repeating throughout the nation, "I just want to see this country once again as pure, and honest, and decent, and truthful, and fair, and confident, and idealistic, and compassionate, as filled with love, as are the American people"?

The Voters' Perceptions: Campaign-Specific Political Images

Neither voters' attributes nor perspectives dictate electoral choices. Rather, voters selectively perceive the parties, candidates, issues, and events in a campaign, give them meaning, and fashion votes accordingly. Through an interpretative process, they take into account not only their attributes and evolving, long-term images but construct short-term images of campaign objects as well.

Party Images. Party images consist of what people believe about each of the major political parties, like and don't like about them, and what they expect the parties to do. They differ from partisan self-images in that they are perceptions of how each party acts in a specific campaign. Thus a person may identify with a particular party, yet not like what that party does.

Party images have several dimensions: the relationship people perceive between a party and its candidate ("I like the Republicans because they nominated Ike," or "Democrats are good because Jimmy Carter is one"); general perceptions of party performance ("they keep us out of war" or "times are never good with them"); references to the interests parties favor ("Democrats are for the little man" or "Republicans always support big business"); and similar expressions. During presidential elections from 1952 to 1972, voters were slightly more positive about the Democratic party than the Republican party. Trilling has found that during the two decades 20 to 25 percent of respondents in nationwide surveys were neutral with respect to their images of the two parties, about 40 percent were pro-Democratic, and slightly less than 40 percent were pro-Republican. Comparing those figures with the data in Table 10-1, it is apparent that the Republicans have been considerably less disadvantaged with respect to Americans' party images over the twenty-year period than they have been in proportions of Americans as party identifiers.

Just as partisan self-images have had lessened influence on voting in recent presidential elections, so has there been a decline in the relationship between party images and how people vote. As Trilling argues, however, the trend need not be irreversible. In fact, party images are particularly responsive to factors operating in a campaign and become more or less important in fashioning electoral choices as these factors change: "In other words, party images effectively play an intermediary role, translating what transpires in the political environment into meaningful terms for the voter. In sum, the likes and dislikes Americans have for their political parties do in fact constitute the meaning of American political parties for American voters."[39]

Candidate Images.   A candidate's political attributes and personal style as perceived by voters form the electorate's image of the office-seeker. We have already noted that some voters choose between candidates on the basis of how close each campaigner measures up to the voters' images of ideal officeholders. We have also remarked that although party loyalties color people's images of candidates, there is no one-to-one correspondence. Moreover, many voters affiliate with parties because they like the candidates nominated. A growing body of evidence thus suggests that in recent elections at a variety of levels—presidential, congressional, statewide—the images people construct of the contenders is a major factor in the electorate's choice. For example, one of the principal reasons that partisans defect from their party's fold in presidential elections is that they form more positive views of the opposition's candidate than of their own. In the 1972 presidential election almost 60 percent of the vote could be explained by how people rated Richard Nixon and George McGovern on a scale designed to measure the warmth or coolness respondents felt for the candidates. In comparison the effects of voters' partisan and ideological self-images were scarcely noticeable.[40]

What features in competing candidates are salient to voters in constructing images? With the exceptions of Barry Goldwater in 1964, George Wallace in 1968, and George McGovern in 1972, Americans in the two decades from 1952 to 1972 were generally positive in their regard for all the various presidential candidates. Within that generally positive content a fairly large number of voters worry about the candidates' personal attributes. This, however, is not their only concern. In fact, only in the cases of Dwight Eisenhower and John Kennedy during the period from 1952 to 1972 did the trait labeled "personal attraction" in survey responses dominate the public image of presidential candidates. More typically, voters search for clues about the candidate's political role—experience, background, and potential as a public official. Here, however, they are normally limited by the raw material available in the campaign media, thus indicating that political communication serves as an important facet of constructing voters' images of candidates.

Political Issues.   There has been a growing debate in the last two decades regarding whether voters take issues into account in making electoral choices. Studies conducted prior to 1964 minimized the importance of issues to voters. Members of the electorate, according to the research of the period, were typically unaware of campaign issues, cared little about them, and did not know where the respective parties and candidates stood on issues. Following 1964, however, students of voting began to revise their earlier estimate of how people perceive issues. Some researchers challenged the view that the failure of voters to express awareness of the issues that researchers thought important indicated a lack of interest in issues. These investigators began to ask in surveys what issues respondents (instead of investigators) deemed important. Other researchers claimed that the concept of "issue" was too narrowly framed. Voters might not, for instance, be able to list specific issues on which the political parties differed, but they could judge the good or bad "nature of the times" and hold political parties responsible for those conditions. Still other scholars reported that there was good reason that voters could not discern differences between candidates and/or parties on issues, which was that candidates and parties purposely obscured issue differences in order to recruit broad support.

Revisionist approaches to the question of issue voting have led to tentative conclusions: (1) There is a higher level of awareness of issues among voters than seemed apparent in earlier voting studies; (2) Voters not only are aware of issues and care about them, they detect differences between the political parties and between the candidates on issues those voters deem important; (3) The growth in awareness of party differences on policy issues extends to large segments of the electorate and is even present among persons of limited formal education. In sum, "the effect of issues on the vote has risen considerably, while the effect of partisanship has decreased."[41]

Although voters apparently do take issues into account in constructing electoral choices—including such matters as taxation, economic questions, defense spending, and even the general nature of the times—revisionist studies generally conclude that events in a political campaign, even events highly dramatized and widely publicized, do not become salient issues to voters. For example, separate studies of the 1972 presidential campaign concluded that such "journalistic blockbusters" as the resignation of Senator Thomas Eagleton from the Democratic ticket as McGovern's running mate, the break-in of Democratic National Headquarters in the Watergate apartment complex, and McGovern's major address on Vietnam policy produced little change in vote decisions in spite of high levels of voters' awareness of such events.[42]

Political Communication and the Voter's Image

Voters do not simply become aware of issues, formulate images of candidates' political attributes and personal styles, and fashion images of political parties by living as isolated hermits. Nor do the perspectives they bring to a campaign predetermine their perceptions of issues, candidates, and parties. Rather, in the time between elections and during specific campaigns, they are exposed to a variety of political media—interpersonal, organizational, and mass. To clarify our picture of the electoral consequences of political communication, we conclude this chapter by examining two matters: (1) the growing potential salience of campaign communication for the choices voters make, and (2) the catalytic function of campaign communication in assisting voters to formulate beliefs, values, and expectations about electoral politics.

The Emerging Potential of Campaign Communication

Given the fact that during elections for president, members of Congress, governor, state legislature, and many lesser offices it is almost impossible for the citizen to shield himself from the appeals of candidates and other campaigners, one would think that campaign communication is a major factor in helping voters reach electoral choices. Early studies of voting included such an assumption. *The People's Choice*, one of the earliest of these inquiries, likened voting to making a decision between competing consumer goods. Just as each of many food products had its own particular qualities to distinguish it from competitors, so did political candidates. As Peter Rossi noted in his critique of the study: "The predispositions (attitudes) of the voter are acted upon by the mass media, just as advertising acts upon the shopper. The voter vacillates between one and the other candidate as propaganda filters down to him. Finally, he comes to a decision, perhaps at the last moment before he enters the polling booth, just as the undecided shopper makes his choice at the food bins in the supermarket."[43]

But early voting studies quickly disabused scholars of such a picture of the voter and of the role of campaign communication. For one thing, at least in major elections, few voters vacillated between candidates. In presidential elections, for example, studies indicated that only about one-third of voters made up their minds during the campaigns; in contrast 40 percent made up their minds before the nominating conventions and the remainder during those conventions. Second, studies indicated that instead of the media working on predispositions, the reverse was more typical. Both social attributes and partisan self-images were particularly resistent to media influence. On the basis of social and party loyalties people selectively monitored campaign communication, reading, listening, and viewing what supported their point of view and avoiding messages that did not. Even those one-third in presidential elections who arrived at choices during the campaign did so primarily on the basis of the perspectives they carried into the campaign rather than as a result of media influence. Finally, the early voting studies disputed the then widely accepted notion of the "hypodermic" quality of media effects—the idea that exposure to communication carried with it automatic effects, so that if voters could be exposed to an appeal a sufficient number of times they would react in the intended direction. Selective attention, perception, and recall worked against such effects. The hypodermic view was replaced with the "rule of minimum effects" which outlined three possible effects of communication upon voting—reinforcement of partisan decisions already made, activation of otherwise indifferent citizens, and conversion of the doubtful. Estimates were that fewer than two in ten voters underwent such campaign conversions.[44]

The conclusions about the effects of campaigns on voting derived from first and second generation voting studies (roughly the BASR and SRC studies cited at the beginning of this chapter) are now challenged by a third generation of investigations of the 1970s.[45] The basis for that challenge lies in several current trends previously alluded to that warrant recapitulation: (1) evidence from nationwide surveys of a decline in the tendency of citizens to identify with political parties, combined with a concurrent increase in the proportion of political independents, especially of "new" independents described earlier; (2) an increase in the proportion of voters who defect from standing party loyalties in specific elections; (3) an increase in levels of split-ticket voting; (4) an increase in turnout rates among independents and weak partisans; and (5) increased levels of media dependence in a complex society, as described in Chapter 10. Two other trends are worthy of brief mention. First, a number of writers comment not only upon the declining strength of social and partisan ties upon voters, and thereby the increased potential for short-term factors in guiding vote choices, but also on the possibilities of major realignments of the Democratic and Republican parties. To the degree that many citizens might be shifting partisan loyalties, the potential of political communication increases for providing the raw material for constructing both evolving and campaign-specific political images.[46] Second, recent contests for the presidency have witnessed a marked rise in the number of statewide presidential primaries; paralleling this proliferation has been an increased emphasis upon already existing primaries for nominating candidates for congressional, statewide, and local offices. These primaries—where long-term perspectives of voters offer less guidance in sorting out a glut of candidates—offer an expanding role for campaign communication in influencing voters' constructions.

The Catalytic Function of Campaign Communication

A catalyst is a substance that precipitates, modifies, and often increases a process or event without being exhausted by doing so. This is certainly one way to think of what political communication does in an electoral campaign. In contemporary campaigns communicated messages provoke the collective process of definition and interpretation through which voters find meaning in competing candidates, parties, and issues. Although produced and consumed at a prodigious rate, the supply of campaign appeals—at least from the citizen's perspective—must seem inexhaustible. It is this catalytic agent, campaign communication, that voters act upon in formulating their beliefs, values, and expectations of campaign objects. In sum, then, campaign communication is a catalyst with cognitive, affective, and conative consequences.

Cognitive Effects.   Insofar as they examined what effects campaigns have for voters, first and second generation voting studies (1) looked primarily for cases of voters changing their minds as a result of media exposure and (2) followed the simple procedure of identifying the influence a given message was intended to have, the people the message was intended to influence, and the effects of the influence on the audience in question. The procedure was analogous to firing field artillery: a missile (media message) strikes a target (audience) with a measurable impact (effect).

Third generation voting studies have different emphases and assumptions. For one, they explore not only possible changes of voters' preferences but also changes of voters' information levels and expectations. For another, contemporary studies adopt the "uses and gratifications" approach to communication research (see Chapter 5) and ask such questions as how people use campaign communication, what rewards they derive from it, how dependent they are upon it, and how much they perceive they are influenced by campaigns. Among the gratifications that people seek from the political content of the media are *guidance* in reaching a voting choice, *reinforcement* and support for a decision already made, *information* as a means of surveillance of the political environment, *excitement* as spectators of the drama of electoral conflict, and *argumentative material* for future debates and discussions. Although there are also reasons why people avoid the political media—such as that they are alienated from politics, are too partisan to expose themselves to threatening, countering messages, or feel that politics interferes with other pursuits—citizens find it increasingly hard to escape political communication entirely. As a result, their exposure to, uses of, and gratifications from political media have several cognitive consequences.[47]

In their study of the 1972 presidential election, Mendelsohn and

O'Keefe posited that voters used the various media to gather four kinds of information: (1) what to look for in the campaign, or agenda-cueing; (2) what the important issues of the campaign were, or agenda-setting; (3) candidates' positions on important issues; and (4) information about candidates' personalities and other attributes. The largest percentage of respondents surveyed making high use of the media for these purposes employed television (a majority following the campaign in October), about one-third used newspapers, and relatively small percentages used radio, magazines, or interpersonal communication. In contrast to the selective exposure revealed in earlier voting studies, Mendelsohn and O'Keefe found Democrats and Republicans almost equally aware of each other's political communication.[48]

The pervasive exposure to television as a source of campaign information throughout all segments of the electorate raises the question of what kinds of information count most, that contained in televised political advertising or that in television news? Available evidence provides an equivocal answer. On the one hand, a study of split-ticket voters gives priority to television newscasts, documentaries, and specials as an information source for ticket-splitters. Other research also stresses the news and editorial content of the media as a source of information for ticket-splitters, although emphasizing that print (newspapers and magazines) provides more substantial portions of information to voters than does television.[49] On the other hand, there are studies reporting that television's political advertising, not news, is the key source of information. McClure and Patterson argue from research of the 1972 presidential election that television news is not an efficient communicator of everyday political information, nor does exposure to television news affect voters' beliefs about candidates' issue positions (although it may influence voters' assessments of candidates' personal qualities and character).[50] However, exposure to televised political advertising immediately and directly influences voters' beliefs about candidates. This is not to say that exposure to televised advertising has hypodermic effects; studies suggest that people frequently distort the contents of political spots, reading into the ads information not directly stated in order to support preconceived views.[51] The meaning, in short, is not the message, but what the viewer chooses to attribute to that message. Finally, Mendelsohn and O'Keefe provide data that different kinds of voters respond to political advertising in different ways. Those who make up their minds in a campaign are less likely to seek information and guidance from televised political advertising than are the late deciders. Late deciders rely less upon other sources of information (political parties, television and print news, etc.) and turn instead to the "noneffort" sources such as political commercials. There is also evidence that those who change their minds during a campaign ("switchers") may also acquire information through televised political advertising.[52]

Affective Responses. Mention that switchers and late deciders use television for information during an election suggests that political communication influences voters' evaluations as well as their levels of knowledge about issues and candidates. One area where this is the case, at least to a marginal degree, consists of the images voters construct of candidates. A review of presidential elections from 1952 to 1972 reveals no overall trends, but does indicate that in specific campaigns voters using different media as an information source did change their images of candidates. For example, in 1952 the image of Adlai Stevenson improved during the campaign among people using a variety of media; Dwight Eisenhower's image declined among newspaper and magazine readers but remained steady among television and radio users. In 1960 the image of John Kennedy became more positive among television viewers, that of Richard Nixon improved among radio listeners. Curiously enough, the greatest improvement in the Kennedy image came among people who reported in surveys that they had not heard about the campaign through any of the mass media. More recently, George McGovern's image in 1972 became more positive among television viewers while Richard Nixon's image changed relatively little, declining slightly, among users of all media.[53]

Whether television provides voters with the raw material conducive to changing their images of candidates depends a great deal on what type of television content voters view and the use they make of it. Television's political advertising is a case in point. An experimental study reveals that spot commercials emphasizing issue content change voters' evaluations of candidates more than do those emphasizing image content (personal qualities, etc.). Spots of five-minute length prove superior to shorter, sixty-second commercials.[54]

The changes in affective orientations toward candidates of voters exposed to other forms of campaign communication vary considerably. There is no convincing evidence, for example, that direct mail campaigns substantially improve the evaluations voters make of an office-seeker; indeed a recent study questions the overall effectiveness of direct mail.[55] Display media, on the other hand, make a difference; the quantity and quality of billboards, yard signs, posters, etc. can increase the amount of information about candidates to create name recognition and have positive effects on voters' evaluations as well.[56] Finally, the effectiveness of organizational communication on voters' evaluations (particularly contact by a political party) is difficult to assess. Usually fewer than one-half of Americans are contacted by any political party during a presidential election; those who tend already to be predisposed to the party that contacts them. There are cases where contact has improved a candidate's image; images of Hubert Humphrey in 1968 and George McGovern in 1972 improved among voters contacted by the Democratic party.[57]

Conative Consequences. How does use of political communication relate to voters' expectations and behavior? One of the few studies examining the relationship between voters' expectations and their exposure to political media is the Mendelsohn and O'Keefe analysis of the 1972 campaign. Very early in the campaign a panel of survey respondents provided answers to questions measuring how much each voter anticipated being influenced by the political media in reaching a choice. Surveys of these respondents at later points revealed that those who expected to be influenced by the media were those actually most influenced. Those scoring highest on expected influence were switchers, i.e., voters changing from one candidate to another during the campaign, who also scored highest in reported influence at the end of the campaign.

With respect to the relationship between campaign communication and voting choices, however, third generation voting studies parallel earlier investigations with respect to whether or not campaigns help people make up their minds. Mendelsohn and O'Keefe reported that 75 percent of their sample of Summit County, Ohio, voters were early deciders, 13 percent late deciders, and 10 percent switchers:

> The role of the mass media as agents of influence during the campaign seems in some ways submerged, and in other ways quite dominant. Campaign media exposure alone was only indicative (and weakly at that) of influence among the already-decided, presumably those seeking justification for their decisions. Exposure was actually negatively related, albeit slightly, to influence, after other factors were controlled for among switchers and late deciders. Hence mere exposure to campaign media was not indicative of influence associated either with voters making up their minds or with their changing them.[58]

Before assuming that the behavioral consequences of political communication are minimal, however, a number of points should be noted. First, Mendelsohn and O'Keefe emphasize that mere exposure and attention to the media do not constitute influence. One must also consider gratifications people receive from the media such as reinforcement, support, or guidance. These enable voters to adjust electoral choices to the ongoing experiences they encounter during their lives, to their specific dispositions, habits, and needs, and to the things they must take into account in constructing meanings for a specific campaign. Second, evidence that voters make up their minds early in a presidential contest does not mean they do so in all electoral races. For instance, available research indicates that voters confronted with more than a single election turn to political media for guidance in whether to vote straight or split tickets; the more the voter pays attention to media for information about both parties' candidates, the greater the likelihood of ticket splitting.[59] And even in presidential contests where the outcome is often likely to be foreordained, as it was in 1972, political media play a greater role in helping voters construct electoral choices, perhaps even defecting from traditional voting habits. For example, in 1968 persons most dependent on television as an entertainment and information medium were those most apt to vote for the third party candidacy of George Wallace.[60] Finally, we should not ignore that aside from mass media, both interpersonal and organizational channels have an impact upon electoral outcomes, a point already discussed in Chapter 5.

Sociopolitical Effects of Political Communication

The focus of this chapter has been primarily on the effects of political communication, particularly campaign communication, upon individual voters constructing personal electoral choices. We should not forget, however, that political communication has more encompassing consequences and transcends the acts of individuals. We alluded to some of these in Chapter 10. In closing this chapter, however, and making a transition to related concerns of the final chapter, we want to reconsider a social and political consequence of campaign communication, that of agenda-setting:

> The power of the press in America is a primordial one. It sets the agenda of public discussion; and this sweeping political power is unrestrained by any law. It determines what people will talk and think about—an authority that in other nations is reserved for tyrants, priests, parties, and mandarins.[61]

Such an observation probably claims too much for political media, yet it is clear that voters must interpret an environment in which political media report what is important about politics and what candidates hold views that may be similar to their own.[62] Two implications flow from such agenda-setting. One is that media agendas alter electoral agendas by selecting some issues for attention and ignoring others. If it is the issues on electoral agendas which motivate people's actions, it follows that the agenda may become a means for social change or preservation of the status quo. Put simply, one political consequence of campaign communication is to shape the agenda of both short- and long-term electoral politics (a point considered again in Chapter 12).

Second, as pointed out several times previously, a large plurality of Americans in an increasing number rely upon television for information about political affairs. To that degree television is the prime agenda-setter in politics. But as noted previously (Part Two), constraints on television make it difficult to communicate the variety and complexity of political information associated with many agenda items (such as the social and environmental impacts of exploiting new energy sources, problems of disposing of nuclear wastes, considerations surrounding a host of new technologies, etc.). Manheim warns that *"as the flow of complex political information declines apace with the increasing reliance on television as a source of political information, first the perceived need, and later the ability, to perform sophisticated intellectual operations on such information, as well as an appreciation for the complexity of politics itself, also declines."*[63] The result, observes Manheim, is a reduction in the quality of political discourse among the mass of Americans, thus opening the way for an elite with the requisite technical knowledge, skills, and resources effectively to manipulate policy making. In short, the sociopolitical consequences of campaign communication extend beyond the electoral context to the policy making arena.

BIBLIOGRAPHY

Several succinct syntheses of the key theories and findings of contemporary voting studies are now available. Among those that provide a useful review for the reader are, first, Herbert Asher, *Presidential Elections and American Politics* (Homewood, Ill.: The Dorsey Press, 1976). Asher not only covers the standard fare of such books—the role of party identification, candidates, issues, etc.—but also discusses the influence on voting of changes in the conduct of election campaigns. Second, readers will want to consult Gerald Pomper, *Voters' Choice* (New York: Dodd, Mead and Co., 1975) for a discussion of dependent and responsive voters, a discussion of generational factors pertaining to voting behavior, and a causal modeling of selected influences on voting. Third, for a review of research findings and a description of the major voting studies, one can turn to William H. Flanigan and Nancy H. Zingale, *Political Behavior of the American Electorate* (Boston: Allyn and Bacon, Inc., 3rd ed., 1972).
As we noted in this chapter, political scientists in the 1970s are beginning to note trends in voting behavior that were not apparent in the 1950s and early 1960s. Pomper's *Voters' Choice* summarizes many of these. In addition the reader should consult two works, each the product of collaboration by leading students of voting and elections: Warren E. Miller and Teresa E. Levitin, *Leadership and Change: The New Politics and the American Electorate* (Cambridge, Mass.: Winthrop Publishers, 1976) and Norman H. Nie, Sidney Verba, and John R. Petrocik, *The Changing American Voter* (Cambridge, Mass.: Harvard University Press, 1976).
Beyond the texts that focus primarily upon individual voting behavior, there are others that examine various institutional features of elections. Gerald Pomper's *Elections in America* (New York: Dodd, Mead and Co., 1968) is one example; readers should compare Pomper's classification of types of voters which appears in this book with that he derives from *Voters' Choice*. A standard work on American elections is Nelson W. Polsby and Aaron Wildavsky, *Presidential Elections* (New York: Charles Scribner's Sons, 4th ed., 1976). There are also books that focus upon specific segments of voting such as issues, candidates, and parties. A widely read book regarding the nature of selected types of issues and their impact on the American electorate is Richard M. Scammon and Ben J. Wattenberg, *The Real Majority* (New York: Coward-McCann, 1970);

Scammon and Wattenberg develop the concept of the social issue and relate electoral strategies both to that issue and to the demographic and attitudinal makeup of the American electorate. A review of the nature of voters' perceptions of candidates and the research related to that phenomenon is Dan Nimmo and Robert L. Savage, *Candidates and Their Issues* (Pacific Palisades, Cal.: Goodyear Publishing Co., 1976). And a useful statement regarding shifting patterns of voting behavior and their impact upon the American party system, especially the New Deal coalition of the Democratic party, is Everett Carll Ladd, Jr. (with Charles D. Hadley), *Transformations of the American Party System* (New York: W. W. Norton Co., 1975).

Readers should also attempt to develop a sense of the evolution of voting studies over recent decades. One way to do this is to sample the three generations of voting studies. The first is exemplified by Paul F. Lazarsfeld, et al., *The People's Choice* (New York: Columbia University Press, 1944) and Bernard R. Berelson, et al., *Voting* (Chicago: University of Chicago Press, 1954). Also published in 1954 but representing in many respects a departure from these studies was an early volume of second generation approaches to the study of voting, Angus Campbell, et al., *The Voter Decides* (Evanston, Ill.: Row, Peterson, 1954). Two important and related volumes are Angus Campbell, et al., *The American Voter* (New York: John Wiley and Sons, 1960) and Angus Campbell, et al., *Elections and the Political Order* (New York: John Wiley and Sons, 1966). Readers will profit by comparing these studies with Ithiel de Sola Pool, et al., *Candidates, Issues, and Strategies* (Cambridge, Mass.: The M.I.T. Press, 1964). The contemporary generation of voting studies is diverse, both from the standpoint of approaches, findings, and quality. Among the volumes that should be consulted are Walter Dean Burnham, *Critical Elections and the Mainsprings of American Politics* (New York: W. W. Norton and Co., 1970); V. O. Key, Jr., *The Responsible Electorate* (Cambridge, Mass.: Belknap Press, 1966); Walter DeVries and V. Lance Tarrance, *The Ticket-Splitter* (Grand Rapids, Mich.: William B. Eerdmans, 1972); Harold Mendelsohn and Garrett J. O'Keefe, *The People Choose a President* (New York: Praeger Publishers, 1976); Thomas E. Patterson and Robert D. McClure, *The Unseeing Eye* (New York: G. P. Putnam, 1976); Gerald C. Wright, Jr., *Electoral Choice in America: Image, Party, and Incumbency* (Chapel Hill, N.C.: Institute for Research in the Social Sciences, 1974); and two studies from The American Institute for Political Communication: *The 1968 Campaign: Anatomy of a Crucial Election* (Washington, D.C.: A.I.P.C., 1970) and *The 1974 Campaign* (Washington, D.C.: A.I.P.C., 1975).

NOTES

1. Robert Abrams, *Some Conceptual Problems of Voting Theory* (Beverly Hills: Sage Publications, 1973).

2. Paul Lazarsfeld, et al., *The People's Choice* (New York: Columbia University Press, 1944), p. 37; see also Bernard Berelson, et al., *Voting* (Chicago: University of Chicago Press, 1954).

3. See each of the following by Angus Campbell, et al.: *The Voter Decides* (Evanston, Ill.: Row, Peterson, 1954); *The American Voter* (New York: John Wiley and Sons, 1960); and *Elections and the Political Order* (New York: John Wiley and Sons, 1966).

4.   See Harold Mendelsohn and Garrett J. O'Keefe, *The People Choose a President* (New York: Praeger Publishers, 1976); Walter DeVries and V. Lance Tarrance, *The Ticket-Splitter* (Grand Rapids, Mich.: William B. Eerdmans Publishing Co., 1972).

5.   Anthony Downs, *An Economic Theory of Democracy* (New York: Harper and Row, 1957).

6.   Berelson, et al., *Voting*, pp. 308–10.

7.   See Seymour Martin Lipset, *Political Man* (Garden City, N.Y.: Doubleday and Co., 1959).

8.   Lazarsfeld, et al., *The People's Choice*.

9.   David L. Swanson, "Some Theoretic Approaches to the Emerging Study of Political Communication: A Critical Assessment." Paper delivered at the annual meetings of the Political Communication Division, International Communication Association, April 14, 1976, Portland, Ore.

10.   Campbell, et al., *The American Voter*, pp. 128, 133.

11.   Gerald Pomper, *Voters' Choice* (New York: Dodd, Mead and Co., 1975), pp. 7–12.

12.   V. O. Key., Jr. and Frank Munger, "Social Determinism and Electoral Decision: The Case of Indiana," in Eugene Burdick and Arthur Brodbeck, eds., *American Voting Behavior* (New York: The Free Press, 1959), pp. 297–98.

13.   V. O. Key, Jr., *The Responsible Electorate* (Cambridge, Mass.: The Belknap Press, 1966), pp. 7–8; quoted by Pomper, *Voters' Choice*, p. 10.

14.   Pomper, *Voters' Choice*, pp. 9, 11 (emphasis added).

15.   Key, *The Responsible Electorate*, pp. 2–3; consult Pomper's partial quote, *Voters' Choice*, p. 9.

16.   Herbert Blumer, "Symbolic Interaction: An Approach to Human Communication," in Richard W. Budd and Brent D. Ruben, eds., *Approaches to Human Communication* (Rochelle Park, N.J.: Hayden Book Co., 1972), pp. 411–12 (emphasis added).

17.   Gregory Casey, "Popular Perceptions of Supreme Court Rulings," *American Politics Quarterly*, 4 (January 1976):4–5.

18.   Herbert Blumer, "Suggestions for the Study of Mass-Media Effects," in Burdick and Brodbeck, eds., *American Voting Behavior*, p. 201.

19.   George Herbert Mead, *Mind, Self, and Society* (Chicago: University of Chicago Press, 1934).

20.   Blumer, "Symbolic Interaction," pp. 406–7.

21.   Bernard N. Meltzer, "Mead's Social Psychology," in Jerome G. Manis and Bernard N. Meltzer, eds., *Symbolic Interaction* (Boston: Allyn and Bacon, 1967), p. 14 (emphasis in original).

22.   Blumer, "Suggestions for the Study of Mass-Media Effects," p. 205.

23.   Walter Dean Burnham, *Critical Elections and the Mainsprings of American Politics* (New York: W. W. Norton and Co., 1970), p. 127.

24.   Walter DeVries and V. Lance Tarrance, *The Ticket-Splitter* (Grand Rapids, Mich.: William B. Eerdmans, 1972).

25.   Robert Axelrod, "Where the Votes Come From: An Analysis of Electoral Coalitions, 1952–1968," *American Political Science Review*, 66 (March 1972):11–20.

26.   Ruth S. Jones and E. Terrence Jones, "Issue Saliency, Opinion-Holding, and Party Preference," *Western Political Quarterly*, 24 (Sept. 1971):501–9.

27.   Harold D. Lasswell and Abraham Kaplan, *Power and Society* (New Haven: Yale University Press, 1950), p. 25.

28.   Dan Nimmo and Robert L. Savage, *Candidates and Their Images* (Pacific Palisades, Cal.: Goodyear Publishing Co., 1976), pp. 140–42.

29.   Herbert Asher, *Presidential Elections and American Politics* (Homewood, Ill.: Dorsey Press, 1976), Ch. 3; *The Gallup Opinion Index*, Rpt. No. 137 (December 1976), p. 21.

30.   Edward C. Dreyer, "Media Use and Electoral Choices: Some Political Consequences of Information Exposure," *Public Opinion Quarterly*, 35 (Winter 1971–1972):544–53.

31.   Mendelsohn and O'Keefe, *The People Choose a President*.

32.   Richard F. Hamilton, *Class and Politics in the United States* (New York: John Wiley and Sons, 1972), pp. 100–101.

33.   Pomper, *Voters' Choice*, Ch. 3.

34.   William Watts and Lloyd A. Free, *State of the Nation 1974* (Washington, D.C.: Potomac Associates, 1974), p. 356.

35.   Pomper, *Voters' Choice*, p. 182.

36.   Nimmo and Savage, *Candidates and Their Images*, Ch. 3.

37.   Roy E. Miller and John S. Jackson, III, "The Role of Candidate Image in Non-Presidential Campaigns." Paper presented at the annual meeting of the Southwestern Political Science Association, April 8, 1976, Dallas, Texas.

38.   Gene Wyckoff, *The Image Candidates* (New York: Macmillan, 1968), p. 208.

39.   Richard J. Trilling, "Party Image and Electoral Behavior," *American Politics Quarterly*, 3 (July 1972):284–314.

40.   See Nimmo and Savage, *Candidates and Their Images*, Ch. 8, and Mendelsohn and O'Keefe, *The People Choose a President*, passim.

41.   Pomper, *Voters' Choice*, p. 185; Asher, *Presidential Elections and American Politics*, Ch. 4.

42.   Mendelsohn and O'Keefe, *The People Choose a President*, Ch. 7; Arthur Miller, et al., "A Majority Party in Disarray." Paper presented to the annual meeting of the American Political Science Association, September 4–8, New Orleans, La.

43.   Peter H. Rossi, "Four Landmarks in Voting Research," in Burdick and Brodbeck, eds., *American Voting Behavior*, p. 16.

44.   For a review of relevant studies see Nimmo and Savage, *Candidates and Their Images*, Ch. 2.

45.   See Mendelsohn and O'Keefe, *The People Choose a President*; DeVries and Tarrance, *The Ticket-Splitter*; and Thomas E. Patterson and Robert McClure, *The Unseeing Eye* (New York: G. P. Putnam, 1976).

46.   For a review of various theories of partisan realignment being discussed by political scientists see Everett Carll Ladd, Jr., and Charles D. Hadley, *Transformations of the American Party System* (New York: W. W. Norton and Co., 1975).

47.   See Lee B. Becker, "Two Tests of Media Gratifications: Watergate and the 1974 Election," *Journalism Quarterly*, 53 (Spring 1976):28–33, 87; Blumer, "Suggestions for the Study of Mass-Media Effects," in Burdick and Brodbeck, eds., *American Voting Behavior;* and Maxwell E. McCombs, "Mass Communication in Political Campaigns: Information, Gratification, and Persuasion," in F. Gerald Kline and Phillip J. Tichenor, eds., *Current Perspectives in Mass Communication Research* (Beverly Hills, Cal.: Sage Publications, 1972), pp. 169–194.

48.   Mendelsohn and O'Keefe, *The People Choose a President*.

49.   L. Erwin Atwood and Keith R. Sanders, "Perception of Information Sources and Likelihood of Split Ticket Voting," *Journalism Quarterly*, 52 (August 1975):421–428; DeVries and Tarrance, *The Ticket-Splitter*.

50.   Robert D. McClure and Thomas E. Patterson, "Television News and Political Advertising," *Communication Research*, 1 (January 1974):3–31; "Print vs. Network News," *Journal of Communication*, 26 (Spring 1976):23–28; Patterson and McClure, *The Unseeing Eye*.

51. Thomas R. Donohue, "Impact of Viewer Predispositions on Political TV Commercials, *Journal of Broadcasting*, 18 (Winter 1973–1974):3–15.

52. Mendelsohn and O'Keefe, *The People Choose a President*.

53. Nimmo and Savage, *Candidates and Their Images*.

54. Lynda Lee Kaid, "Political Television Commercials: An Experimental Study of Type and Length." Paper presented to the annual meeting of the Political Communication Division, International Communication Association, April, 1975, Chicago, Ill.

55. Roy E. Miller and Dorothy L. Robyn, "A Field Experimental Study of Direct Mail in a Congressional Primary Campaign: What Effects Last Until Election Day?" *Experimental Study of Politics*, 4 (December 1975):1–37.

56. David J. Stang, "An Analysis of the Effects of Political Campaigning." Paper presented to the annual meeting of the Southern Society for Philosophy, April 11–13, 1974, Tampa, Fla.

57. Nimmo and Savage, *Candidates and Their Images*.

58. Mendelsohn and O'Keefe, *The People Choose a President*, p. 162.

59. Akiba A. Cohen, "Attention to the Mass Media Among Straight and Split Ticket Voters," *Human Communication Research*, 2 (Fall 1975):75–78.

60. Michael J. Robinson and Clifford Zukin, "Television and the Wallace Vote," *Journal of Communication*, 26 (Spring 1976):79–83.

61. Theodore H. White, *The Making of the President 1972* (New York: Bantam, 1973).

62. Maxwell E. McCombs and Donald L. Shaw, "The Agenda-Setting Function of Mass Media," *Public Opinion Quarterly*, 36 (Summer 1972):176–87.

63. Jarol B. Manheim, "Can Democracy Survive Television?" *Journal of Communication*, 26 (Spring 1976):84–90 (emphasis in original).

chapter 12

Influencing Officials: Consequences of Policy Communication

A key question in closing any discussion of political communication and public opinion must be the degree and conditions of a close correspondence between public opinion and public policy, i.e., between what people think and what governments do. It is a topic referred to by various writers as "government by public opinion" or the "opinion-policy process."[1] At the outset we stress that the subject is best approached, as V. O. Key, Jr., noted, in its complexity rather than simplicity: " . . . One must discard simplistic conceptions, such as the notion that in some way public opinion exudes from the mass of men and produces guidelines for governmental action. A complex interaction occurs, with government (and other centers of influence as well) affecting the form and content of opinion; and, in turn, public opinion may condition the manner, content, and timing of public action."[2]

The purpose of this chapter is to chart the lines of two-way communication joining citizens and officials, what we call policy communication. First we look at the opinion-policy relationship as a process of representation providing alternative modes of popular, mass, and group opinions officeholders take into account in fashioning public policy. Second we examine complications associated with major types of policy communication. We close by considering the problems in maintaining an opinion-policy process in a fragmented, pluralist democracy.

REPRESENTATION: COMMUNICATING ABOUT POLICY

In a classic work on the theory and practice of constitutional government first published more than four decades ago, Carl J. Friedrich defined representation as follows: "The process by and through which the political power and influence which the entire citizenry or a part of them might have upon governmental action is, with their express or implied approval, exercised on their behalf by a small number among them, with binding effect upon the whole community thus represented."[3] This view suggests that representation requires means by which the expressed or implied approval of citizens reaches a smaller number of officials acting on behalf of the community. And if official decisions are to bind everyone, there must be means of informing people of the content of those decisions. Moreover, if we add the requirement that the political arrangement be democratic, then there must also be means for citizens to express their policy preferences to policy makers and "a receptivity of policy makers to all points of view whatever their source, together with a special commitment to the general public as a source of guidance."[4]

In sum, representation occurs when communication lines join public and policy makers in policy making, lines which channel policy preferences, decisions, and approval or rejection. But recall from Part Three that there are at least three faces to public opinion: (1) the popular expressions of many citizens, (2) the symbolic expression of the mass, or one, citizenry, and (3) the unorganized and organized expressions of a relatively few special interests. From these three modes of opinion expression many opinions are called, but few (and sometimes only one) are chosen in policy making. What Friedrich calls the "smaller number" in the representative process are policy makers exercising options; they may take into account the "entire citizenry" (perhaps popular or mass opinion) or only a "part of them" (various opinion publics). Aside from the sources of public opinion they take into account, whether many, one, or few, policy makers also interpret and define the content of opinion. Typically they regard opinions on policy related matters as supporting or vetoing, implicitly or explicitly approving or rejecting, their activities as representatives.

Thus, as does any political actor, a representative constructs through symbolic interaction both relationships with persons represented and meanings for those relations. Although limiting his remarks to congressmen, Dexter's observation applies to others in the representative's role: "We talk frequently of a representative or senator 'representing' or 'failing to represent' his constituents. The fact is the congressman represents his image of the district or of his constituents (or fails to represent his, or our, image of them). How does he get this image? Where does it come from?"[5] To grasp the outlines of policy communication joining public opinion and public policy, and thereby constituents' and representatives' images of one another, let us explore two overlapping matters: (1) the major lines of communication constituting the policy official's sources for constructing images of popular, mass, and group opinion, and (2) the kinds of support or rejection the official perceives in the content of that opinion.

CONSTRUCTING THE POLICY MAKER'S IMAGE: OFFICIALS' SOURCES OF PUBLIC OPINION

In assessing popular feelings, the mood of the masses, and the demands of special interests, policy makers rely upon a variety of sources. We consider each in approximate order of its increasing salience for guiding official conduct.

Officials Look at the Many: Popular Opinion and Public Policy

Two major institutional arrangements, one quite old and the other relatively new, suggest trends in popular beliefs, values, and expectations to public officials: popular elections and polls.

The Electoral Connection

Campaigning in presidential primaries in the 1960s and 1970s, George Wallace urged voters to support his candidacy as a way of communicating dissatisfaction to federal officials over a variety of policies. "Send them a message," Wallace repeated in all geographic regions of the country. He was not the first, nor will he be the last, to use elections to voice demands to policy makers. Nor are politicians alone in taking this view of the electoral process; philosophers and political scientists also remark on the communication function of elections.

There are three general theories regarding the communication role of elections. The first is a theory of the *popular will*. It argues that elections have an important instrumental dimension; they offer voters alternative means of achieving agreed goals within a framework of accepted rules. The theory has a cognitive focus in that voters (1) are oriented toward specific, tangible goals, (2) take an active interest in election campaigns and acquire knowledge regarding important issues, and (3) employ their votes as instruments to obtain those goals by political action. By providing issue-oriented voters (those who vote for candidates and/or parties on the basis of perceived issue stands rather than personality or partisanship) a means of voicing their material concerns and choices, elections discover the popular will and accurately reflect it to policy makers. The distribution of votes is a policy mandate communicated to public officials, supporting some proposals and rejecting others.

The view that elections express the popular will makes a number of assumptions. Some raise problems with the theory itself. For one, there is the premise that the primary function of an election is to resolve conflicts over policy and channel those resolutions to policy makers; through votes citizens make policies and dictate actions to elected officials. Second, the view assumes that candidates and parties take clearly visible, differing postures on policy issues so that voters can make issue choices. Third, the view postulates that voters are interested and informed about issues. Fourth, there is at least the tacit assumption that the problems which elected officials face in carrying out their duties are the same problems which voters resolved at the polls. Finally, there is the postulation that voters' views on issues remain stable, thus permitting elected officials to register a fixed popular will.

We saw in Chapter 11 that there is some disagreement among students of voting behavior regarding the extent of issue voting among the American electorate. Although there is evidence that the proportion of issue-oriented voters is on the rise, it is premature to assert that issues are the sole, or even the dominant, thing that voters take into account. Moreover, evidence that voters discern clear-cut differences between candidates and between parties on issues in presidential elections has not yet been buttressed by a sufficient number of studies of congressional, statewide, and local elections to demonstrate that voters at all electoral levels do so. Finally, there is sufficient variability in popular opinions on changing issues to suggest that elected policy makers cannot simply look to the results of the last election for a mandate on what policy choices they should make in the day-to-day process of governing.

Despite problems which make it difficult to accept the unqualified view that elections transmit popular mandates to policy makers, elections do indicate some popular preferences that policy makers act upon. For instance, one study compared the positions taken by the two major parties on a variety of issues from the period 1844–1968 with governmental policies made with respect to the same issues. Both party positions and national policies were then compared to the aggregate voting patterns of the electorate for and against the two parties. The results indicated that popular majorities did support national policies over extended periods of time and, in that sense at least, governed.[6]

A second theory emphasizes that elections provide a mechanism of *popular control*. The focus of this view is less instrumental than evaluative, less cognitive than affective. Voters choose between candidates and/or parties not to advance specific, tangible goals but to choose who should govern for specified, limited periods. The popular control theory stresses that party-oriented voters (1) make judgments on the basis of partisan and ideological standards, (2) retrospectively evaluate the conduct of policy makers during terms in office as good or bad, and (3) thus decide who should be the "ins" and "outs" among competing office seekers. The purpose of the election is not to communicate a policy mandate to officials but to select a government: "The democratic method is that institutional arrangement for arriving at political decisions in which individuals acquire the power to decide by means of a competitive struggle for the people's vote."[7]

The popular control view also makes assumptions about voters—that they are politically interested and involved, seek out information about how party officeholders conduct themselves, keep abreast of the general lines of policy made by governments, and have reasonably stable biases toward one political party or another. Until recently, voting studies tended to give more credence to this view than to that of the popular will theory. Until the 1970s the distribution of party identification in the nation was fairly stable. Moreover, studies revealed that voters reached general conclusions about the goodness or badness of the times; if times were good, they supported the party in power, but if bad, they held the party responsible.[8] Thus, for example, in 1968 "weak" and "moderate" Democratic partisans joined independents in sufficient numbers to vote the "ins," the Democratic administration, out of office by a narrow margin. There are two difficulties with this theory. One is that in the American party system it is often difficult to know which party should be held accountable for bad or good policy, especially when one party controls the presidency and the other controls Congress. Second, as party loyalties of voters diminish, it is not always clear whether voters respond to elections on the basis of what set of partisans they want to govern or on the basis of issues and personalities.

A third theory is one of *popular support*. Under the theory of popular will, elections communicate policy mandates; under popular control views they communicate approval or disapproval of the sitting government. In the popular support notion the function of elections is to communicate loyalty and devotion to the political community, regime, and procedures. The focus is expressive rather than instrumental or evaluative, cathetic instead of cognitive or affective. A cathetic focus involves releasing emotional tensions rather than acting to reach a tangible goal or to declare what is morally right or wrong. In this view the voter is candidate oriented, responding to the personal qualities of candidates, constructing images of them, and projecting one's own fears and frustrations, hopes and aspirations, self-concepts and self-images upon office-seekers as a means of relieving inner tension and reaffirming self. Elections provide opportunity for symbolic reassurance, to "quiet resentments and doubts about particular political acts, reaffirm belief in the fundamental rationality and democratic character of the system, and thus fix conforming habits for future behavior."[9]

The popular support view emphasizes the role of campaign propaganda, advertising, and rhetoric in promoting participation in a ritual that supports reigning political institutions but has relatively little direct effect upon policy formation, allocating material advantages and disadvantages, and choosing a government. The function of the election is psychological; the purpose is to offer a spectacular drama, appealing actors (for example, Ronald Reagan, Jimmy Carter, and Jerry Brown in the 1976 presidential primaries), and the means for sublimating the inclination toward organized violence to change the status quo.

One need not opt for any of these theories as an exclusive explanation of how elections open communication lines to policy makers. Elections serve instrumental, evaluative, and cathetic communication functions; they provide a partial discovery of popular wills regarding issues salient to some voters, a means of selecting a government, and an outlet for release of inner tensions and displays of regime support. Regardless of their function, elections are sources which policy makers monitor for messages about popular acceptance or rejection.

The Messages of Opinion Polls

Representation implies measurement. In order to act on behalf of the entire community and to gauge whether they have implicit or explicit approval of their constituents, political leaders (Friedrich's "smaller number,") assess popular views. Whether intuitively (by hunch, flying by the seat of the pants) or systematically (through procedures of gathering evidence), representatives look for similarities and differences in what people think; they qualitatively or quantitatively measure popular thoughts, feelings, and inclinations. In recent decades an increasing number of political leaders—officeholders and office-seekers worried about their constituents, professional communicators worried about audiences and clients, and political activists worried about their followers—have turned to opinion polls to find out about popular views. Some widely publicized polls, such as those conducted by George Gallup and Louis Harris, are major sources of popular opinions for policy makers. Other political leaders employ private polls, hiring survey firms for confidential soundings of constituents' sentiments. There are also a large number of academicians using opinion surveys to gather information to explain a wide range of political behavior such as voting, modes of participation, and communication habits. This is not the place to describe the various techniques of polling and survey research. (The reader will find such a discussion in the Appendix.) Rather, considering polls as one form of communication between citizens and officials, we examine two things: (1) how political leaders use polls and (2) the general relationship between opinion, as measured by polls, and what policy makers do.

For what do political leaders employ polls? Political candidates rely upon polls to help answer a variety of questions: to decide whether to run for public office or not, to determine a candidate's strength relative to other candidates, to measure the degree a candidate is known to voters, to locate areas of maximum potential voting strength, to identify general concerns and issues on the minds of voters, to assess the voters' image of the candidate's qualities and issue positions, to identify weaknesses of the opposition, and to publicize a candidacy by releasing the results of favorable surveys.

Officeholders utilize polls for many of the same reasons as do office-seekers, but generally two uses are uppermost—finding out what constituents think on key policy issues and determining whether or not constituents think the public official is doing an adequate job. It is important to distinguish here between the professional poll conducted in accordance with standards discussed in the Appendix and "polls of the district" conducted by many congressmen. Properly conducted, the former provide elective and appointive officials with a detailed profile of what citizens think about local, state, and national needs and such domestic problems as drug abuse, crime, care for the mentally retarded and ill, air and water pollution, transportation, increasing costs of energy, etc. The typical congressman's "polling" of constituents, however, is much more likely to be for the sake of publicity than a tool for information gathering. The normal procedure is for the congressional official's responsible staff member to draw up a brief questionnaire, frequently employing highly loaded questions designed as much to tell a constituent what he *should* think as to find out what the citizen *does* think. Questionnaires are mailed to all of the residents of the congressman's district or a haphazardly drawn sample thereof. On the basis of a very small proportion of questionnaires returned (perhaps as few as one thousand out of an original fifty thousand) the congressman reports in a news release, not surprisingly, that the district agrees with his stands on issues, that they think he is doing a "good job in Washington."

How seriously do policy makers take into account popular opinion as measured by polls when formulating images of what citizens want when making policy choices? It is difficult to say, since available evidence bears more indirectly than directly on the question. A body of research examines the degree of correspondence between popular opinion and public policies in selected areas. One study, for instance, correlated selected factors including popular opinion with policies passed in each of the American states in five areas—public accommodations laws, aid to parochial schools, right-to-work laws, laws regarding the unionization of teachers, and laws regulating ownership and possession of firearms. It concluded that popular policy preferences provide a better explanation of what policies states pass than do factors associated with the social and economic environments or political climates. However, this responsiveness is greater in some areas than in others (specifically greater with regard to public accommodations and aid to parochial schools).[10] In Part Three we saw other evidence that officials do not respond to popular concerns in all policy areas. Recall, for example, that two decades of polls indicate that two-thirds to three-fourths of Americans surveyed generally support passage of a law requiring a person to obtain a permit before buying a gun. Yet, public officials have consistently failed to adopt such legislation.

There is another bit of evidence bearing indirectly upon how seriously public officials take popular opinion. In a study of members of Congress, Roger Davidson explored how each congressman defined his representative style, i.e., whether the official thought it best to follow his own judgment in voting, to rely on the preferences of constituents, or to shift between personal inclinations and constituents' views depending upon issues and circumstances. Less than one-fourth of members of the House of Representatives thought they should follow constituents' opinions, more than one-fourth thought they should follow their own preferences, and the remainder believed in shifting with the issues and circumstances. In comparision, a nationwide survey of a cross section of Americans pertaining to the congressman's style revealed that two-thirds thought members of the House should place the opinions of constituents uppermost when it comes to voting.[11]

Regardless of whether policy makers pay attention to the polls, there is evidence that the polls do communicate to citizens and party leaders, at least when it comes to choosing candidates to run for president of the United States. Beniger examined the relative impact of polls and primary elections in selecting the nominees of the two major parties for president from 1936 to 1972. He found that a candidate's standing in the national preference polls has a strong direct effect on whether that office-seeker obtains his party's nomination. Moreover, standing in the preference polls had a strong direct effect on the candidate's relative success in the various state primary elections. Although Beniger found no evidence of bandwagon effects (voters' rushing to support a candidate doing well in the polls), he did conclude that people respond to a candidate's popularity as measured by polls. However, with the increased number of state presidential primaries (thirty in 1976) and numbers of relatively unknown candidates vying for nominations (neither Jimmy Carter nor Jerry Brown were particularly well known outside their respective states early in 1976), standing in early preferential polls may be less a predictor of success in the future than it has been in the past.[12]

In sum, although sketchy, the evidence suggests that citizens and officials fashioning their images of one another's beliefs, values, and expectations probably pay some attention to popular opinion as measured by polls. How much and how consistently is a question for additional investigation.

Officials Look at the One: Mass Consensus and Public Policy

Chapter 7 characterized the public opinion of the One as an ill-defined, ambiguous, poorly delineated, and sometimes contradictory mass consensus. That consensus is less a uniformity of opinion than a facade masking discord in fundamental political beliefs, values, and expectations. Vague though mass consensus may be, however, policy makers pay heed to it; they define it, interpret it, and symbolize it through appeals to "the public" and "the community." Among the sources public officials turn to as indicators of political consensus, three stand out: shifting levels of mass support for political institutions measured through opinion surveys, the content of the mass media, and the concerns expressed through mass movements.

Mass Support for Policy-Making Institutions

We noted in Chapter 2 that levels of public support for specific political leaders—presidents, congressmen, judicial officers, mayors, governors, etc.—vary with time, circumstance, and what people think incumbents in policy positions do. Policy makers worry about their popularity, but they also worry about how much support people give to the key policy-making institutions, regardless of who may be occupying the office. Presidents worry about their own reputations and about the credibility, faith, and trust people have in the presidency. Congressmen accept the fact that constituents sometimes approve, sometimes reject items of legislation but worry far more when there is evidence of mass distrust of Congress as a whole. In sum, policy makers concern themselves not only with changing levels of short-term support for their specific actions, (specific support), but also with shifts in long-term, relatively stable levels of support for the political community, regime, and authorities, (diffuse support).[13]

Does the mass consensus communicated to policy makers indicate that, at least in an abstract, generalized, and diffuse sense, people give political institutions sufficient support to permit public officials to conduct the day-to-day operation of government? In the broadest sense the answer is yes. After examining a wide variety of data concerning levels of diffuse support for the president, state governors, Supreme Court, and Congress, political scientist Robert Lehnen says that "relatively favorable levels of diffuse support" are "one important contribution that Americans give their public institutions." Most citizens have well-developed notions of support; between one-third and one-half of all citizens "have favorable levels of diffuse support that are almost immune from the day-to-day events of government officials."[14] One consequence of political communication from people to policy makers, therefore, is to provide officials with manueverability and latitude for governing.

Yet there are complications that demand qualifications in this conclusion. For one, as Lehnen notes, Americans are ambivalent about the exercise of public power. They recognize a need for powerful institutions, yet give high levels of diffuse support to institutions only so long as they think those bodies don't exert power over their lives. As government becomes more salient, levels of trust and faith in governing institutions decline (see Chapter 8). Thus in the decade from 1966 to 1976, pollster

Louis Harris found that the proportions of Americans expressing a "great deal of confidence" in the executive branch of the federal government fell from 41 to 11 percent, in Congress from 42 to 9 percent, and in the Supreme Court from 50 to 22 percent.[15] Although the message of mass consensus may have once been favorable, indications are that policy makers are now told a less positive story than that of yesteryear.

The Role of the Mass Media in Policy Communication

Newspapers, newsmagazines, radio, and television have a permanent interest in publicizing private conflicts and turning them into issues for public debate. The media thereby contribute to the processes of constructing public opinion described in Chapter 7. The source of that interest was identified in Chapter 6 as the need to stimulate public attention to build and hold large audiences. Advertising messages are among the many constraints that enter into the construction of news and the part played by the mass media in defining issues and setting agendas.

There are at least two respects in which the mass media serve as a source of messages to policy makers estimating public opinion. The first lies in the tendency of some policy officials to commit the journalistic fallacy of assuming that the news and editorial content of the press is synonymous with public opinion. This is risky because at best the press provides but one possible mode of expressing personal beliefs, values, and expectations in public.

The second way that the mass media act as a source of political messages is via the agenda-setting and building function of the media described in Chapters 5 and 11. Cobb and Elder list five major ways that parties in conflict transmit symbols through the mass media, enlarge political controversies, call them to the attention of policy makers, and enlist support.[16] Through (1) *arousal,* interest groups activate latent support within the community. As people grow increasingly dependent upon the mass media in a society as complex as ours (recall the discussion in Chapters 10 and 11), the media play a highly significant role in defining and creating conflicts, calling attention to issues, and perpetuating concerns among ever widening audiences. Thus the news media aroused a growing interest in events surrounding the break-in at Democratic national headquarters at the Watergate apartment complex during the 1972 presidential campaign. The media thereby contributed to an agenda for public discussion and helped set the stage for the eventual resignation of a president. Parties in conflict also employ the media for (2) *provocation* to goad allies and opponents to action. In 1968 various groups of protestors at the Democratic national convention in Chicago used protest marches to provoke a response from the Chicago police that would win sympathetic support for the demonstrators. Obscene language and attacks on sacred community symbols (such as burning the flag) are examples of provocative acts frequently covered and publicized by the news media. (3) *Dissuasion* consists of using symbols to discourage the opposition and win converts. For example, in campaigning against President Gerald Ford in Tennessee for the 1976 Republican presidential nomination, former California Governor Ronald Reagan spoke against the Tennessee Valley Authority. Ford backers labeled Reagan's remarks as a "plan to sell TVA," a symbol that may have dissuaded many conservative Democrats from crossing party lines in the primary stage to support Reagan. (4) The media can be used to demonstrate strength of *commitment* to a cause. In the civil rights movement of the 1960s, for instance, the news media publicized a march on Washington designed to prove the massive size and solidarity of the movement. However, if a media-covered protest fails to demonstrate strength (as when in 1976 only a handful of demonstrators arrive at Dulles International Airport to protest the first landing of the supersonic aircraft Concorde, which protestors thought a threat to the environment), the results damage the cause. Finally (5) the media engage in *affirmation*. Throughout most of the period of America's manned flights to the moon in the late 1960s and early 1970s, for example, media coverage of the space spectacular often took on the tone of "cheerleading" as well as reporting.

Aside from efforts to detect public sentiment and publicize controversies, policy makers use the news media for their own purposes. The press is especially important to public officials as a source of intelligence regarding what is going on within government. By monitoring the news, policy makers receive information and interpretations of what other officials are doing and saying; hints about the strategies and plans of the opposition; factual information about the timing, substantive content, and impact of proposals; and suggestions and ideas about future trends, both in the thinking of fellow officials and in popular, mass, and group opinions.[17]

Messages in Mass Movements

Policy makers also learn about mass opinions through the emergence and decline of social movements. A social movement consists of widely shared demands for change in some aspect of the social order. Examples are the civil rights movement, the anti-Vietnam war protests, the environmental movement, and the nuclear power protest movement. Although a social movement may have members and partisans, specific programs, and a formal leadership cadre as do the organized interests (discussed later), a social movement differs by its explicit and conscious indictment of all or some aspect of the social order. Pressure groups, political parties, and other organized interests, in contrast, work within the existing social order for special gains.[18]

Mass movements communicate three types of demands to policy makers. First, there are movements aimed at achieving immediate material gains for adherents. An example is the Townsend movement of the 1930s. Originated by Dr. Francis E. Townsend, the movement enrolled millions of supporters on behalf of a plan to redistribute America's wealth on •behalf of the elderly. Every person sixty years of age and over with at least five years of U.S. citizenship would have received, upon application to the U.S. Treasury, an annuity not exceeding $200 per month so long as the person spent the entire check within the month received. A second type of demand which movements communicate to policy makers is that of status. The American temperance movement that resulted in passage of the Eighteenth Amendment to the Constitution was as much devoted to maintaining the ruling status of a white, Anglo-Saxon, Protestant class as to enforcing laws regarding the sale, manufacture, and consumption of alcoholic beverages. Finally, social movements provide expressive outlets. The youth movement of the 1960s, for example, provided many Americans the opportunity to express their identities and their opposition to "the establishment" and "the older generation" through the wearing of unconventional clothes and long hair, smoking marijuana, etc. Some movements, of course, combine instrumental, evaluative, and expressive messages. The women's liberation movement is a case in point. In part women seek material benefits in employment and other opportunities denied them for decades, but they also want equal status as "persons" and to express their individual identities as females.

Officials Look at the Few: Opinion Publics and Public Policy

Of the three faces of public opinion, policy-makers find the visage of the Few most alluring. It comes to them in two guises, as unorganized and organized interests.

The Message of the Unorganized

At previous points, especially in Chapters 8 and 10, we described the principal ways that relatively small numbers of people, compared with the popular and mass citizenry, contribute to the construction of public opinion. One contribution derives from attentive and mobilized publics and issue-minded and ideologically inclined citizens (Chapter 8). Recall that these individuals differ from the general population by virtue of the opinions they hold, their consistency in holding them, their interest in politics, and their relative high levels of political involvement.

Policy makers generally heed more closely the opinions of attentives, the mobilized, issue-minded, and ideologues than they do either popular or mass opinion. By way of illustration, Devine's study of the attentive public revealed that (1) majority support of attentives is generally necessary for policies to be processed by public officials and (2) in some policy areas such as foreign aid, civil rights, allocation of resources to public or private sectors, and others, there is a closer relationship between the opinions of attentives and public policies than between the views of non-attentives or the general public and policy decisions.[19]

A second way that the demands of the unorganized Few reach the ears of policy makers is through the personal contacts between citizens and government. These contacts include mail, telephone, face-to-face communication, and confrontations with officials in public hearings. They may be initiated by the citizen or by the policy maker. The percentage of citizens who contact officials varies with the type of transaction initiated. The proportion of citizens writing letters to public officials is only about one-fifth of adults surveyed in nationwide studies.[20] Yet when investigators ask if people have had contact with a governmental agency in the recent past, about 70 percent reply in the affirmative. The most frequently contacted agencies deal with taxation, education, and social welfare.[21] Most citizens initiate contacts for private reasons; rarely are they interested in influencing general public policy decisions. Usually they seek to clarify or modify the manner in which an existing policy or program affects their daily lives. To be sure, this is important to the citizen involved, but the private character of the communication does not satisfy the criteria we outlined in Chapter 7 of a "public" problem, a transaction that has relatively broad and indirect consequences for people other than the immediate parties to the exchange. In this sense, then, communication through citizen contact constitutes policy communication of a fairly parochial variety.[22]

The Message of the Organized

One key source that policy makers take into account in fashioning an image of public opinion is information from spokespersons for organized interests. This includes communication with three of the varieties of political leaders described in Chapter 2—politicians speaking in the interest of a political party, representatives of pressure organizations, and office-holders in administrative agencies, legislatures, and the courts.

Listening to Political Parties.
Scholars outline a variety of models to describe the relationships between governed and governors. One is the political parties model.[23] It is similar to the popular control view of elections described earlier in this chapter. When parties nominate and offer candidates for office, goes the argument, voters choose between competing party slates rather than between candidates running independently. Parties offer competing platforms and voters judge how each party's stand squares with its own policy preferences, a feature of the

political parties model that makes it also akin to the popular-will view of elections. Finally, if elected, a party mobilizes its officeholders behind passage of the party's platform proposals. Voters hold the majority party accountable for its promises. Failure to carry through may lead voters to turn to the minority party in the next election.

To act as a major line of communication between citizens and officials, political parties must offer (1) competing slates of candidates, (2) distinctive policy positions, and (3) party leaders and candidates supportive of the policy stands of the respective parties. Moreover, (4) voters perceive differences in the policy stands of the parties and act on that basis, (5) each party in power can discipline its members to enact its promised proposals, and (6) voters hold parties accountable for failure to deliver on promises. In some respects American parties meet these criteria; in others, they do not.

First, Republican and Democratic parties typically offer competing slates of candidates to voters. However, the nature of the nominating process in both parties restricts the efforts of the party leaders and the rank and file to control the selection of nominees. Using techniques of campaign communication described in Chapter 5, many candidates win their party's nomination in spite of (rather than with the help of) party leadership and rank and file support. Relying upon private sources of campaign finance, professional political consultants, a combination of interpersonal and mass media appeals, and the support of independents and crossover voters from the opposition in primary elections, candidates with no particular record of either political experience or party loyalty win their party's nomination and in some cases capture their party. (Consider that in 1976 Jimmy Carter won the nomination of the Democratic party by receiving the votes, against numerous opponents, of only 39 percent of persons taking part in the party's presidential primaries; Gerald Ford, however, retained his party's leadership but received a smaller percentage of the Republican primary vote—49 percent—than his unsuccessful challenger Ronald Reagan).

Second, there is evidence from content analyses (see Appendix) of Republican and Democratic presidential election platforms that the parties offer reasonably specific and distinct policy proposals.[24] However, such distinctiveness in party pledges in statewide and local elections is rare or even nonexistent where there is one-party domination, where nonpartisan mechanisms guide the election of officials, or where competing local parties, as products of the same political culture, share the same policy outlooks.

Third, party activists, leaders, and in many cases candidates of the Republican and Democratic parties generally differ in policy preferences. Studies indicate differences in the policy preferences of the two major parties' national convention delegates,[25] local party officials,[26] and candidates for Congress.[27] Insofar as it is possible to generalize, studies find Democrats favoring greater government initiative in dealing with social and economic problems, whereas Republicans rely upon the private sector.

Fourth, we saw in Chapter 11 that today's voters in presidential contests, perhaps less so in congressional races, are more apt to perceive differences in the policy positions of the two major parties and their candidates than were members of the electorate prior to the mid-1960s. Whether the capacity to see such interparty differences penetrates to contests for statewide offices—especially lesser contests for auditor, treasurer, secretary of state, etc.—and local elections is less clear.

Fifth, although conventional wisdom argues that the major political parties have minimal discipline over their legislative officeholders, there is evidence of a degree of party cohesiveness among congressional policy makers. Studies of roll call votes in Congress from 1953 to 1964, for example, reveal that in both House and Senate there are issues where the partisanship of legislators provides an excellent predictor of how they will vote, especially on assistance to agriculture, ways to manage government, and social welfare issues. On other matters, however, including civil liberties and foreign affairs, party cohesion is reduced.[28] Party unity in voting is probably more the exception than the rule; on the average there are sharp partisan divisions on about three or four of every ten roll call votes taken in Congress.

Finally, evidence of voters' desires to hold parties accountable for failure to deliver on promises is mixed. For one thing, as we noted earlier, the general pattern is that parties have delivered, at least in the long run, on their platform promises. Pomper remarks that "legislative or executive action directly fulfills more than half of the planks, and some definite action is taken in nearly three-fourths of the cases. Achievement is even greater for the party in the White House."[29] Another complicating factor is that voters who respond to nebulous assessments of the "goodness" or "badness" of the times turn parties out of office for reasons that have less to do with failure to deliver on specific promises than out of a general uneasiness or dissatisfaction. Further, voters simply differ on how they make up their minds. Some unquestionably vote to enforce accountability. Others, however, take into account loyalty to their partisan self-images, respond favorably to incumbents regardless of their records as officeholders, emphasize personalities of candidates, etc.

In sum, there are some notable differences between the two major parties in the pledges they make to voters, in the political views of their respective activists, leaders, and candidates, and in the voting records of their officeholders. Voters who perceive these differences may well use the parties to "send them a message." Whether parties are a major line of communication to policy makers for more than a few citizens, however, remains problematic.

Listening to Interest Groups.   Research findings reported in Chapter 8 provided a sense of how few Americans use interest organizations as a line of communication to policy makers. Although people generally join organizations, only about 25–30 percent enter those they view as politically involved or in which political discussion occurs.[30] Moreover, people who participate in political interest groups scarcely constitute a representative cross section of either popular or mass opinion. Schattschneider has indicted the pressure system (his term for organized special interest groups) for its clear-cut bias. The very act of mobilizing organizes bias on behalf of people seeking special privileges from the government. In recent years "public" interest groups have been organized to protect and enhance the claims of the general citizenry (for example, Common Cause, and groups organized by consumer advocate Ralph Nader). Yet the pressure system still has an upper-class tendency that disadvantages the less affluent and persons of lower educational and occupational status.[31] And even within special interest groups members do not have equal access to the policy makers. As noted in our discussion of political leadership in Chapter 2, relatively few activists within any organization are spokespersons for group interests. They take initiative in defining group goals, mobilizing resources, forging a group consensus, and contacting officials. In doing so they typically respond to the demands of some group members more than others, sometimes leaving dissident interests completely unrepresented.

Policy makers pay attention to the claims of interest organizations, but this is not to say that they respond to all interests nor that they follow the dictates of lobbyists. Lobbying is communication with policy makers by people claiming to speak on behalf of interests for purposes of influencing governmental decisions.[32] Although the lobbyist's communication to the policy maker is normally direct, the effectiveness of lobbying lies less in pressuring officials to do a group's bidding than in organizing and channeling information. Most lobbyists see only officials who already agree with them.[33] To these friendly officials lobbyists provide relatively straightforward and necessary services—calling problems to the official's attention, clarifying the stands of particular interests, responding to inquiries, gathering factual data (self-serving, to be sure), supporting officials against opponents, protecting policy makers from exhorbitant claims of other lobbyists, and keeping communication lines open through informal efforts that include campaign contributions, entertainment, and social gatherings. Some aspects of lobbying are less direct. There are techniques such as contacting officials through their constituents and friends, publicizing the voting records of recalcitrant legislators, organizing letter writing and telegram campaigns, and conducting public relations programs.

In taking the requests of pressure groups into account (and those of political parties, fellow officials, popular opinion, and mass consensus as well) policy makers have considerably more maneuverability than most people think. It is not a process of pressure groups proposing and officials disposing. Sometimes the alleged pressure is no pressure at all, but simply a request for a fair hearing. In addition policy makers are free to decide what pressures they receive. Congressmen, for example, select the persons within their constituencies on whom to build a following; representatives of interest groups learn this and the image they form influences what kinds of messages any given representative or senator is likely to hear from them. Moreover, the very number and variety of interest groups liberates the policy maker from slavish dependence on any one or few for support, counsel, and assistance. In many instances a policy maker plays interests against one another, thus neutralizing the pressure. Simply put, a policy maker consciously and unconsciously determines what he hears, thus providing considerable discretion in fashioning his image of the public opinion of the Few.[34]

Listening to Fellow Officials. Not all organized interests lie outside the offices of government. Policy makers form alliances to press for advantages on their own behalf, to obtain advice and counsel, and to conduct the work of the departments, agencies, bureaus, legislative bodies, committees, subcommittees, or other offices of which they are members. Frequently policy makers are more sensitive to communication from fellow officials than to messages from the populace, mass, or external organized and unorganized interests.

It is important to keep in mind that policy makers usually have far more in common with one another as fellow politicians and officials than they do with their constituents, party loyalists, or members of pressure groups. For the most part elective, appointive, and career officials are similar in social background (education, social opportunities, etc.); current circumstances of occupation, income, residence, and responsibilities; and even leisure pursuits. Compared to the bulk of the population they are a fairly unrepresentative sampling—older, usually male, better educated, more apt to have professional backgrounds and higher incomes, and more likely Protestant. Certainly they are more politically active, involved, and interested than most of their constituents. And they are likely to hold political beliefs, values, and expectations different from those of the general population.[35]

Although there may be instances where "opposites attract," among policy makers "birds of a feather flock together." Small wonder that they turn to one another for help in constructing images of public opinion and how to act accordingly. Thus, for example, "congressmen develop an implicit roster of fellow congressmen whose judgment they respect, whose viewpoint they normally share, and to whom they can turn for guidance on particular topics of the colleague's competence. Each congressman tends to follow the lead, not of any one person, but of a roster of specific colleagues sorted by topics."[36] Like the fan at the race track who has no possible way to know about all horses before placing his bets, the policy maker cannot know all of the technical aspects and potential consequences of every policy; he relies, therefore, not on the horse, but the jockey—competent colleagues sorted out by topics and including fellow administrators, congressional officials, judicial officers, assistants, staff members, and civil servants.

The principle of separation of powers in the American constitutional structure allocates certain executive and legislative authorities to separate institutions. One result is that policy makers in separated administrative agencies and Congress frequently grapple with identical policy problems such as formulation of energy policy, protection of the environment, defense spending, and myriad other substantive areas. The shared policy interests and responsibilities of officials promote the formation of policy coalitions crossing institutional lines. Members of congressional committees on energy questions, for example, work closely with administrators in the Department of Energy. Members of both policy-making bodies communicate with representatives of the nuclear, natural gas, oil, and other energy-related industries. The consequence of overlapping policy concerns further entangles the lines of communication joining policy makers with the opinions of the One, the Many, and the Few through a network of administrative bureau-congressional committee-interest group transactions.

POLICY MAKING: SELECTIVE CONVERGENCE, SOCIAL CONTROL, OR NEGOTIATION?

Through this book we have discussed three principal answers to the question "how is society possible?" One is that people freely acting as individuals select courses of action from a variety of options; when these self-selections converge, social order results. A second viewpoint argues that political leaders mold order by employing mechanisms of social control such as religious organizations, governments, economic sanctions, force, and propaganda to get members of groups to conform to identical lines of action. A third answer, and the one that best fits many of the arguments about human conduct in these pages, is that people collectively negotiate common meanings of things through their transactions. By fashioning expectations of one another's behavior, constructing their own behavior, and taking societal roles through mutual, reciprocal actions, people develop common images, or significant symbols, of concepts (liberty, equality, fraternity), institutions (presidency, Congress, Supreme Court), and people (leaders and followers). Through the continuous negotiation of significant symbols, therefore, shared meanings provide the substance of social order.

These three views of society parallel three models of how policy communication can be organized and policies made. These are the plebiscitory, rational-comprehensive, and adjustive models.

The Plebiscitory Model

A plebiscite is an election in which people vote directly on a proposal or program submitted to them by policy leaders. The election is more than a communication line between citizens and officials; it is a feature of policy making itself. Presented with the option of accepting or rejecting a policy, each voter makes a choice, and in the manner of converging individual selections, the votes constitute popular choice.

A popular referendum is an example of plebiscitory communication and policy making. In strict definition of the term, a referendum is an election permitting voters to reject a policy passed by a legislature; it stands in contrast to an initiative election offering voters the opportunity to pass laws over the opposition of a hostile legislature. More broadly construed, a referendum is any popular election on proposed policies. The first recorded use of the procedure was in 1780 with the adoption of the constitution of Massachusetts; during the era of the Populist movement at the turn of this century, several states adopted referenda procedures based upon Swiss models. To get an item on the ballot a minimum percentage of voters sign petitions; decision by the electorate follows. Now widely used in states and local communities, referenda place direct popular rule over passage of constitutional and charter amendments, prohibition, taxation, regulation of public utilities, water fluoridation, environmental policies, decisions regarding the construction of nuclear fission power plants, etc.

Given the opportunity to make policy by plebiscite, relatively few citizens avail themselves of it. Referenda elections generally have low turnouts and attract fewer voters than do local elections for public office. Although there are debates on the issues placed before the voters, few of the electorate pay much attention to the mass media or other sources of information about referenda issues. Personal influence exerted through interpersonal channels is slightly greater than the effects of the mass media, but the differences are sometimes negligible. Organizational channels provide potential sources of information as voluntary associations take stands on issues. Typically opposition groups are more visible than support groups. Generally, however, group appeals fail to catch the voters' attention and the impact is largely dependent upon whether voters identify with the groups in question.[37]

To increase the effectiveness of plebiscites in policy communication, advocates of direct democracy propose futuristic approaches utilizing modern media technology. Illustrative is the televote system, in which registered voters receive opposing views on an issue (through the mail, on cable television, in newspapers, etc.). Voters have a period of time, say a week, to declare their preferences by dialing certain numbers on the telephone. Citizens register as televoters by phone or mail and obtain individual televote numbers for dialing to insure that only one vote from each person will be counted.

Pilot projects have tested the televote in various parts of the nation. In San Jose, California in 1973–74, 4 percent of the eligible population (5500 persons) registered as televoters. Televote on nine issues important to the local school district took place in the test year. Voting rates were low, about 13 percent, yet were still greater than generally recorded in popular referenda in the district. Whether televote as a technological augmentation of plebiscitory democracy will encourage popular participation remains to be seen, but along with other futuristic approaches it may breathe new life into a policy-making institution of long duration in this nation.[38]

The Rational-Comprehensive Model

The plebiscitory model does not specify how policy makers arrive at the proposals they place before voters. The rational-comprehensive model purports to describe one way for organizing policy communication to achieve decisions. First, policy makers take into account a problem requiring action, a problem separated from other problem areas. Second, policy-makers clarify the goals, values, and objectives to be achieved in coping with the problem. Third, policy makers identify alternative solutions and investigate each; this investigation considers all information pertaining to the expected consequences of adopting any given solution. Fourth, policy makers weigh the relative costs and benefits of each alternative, compare the options, and choose the alternative that maximizes the goals, values, and objectives already agreed upon. The procedure is "rational" in choosing the most effective means to reach declared ends. It is "comprehensive" in considering every factor relevant to every option.[39]

Once policy makers select an option, they recruit the support of key institutions and opinion publics through propaganda, group leaders, enforcement procedures, etc. Thus, the rational-comprehensive procedure for policy formulation bears a close relationship to the social control approach to achieving order: people "get together to discuss courses of action for their mutual well-being, to share ideas, and to make concessions so that after due consideration they might act collectively. The object was to reach a consensus, agreed to largely by everyone."[40]

The model offers a tidy picture. Whether it is descriptive of how policy makers act or provides an adequate prescription for how they should act is questionable for several reasons. For one, reaching agreement on the critical significant symbols in the process—i.e., a shared meaning of the problem requiring solution, shared understandings of possible solutions, and consensus on the best alternative—is scarcely easy. Images of problems, goals, values, objectives, solutions, ends, and means all arise through communication and do not exist independently of policy makers to be gathered like eggs from a chicken coop. Additionally, the model outlines a comprehensive process of communication in which no information escapes the policy makers who are fashioning reliable expectations of the likely consequences of each policy alternative. Seldom does even the most static- and distortion-free communication technology have such fidelity. Finally, assuming the agreed policy reflects a "best" solution, we know enough about persuasion to realize that convincing the populace of it (so that they will either vote for it in a plebiscite, or simply acquiese to it through obedient behavior) involves more than public instruction on the merits of the policy and the demerits of its alternatives.

The Adjustive Model

The bulk of the day-to-day relationships between policy makers and between them and their constituents, like the everyday lives of most of us, involves bargaining and compromise. This does not imply that policy makers avoid the difficult and time-consuming tasks of specifying problems, clarifying goals, values, and objectives, anticipating consequences, choosing among options, and convincing others of the wisdom of compliance. But all of those activities involve a collective process of people communicating *with* one another rather than *to* one another, of adjusting to subjective judgments rather than coolly assessing objective criteria, discussing the meaning of problems, goals information, solutions, and negotiating compliance rather than imposing it.

The adjustive model accepts the everyday world of contingencies and undiscovered possibilities, of perceived givens and inevitabilities. Bauer et al. sum it up neatly in describing the making of policies respecting foreign trade:

> At some point, it was possible to say that an issue existed, though how it arose was not always clear. . . . Not only may the formulation of a problem not have taken place deliberately, but the decision also may not have been deliberate. Under the pressure of circumstances, a man does something that seems small, and suddenly he finds himself committed to something much larger than he envisioned. He may give a small speech and suddenly find himself a spokesman. Or the actions of subordinates may create conditions which determine his line of action. His decision is to recognize the inevitable.[41]

The adjustive model has many variations, some overlapping, some distinct—"muddling through," incrementalism, mixed scanning, etc.[42] The key feature is that defining problems, selecting ends and means, achieving compliance, and evaluating results all overlap. Policy making is not merely a matter of devising effective means to reach known and shared ends. Rather, it is a simultaneous search for meaningful goals and ways of achieving them under conditions where disagreement on both is widespread. In contrast to rational-comprehensive approaches, the adjustive model posits a search not for "best" policies but for workable ones, asking not what is a good policy but what a policy is good for. There is no pretense that all information regarding policy alternatives and their consequences can be analyzed in detail; only relevant consequences (as imagined by policy makers) can be assessed, and even those only partially. Proposed policies are less likely to be evaluated on a cost-benefit basis than by a process of successively comparing each proposal to perceived successes and failures of existing policies to cope with related problems. Policies are less likely to be perfect than acceptable.

Consideration of the plebiscitory, rational-comprehensive, and adjustive approaches to policy making, including the role that political communication plays in each, raises again the question that must be examined in asking if social order derives from policy making: How clear-cut is the relationship of public opinion to public policy?

THE PROBLEMATIC CHARACTER OF THE OPINION-POLICY RELATIONSHIP

There is no one-to-one correspondence between what people think and what government does, and for reasons touched upon in this and earlier chapters, it is unlikely that there will be, either in the present or distant future. Following is a recapitulation of the principal reasons for the problematic character of a close congruence between public opinion and public policy in the United States.

Expressed Opinions Represent Personal Constructions of Things Taken into Account

Recall from Chapters 1 and 7 that there are at least three overlapping phases in the construction of public opinion—personal, social, and political. Personal and social constructions are especially intertwined. To repeat, human beings act toward objects on the basis of the meaning those objects have for them; at the same time they construct those meanings through their actions. This joint process of constructing acts and meanings is not something a person does in isolation from others. It is a collective enterprise involving social transactions. The personal construction of opinions is joint activity which includes the formation of expectations of how other people act toward things, and acting toward the imagined behavior of others as well as toward the objects themselves. It is in this sense that opinions emerge from personal constructions of things people take into account.

In politics opinions derive primarily from taking into account the persuasive messages of communicators (politicians, professionals, and activists) acting in the role of political leaders. Whether or not expressed opinions represent faithfully the full range of beliefs, values, and expectations that people have about public matters depends initially then upon two factors: (1) what messages political leaders inject into the arena of public discourse, both with respect to the items leaders place on the public agenda and the language and style of talk they use to place them there, and (2) how people take those messages into account—perceive, interpret, and construct meaningful images of them. In sum, personal construction of public opinion is highly selective; it represents neither everything people *opine* nor *opine about* in politics.

The Three Faces of Public Opinion Represent Different, Often Contradictory, Social Constructions

The public opinion of the One, the Few, and the Many offer governing officials considerable latitude in defining and responding to perceived public demands. Moreover, to shift the metaphor, the much acclaimed (in democratic theory) "voice of public opinion" speaks not only with a forked tongue but one with three prongs attached. A one-to-one correspondence between what specialized opinion publics propose and governments dispose does not always imply a similar correspondence between popular opinion and public policy. We have seen examples such as popular support for more strict firearm regulations blunted by the antigun lobby, popular opposition to a policy of forced busing to promote racial integration, etc. Nor are mass and popular voices in unison; popular rejection of the proposition that "I would be willing to have a black family live next door to me" strikes a discordant note to mass consensus that "under our democratic system people should be allowed to live where they please if they can afford it."[43] Thus, the social construction of public opinion is also highly selective, sometimes "sending them a message" from the One, sometimes from the Many, and often from the Few.

Policy Makers Are Selective in the Political Constructions They Take into Account

Policy makers also construct opinions, by constructing images of their constituents and their views. They represent these images in policy making. How well do the policy-makers' images of what their constituents think, feel, and propose measure up to the constituents' opinions? Studies supply tentative answers. Luttbeg reports that political leaders differ from members of the general citizenry on a broad range of beliefs and preferences about issues important to selected local communities such as taxes, metropolitan growth, or recreation facilities.[44] Hedlund and Friesema find that state legislators do not have a very accurate picture of how their constituents feel on referenda issues; moreover, legislators with close ties to political parties and interest groups are scarcely more sensitive to constituents' views than those without close bonds.[45] And studies of congressional policy makers indicate that only on certain kinds of issues— civil rights more than social welfare or foreign policy questions—do congressmen consider their perceptions of what constituents' might think to be important in casting roll call votes.[46] Finally, elections are more likely to be indirect than direct communicators of policy mandates: "In short, the vote per se may not carry much information about citizen preferences, and elections themselves may not be capable of dealing with the vast array of specific problems faced by citizens and groups. . . ."[47] Yet the elected representatives' perceptions and opinions are more strongly associated with the views of people who vote to elect him than they are with the opinions of the constituency as a whole; in addition, roll call votes of defeated incumbents correlate negatively with constituency opinions, those of victors correlate positively. In sum, policy makers' constructions of public opinion vary; in highly selective ways they filter from the chorus of competing voices the tones they find most helpful in the day-to-day orchestration of governing.

Policy Makers Negotiate Policy Views: They Do Not Register Those of Any Single Constituency

The general indifference to plebiscitory policy making by Americans, the difficulties of rational-comprehensive approaches, and day-to-day requirements of getting on with the job of governing result in compromise and bargaining. Even in the unlikely event that policy makers have a clear and accurate view of constituents' opinions, the policy making process itself makes it difficult to follow the perceived dictates or will of public opinion. Representatives negotiate meanings of one another's demands and the relation of those demands to what their constituents want and what their opponents' constituents insist upon. As a result the views reflected in any piece of legislation, executive order, administrative act, or judicial decision are rarely identical to the private views of any single official or interest. A policy, in essence, is more than the sum of its parts.

Policies Influence Personal, Social, and Political Constructions of Public Opinion

If in politics the personal and social construction of public opinion relies in part upon what citizens perceive that political leaders talk about, it stands to reason that governments do more than merely respond to what people think, feel, and propose; governments guide the construction of personal beliefs, values, and expectations as well. Even in the unlikely event of a one-to-one correspondence of public opinion to public policy, one could not say for sure that policy decisions reflect rather than shape public demands.

We have seen in previous chapters (3 and 4 especially) that political communicators acting as policy leaders try to generate favorable citizens' images of government by suggesting (1) that citizens influence policy making: elections of candidates and referenda reinforce such perceptions, exhortive language urges that it is important to take sides on issues, legal language builds public respect for bureaucratic specialists and experts, and bargaining language offers the impression of cooperation between public officials and special interests in public interest; (2) that certain forces —dissidents and "malcontents"—and actions—prostitution, gambling, liquor or marijuana consumption—are evil and must be closely watched; (3) that other groups are friendly, benevolent, or benign—foreign allies, established business, corporate and governing elites, and citizens who respect the law regardless of content; and (4) that political leaders can and will cope in the public interest with issues, forces, and events that concern and bewilder the masses.[48] Beyond trying to recruit the diffuse support of citizens for the political regime, policy makers also strive to sell the public on specific decisions:

> Government, as we have seen, attempts to mold public opinion toward support of the programs and policies it espouses. Given that endeavor, a perfect congruence between public policy and public opinion could be government of public opinion rather than government by public opinion. . . . Yet it is plain that on the American scene congruence between action and public preference results from the flow of influence to as well as from government.[49]

Conclusion: Government by and of Public Opinion: The Discontinuous Continuum Revisited

We return in this discussion to where we began in Chapter 1. The communication-opinion process and its attendant opinion-policy relationship is complex, varying, dynamic, and circular. The relationship of public opinion and public policy is a paradoxical "discontinuous continuum."[50] Some lines of communication between citizens and officials are direct, immediate, and static free. Others are less direct but collaborate in presenting a shared understanding to both citizen and official of each other's meaning. Still others are broken, partial, competing, and overloaded; neither citizen nor official can get through to the other.

Politics, we said, is the regulation of social conduct under conditions of conflict. The character of that regulation is continuing negotiation—

negotiations of the *meanings* of the roles of leaders, followers, and non-followers; of political talk, symbols, and languages; of propaganda, advertising, and rhetoric; of channels, media, and techniques of political communication; of mass, group, and popular opinion; of the political self; of ways of taking part in politics, including voting and elections; and of the choices policy officials face and make. Disputes, disagreements, and conflicts invalidate guarantees of social order, if indeed such guarantees could even be made. Instead of guarantees we have politics, efforts to negotiate significant symbols by thinking, feeling, proposing (i.e., minded) people collectively working for order in their everyday lives.

As is often the case, the novelist expresses it best. In *The Just and the Unjust*, American writer James Gould Cozzens put it this way:[51]

> "Nobody promises you a good time or an easy time. I don't know who it was who said when we think of the past we regret and when we think of the future we fear. And with reason. But no bets are off. There is the present to think of and as long as you live there always will be. In the present every day is a miracle. The world gets up in the morning and is fed and goes to work, and in the evening it comes home and is fed again and perhaps has a little amusement and goes to sleep. To make that possible, so much has to be done by so many people that, on the face of it, it is impossible. Well, every day we do it; and every day, come hell, come high water, we're going to have to go on doing it as well as we can."
>
> "So it seems," said Abner.
>
> "Yes, so it seems," said Judge Coates, "and so it is, and so it will be! And that's where you come in. That's all we want of you."
>
> Abner said, "What do you want of me?"
>
> "We just want you to do the impossible," Judge Coates said.

Have we government by public opinion? Partially. Have we government of public opinion? Partially. Is there perfect congruence between public opinion and public policy? No. Can there be? It is problematic, at least given the character of social conflicts that give rise to policy making. But if such a one-to-one correspondence is even to be approached it will come as a result not of politics as the art of the possible, but of political communication, the art of negotiating the impossible.

BIBLIOGRAPHY

A large number of works attempt to describe the linkages between public opinion and public policy. Far fewer describe the role of communication in policy making, something that is surprising given the current emphasis in political science on the study of public policy. Most of the works in the category of linkages view the opinion-policy relationship primarily as a one-way street, i.e., asking how public opinion influences policy making. For a two-way perspective, however, readers should consult V. O. Key, Jr., and his still insightful text, *Public Opinion and American Democracy* (New York: Alfred A. Knopf, 1961). Readers will also profit from consulting Norman R. Luttbeg's edited volume, *Public Opinion and Public Policy* (Homewood, Ill.: The Dorsey Press, 2nd ed., 1974), especially the introductory essay, pp. 1–10, containing Luttbeg's description of various models of the opinion-policy relationship. For a review of the ideas and works bearing upon how public opinion reaches policy makers, a useful source is the learning module prepared by Philip F. Beach, *Public Access to Policymaking in the United States* (Morristown, N.J.: General Learning Press, 1974). A more recent and lengthy treatment of the problem is Robert Weissberg's *Public Opinion and Popular Government* (Englewood Cliffs, N.J.: Prentice-Hall, 1976). Weissberg explores the congruence between popular opinion (as measured by polls) and public policy in several areas covering a span from 1936 to 1974.

A growing number of monographs, each typically less than 200 pages in length, describe the major outlines of policy making in the United States. One of the first of the genre was Charles E. Lindblom's *The Policy-Making Process* (Englewood Cliffs, N.J.: Prentice-Hall Inc., 1968). Lindblom describes the linkage role of various policy-related institutions—elections, political parties, interest groups, etc. In *An Introduction to the Study of Public Policy* (Belmont, Cal.: Wadsworth Publishing Co., 2nd ed., 1977) Charles O. Jones incorporates notions of John Dewey and Harold Lasswell into the study of public policy. For a review of a variety of approaches to studying policy making (including theories of decision-making, policy analysis, aspects of policy evaluation, etc.) see James E. Anderson, *Public Policy-Making* (New York: Praeger Publishers, 1975).

A few works raise, either explicitly or implicitly, significant questions about how policy makers communicate with one another and with the general public. Readers would do well to consult the useful primer by Roger W. Cobb and Charles D. Elder, *Participation in American Politics: The Dynamics of Agenda-Building* (Boston: Allyn and Bacon, 1972). A detailed account of the role of communication in one area of policy making, foreign trade, is contained in Raymond A. Bauer, et al., *American Business and Public Policy* (New York: Atherton Press, 1963). Readers should also pursue two extremely valuable, succinct accounts: E. E. Schattschneider, *The Semisovereign People* (New York: Holt, Rinehart and Winston, 1960) and J. Leiper Freeman, *The Political Process* (New York: Random House, rev. ed., 1965).

Whether public opinion affects policy making depends in large measure on whether and how it is something officials take-into-account. A principle work dealing with that problem, at least in one area of policy, is Bernard Cohen, *The Public's Impact on Foreign Policy* (Boston: Little, Brown, 1973). In *The Sociology and Politics of Congress* (Chicago: Rand McNally, 1969), Lewis Anthony Dexter tries to answer the question "Whom do congressmen pay attention to?" Also with respect to Congress there are three helpful discussions: Aage R. Clausen, *How Congressmen Decide: A Policy Focus* (New York: St. Martin's Press, 1973); Charles L. Clapp, *The Congressman: His Work as He Sees It* (Washington: The Brookings Institution, 1963); and Roger H. Davidson, *The Role of the Congressman* (New York: Pegasus, 1969). Books describing the relationships between executive, administrative, and judicial arms of government and public opinion are listed in the bibliographies accompanying Chapters 5 and 6 of this text.

NOTES

1. See Bernard C. Hennessy, *Public Opinion* (North Scituate, Mass.: Duxbury Press, 3rd ed., 1975), p. 14, and James N. Rosenau, *Public Opinion and Foreign Policy* (New York: Random House, 1961).

2. V. O. Key, Jr., *Public Opinion and American Democracy* (New York: Alfred A. Knopf, 1961), pp. 409–10.

3. Carl J. Friedrich, *Constitutional Government and Democracy* (Waltham, Mass.: Blaisdell Publishing Co., 4th ed., 1968), p. 278.

4. Philip F. Beach, *Public Access to Policymaking in the United States* (Morristown, N.J.: General Learning Press, 1974). p. 2.

5. Louis Anthony Dexter, *The Sociology and Politics of Congress* (Chicago: Rand McNally and Co., 1969), p. 151.

6. Benjamin Ginsberg, "Elections and Public Policy," *American Political Science Review*, 70 (March 1976): 41–49.

7. Joseph A. Schumpeter, *Capitalism, Socialism, and Democracy* (New York: Harper Torchbook, 1962), p. 269.

8. V. O. Key, Jr., *The Responsible Electorate* (Cambridge, Mass.: Belknap Press, 1966).

9. Murray Edelman, *The Symbolic Uses of Politics* (Urbana: University of Illinois Press, 1964), p. 17.

10. Ronald E. Weber and William R. Shaffer, "Public Opinion and American State Policy-Making," *Midwest Journal of Political Science*, 16 (November 1972): 683–99.

11. Roger H. Davidson, *The Role of the Congressman* (New York: Pegasus, 1969) and "Public Prescriptions for the Job of Congressman," *Midwest Journal of Political Science*, 14 (November 1970): 648–667.

12. James R. Beniger, "Winning the Presidential Nomination: National Polls and State Primary Elections, 1936–1972," *Public Opinion Quarterly*, 40 (Spring 1976): 22–38.

13. David Easton, *A Systems Analysis of Political Life* (New York: John Wiley and Sons, 1965).

14. Robert Lehnen, *American Institutions, Political Opinion, and Public Policy* (Hinsdale, Ill.: Dryden Press, 1976), p. 100.

15. *The Harris Survey*, March 27, 1976.

16. Roger W. Cobb and Charles D. Elder, *Participation in American Politics: The Dynamics of Agenda-Building* (Boston: Allyn and Bacon, 1972), Ch. 9.

17. See Delmer D. Dunn, *Public Officials and the Press* (Reading, Mass.: Addison-Wesley, 1969) and Bernard C. Cohen, *The Press and Foreign Policy* (Princeton: Princeton University Press, 1963).

18. Joseph R. Gusfield, "The Study of Social Movements," *International Encyclopedia of the Social Sciences* (New York: Crowell, Collier, and Macmillan, 1968), 445–52; Lewis M. Killian, "Social Movements," in Robert E. L. Faris, ed., *Handbook of Modern Sociology* (Chicago: Rand McNally, 1964), pp. 426–55.

19. Donald J. Devine, *The Attentive Public* (Chicago: Rand McNally, 1970).

20. Ibid., p. 119.

21. Lehnen, *American Institutions, Political Opinion, and Public Policy*, pp. 185–190.

22. John Dewey, *The Public and Its Problems* (Denver: Alan Swallow, 1927).

23. Norman R. Luttbeg, *Public Opinion and Public Policy* (Homewood, Ill.: Dorsey Press, 2nd ed., 1974).

24. Gerald M. Pomper, *Elections in America* (New York: Dodd, Mead, 1968).

25. Herbert McClosky, et al., "Issue Conflict and Consensus among Party

Leaders and Followers," *American Political Science Review,* 54 (June 1960): 406–27; John W. Soule and James W. Clarke, "Issue Conflict and Consensus: A Comparative Study of Democratic and Republican Delegates to the 1968 National Conventions," *Journal of Politics,* 23 (February 1971): 72–91.

26. Samuel J. Eldersveld, *Political Parties* (Chicago: Rand McNally, 1964).

27. Jeff Fischel, *Party and Opposition* (New York: David McKay, 1973); John L. Sullivan and Robert E. O'Connor, "Electoral Choice and Popular Control of Public Policy: The Case of the 1966 House Elections," *American Political Science Review,* 66 (December 1972): 1256–68.

28. Aage R. Clausen, *How Congressmen Decide: A Policy Focus* (New York: St. Martin's Press, 1973).

29. Pomper, *Elections in America,* p. 202.

30. See Gabriel A. Almond and Sidney Verba, *The Civic Culture* (Princeton: Princeton University Press, 1963) and Sidney Verba and Norman H. Nie, *Participation in America* (New York: Harper and Row, 1972).

31. E. E. Schattschneider, *The Semisovereign People* (New York: Holt, Rinehart and Winston, 1960), Ch. 2.

32. Lester W. Milbrath, *The Washington Lobbyists* (Chicago: Rand McNally, 1963).

33. Dexter, *The Sociology and Politics of Congress,* p. 166.

34. Raymond A. Bauer, et al., *American Business and Public Policy* (New York: Atherton Press, 1963), Part 5.

35. Thomas R. Dye, *Who's Running America?* (Englewood Cliffs, N.J.: Prentice-Hall, 1976).

36. Bauer, et al., *American Business and Public Policy,* p. 437.

37. For a review of findings regarding how people vote in referenda see Alvin Boskoff and Harmon Zeigler, *Voting Patterns in a Local Election* (New York: J. B. Lippincott, 1964).

38. Vincent N. Campbell, *The Televote System for Civic Communication: First Demonstration and Evaluation* (Palo Alto, Cal.: American Institutes for Research, 1974).

39. Charles E. Lindblom, "The Science of Muddling Through," *Public Administration Review,* 19 (Spring 1959): 79–88.

40. William Stephenson, *The Play Theory of Mass Communication* (Chicago: University of Chicago Press, 1967), p. 34.

41. Bauer, et al., *American Business and Public Policy,* p. 482.

42. For a discussion of the variations on the theme see James E. Anderson, *Public Policy-Making* (New York: Praeger Publishers, 1975).

43. Ira Sharkansky, *The United States: A Study of a Developing Country* (New York: David McKay, 1975), p. 116.

44. Norman R. Luttbeg, "The Structure of Beliefs among Leaders and the Public," *Public Opinion Quarterly,* 32 (Fall 1968): 398–409.

45. Ronald D. Hedlund and H. Paul Friesema, "Representatives' Perceptions of Constituency Opinion," *Journal of Politics,* 34 (August 1972): 730–52.

46. Warren E. Miller and Donald E. Stokes, "Constituency Influence in Congress," *American Political Science Review,* 67 (March 1963): 45–56.

47. Verba and Nie, *Participation in America,* p. 326.

48. Murray Edelman, *Politics as Symbolic Action* (Chicago: Markham Publishing Co., 1971), pp. 36–41.

49. Key, *Public Opinion and American Democracy,* pp. 422–23.

50. Oliver Garceau, "Research in the Political Process," *American Political Science Review,* 45 (March 1951): 69–85.

51. James Gould Cozzens, *The Just and the Unjust,* (New York: Harcourt, Brace and World, 1942), p. 434.

Appendix

The Study of Political Communication and Public Opinion

Behavioral scientists examine political communication and public opinion in a variety of ways. They employ numerous methods, techniques, and approaches to enhance understanding of human beliefs, values, and expectations. The purpose of this appendix is not to provide a mini-text in the methods and techniques of social investigation, but to give the reader a background suitable for appraising the plethora of studies cited in this book. A few readers may bemoan the fact that there are so many ways to investigate human conduct, wishing instead that a single mode of analysis were sufficient. Unfortunately that is not the case. Rather, each method, technique, and approach has its special uses. A combination—plus the derivation of new tools of inquiry—is essential to extend comprehension of how people communicate in politics.

DIVERSITY OF METHODS

There are a host of different methods to study political communication and public opinion. We will describe six—aggregate, survey, experimental, ex post facto, content analytical, and ethnomethodological studies. Frequently the methods associated with each overlap and appear in conjunction in a single investigation. After briefly distinguishing the six varieties, the appendix will then describe the principal techniques common to one or more of them, techniques employed to gather, process, analyze, and interpret evidence.[1]

Aggregate Studies

One of the oldest and most useful ways of studing political behavior is through the use of aggregate data, which pertains to collections or categories of individuals (say all persons 18 to 20 years of age) rather than particular individuals. A leading example of this mode of inquiry is "Social Determinism and Electoral Decision: The Case of Indiana," by V. O. Key, Jr. and Frank Munger.[2] One of the authors' concerns was to describe traditional patterns of party voting in Indiana. A way of doing so was to compare the percentage of the total vote received by each of the two major parties in the presidential elections of 1868 and 1900 *in each county*. The units of analysis were thus aggregates of voters, i.e., each Indiana county. In addition to examining partisan voting alignments on a county by county basis, the authors compared these partisan patterns to selected social characteristics of counties, looking at stability and shifts in voting patterns in large and small populated counties, urban and rural counties, predominantly Protestant and Catholic counties, etc. Using aggregate data, Key and Munger demonstrated that social characteristics of the electorate alone are not a sufficient explanation of how voters shift from party to party over a four-year period. This suggested an emphasis on distinctly political factors not directly related to social determinism.

Political scientist Austin Ranney refers to aggregate studies as the "ecological study of electoral behavior" seeking to "understand the interrelationships of political parties and voters with one another and with the social and legal environment in which they act."[3] Researchers typically juxtapose voting patterns with a wide variety of political, social, and economic data about electoral districts and their populations (data most frequently derived from published reports or computer tapes available from the U.S. Bureau of the Census). As Ranney observes, investigators generally attempt to explain political behavior "in terms of what the particular author regards as significant correlations," either of a mathematical or "common sense" variety.[4]

Aggregate methods have advantages and disadvantages. Among the advantages is the fact that aggregate statistics are generally available about a wide variety of electoral units from election and census statistics; the focus is upon how populations actually voted rather than on vote intention, preference, recollections of voting behavior, or related attitudes; and contemporary computer technology makes the processing of vast amounts of aggregate data relatively easy and inexpensive. On the debit side is the inability of researchers to say how individuals think, feel, and act by looking at the behavior of whole populations. To do so risks the "ecological fallacy," the false notion that reliable accounts of individual behavior derive from correlating aggregate data. In a precinct composed of 80 percent Protestants where voters cast 70 percent of their ballots for Republicans, a researcher can speak of the tendency of a Protestant precinct to vote Republican but not of the behavior of any given individual, Protestant or non-Protestant, Republican or Democrat.

Survey Studies

The bulk of information about public opinion comes from studies utilizing survey methods, a means of gathering data about a large number of people by interviewing a few of them.[5] The researcher defines a "population" or group of persons for study (as, for example, all Americans of voting age); then, employing one of several available procedures derives a representative sample of that population. A representative sample assures that the conclusion drawn about people in the sample applies to the whole population (within calculable margins of error) and not merely to persons who happen to be sampled. There are technical problems surrounding survey studies—whom to sample, what to ask them, when to interview and how often, where to conduct a survey, and how to analyze the resulting data. A later section of this appendix examines each of these in detail. It suffices here to say that (a) the focus in survey studies, in contrast to aggregate studies, is usually upon individual beliefs, values, and conduct rather than the behavior of collectivities; but (b) there is often an effort to generalize from sampled opinions to the whole population; and therefore, (c) the accent is upon the distribution of views in a population and the association of those views with selected demographic, social, economic, psychological, political, and other characteristics of individuals. These characteristics make survey studies especially useful in generating self-action and inter-action (see Chapters 1 and 11) interpretations of conduct. The principal disadvantages of large-scale surveys lie in their expense and the tendency to sacrifice in-depth analyses of individual cases to achieve representative sampling or statistical accuracy.

Experimental Studies

The experimental method has been basic to scientific inquiry for so long that many persons equate science with experimental study.[6] In the classical experimental design researchers assign "subjects" to "test" (or "treatment") and "control" groups. (The details of the selection and assignment are in a subsequent section.) Each group's members express their views in interviews, by way of questionnaires, or through some other technique. Investigators then expose test groups to selected stimuli (for example, a persuasive message) but do not expose members of the control group. Finally, both groups are retested to measure the differences in views of each group's members; this provides indicators of any changes in the test group resulting from the exposure to selected stimuli. Researchers must, of course, guard against contamination of the experiment lest uncontrolled, extraneous factors influence the results.

Experiments typically use a relatively small number of subjects in contrast to the larger numbers in survey research. Whereas the costs associated with survey research limit the number of surveys undertaken, experiments can be repeated, each time varying selected subjects, treatments, and conditions. Thus, the experimenter builds confidence in his findings by repetitions under controlled conditions rather than through large numbers of subjects. He is less interested in describing the *distribution* of opinions and attributes of a population than the problem of whether a *given stimulus* under *given conditions* yields a *predicted effect*. The factors which influence changes in beliefs, values, and expectations are especially susceptible to detection through experimentation.[7]

One problem with experiments is that they frequently place persons in artificial situations far removed from the everyday events people take into account in constructing their behavior. It is difficult to translate the findings of many experiments (such as those pertaining to the effects of persuasive communication reported in Chapter 4) into "real world" terms. In political studies, for example, it may be misleading to isolate members of a control group from the world so as to measure effects of political communication upon a test group. To overcome some of these difficulties researchers modify the classical pretest-posttest design and utilize a quasi-experiment without a control group. In many cases field experiments in natural settings are possible. Or it may be necessary to utilize only a posttest (see the description of ex post facto studies below). In sum, experiments can be adjusted to political realities. So long as investigators both explain the problems associated with quasi-experimental research and interpret the findings accordingly, such adjustments do not sacrifice the usefulness of such studies.

Ex Post Facto Studies

Much of the raw material for the study of political communication and public opinion, i.e., human acts, occurs under uncontrolled, even unanticipated, circumstances. Voting, taking part in a political campaign, following public affairs, joining a political group, writing a public official—all are acts researchers seldom control.[8] Moreover, if it is true that the process of interpretation individuals use to construct beliefs, values, and conduct is but a segment of a communication process that cannot be explained simply as the interaction of independent and dependent variables, then researchers need to examine political behavior as they find it and not manipulate what they presume controls it. Finally, the democratic ethic generally frowns upon the notion of direct controls over political behavior, a further impediment to experimentation in the classic manner. It is no surprise, then, that ex post facto studies abound.

As noted, ex post facto studies are related to experimental research, yet there is a basic difference. In experiments researchers deal with the problem of "if x, then y" by predicting y from a controlled x, then observing to see if y occurs. In ex post facto studies, y is observed and the researcher must backtrack to find an x that serves as the most plausible explanation for y.[9] The manipulative control over "independent" variables (x's) that produce changes in "dependent" variables (y's) characterizing the classic experiment is missing from ex post facto studies.

By and large ex post facto studies use combinations of methods outlined in this section (especially with aggregate and survey research). Most of what we know, for example, about the effects of various campaign techniques on voting are derived from surveys and field experiments asking people their vote preferences, correlating preferences with their exposure to the campaign, controlling in a statistical fashion for intervening variables such as standing party loyalties, ideological predilections, etc. Or, a recent study examined the effects upon voting participation of removing the poll tax as a requirement by comparing the voting and registration records of individuals in elections before and after the removal of the poll tax.[10] It thus looked first at the vote and then traced changing rates of participation (y) back to differing registration systems since, obviously, the researchers could not control the shift from one to another x.

Content Analysis

As discussed in Chapters 3 and 4, a key element in communication consists of the languages, symbols, and styles of exchanging messages, the "says what" of the Lasswell formula. Moreover, as Chapters 5 and 6 illustrate, this "says what" is important in interpreting the part played by the communications media in politics. Several studies analyze the content of this "says what" aspect of communications. Content analysis examines the manifest content of message in a systematic and quantitative manner. Studies identify and count the key words, terms and themes of messages to infer what is said, how it is said, changes in appeals, and the motives underlying the message.[11]

Content analysis can examine virtually any communication—speeches, written documents, photographs, newspapers, television programs,[12] body movements.[13] Given readily available data sources, content analysis is widely used. In recent years computer technology has augmented content analysis and made it easier to analyze the entire content of documents rather than samples (for instance all speeches of a political candidate rather than selected speeches or paragraphs of speeches).

As with any method there are limitations to content analysis. Take, for instance, the assumption that the manifest content of a message has the same meaning to its intended audiences as it has for an investigator, i.e., that researchers interpret the words, themes, and other signs as audiences do. This is not always so. Second, there is the assumption that the frequency of occurrences of selected content elements, or the intensity of their appearances, have important effects. This seems a reasonable assumption. Yet, there is no assurance that the "receiver" of a message gives priority either to repetition or intensity. Third, content analysis depends upon the formulation of appropriate categories for classifying words, themes, signs, etc. Content analysis is, therefore, no better than the system of categories that go into it. Finally, if as Marshall McLuhan insists (see Chapter 5) "the medium is the message," the content of the message alone may be less important than the oral, printed, or visual medium that transmits it. Limitations notwithstanding, content analysis is a valuable method for describing communication in a systematic fashion.

Ethnomethodological Studies

Ethnomethodology is a tongue-twisting word. It refers "to the study of the procedures (methodology) employed by everyday man (ethnics) in his effort to meaningfully cope with the world."[14] Ethnomethodologists start with the premise that the proper study of mankind is man. That study begins with finding out how people construct "reality" or the world "out there." In fact, to the ethnomethodologist "reality" does not exist apart from the way people imagine it through their interpretations. The workings of interpretative processes, not a presumed reality, are the subject of ethnomethodological studies.[15] By analyzing the accounts people give of their world (accounts in the form of interviews and questionnaires which the researcher regards as a collaborative effort between investigator and subject rather than an "objective" report), ethnomethodologists strive to find out how people interpret their world, the concepts they use to describe it, and the rules, norms, and meanings people daily take for granted in any social order.

The focus upon personal constructions of opinions is critical to inquiries employing ethnomethodological techniques. There is no effort to describe the social, political, economic, and other determinants of behavior as in aggregate studies. Nor is there an effort to describe the distribution of beliefs, values, and expectations among a large population as in survey research. And there is no attempt to detect the independent variables that change dependent ones as in experimental and ex post facto studies. Rather, interest is in the highly variable quality of personal interpretation. The resulting emphasis is upon a trans-action rather than self-action or inter-action view of human conduct. Compared to the number of studies utilizing other approaches to political communication and public opinion, those of an ethnomethodological perspective are distinctly in the minority.[16] Yet, there are a few. Karl Lamb's study of how members of twelve families in Orange County, California, construct their political opinions is but one example.[17]

Precisely what it seeks to do—i.e., understand personal construction—limits what ethnomethodology can do. The emphasis upon the individual makes it difficult to generalize to larger social units. Moreover, the collaborative relationship of interviewer and interviewee leads to difficulty in replicating findings; indeed, there is no reason to expect, given the assumptions made about human conduct by ethnomethodologists, that any dynamic personal construction or interpretation can be captured in precisely the same way twice. These restrictions aside, the method holds promise for investigating how people make sense of political messages in their daily lives, what they attend to and what they take for granted as the "common sense" of news, public affairs, politics, etc., and how they construct their political behavior.

DIVERSITY OF TECHNIQUES

All of the methods described incorporate specific techniques for gathering, processing, analyzing, and interpreting information. Because many of the techniques are common to more than one method, we present a general discussion of key facets of research techniques, pointing out, as appropriate, variations associated with aggregate, survey, experimental, ex post facto, content analysis, or ethnomethodological studies. Specifically we look at decisions for whom to study, what to ask and how often, where research occurs, and how to do data analysis.

Who: Matters of Sampling

Each method typically used to study some aspect of political communication and public opinion requires that researchers first determine what subjects to examine. In all but content analysis these subjects are people; in content analysis they are selected portions of or total messages. Practical considerations (limited time, resources, etc.) render it unlikely that every participant in political communication—all communicators, messages, media personnel, and audience members—are included in a given study. Hence, researchers normally select a sample of persons to represent the population of participants for a given aspect of the communication process.

All of us pursue our daily lives by sampling portions of our environment. To discuss the views of others, we talk not to everyone but to only a few. And we scarcely watch all television programs, read all newspapers, visit all parts of the country, live in all houses and/or apartments, drive all cars, use all toothpastes, or eat all foods. As the dictionary says, a sample is "a portion, piece, or segment regarded as representative of the whole"; certainly the daily and total life experiences of each of us are but a sampling.

One of the problems with our "personal sampling"[18] is that, although our experiences represent something, we can't say very well what or how well. Our samples are usually haphazard. It is in this critical respect that personal sampling differs from the sampling undertaken by students of the communication-opinion process. Rather than just select anything or anybody for subjects, the latter generally draw samples that permit them to estimate how representative those portions are of the whole. There are two principal techniques for achieving this, probability and purposive sampling. A *probability* sample is selected in a way assuring that any subject has a known probability of being chosen. This criterion assists in estimating the accuracy of the sample and the risk involved in making inferences from it. A *purposive* sample affords no such assurrances about its representative quality. By and large, to make reliable inferences requires probability sampling; where the researcher seeks to study a population to discover new information and insights, purposive sampling suffices.

Employing probability methods, researchers obtain representative samplings of large populations, yet the samples themselves contain relatively few subjects. The key to whether a sample is representative is less the number of subjects selected than the manner of that selection: *"No major poll in the history of this country ever went wrong because too few persons were reached."*[19] There are two general approaches to the selection of subjects for probability samples. Ideally, to assure that every subject in the population has an equal chance of being chosen and that every segment of the population is proportionately represented, a researcher would list every member of the population to be sampled (say every adult of voting age), then draw the necessary number of subjects at random. Such a procedure is a simple random selection. It is rarely employed in studies of public opinion because of the difficulty of obtaining accurate listings of all members of a population. Moreover, from the practical standpoint of sampling people, random selection usually leads to wide geographic dispersal of subjects, thus increasing costs in time and travel for interviews. The second approach is a modification of the simple random technique called cluster sampling. Using this procedure researchers randomly select geographic areas that divide up the population to be sampled. They do this in a series of steps by first selecting large sized geographic clusters (say regions), then smaller areas (such as counties) within the randomly chosen clusters, then even smaller areas (perhaps precincts) within the second stage clusters, and so on until housing units and individuals within them are selected. The American Institute of Public Opinion, for example, uses an elaborate cluster sampling design to select approximately 300 geographic sampling points from 200,000 election districts. At each point there are five interviews, a total sample size of 1500 persons representing the adult civilian population living in the United States (except for those in institutions such as prisons or hospitals).[20]

What is the proper size for a sample? Four factors enter into calculation. First is the amount of variation within the population sampled. Suppose, for instance, we sample a bowl of soup by tasting each spoonful. If we were dealing with vegetable soup consisting of a variety of ingredients including peas, corn, beans, and meats, it would take several spoonfuls before we had tasted all its contents. But if we eat cream of tomato soup with its constancy of ingredients and texture, perhaps one spoonful would suffice to tell us that we wanted no more. Similarly, when a researcher samples a population of people, the more diversity (in partisanship, social class backgrounds, demographic characteristics, beliefs, values, expectations, etc.), the greater the number it takes to have a cross section of that heterogeneous mixture. The greater the variety in the population, therefore, the larger the required sample.

The second factor is the degree of error the researcher wants to tolerate in his sample. For instance, suppose the researcher finds that 20 percent of a sample of vegetable soup consists of peas. Does that figure represent the proportion of peas for the whole bowl? In any sample, no matter how carefully drawn, there is usually some error. For instance, 25 percent of the soup may be peas, although the taster finds only 20 percent. The connoisseur may find such inaccuracy intolerable, but a starving person might care less. The less the amount of error tolerable, the larger must be the sample size.

Third, the researcher must consider the confidence to be placed in concluding that if one drew another sample of the population it would supply approximately the same results as did the first. Confidence and tolerable error are closely related. The latter refers to how accurate the researcher wishes an estimate to be (whether 20 percent of the vegetable soup consists of peas); confidence refers to how certain one wishes to be that the estimate itself is accurate (that 20 percent of *any* spoonful of soup selected would be peas). Generally researchers like to be confident at least 95 percent of the time, preferably 99, that the composition of a sample could be replicated if other samples were selected. The higher the level of confidence desired, the larger must be the sample size.

These three factors in calculating the size of a probability sample can be summarized in a formula: $n = (v)z^2/e^2$ where n refers to the sample size, v the variance of the population, z a measure of level of confidence, and e a measure of tolerable error. As an example, suppose one seeks a sample of the population of a voting district. As an estimate of the diversity of the voting population, take past voting records, which indicate that the district is usually split 50–50 between Democrats and Republicans. To calculate the variance of that population we simply multiply the proportion Democrat (p) times that non-Democrats (q) so that $pq = .5(.5) = .25$. Thus $v = .25$ in the formula. The measure of level of confidence is a z-score. It is not necessary to describe its derivation here. Let it suffice to say that at a 99 percent level of confidence the z-score is 2.5758, 98 is 2.3267, 95 is 1.96 and 90 is 1.645. Assume a 95 percent level of confidence; thus $z = 1.96$ enters the formula. The measurement of tolerable error is simple. Assume that we want an estimate based upon the sample to be no more than ±5 percent in error (thus, if the sample indicates that 45 percent will vote for Candidate Roe, between 40 and 50 percent of the population would vote for Roe). Thereby $e = .05$. Hence, $n = (.25)\ 1.96^2/.05^2$, or $n = (.25)\ 3.842/.0025 = 384$. The required sample size is 384 persons. If we boosted our level of confidence to 99 percent, a sample size of 663 would be required. To have a 95 percent level of confidence, the following sample size would be required for each degree of accuracy: ±1 percent, 9,600; ±2, 2,400; ±3, 1,067; ±4, 600; ±6, 267; and ±7, 196.

The fourth consideration in estimating sample size cannot be entered into a formula. It consists of the cost of the survey to the researcher. Obviously, the more subjects to be studied, the greater the expense for sampling, interviewing (hiring interviewers, travel, etc.), processing data, and so forth. Large-sized sample surveys of several hundred persons are expensive undertakings. Despite what might be the most desirable sampling design, the investigator's research budget restricts what can be examined and how well.

Accurate portrayals of the distribution of opinions and/or attributes among a population require probability sampling. Most survey studies thus depend upon the techniques of probability sampling. By the same token considerations of probability enter into experimental studies. Recall that the classic experiment usually requires that subjects be selected and assigned to test and control groups. A requirement of that selection and assignment process is that it be random. A great deal of research pertaining to beliefs, values, and expectations, however, violates the requirement of random selection of subjects (college students enrolled in the experimenter's classes are frequently "self-selected" rather than randomly selected subjects). Once a set of subjects has been selected, however, random assignment to experimental groups is the norm.

For a variety of reasons (purpose of the research, potential costs, difficulties of drawing probability samples, etc.), purposive samples underlie much research in the communication-opinion process. A widely used technique of purposive sampling in the early days of public opinion polls was the quota sample. Pollsters would determine the general makeup of a population on the basis of estimates from census data. They would then determine what proportion of their sample should consist of people with a given attribute. For instance, if 15 percent of the population was 24 to 29 years of age, that percentage of the sample should be of the same age group. Interviewers were assigned a quota of respondents with specific attributes, something akin to a hunter seeking to bag his limit of quail. Such nonprobability procedures make tests of sample accuracy and levels of confidence inapplicable.

Certain types of purposive samples involving quotas, however, are valuable sources of insights. A leading example is the kind of samples used in conjunction with the research tool known as Q-methodology. In Q, relatively small samples of subjects (typically no more than 100) with known characteristics represent their opinions about a given object (person, event, idea, etc.) by rank-ordering several dozen separate statements pertaining to it according to which items most and least indicate their thoughts, feelings, and orientations.[21] Subjects in Q seldom represent populations in ways that guarantee that the distribution of opinions among the sample reflects a similar distribution in the population. Although one could employ probability techniques for sampling persons in Q studies, the typical approach is purposive. One variation, for instance, is the balanced sample, a sample consisting of an equal number of subjects of desired characteristics rather than a number proportionate to the distribution of attributes in the population. One might, for example, want to explore the possibility that Republicans, Independents, and Democrats construct different images of a political candidate. A Q study would select various statements about candidates that people might use in constructing such an image, then have equal numbers of each of the three partisan groups represent their images by sorting the statements. Through various statistical techniques (see below) the researcher can determine whether or not selected Republicans, Independents, and Democrats hold distinct images of certain candidates. The other frequently employed approach to sampling in Q is one of theoretical sampling. First, the researcher determines what attributes to represent in a sample of subjects. Assume a desire to represent partisanship (Republicans, Independents, and Democrats), sex, age (young, middle-aged, elderly), and income (high, middle, and low). These attributes can be placed in design as follows:

Attribute	Variation		
Partisanship	(a) Republican	(b) Independent	(c) Democrat
Sex	(d) Male	(e) Female	
Age	(f) Young	(g) Middle	(h) Elderly
Income	(i) High	(j) Medium	(k) Low

What the investigator wants to achieve is an equal representation of all possible combinations of these attributes and their varieties. The number of possible combinations is calculable: $3 \times 2 \times 3 \times 3 = 54$. To fill out this "quota" of combinations requires a Republican male who is young and of high income, a Republican female who is young of high income, a Republican male who is middle-aged of high income, and so on until all 54 combinations are present in the sample. For a sample size of 108 the researcher simply includes two of each combination, thus replicating combinations to achieve a sample of any size representative of predetermined attributes.

It is possible to combine the principles of probability and purposive sampling in various ways. Peter Rossi, for example, has argued that for some research purposes it is useful to abandon representative samples in favor of "factorial" samples. These sampling designs obtain specific types of subjects in given populations (much akin to theoretical sampling) without regard to their actual proportion in the total population under study. Random, nonbiased procedures can be used to select the actual subjects. The key is to use techniques that sample specific segments more heavily or lightly than their proportions in the total population warrant. The purpose is to assure that sufficient numbers of subjects of each variety would be included to make statistically reliable estimates of differences in opinions associated with varied attributes.[22]

As indicated earlier, questions of identifying and selecting subjects are relevant to all six categories of studies of political communication and public opinion (not just survey and experimental studies). Aggregate studies require a decision regarding which aggregates to study from among the thousands on which voting, census, and other statistics are available. Both ex post facto and ethnomethodological studies also must have a theory to guide the selection of subjects; the former more frequently employ probability techniques and the latter purposive samples. Finally, although computer technology has alleviated the problems considerably, the content analyst must work with representative portions of political messages, a requirement which again raises questions of sampling both messages and persons (communicators, media personnel, and audience members). With respect to messages, for example, the researcher must sample media (choose newspapers, television programs, radio presentations, speeches, or other sources), dates (the period of time to cover in a study), and content units (such as the paragraphs, sentences, phrases, or other portions of the message). Sometimes content analysis utilizes probability sampling by dividing a message into lines of print or minutes of programming, then randomly selecting portions. In other instances purposive sampling is the key, perhaps by sampling all editorials, all feature stories, all news columns or some combination.

What: The Questions Asked

Whatever the research method, as the investigator designs a sampling plan appropriate for theoretical purposes it is necessary to keep in mind what information is to be sought, i.e., what questions to ask.

There are two types of questions used to obtain data in most studies of political communication and public opinion, *open-ended* and *closed-ended* questions. Open-ended questions raise a general problem but do not suggest in the question itself any structure for the subject's response; people answer in their own language and organize responses freely. In contrast, closed-ended questions use detailed questionnaires with alternative responses so that the subject chooses among the options. Questions of this type yield responses that can be compared relatively easily across all subjects but necessarily force subjects to think in the researcher's categories rather than their own; open-ended questions provide opportunity for more freewheeling discourse, but it is difficult to classify highly diversified responses. The Gallup Poll illustrates the use of both types. A frequently asked open-ended question, for example, is "What do you think is the most important problem facing the U.S. today?" (see Chapter 8). A typical closed-ended question is "Which of these do you think is likely to be true of this year: a year of full employment or a year of rising unemployment?"

Open-ended questions accompany unstructured interviews. There are variations in this respect.[23] For instance, in the "focused" interview, the questioner directs the subject's attention to a topic by first asking a few general questions about it. As the interview proceeds the interrogator asks a planned sequence of questions ("probes" contained in a written "interview schedule") to elicit more specific responses and explore the subject's detailed beliefs, values, and expectations concerning the general topic. A second variation is the "clinical" interview, in which the questioning follows less of a planned pattern; the interviewer attempts to get a subject to talk freely about thoughts, feelings, and life experiences. This form is typical of research devoted to obtaining personal histories of a limited number of subjects, such as in psychiatric clinics. Even more unstructured is the "nondirective" interview. After raising a topic for discussion the interviewer does little more than encourage the subject to talk, occasionally asking "Why?" or suggesting "Tell me more."

Open-ended questioning is appropriate in surveys using both large and small samples (but is more frequent in the latter) and in ex post facto and ethnomethodological studies.[24] Ethnomethodologists such as Garfinkel, however, stress that regardless of how such interviews are structured, the interviewer is very much a part of the transaction between observer and observed.[25] At best the interviewer is only an imperfect recorder; moreover, his very presence is intrusive and an abnormal addition to a subject talking about making daily choices. In any interview the scientific observer runs the risk of imputing ideas to the respondent or the situation. Denzin suggests that "multiple observers and multiple methods, which overcome one another's restrictive biases, become the most valid and reliable strategies of observation" and "any observation based on the triangulation principle will yield data that are more reliable and valid than an investigation that is not so based."[26]

One partial way to triangulate is to combine open-ended and closed-ended questions in interviews. The Survey Research Center/Center for Political Studies of the University of Michigan follows such a procedure in nationwide election surveys. For example, SRC/CPS interviewers ask respondents open-ended questions about the presidential candidates: "Is there anything in particular about the candidate that might make you want to vote *for* him?" and "Is there anything in particular about the candidate that might make you want to vote *against* him?" Later, respondents rate the same candidate on a "feeling thermometer," a device marked in intervals from zero to one hundred degrees, to determine how warm or cool subjects are about office-seekers. The feeling thermometer is but one of many rating scales researchers use in closed-ended questions. A *rating scale,* technically referred to as an "attitude scale," is a set of alternative responses to a question, each of which can be given a numerical score. Only a few of the more commonly used rating scales will be cited here for illustration; for an elaboration of scaling theory and techniques the reader should consult one of many works on the subject.[27]

A principal rating scale used to study beliefs, values, and expectations is the method of summated ratings. The "Likert scale" is a leading example. Generally the interviewer presents the subject with a series of statements, and for each there is a five-alternative response mode: strongly agree, agree, uncertain, disagree, strongly disagree. A scale measuring views on government policies, for instance, might contain such statements as "The government in Washington ought to see to it that everybody who wants to work can find a job," or "The government ought to help people get doctors and hospital care without cost." The response alternatives have scores of 1 through 5 and each subject's score is the sum of that respondent's scores for all items. Depending upon each subject's score and upon the items the scale allegedly measures, respondents can be classified as liberal or conservative, trusting or cynical, pro- or anti-Administration, etc. The SRC/CPS has used a variant of this technique in recent surveys. Respondents indicate their positions on key issues, liberalism-conservatism, and other matters on separate seven-point scales indicating degrees of agreement or disagreement with a stated proposition. Respondents also rate where they think each of competing candidates in an election stand on the same matters. By calculating the difference between a subject's scale score and where that respondent thinks a given candidate stands, it is possible to obtain a measure of the "proximity" of a voter's issue position and perception of each candidate's views.

Another form of rating scale is the "semantic differential," a widely used device in communication studies. Researchers provide subjects with sets of dichotomous adjectives (hot-cold, strong-weak, good-bad, etc.). Subjects rate a political object (such as a president, democracy, or government) with respect to each adjective pair on a seven-point scale. For instance, if the subject thinks democracy is "hot," it may rate a score of 1 or 2, if "cold" a score of 6 or 7, and if "lukewarm" a mark of 3. A variety of statistical techniques are available (see below) for calculating individual scores on the semantic differential.

Such are but a few of the numerous rating scales afforded to students of political communication and public opinion. Many others exist; scalogram analysis, unfolding techniques, latent structure analysis, sociometric techniques, interpersonal checklists, and interaction process analysis constitute only a partial listing. Each has specialized features, uses, limitations, reliability, and validity. The reader interested in applying such techniques should consult the works already cited and mentioned later in the bibliography to this appendix for detailed descriptions.

Rating devices constitute one way of measuring personal opinions. Another set of tools to accomplish this end consists of *ranking* techniques. These require a subject to rank-order a series of items, attributes, characteristics, or statements about a political object, usually in order of agree-disagree, like-dislike, or characteristic-uncharacteristic. *Q*-sorting, the data gathering technique associated with *Q*-methodology, is a sophisticated ranking procedure that permits a subject to portray his perceptions about an object by sorting statements pertaining to it (one statement appearing upon a separate card in a deck containing as many as several dozen statements). *Q*-studies work not only with samples of people (or *P*-samples as described earlier) but with samples of statements about objects (*Q*-samples). *Q*-samples represent a population of statements or items that could pertain to an object under investigation. Such a population can rarely be specified in a precise fashion; hence, the first step in a *Q*-study is often to collect a pool of statements from various sources (open-ended interviews, documents, informal conversation, news reports, speeches, and even some made up by the researcher). For example, a study of how people perceive the president of the United States might begin with collecting a pool of statements they generally make when talking about the president (labeled technically as "self-referent" statements). From this pool a *Q*-sample can be drawn, perhaps at random but more frequently using the principles of theoretical sampling described earlier. A typical *Q*-sample will consist of between fifty and one hundred statements. Sampled subjects sort the statements according to instructions specified by the researcher. For instance, the researcher might ask the subject to sort the items in a *Q*-sample pertaining to the president by informing the respondent that the items pertain to observations people have made about the president, then instructing the subject to sort them from "most" to "least" characteristic of the president. The researcher indicates how many statements should be placed at each interval along a continuum:

	(most characteristic)					(least characteristic)				
Score	+5	+4	+3	+2	+1	0	−1	−2	−3	−4	−5
Number of Statements	3	6	6	8	8	10	8	8	6	6	3

When finished the subject has indicated through sorting the three statements he deems most characteristic of the president, the six next most characteristic, etc., to the ten he feels are neutral, and finally to the three he finds least characteristic. Since each statement has a score derived from sorting, the scores for each subject can be correlated and factor analyzed (see below). The result consists of clusters of persons who have sorted the items in approximately the same fashion; thus each cluster consists of a separated set of perceptions. Q-sorting is one of several such ranking techniques and/or devices based upon self-referent items.[28]

It is, of course, possible to gather data without asking subjects questions at all. One technique, for example, is simple *observation* of what people are doing. In an excellent study of how the routine operations of news organizations affect the content of news stories, Gaye Tuchman simply devoted several months to virtually around-the-clock observation of the everyday activities in first a newspaper office and then a television station,[29] being as unobtrusive as possible so as not to influence the flow of events. Chris Argyris also studied effects on communication of the daily activities of a newspaper (dubbed *The Daily Planet* to hide the organization's identity); the design called for his "intervention" at various points.[30] In addition to obtrusive and unobtrusive observation, there is the technique of participant observation. Here the researcher takes part on a regular basis in the routine and nonroutine activities of those subjects he is studying, either known or unknown to them. In all three varieties of observation the researcher may seek information by asking questions, but rarely is the search in the form of a full-fledged interview either of the open- or closed-ended variety. A leading exception is observation common to certain types of experimental research. Researchers may test experimental and control groups through interviews, provide a stimulus to the experimental group, observe the interaction of both groups' members (either in their presence, through hidden recording devices and/or cameras, or hidden behind fake mirrors), then administer posttests.

Finally, the procedures of content analysis also pertain to asking questions. The questions of content analysis, however, are not directed at persons but at documents, articles, letters, speeches, etc. (just as the questions of aggregate studies are directed at compiled statistics rather than at the people whose attributes and behavior are allegedly captured in those statistics). A content analysis is only as good as its categories classifying and coding content. A researcher may, for example, be interested in analyzing the contents of newspapers to explore how they report appeals candidates make in presidential campaigns. Assuming a representative sampling of news coverage can be assembled, the researcher might classify "content units" (say specific references to the candidates' public appearances) into those that refer to candidates' "policy pronouncements," "political experience," "connections with a political party," "ties to organized interests," or "personality." For the presidential campaign of 1968

Doris Graber conducted an extensive analysis of newspaper coverage along such lines and found that newspapers are more likely to supply the raw material for voters to construct images of candidates' personalities than of candidates' more issue-oriented concerns.[31]

Many studies employing content analysis seek not only to measure the frequency with which communicators employ selected themes, symbols, and appeals but their intensity in doing so. One way to accomplish this is to have several persons act as judges in scaling the intensity of various content units via Q-sorting from the least to most intense expression of message content. The procedure is similar to that discussed earlier in reviewing the use of Q-techniques in small sample surveys.

In framing questions, statistics, or message content researchers must, of course, guard against biasing tendencies in the wording of questionnaires, the structuring of interview schedules, the labeling of statistics as representative of certain kinds of behavior, or categorization of content. Numerous checks and safeguards can be incorporated into communication and opinion studies to increase the validity and reliability of research findings. The researcher must be wary of another tendency, that of assuming he is separate from the "reality" of his observations. As ethnomethodologists argue, data gathered through questionnaires, interviews, observation, statistical records, and content analysis constitute a "reality" created by the scientific observer and his subjects. Failure of the researcher to keep in mind that his data are but one possible reality often contributes to two corollary tendencies. First, there is the potential for imputing, through the use of the observer's measuring instruments, opinions to subjects who have no opinions or whose opinions have different meanings than those construed by the researcher. In fact, an observer may see no meaning at all in the beliefs, values, and conduct of those he observes: "The great difficulty with one observer standing as critic of another's beliefs is that the first may not be able to see the logic of the other's thought processes, that is, one's explanation of why he believes as he does may not be comprehensible to the other."[32] Second, researchers overinterpret their results, overstructure behavior by discovery of patterns that may be, at best, specious, and overapply conclusions, both in the sense of premature application and to cases where such findings are not relevant. Speaking of the use of public opinion polls as a basis for decision making, we repeat a point from Chapter 8: "To reduce ambivalent, subtle, interacting, contingent responses to statistics is to abstract and simplify grossly but not randomly. It is to describe the responses that occur given existing circumstances, a useful enough enterprise. It is to ignore or discount *possibilities* and the response to changed perspectives that political acts might themselves create if the actors were less bemused by popularity polls."[33]

When: How Often to Ask

A researcher using content analysis must not only select which portions of a given message to examine but also which messages to select over time. A single sample in content analysis may contain messages or portions thereof communicated at widely varying times, perhaps years apart. The problem of sampling over time is not unique to content analysis. Each of the six methods of study described at the outset of this appendix deals with the question of how often to seek data, that is, how many cases of behavior to study over time.

Aggregate studies lend themselves to longitudinal analysis, examination of behavior at successive stages of time. For example, by comparing rates of voting in selected precincts, counties, districts, states, etc. over several years, the researcher can study trends, disruptions, and the effects of intervening events. In this respect aggregate studies have quasi-experimental possibilities. Take the case of a researcher wishing to study the effects of a change in voter registration systems on electoral turnout. By comparing voting rates in selected areas before and after statutory changes with areas where no shifts in registration systems occurred, the researcher can derive and/or test theoretical propositions.

The pre- and post-testing phases of classical experimentation are variations on longitudinal analysis, again permitting the researcher to study the effects of a stimulus, treatment, training, event, or experience through "before" and "after" observations. For example, Charles Brownstein sought to determine whether the strategies political candidates use in election campaigns influence voting behavior. He tested experimental subjects before and after treatment, measuring views on law and order, social welfare, candidates, etc. The treatment consisted of a variety of campaign communications and discussion. Brownstein found that varying communication styles were associated with differences in how subjects perceived and evaluated the candidates.[34]

The methods associated with ex post facto investigations normally incorporate those of other studies, especially survey research. This generally means but a single post-event survey. Since each event to be explained ex post facto is unique and the studies employ a single survey or aggregate analysis, ex post facto analyses pose problems for replication. There is rarely an opportunity or effort to repeat the same basic study to check its accuracy. What must normally suffice is replication through study of similar events after they have taken place. Thus, for instance, efforts to explain the origins of social movements, revolution and rebellion, or violent protest generally rely upon comparing several cases of the phenomenon after the fact.[35]

Survey researchers cope with the problems of measuring changes over time, effects of potential influences, and replication in a variety of ways. If the survey employs small balanced or theoretical samples as in Q-method or similar quasi-experimental designs, it is generally possible to repeat the study, with or without variations, over time. A case in point is Steven R. Brown's Q-study of the persistence with which people express consistent beliefs and values in politics. He was particularly interested in whether active citizens are more persistent than the less active. Using a small sample ($n=36$) he administered a Q-sort to an equal number of political "articulates" and "inarticulates." He first administered the sort to all thirty-six subjects. Two weeks later he randomly selected six of the articulates and six inarticulates from the original sample and read-ministered the sort. At the end of four weeks he readministered the sort to six more articulates and inarticulates. Finally, at the end of six weeks he administered the sort to the remaining twelve persons. Using this procedure he discovered no significant differences between the two sets of citizens in the persistency of their political opinions.[36]

Surveys with large samples of several hundred people are expensive, and the researcher seldom has sufficient resources to space several surveys across separate time periods. Firms that make a business out of public opinion polling such as George Gallup's American Institute of Public Opinion, the Roper Center, or the Harris Survey do conduct several surveys in any given year, frequently incorporating identical questions to measure changes in selected opinions over time. A leading example is the Gallup Poll's use for several decades of standard questions asking respondents "Do you approve or disapprove of the way [the incumbent] is handling his job as president?" Using responses to this and other questions, John E. Mueller derived a sophisticated analysis of the factors associated with the rise and fall in the popularity of presidents since the 1940s.[37]

Researchers without the largess of major polling firms, however, use other means to cope with the problem time poses. One is to tap the surveys of the polling firms for data as did Mueller. The researcher thus conducts a longitudinal study by way of a secondary analysis of surveys. Because of their ready availability to most scholars, the election surveys of the Survey Research Center/Center for Political Studies of the University of Michigan have been subjected to numerous longitudinal analyses. Edward Dreyer, for example, conducted a longitudinal analysis of the presidential election surveys of the SRC/CPS from 1952 to 1968 to measure the relationship between voting preference, partisanship, and exposure to campaign communications from election to election, finding a decline in the strength of the relationship between party identification and party voting for each level of exposure.[38] Cohort analysis is also useful for measuring change across surveys conducted at several different times. Cohorts consist of a number of people having a common characteristic. As an illustration, it is possible to take the persons in a sample between the ages of 18 and 22 and examine their perceptions, opinions, and behavior, and four years later to estimate changes by examining the persons aged 22 to 26.[39]

There are various ways, however, of using a single survey to explore questions of changes over time. One procedure is to employ a panel design. This consists of dividing up the total number of subjects in the survey sample into subsamples, or panels. The overall sample is interviewed, then panels are reinterviewed at various points. One of the first major voting studies addressed the question of how voters perceived candidates in the 1940 presidential campaign. In May of that year approximately 3000 persons were interviewed. From that sample four groups of approximately 600 each were formed into panels. Three of those panels were interviewed again, one in July, one in August, one in October; the fourth was interviewed once each month, May to November. By comparing responses of different panels over time, changes in perceptions could be detected.[40] The possibility that interviewing people repeatedly may itself influence their opinions necessitates using control panels with only one interview with each person as checks for contamination. A variant upon the panel technique is the procedure of conducting both preelection and postelection interviews. In some instances subjects are questioned at both times, in others only before or after the election. Analyses of such data permit researchers to estimate the effects of the election upon how people construct their images of candidates, views on issues, and perceptions of political parties as a result of the victory or defeat of one of the candidates.[41] Finally, it is often possible to measure change by creating artificial or quasi panels of subjects interviewed in a single survey. For instance, John Kessel partitioned the interviews conducted in the SRC/CPS 1964 election survey into three groups by using the dates interviews occurred. The SRC/CPS normally interviews over at least a two-month period prior to the election. Kessel divided the total sample into three subsamples—those interviewed primarily in September, those the first two weeks in October, and those in the final days before the election. Following this procedure enabled him to draw conclusions regarding the impact of the strategies of the two major political parties upon the presidential campaign.[42]

Where: A Problem of Contact

How intimate should be the relationship of a researcher to his subjects? Some investigators argue for unobtrusive observation, others for close contact within the subject's natural setting. Of the methods reviewed aggregate analysis is perhaps the least obtrusive. The analyst works with recorded attributes and behavior, usually a statistical record of characteristics and behavior. This is not to say, however, that the data merely "speak for themselves." For one thing records themselves are the creation of human selectivity, judgment, and error. Census statistics, for example, are based upon personal interviews and mailed questionnaires; and voting records are only as accurate as the discretion of election judges permit. A nonpolitical illustration aptly makes the point that officially recorded facts may not be factual at all. One way agribusiness officials estimate the number of cattle that will come to market in any given year is through a regular census of newborn steers and heifers. But many farmers are reluctant to report to census takers the numbers of their livestock, in part because they may fear such information could restrict their flexibility in filing later statements of income for tax purposes. Hence, underreporting and underestimation of numbers of cattle for market occur, much to the chagrin of all concerned.

Contact between observer and observed in aggregate studies is more than passive in other respects. No statistic simply stands for itself; it derives meaning by a researcher's interpretation. Differing meanings flow from different labels. For instance, researchers and officials decide when a person out of work qualifies as "unemployed," when a death is "suicide," when a cancer patient is "cured," when a juvenile offender is "delinquent," and when one who doesn't vote is "apathetic" or "apolitical." It is not that "figures don't lie but liars figure"; rather, documents, records, statistics, etc. are creations of human definition, accumulation, and interpretation.

So long as practitioners of aggregate study (and content analysts of documents) keep in mind that the contact with their data is discretionary, they can utilize numerous sources of recorded information. Several archives store aggregate statistics, data derived from personal interviews, and documents—libraries, interuniversity consortia, the Bureau of the Census, private and public polling firms, and many others. In recent years the opportunities for secondary analyses of data gathered in opinion surveys have grown enormously. Among the archival sources available are the Inter-University Consortium for Political Research at the University of Michigan, the Roper Public Opinion Research Center, and the Louis Harris Political Data Center. As Norval Glenn points out, secondary analyses offer vast potential and pitfalls. (Readers would do well to consult Glenn's discussion.)[43]

Survey studies deal with the question of intimacy between observer and observed in a direct way with the decision regarding what interview technique to employ. Three general interview situations are available for obtaining responses from subjects. The first (and generally preferred because of the opportunities it offers for validating sample accuracy) is the face-to-face interview conducted within the subject's home, work place, on streetcorners, in supermarkets, public conveyances, etc. Face-to-face interviews afford opportunity for in-depth questioning, taking nonverbal as well as verbal responses into account, and yield a helpful rapport between interviewer and interviewee. But face-to-face interviews are expensive: relatively few interviews can be conducted by a single person in a given period; travel costs are considerable; and specific subjects are frequently hard to locate, thus requiring time-consuming and expensive callbacks. To cut costs many researchers employ either telephone interviews or mail questionnaires. But there is a price to pay for lowered monetary expense: researchers generally must restrict themselves to a relatively few, tightly structured, closed-ended questions; moreover, not everyone in a population that a researcher might want to sample has a telephone or a listed number.[44] Despite the limitations, several major polling firms use telephone interviews extensively, including Sindlinger and Company and Decision Making Information. Telephone interviewing simplifies dealing with callback problems. (Sindlinger reports that on an average of 1000 calls, 600 interviews are completed on the first try, 50 people refuse to be interviewed, and the remaining 350 require callbacks.) Moreover, telephone polling permits sampling via random digit dialing, continuous seven-day-per-week interviewing, and interviewing most of the waking hours; computerizing permits random sampling from directories and dialing via punchcards, and responses can be directly punched onto computer cards for processing. The hidden cost of mailed questionnaires is, of course, the failure of many subjects to return them, thus creating the dilemma of just what population the subsample of returned questionnaires represents. Various tactics can be employed to maximize return rates (follow-up letters, enclosing preaddressed envelopes with return postage, delivering questionnaires personally, etc.). Generally if the sampled population is homogeneous, high response rates are less a requirement for mail surveys than if the population is diversified in characteristics and opinions.[45]

Experimental scientists also cope with the contact problem. Realizing that the experimenter is a potential source of contamination, researchers employ strategies to control experimenter effects, such as using control groups; masking the motives and purposes of the experimenter; covert observation; using collaborators, replications, triangulation procedures, etc. The opportunities for employing safeguards are greater in laboratory than in field experiments. The laboratory experiment attempts to minimize the influence of all variables that are irrelevant to the researchers' purposes by isolating the research in a physical setting apart from the subject's routine of daily living. A field experiment takes place in a situation more in keeping with daily routines, opting for more realistic climates at the expense of some loss of experimental control. In both types of experiment the researcher not only observes effects but manipulates and controls factors to generate tests and their effects. At best, then, the difference in intimacy between researcher and researched is a matter of degree in laboratory versus field experimentation.

Many students of communication argue that the complexity of the process (both with respect to the object of study, communication, and the realization that research itself is communication) makes it impossible to manipulate and control for all factors producing intimacy between the investigator and his subjects. Efforts to do so, they say, interfere with gathering insightful data. Regarding laboratory and/or field experimentation as premature, they opt instead for "naturalistic" observation. Thus Ray L. Birdwhistell, a leading student of nonverbal communication, makes the point: "The methods to which I am wedded by training emphasize observation, description, and comparison. This methodology demands systematic rather than random observation, explicit rather than impressionistic description, and is dependent upon relative comparative data. The controlling elements of systematic observation, the conditions and conventions of description, and the cogent orders of relevancy cannot be predefined. They are functions of the theoretical position from which is drawn the hypotheses which would be tested in further investigation."[46] Naturalistic observation, then, consists of close, precise, systematic observation of subjects in their natural setting in accordance with theoretical design. In addition to Birdwhistell's work with body motion communication, examples include nonpolitical research (Charles Darwin's voyage on the *Beagle*) and such studies of potential political relevance as Jean Piaget's study of the cognitive development of children by observing them as they play marbles (see Chapter 9) and the quasi-experimental, field study variants on naturalistic observation of ethnomethodologists.[47]

How: Problems of Data Analysis

Just as studies employ different techniques for selecting subjects, inquiring about them (both respecting the content and frequency of that inquiry), and coping with problems associated with contact between observer and observed, there are wide differences in techniques of data analysis. What is basically at issue is how researchers measure similarities and differences, both among their subjects and over time.

Measurement is, according to Abraham Kaplan, "the assignment of numbers to objects (or events or situations) in accord with some rule."[48] Readers should regard "number" broadly enough to include that of "category." The reason lies in what Lazarsfeld and Barton label the "continuum of measurement" whereby at one pole lies "the formation of the categories in terms of which the objects under study are to be classified or measured," i.e., the *qualitative* aspects of measurement, and at the other end of the continuum lies the formation of *quantitative* indices.[49] In measurement therefore two procedures shade into one another: first, the derivation of categories of phenomena (qualitative measurement) and, second, the assignment of numbers (quantitative measurement). Methods for studying political communication and opinion offer illustrations of both qualitative and quantitative measurement: aggregate analyses utilize two categories of voting districts, Republican and Democratic (qualitative), according to which party received more votes in the district, and assign measures of partisanship by employing specific percentages of a party's vote (quantitative); surveys create categories of high, medium, and low income families to group respondents (qualitative) and analyze specific income figures (quantitative); analyses of communication content formulate categories for the coding of content units (qualitative) and measure intensity of messages (quantitative).

Ranged along the qualitative-quantitative continuum are four ways to assign numbers to phenomena. Toward the qualitative side are *nominal* measurements, i.e., simply assigning names to various categories (such as "Democrat" and "Republican" precincts or "male" and "female" categories); numbers instead of names may be assigned to the categories (as when sets of numbers are preserved on football teams for the jerseys of quarterbacks, other sets for running backs, others for defensive backs, etc.), but the numbers have no arithmetical qualities (one could not add a quarterback wearing number 6 to a halfback wearing number 44 and get another player with number 50). In nominal measurement the derivation of categories is typically based upon the presence of a *dichotomous attribute,* an attribute belonging to one object but not another, a quality of "this-ness" or "that-ness" (e.g., male or female). Greater quantification comes into play working with *continuous variables,* attributes no longer simply dichotomous but with numerous gradations (for instance, a person's annual income in dollars and cents). When phenomena can be ordered from the object with the most of an attribute to that with the least, the researcher has *ordinal* measurements. (Recall that the *Q*-sort in *Q*-method relies upon such orderings.) If the researcher not only knows that a given object has more or less of this or that attribute than another but can say how much in a numerical way, the numbers express relative differences permitting *interval* measurement. Thus, for instance, the interval between 20 years of age and 30 (10 years) is the same as between 40 and 50. Finally, when numbers can be used to compare objects via a ratio (as when Ms. Smith who earns $20,000 per year has twice the salary of Mr. Roe who earns $10,000), the researcher has *ratio* measurement. As noted, arithmetical operations on nominal measures are limited to the degree that two nominal scores cannot be added, subtracted, multiplied, or divided (although the cases in categories can be counted and compared; for instance, 20 Republicans are twice as many as 10 Democrats). Ordinal measures also cannot be added, subtracted, multiplied, or divided but the researcher can make greater-than and less-than comparisons. Both interval and ratio measurements permit elaborate statistical operations (thus the total income of Ms. Smith and Mr. Roe is $30,000, Mr. Roe earns $10,000 less than, or half as much as, Ms. Smith, etc.).

It goes far beyond the purpose and scope of this appendix to discuss in detail the various technical operations students of political communication and public opinion use in reducing the vast array of information they gather to the few summary statistics that describe it. Here there will be a brief account of each of the most widely used. (The reader should sample the works cited in the accompanying bibliography for details). Among these, first of all, are those employed to describe a single variable. The chief one is the *mean* or calculated average, a measure of central tendency. The procedure is familiar to everyone: add the numerical values of each case and divide by the total number of cases. (Thus, ten persons make the following respective scores on an exam: 80, 70, 90, 100, 100, 90, 70, 80, 60, 70 with total score of $810/10 = 81$.) Other measures of central tendency are the mode, the numerical value appearing most frequently, and the median or center value in a set of data arrayed from highest to lowest. Around any central tendency in a body of data the difference between any given numerical value and the central tendency may vary considerably. The most widely used statistic summarizing such variations is the *standard deviation,* which is the square root of total squared deviations from the mean divided by the total number of cases. Means and standard deviations are necessary not only for summarizing central tendencies and variations in data regarding a single variable; their calculation is essential to more complex statistics discussed later—correlation, regression, factor analysis, and analysis of variance.

Another simple way of describing a body of data is through *frequency distribution,* which is nothing more than the number of cases in a particular category (as when out of a sample of 1000 people, 450 display trust in government, 300 distrust, and 250 express no opinion). *Relative frequency* is a more commonly used statistic; it merely translates the raw totals in the various categories to proportions of the total (as, in the example above, when 450 of the $n = 1000$ sample provides 45 percent). Frequencies and relative frequencies can be cross-tabulated. For example, of the 450 persons who express trust in government, suppose 200 are Democrats and the remainder Republicans; of the 300 distrusting, suppose they are evenly divided in party preference, and of those with no opinion 100 are Democrats, 150 Republicans. The cross-tabulation would be as follows.

Opinion	Party Preference	
	Democrat	Republican
Trust	200 (20%)	250 (25%)
Distrust	150 (15%)	150 (15%)
No opinion	100 (10%)	150 (15%)

Thus 20 percent of the sample are trusting Democrats, 15 percent are distrusting Democrats, etc. It is simple to calculate the proportion of all Democrats or Republicans who are trusting and/or distrusting. Moreover, the researcher could add a third attribute (sex, perhaps) and compare the relationship between trust, partisanship, and sex. The researcher might go on to ask whether one set of partisans are more or less trusting because they are Republican or Democrat or because they are male or female. This requires a "control" for sex by sorting out males and females and looking separately at each category's trust/distrust and partisanship. There are procedures and tests to calculate the relative strength of derived relationships and whether they derive from actual differences between groups or from chance.[50]

Several other statistical devices measure relationships between two or more variables. Among those most frequently employed in communication and/or opinion studies is *correlation,* a measure of the interrelationship between two or more quantitative variables which reveals the extent to which an increase in the magnitude of one or more variables is associated with an increase or decrease in the magnitude of others. The statistic used in correlation is the coefficient of correlation, a number that ranges from $+1.00$ (as when two variables are positively associated in a one-to-one correspondence, e.g., what might exist if each ounce of beer a person drinks increases drunkenness by a measurable increment) through zero (0), for no association between variables, to -1.00 (a case in which, though hard to imagine, each ounce of beer consumed would be associated with an increment of increased sobriety). Such coefficients can be calculated for data measured in intervals (the result being a Pearsonian product-moment coefficient) or for original data (that is, the relative ranking of objects on two sets of attributes can be calculated resulting either in a Spearman or Kendall tau coefficient). Simple correlation deals with relationships between two variables—age and party preference, income and voting rates, partisanship and trust in government, etc. Multiple correlation is a measure of the relationship between a dependent variable and a combination of one or more factors (independent variables). Partial correlation measures the degree of relationship between two variables when the effects of one or more related factors are removed (i.e., controlled).

To round out this snapshot of selected statistics researchers employ in dealing with the multiplicity of factors entering into communication, four additional techniques deserve mention. The first, *multiple regression,* appears primarily in aggregate and survey studies. Multiple regression is a statistical procedure that permits a researcher to infer the most powerful independent variable influencing a dependent one, then the relative influence of other less powerful independent variables. Whereas correlation provides a summary statistic of the total relationship between several variables, regression provides a step-by-step summary of how much change in a dependent variable occurs with the addition (and control) of each of many possible influences. Thus, for instance, using regression techniques, researchers estimate how much variation in voting (a dependent variable) follows from socioeconomic position, partisanship, voters' perceptions of issues and/or candidates, communication in the election campaign, events, etc.[51].

A second technique, *factor analysis,* has been used in aggregate studies, large and small sample surveys, content analysis, experimental and quasi-experimental research, and all manner of ex post facto investigations. Factor analysis is a statistical procedure for reducing a large number of measures to a smaller number of components, called factors, consisting of variables arrayed along a common dimension. Communication and/or opinion studies typically employ two varieties of factor analysis (technically designated as "R" and "Q" factor analysis). In their study of *Participation in America,* for example, Sidney Verba and Norman Nie used a nationwide probability survey to measure rates of political participation by Americans in twelve specific ways (such as voting, persuading others how to vote, and giving money to candidates).[52] In addition to calculating simple correlation coefficients between pairs of each of the twelve activities, the researchers factor-analyzed the correlations to reduce the twelve activities to four principal categories or classes of participation—those relating to voting, political campaigning, cooperative community activity, and private contact of public officials (see Chapter 10). In contrast to the R-factor analysis of Verba and Nie, which uncovers categories of activity, opinions, beliefs, values, etc., Q-factor analysis reduces large bodies of data to categories of people. Q-factor techniques are usually, but not always, associated with Q-methodology. Recall that in Q-method people rank-order a sample of statements pertaining to an object. The rank-ordered sorts of all pairs of persons are correlated, the resulting correlations factor-analyzed, and the results are factors or classes of people having sorted opinion statements in approximately the same ways (and thus having approximately the same general opinions).

A third technique has been adapted to communication research by an increasing number of scholars in recent years. *Multidimensional scaling* uses the judgments that people make about objects—such as political candidates—to calculate the degree of similarity people perceive in those objects, represent the judgments in a spatial way, and map those judgments along several dimensions such as liberal or conservative, Democrat or Republican, etc. A study conducted in 1976, for example, asked 1500 voters to evaluate various contenders for the presidency on a 0 to 100 degree feeling thermometer; through multidimensional scaling the relative ratings of all candidates by all sampled voters were compared. All voters were placed on a two-dimensional map showing voters' relative positions compared with their views of the candidates. Investigators could then visualize the relative support for, say, Gerald Ford and Jimmy Carter, along a left-right ideological spectrum and a party loyalty dimension. Early surveys indicated voters clustering in the same dimensional space as Jimmy Carter; as the campaign progressed later surveys indicated their perceptions of Ford moving toward their dimensional space and Carter slightly away from the bulk of voters. The study provided clues used by Ford forces to plan campaign tactics.[53]

The fourth key technique is *analysis of variance* used in both experimental and survey research. This procedure is a way of determining the amount of total variance in statistical data attributable to various component sources: to variations *within* a given set of variables and to variations *between* sets of variables. For illustration take a nonpolitical case. Let us assume that a person devotes his life to concocting the "perfect" martini. (This is not so nonpolitical as might seem; several notable political figures have sung the praises of the martini, including President Franklin Roosevelt; a candidate for president, Eugene McCarthy; and a former Secretary of State in the Eisenhower administration, Christian Herter.) The ingredients, to keep it simple, are gin and vermouth, each a variable tasting intoxicant in itself. Assuming a person has finally discovered the formula for perfection, then, how much of that perfection is due to variations in the quality and proportions of gin, variations in the quality and proportions of vermouth, and the interaction of gin with vermouth? Or, to use a political case, a researcher might want to know how much of what people think of a political candidate depends upon their partisanship, their ideology, and their partisanship working in concert (or cross purposes) with ideology. Such problems as these are the riddles for analysis of variance.

APPROACHES TO UNDERSTANDING: A PREFERENCE FOR DIVERSITY

The numerous methods of study, techniques for selecting, contacting, and questioning subjects, and alternative modes for analyzing data discussed should give the reader the impression that there is considerable diversity in the study of political communication and public opinion. In a sense this impression is correct. In fact, in addition to diverse methods and techniques, researchers also employ a variety of approaches, i.e., ways of defining subject matter, deciding questions to ask, and suggesting relevant data. Among the many approaches to communication-opinion analysis investigators use are: a focus on the historical settings of various sets of opinions (historical approach);[54] cultural development through communication (developmental approach);[55] a sociological approach emphasizing the class bases of public opinion;[56] a psychological approach locating the sources of personal opinions in attitudes, personalities, human needs, etc.;[57] examinations of the formation of public opinion through social disputes (the conflict approach);[58] the role of constitutional arrangements (an institutional approach)[59] and formal laws (a legal approach)[60] in the opinion process; consideration of the bases, wielders, and uses of power in human affairs (the power approach);[61] a focus upon opinion as reflected in the struggle of competing interests (the group approach);[62] the resolution of opinion differences through policymaking (a decision making approach);[63] expansion of the scope of inquiry to the entire interactive system within which opinions form and take expression (a general systems approach);[64] and the process approach outlined in the introduction of this text.

Despite the marked variety in methods, techniques, and approaches for examining political communication and public opinion, there is yet a sense in which convention and orthodoxy reign. Herbert Blumer has argued that virtually all focuses on the study of human behavior tread the path of "variable analysis," i.e., the effort to reduce human life to "variables and their relations." Notes Blumer: "There seems to be little limit to what may be chosen or designated as a variable. One may select something as simple as a sex distribution or as complex as depression; something as specific as a birth rate or as vague as social cohesion; something as evident as residential change or something as imputed as a collective unconscious; something as generally recognized as hatred or as doctrinaire as the Oedipus complex; something as immediately given as a rate of newspaper circulation to something as elaborately fabricated as an index of anomie."[65] A principal limitation of variable analysis, argues Blumer, is a chaotic condition that prevails in the selection of variables, a selection that occurs in the conspicuous absence of rules, guides, limitations, and prohibitions to govern choice. But the basic weakness of variable analysis for Blumer lies in its failure to come to grips with what he believes is the key to human conduct, which is the process of interpretation or definition by which people construct meaningful, minded behavior. Variable analysis limits itself to factors impinging upon, influencing, even allegedly causing human behavior, but ignores the processes of personal imagery that lie in between. The idea that in human relations "the independent variable automatically exercises its influence in the dependent variable is, it seems to me, a basic fallacy. There is a process of definition intervening between the events of experience presupposed by the independent variable and the formed behavior represented by the dependent variable."[66]

Given the view of political communication and public opinion taken in this text, the author agrees with Blumer that more than mere variable analysis—regardless of the diversity of its methods, techniques, and approaches—is required to increase our understanding. Blumer offers no label comparable to "variable analysis" for the study of interpretative processes, but Kenneth Boulding does. More than two decades ago Boulding called for the study of the *message-image relationship,* a study of the transaction and reciprocal effects of communication and constructed, meaningful behavior. He dubbed the study "eiconics." We suspect that a full understanding of political communication and public opinion will require both variable and eiconic analysis.[67]

It will demand other things as well. Two examples will suffice. First, to advance understanding, researchers need to achieve representative samples of more than just people and messages. Large, cross-sectional surveys do well at obtaining representative samples of persons. *Q*-studies and content analysis are useful ways of representing populations of opinion statements and messages. But how representative of the daily routines and everyday lives of subjects are the settings in which studies occur? Here the critiques by ethnomethodologists of conventional methods of studying human behavior must be taken seriously and even more ways found to represent the routine and taken-for-granted aspects of opinion formation as well as the life circumstances examined through surveys, experiments, quasi-experiments, etc. Second, although a wide range of methods, techniques, and approaches appear in the many diverse communication and opinion studies, researchers would do well to follow Eugene Webb and his colleagues and increase the variety and diversity of investigatory modes within a single study as well as by conducting several studies. As they point out, if no single scientific mode is perfect, neither is it totally useless: "The most persuasive evidence comes through a triangulation of measurement processes. If a proposition can survive the onslaught of a series of imperfect measures, with all their irrelevant error, confidence should be placed in it."[68]

In sum, methodological pluralism, not purism, should underlie explorations of what people believe, value, and expect from their acts. To foreclose the possibility of discovering useful approaches, methods, and techniques because they fail to square with current orthodoxies, fads, fashions, or schools of thought is a form of monism that flies in the face of a preference for diversity. Writing in 1908, Arthur Bentley asked if it was desirable in advance of an investigation to distinguish between government and other varieties of social activity. His reasons for saying emphatically no are worth recalling, for they also apply to efforts to establish methodological purity by prematurely closing alternative avenues of investigation. Said Bentley, "Many a child, making paper toys, has used his scissors too confidently and cut himself off from the materials he needs. That is an error to avoid." Moreover, he noted, "Who likes may snip verbal definitions in his old age, when his world has gone crackly and dry."[69]

BIBLIOGRAPHY

In the last decade dozens of behavioral scientists have published books covering all aspects of the methodology underlying the study of human conduct—the philosophy of social science, alternative approaches, methods of study, and techniques for identifying, gathering, processing, and analyzing data. Added to those that existed prior to the 1960s, these works provide far more information than any interested reader may want to consult. Like the lengthy treatise on alligators read by the young girl, the many volumes on behavioral methodology contain more than most people ever want to know. Be that as it may, this note will be highly selective and cover three areas—general methodological concerns related to the study of political communication and public opinion, primers of methods and techniques, and works concerning specialized problems of inquiry.

One of the best single works covering the general picture of what behavioral science methodology is all about is Abraham Kaplan's *The Conduct of Inquiry* (San Francisco: Chandler Publishing Co., 1964). Kaplan provides in a single volume a carefully organized and readable introduction to the nature of concepts and meaning; the role of scientific laws, experimentation, and measurement; the part played by statistics, the nature of models and theories; what explanation is all about; and the problem of values. His perspective is representative of the conventional concerns and views of behavioral scientists. Less conventional, and even more controversial in some quarters, is the perspective of Barney G. Glaser and Anselm L. Strauss, *The Discovery of Grounded Theory: Strategies for Qualitative Research* (Chicago: Aldine Publishing Co., 1967). Glaser and Strauss are interested in how theory can be discovered through working closely with data and, as the subtitle indicates, they are especially interested in working with qualitative data. Primarily instructive are their chapters on theoretical sampling, comparative analysis, and the theoretical elaboration of quantitative data. Two articles are particularly useful in orienting the reader to general problems of measurement in the behavioral sciences and the nature of thinking about those problems from the viewpoint of a qualitative-quantitative continuum: Paul F. Lazarsfeld, "Evidence and Influence in Social Research," *Daedalus,* 87 (Fall 1958): 99–103, and Paul F. Lazarsfeld and Allen H. Barton, "Qualitative Measurement in the Social Sciences: Classification, Typologies, and Indices," in Daniel Lerner and Harold D. Lasswell, *The Policy Sciences* (Stanford: Stanford University Press, 1951), pp. 155–92. Still the single best anthology of articles related to general questions of behavioral methodology is Paul F. Lazarsfeld and Morris Rosenberg, *The Language of Social Research* (New York: The Free Press, 1955).

One concern of students of political behavior has been to relate their study to that of cognate disciplines. Two works that endeavor to do this in a summary way are Monte Palmer, et al., *The Interdisciplinary Study of Politics* (New York: Harper and Row, 1974) and Rollo Handy and Paul Kurtz, *A Current Appraisal of the Behavioral Sciences* (Great Barrington, Mass.: Behavioral Research Council, 1964).

A number of primers introduce readers to various aspects of research approaches, methods, and techniques. One of those with the most general concerns is Fred N. Kerlinger, *Foundations of Behavioral Research* (New York: Holt, Rinehart and Winston, 1964); Kerlinger ranges over the nature of science, hypotheses, variables, and meaning, but also includes a lengthy discussion of probability and statistical inference (including matters of research design, sampling, and experimentation) as well as the technical aspects of correlation, factor analysis, analysis of variance, Q-methods, etc. In addition to Kerlinger readers will find two volumes sufficiently devoid of complexity to be useful introductions to the same kinds of questions: Claire Selltiz, et al., *Research Methods in Social Relations* (New York: Henry Holt and Co., Rev. 1 vol. ed., 1960) and a handy paperback, John Madge, *The Tools of Social Science* (Garden City, New York: Anchor Books, 1965). Neither of these two works, however, is as comprehensive in coverage as Kerlinger's volume. A very useful guide to research design, alternative methods, statistical analysis, and scaling is the second edition of Delbert Miller's *Handbook of Research Design and Social Measurement* (New York: David McKay Co., 1970). Finally, there are two excellent works written primarily for students of politics: the first is essentially introductory, E. Terrence Jones, *Conducting Political Research* (New York: Harper and Row, 1971), while the second is at a more sophisticated level, David C. Leege and Wayne L. Francis, *Political Research* (New York: Basic Books, Inc., 1974).

Several texts introduce readers to approaches used by political scientists in examining phenomena. One that covers a wide variety is M. Margaret Conway and Frank B. Feigert, *Political Analysis* (Boston: Allyn and Bacon, 2nd ed., 1976); although some portions of the work suffer from lack of detail, especially the discussion of communications, the authors describe personality, attitudinal, socialization, role, group, decision-making, and systems perspectives. An older edited volume is Roland Young, ed., *Approaches to the Study of Politics* (Evanston: Northwestern University Press, 1958); students of the opinion process especially concerned with how people construct meaning should consult Charles E. Osgood's essay in the Young volume, "Behavior Theory and the Social Sciences," pp. 217–43. Another work which provides coverage of selected approaches is Robert T. Golembiewski, et al., *A Methodological Primer for Political Scientists* (Chicago: Rand McNally and Co., 1969).

As pointed out in our discussion of "Diversity of Techniques," many relative specialized and technical matters arise pertaining to sampling, gathering, processing, and analyzing data. Two general categories of works are especially concerned with such matters as related to studying communication and opinion. The first consists of selected volumes of the second edition of *The Handbook of Social Psychology* edited by Gardner Lindzey and Elliot Aronson (Reading, Mass.: Addison-Wesley Publishing Co., 1968). The second includes the volumes published in the "Handbooks for Research in Political Behavior" series published by Northwestern University Press under the general editorship of James A. Robinson. For instance, Lee F. Anderson, et al. in *Legislative Roll-Call Analysis* (1966) include a brief discussion of R- and Q-factor analysis; there is Robert C. North, et al., *Content Analysis* (Evanston, Ill.: Northwestern University Press, 1963): Thomas Wm. Madron includes discussions of sociometric techniques in his *Small Group Methods* (1969); Kenneth Janda describes various techniques of *Data Processing* (2nd ed., 1969); and Charles H. Backstrom and Gerald Hursh's *Survey Research* (1963) remains one of the best of the succinct introductions to that technique. One of the most comprehensive discussions of survey research is *Sampling Opinions* by Frederick F. Stephan and Phillip J. McCarthy (New York: John Wiley and Sons, Science Editions, 1963). Two more readable introductions are Philip Meyer, *Precision Journalism* (Bloomington: Indiana University Press, 1973); as a journalist himself Meyer introduced social science research techniques to journalists and prospective journalists—surveys, field experiments, documentary research, etc. Readers should also examine the brief discussion of Richard P. Devine and Lawrence L. Falk, *Social Surveys: A Research Strategy for Social Scientists and Students* (Morristown, N.H.: General Learning Press, 1972).

In addition, readers might want to examine works pertaining to related technical matters of data analysis. Factor analysis is discussed by a political scientist in R. J. Rummel's lengthy tome, *Applied Factor Analysis* (Evanston: Northwestern University Press, 1970). Two works will be helpful to readers interested in scaling techniques: Marvin E. Shaw and Jack M. Wright, *Scales for the Measurement of Attitudes* (New York: McGraw-Hill Book Co., 1967) and Gene F. Summers, ed., *Attitude Measurement* (Chicago: Rand McNally and Co., 1970). Experimental research receives a thorough discussion in *Experimental and Quasi-Experimental Designs for Research* (Chicago: Rand McNally and Co., 1966) by Donald T. Campbell and Julian C. Stanley. As noted earlier, Herbert Garfinkel in *Studies in Ethnomethodology* (Englewood Cliffs, N.J.: Prentice-Hall, Inc., 1967) raises ethnomethodological concerns. Finally, *Q*-methods and techniques are introduced in Steven R. Brown, *Small Sample Behavioral Research* (Kent, Ohio: Dept. of Political Science, Kent State University, no date). The seminal work, however, is William Stephenson, *The Study of Behavior: Q-Technique and its Methodology* (Chicago: University of Chicago Press, 1953).

The argument for using plural techniques in research, i.e., the triangulation principle, appears in Eugene J. Webb, et al., *Unobtrusive Measures: Nonreactive Research in the Social Sciences* (Chicago: Rand McNally and Co., 1966). Readers interested in considering the philosophical underpinnings of a broader intellectual and methodological pluralism would do well to begin with the works of William James, especially his discussion of radical empiricism in *The Will to Believe* (London: Longmans, Green, and Co., 1897).

NOTES

1. Readers interested in drawing distinctions between research approaches, methods, and techniques should consult the following: Abraham Kaplan, *The Conduct of Inquiry* (San Francisco: Chandler Publishing Co., 1964); Eugene J. Meehan, *The Theory and Method of Political Analysis* (Homewood, Ill.: Dorsey Press, 1965); Robert T. Golembiewski, et al., *A Methodological Primer for Political Scientists* (Chicago: Rand McNally and Co., 1969); and John Madge, *The Tools of Social Science* (Garden City, N.Y.: Anchor Books, 1965).

2. V. O. Key, Jr. and Frank Munger, "Social Determinism and Electoral Decision: The Case of Indiana," in Eugene Burdick and Arthur J. Brodbeck, eds., *American Voting Behavior* (Glencoe, Ill.: The Free Press, 1959), pp. 281–99.

3. Austin Ranney, "The Utility and Limitations of Aggregate Data in the Study of Electoral Behavior," in Austin Ranney, ed., *Essays on the Behavioral Study of Politics* (Urbana: University of Illinois Press, 1962), p. 93.

4. Ibid., p. 94.

5. A useful primer on survey designs is Charles H. Backstrom and Gerald D. Hursh, *Survey Research* (Evanston, Ill.: Northwestern University Press, 1963).

6. See Donald T. Campbell and Julian C. Stanley, *Experimental and Quasi-Experimental Designs for Research* (Chicago: Rand McNally and Co., 1963).

7. On the different results obtained through survey and experimental methods see Carl I. Hovland, "Results from Studies of Attitude Change," in Bernard Berelson and Morris Janowitz, eds., *Reader in Public Opinion and Communication* (New York City: The Free Press, 2nd ed., 1966) pp. 654–69 and reprinted from *The American Psychologist*, 14 (1959): 8–17.

8. Experimental research in this area is possible; see Samuel J. Eldersveld, "Experimental Propaganda Techniques and Voting Behavior," *American Political Science Review*, 50 (March 1956): 154–65.

9. Fred N. Kerlinger, *Foundations of Behavioral Research* (New York: Holt, Rinehart and Winston, 1964), Ch. 20.

10. Dan Nimmo and Clifton McCleskey, "Impact of the Poll Tax on Voter Participation: The Houston Metropolitan Area in 1966," *Journal of Politics*, 31 (August 1969): 682–99.

11. See Bernard Berelson, *Content Analysis in Communication Research* (Glencoe: The Free Press, 1952) and Robert C. North, et al., *Content Analysis* (Evanston, Ill.: Northwestern University Press, 1963); Ole R. Holsti, "Content Analysis," in Gardner Lindzey and Elliot Aronson, eds., *Handbook of Social Psychology*, (Reading, Mass.: Addison-Wesley Publishing Co., 1969) vol. 2, Ch. 16.

12.   Richard A. Pride and Barbara Richards, "Denigration of Authority? Television News Coverage of the Student Movement," *Journal of Politics*, 36 (August 1974): 637–61; Edith Efron, *The News Twisters* (Los Angeles: Nash Publishing 1971); American Institute for Political Communication, *The Nixon Administration-Mass Media Relationship* (Washington: AIPC, 1974).

13.   Ray L. Birdwhistell, *Kinestics and Context: Essays on Body Motion Communication* (Philadelphia: University of Pennsylvania Press, 1970).

14.   Stanford M. Lyman and Marvin B. Scott, *A Sociology of the Absurd* (New York: Appleton-Century-Crofts, 1970), p. 25.

15.   Norman K. Denzin, "Symbolic Interactionism and Ethnomethodology: A Proposed Synthesis," *American Sociological Review*, 34 (December 1969): 922–34.

16.   Erving Goffman, *Behavior in Public Places* (New York: The Free Press, 1963) and *Frame Analysis* (Cambridge, Mass.: Harvard University Press, 1974).

17.   Karl Lamb, *As Orange Goes* (New York: W. W. Norton Co., 1974).

18.   W. Phillips Davison, "The Public Opinion Process," *Public Opinion Quarterly*, 22 (Summer 1958): 91–106.

19.   George Gallup and Saul Forbes Rae, *The Pulse of Democracy* (New York: Simon and Schuster, Inc., 1940), p. 68, (italics in original).

20.   George Gallup, *The Sophisticated Poll Watcher's Guide* (New York: Princeton Opinion Press, 1972).

21.   William Stephenson, *The Study of Behavior: Q-Technique and its Methodology* (Chicago: University of Chicago Press, 1953).

22.   Peter Rossi, "Four Landmarks in Voting Research," in Burdick and Brodbeck, eds., *American Voting Behavior,* pp. 45–46. See also David Willer, *Scientific Sociology* (Englewood Cliffs, N.J.: Prentice-Hall, 1967), especially Ch. 6 concerning "Conditional Universals and Scope Sampling"; and Barney G. Glaser and Anselm L. Strauss, *The Discovery of Grounded Theory* (Chicago: Aldine Publishing Co., 1967), especially Ch. 3, "Theoretical Sampling."

23.   Claire Selltiz, et al., *Research Methods in Social Relations* (New York: Henry Holt and Co., Inc. Rev. ed., 1960), pp. 263–68; see also Arnold Brecht, *Political Theory* (Princeton: Princeton University Press, 1959), pp. 38–42; and Robert K. Merton and Patricia L. Kendall, "The Focused Interview," Paul F. Lazarsfeld and Morris Rosenberg, eds., *The Language of Social Research* (New York: The Free Press, 1955), pp. 476–89.

24.   Lamb, *As Orange Goes.*

25.   Harold Garfinkel, *Studies in Ethnomethodology* (Englewood Cliffs, N.J.: Prentice-Hall, Inc., 1967).

26.   Denzin, "Symbolic Interactionism and Ethnomethodology," p. 933; see also Eugene J. Webb, et al., *Unobtrusive Measures* (Chicago: Rand McNally Co., 1966).

27.   See, for example, Marvin E. Shaw and Jack M. Wright, *Scales for the Measurement of Attitudes* (New York: McGraw-Hill, 1967); Delbert C. Miller, *Handbook of Research Design and Social Measurement* (New York: David McKay Co., Inc., 2nd ed., 1970); John P. Robinson, et al., *Measures of Political Attitudes* (Ann Arbor: Institute for Social Research, University of Michigan, 1968); and Charles M. Bonjean, et al., *Sociological Measurement: An Inventory of Scales and Indices* (San Francisco: Chandler Publishing Co., 1967).

28.   For examples of other self-referent techniques see Carolyn W. Sherif, et al., *Attitude and Attitude Change* (Philadelphia: W. B. Saunders and Co., 1965), especially Chapter 4, "The Individual's Own Categories for Evaluation"; and George Kelley, *The Psychology of Personal Constructs* (New York: Norton, 1955).

29.   See Gaye Tuchman, "Objectivity as Strategic Ritual: An Examination

of Newsmen's Notions of Objectivity," *American Journal of Sociology*, 77 (January 1972): 660–70.

30. Chris Argyris, *Behind the Front Page* (San Francisco: Jossey-Bass Publishers, 1974).

31. Doris Graber, "Personal Qualities in Presidential Images: The Contribution of the Press," *Midwest Journal of Political Science*, 16 (November 1972): 46–76.

32. Steven R. Brown, "Consistency and the Persistence of Ideology: Some Experimental Results," *Public Opinion Quarterly*, 34 (Spring 1970): 68.

33. Murray Edelman, *The Symbolic Uses of Politics* (Urbana: University of Illinois Press, 1964).

34. Charles Brownstein, "Communication Strategies and the Electoral Decision Making Process: Some Results from Experimentation," *Experimental Study of Politics*, 1 (July 1971): 37–51.

35. Ron Roberts and Robert Marsh Kloss, *Social Movements* (St. Louis: C. V. Mosby Co., 1974); *Report of the National Advisory Commission on Civil Disorders* (New York: Bantam Books, 1968); Ted Robert Gurr, *Why Men Rebel* (Princeton: Princeton University Press, 1970). Compare Leon Festinger, et al., *When Prophesy Fails* (New York: Harper Torchbook, 1964).

36. Brown, "Consistency and the Persistence of Ideology," pp. 60–68.

37. John E. Mueller, *War, Presidents and Public Opinion* (New York: John Wiley and Sons, 1973).

38. Edward Dreyer, "Media Use and Electoral Choices: Some Political Consequences of Information Exposure," *Public Opinion Quarterly*, 35 (Winter 1971–1972): 544–53.

39. See, for example, Norval D. Glenn, "Class and Party Support in the United States: Recent and Emerging Trends," *Public Opinion Quarterly*, 37 (Spring 1973): 1–20.

40. Paul Lazarsfeld, et al., *The People's Choice* (New York: Columbia University Press, 1944).

41. Dan Nimmo and Robert L. Savage, *Candidates and Their Images* (Pacific Palisades, Cal.: Goodyear Publishing Co., 1976).

42. John Kessel, *The Goldwater Coalition* (Indianapolis: Bobbs-Merrill Co., 1968).

43. Norval Glenn, "Archival Data on Political Attitudes: Opportunities and Pitfalls," in Dan Nimmo and Charles M. Bonjean, eds., *Political Attitudes and Public Opinion* (New York: David McKay, 1972), pp. 137–46.

44. David A. Leuthold and Raymond Scheele, "Patterns of Bias in Samples Based on Telephone Directories," *Public Opinion Quarterly*, 35 (Summer 1971): 249–57.

45. Larry L. Leslie, "Are High Response Rates Essential to Valid Surveys?" *Social Science Research*, 1 (September 1972), 323–34.

46. Birdwhistell, *Kinesics and Context*, p. 61.

47. Garfinkel, *Studies in Ethnomethodology*.

48. Kaplan, *The Conduct of Inquiry*, p. 177.

49. Paul F. Lazarsfeld and Allen H. Barton, "Qualitative Measurement in the Social Sciences: Classification, Typologies, and Indices," in Daniel Lerner and Harold D. Lasswell, eds., *The Policy Sciences* (Stanford, Cal.: Stanford University Press, 1951), p. 155.

50. Such techniques are discussed in understandable form in Miller, *Handbook of Research Design and Social Measurement;* Abraham N. Franzblau, *A Primer of Statistics for Non-Statisticians* (New York: Harcourt Brace, and World, 1958); and Terrence Jones, *Conducting Political Research* (New York: Harper and Row, 1971).

51. On applications of regression analysis to aggregate studies see V. O. Key, Jr., *A Primer of Statistics for Political Scientists* (New York: Thomas Y. Crowell, 1954), Ch. 3.

52. Sidney Verba and Norman Nie, *Participation in America* (New York: Harper and Row, 1972).

53. James M. Perry, "AMDAHL Speaks: Carter Really Won the Election," *The National Observer*, February 12, 1977, p. 5. For a sophisticated application see George A. Barnett et al., "Campaign Communication and Attitude Change: A Multidimensional Analysis," *Human Communication Research,* 2 (Spring 1976): 227–44.

54. John Bowle, *Politics and Opinion in the Nineteenth Century* (New York: Oxford University Press, 1961); Doris A. Graber, *Public Opinion, The President, and Foreign Policy* (New York: Holt, Rinehart and Winston, 1968).

55. Thomas Landon Thorson, *Biopolitics* (New York: Holt, Rinehart and Winston, 1970).

56. Richard F. Hamilton, *Class and Politics in the United States* (New York: John Wiley and Sons, 1972).

57. Fred I. Greenstein, *Personality and Politics* (Chicago: Markham Publishing Co., 1969).

58. Lewis A. Coser, *Continuities in the Study of Social Conflict* (New York: The Free Press, 1967).

59. Carl J. Friedrich, *Constitutional Government and Democracy* (Waltham, Mass.: Blaisdell Publishing Co., 4th ed., 1968).

60. Foster H. Sherwood, "The Role of Public Law in Political Science," in Roland Young, ed., *Approaches to the Study of Politics* (Evanston: Northwestern University Press, 1958), pp. 86–95.

61. C. Wright Mills, *The Power Elite* (New York: Oxford University Press, 1957).

62. David B. Truman, *The Governmental Process* (New York: Alfred A. Knopf, 1958).

63. Richard C. Snyder, "A Decision-Making Approach to the Study of Political Phenomena," in Roland Young, ed., *Approaches to the Study of Politics* (Evanston: Northwestern University Press, 1958), pp. 3–37.

64. Contrast David Easton, *A Systems Analysis of Political Life* (New York: John Wiley and Sons, 1965) and Karl Deutsch, *The Nerves of Government* (New York: The Free Press of Glencoe, 1963).

65. Herbert Blumer, "Sociological Analysis and the 'Variable,'" *American Sociological Review*, 21 (December 1956): 683.

66. Ibid., p. 687.

67. Kenneth Boulding, *The Image* (Ann Arbor: University of Michigan Press, 1956), Ch. 10.

68. Webb et al., *Unobtrusive Measures, p.* 3.

69. Arthur Bentley, *The Process of Government* (Cambridge: The Belknap Press, 1967), p. 199.

INDEX